THE HEART
OF THE
BIBLE

THE HEART OF THE BIBLE

OF THE

BIBLE

AS REVEALED IN THE OLD TESTAMENT

STEPHEN SCIORTINO

XULON PRESS

Xulon Press
2301 Lucien Way #415
Maitland, FL 32751
407.339.4217
www.xulonpress.com

Unless otherwise indicated, Scripture quotations taken from the Holy Bible, New International Version (NIV). Copyright © 1973, 1978, 1984, 2011 by Biblica, Inc.™. Used by permission. All rights reserved.

Paperback ISBN-13: 978-1-6628-4126-2
Dust Jacket ISBN-13: 978-1-6628-4127-9
Ebook ISBN-13: 978-1-6628-4128-6

TABLE OF CONTENTS

CONFESSION OF FAITH

After spending my entire career as an economist in the electric utility industry, my wife Susan jokingly asked, "What are you going to do with all those brains now that you're retired?" Not having a real plan, she and I attended several Bible study classes where I discovered that I could focus my time and thoughts on a critical area for my soul and salvation. I could take on a more academic study of the Bible, to better know the Holy Trinity and open my heart and mind to all God has spoken to me from His Word, the Bible.

As background for my undertaking these studies, I confess to believe in the Bible as the Word of God, inspired by the Holy Spirit. I believe that Jesus Christ is the Son of God who came down from heaven and became man to die for our sins as the perfect sacrifice to save all those who believe in Him, which will lead us to enjoy everlasting life with Him in Heaven.

I am a literalist; I believe everything in the Bible to be true and factual. It is a slippery slope when those of a different mindset pick apart the Bible and accept some things as truth, some things as stories, and others as metaphors for how to live. The inherent danger is knowing where to draw the line and deciding into what categories various parts of the Bible fall. When you start cherry-picking verses, it's easy to get comfortable with the idea that anything in the Book can be questioned or taken for less than God's Word to and for us.

As I educate myself through study, prayer, and reading, I become more aware of what the Bible has in it. As I reread the Bible, I continue to find connections between verses, chapters, and books. Early in life, I had several misconceptions about the Bible. I thought our existence on earth was somewhat of a test: how will you spend your live on earth to show you are worthy? How can you earn your way into heaven through good acts alone? Sadly, that thinking was the result of my Catholic upbringing in the 1960s.

Now that I know Christ as my Savior, I understand that it is only through God's grace and belief in Jesus that we are saved, not through acts or works. Our obedience and good works are the result of our faith is Jesus Christ. As St. James wrote, "You foolish person, do you want evidence that faith without deeds is useless?" (Jas 2:20). As I grow in the grace and knowledge of our Lord and Savior, what He teaches in the New Testament stays with me, and I continually try to apply those words in my life.

One of the messages Jesus gave us that inspired me to write this book was, "'Do not be afraid, little flock, for your Father has been pleased to give you the kingdom. Sell your possessions and give to the poor. Provide purses for yourselves that will not wear out, a treasure in heaven that will never fail, where no thief comes near and no moth destroys. *For where your treasure is, there your heart will be also*'" (Luke 12:32–34, emphasis mine).

"For where your treasure is, there your heart will be also." That is how I have tried to live my life. Not to dedicate my life to what I could accumulate here on earth, but to focus on my spiritual treasures. More importantly, *where my heart is* was a fulcrum for my behavior and actions, both to God and how I interacted with those around me.

As I grew more familiar with the Scriptures, I noticed that references to the heart ran throughout: sometimes as direct quotes and other times by actions of various people that reflected their heart. Itw occurred to me that these references struck a level of consistency and the more references I picked up, the more I reflected on how they had a common theme. It is this one verse that drove me to draft an outline of the scriptural heart to show what I believe God wants us to know about: the heart and how to act accordingly. From this verse, I began my research to piece together my thoughts on what God has infused in us from the beginning.

My plan was to cover this theme throughout the whole Bible. As the document grew too large, I realized that it should be split into two books: Volume I covering the Old Testament and Volume II covering the New Testament. In this volume, I sought to capture the heart of individuals described in the Old Testament to demonstrate that despite sin, spiritual hearts in obedience and faith in God were alive and well.

When we get to the New Testament in Volume II, the focus will be on the teachings and parables provided by Jesus in the Gospels that emphasize how important it is to live your life by the Two Great Commandments. As He walked among us to show us the way to salvation, He often relied on these Two Commandments to show how eternal life is to be reached, with the added ingredient that belief in Him was the final ingredient for our ultimate spiritual heart. The Epistles continue with these teachings, especially regarding obedience to God and the importance of having Jesus as an integral part of our heart. I offer this discussion which I suggest is the means of getting us back to our original design as God created us; the pure and perfect hearts that would reflect His image and likeness.

Being created in God's image, we were given pure and holy spiritual hearts with the inherent ability to love God and our fellow man in the manner God desired. Because of sin, that heart lost its original capabilities, but the core ingredients to reflect those qualities were still there. I will use the Old Testament to demonstrate that the imperfect heart still showed obedience and faith to God and I will contrast them with those who rejected God's word. As it mainly covers the history of Israel, we find that God's plan for our salvation was revealed to the prophets and was promised through His Son Jesus, who came to die for our sins and provide the path to restore our hearts to God and mankind.

Before you dive into The Heart of the Bible, Volume I, there are a few style issues I'd like to point out. First, I majored in economics and mathematics for good reason, so those of you with better literary skills, please indulge me. Second, I was raised as a Catholic, so I prefer to capitalize all pronouns used for the Godhead out of reverence, but also to clarify for whom the pronoun is being used. Third, I provide the scripture reference and verses in my writing from the NIV Bible unless otherwise noted. In my research, I found that the more knowledgeable authors often referenced chapter and verse; I expect they have a better handle on quoting Scripture. I often found that I lost my tempo if I had to interrupt my reading to look up Scriptures, so I thought it might help you, too, if I include them in the text.

I am not a theology student, nor have I had any significant academic training in studying the Bible in a formal setting. I researched my topic by gathering selective scattered crumbs from the banquet table of professional academic biblical theology authors and readily admit my scholastic naivety. This started out as a research project of my own undertaking, without much outside counseling. Therefore, my targeted audience is not academics, but those with a layman's knowledge of the Scriptures like me.

With that in mind, I hope this text brings to light elements of Scripture that inspire you to study God's Word with renewed vigor. My fondest hope is that you enjoy reading it as much as I enjoyed putting it together.

ACKNOWLEDGMENTS

I want to thank Dean Bobar, assistant pastor at Christ Pacific Church in Huntington Beach, California, for providing me with the inspiration to elevate my studies to a more academic level. Before undertaking this research, Dean led a Bible study on the book of Revelation, which Susan and I attended. Dean was working on his PhD dissertation at the time and was beyond brilliant. He was the catalyst for me diving into biblical theology and putting together this book, particularly in addressing the concept of the 'circumcised' heart.

A big debt of gratitude to Michelle Gardner, a friend and neighbor who just happens to be a professional editor. Her markups were a constant reminder of why I did better in mathematics. Given the number of changes she's made, I sometimes felt English must have been a second language to me. With her help, the paragraphs are limited in their redundancy.

Thanks to my brothers Lou and Guy for their spiritual help. Guy helped review an earlier version of this book and, while we tend to agree with each other 95% of the time, we spent many hours arguing over the last 5%.

And thanks to my wife Susan who continues to be my biggest and best advocate. She had no problem with me spending hours on this project as she spent her time developing her watercolor painting talents. We're both novices but she seems to have a better talent for her craft. But she did take the time to read some of the manuscript and often pointed out interesting perspectives to include.

Chapter 1

An Outline of the Heart

Defining the Heart by Way of the Commandments

In defining our spiritual heart, I would like to begin with one of the basic tenets of Scripture regarding God's direction for us: the Ten Commandments. Living a life that sincerely and willingly abides by these commandments would demonstrate our spiritual intimacy with God and a loving connection to those with whom we live. Our spiritual heart, then, would have the ability and desire to follow God's commandments and reflect that obedience.

God provided the Ten Commandments to Moses as a covenant with the Israelites at a time they needed it most.[1] God would take them out of slavery in Egypt, lead them to the Promised Land, and He would be their God. The Israelites would be His chosen people and they would obey His commandments. This covenant was a continuation of God wanting to stay close with His people. "I will put my dwelling place among you, and I will not abhor you. I will walk among you and be your God, and you will be my people" (Lev. 26:11–12).

As God's chosen people, they were to be His priests and represent God to all other nations; they were to reflect His presence here on earth. They were to be holy and pure, making their spiritual hearts an example for the rest of the world. This was what God intended for Adam and Eve, but sin prevented them from fulfilling that role. There were several individuals between Adam and Moses who may

---

[1]How God uses Moses and the Law to provide the Israelites a template to restore their hearts for Him is discussed in Chapter 5.

have fit the bill, but God chose an entire nation to be set apart from the world. "Now if you obey me fully and keep my covenant, then out of all nations you will be my treasured possession. Although the whole earth is mine, you will be for me a kingdom of priests and a holy nation" (Exod. 19:5–6).

The Ten Commandments can be summarized into two simple concepts: "The LORD our God, the LORD is one. Love the LORD your God with all your heart and with all your soul and with all your strength" (Deut. 6:4–5), and "Do not seek revenge or bear a grudge against anyone among your people but love your neighbor as yourself. I am the LORD" (Lev. 19:18). These verses were ingrained in the minds of the Israelites. These are later referred to in the New Testament as the Two Great Commandments.

The first and greatest commandment requires us to love God with all our heart, soul, and strength. This is our spiritual heart reflecting our love for God. To love God in this all-out manner demonstrates our total dedication and obedience to His will and commands, our faith and trust in Him, and our gratitude to and worship of Him. This vertical relationship is to love Him as our Father and Creator. This closeness to Him and reliance upon Him results in humility and selflessness. In contrast, the lack of a spiritual heart leads to pride, arrogance, and rebellion against God (sin).

Richard Patterson and Hermann Austel present a formula for showing God our love for Him. They stress that there is "... the paramount value placed on the preparation of our hearts to pursue God in fellowship and obedience.[2]...Setting our heart to seek God goes hand in hand with serving God with all our hearts[3] laying up God's Word in our hearts and applying our hearts to understanding and walking

---

[2]"But if from there you seek the LORD your God, you will find him if you seek him with all your heart and with all your soul" (Deut. 4:29).

[3]"I have hidden your word in my heart that I might not sin against you" (Ps. 119:11).

in God's ways."[4,5] It is, then, through and from our hearts that we show our obedience and love for God as required in the First Great Commandment.

The Second Great Commandment regarding our ability to love our neighbor as ourselves is similar to the first, only it is a horizontal relationship. Here, the spiritual heart is characterized by qualities that include, but are not limited to, charity, compassion, mercy, consideration, kindness, the ability to forgive and ask forgiveness from our fellow man, to have harmony in our fellowship, and be void of jealousy and envy. This is God's desire for our relationships with our fellow man.

Following these two commandments establishes the actions of our spiritual heart. In the Old Testament, righteousness is demonstrated in God's gracious, covenant relationship with His people and their behavior toward each other. As George Ladd describes, "Righteousness is not primarily an ethical quality, but a right relationship, the divine acquittal from the guilt of sin...Righteousness in Jewish thought was a human activity. The rabbis taught that it was a human obedience to the Law and acts of mercy."[6]

In New Testament times, righteousness is the result of living in obedience to God. Ladd continues, "Jesus taught that it was both God's demand and God's gift. A righteousness exceeding that of the scribes and the Pharisees...This righteousness includes freedom from anger, from lust, from retaliation."[7]

Christopher Wright defines righteousness as "the right response of the person who chooses to live as befits his or her membership of the covenant community of Yahweh. It does not mean moral perfection,

---

[44] "And now, Israel, what does the LORD your God ask of you but to fear the LORD your God, to walk in obedience to him, to love him, to serve the LORD your God with all your heart and with all your soul" (Deut. 10:12).

[5] Richard Patterson and Hermann Austel, *The Expositor's Bible Commentary — 1 and 2 Kings*, 2009, p. 215.

[6] George Ladd, *A Theology of the New Testament*, 1974, p. 77.

[7] Ibid., p. 78.

but it certainly implies moral commitment...It is a term of allegiance and obligation, not of achievements."[8]

Our ability to love God and our neighbors is clearly a key element of the Scriptures. In later chapters, I will explain how having the heart to love in this manner is demonstrated throughout the Old Testament, and I'll compare and contrast various individuals through their words and actions.

Sampling of the Heart in the Old Testament

Having God alive in our hearts is the basis of this book. What does it mean to have God in our hearts? Is it our frame of mind or attitude? Is it how we act toward others? How does it describe our relationship with God and our fellow man? Our faithfulness and obedience to God's will and showing kindness and mercy to others are keys to these relationships.

While the New Testament has a lot to say about obedience and faith to Jesus's mission and message, I will save that for The Heart of the Bible, Volume II. Here in Volume I, I will expound on Old Testament characters who demonstrated a heart for God and contrast them with those who did not. It's important to remember that, of those who did have a heart for God, none of them showed complete or perfect obedience to Him and that imperfection was caused by sin. Still, the Old Testament is brimming with special relationships with God despite impure hearts. These Old Testament characteristics are examples of how we can return to God's original design for our hearts through our faith in Jesus Christ.

To love God according to the First Great Commandment encompasses myriad characteristics that are found in the Old Testament. Having faith in God and being obedient to His will are key to a close relationship with Him; however, they are not exclusive characteristics of a spiritual heart for Him.

---

[8]Christopher Wright, *The Message of Ezekiel*, 2001, p. 194.

As to faith, Paul remarked in Romans, "What does Scripture say? 'Abraham believed God, and it was credited to him as righteousness'" (Rom. 4:3). He was referring to Genesis 15:6, "Abram believed the LORD, and he credited it to him as righteousness." Paul cited Abraham as an example of faith in God and argued that it was faith combined with obedience—and not strict adherence to the Jewish law of his time—that one is found righteous in God's eyes. He also argued that righteousness through faith was established long before God gave Moses the Ten Commandments. Faith and obedience superseded strict adherence to the laws, which is what the religious leaders of his time taught would constitute righteousness in a legalistic sense.

Paul cited the prophet Habakkuk who made the same observation regarding a life of faith, "See, the enemy is puffed up; his desires are not upright—but the righteous person will live by his faithfulness" (Hab. 2:4). Paul and Habakkuk agree that the measure of one's faith defines his relationship with God, and that it is His image in us that enables our faithfulness to Him. Bruce Waltke uses a quote from Blaise Pascal that ties the heart and the attribute of faith together: "It is the heart that perceives God and not the reason. That is what faith is; God perceived by the heart, not by reason."[9]

Again, faith is key to a life of righteousness. Relying on God's protection, depending on His assistance, and believing in His promises are all elements of faith that we find in the Scriptures. The writer of Hebrews echoes this as he commends the faithfulness of several Old Testament individuals: "Now faith is confidence in what we hope for and assurance about what we do not see. This is what the ancients were commended for. By faith we understand that the universe was formed at God's command, so that what is seen was not made out of what was visible. And without faith it is impossible to please God because anyone who comes to him must believe that he exists and that he rewards those who earnestly seek him" (Heb. 11:1–3, 6). The writer cites Abel, Enoch, Noah, Abraham, and Sara as examples of their faith in God and what was accomplished and rewarded to them as a result.

---

[9]Bruce Waltke, *An Old Testament Theology,* 2007, p. 334.

Obedience and faith give us a spiritual heart for God. A prime example of a heart for God was King David. His story helped inspire this book.[10] In 2 Samuel 22:21–25 (ESV), David reflected on his relationship with God toward the twilight of his life, "The LORD dealt with me according to my righteousness; according to the cleanness of my hands he rewarded me. For I have kept the ways of the LORD and have not wickedly departed from my God. For all his rules were before me, and from his statutes I did not turn aside. I was blameless before him, and I kept myself from guilt. And the LORD has rewarded me according to my righteousness, according to my cleanness in his sight."

Here, David acknowledged that it was his lifelong obedience to God's laws and statutes that God rewarded him. Not that David was perfect, but he strove to stay in God's grace by obeying His will and dedicating his heart and life to do what was right in God's eyes. While he did stray, as we all do, he was quick to recognize the errors of his ways and turned back to God. This will be clear as I share the differences between Saul and David in Chapter 8. For now, it is important to point out that David's actions and thoughts were driven by a heart that was devoted to God's will.

As the author of many Psalms, David defined the character of heart that God desires and how it will be rewarded. It ties in to the First Great Commandment through being obedient to His will.

In Psalm 18, David prayed, "The LORD has dealt with me according to my righteousness; according to the cleanness of my hands he has rewarded me. For I have kept the ways of the LORD; I am not guilty of turning from my God. All his laws are before me; I have not turned away from his decrees. I have been blameless before him and have kept myself from sin. The LORD has rewarded me according to my righteousness, according to the cleanness of my hands in his sight. To the faithful you show yourself faithful, to the blameless you show yourself blameless, to the pure you show yourself pure, but to the devious you

---

[10]A fuller description of David's heart is provided in Chapters 8 and 9. I highlight David's words here first because God referred to David as a man after His own heart. With that endorsement, David captured his relationship with God through many of the Psalms, which provided the inspiration to help define the "heart" in this project.

show yourself shrewd. You save the humble but bring low those whose eyes are haughty" (vv. 20–27).

David recognized that a life of righteousness was important for keeping God's commands. He understood that God's rules were provided to steer us away from sin and that is what kept David blameless in God's sight. He advised us to remain faithful to God, to be pure of heart, and to be humble without pride or haughtiness. This is the heart to which I refer: turning away from our earthly desires and maintaining a lifestyle that is true to God's commands. It's easier to obey God's will when you are not pursuing a life of self-indulgence.

In Psalm 15, we find additional characteristics of righteous living and in this case, David focused on actions that demonstrate loving your neighbor as yourself, the Second Great Commandment. "Lord, who may dwell in your sacred tent? Who may live on your holy mountain? The one whose walk is blameless, who does what is righteous, who speaks the truth from their heart; whose tongue utters no slander, who does no wrong to a neighbor, and casts no slur on others; who despises a vile person but honors those who fear the Lord; who keeps an oath even when it hurts and does not change their mind; who lends money to the poor without interest; who does not accept a bribe against the innocent. Whoever does these things will never be shaken" (vv. 1–5).

David urges us to treat our neighbor with grace and love, not with slander or hatred; to speak honestly and sincerely, not with malice or deceit; and to show honor, respect, kindness, and generosity. This is being faithful and obedient to God. To dwell in His sacred tent and live on His holy mountain, we must be holy as He is holy. That is our reward for having the right heart.

In contrast, David warned that God is ever watchful and knows what's in our hearts. Those who follow an evil path will be punished, but those who follow His guidelines for a righteous life shall be with Him. David writes, "The Lord is in his holy temple; the Lord is on his heavenly throne. He observes everyone on earth; his eyes examine them. The Lord examines the righteous, but the wicked, those who love violence, he hates with a passion. On the wicked he will rain fiery coals and burning sulfur; a scorching wind will be their lot. For the LORD is righteous, he loves justice; the upright will see his face" (Ps. 11:4–7). God is aware of our thoughts, both good and evil. He judges men accordingly as will be demonstrated in the next several chapters.

David continued to show examples of his obedience to the Two Great Commandments: "Vindicate me, LORD, for I have led a blameless life; I have trusted in the LORD and have not faltered. Test me, LORD, and try me, examine my heart and my mind; for I have always been mindful of your unfailing love and have lived in reliance on your faithfulness. I do not sit with the deceitful, nor do I associate with hypocrites. I abhor the assembly of evildoers and refuse to sit with the wicked. I wash my hands in innocence, and go about your altar, LORD, proclaiming aloud your praise and telling of all your wonderful deeds. LORD, I love the house where you live, the place where your glory dwells. Do not take away my soul along with sinners, my life with those who are bloodthirsty, in whose hands are wicked schemes, whose right hands are full of bribes. I lead a blameless life; deliver me and be merciful to me. My feet stand on level ground; in the great congregation I will praise the LORD" (Ps. 26:1–12).

David was asking God to confirm his obedience and faithfulness by examining his heart and mind. He gave thanksgiving and praise to the Lord and, as we find in the Lord's Prayer, David asked God to deliver him from all evil. Giving thanks to God for the blessings He bestows upon us is another way to show our love for Him. It's easy to forget the troubles He has pulled us out of, or to take for granted what He has given us. It takes but a moment to give Him thanks and praise.

In Psalm 112, the Psalmist describes how having trust in the Lord will provide a firm foundation for your life. Combined with righteousness and obedience to the Two Great Commandments, you can rest in the calm assurance of God's grace. This peace in the Lord strengthens our hearts and keeps fear at bay when things go bad or when evil befalls us. "Praise the LORD. Blessed are those who fear the LORD, who find great delight in his commands. Their children will be mighty in the land; the generation of the upright will be blessed. Wealth and riches are in their houses, and their righteousness endures forever. Even in darkness light dawns for the upright, for those who are gracious and compassionate and righteous. Good will come to those who are generous and lend freely, who conduct their affairs with justice. Surely the righteous will never be shaken; they will be remembered forever. They will have no fear of bad news; their hearts are steadfast, trusting in the LORD. Their hearts are secure, they will have no fear; in the end they will look in triumph on their foes. They have freely scattered their gifts to the poor, their righteousness endures forever; their horn will be lifted high in honor. The wicked will see and be vexed, they will gnash their teeth and waste away; the longings of the wicked will come to nothing" (vv. 1–10).

In Proverbs, Solomon advises, "Above all else, guard your heart, for everything you do flows from it" (Prov. 4:23). We see here that the heart is central to our emotions and will. It is the very core that drives all our actions and behavior.

In the New Testament, Jesus addressed this very concept when the Pharisees accused His disciples of disobeying the law by not washing their hands before eating. "Don't you see that whatever enters the mouth goes into the stomach and then out of the body? But the things that come out of a person's mouth come from the heart, and these defile them. For out of the heart come evil thoughts—murder, adultery, sexual immorality, theft, false testimony, slander. These are what defile a person; but eating with unwashed hands does not defile them" (Matt. 15:17–20).

For it is our hearts that defines our motives and guides our actions and behavior; it speaks of our integrity or deceit, our love or anger, our obedience or rebellion. Our hearts reflect who and what we are. In Proverbs we find, "As water reflects the face, so one's life reflects the heart" (Prov. 27:19). In his commentaries on Proverbs, David Guzik remarks, "The feelings and thoughts that come from our heart reveal us as the reflection in smooth water reveals the face. Who we are will eventually be evident to others as our words and actions reveal our heart."[11]

The quest for a more holy and pure heart is the exercise of our life. God gave us those qualities when we were first created; but with sin, we have lost that purity. There is a path for us to return to that original design. Scriptures give us the spectrum of where our hearts have been; we have examples to follow and some to avoid.

Our Spiritual Hearts: In the Image and Likeness of God

Maintaining a spiritual heart requires adherence to the Two Great Commandments. "Love the LORD your God with all your heart and with all your soul and with all your strength" (Deut. 6:5) and "...love your neighbor as yourself" (Lev. 19:18) were provided to Moses and the Israelites over 3,500 years ago and reiterated by Jesus over 2,000 years ago, so those instructions have been with us all this time. But what about the time from when Adam and Eve were created to the time of Moses when the Ten Commandments were carved in stone, so to speak? What maintained man's relationship with God and the status of the heart during those 2,500 years? (I make no apologies for being a Biblical literalist.)

While the commandments are not formalized until Moses's time, close relationships with God were demonstrated throughout Genesis, which we read about in Hebrews 11. In fact, it seemed these relationships with God were much more personable. God spoke directly to some individuals in Genesis, whereas after Moses and Joshua, most of God's interactions were limited (for example, David and Solomon) and accomplished through the prophets. So, how did Enoch, Noah, and others find favor with God prior to circumcision (Abraham's requirements) or keeping the Sabbath (from Moses forward)?

---

[11]David Guzik, "Study Guide for Proverbs 27 by David Guzik," Blue Letter Bible, last modified February 21, 2017, https://www.blueletterbible.org/Comm/guzik_david/ StudyGuide 2017-Pro/Pro-27.cfm.

We were given the ability to love God and mankind at the onset of creation. One of the key elements from the creation story in the first chapter of the Bible is when God said, "'Let us make mankind[12] in our image, in our likeness, so that they may rule over the fish in the sea and the birds in the sky, over the livestock and all the wild animals, and over all the creatures that move along the ground.' So, God created mankind in his own image, in the image of God he created them; male and female he created them. God saw all that he had made, and it was very good. And there was evening, and there was morning—the sixth day" (Gen. 1:26–27, 31).

By creating us in His image, it seems logical that God wanted us to have pure, loving, and holy hearts, and to love Him as the First Great Commandment instructs. This ability was innate in Adam and Eve, and I believe God wrote these instructions within their hearts. God saw that what He created was good and that this original design could follow the guidance provided by the Two Great Commandments without having them formalized in writing. Adam and Eve were "wired" with pure and holy hearts to love God and, eventually, to love their fellow man with the same sense of purity. Because of sin, the wiring got crossed and we lost some of that purity and holiness of heart. The good news is, we all maintain some remnant of that purity; it wasn't totally lost because of sin.

There is a wealth of literature by theologians who have defined the image and likeness of God. I don't pretend to have done an extensive study on this subject, nor do I intend to reinvent the wheel here; however, there are certain aspects from different sources that help to develop this theme of our pure and holy hearts. That is, how God

---

[12]Initially, God designed "*mankind in our image*" (Gen. 1:26, emphasis mine). In his text, *Seriously Dangerous Religion,* Provan makes the convincing argument that in mentioning mankind before the designation of male and female indicated that God intended to treat both men and women equally; that they were both created with no hierarchy in mind, but that they shared equally in His image and with equal duties here on earth (pp. 80–92). "No reading of Genesis 2 about the creation of male and female can be accepted as correct, I suggest, that does not take seriously the claim that *'adam*, male and female, is created in the image of God and given joint dominion over creation'" (p. 92).

originally designed our hearts; not to describe the image and likeness of God in its entirety, but how it applies to our spiritual heart.

Thus, it is our nature or non-physical makeup that His likeness in us is reflected. James Borland, in his review of Christophanies,[13] remarks "...in Genesis 1:26, the triune God said, 'let us make man in *our* image after *our* likeness.' Man was not patterned *solely after* the 'perfect, spiritual' or quasi-physical form or the preincarnate Christ, but after the image of the immaterial triune God. The *imago dei* should not be interpreted as something physical but rather it concerns man's likeness to God in areas of personality, intellect, communication, emotions and power of the will."[14]

In David Guzik's commentary on Genesis 1, we find this image is strictly ours. "In Our image" means there is "an unbridgeable gap between human life and angelic life. Nowhere are we told the angels are made in the **image** of God. Angels cannot have the same kind of relationship of love and fellowship with God we can have."[15] So, we are special to God by having this relationship.

Guzik also describes something that hadn't occurred to me: "This means the incarnation was truly possible. God (in the Second Person of the Trinity) could really become man, because although deity and humanity are not the same, they are compatible."[16] Because we are made in His image, the incarnation of Jesus was a natural transition because of that compatibility. That's an interesting explanation of how Jesus's incarnation would be a natural transition to his humanness, even though God can make all things possible.

You could even say that God had this all planned out; He knew mankind would fail and need a Savior and, with Jesus coming to earth

---

[13]A Christophany is the appearance of Jesus on earth reflected in human form prior to His incarnation. In the Old Testament, this is referenced as the angel of the Lord.

[14]James Borland, *Christ in the Old Testament,* 2010, p. 91.

[15]David Guzik, "Study Guide for Genesis 1 by David Guzik," Blue Letter Bible, last modified February 21, 2017, https://www.blueletterbible.org/Comm/guzik_david/StudyGuide 2017-Gen/Gen-1.cfm.

[16] Ibid.

to die for our sins, the transition was thought out from the very beginning.[17] You might say, "God has perfect knowledge. Why couldn't He have planned this from the very beginning?" I just didn't realize the implications! We can say this in reverse when discussing the New Testament. We can use our core image to be like Jesus; that is, because of Him, we can revitalize our sinful hearts to come close to God's original design for us.

The other point Guzik makes—which supports my spiritual heart concept—is that the image reflects personality, morality (judgement and conscience), and spirituality. The latter, Guzik states, allows us to be in "communion with God. It is on the level of spirit we communicate with God."[18]

In Matthew Henry's commentary,[19] he speaks of the original man in the purest sense, prior to Adam and Eve's sin. Like the others mentioned above, he highlights that "...we were created in the initial state of purity and holiness." That is, made unique from animals and in God's likeness, consisting of God's "nature and constitution, not those of his body (for God has not a body), but those of his soul... The soul of man, considered in its three noble faculties, understanding, will, and active power, is perhaps the brightest clearest looking glass in nature, wherein to see God." In addition, Henry notes the image reflects God's authority here on earth, "As he has the government of the inferior creatures, he is, as it were, God's representative, or viceroy, upon earth..." Most importantly, for the purposes of this text, Henry

---

[17]"For he chose us in him before the creation of the world to be holy and blameless in his sight" (Eph. 1:4), and "All inhabitants of the earth will worship the beast—all whose names have not been written in the Lamb's book of life, *the Lamb who was slain from the creation of the world*" (Rev. 13:8, emphasis mine).

[18]David Guzik, "Study Guide for Genesis 1 by David Guzik," Blue Letter Bible, last modified February 21, 2017, https://www.blueletterbible.org/Comm/guzik_david/StudyGuide 2017-Gen/Gen-1.cfm.

[19]Matthew Henry is the author of the six-volume *Exposition of the Old and New Testaments* written from 1708–10.

notes the likeness reflects God's "purity and rectitude. God's image upon man consists in knowledge, righteousness, and true holiness."[20]

The governance and authority that Henry mentions is enlightening. God entitled Adam and Eve to have dominion over the earth; they had total control over all things, but this was lost because of their disobedience. This will be explored later in the text, but it is interesting that Henry declares we were intended to rule all things on earth.

John Calvin commentaries relate to a perfection of man's creation, with a particular reference to the gifts and endowments God bestows on man at the outset. These gifts reflect the spiritual heart: the ability to obey and trust God's will, understand, and revere His authority as our Creator, and love our fellow man by showing kindness, mercy, and compassion. These gifts reflect the best characteristics of our nature. This constitutes what Anthony Hoekema characterizes as the basic ingredients of our **structural** spiritual makeup, which I will address shortly.

Calvin's commentary continues, "Let us make man[21]... God has been introduced simply as commanding; now, when he approaches the most excellent of all his works, he enters into consultation. God certainly might here command by his bare word what he wished to be done: but he chose to give this tribute to the excellency of man, that he would, in a manner, enter into consultation concerning his creation... so now, for the purpose of commending to our attention the dignity of our nature, he, in taking counsel concerning the creation of man, testifies that he is about to undertake something great and wonderful...man

---

[20]Matthew Henry, "Commentary on Genesis 1 by Matthew Henry," Blue Letter Bible, last modified March 1, 1996, https://www.blueletterbible.org/Comm/mhc/Gen/Gen_001.cfm.

[21]Most commentaries point out prior to this God commanded the creations directly. He now takes counsel in creating mankind, a separate design from the earlier days of creation where God plainly commands the elements to be created. In taking counsel, it is commonly understood that God is addressing the Son and the Holy Spirit and not addressing angels in this statement.

is, among other creatures, a certain preeminent specimen of Divine wisdom, justice, and goodness."[22]

H. C. Leupold states, "Those that hold that a reference to the Trinity is involved do not mean to say that the truth of the Holy Trinity is here and plainly revealed."[23] As to counter the argument God is addressing angels, Leupold mentions that Scriptures note on occasion, "Angels are found standing in his presence...But never once does God actually counsel with them...man is not considered in the Scriptures of be made in the image of angels."[24]

As a professor at Calvin Theological Seminary, it is no coincidence that Anthony Hoekema reiterates John Calvin's concept that God was in consultation when He created man. "This indicates that the creation of man is in a class by itself, since this type of expression is used of no other creature...It should also be noted that a divine counsel or deliberation preceded the creation of man...This again makes out the uniqueness of man's creation. In connection with no other creature is such a divine counsel mentioned."[25]

Continuing with Calvin, "'In our image.' Interpreters do not agree concerning the meaning of these words...They who would define the subject briefly, say that in the image are contained those endowments which God has conferred on human nature at large, while they expound likeness to mean gratuitous gifts...Paul says that we are transformed into the image of God by the gospel. And, according to him, spiritual regeneration is nothing else than the restoration of the same image...That he made this image to consist in 'righteousness and true

---

[22]John Calvin, "Commentary on Genesis 1 by John Calvin," Blue Letter Bible, last modified March 1, 1996, www.blueletterbible.org/Comm/calvin_john/Gen/Gen01. cfm?a=1001.

[23]H. C. Leupold, *Exposition of Genesis: Volumes 1 and 2*, 1942, p. 86.

[24] Ibid., p. 87.

[25]Anthony Hoekema, *Created in God's Image,* 1989, p. 12.

holiness,' is by the figure synecdoche; for though this is the chief part, it is not the whole of God's image."[26]

The idea of our spiritual regeneration by way of the gospel will be addressed in The Heart of the Bible, Volume II. The spiritual heart we were given at creation was corrupted by sin, but the spiritual nature is still within us; we are able to restore our hearts, as it is not totally lost as of result of sin.

Concluding with Calvin, "'And let them have dominion.' Here he commemorates that part of dignity with which he decreed to honour man, namely, that he should have authority over all living creatures. He appointed man, it is true, lord of the world; but he expressly subjects the animals to him, because they having an inclination or instinct of their own, seem to be less under authority from without. The use of the plural number intimates that this authority was not given to Adam only, but to all his posterity as well as to him."[27]

From his lectures on the summary of the Old Testament at Gordon-Conwell Theological Seminary, Dr. Douglas Stewart discussed the image of God. He said one way to think of it was that we have the ability to think, reason, imagine, and plan, not that we resemble Him per se, but we are to do His work here on earth. We are to represent God in doing His will; to do what He wants or asks us to do.

When God created Adam and Eve, He gave them their first assignment: "The LORD God took the man and put him in the Garden of Eden to work it and take care of it" (Gen. 2:15). Adam and Eve oversaw caring for Eden, cultivating it, and maintaining it. And, with Eve's help, Adam was to populate the earth, have dominion over all things, and rule over it. "God blessed them and said to them, 'Be fruitful and increase in number; fill the earth and subdue it. Rule over the fish in the sea and the birds in the sky and over every living creature that

---

[26] John Calvin, "Commentary on Genesis: Chapter 1 by John Calvin," Blue Letter Bible, last modified January 1, 2001, https://www.blueletterbible.org/Comm/calvin_john/Gen/Gen01 .cfm.

[27] Ibid.

moves on the ground'" (Gen. 1:28). God honored us by making us in His image, and our purpose is to do His work.

Hoekema's book, *Created in God's Image*, helped me put my thoughts into words. The image and likeness adjectives, according to Hoekema, are interchangeable, but with some slight differences. "The two words together tells us that man is a representation of God, who is like God in certain aspects."[28] This is not to say that we are exactly like God in all ways, but more of a reflection of traits we recognize in God, and I want to focus on those of the heart: charity, love, obedience, faithfulness, and humility.

Hoekema provides a historic summary of various biblical theologians and how they interpret the image-and-likeness concept, particularly with respect to aspects kept or lost after Adam's sin. It can be argued that the image of God is corrupted or distorted because of man's sin. Did we lose this integrity after Adam sinned? There is universal agreement among Christians that through Jesus, we can be restored or renewed, but that won't happen until the final judgement.

I agree with Hoekema's summary: "The image of God must, therefore, be seen as involving both the *structure* of man (his gifts, capacities and endowments), and the *functioning* [emphasis mine] of man (his actions, his relationships to God and to others, and the way he uses his gifts.) To stress either of these at the expense of the other is to be one-sided. We must see both, but we need to see the structure of man as secondary and his functioning as primary. God has created us in his image so that we may carry out a task, fulfill a mission, pursue a calling."[29] God has given us the tools we need (one of which is the spiritual heart) to be like Him. As Hoekema would say, this is the structure of man. The core ingredients for the heart remain after sin, but the key to restoring the heart depends on whether it is acted upon or not.

Putting our hearts to use is similar to what James states in his epistle regarding acting on our faith. "What good is it, my brothers and sisters, if someone claims to have faith but has no deeds? Can such

---

[28]Anthony Hoekema, *Created in God's Image*, 1989, p. 13.

[29] Ibid., p. 73.

faith save them? Suppose a brother or a sister is without clothes and daily food. If one of you says to them, "Go in peace; keep warm and well fed," but does nothing about their physical needs, what good is it? In the same way, faith by itself, if it is not accompanied by action, is dead." (James 2:14-17) In the same manner, we find out later in the text what the consequences were for those who did not act on the core ingredients of the heart.

George Ladd refers to this innate structure as one's conscience, but his characterization sounds very much like the core ingredients described above. "God has implanted in all human beings a moral instinct that gives them a sense of right and wrong."[30] He then discusses Paul's letter to the Romans to make this point. Paul argued that it is faith that makes one righteous, not strict adherence to the Law. Faith was exhibited before the Law was formally established, which reinforces the thought that our core ingredients of being created in God's image drives us to be faithful, even without the instructions given to us in the Ten Commandments.[31]

As further evidence of this innate ability to demonstrate obedience to God, Paul speaks of the Gentiles who did not grow up in an atmosphere of faith (defined by God's covenant with Israel) as did the Jews he was addressing. Their behavior, without knowledge of the law, according to Paul, demonstrated that the basic ingredients of the spiritual heart was revealed not by religious affiliation, but **by our** innate characteristics. Paul writes, "For it is not those who hear the law who are righteous in God's sight, but it is those who obey the law who will be declared righteous. (Indeed, when Gentiles, who do not have the law, do by nature things required by the law, they are a law for themselves, even though they do not have the law. They show that the requirements of the law are written on their hearts, their consciences also bearing witness, and their thoughts sometimes accusing them and

---

[30]George Ladd, *A Theology of the New Testament*, 1993, p. 444.

[31]The point of the next three chapters is to demonstrate this very concept. I discuss several individuals who were righteous by faith before Moses and the Law. From where did that faith emanate? It was innately part of that spiritual heart that was given to them.

at other times even defending them)" (Rom. 2:13–15). Paul says the Gentiles do by *nature* things required by law. What is that nature? It is the image of God that is innate in us all and what allowed the Gentiles to act in accordance with the Law.

As we are the image of God, we are to represent Him and do His work here on earth. This demonstrates the characteristics of the heart. Hoekema states that the functioning of the heart is of primary concern because that is what puts our gifts to use. In our relationship with God, love flows in both directions. When He created Adam and Eve, the relationship was pure, but their sin disrupted the relationship. Our disrupted relationship with God requires an intercession: Jesus.

Hoekema reminds us that "God saw all that He had made, and it was very good" (Gen. 1:31), including man. "Man, therefore, as he came from the hands of the Creator, was not corrupt, depraved or sinful: he was in a state of integrity, innocence and holiness."[32]

Finally, Leupold characterized "in our image" as "to assert with emphasis that man is to be closely patterned after his Maker...the singular dignity of man: Man is not only made after the deliberate plan and purpose of God but is also very deliberately patterned after Him."[33] Referring to Ephesians and Colossians,[34] he adds, "The reformers clearly saw that the most important thing involved was a proper attitude of heart in faith. Luther says, "I understand this image of God to be...that Adam not only knew God and believed in Him that he was gracious but that he also led an entirely godly life.""[35]

This is reflective of the heart's core ingredients that allowed Adam and Eve to lead righteous lives before their sin, but also is maintained by mankind even under the curse of sin.

---

[32]Anthony Hoekema, *Created in God's Image,* 1989, p. 15.

[33]H. C. Leupold, *Exposition of Genesis: Volumes 1 and 2,* 1942, pp. 89–90. Of all the components that the image of God reflects, Leupold's opinion is that the spiritual and inner side of the image of God was the most important one.

[34]"And to put on the new self, created to be like God in true righteousness and holiness" (Eph. 4:24), and "...have put on the new self, which is being renewed in knowledge in the image of its Creator" (Col. 3:10).

[35]H. C. Leupold, *Exposition of Genesis: Volumes 1 and 2,* 1942, p. 91.

In the beginning, then, Adam and Eve were without sin, but as Hoekema points out, "...the integrity Adam and Eve exhibited before the Fall was not a state of consummate and changeable perfection. Man, to be sure, was created in the image of God at the beginning, but he was not yet a 'finished product.' He still needed to grow and be tested. God wished to determine whether man would be obedient to him freely and voluntarily, in the face of an actual possibility of disobedience."[36]

What happened to this image of God after Adam and Eve sinned? The spiritual heart is now flawed and imperfect. I like G. K. Beale's perspective that "God's image in unbelieving humanity has not been erased but blurred."[37] I believe there is a difference between the heart of sinful man and unbelief, but the spiritual heart has not been extinguished. There are traces of the spiritual heart that prevent us from completely missing out on God's presence. Those embers can be restored, but not to the extent of the original design. The heart is replete in the Old Testament when the Israelites return to God after having fallen out of obedience to Him, but the path to a longer-lasting state will only be revealed through Jesus. In the last three chapters, we'll hear the prophets' messages of this promised salvation; the fulfillment of the promise will be discussed in detail in Volume II.

I don't want to skip ahead too far, but following the sin of Adam and Eve, much can be gained by our continued faith and obedience to God and love for our fellow man. We still have the ingredients of the heart to maintain those attributes. Paul said, "For we maintain that a man is justified by faith apart from observing the law" (Rom. 3:28). Paul is referring to faith in Jesus, but I believe it also applies to those in the Old Testament. We are not like God's original creation; we are all imperfect in many ways. But therein lies hope, God's everlasting love and forgiveness of our imperfections. Hoekema quotes John Calvin who said, "our imperfect obedience will be accepted by God as if it

---

[36]Anthony Hoekema, *Created in God's Image,* 1989, p. 83.

[37]G. K. Beale, *We Become What We Worship,* 2008, p. 29.

were perfect, since he readily forgives the many imperfections that still cling to our very best deeds."[38]

While all of mankind has the structural image of God in their hearts, it is the functioning of that heart that allows it to grow closer to its original design. The Old Testament focuses primarily on Abraham and his descendants, but that does not preclude anyone else from demonstrating that heart. For example, Tamar, Rahab, and Ruth were not of the Jewish faith, but they demonstrated a sense of moral standards.

Obedience is what gives us the ability to demonstrate our love for God and our fellow man. We will see these core ingredients in individuals throughout the first three chapters who loved and obeyed God prior to the Law being recorded.

It is with the imperfect heart that we navigate through the Old Testament to find examples of those who lived by the Two Great Commandments and those who didn't.

---

[38]Anthony Hoekema, *Created in God's Image,* 1989, p. 240.

Chapter 2

Initial Contrast
of Hearts

In the beginning, God created a world that was in total harmony. Everything fulfilled a specific and perfect purpose; all elements of nature interacted in perfect order with each other. At the end of each day of creation, Scriptures note God viewed His work and "He saw that it was good." All this was intended for His final creation, mankind, whom He created in His image. As described at the outset, this image included creating the spiritual heart that had the capability to love Him[39] as well as our fellow mankind in a true, sincere, and perfect manner.

Graeme Goldsworthy noted that the design of creation not only brought things into physical existence, but "[i]t actually establishes the structure of the kingdom of God: God's people dwelling with God in the place he has prepared for them, submitting to his lordship, and reflecting it in their dominion over creation."[40]

Living in harmony with God and our fellow human beings while here on earth was the goal. God created the Garden of Eden, the perfect environment for us to live and dwell with Him. Initially, Adam and Eve were pure in body, without sin and hence, had the capability of being directly in God's presence without harm. That He physically walked with Adam and Eve regularly demonstrated His intent to dwell

---

[39]Here, my reference to God is not intended to be limited to God the Father, but the Trinity of the Father, Jesus, and the Holy Spirit.

[40]Graeme Goldsworthy, *The Son of God and the New Creation*, 2015, p. 85.

among His creation. It makes no sense to think that God would create all this and just sit on His throne in heaven, remotely observing His works. He created us so that we could interact with Him on a personal level, and originally, as a physical experience.

The intention of His physical presence with mankind was implicit as Scriptures tell us that when Adam and Eve had sinned, God appeared to walk once again with them. "Then the man and his wife heard the sound of the LORD God as he was walking in the garden in the cool of the day, and they hid from the LORD God among the trees of the garden" (Gen. 3:8). In his commentary on Genesis, H. C. Leupold makes this point: "Yahweh God is represented as 'walking about the garden.' This almost casual way in which this is remarked indicates that this did not occur for the first time just then. The assumption that God had repeatedly done this is quite feasible."[41]

While in their presence, God gave Adam and Eve their first mission: to populate the earth and be stewards over all things. "God blessed them and said to them, 'Be fruitful and increase in number; fill the earth and subdue it. Rule over the fish in the sea and the birds in the sky and over every living creature that moves on the ground'" (Gen. 1:28).

G. K. Beale notes that, in their commission, "They were to reflect God's kingship by being his vice-regents on earth."[42] In an earlier text, Beale states that one of Adam's tasks was to serve and worship God and that this role included one of a priestly nature. In maintaining the concept that Eden represented the initial temple for worship, he states, "This is an indication that the task of Adam in Genesis 2:15 included more than mere spadework in the dirt of a garden... It is apparent that priestly obligations in Israel's later temple included the duty of 'guarding unclean things from entering'...and this appears to be relevant for Adam, especially in view of the unclean creature lurking on the perimeter of the garden and who then enters."[43]

---

[41]H. C. Leupold, *Exposition of Genesis: Volumes 1 and 2*, 1942, p. 155.

[42]G. K. Beale, *We Become What We Worship*, 2008, p. 128.

[43]G. K. Beale, *The Temple and the Church's Mission*, 2004, p. 69.

Along with this initial mission, God instructed Adam and Eve to work for their sustenance, subject to a single caveat. "The LORD God took the man and put him in the Garden of Eden to work it and take care of it. And the LORD God commanded the man, 'You are free to eat from any tree in the garden; but you must not eat from the tree of the knowledge of good and evil, for when you eat from it you will certainly die'" (Gen. 2:15–17).

Here, God set the consequences of disobedience. The active step of rebellion (disobedience) is sin, which separates us from God and life. Death is the ultimate outcome, both spiritually and physically. God was not saying that their eating of the forbidden fruit would bring about instantaneous death. Rather, a death, which was not initially contemplated, would now eventually occur. While physical death is never overcome in this world, spiritual death will be overcome when God sends Jesus to die on behalf of all sins, making a path for eternal live.

As Dwight Pentecost notes, "The prohibition against eating of the tree of knowledge of good and evil was given to test man's recognition of and subjection to the authority of God. Man was not to assume that, because he had been given delegated authority to rule, as God's administrator in the theocracy, he was independent of God or not responsible to God's law."[44]

The unclean creature referenced above by Beale, now arrives on the scene; that creature was the serpent that deceived Eve. I don't think it's a stretch to say that Satan was the serpent, or that the serpent represented Satan. Jesus referred to Satan's deception from the beginning. In refuting the religious leaders' self-righteous attitude of "Abraham is our father," Jesus retorts, "You belong to your father, the devil, and you want to carry out your father's desires. He was a murderer *from the beginning, not holding to the truth*, for there is no truth in him. When he lies, he speaks his native language, for he is a liar and the father of lies" (John 8:44, emphasis mine).

---

[44]J. Dwight Pentecost, *Thy Kingdom Come*, 1995, p. 35.

The serpent told Eve that, if they ate from the tree, they wouldn't die but instead be like God, knowing good from evil. "When the woman saw that the fruit of the tree was good for food and pleasing to the eye, and also desirable for gaining wisdom, she took some and ate it. She also gave some to her husband, who was with her, and he ate it" (Gen. 3:6). Their eyes were immediately opened to the fact that they were naked, so they hid. I have an unfounded thought about this. What if Adam and Eve were given glorified bodies that shone like Moses's face after being in God's presence? Or in the manner that Jesus's face "shone like the sun, and his clothes became as white as the light" in His transfiguration (Matt. 17:2)?[45] What if their bodies shone so that they didn't see that they were naked, but when they sinned, the glory was removed, and that truth was revealed?

Either way, their disobedience to God's one rule caused their perfect being to become corrupted and their purity of heart was removed. Rather than taking dominion over the serpent and casting it out of the garden, they were deceived by it. Iain Provan writes, "Though Genesis 2–3 does not explicitly say Adam's ruling and subduing task was to guard the Garden from the satanic snake, the implication is there."[46] Whatever the case, Beale adds, "Thus, Adam did not guard the Garden but allowed a foul snake to enter, which brought sin, chaos and disorder into the sanctuary and into Adam and Eve's lives. He allowed the serpent to rule over him rather than ruling over it and casting it out of the Garden."[47]

One may wonder why Adam, after naming all the animals in the garden, did not find it suspicious that the snake could speak and conclude that something out of the ordinary was happening. Most commentators agree that Adam was provided with an implicit superiority or authority in providing names to all the animals. Provan

---

[45]"After six days Jesus took with him Peter, James, and John the brother of James, and led them up a high mountain by themselves. There he was transfigured before them. His face shone like the sun, and his clothes became as white as the light" (Matt. 17:1–2).

[46]Iain Provan, *Discovering Genesis*, 2015, p. 63.

[47]G. K. Beale, *We Become What We Worship*, 2008, p. 132.

notes that "… in naming the creatures in Genesis 2, 'adam is joining with God in *creating the world*, not least by assigning the other creatures' *role* in the world. Their names speak not so much of what they are as of where they *fit* in the cosmos."[48]

Adam should have had the intelligence to discern that snakes didn't possess the ability to speak and should have acted with authority rather than submission to the snake's deception. Stephen Dempster comments on this aspect: "The snake is a bizarre aberration in the garden, with its ability to do what only humans and God can do (namely speak) and its attempt to rule the rulers. In consonance with its slippery nature, it subtly renames the tree of knowledge of good and evil as the tree of life instead of death."[49]

Goldsworthy sees that this deception was designed to convince them that in eating the forbidden fruit, Adam and Eve would be equal to God. "…he [the snake] does not suggest that the humans transfer their allegiance from God to himself, but only that they themselves should consider and evaluate God's claim to the truth…They rebel against God not by making Satan their new final authority but by taking that function to themselves."[50]

When questioned by God about their disobedience, they both made excuses for themselves rather than taking responsibility for their actions; Eve blamed the serpent for her action and Adam blamed Eve for his. Adam's excuse showed less accountability than Eve's, "The man said, 'The woman you put here with me—she gave me some fruit from the tree, and I ate it'" (Gen. 3:12). He blamed Eve, but he also blamed God for giving him Eve in the first place. Leupold notes, "It is a reply

---

[48]Iain Provan, *Seriously Dangerous Religion: What the Old Testament Says and Why It Matters*, 2014, p. 88.

[49]Stephen Dempster, *Dominion and Dynasty: A Theology of the Hebrew Bible*, 2003, p. 67.

[50]Graeme Goldsworthy, *According to Plan: The Unfolding Revelation of God in the Bible*, 1991, p. 104.

that in cowardly fashion lays the blame for it all first on his wife and then by a wicked charge upon God Himself."[51]

There was no sense of remorse, nor did they ask for forgiveness. Because of sin, they lost Eden and their role as priest—or regents—over the earth.[52] In sinning, Adam and Eve lost God's glory and their physical purity was contaminated. The spiritual heart was seriously damaged but not totally switched off. The ability to remain within God's physical presence would quickly come to an end and, to compound the consequences, spiritual and physical death was now the reality. Mankind would suffer from all the instabilities of nature as well as the bodily imperfections that would slowly evolve. Sin became the major factor impeding our relationship with God and the callouses of worldly pleasure and personal desires now form over our uncircumcised hearts.

Much literature is dedicated to the motivation or reason for why Adam and Eve disobeyed God. For example, Leupold offers that in molding man "from the dust of the ground" (Gen. 2:7), this lowly component of our makeup accounted for our inability to maintain a holy state. He argues that "in spite of the high station involved in being made in the image of God, man has a constituent part of his makeup, which forever forbids unseemly pride on his part...Without this fact to reckon with we could hardly have been in a position to understand how a temptation and fall were even possible."[53]

Adam and Eve lacked total trust and faith in God to feel at ease with the role He had given them. To be so easily talked out of it by the serpent showed their weakness even though God gave them the authority to take charge of the situation. While God gave them pure and holy hearts, they weren't spiritually seasoned to take on the challenge of temptation.

---

[51]H. C. Leupold, *Exposition of Genesis: Volumes 1 and 2*, 1942, p. 159.

[52]In later chapters, we will see how this role is somewhat revived in the patriarchs and eventually the nation of Israel, but in both cases, the revival will be short-lived; Israel will fall to idolatry just like Adam and Eve.

[53]H. C. Leupold, *Exposition of Genesis: Volumes 1 and 2*, 1942, p. 116.

Anthony Hoekema notes that the fruit of the Holy Spirit in Christian spiritual development takes time to mature; it's not an immediate transformation. It seems reasonable to make the same assessment of Adam and Eve. God gave them all the gifts they needed, but they were spiritual infants with no experience to rely upon when they were tempted. With respect to newborn Christians, Hoekema states that "...there must be time for ripening and maturing. Producing the fruit of the Spirit must, therefore, not be thought of as a single, climatic, datable happening...but rather as a continuing process of spiritual growth."[54]

If Adam and Eve hadn't grown spiritually, it's no wonder they fell prey to the serpent's deception. They certainly had intelligence; after all, Adam named all of the animals God created. They had to be aware of God's love and blessings placed upon them, but perhaps they were unaware of the full power and authority He had granted them. Their spiritual development was incomplete; hence, they disobeyed God, losing paradise and God's close presence with them.[55] Provan makes a similar observation: "In the same way that a child grows up and becomes an adult, 'knowing good and evil' and having wisdom or insight, human beings were scheduled one day to 'know good and evil.' The emphasis on Genesis 3 lies on the *grasping* after knowledge, in independence of God, prior to the right time."[56]

The consequences of their disobedience were many; they led to being expelled from Eden and having to work the soil to eat, rather than eating freely from any tree; childbirth would be painful; but more importantly, their separation from God meant they could not commune with Him. Sin introduced death and the loss of eternal life.

God banished them from the garden and posted an angel to guard the way to the tree of life. In creating the garden of Eden, God included

---

[54]Anthony Hoekema, *Saved by Grace*, 1994, p. 45.

[55]In the chapters that follow, I will describe how individuals that God chose for His long-term plan of redemption faced situations that allowed them to grow spiritually to fulfill the task that God had for them.

[56]Iain Provan, *Discovering Genesis*, 2015, p. 75.

the tree of life, representing eternal life. "The LORD God made all kinds of trees grow out of the ground—trees that were pleasing to the eye and good for food. In the middle of the garden were the tree of life and the tree of the knowledge of good and evil" (Gen. 2:9).

Now that they had sinned, Adam and Eve were kept from the tree of life, hence the banishment from the garden. "And the LORD God said, 'The man has now become like one of us, knowing good and evil. He must not be allowed to reach out his hand and take also from the tree of life and eat and live forever'" (Gen. 3:22).

Allen Ross explains the potential danger of this action. "And yet, even forgiven sinners could not remain in the presence of this Holy God, in his garden sanctuary. They had now become aware of good and evil in a dangerous way—by disobedience. If they ate from the tree of life, they would live forever in this condition."[57]

In addition to losing Eden and having to work the soil for survival, all the purity and holiness of their original design was lost for all mankind. It was only when Jesus saved us all through his death on the cross and resurrection that a path to return those original characteristics was provided. God promised this salvation to Adam and Eve when He issued His punishment to them and in His judgement over the serpent: "And I will put enmity between you and the woman, and between your offspring and hers; he will crush your head, and you will strike his heel" (Gen. 3:15). The offspring God spoke of was Jesus; the serpent would be crushed after Jesus has been resurrected.

Cain and Abel: Angry vs. Righteous Hearts

After Adam and Eve's sin of disobedience, the book of Genesis continues with the narrative of Cain and Abel, the first of Adam and Eve's children. "Now Abel kept flocks, and Cain worked the soil. In the course of time Cain brought some of the fruits of the soil as an offering to the LORD. And Abel also brought an offering—fat portions from some of the firstborn of his flock. The LORD looked with

---

[57]Allen Ross, *Cornerstone Biblical Commentary – Genesis, Exodus*, 2008, p. 57.

favor on Abel and his offering, but on Cain and his offering he did not look with favor" (Gen. 4:2–5). It was deemed that Abel lived a righteous life, having a good, spiritual heart, which was one reason his offering was pleasing and acceptable to God. Though not directly addressed, God knew the hearts of both men. We find out shortly that Cain had evil smoldering in his heart and that his offering was spurned by God because of it.

Matthew Henry notes that "Abel chose that employment which most befriended contemplation and devotion, for to these a pastoral life has been looked upon as being peculiarly favourable. Moses and David kept sheep, and in their solitudes conversed with God."[58] Allen Ross suggests "...the narrative gradually begins to unveil Cain—first associating him with the curse because he worked the soil, whereas Abel's herding stood close to God's original purpose that mankind have dominion...One man was living according to the original instruction of God, ruling over living creatures, the other was living according to the decree of the curse, working the ground from which they were taken."[59]

We get additional information of Abel's righteousness from the writer of the book of Hebrews which plainly states why the offering of Abel was accepted and the offering of Cain was rejected. "By faith Abel brought God a better offering than Cain did. By faith he was commended as righteous when God spoke well of his offerings. And by faith Abel still speaks, even though he is dead" (Heb. 11:4). Cain's offering was obviously an effort that did not demonstrate his faith, while Abel's offering was made in faith in a desire to worship God in spirit and in truth. Hebrews tells us Abel's faith was deemed righteous in God's eyes; he was obedient to His will. Abel's relationship with God was one of worship and praise, and as he wanted to give God his

---

[58]Matthew Henry, "Commentary on Genesis 4 by Matthew Henry," Blue Letter Bible, last modified March 1, 1996, https://www.blueletterbible.org/Comm/mhc/Gen/Gen_004.cfm.

[59]Allen Ross, *Cornerstone Biblical Commentary – Genesis, Exodus,* 2008, p. 59.

best. God was pleased with Abel's offering because it came from Abel's heart in sincerity and love for his Lord.

The fat of the animal was prized and was to be given to God when the animal was sacrificed. We find this described later when Moses established the function of sacrifices when worshiping God. "The priest is to splash the blood against the altar of the LORD at the entrance to the tent of meeting and *burn the fat as an aroma pleasing to the LORD*" (Lev. 17:6, emphasis mine). This effort to please God with the first-born of his flock revealed the motivation of his heart and showed that Abel's offering was the type of offering God expected from His chosen people.

Malachi relayed God's displeasure with second-best offerings. "But you say, 'How have we despised your name?' By offering polluted food upon my altar. But you say, 'How have we polluted you?' By saying that the LORD's table may be despised. When you offer blind animals in sacrifice, is that not evil? And when you offer those that are lame or sick, is that not evil? Present that to your governor; will he accept you or show you favor? says the LORD of hosts" (Mal. 1:6–8, ESV).

We must offer Him our best, not something we don't cherish or revere for ourselves. Abel did right in God's view by offering his very best and this nature of Abel's heart is why God found his sacrifice pleasing.

In contrast to Abel's righteousness, Cain's heart was clouded with pride and envy, and in the case of his sacrifice, perhaps an indifference to God. While it was not the sacrifice itself that God was displeased with, it was the Cain's attitude in his presentation. Provan highlights that "...Cain brings to God only *some of the fruits of the soil*'... The remainder of the Old Testament makes clear that sacrifices are not really sacrificial if they do not cost the worshipper much."[60]

John Sailhamer concurs that this contrast between the brothers' offerings is a lesson in worship. "What kind of worship is pleasing to God? Worship pleasing to God is worship that springs from a pure

---

[60]Iain Provan, *Seriously Dangerous Religion: What the Old Testament Really Says and Why It Matters*, 2014, p. 193.

heart."[61] Cain's offering may have been perfunctory; that is, more of a routine practice of obligation than one that sincerely emanated from the heart. It was his motivation—or lack thereof—that God found displeasure with his offering. This is the very premise of the text; the nature of your heart drives the motivation for your actions.

T. W. Manson says that God looks at our heart for the motivation of our actions as he summarizes the message behind the Sermon of the Mount. "There are a number of cases in the Sermon of the Mount (Matthew 6) where it is emphasized repeatedly that the Father sees in secret, that is, looks to the heart and the motive rather than the outward act. As Father, it is impossible that he should be satisfied with the mere outward observances of piety and righteousness; rather he seeks that inner affection and devotion of which the outward act may be a token but for which it can never be a substitute."[62] This clearly applies to what God found wanting in Cain's heart.

Walter Kaiser makes the same point. "God valued the heart condition of the one making the offering more than the gift that was brought."[63] Just as God examines the transgression of us all, He saw through Cain's offering and identified the lack of spiritual heart behind his gift. This inner inspection of man's spiritual heart and the resulting motivations for actions and behavior then, was recorded from the very beginning.

The evil traits of Cain's heart were left unchecked and led to wickedness that would be renowned throughout the Scriptures. In his epistle, Jude warned his contemporaries to protect themselves against the ways of sinful people who could be a threat to their spiritual health. He likens those sinners to the more infamous characters from Israel's history. "Woe to them! They have taken the way of Cain; they have rushed for profit into Balaam's error; they have been destroyed in

---

[61]John Sailhamer, *The Expositor's Bible Commentary – Genesis*, 2008, p. 97.

[62]T. W. Manson, *The Teachings of Jesus: Studies in Form and Content*, 1963, pp. 114–115.

[63]Walter Kaiser, *The Promise-Plan of God: A Biblical Theology of the Old and New Testaments*, 2008, p. 44.

Korah's rebellion" (Jude 1:11). Note that Cain was the first name mentioned.

Similarly, in describing those in the New Testament who failed to show love to each other, Thomas Schreiner also makes a comparison to Cain's characteristics. "... they were in darkness, indicating that they are not believers. The kind of hatred that Cain demonstrated for Abel shows that he did not belong to God."[64] He cites the message in John's first letter, where John addresses our need to love one another. In the letter, John warned: "Do not be like Cain, who belonged to the evil one and murdered his brother. And why did he murder him? Because his own actions were evil and his brother's was righteous" (1 John 3:12).

As he witnessed God's acceptance of Abel's gift and rejection of his own, Cain's reaction was not surprising given the nature of his heart. "So, Cain was very angry, and his face was downcast. Then the LORD said to Cain, 'Why are you angry? Why is your face downcast? If you do what is right, will you not be accepted? But if you do not do what is right, sin is crouching at your door; it desires to have you, but you must rule over it'" (Gen. 4:5–7).

John Sailhamer writes, "Cain is angry with God and angry against his brother. It is a pure heart that is required in worshipping God that is central here, not the nature of the offering itself."[65] God was aware of the anger and pride that was welling in Cain's heart. Cain was jealous and hurt, and he sulked because his gift was not pleasing to God. In direct contrast to Abel's heart, Cain's heart was full of bitterness, and he was not willing to please the Lord. He evidenced a total lack of spiritual development. He was concerned only with his pride. If his heart had any goodness in it, he might have asked God how he could have done better. Bruce Waltke notes, "Instead of repenting for his failure to please God, he becomes angry with God, expecting God to

---

[64]Thomas Schreiner, *New Testament Theology: Magnifying God in Christ*, 2008, p. 566.

[65]John Sailhamer, *The Expositor's Bible Commentary – Genesis*, 2008, p. 97.

change to accommodate his sacrifice instead of his changing his sacrifice to please God."[66]

In fact, God consoled and counseled Cain to show him what he needed to do to be righteous and obedient, and to clean up his heart. God warned Cain that he must conquer his sinful urges, or he would succumb to the evilness in his heart. With this dialogue, God did not condemn Cain but gave him an opportunity to overcome his pride and hurt feelings, a second chance to grow spiritually. In His grace and mercy, He gave Cain the opportunity to be righteous like his brother Abel.

Alas, God's advice was in vain. Cain never recovered the goodness that God had intended for him. In the words of Matthew Henry, "Cain was a wicked man, led a bad life, under the reigning power of the world and the flesh; and therefore his sacrifice was an abomination to the Lord."[67] In what may have been defining the criteria behind the heart of worshiping God, Solomon wrote, "The LORD detests the sacrifice of the wicked, but the prayer of the upright pleases him" (Prov. 15:8).

Perhaps this was what Jesus had in mind when He warned His disciples against having anger in their hearts when He delivered the Sermon on the Mount. "You have heard that it was said to the people long ago, 'You shall not murder, and anyone who murders will be subject to judgment.' But I tell you that anyone who is angry with a brother or sister will be subject to judgment. Again, anyone who says to a brother or sister, 'Raca,' is answerable to the court. And anyone who says, 'You fool!' will be in danger of the fire of hell" (Matt. 5:21–22).

One could ask of Cain, was he always jealous of Abel and was this festering in his heart for a long time? Did he always have anger in his heart prior to their respective offerings? Maybe so, since it seems that he plotted in advance in taking his brother's life rather than some spontaneous reaction to God's rejection.

---

[66]Bruce Waltke, *An Old Testament Theology,* 2007, p. 270.

[67]Matthew Henry, "Commentary on Genesis 4 by Matthew Henry," Blue Letter Bible, last modified March 1, 1996, https://www.blueletterbible.org/Comm/mhc/Gen/Gen_004.cfm.

Anger starts in the heart and Jesus warned that those thoughts, left unchecked, can lead to the same result as actions. Better to show mercy and kindness than to let anger and hate build up and consume your heart. Jesus continued with another implicit consideration that coincides with Cain's situation. "Therefore, if you are offering your gift at the altar and there remember that your brother or sister has something against you, leave your gift there in front of the altar. First go and be reconciled to them; then come and offer your gift" (Matt. 5:23–24).

In reference to this verse, D. A. Carson notes, "The 'altar' is the one in the inner court. There amid solemn worship, recollection of a brother with something against one should in Christ's disciples prompt immediate efforts to be reconciled. Only then is formal worship acceptable."[68] Jesus is clearly saying that anger toward a brother must be reconciled; otherwise, worshiping with an angry heart would not be acceptable to God. This is clearly the case for Cain.

Abel's heart was upright, and his life was pious; he obviously found favor in God's sight. Abel offered in faith and Cain did not. That was the difference between their hearts. Matthew Henry stated that Abel offered knowing that God's will ruled his life, but Cain did not offer in faith, and so it turned into sin and made him capable of killing his brother.

"Now Cain said to his brother Abel, 'Let's go out to the field.' While they were in the field, Cain attacked his brother Abel and killed him. Then the LORD said to Cain, 'Where is your brother Abel?' 'I don't know,' he replied. 'Am I my brother's keeper?'" (Gen. 4:8–9).

In convincing his brother to follow him into the field, it's obvious that Cain made the plan well ahead of time to kill his brother away from the watchful eyes of their parents. We now have our first recording of a premeditated murder. His anger and hatred for his own brother is difficult to comprehend. How could this take place so soon after God's good, created work? How long did that anger fester before he acted on it? And for what reason? God gave Cain a chance to turn from sin, but he wasn't spiritually connected to God to redeem his behavior.

---

[68]D. A. Carson, *Expositor's Bible Commentary: Matthew,* 2010, p. 183.

Referencing the concept of man being created in God's image, Anthony Hoekema comments on the seriousness of Cain's crime. "The reason that murder is here said to be such a heinous crime, that it must be punished by death is that the man who has been murdered is someone who imaged God, reflected God, was like God, and represented God...to kill the image of God is to do violence to God himself."[69]

Murder was bad enough, but then God came to Cain and asked where his brother was. Cain's response revealed the total depravation of his heart. God was already aware of what transpired but in asking the question, God gave Cain an opportunity to confess his sin. We know that God is willing to forgive a repentant and humble heart when we confess to our sins. That would be the characteristic of a right heart.

But Cain eschewed the opportunity to show any righteousness at all. Rather, he responded in a manner that gave the appearance of an innocent; lying to God about what transpired by feigning ignorance. He did not take responsibility or ownership of his actions, nor did he show any remorse. With defiance and disrespect Cain answered, "Am I my brother's keeper?" He denied his actions and showed ambivalence as to the welfare of his brother. That was the answer of a prideful, evil man, who showed no humility or reverence to God.

In response to Cain's rebellious attitude and flippant response, God passed judgement on Cain's actions and his sinful nature. "The LORD said, 'What have you done? Listen! Your brother's blood cries out to me from the ground. Now you are under a curse and driven from the ground, which opened its mouth to receive your brother's blood from your hand. When you work the ground, it will no longer yield its crops for you. You will be a restless wanderer on the earth'" (Gen. 4:10–13).

Here was another opportunity for Cain to show remorse, beg forgiveness, and turn his heart back to the Lord. Instead, when faced with the consequences of his actions, like King Saul depicted later, Cain

---

[69]Anthony Hoekema, *Created in God's Image*, 1989, p. 16.

lamented that the punishment wasn't fair; it was too harsh and unjustified. The irony was that Cain feared the same fate that he laid on his own brother and whined to God about it. "Cain said to the LORD, 'My punishment is more than I can bear. Today you are driving me from the land, and I will be hidden from your presence; I will be a restless wanderer on the earth, and whoever finds me will kill me.' But the LORD said to him, 'Not so; anyone who kills Cain will suffer vengeance seven times over.' Then the LORD put a mark on Cain so that no one who found him would kill him. So, Cain went out from the LORD's presence and lived in the land of Nod, east of Eden" (Gen. 4:13–16).

Despite his wickedness and sinful nature, God showed great kindness and mercy toward Cain. God heard his plea for protection from suffering the same fate as Abel and promised His protection. The greater punishment, however, was Cain going out from God's presence for the remainder of his life. As Leupold points out, "...it must be admitted that banishment from God's presence was the heaviest punishment of all, heavier than the loss of life, and this heavier punishment Cain knows he has suffered."[70]

As he departed from his family, Cain still didn't get the idea of repenting and turning back to the Lord. He did, however, recognize that in his banishment, he would be hidden from God's presence, but only in the fear that he would come to harm, which reflected his selfish attitude for his own self-preservation.

Lamech and Enoch: Following After the Heart of Their Lineage

There was a similar contrast in spiritual hearts in the lives of Lamech (a descendant of Cain six generations down) and Enoch (a descendant of Seth, another brother of Cain's, six generations down). Abel was killed before a lineage could be established, but Seth exhibited faith like Abel. Although Lamech is not as well-known, he does

---

[70]H. C. Leupold, *Exposition of Genesis: Volumes 1 and 2*, 1942, p. 212.

present a contemporary contrast to Enoch, who was so faithful and obedient that God called him home without experiencing death.

God judged Cain's murder of his brother Abel by banishing him to the wilderness and—even more detrimental to Cain—depriving him of His presence even though he still had God's umbrella of protection. As a result of this judgement and of Cain's own evil life, he was secluded from the rest of Adam's family and driven to a very secular existence. There was no relationship with God nor a moral compass for Lamech six generations later and his behavior and actions reflected the complete absence of God's love. His evil heart was even more exaggerated than Cain's.

In contrast, Seth remained with the extended family and maintained a strong relationship with God. We get a sense of community worship in the family from one generation to the next. Enoch's obedience and love for God was so strong that it reflected the relationship God had with Adam and Eve before they sinned. His spiritual heart must have been close to the original design and, after 350 years on earth, God called him to heaven. (Enoch and Elijah are the only two in the Scriptures who didn't experience death.) It is safe to conclude that Lamech and Enoch were on opposite extremes of the spiritual-heart spectrum.

Lamech: A Heart Absent of God

It is interesting to see how the descendants of Cain followed in the direction of his wicked heart, as exemplified through Lamech six generations later. To help explain the trail of Cain's wickedness, let's go back to his banishment from God and the area where his family settled. "Cain made love to his wife, and she became pregnant and gave birth to Enoch. Cain was then building a city, and he named it after his son Enoch" (Gen. 4:17). Cain's relationship with God was non-existent and there was no mention of his connection or faithfulness with God. He built a city, not for the glory and honor of God, but for the benefit of his son, Enoch.

Graeme Goldsworthy writes, "Cities come to figure prominently in the Bible as the expression of human wickedness. Babel, Sodom and Gomorrah, the cities of Egypt and Canaan, and finally, Babylon and Rome all represent concentrations of human godlessness."[71]

Iain Provan writes, "By building a city, Cain has, in fact, refused the life of wandering God has prescribed. City building under these circumstances suggests that once again, Cain is self-reliant, not someone who trusts in God's goodness and in his ability to protect."[72]

Cain demonstrated once again that he was a man of the earth and not one in connection with God. Josephus noted that Cain did not amend his behavior after God cast him out, "but only to increase his wickedness; for he only aimed to procure everything that was for his own bodily pleasure, though it obliged him to be injurious to his neighbors. He augmented his wealth by plunder and violence; he urged his followers to procure pleasures and spoils by robbery and became a great leader of men into wicked courses."[73]

This same wickedness and prideful heart reared up in Lamech. In a very brief reference, we read, "Lamech said to his wives, 'Adah and Zillah, listen to me; wives of Lamech, hear my words. I have killed a man for wounding me, a young man for injuring me. If Cain is avenged seven times, then Lamech seventy-seven times'" (Gen. 4:23–24).

It is revealing to see how within a few generations, the pride demonstrated in Cain's heart was exaggerated in Lamech's heart. As each generation before Lamech was further removed from God's influence and guidance, they turned more and more to secular behavior until wickedness was the rule of the day. On the other hand, Seth's lineage remained with Adam and Eve and continued their relationship with God and showed reverence and obedience to Him.

---

[71]Graeme Goldsworthy, *According to Plan: The Unfolding Revelation of God in the Bible,* 1991, p. 108.

[72]Iain Provan, *Seriously Dangerous Religion: What the Old Testament Says and Why It Matters,* 2014, p. 202.

[73]Josephus, *Jewish Antiquities,* 2.61–62.

In his account of Lamech's generation and their lack of morality, Josephus said that "...the prosperity of Cain had become exceedingly wicked, everyone successively dying, one after another, more wicked than the former. They were intolerable in war, and vehement in robberies; and if anyone were slow to murder people, yet he was bold in his immoral behavior, in acting unjustly, and doing injuries for gain."[74]

Lamech appeared to be a wicked man, but that comes as no surprise. Firstly, Lamech had two wives, a transgression of God's original design of marriage: "...a man leaves his father and mother and is united to his wife, and they become one flesh" (Gen. 2:24). God's intention for marriage is repeated by Jesus in the New Testament (Matthew 19:5 and Mark 10:8).

It may be that having multiple wives was an accepted practice in Lamech's time, or perhaps there was an unawareness or indifference to God's original plan regarding marriage between one man and one woman. It seems there was no moral code or awareness of conscience behavior. Lamech decided how he would live his life. Just like the end of the book of Judges, there was no sense of moral direction. "In those days Israel had no king; everyone did as they saw fit" (Judg. 21:25). In Lamech's case, we could say he had no God, so he did as he saw fit.

Secondly, Lamech openly boasted that he committed murder with no sense of remorse. In fact, there was a sense of pride in the act, and he felt justified in taking a life. He demonstrated "an exaggerated sense of self-worth and a wounded self-esteem constantly in search of satisfaction."[75] Allen Ross writes, "Lamech killed a youthful warrior who had apparently insulted or harmed him in some manner. Showing no remorse over the act, he actually gloated about it...Not only did Lamech exact revenge—a fate Cain had feared—but he demanded greater leniency than that which was afforded to Cain."[76]

H. C. Leupold sheds light on Lamech's boast: "Zillah [Lamech's wife] also had a son, Tubal-Cain, who forged all kinds of tools out

---

[74] Ibid., p. 66.

[75] Iain Provan, *Seriously Dangerous Religion*, 2014, p. 203.

[76] Allen Ross, *Cornerstone Biblical Commentary: Genesis, Exodus*, 2008, p. 62.

of bronze and iron" (Gen. 4:22). Leupold indicates that Tubal-Cain constructed a sword which likely was a unique weapon at the time. Lamech's words in verses 23 and 24 are referred to as his "Sword Song." Upon receiving the sword from his son, Lamech may have swung it in boastful arrogance.

Leupold says that this poem "is a glorification of the sword. But penetrating deeper into its character, we find it to be a glorification of the spirit of personal revenge. So, the poem has an unholy savor and reflects admirably, the spirit of those who have grown estranged from God and His Word."[77]

If Lamech had possession of the only sword in town, then his boast can be construed as cowardice as well. He would clearly have had the advantage in any conflict with the weapon, so it was only by way of its possession that Lamech felt comfortable enough to make his boast. Without it, would he have shown such bravado?

Perhaps not surprisingly, Lamech was more prideful and arrogant than Cain. Notice his boastfulness as he addressed his wives in verse 23: "... wives of Lamech, hear my words." Matthew Henry observes it's "no marvel that he (Lamech) who had broken one law of marriage, by taking two wives, broke another, which obliged him to be kind and tender to those he had taken, and to give honour to the wife as to the weaker vessel."[78] The wives may have been subservient to Lamech and maybe they were in fear of his temper.

His viciousness and cold-heartedness in "I have killed a man for wounding me, a young man for injuring me," made him come across as a man of a fierce and cruel disposition, one that showed no mercy, and would kill anybody who confronted him. Again, Matthew Henry states, "Some think, because (v. 24) he compares himself with Cain, that he had murdered some of the holy seed, the true worshippers of God, and that he acknowledged this to be the wounding of his

---

[77]H. C. Leupold, *Exposition on Genesis: Volumes 1 and 2*, 1942, pp. 222–223.

[78]Matthew Henry, "Commentary on Genesis 4 by Matthew Henry," Blue Letter Bible, last modified March 1, 1996, https://www.blueletterbible.org/Comm/mhc/Gen/Gen_004.cfm.

conscience and the hurt of his soul; and yet that, like Cain, he continued impenitent, trembling and yet unhumbled."[79]

Lamech was self-centered and didn't care if anyone hated him as long as he was feared by the threat of death if anyone confronted him. Walter Kaiser writes, "Already a proud Lamech had begun to distort the purpose of government with his boastful tyranny and polygamy. According to his thinking, he was not to be challenged or rebuked by anyone."[80] He was presumptuous and assumed God was going to protect him in his heartless ways just as He protected Cain. Lamech heard that Cain should be avenged seven-fold and made an egotistical evaluation that if anyone should kill him for the murders he had committed, God would avenge his death more than ten times the amount reserved for Cain's murderer.

This was the opposite of Jesus's teaching on forgiveness. When Peter asked Jesus, "'Lord, how many times shall I forgive my brother or sister who sins against me? Up to seven times?' Jesus answered, 'I tell you, not seven times, but seventy-seven times'" (Matt. 18:21–22). Charles Scobie writes, "While this figure really constitutes a call to infinite forgiveness, it also represents a total reversal of Lamech's seventy-sevenfold vengeance."[81]

Lamech's arrogance led him to believe that God's assurance of vengeance—for reasons specific to Cain—were also meant for Cain's descendants, or at least for himself. This was delusional thinking from a depraved, murderous mind that had no moral or ethical values.

In just two verses, we saw Lamech's disobedience to God's law on marriage, exaggerated pride and arrogance, a willingness to inflict wounds on anyone who defied him, and a promise to take vengeance on all who threatened him.

While addressing the sinful people of Israel, Isaiah could have easily been addressing Lamech. "But your iniquities have separated you from

---

[79] Ibid.

[80] Walter Kaiser, *The Promise-Plan of God: A Biblical Theology of the Old and New Testaments,* 2008, p. 44.

[81] Charles Scobie, *The Ways of Our God: An Approach to Biblical Theology,* 2003, p. 251.

your God; your sins have hidden his face from you, so that he will not hear. For your hands are stained with blood, your fingers with guilt. Your lips have spoken falsely, and your tongue mutters wicked things. No one calls for justice; no one pleads a case with integrity. They rely on empty arguments, they utter lies; they conceive trouble and give birth to evil" (Isa. 59:2–4).

How disappointing it is to see Cain's lineage corrupted to this level of immorality and self-centeredness. Let that be a lesson to us to cherish God's presence and His command to maintain love for our fellow man.

Enoch: A Heart in Total Faithfulness to God

"Adam made love to his wife again, and she gave birth to a son and named him Seth, saying, 'God has granted me another child in place of Abel, since Cain killed him.' Seth also had a son, and he named him Enoch. At that time people began to call on the name of the LORD" (Gen. 4:25–26).

There were no descendants of Abel, but the descendants of Seth, Adam and Eve's third child, are a sharp contrast to those of Cain. Seth's lineage can be traced all the way down to Jesus (see Luke 3:23–38).

The impenitence and apostasy of Cain must have caused great remorse to Adam and Eve. Their sin had removed them from a close relationship with God and disappointment was compounded by the loss of Abel at the hand of Cain. However, they stayed faithful and obedient to God's command to be fruitful and increase in number, to fill the earth and subdue it, by having more children, starting with Seth. God assured them that, while they sinned, they would still receive His mercy, forgiveness, and grace.

Verse 26 ends with, "At that time people began to call on the name of the Lord." To call on God's name means to express trust and confidence in the God who has revealed his character.[82] "And everyone who

---

[82]Graeme Goldsworthy, *According to Plan: The Unfolding Revelation of God in the Bible,* 1991, p. 113.

calls on the name of the LORD will be saved; for on Mount Zion and in Jerusalem there will be deliverance, as the LORD has said, even among the survivors whom the LORD calls" (Joel 2:32). This is an indication of formalized community worship, not so much a formal religious ceremony, but more like communal worship and praise.

Faith and obedience continued in Seth's lineage, and it thrived in God's presence. A faithful environment existed here, unlike the void that enveloped Cain's lineage. We have a sense of spiritual renewal, a connection and relationship with God. Since there is a reference to "people" in the verse, it may be that Seth's descendants worshiped God in public and solemn assemblies. Their spiritual hearts were healthy.

Matthew Henry notes, "The worshippers of God began to distinguish themselves...Now that Cain and those that had deserted religion had built a city, and begun to declare for impiety and irreligion, and call themselves the *sons of men,* those that adhered to God began to declare for him and his worship and call themselves the *sons of God.*"[83]

This religious practice and worship of God continued through Seth's descendants. Then, six generations later, there was Enoch. "When Enoch had lived 65 years, he became the father of Methuselah. After he became the father of Methuselah, Enoch walked faithfully with God 300 years and had other sons and daughters. Altogether, Enoch lived a total of 365 years. Enoch walked faithfully with God; then he was no more because God took him away" (Gen. 5:21–24).

In these few verses, we see that Enoch was dedicated to God his entire life. The religious atmosphere that remained within Seth's lineage allowed his descendants to maintain their relationship with God; their faithfulness and obedience were still the order of the day. Humility and worship of God continued through Enoch whose name meant "teaching" or "consecrated one," so he must have been well-versed in God's way and was blessed by God.

Enoch was a man whose lifestyle was in step with God and, except for Elijah the prophet, Enoch was the only other person who didn't

---

[83]Matthew Henry, "Commentary on Genesis 4 by Matthew Henry," Blue Letter Bible, last modified March 1, 1996, https://www.blueletterbible.org/Comm/mhc/Gen/Gen_004.cfm.

experience death. The book of Hebrews describes this extraordinary event and the strength of his faith. "By faith Enoch was taken from this life so that he did not experience death: 'He could not be found, because God had taken him away.' For before he was taken, he was commended as one who pleased God" (Heb. 11:5).

Enoch walked with God and demonstrated that his heart was close with Him. In his commentary on the book of Zechariah, George Klein writes that "walk" is "the metaphorical sense of living one's life...in a moral and spiritual fashion, abiding by the Lord's decrees."[84] That he was especially mentioned as walking faithfully with God, Enoch would have demonstrated the righteousness and obedience that marked the heart for God as defined in this text. John Sailhamer notes that "Enoch's escape from death is tied directly to the fact that 'he walked with God.' This phrase 'walked with God' describes a life of faithfulness and obedience with God."[85]

Enoch had a true relationship with God, much like Adam and Eve had while they were in the Garden of Eden. In our definition of the heart, to walk with God is to live a life based on humility and selflessness. It is a life of communion with God and following His will. To love God with our whole heart, mind, and strength is to make God's word our rule and glorify Him with our actions. We are to please God and do nothing to offend him. These traits were characterized in Enoch's life.

I'd like to think that his faithful walk with God could be taken literally and figuratively. Enoch was so obedient and faithful to God that the Lord may have physically walked with him as He used to walk with Adam and Eve in Eden before they sinned. Obviously, he kept God's commands and it appears his relationship with God was personal like that of Abraham and Moses. That he walked faithfully with God for 300 years is remarkable. He did not waiver in his faithfulness, nor did he ever fall out with God.

---

[84]George Klein, *The New American Commentary – Zechariah,* 2008, p. 141.

[85]John Sailhamer, *The Expositor's Bible Commentary – Genesis,* 2008, p. 108.

David Guzik writes that Enoch was a godly man without peers in his generation. "It seems Enoch began to walk with God in a special way after the birth of **Methuselah**. The name Methuselah means, *When he is dead, it shall come.* At the birth of Methuselah, Enoch had a special awareness from God that judgment was coming, and this was one of the things that got him closer in his walk with God."[86] This was the revelation of the flood, which did not begin until after Methuselah died.

In the *First Book of Enoch*[87] (from the collection of books translated by Joseph Lumpkin), Lumpkin writes of the prediction of the flood, "And in those days, punishment will come from the Lord of spirits, and he will open all the storehouses of waters above the heavens, and all the fountains which are under the surface of the earth. And all the waters shall come together (flow into or be joined) with the waters of heaven (above the sky)...And they shall destroy all who live on dry land and those who live under the ends of heavens."[88]

Notice Lumpkin's depiction of the flood compared to what we read in Genesis 7: "In the six hundredth year of Noah's life, on the seventeenth day of the second month—on that day all the springs of the great deep burst forth, and the floodgates of the heavens were opened" (v. 11). They depict the same result of the flood: "Everything on dry land that had the breath of life in its nostrils died. Every living thing on the face of the earth was wiped out; people and animals and the creatures that move along the ground and the birds were wiped from the earth. Only Noah was left, and those with him in the ark" (vv. 22–23).

In the *First Book of Enoch*, we find that Enoch is taken up to heaven and is witness to the many warehouses containing the snows, rains,

---

[86]David Guzik, "Study Guide for Genesis 5 by David Guzik," Blue Letter Bible, last modified February 21, 2017, https://www.blueletterbible.org/Comm/guzik_david/StudyGuide 2017-Gen/Gen-5.cfm.

[87]The First Book of Enoch is not within the canon of the Bible. It was likely written between 300–100 BC, but much like Josephus's writing or the Book of Jubilees, it is an interesting reference in Jewish history.

[88]Joseph Lumpkin, *The Books of Enoch: The Angels, The Watchers, and The Nephilim*, 2011, p. 72.

and other weather conditions stored up. It is also revealed to him how those who lived in righteousness are now joined in heaven, and Jesus (referred to as the Elite One) judges the righteous and the wicked. This is clear perspective on the concept of resurrection and judgement at the end of time. "And after that I saw all the secrets of the heavens, and how the kingdom is divided, and how the actions of men are weighed in the balance. And there I saw the mansions of the elect and the mansions of the holy, and my eyes saw all the sinners being driven from there which deny the name of the Lord of spirits, and they were being dragged off; and they could not live there because of the punishment which proceeds from the Lord of spirits" (41:1–2).

Enoch was shown mansions in heaven that were reserved for the elect and the holy. This was the same characterization Jesus used several centuries later to describe the reward His apostles would receive for leaving *their* earthly homes and livelihoods to follow Him. "'Let not your heart be troubled; you believe in God, believe also in Me. In My Father's house are many mansions; if it were not so, I would have told you. I go to prepare a place for you. And if I go and prepare a place for you, I will come again and receive you to Myself; that where I am, there you may be also'" (John 14:1–3 NKJV).

In the *First Book of Enoch*, Enoch also refers to Jesus as the Son of Man later in his vision of heaven. "And I asked the angel who went with me and showed me all the hidden things, concerning that Son of Man, who he was, and where he came from and why he went with the Ancient One? And he answered and said to me: This is the Son of Man, who hath righteousness, with whom dwells righteousness, and who reveals all the treasures that which is hidden because the Lord of spirits hath chosen him...and this Son of Man whom you have seen shall raise up the kings and the mighty from their seats, and the strong from their thrones...and this Son of Man shall put down the kings from their thrones and kingdoms because they do not exalt and praise Him, nor humbly acknowledges who bestowed their kingdom on them" (Chapter 46:2–5).[89]

---

[89] Ibid., p. 65.

F. F. Bruce reiterates the connection of the Son of Man to Jesus, referring to *The First Book of Enoch* later in the text. Enoch is again called to heaven where, up to this point, the name for the Son of God is "kept secret until near the end of the of the *Similitudes.*"[90] Bruce continues that in Chapter 71 of the *First Book of Enoch*, he was greeted by God and met with these words. "Thou art the son of men who art born for righteousness; righteousness abides over thee and righteousness of the Head of days forsakes thee not (71:14)."[91] While the *First Book of Enoch* was written closer to the second century BC, Bruce makes it clear that this writing was not one of a Christian so that it remained a prophetic revelation.

In a letter to his generation warning against the mistakes Enoch recognized during his time, Jude writes, "Enoch, the seventh from Adam, prophesied about them: 'See, the Lord is coming with thousands upon thousands of his holy ones to judge everyone, and to convict all of them of all the ungodly acts they have committed in their ungodliness, and of all the defiant words ungodly sinners have spoken against him.' These people are grumblers and faultfinders; they follow their own evil desires; they boast about themselves and flatter others for their own advantage" (Jude 1:14–16).

Jude's letter revealed Enoch's testimony against the practices during his time. H. C. Leupold adds, "Luther rightly contends that Enoch's communion with God was coupled with the aggressive testimony to the unbelievers of his own generation and therefore, he is to be regarded as a man who manifested 'great boldness in testifying for the Lord and His church against Satan's church and that of the Cainites.'"[92]

During His "walks" with Enoch, perhaps God discussed how things on earth were to play out. This may also be what Jude had in mind when he wrote that Jesus would come in judgement and the wicked would be convicted by their actions, words, and attitudes. Those that

---

[90]F. F. Bruce, *New Testament History,* 1969, p. 132.

[91] Ibid.

[92]H. C. Leupold, *Exposition of Genesis: Volumes 1 and 2,* 1942, p. 243.

boast about themselves bear a striking resemblance to Lamech. Jude's point was that Enoch prophesied Jesus's coming in judgement long before the flood, which implied that this was another conversation God had with Enoch in their walks. Enoch was given a lot of information about what the future would bring. A prophet long before Moses, Enoch's relationship with God was revealed to be very special because of his devotion, obedience, and faith in God. His heart must have been as pure and holy in His image as his relationship with God reflected that of Adam and Eve before they sinned. He received the ultimate reward for his purity of heart.

Chapter 3

Abraham: The Evolution of an Obedient Heart

braham is one of the most revered names from the Old Testament. God made His covenant with Abraham to make his descendants as numerous as the stars, to make his name well-known throughout the ages and through him, all nations would be blessed: the father of many nations (Gen. 17:4–8). It was Abraham's direct descendants that God chose to be His people and in 400 years, He delivered them out of Egypt and made them a nation of priests, and He was their God. This covenant reset God's plan to dwell with His people like the arrangement originally intended for Adam and Eve. They served as regents and priests of the land and were His holy representatives here on earth. Abraham was selected to be at the core of God's plan. As Paul House notes, "It is impossible to measure the significance of Abraham. He begins the Jewish race. He receives the eternal promises of God. Through him three major religions—Judaism, Christianity, and Islam—trace their roots...all that God intends to do for [93] [94]

Abraham was a man of great faith in an otherwise secular environment and his obedience to God caused the prophet Isaiah to count him as a friend to God. "'But you, Israel, my servant, Jacob, whom I have chosen, you descendants of Abraham my friend'" (Isa. 41:8). His obedience to God serves as one of the more familiar examples of the spiritual heart, and his faith caused Paul to recall Abraham

---

[93]

[94]Paul House, *Old Testament Survey,* 1992, p. 38.

in his letter to the Romans as righteous. "What does Scripture say? 'Abraham believed God, and it was credited to him as righteousness'" (Rom. 4:3). In his epistle, James concurred with Isaiah and Paul. "And the scripture was fulfilled that says, 'Abraham believed God, and it was credited to him as righteousness,' and he was called God's friend" (Jas 2:23).

Anthony Petterson writes, "Relationship with God is not earned through obedience; rather, obedience is the sign of being in right relationship with God."[95] As will be noted throughout the text, it is through God's grace that we have our relationship with Him; we do not earn it. This will be reflected in Volume II where we discuss how the Jewish leaders felt entrance into God's kingdom was earned through good acts. It was not the action of obedience that Abraham earned the right to be called a friend to God, but it was a natural result of the reflection in His image that is seen through Abraham's story.

Despite the nature of his ever-evolving spiritual heart, the obedience of Abraham is perhaps the most exemplary in the Old Testament. On two occasions he demonstrated total submission to God's will. First, he obeyed God's command to leave the place he was born to go to a new land that God would show him. This meant leaving Ur of the Chaldeans, a highly developed city, to go to the unfamiliar land of Canaan. With his total trust in God to move to an unknown territory, Abraham's obedience resulted in his being a chosen one for a special role in God's plan of salvation for humankind.

Second, he obeyed God's command to offer his one and only son Isaac as a sacrifice despite waiting 100 years for Isaac to be born. This was the ultimate test for Abraham to place his utmost trust into God's hands and demonstrated his obedience regardless of what God required of him. Abraham was about 125 years old before this final test was met successfully. It can take a lifetime to develop a trust in total obedience to God's will, a lesson of patience for us all. Abraham was very close with God; he was considered His friend and he was

---

[95]Anthony Petterson, *ESV Expository Commentary (Volume 7): Daniel–Malachi (Zechariah)*, 2018, p. 635.

blessed. Like Abraham, none of us are prefect and need fine tuning now and again. It is important to remember that God's love, mercy, and patience for us is no less than what he showed Abraham.

Though Abraham's obedience is well documented, he occasionally took matters into his own hands rather than trust God for everything. Bruce Waltke notes, "The Bible does not, however, paint a picture of a man of perfect faith, but of a man who stumbles and gets hurt. He is slow to leave his homeland for an unseen land; when he arrives, he walks right through it to feast on Egypt's bread; and he obeys Sarah and seeks at first to fulfill the divine promise of a seed through his own, not God's empowering. Finally, just before the birth of Isaac, he pulls the same 'sister' deception he had used in Egypt. Thus, even the greatest hero of faith sometimes fails."[96]

His story, however, demonstrates the gradual evolution of his heart and God's mercy and patience to wait on Abraham's spiritual growth. By the time God instructed him to sacrifice Isaac, Abraham had developed such a strong trust that he proceeded willingly, without question. He finally realized that by believing in God's promises and blessings, he could leave everything in His hands.

In the method of contrasting hearts, we can draw some comparison of Abraham's spiritual development to that of his nephew Lot, who traveled with Abraham early in their journey from Ur to Egypt and back to the land of Canaan. We will focus on what was in their hearts that determined how each man would make decisions in their lives. Lot's heart was not in direct contrast as described in the previous chapter; he was not wicked or evil like Cain and Lamech. But Lot's motivation for decision-making contrasted with Abraham's.

While Lot had faith in God, he made decisions based on earthly circumstances and didn't follow God's direction. He was living in Sodom when God chose to destroy it and the city of Gomorrah for their wicked and evil ways. But Lot tried to maintain some level of spirituality during the event. In his second epistle, Peter noted the positive side of Lot: "and if he rescued Lot, a righteous man, who was

---

[96]Bruce Waltke, *An Old Testament Theology,* 2007, p. 333.

distressed by the depraved conduct of the lawless (for that righteous man, living among them day after day, was tormented in his righteous soul by the lawless deeds he saw and heard)—" (2 Peter 2:7–8). Lot's dilemma was that he tried to straddle both earthly and spiritual worlds, but with no success in either.

Abraham, however, displayed a steady improvement in his obedience to God, eschewing the city life of Ur and Sodom. He gave God the credit for his blessings and rewards. He followed God's direction, not always perfectly but always willingly. And, as described in Chapter 1, Abraham had the core ingredients to display the image of God through his morality and integrity.

Background

Chapter 2 ended with comparing the spiritual hearts of Enoch and Lamech. As we continue our way through the early chapters of Genesis, we find that disobedience against God was spreading like a cancer throughout humanity. It would be centuries before God called upon Abraham to start things anew. Meanwhile God had to deal with the disappointing behavior of mankind.

It was another 550 years after Enoch was taken up by God when Noah was told to build the ark. During that interlude, the spiritual heart of mankind was in a deadly decline. Evil spread to such an extent that God planned to bring floodwaters on the earth that would doom all mankind except for Noah and his family. "The LORD saw how great the wickedness of humanity had become on the earth, and that every inclination of the thoughts of the human heart was only evil all the time. The LORD regretted that he had made human beings on the earth, and his heart was deeply troubled. So, the LORD said, 'I will wipe from the face of the earth the human race I have created—and with them the animals, the birds and the creatures that move along the ground—for I regret that I have made them'" (Gen. 6:5–7). God's course of action was to wipe everything out by flooding the earth and start anew.

The whole earth was corrupt, and violence ruled the day, much like it was in Lamech's time. All connections with God were extinguished; there was no mention of worship or reverence to God at all. In all of this, only Noah was blameless in God's eyes; he was righteous and walked with God in the same manner as Enoch. "But Noah found favor in the eyes of the LORD. This is the account of Noah and his family. Noah was a righteous man, blameless among the people of his time, and he walked faithfully with God" (Gen. 6:8–9). Because of his devotion to God, Noah and his family were spared God's wrath against the evil that had extended to the entire population.

God commanded Noah to build an ark to house pairs of animals that He would spare along with Noah's family. The enormity of the project took several decades to complete. Scriptures say that Noah was 500 years old when he had his sons Seth, Ham, and Japheth (Gen. 5:32) and God's instruction to bring "you and your sons and your wife and your sons' wives with you" (Gen. 6:18) imply his sons were old enough to be married. We read that Noah was 600 years old when he entered the ark, so it must have taken Noah at least 50 years to complete the construction.

During this period, Noah's time was not solely dedicated to building the ark. In his second letter, Peter identified Noah as a preacher: "if he [God] did not spare the ancient world when he brought the flood on its ungodly people, but protected Noah, a preacher of righteousness, and seven others..." (2 Peter 2:5). Noah's preaching was to get people to realize their sins and turn back to God. Otherwise, like Sodom and Gomorrah, God's wrath would destroy everyone. In those two cities, only Lot and his two daughters were spared; in the flood, only Noah and his family were spared for their righteousness.

Noah built the ark per God's instructions and faithfully obeyed all that God had commanded him. When God told Noah to board the ark with the animals and his family, the heavens and earth opened up and flooding commenced. "In the six hundredth year of Noah's life, on the seventeenth day of the second month—on that day all the springs of the great deep burst forth, and the floodgates of the heavens were opened" (Gen. 7:11). Rain fell on the earth for 40 forty days and 40 forty nights and it covered the entire earth. So high were the waters that the mountains were some 20 feet under water. Every living creature was blotted out and God began anew with Noah and his family. A little over a year later, when the waters finally receded and Noah was on dry land, he built an altar and made a sacrifice in worship and thanks to God.

God was happy with the sacrifice. "The LORD smelled the pleasing aroma and said in his heart: 'Never again will I curse the ground because of humans, even though every inclination of the human heart is evil from childhood. And never again will I destroy all living creatures, as I have done'" (Gen. 8:21). It is comforting to note once again, that God overlooks the sinful nature of our hearts to bestow His grace and mercy.

God then assigned Noah the same mission that was given to Adam. "Then God blessed Noah and his sons, saying to them, 'Be fruitful and increase in number and fill the earth'" (Gen. 9:1). God also gave Noah authority to rule over all the animals and allowed all the plants and animals for food just as Adam and Eve were given food in Eden (the exception being Noah and his descendants could eat animals as well as plants).

God made a covenant with Noah that He would never repeat man's destruction by way of flood, regardless of the evilness of man's heart. The covenant also included rules for preserving the lives of man and animal. "'And for your lifeblood I will surely demand an accounting. I will demand an accounting from every animal. And from each human being, too, I will demand an accounting for the life of another human being. Whoever sheds human blood, by humans shall their blood be shed; for in the image of God has God made mankind'" (Gen. 9:5–6). Allen Ross writes, "The Noahian covenant then was installed to ensure the stability of life and of nature. It recorded God's guarantee of the order of the world. People would learn here that law was necessary for preserving life and punishing wickedness if social order was to survive.

So, a basic principle of human government was established with this covenant."[97]

There was an incident following this high note of Noah's spiritual closeness with God that is worth noting. Scriptures recount later, that in cultivating the land, Noah got drunk from wine he had made from the grape harvest and was found naked in his tent by his son Ham. "When he drank some of its wine, he became drunk and lay uncovered inside his tent. Ham, the father of Canaan, saw his father naked and told his two brothers outside...When Noah awoke from his wine and found out what his youngest son had done to him, he said, 'Cursed be Canaan! The lowest of slaves will he be to his brothers'" (Gen. 9:21–22, 24–25). It was not long before Noah's spiritual goodness started to sour. Paul House comments, "Any hope that the promises in Genesis 8 will lead to the elimination of sin is dashed...Noah himself becomes drunk and lies uncovered in his tent. While in this condition, Noah's son Ham defiles his father."[98]

While the nature of the defilement was not specified, some have speculated that it may have been sexual in nature. David Guzik says, "It may be Noah was abused sexually by one of his sons or relatives. The phrase 'became uncovered' and the idea of nakedness are sometimes associated with sexual relations (Leviticus 18:6–20)."[99]

When Noah woke up, he realized what his son had done and cursed both Ham and his grandson, Canaan. Again, from David Guzik, "It seems strange that if Ham sinned against Noah, that Canaan (Ham's son) is cursed. Perhaps Canaan was also involved in this sin against Noah in a way not mentioned in the text. Perhaps the strongest punishment against Ham was for Noah to reveal prophetically the destiny of his son Canaan."[100]

---

[97] Allen Ross, *Cornerstone Biblical Commentary: Genesis, Exodus,* 2008, p. 78.

[98] Paul House, *Old Testament Survey,* 1992, p. 33.

[99] David Guzik, "Study Guide for Genesis 9 by David Guzik," Blue Letter Bible, last modified February 21, 2017, https://www.blueletterbible.org/Comm/guzik_david/StudyGuide 2017-Gen/Gen-9.cfm.

[100] Ibid.

Whatever action Ham took against his father, it was sinful in nature. He lacked the obedience of a spiritual heart. This curse on Canaan may not have been targeted to Noah's grandson directly but may be seen as a prophecy against the descendants of Canaan, which is Allen Ross's contention. The curse against Canaan was a prophecy of "...what would become of the descendants of his three sons...Ham's act of hubris and moral abandon would necessarily have extensive repercussions...thus a curse would be on his descendants...Only one line of Ham's family—the Canaanites—was singled out for this curse because they would be the most corrupt and contaminating of all people that Israel had to deal with when they entered the land."[101] This is borne out in the later chapters of this text; by the time the Israelites reached the Promised Land, the land occupied by Canaan's descendants was a nation of pagans with a reputation of immorality that would plague Israel for centuries.

About 100 years after Noah and his family disembarked from the ark and were told to multiply and fill the earth, there was yet another act of disobedience to God's command. Rather than continue to fill the earth as directed, the people that migrated eastward stopped at a plain in Shinar to settle and planned to build a city. From Genesis 10:10, this area was referred to as the city of Babylon: "The first centers of his kingdom were Babylon, Uruk, Akkad and Kalneh, in Shinar." So, it was the tribe of Nimrod (the grandson of Ham) that settled the land under his direction. In translating the meaning of the word Nimrod, H. C. Leupold identifies it as a tyrant, a hunter of men. As noted by Josephus in a later footnote, "...(Nimrod) came to be the first tyrant upon the earth, oppressing others and using them for the furtherance of his own interests."[102]

"Then they said, 'Come, let us build ourselves a city, with a tower that reaches to the heavens, so that we may make a name for ourselves; otherwise, we will be scattered over the face of the whole earth'" (Gen. 11:4). Recall from the previous chapter that Cain built a city

---

[101]Allen Ross, *Cornerstone Biblical Commentary: Genesis, Exodus*, 2008, p. 82.

[102]H. C. Leupold, *Exposition of Genesis: Volumes 1 and 2*, 1942, p. 366.

and named it after his son rather than make any reference or homage to God. The people here were motivated by similar self-interests. And recall the nature of Cain's heart; these people were just as self-invested as Cain. Matthew Henry writes, "It is observable that the first builders of cities, both in the old world [citing Cain's action in Genesis 4:17], and in the new world here, were not men of the best character and reputation: tents served God's subjects to dwell in; cities were first built by those that were rebels against him and revolters from him."[103]

Iain Provan makes a similar observation: "...the true and living God does not enjoy a settled existence in Babylonia with a people whose primary interest is in their own reputation. The true and living God is rather to be found traveling with an obscure people, the family of Abraham, who embark on a long pilgrimage with God throughout the world, leaving Babylonia because God tells them to...In the course of traveling with God, they bless other people, rather than building up their own imperial self-esteem."[104]

Building a city likely involved fortification of some sort for protection from potential enemies, another action that relied less on God's protection and more on man's own devices. They stopped and built a city instead of continuing to fill the earth as commanded by God. Apparently, the consequences of disobedience (the flood) were totally forgotten. And to indicate their level of arrogance, they built a tower to reach the heavens.

Their self-centered attitude to make a name for themselves was to ensure that any neighboring tribe would fear them rather than wage war against them. Their need to stop migrating and build a fortified city was based on their fear of being dispersed over the face of the earth, instead of being dispersed to fill the earth. This behavior showed no obedience or faith in God that He would protect them. H. C. Leupold notes that this signifies their desire to "acquire fame or a reputation...

---

[103]Matthew Henry, "Commentary on Genesis 11 by Matthew Henry," Blue Letter Bible, last modified March 1, 1996, https://www.blueletterbible.org/Comm/mhc/Gen/Gen_011.cfm.

[104]Iain Provan, *Seriously Dangerous Religion: What the Old Testament Says and Why it Matters*, 2014, p. 172.

Nothing shall deter these men, so greedy of enhancing the glory of their own name."[105] And the tower to reach heaven? Perhaps they wanted to be on equal terms with God rather than be subservient to His will; or maybe it was a monument to themselves. It certainly was arrogant.

Building the tower was quite an undertaking. Ruins discovered later indicated that the tower may have been the Tower of Jupiter Belus. It was a quarter mile square at the base and was eight stories (650 feet) high. In the *Book of Jubilees,* there is a detailed account of the tower's construction:

> "They began to build, and in the fourth week, they made a brick with fire and the bricks served them for stone, and the clay with which the cemented them together was asphalt which comes out of the sea, and out of the fountains of water in the land of Shiner. They built it, forty-three years were they building it. Its breadth was 203 bricks, and the height of a brick was a third of one; its height amounted to 5,433 cubits and two palms, and the extent of one wall was thirteen times 600 feet and the other thirty times 600 feet."[106]

In his *Antiquities of the Jews,* Jewish historian Flavius Josephus (94 AD) explains that the construction of the tower was a hubristic act of defiance against God ordered by the arrogant tyrant Nimrod, the grandson of Ham. According to his account, Josephus indicated Nimrod persuaded his people not to ascribe the tower to God, as if it were through His means they were happy, but to believe that it was their own courage which procured that happiness. Nimrod gradually changed the government to one of tyranny, preventing his people from revering God and bringing them to totally depend upon his power. Josephus adds that the people were very ready to follow the determination of Nimrod and to esteem the tower a piece of cowardice to

---

[105]H. C. Leopold, *Exposition of Genesis: Volumes 1 and 2,* 1942, p. 367.

[106]Joseph Lumpkin, *The Book of Jubilees,* 2006, p. 68

submit to God. "When God saw that they acted so madly, he did not resolve to destroy them utterly, since they were not grown wiser by the destruction of the former sinners from the Flood."[107]

God saw the wickedness of this disobedience and as Josephus recounts, there were no lessons learned by the flood; wickedness and selfishness continued. Note that God kept His covenant. Rather than destroy these people outright, He caused them to speak in different languages so they could no longer understand one another. Until that time, everyone spoke just one language. Rather than being unified in defiance to God and doing what they thought was right, God's actions caused them to do the very thing they feared. "So, the LORD scattered them from there over all the earth, and they stopped building the city" (Gen. 11:8). Thus, another setback in mankind's journey to restore their spiritual hearts.

The condition of mankind's spiritual relationship with God that began with Adam and Eve slowly deteriorated over time. Despite clearing out evil and starting anew with Noah's family, the new beginning was not a remedy to correct sinful behavior. Quoting from Gentry and Wellum, "As Bruce Waltke aptly notes, the covenant with Noah is instructive because it shows that being given a fresh start and a clean slate is not a sufficient remedy for the human plight."[108] The story of Noah's drunkenness, Ham's subsequent behavior, and the episode of the Tower of Babel 100 years later proved that the lesson of the flood was quickly forgotten.

Once again, man's ability to be faithful and obedient to God appeared tenuous at best. However, God's steadfast love for His creation endures forever. He would await the arrival of his obedient servant Abraham to continue with His plan for mankind's salvation.

---

[107]Josephus, *Jewish Antiquities,* Book 1, Chapter 4, vv. 113-116.

[108]Peter Gentry and Stephen Wellum, *Kingdom Through Covenant,* 2018, p. 208. Note the same result occurs in the discussion from Chapter 5 when God tried to restart the nation of Israel by preventing the first generation of Jews leaving Egypt from entering the promised land. While the second generation kept their end of the covenant, shortly after that generation dies out, the next generation starts with rejecting God almost immediately.

God's plan to raise a nation of holy and faithful people came from the seed of this one man of faith.

Abram and Lot: Choices Made, Lives Dictated

Out of this previous plague of human condition, God selected Abraham, a righteous man, as a "reset button" to restore His relationship with His creation. As N.T. Wright notes, "Abraham emerges within the structure of Genesis as the answer to the plight of all mankind. The line of disaster and the 'curse' from Adam, through Cain, through the Flood to Babel, begins to be reversed when God call Abraham and says, 'in you shall all the families on earth be blessed.'"[109]

Abram (God renames him Abraham later in recognition of his faith) was born about 350 years after the flood and was a descendant of Noah's son, Shem. Abram's father, Terah, had two other sons, Nahor and Haran. It is likely that their faith in God was maintained much like Seth's lineage remained faithful to God's obedience. They all lived in the city of Ur, a large, progressive metropolis of the time. A thriving commercial and political center, its population in Abram's day could have been 250,000 residents.[110] And, as a major city, it's not likely that it was a spiritual hotbed for God's obedient servants, as we discovered in prior accounts of the nature of hearts dwelling in cities. Polytheism and pagan worship were predominant in Ur.

Terah was a man of means and, as a result, Abram was very well educated growing up in Ur. Josephus records that this education was evident in Abram's first trip to Egypt, where Abram conversed with the Egyptians. He was seen as "...a very wise man, and one of great sagacity, when he discoursed on any subject he undertook; and this not only in understanding it, but in persuading other men also to assent to him. He communicated to them arithmetic and delivered to them the science of astronomy; for before Abram came into Egypt,

---

[109]N. T. Wright, *The New Testament and the People of God*, 1992, p. 262.

[110]Nelson Keyes, *Story of the Bible World*, 1959, p. 16. Ur was a city in southern Mesopotamia; nowadays, the country of Iraq.

they were unacquainted with those parts of learning; for that science came from the Chaldeans into Egypt, and from thence to the Greeks also."[111]

While the family was still in Ur, all three sons were married, and Abram's brother Haran had a son named Lot. Abram married Sarai and the Scriptures tell us right away that Sarai was barren, which became a major focal point of God's plan for Abram's spiritual development. While still in Ur, Abram's brother Haran died; Abram took Lot under his wing and Lot traveled with Abram for many years.

At some point, Terah took Abram, Sarai, and Lot out of Ur to make their way to Canaan. However, they stopped at Harran, some 600 miles north of Ur and settled in this city rather than continuing to Canaan. The reason for their departure from Ur may be found in the disciple Stephen's defense speech presented to the Sanhedrin in the New Testament. In his trial before the religious leaders shortly after Jesus's death, he referenced God's first appearance to Abram taking place while the family was still in Ur. "...'Brothers and fathers, listen to me! The God of glory appeared to our father Abraham while he was still in Mesopotamia, before he lived in Harran. "Leave your country and your people," God said, "and go to the land I will show you." So he left the land of the Chaldeans and settled in Harran. After the death of his father, God sent him to this land where you are now living'" (Acts 7:2–4).

That God directed Abram to leave his country while still in Ur is also found in Nehemiah: "You are the LORD God, who chose Abram and brought him out of Ur of the Chaldeans and named him Abraham. You found his heart faithful to you, and you made a covenant with him to give to his descendants the land of the Canaanites, Hittites, Amorites, Perizzites, Jebusites and Girgashites. You have kept your promise because you are righteous" (Neh. 9:7–8). Nehemiah also referenced Abram's faithful heart as a reason he was called by God. The covenant that Nehemiah mentioned is explored in more detail later in this text.

---

[111]Josephus, *Jewish Antiquities,* Book 1, Chapter 8, v. 167–168.

Perhaps Abram convinced his father to leave Ur because of God's direction. God was obviously directing this faithful family away from the influence of city life, to separate them and to keep them pure. God's desire is that the people He chooses to represent Him be removed from pagan cultures to be holy and obedient. Later in the Old Testament, the influence of their pagan surroundings got increasingly worse for the nation of Israel.

According to Josephus, another explanation for their departure was to demonstrate Abram's strong belief in God. He said that Abram played the part of a missionary, working to convince the polygamists in Ur that "there was but one God, the Creator of the universe; and that, as to other [gods], if they contributed anything to the happiness of men, that each of them afforded it only according to his appointment, and not by their own power."[112] Josephus continues to say that Abram preached that if other gods existed, any power they demonstrated would have to come from God "...to whom alone we ought justly to offer our honor and thanksgiving. For which doctrines, when the Chaldeans, and other people of Mesopotamia, raised a tumult against him, he thought fit to leave that country."[113]

For whichever reason Terah moved from Ur, Stephen's account may indicate that Abram did not obey God's command right away. Abram left the country but not his people. They settled in Harran and not in Canaan, the land to which God was leading Abram. While Abram was faithful, he was not on God's schedule. This was not the only time Abram made decisions on his own; but in His mercy, God worked on strengthening Abram's obedience and trust.

After they settled in Harran, Terah died and the Scriptures report that God directed Abram, who was then 75 years old, to leave his father's household and go to a land that God would show him (the land of Canaan). "The LORD had said to Abram, 'Go from your country, your people and your father's household to the land I will show you. I will make you into a great nation, and I will bless you; I will make your

---

[112] Ibid., Chapter 6, v. 157.

[113] Ibid.

name great, and you will be a blessing. I will bless those who bless you, and whoever curses you I will curse; and all peoples on earth will be blessed through you'" (Gen. 12:1–3). Either God was repeating what He said to Abram in Ur, or Abram remembered God's command and, when his father passed away, decided to continue to Canaan.

David Guzik points out, "These are *God's* promises; notice how often God says **I will** in these verses." He then contrasts this with the story of the Tower of Babel being all about the plans of man while "Genesis chapter 12 [the promises made to Abram] is all about the plans of God."[114] Peter Gentry and Stephen Wellum make a similar comparison. In quoting Bill Arnold, they note, "Yahweh will make Abram's name 'great' which is more than a promise of renown or acclaim. Rather, in contrast to the tower-builders at Babel, who pathetically strove for the permanence themselves by building a name in their own strength (11:4), to have a great name given to one by God in the Hebrews Scriptures is to be viewed as a royal figure."[115]

God was aware of Abram's faithful heart and, on account of his obedience (albeit, still in the developing stages), God promised this unique relationship. God established a nation from His chosen people and made Abram's name known through the ages. Making a great nation from Abram's descendants was an indicator of the protection and relationship Abram had with God. And best of all, God promised that all nations would be blessed through Abram. Thus, God opened the door to His kingdom not only for Abram's descendants, but even the Gentiles in faith. As Paul wrote to Galatia centuries later, "Scripture foresaw that God would justify the Gentiles by faith and announced the gospel in advance to Abraham: 'All nations will be blessed through you.' So those who rely on faith are blessed along with Abraham, the man of faith" (Gal. 3:8–9).

---

[114]David Guzik, "Study Guide for Genesis 12 by David Guzik," Blue Letter Bible, last modified February 21, 2017, https://www.blueletterbible.org/Comm/guzik_david/StudyGuide 2017-Gen/Gen-12.cfm.

[115]Peter Gentry and Stephen Wellum, *Kingdom Through Covenant*, 2018, p. 272.

The book of Hebrews also credits Abram's faith to follow God's commands without reservation, to leave the comfort and familiarity of his family, and to go to another land, not knowing anything about his final destination. "By faith Abraham, when called to go to a place he would later receive as his inheritance, obeyed, and went, even though he did not know where he was going. By faith he made his home in the Promised Land like a stranger in a foreign country; he lived in tents, as did Isaac and Jacob, who were heirs with him of the same promise. For he was looking forward to the city with foundations, whose architect and builder is God" (Heb. 11:8–10).

Abram lived in tents for the remainder of his life once he left Ur. I commented in Chapter 2 how God preferred those who tended livestock (like Abel, Moses, and David), and lived away from the distractions and contamination of city life. Abram and his immediate family (Isaac and grandson Jacob) lived similarly. Later, we find that Lot chose a more urban lifestyle, which drew him away from God's presence.

It is revealed in the last verse of Hebrews 11 that Abram was looking forward to the city built by God; not one of this world, but a heavenly one. This may also explain why Abram was satisfied living in tents. In N.T. Wright's New Testament commentary on Hebrews, he notes "...it is the focal point of the promise about the land. In [Hebrews 12:22 [116]] it is the heavenly Jerusalem...the establishment of the final city of God."[117] T. Desmond Alexander makes a similar observation: "The writer [of Genesis] obviously believes that God had promised Abraham that one day the patriarch would dwell in a divinely constructed city, which he inherits after death."[118]

Abram left his extended family behind and trekked about 400 miles to Canaan. When he got to Bethel, he built an altar to God to worship Him. (Decades later, Abram's grandson Jacob built an altar in Bethel when he saw visions of angels ascending and descending

---

[116]"But you have come to Mount Zion, to the city of the living God, the heavenly Jerusalem. You have come to thousands upon thousands of angels in joyful assembly."

[117]N. T. Wright, *Hebrews for Everyone*, 2004, pp. 133–34.

[118]T. Desmond Alexander, *From Eden to the New Jerusalem*, 2008, p. 74.

a ladder to and from heaven). The Lord was pleased with Abram's offering and confirmed that this was the land of His promise.

Though God promised to make a nation from his descendants, Sarai was still barren, yet Abram proceeded without question. He firmly believed that God would fulfill His promise. Abram's only failure was that he didn't completely leave his family behind; his nephew Lot continued with him and there were consequences for Abram not following God's commands to the letter.

After some time, there was a famine in the land and Abram went to Egypt. As we will see throughout the Old Testament, there were repercussions any time Egypt was involved when not under God's direction. This was the first of those circumstances. Abram feared that because Sarai was so beautiful (she was over 65 years old by then), the Egyptians would kill him to possess her. When they entered Egypt, Abram and Sarai agreed to tell everyone they were brother and sister.

Abram's prediction was accurate. Egyptians were captivated by her beauty and Sarai was brought to Pharaoh's palace. Pharaoh treated Abram well and supplied him with livestock. However, instead of trusting God to make good on His promises, Abram relied on his own plan. First, he left the land God promised him because of the famine. He did this without inquiring of God. Rather than trust the promises God made, he took matters into his own hands and fled to Egypt. Second, God promised to make a nation from Abram's descendants; specifically, he would have a child through Sarai. By passing his wife off as his sister, Abram risked Sarai being taken as the wife of an Egyptian and bearing children under those circumstances.

As H. C. Leupold notes, "...there is something cowardly and meek about expecting Sarai to encounter the hazards in order that Abram might avoid danger...Sarai's acquiescence, however, seems to grow out of the idea that there actually is no other safe course to follow. She was as sadly deficient in faith as he himself on this occasion."[119] Worse yet, Abram's fear of the Egyptians was unfounded; he forgot that God also

---

[119]H. C. Leupold, *Exposition of Genesis: Volume 1*, 1942, pp. 424–25.

promised to protect him. By acting on his own, Abram's decisions were in direct conflict with God's plans for him.

Of course, God intervened before things went too far by sending a plague on Pharaoh's household. Pharaoh realized this was due to Abram's arrival and was furious with Abram's deceit when the truth of the situation came out. Pharaoh demanded to know why Abram passed Sarai off as his sister. He was offended that Abram thought so little of his host. As one might say today, never accuse anyone of your own imaginations. Abram provided no answer and might have recognized that he deserved the Pharaoh's frustration. Pharaoh ordered Abram to take Sarai and all their possessions and leave Egypt immediately. That was one step forward and two steps back for Abram's obedient heart.

Abram returned to Bethel with Sarai and Lot. There, he built an altar and called on the name of Lord in worship. Despite his lack of trust by going to Egypt, he remained strong in his faith. At this point, he and Lot had increased their wealth and livestock to the point that the land could not support them both. Quarrels began to erupt between their herdsmen and Abram told Lot that they needed to part company to prevent any hardship between them. From the high hills at Bethel, about 20 miles south of Sechem, they surveyed the land and Abram gave Lot the first choice of where to settle. Abram would go in the opposite direction.

Abram's spiritual heart and selflessness were showing, and he was content to take what Lot did not choose. He felt blessed by the Lord and had no reason to greedily take the best land, even though as the elder, he would have first choice. "Lot looked around and saw that the whole plain of the Jordan toward Zoar was well watered, like the garden of the LORD, like the land of Egypt. [This was before the LORD destroyed Sodom and Gomorrah.] So, Lot chose for himself the whole plain of the Jordan and set out toward the east. The two men parted company" (Gen. 13:10–11).

Lot chose the superior site which was very close to the city of Sodom. His thoughts were on earthly rewards, picking the better land to increase his possessions rather than rely on God for continued support or blessings. This is not to say that Lot was greedy; he still had a good, moral heart. It may be that he sought more comfortable urban surroundings, perhaps like Ur where he grew up. He was straddling both worlds; still having faith yet allowing the trappings of the world to pull him down.

After Abram pitched his tents in Canaan, the Lord promised him that the land around him would be for his descendants who would be as numerous as the stars. Abram built another altar to God in thanks. Abram chose the way of God while Lot chose the way of men.

Lot's Heart Chooses This World

At first, Lot settled outside of Sodom, but Scriptures tell us that eventually he would be found sitting at the gate inside the city and that he had a house within Sodom itself. He got drawn into city surroundings and its politics (it is likely he was a judge at the gate). Lot maintained his moral compass as best he could, given that everyone living there was motivated by worldly things, immoral behaviors, and depravity. It's hard to say why this corrupt environment appealed to Lot. Until he parted from Abram, he enjoyed the spiritual benefit of Abram's company. Even though Abram hadn't fully developed his trust in God, he was a spiritual and devoted man and exposed Lot to that faith. The years Lot spent with his uncle must have contributed to his spiritual education and had a great influence on his own spiritual development, as Peter noted in his epistle. But Lot's weaknesses in his own heart prevented him from relying totally on God; instead, he relied on the ways of men.

Lot's difficulties in Sodom began about five years after he settled there. Sodom and the surrounding region had been in servitude to the Assyrians, the military power at the time who controlled much of the Middle East. The Assyrians had defeated the five kings of the region, including the kings of Sodom and Gomorrah. For 12 years, these five kings paid tribute to the Assyrians but at this point, they decided to rebel against the Assyrian control and led their armies to the Valley of Sidon.

The Assyrian army (led by four kings of their own) met the five rebel kings in battle and the latter were soundly defeated. The kings of Sodom and Gomorrah fled from the battle and much of their armies were taken captive, including Lot who had given his assistance to the Sodomites. Scriptures note that, "The four kings seized all the goods of Sodom and Gomorrah and all their food; then they went away. They also carried off Abram's nephew Lot and his possessions, since he was living in Sodom" (Gen. 14:11–12).

Thus begins the consequence of Lot choosing to go the way of man, dwelling in city life rather than communing with God, living in tents, and tending herds like his uncle. To say that the Sodomites were ungodly people is an understatement. Lot went to Sodom with some level of wealth and education. Sitting at the city's gates, he was in a government position or one like a judge. When rebelling against the Assyrians became a rallying cry in the surrounding cities, he chose to enlist in the battle. He was taken captive and lost all the possessions he accumulated while in Sodom. There was no indication that he sought God's protection during the military defeat. God, however, used Abram to rescue Lot.

Fortunately for him, word got to Abram that Lot was among those captured in battle. Abram gathered 318 warriors, some of whom were friends and allies, and fought against the Assyrians holding the captives. Abram's men routed the Assyrians, who fled as far north as Damascus. Lot was rescued along with the other captives and their possessions.

Witness the power of God through Abram. He attacked the Assyrian army—who had just routed five other armies—with a very small force of his own, causing the Assyrians to flee several miles from the battle scene.

This was the first of many times in the Old Testament where God defeated the enemies of His people against huge odds to demonstrate His power. One memorable occurrence took place in the book of Judges when Gideon and an army of just 300 men defeated the combined armies of the Midianites and Amalekites. No number for the size of their force is given, but Scriptures note, "The Midianites, the Amalekites and all the other eastern peoples had settled in the valley, thick as locusts. Their camels could no more be counted than the sand on the seashore" (Judg. 11:7).

After rescuing Lot, Abram returned home in peace while Lot returned to Sodom. It must not have occurred to Lot that God was behind his rescue. He returned to his familiar life in Sodom, rather than asking to return with Abram where he could renew his spiritual condition. Lot lost much of his livestock at this point, so having too much livestock in one spot was no longer a concern. If Lot experienced any awakening from his lost wealth and short captivity, he might have chosen to go the spiritual route and returned to live with Abram under God's blessing and protection. Returning to the secular, sinful world of Sodom, his spiritual heart continued to fade.

The next mention of Lot came with God's judgement of the evil and wicked Sodom and Gomorrah. The Lord visited Abram (now called Abraham) and Sarai (now called Sarah) with two angels to give him the news that they would have a child within a year. During that visit, the Lord considered whether He should share His intention regarding the two sinful cities, knowing full well Lot was still there. "Then the LORD said, 'Shall I hide from Abraham what I am about to do?'" (Gen. 18:17). He decided to share with Abraham what was about to happen. "Then the LORD said, 'The outcry against Sodom and Gomorrah is so great and their sin so grievous that I will go down and see if what they have done is as bad as the outcry that has reached me. If not, I will know'" (vv. 20–21).

As to the moral condition of the cities, they became the "poster child" of evil and depravity throughout Scriptures. Condemning the practices of Israel and Judah that occurred during his time, the prophet Ezekiel exclaimed they exceeded the sins of Sodom. Their deprivation, in his words, exceeded the evil behavior from those of Sodom, which he described in some detail. "'As surely as I live, declares the Sovereign LORD, your sister Sodom and her daughters never did what you and your daughters have done. Now this was the sin of your sister Sodom: She and her daughters were arrogant, overfed, and unconcerned; they did not help the poor and needy. They were haughty and did detestable things before me. Therefore, I did away with them as you have seen'" (Ezek. 16:48–50).

In Josephus' account of the moral deprivation in Sodom, he notes, "About this time the Sodomites grew proud, on account of their riches and great wealth; they became unjust toward men, and impious toward God, insomuch that they did not call to mind the advantages they received from him: they hated strangers and abused themselves with Sodomitical practices. God was therefore much displeased at them, and determined to punish them for their pride, and to overthrow their city, and to lay waste their country, until there should neither plant nor fruit grow out of it."[120] Iain Provan[121] summarizes the transgressions cited in Scriptures to include, a lack of justice,[122] idolatry,[123] arrogant disregard for the poor, (see Ezekiel 16:48–50 above), and sexual perversity.[124]

As His angels left for Sodom, the Lord remained with Abraham, who now realized that Sodom would be doomed, including his

---

[120]Josephus, *Jewish Antiquities,* Book 1, Chapter 11, v. 194–195.

[121]Iain Provan, *Discovering Genesis,* 2015, p. 141.

[122]"Unless the LORD Almighty had left us some survivors, we would have become like Sodom, we would have been like Gomorrah. Hear the word of the LORD, you rulers of Sodom; listen to the instruction of our God, you people of Gomorrah! ... When you come to appear before me, who has asked this of you, this trampling of my courts?" (Isa. 1:9–10, 12). "'The look on their faces testifies against them; they parade their sin like Sodom; they do not hide it. Woe to them! They have brought disaster upon themselves" (Isa. 3:9).

[123]" How could one man chase a thousand, or two put ten thousand to flight, unless their Rock had sold them, unless the LORD had given them up? For their rock is not like our Rock, as even our enemies concede. Their vine comes from the vine of Sodom and from the fields of Gomorrah. Their grapes are filled with poison, and their clusters with bitterness" (Deut. 32:30–32).

[124]"In a similar way, Sodom and Gomorrah and the surrounding towns gave themselves up to sexual immorality and perversion. They serve as an example of those who suffer the punishment of eternal fire" (Jude 1:7).

nephew Lot. Abraham advocated for the sinners of the cities to save them from God's wrath, especially his nephew.[125]

Abraham set the first example of advocacy by asking God to spare His wrath if 50 righteous people could be found in Sodom. The Lord agreed and Abraham, in his realization of the conditions there, continued to renegotiate the number until he gets down to just 10 righteous people, all the while attempting not to try the Lord's patience through the process. He tried hard not to press the issue too far because he knew finding even 10 righteous men in Sodom would be a challenge.[126]

When the two angels arrived in Sodom that evening, they found Lot sitting by the gate. David Guzik notes that his being there indicated he was a civic leader. "The gate area of an ancient city was sort of a town-hall, where the important men of the city judged disputes, conferred with one another, and supervised those who entered and left the city."[127] It was no coincidence that Lot was the only one sitting at the gate on that particular evening. It's not known what his schedule was or what other civic leaders could have been there to meet the angels

---

[125]There will be others in the Scriptures with strong spiritual hearts that will act as advocates before the Lord for the sinners in their midst; Moses clearly does so when his people worship false gods while the Lord is giving him the Ten Commandments. And as will be discussed in the New Testament chapters, Jesus is the ultimate advocate for all of us. Here, Abraham's negotiations with the Lord are the first advocacy before God for sinners noted in the Scriptures.

[126]As it turns out, the angels could only find Lot, his wife and two daughters who were righteous, so both cities are destroyed, as well as some of the smaller cities in the vicinity. While it seems disheartening to hear there were so few righteous people to be found, it was even more condemning much later in the Israelites' history. That occurred at the fall of the nation of Judah by the Babylonians several centuries later. In that instance, God asked the prophet Jeremiah if he could find just one honest man in all Jerusalem then He would spare it from destruction. "Go up and down the streets of Jerusalem, look around and consider, search through her squares. If you can find but one person who deals honestly and seeks the truth, I will forgive this city" (Jer. 5:1). Unfortunately, he couldn't, and the city and the temple are both destroyed.

[127]David Guzik, "Study Guide for Genesis 19 by David Guzik," Blue Letter Bible, last modified February 21, 2017, https://www.blueletterbible.org/Comm/guzik_david/StudyGuide 2017-Gen/Gen-19.cfm.

instead. The timing was right; God knew that Lot was the only righteous person living in Sodom and the angels were sent there to deliver him from the destruction that was about to take place.

Lot saw the angels coming and greeted them, bowing with his face to the ground. He didn't realize they were angels, but he did recognize that they were men of character; he addressed them as "my lords." He invited the angels into his house to wash their feet and to spend the night with him, allowing them to go on their way in the morning. This was hospitable and typical of the Middle Eastern culture at the time.[128] We'll soon see that such hospitality was atypical for the people of Sodom. As a side note, Lot was probably pleased to meet people of character; surely, he could discern the difference.

The angels initially declined his offer, but Lot knew it would be too dangerous for the strangers to remain in the square overnight and insisted that they come with him. They finally agreed and Lot took them home and prepared a meal for them. Lot played the host on his own; his wife did not participate, which is in contrast to when the angels first appeared with the Lord to Abraham and Sarah.

Lot's concern for the safety of the angels was quickly realized. The men of the town heard of their arrival and surrounded Lot's house, demanding that he let the angels out so they could have sex with them. That was the level of depravity that Sodom had reached. Jude referred to it in his epistle. "In a similar way, Sodom and Gomorrah and the surrounding towns gave themselves up to sexual immorality and perversion. They serve as an example of those who suffer the punishment of eternal fire" (Jude 1:7).

In the culture of the Middle East at that time, the safety and protection of guests was tantamount to a host with character. Lot's desire to protect his guests from being sexually assaulted by the townsmen set him apart from those in the city. He maintained some level of morality and his protection of the angels was an indication that he hadn't totally lost his righteousness.

---

[128]Lot's hospitality is not unlike Abraham's when the angels and the Lord arrive at Abraham's tent prior to going on to Sodom.

Lot pled with the townsmen not to undertake such a wicked deed and he offered his virgin daughters instead. Though women occupied a low social standing, giving up his daughters to the angry, depraved crowed made Lot's decision-making morally questionable. His circumstance was a direct consequence of choosing to stay in Sodom.

No amount of moral suasion would stop these men from their evil and wicked ways. "'Get out of our way,' they replied. 'This fellow came here as a foreigner, and now he wants to play the judge! We'll treat you worse than them.' They kept bringing pressure on Lot and moved forward to break down the door" (Gen. 19:9). What's interesting is the attitude they had toward Lot. He lived in Sodom for about 15 years by now and they still considered him to be a foreigner. Worse still was the threat of harm if he didn't get out of their way. This lack of social recognition is likely the result of his morality in the midst of a sinful city. His life wasn't worth much to the Sodomites.

As the men got more and more forceful, the angels pulled Lot into his house before anything happened to him. He was delivered from danger once more by divine intervention, but he wasn't aware of it. Lot was too busy trying to control the situation on his own and didn't reach out to God. He let his spiritual heart wane and relied on his own wits to get out of a dangerous situation.

The angels inflicted blindness on the men outside, but they still groped around trying to get to the door. Such were their evil desires; even blindness would not thwart their actions.

The angels told Lot to flee the city at dawn and to take anyone belonging to him because the city would be destroyed. Lot's soon-to-be sons-in-law laughed at the thought of the whole city being destroyed. He obviously was not a spiritual influence in their lives even though they would soon be a part of the family.

At dawn, Lot continued to straddle spiritual wellbeing against physical comforts. From H. C. Leupold, "Lot, though a saint, is a specimen of weak godliness. He lacks the decision and wholehearted obedience of Abraham. The thought of sacrificing house and home and all his goods makes the departure difficult."[129]

The angels grasped the hands of Lot, his wife, and his two daughters and led them safely out of the city "for the Lord was merciful to them" (Gen. 19:16). The angels told him to flee to the mountains and to not look back, but Lot still didn't understand that God was trying to protect him. He argued that fleeing to the mountains might not be far enough from the destruction to be protected and asked to flee to a small town nearby instead. The angels allowed him to flee to Zoar and spared that town from the oncoming destruction. Against the warnings of the angels to not look back upon the cities when God sent burning sulfur to destroy them, Lot's wife looked back to watch and turned into a pillar of salt. She didn't totally give up her life as a Sodomite and as a result of her disobedience, she suffered the same fate as her townspeople.

From D. A. Carson's footnotes, he observes that "Lot's rescue emphasizes God's concern for the righteous in the midst of a world that stands condemned for its sinfulness."[130] Despite being rescued several times by God's intervention (based on Abraham's prayers for him), Lot's heart for the Lord was not strong at all. He left Zoar despite his plea to the angels to let him go there and went to the mountains anyway because he was afraid to live in the city. He never quite understood that God would have protected him all along.

John Sailhamer adds the other reason for Lot's rescue. He summarizes the nature of Lot's heart: "The picture of Lot, then, is that of a righteous man living amid the unrighteous—a righteous man being rescued from the fate of the wicked through divine intervention. Moreover, not surprisingly, the basis of God's rescue of Lot is not Lot's righteousness, but the Lord's compassion."[131] The reality is that Lot was saved for Abraham's sake, not for his own righteousness.

---

[129]H. C. Leupold, *Exposition of Genesis, Volume 1*, 1942, p. 564.

[130]D. A. Carson, *NIV Zondervan Study Bible*, 2015, p. 68.

[131]John Sailhamer, *The Expositor's Bible Commentary – Genesis*, 2008, p. 198.

Lot's chapter ended on a moral nadir. Living in a cave, his daughters somehow assumed they were the only three survivors (despite having just left the town of Zoar). In a misguided attempt to repopulate the family, they each got Lot drunk and slept with him to preserve the family line. That they had been influenced by the heart of their mother rather than a moral leaning from Lot is apparent. Perhaps their life in Sodom made the idea seem practical and not immoral. In any event, they did not trust that God could provide for the family. Both daughters became pregnant by their father, and each has a son: the oldest named her son Moab, whose descendants became the tribe of Moabites, and the youngest named her son Ben-Ammi, whose descendants become the tribe of the Ammonites.

The tribes of these sons later became the moral thorn in the side of the Israelites for centuries to come. They were the epitome of pagan idol worshipers that would draw the Hebrews away from God with temple practices that included male and female prostitutes, child sacrifice, and other abominations. It was this infestation of pagan culture into Israel's society that would eventually lead to the nation's ultimate destruction and their captivity by the Assyrians and Babylonians. This will be discussed in Chapter 10.

The lineage from Lot's daughters continued the concept that wickedness follows wickedness, as we saw with Cain and his descendant Lamech. Later, we find it was Balak, the Moabite king, who hired the prophet Balaam to curse Israel to ensure Balak would be victorious in battle against them. The Moabites also got some of the Israelites to practice idolatry during their 40 years in the wilderness. This was the same Hebrew generation that did not learn their lesson when they worshiped the golden calf created by Aaron. "While Israel was staying in Shittim, the men began to indulge in sexual immorality with Moabite women, who invited them to the sacrifices to their gods. The people ate the sacrificial meal and bowed down before these gods" (Num. 25:1–2).

As for the Ammonites, Israel would contend with them as a warring enemy just like the Philistines from the time they settled in the Promised Land under Joshua until King David's rule. Even King

Solomon, when he fell prey to idol worship, returned to the pagan practices of both tribes. "On a hill east of Jerusalem, Solomon built a high place for Chemosh the detestable god of Moab, and for Molek the detestable god of the Ammonites" (1 Kgs. 11:7). Thus, Lot's lack of spiritual conviction yielded consequences for centuries to come.

God's Promises for Abram's Faithfulness

Sodom and Gomorrah were the epitome of immorality and wickedness; the cities represented all that was evil in the world. In Genesis 14, after Abram's men defeated the Assyrian army and rescued Lot, the king of Sodom and the other defeated kings met him at the Valley of Shaveh. Abram was also greeted by Melchizedek, the king of Salem and priest of God Most High, who brought bread and wine to the victorious Abram. He blessed God and Abram and acknowledged that it was God who delivered Abram's enemies into his hands. In return for the blessings, Abram gave Melchizedek a tenth of all his possessions.

"By contrast, the king of Sodom and the other kings gave no sign of gratitude for their rescue, no reference to God or blessings, but offered Abram all the goods they plundered as long as Abram returned their men who were held captive."[132] Abram declined, declaring that it is God's blessings that are important, not man's worldly possessions. Abram refused the spoils of war; he was only out to save the life of his nephew.

Abram showed the character of his heart; he relied on God for His protection and blessings, which God provided all along and implicitly, Abram was conscious of God's promises to him. We get a bit more detail from the account given by Josephus:

"Now this Melchisedec supplied Abram's army in a hospitable manner and gave them provisions in abundance; and as they were feasting, he began to praise him, and to bless God for subduing his enemies under him. And when Abram gave him

---

[132]T. Desmond Alexander, *From Eden to the New Jerusalem*, 2008, p. 81.

the tenth part of his prey, he accepted of the gift: but the king of Sodom desired Abram to take the prey but entreated that he might have those men restored to him whom Abram had saved from the Assyrians, because they belonged to him. But Abram would not do so; nor would make any other advantage of that prey than what his servants had eaten; but still insisted that he should afford a part to his friends that had assisted him in the battle. The first of them was called Eschol, and then Enner, and Mambre."[133]

Abram did not rely on help from men or on worldly wealth as a motivator. He demanded that all credit for the victory be given to God alone. "But Abram said to the king of Sodom, 'With raised hand I have sworn an oath to the LORD, God Most High, Creator of heaven and earth, that I will accept nothing belonging to you, not even a thread or the strap of a sandal, so that you will never be able to say, 'I made Abram rich'" (Gen. 14:22–23).

As to the greetings between Abram and Melchizedek, David Guzik observes that the two holy men appear to try to outdo each other in their exchange. "Melchizedek blessed Abram out of his resources, and Abram blessed Melchizedek out of his resources. This is a great attitude for us to have in the community of believers."[134] It is an act of homage and some humility to give thanks to and for one another. In a sense, this is the virtue we observe in the Second Great Commandment, "love your neighbor as yourself." The "image of God" was fondly demonstrated by both men's mutual respect and consideration for each other. Kindness was returned with kindness. Witnessing the king of Sodom's worldly offer seemed awkward in light of their character and paled in comparison.

[133]Josephus, *Jewish Antiquities*, Book 1, Chapter 10, v.182.

[134]David Guzik, "Study Guide for Genesis 14 by David Guzik," Blue Letter Bible, last modified February 21, 2017, https://www.blueletterbible.org/Comm/guzik_david/StudyGuide 2017-Gen/Gen-14.cfm.

By affirming the truthfulness of what Melchizedek had to say and rejecting the offer of the king of Sodom, Abram indicated his own commitment to be a righteous priest-king. Abram did not inherit the earth through the use of aggressive military power, although clearly his defeat of the eastern kings indicated he had the capacity to do so; certainly, with God's assistance. Rather, he looked to God to provide for his future well-being.[135]

It is at this point in the narrative that John Sailhamer notes that "the author [of Genesis] intends to show that Abram is living a life in harmony with God's will even though he lived long before the revelation at Sinai. Abram is one who pictures God's law as written on his heart. He obeys the law, even though the law has not yet been given. In this respect, the picture of Abraham that emerges...is much like that of the 'new covenant' promise in Jeremiah 31:33, where God promises to write the Torah on the hearts of the covenantal people so that they will obey it from the heart."[136]

Sailhamer's observation is aligned with the theme of this text. Recall that in Chapter 1, I noted that the ability to be obedient and faithful to God was inherent in our originally created "image and likeness of God." We were designed to have a pure heart, to be faithful, and to be obedient. While that structure was altered after the fall of Adam and Eve, it was not extinguished. This review of individuals in the Old Testament reveals those like Abraham who had the ingredients of a spiritual heart not to stray far from the original intent of our creation.

Sailhamer's point also falls in line with the apostle Paul's perspective that it wasn't adherence to the Law given to Moses at Mount Sinai that one demonstrated a spiritual heart, but God's image within us. In fact, we see that some level of the spiritual heart was demonstrated before the Law was given to Abraham. Sailhamer connects God's promise through the prophets that His law will be written in

---

[135]T. Desmond Alexander, *From Eden to the New Jerusalem*, 2008, p. 82.

[136]John Sailhamer, *The Expositor's Bible Commentary – Genesis*, 2008, p. 167.

the heart as spoken through Jeremiah and Ezekiel's prophesies.[137] The running theme here is that what was given to us as God's image at creation is maintained in some degree in the hearts of individuals prior to the codification of God's commandments.[138] By staying in God's presence and following His will in obedience, Abraham's heart maintained his righteousness. Lot, on the other hand, wandered away from God, and suffered the consequence of his focus on the things of this world.

God appeared to Abram (note that God will later rename him as Abraham when he accepts God's covenant) in a vision to reiterate His promises. Several years had passed, and Abram was concerned that he still did not have an heir. God reassured Abram that his heir would be his own flesh and blood, then led him outside to show him the stars in the sky: they were countless, as would be Abram's descendants. At this, "Abram believed the LORD, and he credited it to him as righteousness" (Gen. 15:6). Abram's faith made him right with God. God told Abram that he would possess all the land around him, and God asked for a sacrifice to show Abram He would keep his promise, which Abram immediately obeyed.

God revealed His long-term plan for Abram's descendants. "Then the LORD said to him, 'Know for certain that for four hundred years your descendants will be strangers in a country not their own and that they will be enslaved and mistreated there. But I will punish the nation they serve as slaves, and afterward they will come out with great possessions. You, however, will go to your ancestors in peace,[139] and be buried at a good old age. In the fourth generation your descendants

---

[137]I will discuss the prophets' concept of the "new creation, God's writing the law into our hearts in Chapter 14.

[138]Of course, the improvement of our spiritual heart can only be amplified by Jesus dying for our sins and having God's law written in our hearts by accepting His sacrifice and the infusion of the Holy Spirit. However, with respect to these righteous examples from the Old Testament, suffice it to say that the spiritual heart still functioned to some degree.

[139]H. C. Leupold notes, "The expression, 'you shall go to your [ancestors] in peace' must involve more than having his own dead body laid beside the dead bodies of the fathers. We find here a clear testimony to belief in an eternal life in patriarchal age" (*Exposition of Genesis: Volume 1*, 1942, pp. 485–86).

will come back here, for the sin of the Amorites has not yet reached its full measure'" (Gen. 15:13–16).

God laid out His plan to build a nation from Abram's descendants. While not mentioned explicitly, the land in which his descendants would serve and be afflicted included their time in Egypt and their captivity prior to Moses leading them to the Promised Land. God would judge the nation (Egypt) with ten plagues until Pharaoh released the people. That "they will come out with great possessions" occurred when the Egyptians gave the Hebrews jewels and gold upon their departure, likely because they were glad to be rid of the cause of the plagues. "The Israelites did as Moses instructed and asked the Egyptians for articles of silver and gold and for clothing. The LORD had made the Egyptians favorably disposed toward the people, and they gave them what they asked for; so, they plundered the Egyptians" (Ex. 12:35–36). Events of the captivity and exodus from Egypt will be described in Chapter 6.

In Chapter 5, I will discuss how Joseph (Abram's great-grandson) arrived in Egypt and how Jacob (Abram's grandson) and his 70 family members were brought to Egypt and fulfilled God's promise to Abram. From the time Jacob arrived in Egypt until the Israelites reached the Promised Land was approximately 215 years.[140]

The Lord said to Abram, "In the fourth generation your descendants will come back here, for the sin of the Amorites has not yet reached its full measure" (Gen. 15:16). The Amorites were either synonymous with the nation of Canaanites or a subset of the group. As Allen Ross notes, "In order to give the Promised Land to Israel, the inhabitants of the land had to be dispossessed—it was part of the curse on Canaan." The reference here is from Noah's story in Genesis 9:25: "he said, 'Cursed be Canaan! The lowest of slaves will he be to his brothers.'" Ross contends this is a prophecy that God would wait until the sin of the Amorites grew so great, judgement would fall on them. This judgement allowed the Israelites to drive them out, but not wipe them out completely. This occurred when Saul was king of Israel and

---

[140]The calculation for this amount of time is provided in Appendix A.

the prophet Samuel commanded Saul to destroy the Amalekites as described in Chapter 8. God would tolerate the sins of the Amalekites until they were fully deserving of judgement.[141]

Jacob and his family numbered 70 members when they first entered Egypt and by the time God's chosen people were allowed to leave Egypt, there were more than 620,000 Jewish males above 20 years of age. There may have been 2 to 3 million people coming from Jacob's small family. God left His people in Egypt long enough for Abram's descendants to be as countless as the stars; they were, indeed, a nation. Abram was told all this centuries before the details of God's plan came to fruition.

After living in Canaan for 10 years (Abram is 85 years old and Sarai is 75), Sarai was desperate to give her husband a child. She decided to take control of the situation rather than wait upon the Lord's promise. She gave Abram her Egyptian handmaiden, Hagar, to bear a child as her surrogate. Hagar most likely was one of the gifts Pharaoh gave them when they first arrived in Egypt. This is another action not directed by God that would have serious consequences for His people. Abram's trust in God's promise got wobbly when he agreed to this earthly arrangement. In fact, Abram was working against God instead of with Him.

John Sailhamer notes a recurring theme in Genesis, "namely the attempt and failure of human effort in obtaining the blessing that only God can give. God promised humankind a blessing, and human beings put it aside in favor of their own attempts to obtain blessing."[142] D. A. Carson concurs that the human attempt to fulfill God's plan fails; God fulfills His promise when Sarai gives birth to Isaac several years later.[143]

One of the problems with multiple wives (including concubines such as Hagar) is the possible rivalry in childbearing and the nature of selfish hearts that arises from competition. "He slept with Hagar,

---

[141]Allen Ross, *Cornerstone Biblical Commentary: Genesis Exodus,* 2008, p. 112.

[142]John Sailhamer, *The Expositor's Bible Commentary – Genesis,* 2008, p. 176.

[143]D. A. Carson, *NIV Zondervan Study Bible,* 2015, p. 52.

and she conceived. When she knew she was pregnant, she began to despise her mistress" (Gen. 16:4). I will note later how Rachel and Leah, wives of Jacob, were so competitive in providing children to Jacob that they each gave their servants to their husband to be surrogates of sorts, showing that selfish attitudes could be bred. The rivalry between Sarai and Hagar was one of the first examples of how competing for a husband's attention gets out of control. It was for a very good reason God insisted on one man and one woman for a marriage and why polygamy would be problematic and immoral.

When she got pregnant, Hagar made it clear to Sarai that Abram was not the problem; it was Sarai who couldn't conceive and Hagar ridiculed Sarai. Hagar's attitude infuriated Sarai, who now blamed her husband for the whole situation even though it was her idea. Abram washed his hands of the situation by telling Sarai to do what she wished with Hagar, as it was her handmaiden. Both parties viewed the situation in a worldly manner.

Sarai banished the pregnant Hagar to the desert. Through God's mercy and compassion, Hagar was rescued by the Angel of the Lord[144] who promised to protect her, and her son would live to have many descendants. "The angel added, 'I will increase your descendants so much that they will be too numerous to count'" (Gen. 16:10).[145] He also instructed Hagar to return to Sarai in submission, which she did. She bore a son and named him Ishmael. D. A. Carson says that "Recognizing Ishmael as his heir, Abram must have believed that here was God's solution to the continuation of his family and the fulfillment of the divine promise."[146] Of course, it was not; God's promise

---

[144]I agree with several authors that the title "Angel of the Lord" is a pre-incarnation earthly visit in physical form by Jesus, known as a Christophany. This is one of several accounts in the Old Testament of a brief visit by Jesus's physical presence here on earth prior to His mission.

[145]That He promises Hagar to increase her descendants is an action of God, not an angel. For a full description of this and other accounts of potential Christophanies, see James Borland, *Christ in the Old Testament: Old Testament Appearances of Christ in Human Form.*

[146]D. A. Carson, *NIV Zondervan Study Bible*, 2015, p. 53.

was fulfilled through Sarai, not from a plan concocted by Sarai. Carson describes the difference between man's plan and that of God's: "From Paul's letter to the Galatians [vv.21–31], this contrast between the son of the promise [Sarah's child] and the son of the slave woman [Hagar].

Covenant for Abraham's Obedience

The lack of trust on Abram and Sarai's behalf delayed God's promise another 13 years. His plan was not to be thwarted or modified, but to be trusted. They both came to understand this in time. They continued to wait, but their trust and obedience had to grow to fully believe in His promise. When Abram was 99 years old, the Lord appeared to him and announced. "'I am God Almighty; walk before me faithfully and be blameless. Then I will make my covenant between me and you and will greatly increase your numbers'" (Gen. 17:1–2). In asking him to walk faithfully and be blameless, God communed with Abram in the same manner as He did with Adam and Eve in Eden and with Enoch. God renamed him Abraham, the father of nations.

John Sailhamer said that this walk with God represents Abram's trust and obedience with Him. Abram's faithful heart continued to evolve, and God revealed His covenant for Abram's descendants: He would be their God and they would be His people and live in the land that God has promised.[147] "I will establish my covenant as an everlasting covenant between me and you and your descendants after you for the generations to come, to be your God and the God of your descendants after you. The whole land of Canaan, where you now reside as a foreigner, I will give as an everlasting possession to you and your descendants after you; and I will be their God" (Gen. 17:7–8).

As an indication of their commitment to God's covenant, all the males (starting with Abraham) would be circumcised. "Then God said to Abraham, 'As for you, you must keep my covenant, you, and your descendants after you for the generations to come. This is my covenant with you and your descendants after you, the covenant you

---

[147]John Sailhamer, *The Expositor's Bible Commentary – Genesis*, 2008, p. 179

are to keep: Every male among you shall be circumcised. You are to undergo circumcision, and it will be the sign of the covenant between me and you'" (vv. 9–11). Allen Ross states, "The rite of circumcision is a symbol of purity, of loyalty to the covenant, and a separation from the life of the world."[148]

H. C. Leupold notes that the practice represents "...what obligations are laid upon those who stand in covenant relation with God, namely, primarily to put away the foreskin of their heart (Jer. 4:4),[149] to circumcise the heart and no longer be stiff-necked...(Deut. 10:16)[150]...Secondly, this rite is tied up closely with the Messianic hope. For if it indicates the purification of life at its source, it in the last analysis points forward to Him through whom all such purification will be achieved..."[151] From God's perspective, Stephen Dempster adds, "Just as the rainbow (the sign of the war bow pointing in the sky) reminds God of his promise to preserve creation from another judgement by flood, so circumcision (the sign of the knife in the flesh) is to remind him of his promise of descendants in the face of the curse of sterility and death."[152]

God reiterated His promise that Sarai, who was then called Sarah, would be blessed, and would bear him a son: "'I will bless her and will surely give you a son by her. I will bless her so that she will be the mother of nations; kings of peoples will come from her'" (Gen. 17:16). Abraham fell face down in respect and reverence, but laughed to himself, more in amazement than being disrespectful. He was almost 100 years old, and Sarah was 10 years younger; how could this happen? His trust still needed evolving as he didn't quite understand that with

---

[148] Allen Ross, *Cornerstone Biblical Commentary: Genesis, Exodus,* 2008, p. 122.

[149] "Circumcise yourselves to the LORD, circumcise your hearts, you people of Judah and inhabitants of Jerusalem, or my wrath will flare up and burn like fire because of the evil you have done—burn with no one to quench it." Circumcision of the heart is discussed in more detail in Chapter 11.

[150] "Circumcise your hearts, therefore, and do not be stiff-necked any longer."

[151] H. C. Leupold, *Exposition of Genesis: Volume 1,* 1942, p. 520–21.

[152] Stephen Dempster, *Dominion and Dynasty,* 2003, p. 81.

God, anything is possible in faith. He then asked if Ishmael would be the one through whom the blessings would fall, again, showing his human thought process into God's plan.

"And Abraham said to God, 'If only Ishmael might live under your blessing!' Then God said, 'Yes, but your wife Sarah will bear you a son, and you will call him Isaac. I will establish my covenant with him as an everlasting covenant for his descendants after him. And as for Ishmael, I have heard you: I will surely bless him; I will make him fruitful and will greatly increase his numbers. He will be the father of twelve rulers, and I will make him into a great nation. But my covenant I will establish with Isaac, whom Sarah will bear to you by this time next year'" (Gen. 17:18–21). With those reassurances, God departed from Abraham's presence.

Immediately after he was left alone, Abraham circumcised every male member of his family and his servants. Abraham was obedient to the terms of the covenant with no hesitation. He took the lead despite the physical pain and discomfort.

Shortly after this meeting, the Lord approached Abraham again, along with two angels (another Christophany).[153] This was the occasion that immediately preceded the judgement against Sodom and Gomorrah noted in the previous section regarding Lot. Abraham was sitting in the front of his tent in the heat of the day, recognized the Lord, and ran to the visitors. He bowed to the ground in respect and reverence and asked if they would stay to be his guest. They agreed to stay, so Abraham ran to tell Sarah to prepare the bread and he ran to his servants to quickly prepare the meat.

Abraham was very eager to wait on the Lord. His reverence for God was clear; he did everything he could to make his guests comfortable. Bear in mind, Abraham was a man of wealth and authority; in fact, when he rescued Lot from the Assyrian forces, the five kings returned from their defeat to honor Abraham and treated him as a contemporary. Abraham's social standing was equivalent to a king. I

---

[153] Another recorded instance of a Christophany. See James Borland, *Christ in the Old Testament*, 2010, p. 68.

point this out because men of social status and wealth in Abraham's time did not run anywhere, to anyone. But there he was, running everywhere to ensure God's comfort. Given his age, he may not have been in great condition to hurriedly wait on his guests. This speaks to his increasing obedience to God. Just as he greeted Melchizedek in humility, he extended his humility here to see to his guests' needs personally.

The guests asked where his wife Sarah was. Abraham said she was in the tent. Then the Lord said, "'I will surely return to you about this time next year, and Sarah your wife will have a son'" (Gen. 18:10). While Abraham had grown to trust in God's promise. Sarah overheard Him (probably for the first time getting the news from God's lips) and laughed to herself. "'After I am worn out and my lord is old, will I now have this pleasure?'" (v. 12). The Lord knew her thoughts and asked Abraham why Sarah laughed at the news. He reminded them both there is nothing God cannot accomplish.

There are many instances in the Old Testament where God's power and grace are made very clear to us; in Abraham's story, we find several. He used Abraham's small forces of only 318 men to defeat the entire Assyrian army, His power to destroy Sodom and Gomorrah, rescuing Lot from certain death and now, waiting until Abraham was almost 100 years old and Sarah at 90 to show He can deliver His promise for them to have a child in old age. This is just a small sampling of what God will do to fulfill His plan, even if it seems impossible to mankind that such things can happen.

The Ultimate Test of Trust

Soon after this encounter and shortly after God destroyed Sodom and Gomorrah, Abraham and Sarah traveled to Gerar in the land of the Philistines, where Abimelek was king. As he did in Egypt, Abraham introduced Sarah as his sister. Like Pharaoh before him, Abimelek took Sarah into his court. That night, God appeared to Abimelek in a dream and said, "'You are as good as dead because of the woman you have taken; she is a married woman'" (Gen. 20:3). Terrified, Abimelek pled his innocence, stating that Abraham and Sarah passed themselves off as brother and sister. God acknowledged his argument, stating it was He who prevented Abimelek from sinning against Him. God told Abimelek to return Sarah to Abraham, as he is a prophet; otherwise, He would kill Abimelek and his entire family.

Abimelek got up early in the morning and told his court what transpired; everyone was in fear. He called Abraham and rebuked him for putting the king and his people in such an awkward and dangerous position. He demanded to know what Abraham was thinking to do this. "Abraham replied, 'I said to myself, "There is surely no fear of God in this place, and they will kill me because of my wife." Besides, she really is my sister, the daughter of my father though not of my mother; and she became my wife. And when God had me wander from my father's household, I said to her, "This is how you can show your love to me: Everywhere we go, say of me, 'He is my brother'"'" (Gen. 20:11–13).

When Abraham finished with his reasoning, Abimelek returned Sarah and gave him gifts of livestock slaves, and land; he also provided Sarah with a thousand shekels to cover any offense she may have experienced privately or publicly. "Then Abraham prayed to God, and God healed Abimelek, his wife and his female slaves so they could have children again, for the LORD has kept all the women in Abimelek's household from conceiving because of Abraham's wife Sarah" (vv. 17–18).

There are a few points to make in this account of Abraham's life. First, God intervened with Abimelek for the same reason He did with Pharaoh. His plan for Abraham and Sarah to have their own child would not be derailed no matter how Abraham tried to take matters into his own hands, so that the covenant would not be abrogated. Both kings were prevented from taking Sarah as a wife by God just at the right moment.

Second, both Pharaoh and Abimelek were operating in good faith based on the half-truth they were given. Abimelek's integrity protected him, along with not knowing that Sarah was Abraham's wife, or that Abraham was a prophet of God.

Third, Abraham wrongly thought his neighbors would do him harm if they knew Sarah was his wife. He assumed there was no respect for God because they were pagans, and his life would certainly be endangered. While Abraham is technically correct, his fear was unfounded. Abimelek showered Abraham with gifts to compensate for any offense he may have caused. His actions proved more righteous than Abraham's.

Didn't Abraham realize he was making the same mistake he made in Egypt? Did he not consider he was jeopardizing the covenant God made with him? He was essentially blaming God for his passing Sarah off as his sister when he said that God made him wander from his father's household. Abraham should have known by then that God would protect him against the Egyptians and the Philistines. At the very least, he could have trusted the Philistines by not making the same wrong assumptions he made regarding the Egyptians.

Abraham did, however, turn things around spiritually when he prayed to God to restore Abimelek's wife and female slaves' fertility. As a prophet (the first time in the Old Testament the title is used), Abraham was able to intercede for Abimelek, just as he tried to be an advocate for Lot and any righteous people that could be found in Sodom and Gomorrah.

Despite this bump in Abraham's journey toward a trusting heart, God showed His continued mercy and forgave Abraham's mistakes, just as He overlooks the imperfections of all his righteous and faithful people. As noted by John Calvin in Chapter 1, God lovingly accepts our imperfect obedience and in Abraham's case, God's promise was going to proceed as planned. David Guzik says, "Despite Abraham's failure to really trust God in the situation, God was not going to abandon him. He would not *let* Abimelek touch Sarah. That womb was going to bring forth the son of promise, who would eventually bring forth God's Messiah. God would not leave this matter up to man."[154]

---

[154]David Guzik, "Study Guide for Genesis 20 by David Guzik," Blue Letter Bible, last modified February 21, 2017, https://www.blueletterbible.org/Comm/guzik_david/StudyGuide 2017-Gen/Gen-20.cfm.

As God promised, Sarah became pregnant and delivered their son Isaac. The writer of Hebrews reminds us of Sarah and Abraham's faith and that this was the beginning of the fulfillment of God's covenant with Abraham. "And by faith even Sarah, who was past child-bearing age, was enabled to bear children because she considered him faithful who had made the promise. And so from this one man, and he was as good as dead, came descendants as numerous as the stars in the sky and as countless as the sand on the seashore. All these people were still living by faith when they died. They did not receive the things promised; they only saw them and welcomed them from a distance, admitting that they were foreigners and strangers on earth" (Heb. 11:11–13).

The prophet Isaiah mentioned the blessings that were extended to the sons of Abraham: "Listen to me, you who pursue righteousness and who seek the LORD: Look to the rock from which you were cut and to the quarry from which you were hewn; look to Abraham, your father, and to Sarah, who gave you birth. When I called him, he was only one man, and I blessed him and made him many" (Isa. 51:1–2). According to G. K. Beale, this passage "...alludes to the Abrahamic blessing as a basis for the forthcoming prophesied restoration from captivity," including the Gentiles when God's Holy Spirit comes to them following the resurrection.[155]

The *Book of Jubilees* states that Abraham and his family and servants celebrated in thanks to God for the birth of Isaac. He built an altar to the Lord and offered a sacrifice of oxen, sheep, and goats in worship. "And he celebrated this feast seven days, rejoicing with all his heart and with all his soul, he and all those who were in his house... He blessed his Creator who created him in his generation, for He had created him according to His good pleasure. God knew and perceived that from him would arise the plant of righteousness for the eternal generations, and from him a holy offspring, so that it should become like Him who made all things."[156] Abraham ensured that Isaac was

---

[155]G. K. Beale, *A New Testament Biblical Theology*, 2011, p. 307.

[156]Joseph Lumpkin, *The Book of Jubilees*, 2006, pp. 94–95.

circumcised on the eighth day after his birth, as God required in His covenant. Abraham remained faithful and obedient because he saw God's promises come to fruition.

An interesting anecdote after Isaac was born reveals how meticulous God's long-term plans are. Scriptures say that when Isaac was to be weaned (probably three years of age), Abraham decided to prepare a celebratory feast, but then Sarah saw Hagar and Ishmael mocking Isaac, which enraged her. She said to Abraham, "'Get rid of that slave woman and her son, for that woman's son will never share in the inheritance with my son Isaac.' The matter distressed Abraham greatly because Ishmael was still his son. But God said to him, 'Do not be so distressed about the boy and your slave woman. Listen to whatever Sarah tells you, because it is through Isaac that your offspring will be reckoned. I will make the son of the slave into a nation also because he is your offspring'" (Gen. 21:10–13).

Sarah had certainly lost sight of the attributes behind the Second Great Commandment; the memory of Hagar's earlier taunts was not forgotten nor forgiven.[157] She must have let those feelings fester in her heart. The joy of finally bearing a son and the festive mood of the day transformed into intense anger. Her demand to remove Hagar and Ishmael from the camp without any means of support was punishment exceeding the offense (most likely fatal, as they would be forced into the desert) and Abraham knew it. However, in God's mercy and providence, He directed Abraham to heed Sarah, and He would care for them in the desert. True to His Word, Hagar and Ismael are rescued and God remained with Ismael as he grew up, providing him with descendants as He promised.

Interestingly, three generations from Ishmael, his descendants were the very clan that Joseph's brothers would sell him to, which is how

---

[157]In Chapter 7, when Hannah suffers the same humiliation from Peninnah over a period of several years, we see a contrast in Hannah's ability to overcome that pain and anguish (1 Sam. 1:16-17). Rather than condemn her rival or seek vengeance, she turns to God in a plea to provide her a son, which God does, giving her Samuel. In this regard, Hannah's heart is superior to Sarah's who essentially gives Hagar a death sentence, banishing her and Ishmael to the desert.

Joseph got to Egypt.[158] "As they sat down to eat their meal, they looked up and saw a caravan of Ishmaelites coming from Gilead. Their camels were loaded with spices, balm, and myrrh, and they were on their way to take them down to Egypt....Come, let's sell him to the Ishmaelites and not lay our hands on him; after all, he is our brother, our own flesh and blood" (Gen. 37:25, 27). The brothers sold Joseph to the Ishmaelites for twenty shekels of silver.

It is no coincidence that Joseph was sold to this particular caravan; it fit neatly into God's plan for the nation of Israel. If Sarah hadn't given Hagar to Abraham to provide an heir, if God had not allowed the conception and birth of Ismael, and if He hadn't intervened to save Hagar both times she was sent out of the camp, the tribe of Ishmaelites may not have existed and who knows what caravan Joseph's brothers would have sold him to and whether the caravan would be headed for Egypt. However, all of this was carefully planned out by God. Hagar's purpose was not merely to test Abraham's trust in God's plan to provide his heir, but it paved the way to get Joseph to Egypt and hence, the birth of the nation of Israel. God truly works in marvelous ways, but that should be no surprise to the student of the Scriptures.

It was several years later (in Josephus' account, he put Isaac's age at 25 years old)[159] when the Lord tested Abraham once again. "He said to him, 'Abraham!' 'Here I am,' he replied. Then God said, 'Take your son, your only son, whom you love—Isaac—and go to the region of Moriah.[160] Sacrifice him there as a burnt offering on a mountain I will show you'" (Gen. 22:1–2). There began the ultimate

---

[158] Allen Ross, *Cornerstone Biblical Commentary: Genesis, Exodus,* 2008, p. 118.

[159] Josephus, *Jewish Antiquities,* Book 1, Chapter 13, v. 227.

[160] The place where Abraham was to sacrifice Isaac was the site God instructed David to place the Temple of Jerusalem, which was constructed under Solomon's reign. More on that in Chapter 9.

test of Abraham's obedience to God.[161] Had his heart evolved enough to place everything in his life into God's hands? Would he obey God no matter what was asked of him? He was told to sacrifice his only son and heir—the one he and Sarah waited years to have—in order to obey God's will. How can God's promise of having a nation of people from his descendants be true if Abraham sacrificed his only son? Total trust in God to obey His will was not without some reciprocity on God's part. H. C. Leupold and others recognize the test of Abraham to sacrifice his only son reflected what Jesus did for mankind. "The starting point for this consideration may well be the simple fact that God does not expect man to do for Him what He is not ready to do for man. Abraham and all men are expected to give up their dearest possession to God. God on his part gives up His dear Son."[162]

Abraham dutifully collected all that was required for the sacrifice, left his camp with Isaac and two servants, and traveled three days to the place God directed him to go. D. A. Carson estimates that the trip from Beersheba, the starting point, to the region of Moriah, the place of sacrifice, was about 45 miles.[163]

There is no hint of what Abraham was thinking at this point, as the Scriptures are silent to any conversation between Abraham and his son. We do know that there were no questions asked, no alternative plans, and no hesitation. Abraham responded directly to God's command.

We could assume that Abraham relied on God's promise to use Isaac and his descendants to carry out the covenant to create a nation. God had fulfilled all His other promises; Abraham finally reached that

---

[161]One explanation of God's test for Abraham is suggested In the *Book of Jubilees*. In this account, Satan comes before God, accusing Abraham of loving Isaac more than God Himself. Satan suggests that if Abraham was truly faithful to God, he would obey God's command to offer Isaac as a sacrifice. God knew that Abraham was faithful, so God had no reservations about putting Abraham through such a test. (Lumpkin, pp. 97–98). This account is similar to the story of Job, where Satan thinks Job is only faithful because God protected him with wealth and health. In both cases, their faith was successfully tested, and Satan was proved wrong each time.

[162]H. C. Leupold, *Exposition of Genesis: Volume 2,* 1942, p. 636.

[163]D. A. Carson, *NIV Zondervan Study Bible,* 2015, p. 61.

point where his heart could totally rely on God and not on his own strategy or thinking.

We get a hint of Abraham's trust when they arrived at their destination. "He said to his servants, 'Stay here with the donkey while I and the boy go over there. We will worship and then we will come back to you'" (Gen. 22:5). By stating "we will come back to you," Abraham revealed his confidence in God's plan that, no matter what happened on the mountain, Isaac would return with him.

In recounting this scene, the writer of Hebrews wrote that Abraham may have thought God would restore Isaac back to life if he carried this action through its conclusion. "By faith Abraham, when God tested him, offered Isaac as a sacrifice. He who had embraced the promises was about to sacrifice his one and only son, even though God had said to him, 'It is through Isaac that your offspring will be reckoned.' *Abraham reasoned that God could even raise the dead, and so in a manner of speaking he did receive Isaac back from death*" (Heb. 11:17–19, emphasis mine).

Abraham continued up Mount Moriah with Isaac, who at this point, had no idea what was about to take place. No other words were exchanged as Isaac and his father made their way up the mountain. Breaking the silence, Isaac spoke up. "'Father?' 'Yes, my son?' Abraham replied. 'The fire and wood are here,' Isaac said, 'but where is the lamb for the burnt offering?' Abraham answered, 'God himself will provide the lamb for the burnt offering, my son.' And the two of them went on together" (Gen. 22:7–8). Isaac noticed they were missing the key element of worship, the sacrificial lamb. Abraham's response was either his continued trust in God or a statement to reassure Isaac; most likely it was both.

Abraham built an altar, arranged the wood for the fire, then bound Isaac and put him on the altar to carry out God's will. Isaac must have been compliant and obedient to have allowed Abraham to bind him and place him in the spot of the sacrifice. The Scriptures are silent in this regard, but perhaps Isaac had the same obedience to his father as Abraham had to God. He was raised in the same spiritual environment as Lot, only in Isaac's case, he stayed spiritually close to God the remainder of his life. There is no resistance from Isaac to his father, or Abraham to God's command.[164]

As Abraham took the knife to slay his son, the angel of the Lord called out to him. "'Do not lay a hand on the boy,' he said. 'Do not do anything to him. Now I know that you fear God, because you have not withheld from me your son, your only son'" (v. 12). Abraham passed his final test of trust and obedience to God. He was ready to follow through with the sacrifice of his son with no hesitation. His heart was fully dedicated to God's will no matter what was asked of him.

An obvious comparison between Isaac and his father is Jesus and His Father. Abraham was prepared to sacrifice his only son to demonstrate his love for God, and God sacrificed His only Son to demonstrate His love for mankind. Like Isaac, Jesus offered His life in obedience to his Father.

After releasing Isaac from his bonds, Abraham saw a ram caught in the bushes (God provided the substitute), which he used to complete their worship.

Abraham's spiritual evolution is complete. G. K. Beale notes that Abraham is "...vindicated not only by faith but also by the evidence of the works he did, that is, Abraham's offering of Isaac. Abraham's obedience indicated to God that he had true vindicating faith..."[165] In his New Testament letter, James writes, "Was not our father Abraham considered righteous for what he did when he offered his son Isaac on the altar? You see that his faith and his actions were working together, and his faith was made complete by what he did" (Jas 2:21–22).

Because he followed God's will to the very end, God blessed him once again. "The angel of the LORD called to Abraham from heaven

---

[164]In Book 1, Chapter 13 v. 232 of his *Jewish Antiquities,* Josephus writes that Abraham reveals to Isaac what is in store for him prior to sacrificing him. Abraham states that while he has done everything for Isaac in raising him and would like nothing more than to see him grown to leave his estate, that it was God's will to be sent to Him in the nature of a sacrifice. Isaac was pleased with Abraham's explanation, thinking it unjust if "he had not obeyed even if his father alone had so resolved," let alone God's will. "So, he went immediately to the alter to be sacrificed."

[165]G. K. Beale, *A New Testament Biblical Theology,* 2011, p. 521.

a second time and said, 'I swear by myself, declares the LORD, that because you have done this and have not withheld your son, your only son, I will surely bless you and make your descendants as numerous as the stars in the sky and as the sand on the seashore. Your descendants will take possession of the cities of their enemies, and through your offspring, [166] all nations on earth will be blessed, because you have obeyed me'" (Gen. 22:15–18).

God reiterated the promise he made to Abraham years before: to fulfill His promise based on Abraham's obedience, and Abraham proved himself to God.

God's final blessing applies to all who have faith in Him; it is not exclusive to the Israelites. G. K. Beale writes, "The mention of 'all the nations of the earth' being blessed by Abraham's seed alludes to a renewed human community bearing God's image and filling the earth with regenerated progeny who also reflect God's image..."[167] (I will discuss this in more detail in Volume II where this applies to both Jew and Gentile and the nation of Israel is redefined accordingly). As Douglas Stewart indicates in his lecture notes on *Fathers of the Chosen*, "All peoples of earth will be blessed through Abraham, a promise of redemption for all people. Anyone can be eligible if you accept Christ."

In Paul's epistle to the Galatians, he wrote that this blessing would be available to both the Jews and the Gentiles, but that the blessing was contingent upon one's faith. Paul specifically referred to this promise being fulfilled through faith in Jesus: "Scripture foresaw that God would justify the Gentiles by faith and announced the gospel in advance to Abraham: 'All nations will be blessed through you.' So those who rely on faith are blessed along with Abraham, the man of faith...The promises were spoken to Abraham and to his seed. Scripture does not say 'and to seeds,' meaning many people, but 'and to your seed,' meaning one person, who is Christ" (Gal. 3:8–9, 16).

Peter made the same reference when he preached in the temple shortly after receiving the Holy Spirit at Pentecost. "'And you are

---

[166]Some Bible translations use the word 'seed' for offspring.

[167]G. K. Beale, *The Temple and the Church's Mission*, 2004, p. 114.

heirs of the prophets and of the covenant God made with your fathers. He said to Abraham, "Through your offspring all peoples on earth will be blessed." When God raised up his servant, he sent him first to you to bless you by turning each of you from your wicked ways'" (Acts 3:25–26).

This blessing was not solely for the direct descendants of Abraham (the people of Israel), but it is available for the whole world. Graeme Goldsworthy writes, "The election and calling of Abraham does not alter this reality that the one man is chosen ultimately to bring blessings to all nations of the world."[168] Understand, then, that those who have faith and obey God's will are all children of Abraham. Scripture foresaw that God would justify the Gentiles by faith and announced the gospel in advance to Abraham: "All nations will be blessed through you." Those who rely on faith are blessed along with Abraham, the man of faith. Paul wrote in his letter to the Galatians, "He redeemed us in order that the blessing given to Abraham might come to the Gentiles through Christ Jesus, so that by faith we might receive the promise of the Spirit" (Gal. 3:14).

As the Scriptures complete Abraham's story, we find that he continued to pastor his family as he did in Ur. Not only does Isaac follow in his father's righteousness, but his servants and workers also find faith in God. It was unfortunate that Lot's spiritual heart faded once he parted company from Abraham. The longer he remained on his own, away from Abraham's influence, the more he was trapped by the wicked ways of the world. It was Lot's choice to go in that direction. Paul wrote of the struggles between the flesh and the spirit. The reality is Lot was saved for Abraham's sake, not for his own righteousness. While Abraham's heart was being honed by God, Lot's spiritual heart slowly faded as he found himself too absorbed in "being of this world." God rescued Lot from the physical trappings of this world twice and each time he could have returned to Abraham's spiritual umbrella, but each time he returned to his worldly ways.

---

[168]Graeme Goldsworthy, *Christ-Centered Biblical Theology*, 2012, p. 60.

Chapter 4–

JOSEPH AND HIS CHRIST-LIKE HEART

The story of Joseph may be one of the more familiar stories from the Old Testament. The multi-colored robe given to him by his doting father, his jealous brothers selling him into slavery and his ensuing trials, his ability to interpret dreams that led to his rise as the second most powerful man in Egypt, and his reconciliation with his brothers all contain many life lessons and are what make the Bible a book for all generations. The accounts of his life are intermingled with those of his brothers, so their contrasting hearts are readily identified. Together, they were the twelve sons of Jacob (God renamed him Israel because he was obedient to His will), the grandson of Abraham through whom the promise of God's covenant continued. It was Jacob's sons who established the twelve tribes that became the nation of Israel.

Joseph's actions and behavior were a prime example of a spiritual heart in the Old Testament. In fact, my personal conviction is Joseph demonstrated one of the strongest elements of faith and compassion in all Scriptures, reflecting the best of both Great Commandments.[169] H. C. Leupold would take exception to this characterization stating that, in the chapters related to Joseph's life, "...though Joseph is prominent, he is not to be estimated too highly. God never appeared to him as he did to his father Jacob, or to Isaac and to Abraham. Joseph dare not be ranked higher on the level of faith than his forefathers...In contrast

---

[169] We get a full dimension of all aspects of the spiritual heart in David, where we not only witness those traits that are similar to Joseph, but also the examples of true recognition and repentance of sin.

98

with non-Israelites Joseph surely achieved prominence, but for the inner, spiritual history of the kingdom of God he does not come up to the level of his fathers." Despite this comparison, Leupold immediately follows: "In a more distinct way than in the lives of his fathers, Joseph stands out as a type of Christ."[170] With that admission, I totally agree.

Joseph demonstrated love and obedience to God, especially in the face of the many calamities he endured. Even though his brothers' hatred for him was the catalyst for his trials early in his life, Joseph harbored no resentment against their actions. He readily forgave them, witnessed the atonement of their sin against him, and helped to restore their spiritual hearts. But even with this example of the spiritual heart, Sailhamer notes, "This is not a story of the success of Joseph; it is a story of God's faithfulness to His promises."[171]

Even though he suffered many hardships in his early life, those events only led to further growth in Joseph's spiritual walk with God. Joseph was rewarded for his faith, and, because of the position given to him by Pharaoh, he was able to deliver his family from a long-term famine and provided for their safety and wellbeing for the rest of his life. In this capacity, he brought his brothers back into faith and obedience to God just as Jesus's mission for mankind was to restore our hearts to God. All of this, of course, was God's ultimate plan for bringing Abraham's descendants out of Egypt and to the Promised Land.

Unlike other pillars of the Old Testament, Joseph's character had no serious deficiencies in his obedience and faith in God. In Sailhamer's commentary on Genesis, he writes, "We have seen in the preceding narratives that Abraham, Isaac, and Jacob repeatedly fell short of God's expectations, though of course, they continued to have faith in God. In the narratives of Joseph, however, we do not see him fall short. On the contrary, Joseph is a striking example of one who always responds in total trust and obedience to the will of God."[172]

---

[170]H. C. Leupold, *Exposition of Genesis: Volume 2,* 1942, p. 950.

[171]John Sailhamer, *The Expositor's Biblical Commentary – Genesis,* 2008, p. 280.

[172] Ibid.

I think of Joseph's nature and high moral standard as being a forerunner to Jesus; not in His mission, perfection, or deity, but in his obedience to God's plan for him, overcoming the many adversities that befell him early on. In the spirit of the Second Great Commandment, Joseph not only forgave his brothers for their murderous intentions, but he showed compassion, kindness, and mercy toward them, not revenge or retaliation. Those are the very traits that Jesus encouraged during His mission and by which we should all live.

Joseph shared several life experiences that were similar to those of Jesus. Both have Egypt as a focal point in their lives. When he was a young child, Jesus and His family fled to Egypt because of Herod's intent to kill Him. Joseph was taken to Egypt to ultimately save the lives of his family from the seven-year famine. Jesus resisted the temptations thrown at Him by Satan (food, life, and the kingdoms of the world). Joseph resisted the physical pleasure of sleeping with Potiphar's wife. Both Jesus and Joseph were innocent of the false accusations made against them and they were both imprisoned. Jesus's mission was to save His family's spiritual lives (all of us) and begin a new creation. Joseph's mission was to save his family's physical lives and begin a new nation (Israel). Jesus teaches that we should love our enemies. Joseph led his life by those words.

Another similarity between Jesus and Joseph was that they were rejected by the very people they were sent to save. Jesus's teachings were either misunderstood or ignored by many of the Israelites and a majority of the religious leaders of His time. The nation of Israel, which He came to redeem and restore, rejected His preaching, and ultimately put to Him death.

Joseph suffered a similar fate. He was rejected by his own brothers because of their jealousy and was thrown into a pit with the intention of killing him. When Stephen testified to the religious leaders for the charge of speaking against the temple and the laws, he cited several occasions in Jewish history where God was rejected by his people, and he included Joseph. "Because the patriarchs were jealous of Joseph, they sold him as a slave into Egypt. But God was with him and rescued him from all his troubles. He gave Joseph wisdom and enabled him to gain the goodwill of Pharaoh king of Egypt. So pharaoh made him ruler over Egypt and all his palace" (Acts 7:9–10). You could equate the patriarchs with Israel since they represent the twelve tribes of the nation on a micro level, so in a sense, Israel rejected both Jesus and Joseph.

This view of Joseph being much like Jesus is echoed by David Guzik, quoting Boice: "He was loved and hated, favored and abused, tempted and trusted, exalted and abased. Yet at no point in the one-hundred-and-ten-year life of Joseph did he ever seem to get his eyes off God or cease to trust him. Adversity did not harden his character. Prosperity did not ruin him. He was the same in private as in public. He was a truly great man."[173] Guzik himself adds, "Enoch shows the *walk* of faith, Noah shows the *perseverance* of faith, Abraham shows the *obedience* of faith, Isaac shows the *power* of faith, and Jacob shows the *discipline* of faith. Along these lines we could say that Joseph shows the *triumph* of faith. Joseph never complained and he never compromised. Joseph is also a remarkably powerful picture of Jesus."[174]

Matthew Henry makes a similar comparison. "His story is so remarkably divided between his humiliation and exaltation that we cannot avoid seeing something of Christ in it, who was first humbled and then exalted, and, in many instances, so as to answer the type of Joseph."[175]

Up to this point, I've contrasted the spiritual hearts of two individuals. Here, the comparison is between Joseph and his brothers. No matter what calamity fell upon Joseph, he remained strong in his faith and never wavered. In contrast, his brothers fell victim to jealousy and envy to the point of plotting to kill their brother. They were dragged into the ways of the world and did not rely on God's protection during

---

[173]David Guzik, "Study Guide for Genesis 37 by David Guzik," Blue Letter Bible, last modified February 21, 2017, https://www.blueletterbible.org/Comm/guzik_david/StudyGuide 2017-Gen/Gen-37.cfm.

[174] Ibid.

[175]Matthew Henry, "Commentary on Genesis 37 by Matthew Henry," Blue Letter Bible, last modified March 1, 1996, https://www.blueletterbible.org/Comm/mhc/Gen/Gen_037.cfm.

bad times. But in the end, the brothers' spiritual hearts were healed and restored; not to the level we see through Joseph's actions, but they do make progress in the right direction.

Background

In the last chapter, God revealed to Abraham that He would make a nation from his seed and that his descendants would inherit the Promised Land. God passed this promise to Abraham's son Isaac, and then through Isaac's second son Jacob. When God revealed His promise to Jacob, he was fleeing for his life. His twin brother Esau (the older of the two) was furious that Jacob gained both his birthright and inheritance through cunning and deception. On the urgent advice of his mother Rebekah, he fled to the land of her brother Laban in Haran.

When Jacob stopped in Bethel, God appeared to him in a dream. "'I am the LORD, the God of your father Abraham and the God of Isaac. I will give you and your descendants the land on which you are lying. Your descendants will be like the dust of the earth, and you will spread out to the west and to the east, to the north and to the south. All peoples on earth will be blessed through you and your offspring. I am with you and will watch over you wherever you go, and I will bring you back to this land. I will not leave you until I have done what I have promised you'" (Gen. 28:13–15).

When Jacob arrived in Haran, he met and fell in love with Rachel, the youngest daughter of his uncle Laban. After working for Laban for a month, his uncle asked what wages Jacob would like for his work. "Jacob was in love with Rachel and said, 'I'll work for you seven years in return for your younger daughter Rachel'" (Gen. 29:18). Laban accepted this agreement, but when the pact was completed, Jacob was tricked into marrying Leah, Rachel's older sister. Laban wanted to follow the tradition of getting the oldest daughter married first. He substituted Leah on the wedding day and since she wore a veil, Jacob didn't realize he married Leah until the wedding was over. Upset that he was tricked by his uncle, Laban allowed Jacob to marry Rachel a week later, as long as Jacob agreed to work another seven years for

Laban. He agreed because he truly loved Rachel. Scriptures do not condemn polygamy, but again, there was a rivalry between Jacob's wives regarding childbirth just as there was with his grandfather, Abraham.

While employed by Laban, Jacob's faithfulness to God was rewarded and he prospered greatly, which spilled over to Laban. Jacob had four sons through Leah while Rachel remained childless. In those days, a woman's success and blessings were based on the number of children she bore. Being barren was a social stigma and there was pressure on Rachel to have a child, especially since her sister had quite an advantage. In fact, Rachel blamed Jacob for her inability to conceive. Jacob angrily responded that he was not God, who was the Creator of life. Leupold notes that Jacob didn't show compassion to comfort his wife; rather, Jacob "was not sufficiently strong in faith to bring the problem to God in prayer together with his wife. Isaac's (Jacob's father) example should have taught him what was to be done in such a case."[176] "Isaac prayed to the LORD on behalf of his wife because she was childless. The LORD answered his prayer, and his wife Rebekah became pregnant" (Gen. 25:21).

Competition between Leah and Rachel got out of hand as each of them gave Jacob their servant to bear children on their behalf, reminiscent of Sarah giving her servant Hagar to Abraham. Jacob had four more sons through these two servants and two more through Leah until Rachel's prayers were finally answered and she bore Joseph. She later bore Benjamin, the last son for Jacob, but she died during labor.

Between his wives and their servants, Jacob had twelve children. He finally returned to his homeland after 20 years working for his uncle. When he neared his home, despite his fears of retribution, Esau greeted him eagerly and the brothers were reconciled; both blessed by God with great wealth.

---

[176]H. C. Leupold, *Exposition of Genesis: Volume 2,* 1942, p. 805.

Joseph's Brothers with Cain-Like Hearts

I share this background as the basis for why Joseph was favored by Jacob over all his sons. As Joseph's story begins, Scriptures tell us, "Now Israel [Jacob] loved Joseph more than any of his other sons, because he had been born to him in his old age; and he made an ornate robe for him. When his brothers saw that their father loved him more than any of them, they hated him and could not speak a kind word to him" (Gen. 37:3–4). Joseph was the first son born to Jacob by Rachel, his true love. The long wait for Joseph because of Rachel's barrenness made him special in Jacob's eyes. Since Rachel died after giving birth to Benjamin, it's likely that Joseph would be the only memory of Rachel that Jacob would have, and he favored Joseph because of it.

The special treatment is seen early on. Joseph is 17 years old when the story begins, and his father gives him an ornate robe. A gift like this typically indicates the firstborn, which should have been reserved for Rueben, the eldest brother. The robe set Joseph apart from his brothers. David Guzik writes, "Jacob's favoritism of Joseph was plain to all, including Joseph and his brothers. As an outward display of this, he gave Joseph a tunic of many colors. This signified a position of favor, princely standing, and birthright. It was a dramatic way of saying he was the son to receive the birthright...This was not what a workingman wore. It was a garment of privilege and status."[177]

Beale concurs and suggests that in the days of the Old Testament, certain religious ceremonies that involved such garments indicated the acquisition of inheritance rights. He cites the "...divine provision of clothing to Adam and Eve in Genesis 3:21 appears to indicate a gracious reaffirmation of their inheritance rights over creation, despite their former rebellion."[178] G. K. Beale cites Joseph's tunic as another

---

[177]David Guzik, "Study Guide for Genesis 37 by David Guzik," Blue Letter Bible, last modified February 21, 2017, https://www.blueletterbible.org/Comm/guzik_david/StudyGuide2017-Gen/Gen-37.cfm.

[178]G. K. Beale, *The Temple and the Church's Mission,* 2004, p. 30.

example, so Joseph is clearly being identified by his father as one with honors traditionally reserved for the firstborn.

Of course, this special treatment did not sit well with his older brothers. With his father doting over him, Joseph's brothers "hated him and could not speak a kind word to him" (Gen. 37:4). Envy and jealousy were swelling in the minds of his brothers to the point of hatred. H. C. Leupold notes that another bone of contention from some of the brothers would be that the sons of Jacob's concubines (Dan, Naphtali, Gad, and Asher) would be seen as "slightly inferior in social standing" than the sons of Leah and Rachel, including Joseph.[179] With that type of anger, they didn't speak to him kindly, if at all. He was an outsider to them. Their bad hearts were only beginning to cause a problem. The unchecked anger in the hearts of Joseph's brothers was similar to the resentment Cain had toward his brother Abel, which led to the murder of Abel.

This animosity toward Joseph did not start with the gift of the garment. In Genesis 37, Joseph was tending sheep with his brothers and delivered a bad report to his father about them. Given Joseph's moral character and the lack of morality in his brothers, it is likely that Joseph did not lie about their behavior just to get them in trouble. In fact, Matthew Henry says that Joseph may have made the report "not as a malicious tale-bearer, to sow discord, but as a faithful brother, who, when he durst not admonish them himself, represented their faults to one that had authority to admonish them."[180]

As the report of their dereliction of duty was revealed to his father, Joseph was operating at a higher moral behavior than his brothers. Anyone with younger siblings might understand how older brothers would react to being ratted out, especially when that younger sibling can do no wrong in the eyes of the father. Compound that with the

---

[179]H. C. Leupold, *Exposition of Genesis, Volume 2,* 1942, p. 954.

[180]Matthew Henry, "Commentary on Genesis 37 by Matthew Henry," Blue Letter Bible, last modified March 1, 1996, https://www.blueletterbible.org/Comm/mhc/Gen/Gen_037.cfm.

robe of inheritance and it's not hard to imagine how this led to them taking malicious actions against Joseph.

The animosity continued to build. Joseph revealed to his brothers a dream that foretold his superior position among them. "He said to them, 'Listen to this dream I had: We were binding sheaves of grain out in the field when suddenly my sheaf rose and stood upright, while your sheaves gathered around mine and bowed down to it.' His brothers said to him, 'Do you intend to reign over us? Will you actually rule us?' And they hated him all the more because of his dream and what he had said" (Gen. 37:6–8).

Some commentators view this as a moment of pride or arrogance by Joseph, a chink in the armor, so to speak. I see this as nothing more than an innocent teenager revealing youthful, naive enthusiasm telling them the dream, rather than rubbing their noses in the revelation. When he said, "Listen to this dream I had," he was excited to share it without thinking about the impact on his audience. If he had said it with any amount of pride or "aha, get this, guys," I'm thinking (as one with four brothers of my own) he would have gotten more of a physical response from his brothers. As it was, it made their hatred for him grow even more.

Later, Joseph revealed a second dream to the entire family, similar to the first: "Then he had another dream, and he told it to his brothers. 'Listen,' he said, 'I had another dream, and this time the sun and moon and eleven stars were bowing down to me'" (Gen. 37:9). This dream was shared with his father as well, who rebuked Joseph and asked if he seriously believed the whole family would bow to him. The rebuke in front of his other sons did not abate their jealousy.

Commentators have reacted to the second dream as a lack of discretion on Joseph's behalf, that he should have realized it would exasperate his brothers even more. However, neither the brothers nor Jacob himself realized that God was speaking prophecy through Joseph's dreams; they were only thinking of the earthly circumstances. Joseph was almost the youngest in the family; how could he possibly lead the family? God obviously had not revealed to Jacob what He was intending for Joseph, nor did Jacob understand the divine origins. He did, however, keep this revelation in the back of his mind. Given his personal walk with God, it is curious that Jacob didn't see how this may be part of God's promise to him. The brothers, meanwhile, were too consumed by jealousy to see God's hand in this because their spiritual development was clouded by their poisoned hearts.

What is interesting here is that Joseph's two dreams revealed the same meaning: he would rule over his family. Notably, while captive in Egypt, Joseph was sent to interpret two dreams of similar nature for Pharaoh. Joseph told Pharaoh, "The reason the dream was given to Pharaoh in two forms is that the matter has been firmly decided by God, and God will do it soon" (Gen. 41:32). By that time, Joseph's spiritual development had greatly progressed, and he understood the relevance of having similar dreams. But at 17, he didn't have the same understanding.

Interestingly, the additional elements Joseph described in the second dream were the sun, moon, and eleven stars. This could be the prediction of the nation of Israel centuries later and how that nation eventually gave rise to Jesus. The reference is similar to the one found in Revelation 12: "A great sign appeared in heaven: a woman clothed with *the sun, with the moon under her feet and a crown of twelve stars on her head* [my emphasis]. She was pregnant and cried out in pain as she was about to give birth. The dragon stood in front of the woman who was about to give birth, so that it might devour her child the moment he was born. She gave birth to a son, a male child, who 'will rule all the nations with an iron scepter.' And her child was snatched up to God and to his throne" (vv. 1–2, 4, 5). God revealed not only the short run prediction of Joseph's role in the nation of Israel's rise, but also the twelve tribes and the coming of the Savior.

While his older sons were tending the flocks quite a distance from home, Jacob sent Joseph to check on them once again. As Joseph neared their location, they saw him coming, probably on account of his royal garment. "But they saw him in the distance, and before he reached them, they plotted to kill him. 'Here comes that dreamer!' they said to each other. 'Come now, let's kill him and throw him into one of these cisterns and say that a ferocious animal devoured him. Then we'll see what comes of his dreams'" (Gen. 37:18–20).

Their attitude was very similar to Cain's consuming anger. Cain and Joseph's brothers were angered by the favoritism shown to their younger brothers and made conscience plans to kill them. Both plots were contrived away from home, out of the sight of protecting parents. Cain and Joseph's brothers were given the opportunity to repent and restore their hearts to God. While Cain eschewed the opportunity to return to God's favor and didn't repent, Joseph's brothers eventually saw the errors of their sinful hearts, repented, and restored their hearts back to God.

As the brothers continued with their plan, Reuben—the oldest—acted as the collective conscience regarding the seriousness of their intentions. He convinced the others to throw Joseph into a cistern, thinking he could rescue Joseph later without them being aware. "When Reuben heard this, he tried to rescue him from their hands. 'Let's not take his life,' he said. 'Don't shed any blood. Throw him into this cistern here in the wilderness, but don't lay a hand on him.' Reuben said this to rescue him from them and take him back to his father" (Gen. 37:21–22).

They agreed, stripped him of his cloak, and threw him in. While Reuben was away (though we don't know where or why), a caravan heading for Egypt arrived on the scene. Judah came up with the idea to sell Joseph to the caravan[181] arguing, "'What will we gain if we kill our brother and cover up his blood? Come, let's sell him to the Ishmaelites and not lay our hands on him; after all, he is our brother, our own flesh and blood.' His brothers agreed" (Gen. 37:26–27).

This plan sounds worse than killing Joseph outright, which would end any misery he would experience immediately. Selling him as a slave would result in losing his family and who knows what evil would befall Joseph in captivity. Even worse, Judah and his brothers couldn't

---

[181]Recall from the previous chapter that the caravan was of the tribe of Ishmael, descendants of the child between Hagar and Abraham. God used them to take Joseph to Egypt where his descendants grew to become the nation that God led to the promised land.

care less; they sold Joseph for twenty shekels of silver (Judas would sell out Jesus for 30 pieces of silver). Judah's absolution regarding Joseph's fate echoed Pilate in Matthew 24: "'I am innocent of this man's blood'" (v. 24). There was no love at all in the hearts of these men.

When Reuben returned to the cistern, he found that Joseph was gone. Remorseful, he ripped his garments in anguish. As the oldest brother, he likely felt ultimately responsible. "'The boy isn't there. Where can I turn now?'" (Gen. 37:30). Despite Rueben's concern for Joseph's fate, the duplicity of the brothers continued. They dipped Joseph's robe in blood to make it appear that Joseph was killed by wild animals. When they returned home, they showed the garment to Jacob and asked if it was Joseph's. They acted innocent and feigned ignorance as to whether it was their brother's. Even if the brothers were not involved in his disappearance, they knew full well the robe was his.

Of course, Jacob recognized it immediately. They let Jacob think that Joseph has been killed and devoured by wild animals; otherwise, a dismembered body would have been available as evidence. Jacob's reaction for the loss of his favorite son was understandable; he tore his garments, put on sackcloth, and mourned for many days. Scriptures say that Jacob refused to be comforted by anyone who tried to console him, including his sons. Along with attempted murder, selling their brother into slavery, and duplicity, we can add hypocrisy to their list of failings.

This episode was not the first account of the brothers' spiritual failings. Scriptures record that there was earlier evidence of their lack of morality, which was surprising given Jacob's close relationship with God. For example, when the family first settled into Bethel, Rueben slept with one of his father's concubines which, in those days, was equivalent to sleeping with his father's wife. H. C. Leupold calls this a sad testimony to the demoralization of Jacobs sons. "Vile, incestuous lust here has its sway among men who should have been worthy to bear the honorable title sons of Israel."[182]

---

[182]H. C. Leupold, *Exposition of Genesis: Volumes 1 and 2,* 1942, p. 927.

Centuries later, God gave instructions to Moses and the Israelites regarding sexual immorality, particularly in regard to incest, but even in Jacob's time it was considered an act of immoral behavior and a betrayal to his father. David Guzik says that Rueben, as the firstborn son, should have set the bar of morality for his younger brothers. "We might expect the best conduct from him and might expect him to most seriously receive the covenant of his fathers. Yet, here he sinned in a most offensive way against his father and entire family."[183] Jacob did not forget the sin. On his deathbed, he told Rueben that he lost his birthright of inheritance because of his immoral actions.

There was no need for Reuben's power play to take over family leadership since he was already entitled to the inheritance. Still, this transgression was not unique in the Old Testament; there were two similar events involving the sons of King David. When David's son Absalom[184] tried to overthrow his father to take the throne, he was advised to sleep with David's concubine when David fled Jerusalem. "'Sleep with your father's concubines whom he left to take care of the palace. Then all Israel will hear that you have made yourself obnoxious to your father, and the hands of everyone with you will be more resolute.' So they pitched a tent for Absalom on the roof, and he slept with his father's concubines in the sight of all Israel" (2 Sam. 16:21–22). The act was clear contempt for David and a pointed claim to the throne.[185]

When David died, his son Adonijah attempted the same sin, only it resulted in his death when he asked King Solomon (his younger brother) for one of David's former concubines. Solomon saw the

---

[183]David Guzik, "Study Guide for Genesis 35 by David Guzik," Blue Letter Bible. last modified February 21, 2017, https://www.blueletterbible.org/Comm/guzik_david/StudyGuide 2017-Gen/Gen-35.cfm.

[184]Absalom was third in line as successor to David. However, the oldest son, Amnon was murdered by Absalom in revenge for raping his sister Tamar, which is discussed in Chapter 7. The second son Kilead (Chronicles 3:1 refers to him as Daniel) must have died earlier as there is no other reference to him in Scriptures. So, at this point, Absalom would have been the direct successor in order of birth.

[185]D. A. Carson, *NIV Zondervan Study Bible*, 2015, p. 573.

request as an endplay to give Adonijah a right to claim succession to the throne and put him to death.[186]

Simeon and Levi, Jacob's next two sons in line for birthrights, also lost their claim on the inheritance because of their murderous behavior. While in Shechem, Jacob bought land and set up camp. His daughter Dinah went to visit some women in town and was raped by Shechem son of Hamor, the Hivite king. Shechem said he loved Dinah and wanted her as his wife. The king, ignoring the violation of the girl, discussed an arrangement for marriage with Jacob that would include allowing Jacob's family to settle in the land. According to H. C. Leupold, "...the Canaanite laxity of morals is apparent in both the father's and the son's words: neither admits that a wrong has been committed...They feel that Jacob's clan should feel honored at the proposal of a matrimonial alliance with their own princely line."[187]

The brothers were furious that their sister was defiled by these pagans, but they agreed to the marriage on one condition: all the men of the city must be circumcised in order to be religiously acceptable. Hamor and his son convinced the men of the city to agree to circumcision in exchange for Jacob and his people trading in the land, intermarrying, and thinking their livestock, property, and animals would become theirs.

Before the men fully healed, Simeon and Levi attacked the city and killed every male. They took all the wealth of the town, including livestock and women and children as plunder.

Jacob was horrified by their actions. "Then Jacob said to Simeon and Levi, 'You have brought trouble on me by making me obnoxious to the Canaanites and Perizzites, the people living in this land. We are few in number, and if they join forces against me and attack me, I and my household will be destroyed.' But they replied, 'Should he have treated our sister like a prostitute?'" (Gen. 34:30–31). John Lennox observes that Jacob's reprimand was somewhat weak. "There is no evidence that he tried to exercise any moral discipline on them, a weak

---

[186] Discussed in Chapter 9.

[187] H. C. Leupold, *Exposition of Genesis: Volumes 1 and 2*, 1942, p. 902.

trait that became more evident as he and the sons grew older. Jacob appeared only to be concerned with 'I, me, and my.'"[188]

D. A. Carson notes that while the crime of rape was serious, it did not warrant the murder of every man in the city, all of whom but Shechem were innocent of any reason for "...such brutal retaliation. The punishment far exceeds Shechem's crime...Although Simeon and Levi did the killing, the brothers join them in looting the city. The whole event is a shameful episode for Abraham's descendants."[189]

William Barclay references this extreme action of vengeance as the reason Moses included in the law a limit on how far one should take it. "But if there is serious injury, you are to take life for life, eye for eye, tooth for tooth, hand for hand, foot for foot, burn for burn, wound for wound, bruise for bruise" (Ex. 21:23–25).[190] Barclay states, "In the very earliest of days, the vendetta and the blood feud were characteristic of tribal society. If a man of one tribe injured a man of another tribe, then at once all the vengeance on all the members of the injured man were out to take vengeance on all the members of the tribe of the man who committed the injury; and vengeance desired was nothing less than death."[191]

This is precisely the action taken by Simeon and Levi. Murder and retaliation for the revenge of one being harmed was reminiscent of Lamech's behavior discussed in Chapter 2. Added to this raging vengeance was using something holy to enact their revenge; the brothers used God's covenant symbol of circumcision as a tool to ravage the male population. As Allen Ross notes, "But because of their unbridled passion, a whole group of people are slaughtered. Worse than that, they dangled the covenant before the Canaanites to deceive them. It is one thing to trick the Canaanites...but it was another matter to use the covenant and its rites deceitfully—that is sacrilegious."[192]

---

[188]John Lennox, *Joseph*, 2019, p. 63.

[189]D. A. Carson, *NIV Zondervan Study Bible*, 2015, p. 84.

[190]See also Leviticus 24:19–20 and Deuteronomy 19:21.

[191]William Barclay, *Gospel of Matthew, Volumes 1 & 2*, 1975, p. 180.

[192]Allen Ross, *Cornerstone Biblical Commentary: Genesis, Exodus*, 2008, p. 198.

As with Reuben, Jacob remembered Simeon and Levi's sin on his deathbed. As he gave each son a separate blessing, these two were also removed from the line of inheritance. It finally fell on Judah, which was God's long-term plan. David and Jesus were a continuation of Judah's line as it was prophesied.

In another episode demonstrating a lack of spiritual development, Judah failed to care for his daughter-in-law Tamar after his two oldest sons married her and died before leaving an heir. He moved away from the family to a town about 12 miles from Hebron and married a Canaanite woman. Not following the examples of his father or grandfather, he married outside of his faith. "This marriage outside the clan, particularly to a Canaanite, was reprehensible to patriarchal sensibilities, as is clear from the careful efforts of both Abraham and Isaac to secure wives for their sons among their own kinfolks. The refusal of Jacob's sons to permit Dinah to marry Sechem, even after he had violated her, also reveals this spirit."[193]

He had three sons in this marriage, Er, Onan, and Shelah, and he arranged a marriage for his oldest son Er with yet another Canaanite woman, Tamar. With no explanation in Scriptures, God found Er to be wicked, and he was killed.

As was the tradition of the time, Judah told his second son Onan to marry Tamar to preserve the lineage, but Onan refused to consummate their relationship, as the offspring would be heir to Judah's estate and not Onan's. Because of his selfishness, he also came to an early death. Rather than care for the grieving widow, Judah sent Tamar back to her father until his youngest son Shelah was old enough to marry her. "Judah then said to his daughter-in-law Tamar, 'Live as a widow in your father's household until my son Shelah grows up.' For he thought, 'He may die too, just like his brothers.' So, Tamar went to live in her father's household" (Gen. 38:11). Concerned by the death of his two oldest boys, Judah had no intention of having his last surviving son marry Tamar. He reneged on his promise to take care of her and withheld his last son for fear of losing his dynasty. Whatever

---

[193]Eugene Merrill, *Kingdom of Priests*, 2008, p. 64.

faith in God's protection that Jacob tried to instill in his sons did not take hold in their hearts.

Tamar was told that her father-in-law was coming to Timnah to shear his sheep, so she took off her widow's cloths, covered herself with a veil, and waited for him to arrive. When he saw her, Judah did not recognize her as his daughter-in-law, and he solicited her as a prostitute. Judah's wife had died at this point, but he didn't hesitate to have sex with a prostitute. She asked what he would give her to sleep with him and he offered her a young goat. She asked for his seal and its cord as collateral to keep his pledge. When they were finished, Judah left to return with his payment, but Tamar was nowhere to be found.

Later, Tamar was discovered to be with child (by Judah!) and she was brought before Judah to judge her immorality. He was enraged that his daughter-in-law would get pregnant outside of marriage and he ordered her to be burned to death. John Lennox notes the irony of the situation. "This is a horrific example of double standards. On the one hand, the man himself behaves like a Canaanite in using the services of a prostitute and then, on the other hand, condemns his own daughter-in-law to death for behaving like one."[194] Fortunately, Tamar was much more astute than Judah and was prepared for this. She told Judah she could identify the father and showed Judah's seal and cord as proof it was him. Shamed by the evidence of his own sin, Judah admitted that Tamar was more righteous than he was. In his conviction, he reversed his judgement and allowed her to go free.

Thus, you can see that the hearts of Joseph's brothers were in stark contrast to the kindness and forgiveness Joseph later displayed. In fact, until they were confronted by the guilt of their actions, there was no display of any faithfulness or obedience to God by the brothers. They were consumed by worldly passions and behavior.

---

[194]John Lennox, *Joseph*, 2019, p. 103.

Joseph's Faithful Heart Maintained Through Adversity

Joseph's trials began when his brothers threw him into the cistern. They changed their minds about killing him, but not their hearts about selling him as a slave to a caravan heading for Egypt. While the Scriptures make clear the nature of his brothers' hearts through their actions and words, the only information given regarding Joseph's reaction to his abandonment by his brothers was a plea for mercy. The pleas went unheard and off to Egypt he went. There was no mention of Joseph cursing his brothers or blaming God for his fate. As the story unfolded, this and other disasters in his early days only made his heart grow stronger and more mature.

God had a mission for Joseph and as his story revealed, God selected Joseph on the basis of his strong faith and obedience. It was already revealed to Joseph in his dreams that great things awaited him; what was not revealed to him were the trials he would endure to get there. He was just a youth as the story began and it is reasonable to think that the trials were meant to spiritually season him and not punish him for being errant in his ways. I mentioned in Chapter 2 that one reason for Adam's failure to carry out his mission was that he was not spiritually developed enough to resist Satan's deception and temptation. Trials affect us all; for the spiritual heart, trials can be used to strengthen our faith by relying on God to help see us through. Joseph soon came to realize this.

When the caravan reached Egypt, Joseph was sold to Potiphar who was one of Pharaoh's officials. This was no coincidence; Joseph could have been sold to anyone of means anywhere in Egypt, but he was sold to a high-ranking officer in Pharaoh's court. This put him in a position to learn the ways of the Egyptian court which served him well later. The Scriptures state that the Lord was with Joseph and, while he was in Potiphar's service, he prospered and was allowed to live in Potiphar's house, a rare occasion for a slave, especially a Hebrew slave.

Joseph was diligent and industrious in his work and as a result of his faith and obedience, he was rewarded; he gained Potiphar's trust over time and eventually was put in charge of the entire household.

God gave Joseph success in all he did, with his prosperity extending to Potiphar's household as well. This success to his master was similar to the success God rewarded his father Jacob when he served his uncle Laban; God extended his blessings to everyone in His chosen's presence.

He gained success and favor with his master Potiphar, but because of his youth and handsome appearance, Potiphar's wife repeatedly tried to convince Joseph to sleep with her, which he refused to do each time. He kept her advances at bay and did his best to avoid her. It would be especially dangerous for Joseph to be in a situation where they would be alone in the house together. He understood that if he acted on her advances, it would betray the confidence, trust, and gratitude of his master, but more importantly, it would be a sin against God. Again, another Christ-like attribute.

He rebuffed her advances, stating, "No one is greater in this house than I am. My master has withheld nothing from me except you because you are his wife. How then could I do such a wicked thing and sin against God?" (Gen. 39:9). Unlike his brothers Rueben and Judah, Joseph had no difficulty in refusing to act immorally by having sex outside of marriage.

In her last advance, Potiphar's wife grabbed his garment to seduce him when no one was around. He escaped her grasp, leaving the cloak in her hand. Probably out of embarrassment or being scorned, she screamed for help, accusing the "Hebrew slave" of trying to rape her. When Potiphar arrived, she convinced him of Joseph's "advances," producing his cloak as "evidence." Potiphar was enraged by the circumstances and Joseph was sent to prison.

Falsely accused and imprisoned, through no wrongdoing of his own, Joseph's circumstances were similar to Jesus's last days. Joseph was faced with another calamity and the Scriptures are silent as to his reaction. He was innocent of the charges and shouldn't have been in prison, but there was no complaining or cursing God for his fate. By now he must have understood God was with him as He had been all along. As captain of the guard, Potiphar had the authority to place him anywhere in Egypt's prison system, but he put Joseph in the prison where the king's prisoners were confined. Despite his anger for Joseph's alleged crime, he may not have been totally convinced by his wife's accusations based on the loyalty and effective management Joseph had displayed to that point. However, this special treatment was not coincidental. It was all part of God's plan for Joseph.

The same quality of character and workmanship he displayed with Potiphar carried over to the prison. Just as his diligence won over Potiphar, Joseph soon gained the trust of the warden and prison guards. In fact, he was left in charge of the other prisoners. "The warden paid no attention to anything under Joseph's care, because the LORD was with Joseph and gave him success in whatever he did" (Gen. 39:23). Joseph's faith and obedience to God was unaltered by the disasters that befell him, and God continued to be with him.

While in prison, Joseph found himself caring for Pharaoh's official cupbearer and baker, members of the king's royal court who had fallen out of favor. During their imprisonment, each of them had disturbing dreams and God revealed to Joseph the meaning of each of them. Joseph told the cupbearer he would be released and restored to his former position while the baker would hang for his crimes. Both events were to take place in three days. Both predictions came true. As the cupbearer was being released, Joseph said to him, "'But when all goes well with you, remember me and show me kindness; mention me to Pharaoh and get me out of this prison. I was forcibly carried off from the land of the Hebrews, and even here I have done nothing to deserve being put in a dungeon'" (Gen. 40:14–15). But the cupbearer soon forgot his benefactor of good news and Joseph remained in prison.

Two years later, Pharaoh himself had two dreams that were similar in nature. In the first, he dreamt of seven fat cows coming out of the Nile followed by seven lean cows, who devoured the fat cows. The dream woke Pharaoh in a fright, but he fell back to sleep and had the second dream; seven full ears of corn on a single stalk were devoured by seven dried up, scorched ears. Pharaoh was troubled by the dreams and in the morning, he called the magicians and wisemen of the court asking if they could explain the dreams to him. No one in his court was able to interpret the dreams.

Then the cupbearer remembered Joseph's abilities and told Pharaoh how his dream was correctly predicted by the Hebrew prisoner. Joseph was immediately taken out of prison, cleaned up, and presented to Pharaoh, who asked Joseph to interpret his dreams. "'I cannot do it,' Joseph replied to Pharaoh, 'but God will give Pharaoh the answer he desires'" (Gen. 41:16).

H. C. Leupold observes Joseph's humility and faithfulness to God by his refusal to take credit for this gift of interpretation. "We may well be astounded at the downright honesty which refuses to profit even in an emergency by a slight distortion of truth. As far as Joseph was concerned, absolute truthfulness in grading God's honor was far more important than personal advantage."[195]

Joseph's refusal to take credit for interpreting dreams is the same humility and homage to God that Daniel demonstrated when the king of Babylon needed his dream interpreted. "Daniel replied, 'No wise man, enchanter, magician, or diviner can explain to the king the mystery he has asked about, but there is a God in heaven who reveals mysteries. He has shown King Nebuchadnezzar what will happen in days to come'" (Dan. 2:27–28).

Joseph explained the meaning of the dreams: God was revealing to the king that there would be seven years of great production of crops followed by seven years of famine that would ravage the land. Joseph then told Pharaoh what he should do to prepare for this revelation. Pharaoh should appoint an administrator to collect 20% of the crops each year during the seven good years and store the grain in the cities for distribution during the famine. Storing the grain would ensure there was enough to last the nation and surrounding populace during the years of famine.

Pharaoh was impressed with this information and marveled to his court about Joseph's astute interpretation and logical solution to the impending famine. "So Pharaoh asked them, 'Can we find anyone like

---

[195]H. C. Leupold, *Exposition of Genesis: Volumes 1 and 2*, 1942, pp. 1025–26.

this man, one in whom is the spirit of God?'" (Gen. 41:38). Pharaoh recognized the influence of the Hebrew God and was pleased by Joseph's revelation. John Sailhamer points out that of all those mentioned as obedient and faithful to God, "only Joseph is described as one who is filled with the Spirit of God."[196]

Because of his humility, it didn't occur to Joseph to recommend himself as the administrator of the plan; however, because Pharaoh was so relieved and impressed by his wisdom, he appointed Joseph to this role. As a result, Joseph became the most powerful man in Egypt under Pharaoh.[197] Pharaoh provided him with an Egyptian name and a wife—his own daughter, no less—so that socially, no one would show animosity toward him as a foreigner. He was only 30 years old at the time and God continued to reward Joseph's faith, which had only grown stronger despite living 13 years in one of the most polytheistic nations of his time.

During the seven good years, Joseph established the system of collection, storage, and record keeping so that there was ample food to last during the famine years. Each major city in Egypt was set up for storage, so the distribution was logistically more manageable. When the famine began, Joseph was in charge of the distribution of the stored grain. First Egypt and then the surrounding regions were affected by the famine; everyone had to go to Joseph for relief. Joseph's status in Egypt soared; from Hebrew slave to prisoner, then second to only Pharaoh in the greatest nation in that region. God was with Joseph the entire time and His plan to grow the nation of Israel began to take

---

[196]John Sailhamer, *The Expositor's Bible Commentary – Genesis*, 2008, p. 281. He also notes "Joseph's interpretation of Pharaoh's dreams differ from Daniel's in that not only does he have to forecast from the dreams what is to happen, but, more importantly, he must advise Pharaoh how to prepare for what is to come." Joseph's wisdom (planning and administration) was as important as his ability to interpret the dream.

[197]This fulfills God's promise to Joseph when he was a teenager: "and he sent a man before them—Joseph, sold as a slave. They bruised his feet with shackles, his neck was put in irons, till what he foretold came to pass, till the word of the LORD proved him true. The king sent and released him the ruler of peoples set him free. He made him master of his household, ruler over all he possessed, to instruct his princes as he pleased and teach his elders wisdom" (Ps. 105:17–22).

shape. Joseph's character during those 13 years was the same: he was neither dejected during the bad times nor pompous or proud during his prosperous times. He remained obedient and faithful to God. He was able to save the seeds of the nation of Israel and restore the spiritual hearts of his brothers; both of which were God's plan from the beginning of his story.

Repentance, Restoration, and Reconciliation

Since the region of Canaan was also affected by the famine, Jacob sent his ten sons to Egypt to buy grain and food. The youngest, Benjamin, was kept behind for safety since he was the only one left of Rachel's two children. When they arrived in Egypt, they had to go before Joseph who was administering the rationed storage. They did not recognize him because he had the appearance and garments of a high Egyptian official, and they never expected to see him. It had been 20 years since they last saw him, and they must have assumed that he died. At any rate, Joseph immediately recognized them and remembered the two dreams God revealed to him all those years ago; both had come to fruition.

Paul House states that this scenario defined Joseph's greatest test of faith. "He could take revenge on them, or he could sell them grain and not tell them who he is, and that more famine will come. [Because of the nature his spiritual heart, he doesn't do either nor does he intend to do them harm, but he did] decide to test his brothers to see if they have changed."[198] Joseph denied them grain, telling them (through an interpreter because he was holding back on revealing his true identity) that they must be spies, trying to determine Egypt's weaknesses.

Terrified and afraid for their lives, the brothers denied being spies and said they came from an honest family of twelve brothers from Canaan, the youngest one at home with their father and another who was no longer living. Joseph continued to play a heavy hand and put them in prison for three days. When they were released, he told them

---

[198]Paul House, *Old Testament Survey,* 1992, p. 43.

to return home and bring the youngest brother to him to prove they were not sent as spies. He also held Simeon in prison as collateral to ensure they would come back as ordered.

The day of reckoning for the brothers had arrived. They were imprisoned three days and easily cracked under minimal pressure and discomfort. The guilt of their actions against Joseph must have haunted them all those years. "They said to one another, 'Surely we are being punished because of our brother. We saw how distressed he was when he pleaded with us for his life, but we would not listen; that's why this distress has come on us.' Reuben replied, 'Didn't I tell you not to sin against the boy? But you wouldn't listen! Now we must give an accounting for his blood'" (Gen. 42:21–22).

This was the first admission of sin in the Old Testament. It was the first step toward restoring their spiritual hearts; however, Reuben's "I told you so" did little to improve the situation. As the oldest, he should have stopped the situation from happening at the start instead of planning to rescue Joseph when his brothers were not aware. As we know, all of this took place to fulfill God's plan for Joseph: a stronger faith on behalf of his brothers and ultimately, the birth of the nation of Israel.

Repentance starts with the ability to recognize sin. The brothers' sin against Joseph was brought to the forefront. It must have weighed on them all those years for them to bring it up as the only cause for their dilemma. I pointed out their earlier transgressions against God, but it was their treatment of Joseph and deceiving their father that weighed on their conscience now. They needed to atone for this sin. Confronted by punishment likely originating from God, Joseph's brothers realized how horribly they treated him and showed sincere remorse.

While they argued amongst themselves in front of him, they had no idea that Joseph understood everything they were saying. Seeing his brothers remorseful for their actions against him moved Joseph to tears and he removed himself from their presence to weep. I think his tears were a result of the love he held for them. He hadn't seen his family in 20 years and instead of holding a grudge or nursing the hurt they caused, he never stopped loving them. To see that they were sorry for his "demise," it was too much for him to witness. Joseph truly demonstrated a forgiving spiritual heart.

Joseph kept Simeon in prison and released the rest of the brothers to return to Canaan with the grain and food they purchased. He ordered his steward to hide in their sacks of grain the money they used to the buy the food. It was an act of love and generosity that his brothers did not discover until they returned home and opened them. Instead of recognizing the blessing of forgiveness, they looked at each other in horror asking, "'What is this that God has done to us?'" (Gen. 42:28). Their guilt was not removed, and they didn't know they were forgiven. They thought, if discovered, the Egyptians would believe they stole the money and would be punished for it.

When the brothers returned home, even Jacob displayed a momentary lapse in faith. When his sons told him what had transpired, including the command to return to Egypt with Benjamin (now Jacob's most favored and endeared son), Jacob lamented, "'You have deprived me of my children. Joseph is no more, and Simeon is no more, and now you want to take Benjamin. Everything is against me!'" (Gen. 42:36). Again, as John Lennox noted earlier, Jacob was still "all about me," so his faith was withering against this bad news.

In an effort to ease his father's troubled mind, Rueben impetuously volunteered to sacrifice his two sons if they returned from Egypt without Benjamin. This would do no one any good; murdering his two sons if he returned without Benjamin was no indication that any lessons were learned. Rueben was thinking in worldly terms, and no one thought to pray to God for assistance or guidance. But Jacob was adamant; if Benjamin went, the grief of losing his only surviving son of Rachel would kill him. Even Jacob did not see God's plan in any of this. If he had, he could have trusted that God would protect them all and that His promise to Jacob was still intact.

The famine continued, the conditions were getting worse for Jacob's family, and the topic of returning to Egypt came to the fore-front. The brothers reminded Jacob of the conditions for Simeon's release and the additional provisions they purchased were contingent upon them returning with Benjamin (meanwhile, Simeon remained in prison all this time). Jacob rebuked them for giving the Egyptian (a.k.a. Joseph) all that information in the first place.

At that juncture, they may have forgotten God's covenant with Abraham, which was repeated to Isaac and to Jacob. When Jacob arrived in Bethel all those years ago, he had a dream where God spoke of His promise to Abraham and his descendants. Rather than submitting to his earthly fears, Jacob should have remembered God's promise to protect him and his family, which He had already demonstrated several times. Jacob experienced a memory lapse or a gap in faith, but that is the beauty of the Scriptures; everyone in the Bible reflects our sinful, modern-day humanity. The Bible doesn't hide the frailties of the patriarchs. Who among us doesn't have worldly crises that cause us to forget we have God to protect us and provide comfort?

Finally, Judah stepped up to take control of the situation and promised Benjamin's safe return. He reminded Jacob that the entire family would die if they didn't make the trip. Rather than offering his children as a pledge like Reuben did, Judah made a more level, humane offer to take responsibility for Benjamin's safety. If anything happened to him, Judah would bear the blame. Recognizing that the entire family would die of starvation if they didn't make the trip, Jacob finally capitulated. He instructed them to take twice the money (in case the Egyptians realized they hadn't been paid on the first trip) and they made their way back to Joseph.

When Joseph saw that they returned with Benjamin, he told his steward to prepare a meal for everyone and to invite them to his royal home to dine. The brothers thought they were in trouble for not paying for the grain from the last visit, so they approached the steward, confessed to finding the silver in their sacks, and promised to pay it back in full. "'It's all right,' he said. 'Don't be afraid. Your God, the God of your father, has given you treasure in your sacks; I received your silver.' Then he brought Simeon out to them" (Gen. 43:23). It was a moment of honesty on the brothers' part to repay for the grain purchased earlier. It may have been driven by their fear of consequences; however, their hearts were moving in the right direction.

Although Joseph instructed the steward to return the money in their sacks, it appeared that the steward was more familiar with God's blessings and forgiveness than the brothers were. He must also have been familiar with some of the nuances of their faith through Joseph, who continued in his faith despite living in a pagan culture for the last 20 years. The steward must have been aware of Joseph's good nature as well, since he understood Joseph's plans.

When the brothers arrived for the meal, Joseph greeted them, inquired of the health of their (and his) father, and saw his younger brother for the first time in 20 years. Again, Joseph was emotionally overwhelmed and hurried out to weep in seclusion. When he returned, the meal was served with Joseph—maintaining the illusion he was an Egyptian—eating in a separate room because Hebrews were detestable to Egyptians. The brothers were amazed that the seating arrangement had them in order of their ages.

Joseph tested their reactions when Benjamin was given a portion of food that was five times the portion of the others. He wanted to see if any jealousy remained when it appeared the youngest received favored treatment (like Joseph's robe of many colors). The brothers passed this test, and everyone enjoyed the meal, which was another indication that their hearts were overcoming thoughts of envy and jealousy.

When it came time for the brothers to buy grain and food and return home, Joseph set up one final test to see how far they had come in restoring their hearts. He instructed his steward to fill the sacks with grain along with the silver they used to purchase the grain. The steward was also told to put Joseph's silver cup into Benjamin's sack. Paul House writes, "Joseph has a cup placed in Benjamin's sack to make him look like a thief. Why? To see if they will protect Benjamin. All is lost if they treat him as they did Joseph."[199] After the brothers started for home, the steward and the court guards caught up to them and accused them of stealing the Governor's silver cup, essentially returning evil for the good that was shown to them.

---

[199]Paul House, *Old Testament Survey,* 1992, pp. 43–44.

The brothers were adamant about their innocence and suggested that whoever was found to have it would die and the others would return as slaves. This was more severe punishment than what the steward levied; only the one with the cup would be taken as a slave, the rest could return home. When the cup was discovered in Benjamin's sack, the brothers tore their garments in anguish and remorse. They realized that, like the silver, God had a role in this, but they were still in the dark. They loaded up their donkeys and returned to the city with the steward and Benjamin.

The steward's punishment was for Benjamin to return as his slave and the rest could return home. Unlike deserting Joseph when they sold him to the caravan, the brothers would not abandon Benjamin. They would not return home without him while he endured the punishment, and knowing full well how all this would affect their father.

They knew Benjamin couldn't have stolen the Governor's cup and they were willing to give up their freedom to defend Benjamin's innocence. Their selfish behavior was behind them; regardless of the risk to their own lives, they vowed to protect their youngest brother, the one most loved by their father. They could have taken the easy way out and let Benjamin go back to the Governor as a slave (like Joseph had become) while they returned home, but their love for their father and for Jacob's favored son meant they would rather give up their freedom than allow harm to come to Benjamin. Their spiritual hearts were getting stronger.

They threw themselves before Joseph for mercy. Joseph feigned anger and asked how they could do such a thing to him; weren't they aware of his ability to find them out? Judah, not Reuben the oldest, pled on behalf of Benjamin. "'How can we prove our innocence? God has uncovered your servants' guilt. We are now my lord's slaves—we ourselves and the one who was found to have the cup'" (Gen. 44:16). Judah and his brothers recognized that this whole scenario was the result of their sin against Joseph all those years ago and they were ready to accept the consequences of those actions to protect Benjamin and become Joseph's slaves.

Interestingly, the brothers endured the same hardships that Joseph did after being sold to the caravan: they were imprisoned and accused of a crime they did not commit (the brothers for stealing the cup and Joseph for the attempted rape of Potiphar's wife). As Joseph was a slave to Potiphar, the brothers agreed to become slaves to protect Benjamin. Their repentance has restored their hearts; they were suffering similar consequences that befell Joseph and were willing to accept the consequences for their past sin.

Joseph pushed the envelope by refusing to take them all as slaves; only Benjamin would remain behind while the rest were free to go. From John Lennox, "Robert Sacks gets it exactly right when he says, 'Joseph has now decided to put his brothers to the final test. He will place them in a position where they will be strongly tempted to treat Benjamin as they had treated him. The point of Joseph's trial is that repentance is only complete when one knows that if he were placed in the same position, he would not act in the way he had acted before.'"[200]

Judah took on the leadership and made one of the most impassioned speeches in the Old Testament[201] as he pled for Benjamin and appealed to the Governor's mercy. "For depth of feeling and sincerity of purpose it stands unexcelled. What makes it most remarkable, however, is the fact that it comes from the lips of one who once upon a time was so calloused that he cared nothing about the grief he caused his father."[202]

Judah detailed how Benjamin was loved by their father as the only son left from Rachel, his true love; the other brother died. Judah related Jacob's remorse over the son who was torn to pieces by wild animals and the hardship to him if anything should happen to Benjamin. He related the personal pledge he made to Jacob to ensure Benjamin's safety and how, if they returned without Benjamin, their father would surely die of grief. He offered himself as a sacrifice in the place of

---

[200]John Lennox, *Joseph*, 2019, p. 192.

[201]Lennox goes a step further in describing Judah's speech: "Judah then steps in and embarks on one of the greatest and most moving speeches in all literature." Ibid., p. 193.

[202]H. C. Leupold. *Exposition of Genesis: Volumes 1 and 2*, 1942, p. 1086.

Benjamin: "'Now then, please let your servant remain here as my lord's slave in place of the boy and let the boy return with his brothers. How can I go back to my father if the boy is not with me? No! Do not let me see the misery that would come on my father'" (Gen. 44:33–34).

Iain Provan describes Judah's earlier characteristics: "...Judah is presented as someone who does not care about other people, even in his own family...He does not mourn for any of the three deaths [his wife and two oldest sons], and upon the death of his wife, in fact, he goes straight off to a prostitute...Later, he condemns the widow Tamar for having illicit sex, even though he as a widower has just done the same thing."[203] But that Judah was now gone; the new Judah, the Judah whose spiritual heart had been restored, was now full of compassion and selflessness.

It was Judah's idea to sell Joseph to the caravan, now he was willing to sacrifice everything so that his younger brother would not endure the same fate he assumed had befallen his brother Joseph. Although not explicitly stated, the rest of the brothers were willing to join Judah. The jealousy of their father's special child was completely wiped out of the brothers' hearts. Even though Judah took the lead, they were all before the Governor willing to suffer in Benjamin's place. They made great strides in restoring their hearts. Judah and his brothers' spiritual hearts reached a zenith. H. C. Leupold adds, "No doubt the entire attitude of all the rest showed as clearly that Judah was speaking the most inner thoughts of their heart. There could be no more doubt as to whether the brethren were minded toward their father and his most dearly beloved son as they once were. They were all transformed men."[204]

Judah's tender and heart-wrenching speech of love and remorse was too much for Joseph; he couldn't hold back his love for his brothers any longer. He ordered all the Egyptians to leave them alone, then revealed to his brothers that he was Joseph. It took time for them to comprehend this astounding revelation, but Joseph gathered them

---

[203]Iain Provan, *Discovering Genesis,* 2015, pp. 187–88.

[204]H. C. Leupold, *Exposition of Genesis: Volumes 1 and 2,* 1942, p. 1088.

together to console them and told them not to be angry with themselves for selling him to Egypt. He revealed that it was all part of God's plan to save the family from the famine (it still had five more years before it would end) so that His covenant with the family could continue. Joseph did not condemn them or hold a grudge against them. The brothers' actions were meant for evil, but God allowed it for their benefit. Was this not the very ideal of forgiveness and love Jesus taught during his mission? Displaying the epitome of the Second Great Commandment, Joseph harbored no ill will toward his brothers and, on forgiving their malice toward him, he brought everyone under his protective wing in Egypt.

When Pharaoh heard the news of Joseph's family reunion, he gave gifts and provisions to the brothers for their journey to collect the rest of the family and return to Egypt. Joseph sent his brothers to Canaan and told them not to quarrel on the way. When they arrived home, they told Jacob that Joseph was alive and in charge of all Egypt. At first, he didn't believe the news, but when he was shown the gifts they brought back, his spirit was revived. He may have forgotten Joseph's dreams and Jacob's own faith must have been shaken all those years, but he was happy to know Joseph was alive.

God appeared to Jacob the night before they departed telling him not to be afraid to return to Egypt, because it was part of His plan to make a great nation from him, as He promised Abraham. When they arrived in Egypt, Jacob was greeted by Joseph, and it was a tearful but joyous reunion. Joseph settled his family in Goshen where the land was ideal for raising livestock (the family trade) and away from the main population of Egyptians; the profession and culture of the Israelites was disdainful to the locals. It would turn out to be geographically advantageous when, as we'll see in the next chapter, the Israelites were spared from the plagues God sent upon Egypt to free His people.

As the famine continued, so did Joseph's fame and wealth because of how he administered provisions. When the famine ended and conditions returned to normal, the family was also blessed with wealth. When their father died 17 years later, the brothers wondered if Joseph still held a grudge and would punish them now that their father was gone. It should have been clear from Joseph's actions when he revealed his identity to them that he had forgiven them, but they still hadn't learned the lesson of true forgiveness. Sins forgiven are sins forgotten. Perhaps they were thinking on their own level of limited spiritual growth and feared his reprisal.

To compound this lack of faith and trust, they created another act of deception by stating Jacob left instructions for Joseph before he died to forgive his brothers the sins and wrongs they committed in treating him so badly. When Joseph read this message, he wept because they did not understand that he had forgiven them long ago. He was disheartened to see that his brothers did not realize the nature of his heart and that all was forgiven and forgotten.

When Joseph's brothers came to him, they still felt their guilt and threw themselves before him as slaves. Joseph tried to console them once again, saying he was not in the place of God to judge or condemn them. He reminded them that, while they intended to do him harm, God allowed it for the good that it accomplished, saving the family and continuing God's covenant. "So then, don't be afraid. I will provide for you and your children.' And he reassured them and spoke kindly to them" (Gen. 50:21).

Joseph showed compassion, generosity, mercy, and kindness toward his brothers. In fact, after he was empowered by Pharaoh, he did not seek revenge against the cupbearer for forgetting him and causing Joseph to remain there two more years, nor did he seek vengeance against Potiphar or his wife for putting him there on false charges. Given the culture of the time, revenge and retaliation were the norm, as we witnessed by his brothers' earlier actions. Joseph's kindness, compassion, and forgiveness were the characteristics Jesus would impart in His teaching centuries later. Joseph was ahead of his time in demonstrating that component of his heart.

Joseph's trust in God throughout his trials in his early life—without complaint or shaken faith—demonstrated the quality of obedience and faith that are core elements of the First Great Commandment. Going through trials in his life while maintaining a strong faith was what the prophet Habakkuk wrote about centuries later. "Though the fig tree does not bud and there are no grapes on the vines, though the olive crop fails, and the fields produce no food, though there are no sheep in the pen and no cattle in the stalls, yet I will rejoice in the LORD, I will be joyful in God my Savior" (Hab. 3:17–18). Joseph was the epitome of the spiritual heart designed by God; he wasn't perfect, but he was one of finest examples of God's image in the Old Testament.

In contrast, his brothers took a savage revenge for the rape of their sister, demonstrated sexual moral lapses, and showed extreme jealousy of Jacob's favoritism toward Joseph. Retaliation for harm was so ingrained in them that they never understood Joseph's approach of forgiveness, kindness, and mercy that related perfectly to the love Jesus preached. Joseph demonstrated exactly the spiritual heart I defined at the outset; not perfectly pure before the original sin, but very close to what God intended for our lives.

Forgiveness does not harbor resentment, but overcomes the hurt and moves on, forgetting the offense. When you are forgiven, your sin is forgotten, not to be brought up as a constant reminder of the offense. Joseph's brothers could not rid themselves of the guilt even though Joseph told them many times they were forgiven and continued to treat them with kindness and mercy. This behavior was exactly what Jesus spoke about centuries later.

I would like to think that the brothers had their spiritual hearts restored, that they recognized their sin, sought forgiveness, turned back to God, and had compassion for one another. With their hearts restored, they could live under Joseph's authority and enjoy the riches and prosperity of Egypt. Not that this is a worldly endowment, but it does reflect how God protects and blesses His people. Just as we trust our lives to Jesus, the brothers relied on Joseph and lived in a "heavenly" land. What a contrast to almost losing their lives to the famine!

A lesson modern-day Christians can learn from Joseph's story is that, as sinners, we are forgiven, and we don't need to hang on to guilt. God doesn't hold our sin over us in punishment. When Isaiah was shown God's glory early in his mission, he was overwhelmed; he didn't feel worthy to be in God's presence. One of the seraphim in his vision brought a live coal from the altar before the Lord, and with it "he touched my mouth and said, 'See, this has touched your lips; your guilt is taken away and your sin atoned for'" (Isa. 6:7). And the writer of Hebrews advises, "let us draw near to God with a sincere heart and with the full assurance that faith brings, having our hearts sprinkled to cleanse us from a guilty conscience..." (Heb. 10:22).

On his deathbed at the age of 110, Joseph reminded his entire family of God's promise to Abraham's descendants. He reiterated the agreement of the covenant, saying that God would come to their aid and take them out of Egypt to the land He promised on oath to Abraham, Isaac, and Jacob.

Chapter 5

GUIDELINES FOR THE
NEW NATION'S HEART

I n the first several chapters, we examined the lives and hearts of individuals with varying degrees of spiritual development in the book of Genesis. At this juncture, I'll discuss how God provided guidance and instruction to develop the spiritual heart of an entire nation. Following Jacob's reunion with Joseph and after years of living in Egypt, their descendants grew into a small nation. As God promised Abraham, He would deliver His people out of Egypt to the Promised Land where He would be their God and they would be His people. In the next several books of the Bible, God filled His promise, but He had to hone His people to be ready for this unique relationship with Him.

Part of this education came in the form of hardships to test their resolve and evaluate their level of trust and obedience. Another part came in the form of commandments and rules (the Law) that God relayed to His people through Moses and thus, the Law has guided the Jewish faith ever since. The Law provided a blueprint for the nation to develop the spiritual hearts they would need to be His representatives on earth and to fulfill the role originally designed for Adam. God would dwell with His people, provide them protection against enemies, and make them prosper if they were faithful and obedient to Him. Anthony Petterson states the purpose of the Law: "The law was never a means of salvation; rather it was the means by which God's people were to live out their salvation to reflect the character of God in the world. This relationship is formalized in a covenant as the people commit themselves to obedience in view of all God had done to initiate the relationship and save them."[205]

Beyond the need to set the groundwork to develop the Israelites' hearts, God was preparing them to be His representatives and set the moral bar for others. Eugene Merrill writes, "Their role thenceforth would be to mediate or intercede as priests between the holy God and the wayward nations of the world, with the end in view not only declaring his salvation but also of providing the human channel in and through whom this salvation would be effected."[206]

Settling in the Promised Land of Canaan was deliberate in terms of its prime location in the Middle East for this priestly role to be fulfilled. Not only was the land fertile for agricultural purposes for the Israelites' prosperity, it was also the primary location of the major trading route or corridor between Egypt and points going east. This was the link to other nations for God's people to shine as His beacon. From Peter Gentry and Stephen Wellum, "All the communication, commerce and trade back and forth between Egypt and Mesopotamia will pass through Canaan. And when it does, what are the travelers and traders supposed to see? They are supposed to witness a group of people who demonstrate a right relationship to the one and only true God, a human way if treating each other, and a proper stewardship of the earth's resources."[207]

I mentioned in Chapter 2 that Adam was to be God's agent and have sovereignty over the earth, but in their sin, he and Eve lost the position that God intended for them. The nation of Israel was to reinstate Adam's role on a large scale. Walter Kaiser reinforces their role: "Israel was to be separate and holy; she was to be separate and as no other people on the face of the earth. As an elect or called people now being formed into a nation under God, holiness was not an optional feature. Israel had to be holy; as such, they could not be consecrated

[205]Anthony Petterson, *ESV Expository Commentary (Volume 7): Daniel–Malachi (Zechariah)*, 2018, p. 635.

[206]Eugene Merrill, *Kingdom of Priests*, 2008, p. 98.

[207]Peter Gentry and Stephen Wellum, *Kingdom Through Covenant*, 2018, pp. 297–98.

or set apart any further to anything or person or enter into any rival relationships."[208]

As we'll see, God's method of delivering them out of Egypt was to demonstrate His power and glory so they would understand His love and protection for them. His intentions to form a covenant with His people were described to the Israelites by Moses after He brought them out of Egypt. "'You yourselves have seen what I did to Egypt, and how I carried you on eagles' wings and brought you to myself. Now if you obey me fully and keep my covenant, then out of all nations you will be my treasured possession. Although the whole earth is mine, you will be for me a kingdom of priests and a holy nation'" (Exod. 19:4–6). James Boice summarizes, "He was taking a nation of slaves with no discipline, no law, and no religion, and He was giving them all three of those things. He was beginning to train a rabble to become a nation, as well as the kind of fighting force that would one day be able to conquer the land of promise."[209]

This training was expansive and considered information from the books of Exodus, Leviticus, Numbers, and Deuteronomy. The four books (in brief) provide instructions for worshiping God, setting up the priesthood and their functions, defining a moral code for the people to live by, and constructing the ark and tabernacle as God's "temporary housing" when He dwells among His people. That is a lot of material to survey, but I will limit the discussion to the foundation and structure of the spiritual heart of the nation and how the Hebrews rebel or respond to God's instructions.

Background

In Chapter 3, I shared how God revealed to Abraham that his descendants would be led to the Promised Land of Canaan. God told Abraham that these descendants would first suffer oppression by other nations, but God promised He would deliver them from servitude and

---

[208]Walter Kaiser, *The Promise-Plan of God,* 2008, p. 78.

[209]James Boice, *The Life of Moses,* 2018, p. 218.

lead them back to Canaan. Three generations later, Joseph brought his family into Egypt to escape the famine, which began God's plan to bring them out of Egypt several generations later. Initially, Joseph's family prospered in Egypt. Scriptures say that Jacob was 130 years old, and Joseph was about 40 when Jacob arrived in Egypt with his family. Joseph lived another 70 years, during which the family expanded and prospered. It was after his death that fortunes changed for the Israelites; in fact, the oppression God spoke about was the internment and slave conditions they would experience over the next 145 years before Moses would lead them out of Egypt and to the Promised Land.[210]

Despite the pagan environment of Egypt and decades of enslavement, Jacob's descendants maintained their faith. There was no mention of corporate worship, but God's promise to deliver Abraham's descendants to the Promised Land was passed down to each generation. When the oppression reached intolerable levels, their collective cry to God indicated they were still cognizant of their relationship with Him and of His promises passed down through Abraham, Isaac, and Jacob.

The preservation of faith may have been a result of their isolated location in Egypt. Regarding Joseph and his family settling in Goshen, away from the main populous of Egypt, H. C. Leupold writes, "The Israelites were, therefore, isolated geographically and nationally as long as they were in Egypt. Intermarriage with Israelites was out of the question...At the same time Israel was guarded against falling into idolatry of its neighbors as a nation. For the strict isolation of the nation as long as it was in Egypt naturally extended also to matters of religion. Safeguarded thus against idolatry, Israel was at the same time outside the reach of Canaanite immortality and its contamination." [211]

The Egyptians detested the Hebrews despite Joseph rescuing the nation from the famine and his prominence in Pharaoh's court. As shepherds, a trade the Egyptians felt was beneath them, Joseph carved

---

[210]The 145 years after Joseph's death to the time Moses leads the Israelites out of Egypt is calculated in the discussion in Appendix A.

[211]H. C. Leupold, *Exposition of Genesis: Volumes 1 and 2*, 1942, p. 1105.

out the area of Goshen where the family settled. It was no accident this isolation from the general Egyptian population occurred; it was part of God's plan. First, God protected them from the impact of most of the plagues. Second, when Moses prepared to lead them out of Egypt, they were in one location and easier to gather than if they were scattered throughout the land. Third, and most importantly, they practiced their faith without assimilating the pagan practices of the Egyptians' polytheistic religion.[212]

Exodus: Escape from Egypt

In his commentary on the Book of Exodus, Walter Kaiser notes, "Preeminently, it (Exodus) lays the foundations for a theology of God's revelation of his person, his redemption, his laws and his worship. It also initiates the great institution of the priesthood..."[213]

The book of Exodus begins long after Joseph and his family had passed and there was a new Pharaoh who did not know of Joseph and the contribution he made to Egypt as a Hebrew. The Hebrew population had grown so large that Pharaoh feared their size. They were an important element to Egypt's economy since they were relied upon for slave labor, but they also posed a military dilemma. If Egypt was attacked and the Hebrews were to join forces with the enemy, Egyptian security would be jeopardized. Kaiser adds, "The situation calls for an extremely delicate balance: Pharaoh needs to maintain the Israelite presence as an economic asset without thereby jeopardizing Egypt's national security."[214] With these concerns in mind, Pharaoh and his court devised a plan to manage the growing population of

---

[212]That is not to say the Hebrews were unaware of the Egyptians' pagan practices. Elements of the Egyptian culture were ingrained in the Hebrews that led to idolatry and plagued them for centuries. God caused them to wander in the desert for 40 years to allow that generation to die out and cleanse them of the Egyptian influence. But as we'll see in this and subsequent chapters, paganism comes back to haunt the Hebrews until they return from Babylonian captivity some 1,000 years later.

[213]Walter Kaiser, *The Promise-Plan of God,* 2008, p. 342.

[214] Ibid., p. 352.

the Israelites. "So, they put slave masters over them to oppress them with forced labor, and they built Pithom and Rameses as store cities for Pharaoh" (Exod. 1:11). Scriptures describe the level of oppression the Israelites endured as slaves to the Egyptians. However, the more they were oppressed, the more their population increased, which proved problematic for Pharaoh; his plan seemed to have backfired, but God's plan for Abraham's descendants to be as numerous as the stars in heaven stays on course.

As the Hebrew population continued to expand unabated, Pharaoh devised another plan. He gave orders to the Hebrew midwives to kill any male child born to the Israelite women. Thankfully, the midwives had more religious conviction than fear of Pharaoh, so they disobeyed Pharaoh's edict and protected the male children.

When Pharaoh demanded to know why the population continued to grow, the midwives explained that Hebrew women were giving birth faster than the midwives could get there. Once again, God's plan prevailed and Pharaoh's plan to limit the Hebrew threat was frustrated. The midwives were rewarded for their faith. "So God was kind to the midwives and the people increased and became even more numerous. And because the midwives feared God, he gave them families of their own" (vv. 20–21).[215] Seeing that his orders did not result in the change he sought, Pharaoh issued an edict to all his people that any male Hebrew child born must be thrown into the Nile River to its death, but the girl babies may be spared.

Not that I want to give Satan a lot of ink, but throughout the Bible, he does everything he can to confuse mankind and thwart God's ultimate plan for our salvation. His evil actions started with deceiving

---

[215]Defying the king's edict in order to stay faithful to God occurs again in the Book of Daniel. Daniel's three friends, Shadrach, Meshach, and Abednego are brought before the king who demands to know why they refuse to worship his statue. Responding to the consequences of their defiance, they said, "'If we are thrown into the blazing furnace, the God we serve is able to deliver us from it, and he will deliver us from Your Majesty's hand. But even if he does not, we want you to know, Your Majesty, that we will not serve your gods or worship the image of gold you have set up'" (Dan. 3:17–18). Furious over their defiance, the king throws all three into the fiery furnace, but God protected them in the same sense that He blessed the midwives for their faith.

Adam and Eve in the Garden, causing all mankind to struggle in an imperfect world. This deception continued throughout the Scriptures, including tempting Jesus in the desert with physical and earthly pleasures. It's not difficult to see that Satan was behind Pharaoh's plan to kill all the male Hebrew newborns, which would eventually include Moses. Without Moses, there wouldn't be an Exodus, hence no nation of Israel. If there was no Israel, there would be no nation for Jesus to return to at His second coming. This was Satan's attempt to dislodge God's plan.

Pharaoh's motivation was not unlike Herod's when he ordered all the male children under two years of age in Bethlehem to be killed after Jesus was born. Like Pharaoh's concern for threats against his empire,[216] Herod was equally obsessed with threats to his authority given the prophecy that a new king would be born in Bethlehem.[217] Herod refused to think he had to share or give up his reign. "When Herod realized that he had been outwitted by the Magi, he was furious, and he gave orders to kill all the boys in Bethlehem and its vicinity who were two years old and under, in accordance with the time he had learned from the Magi" (Matt. 2:16). As he was likely the catalyst for Pharaoh's motivation, Satan was behind the scenes with Herod to kill Jesus before He got to His ministry. James Boice writes, "We have to see the hand of Satan in anti-Semitism throughout history. He moved the pharaoh to kill the male babies. He did the same thing

---

[216]Josephus writes that some of the sacred scribes to Pharaoh forewarned the king that "about this time, a child would be born to the Israelites, who, if he [that is, Moses] were reared, would bring the Egyptian dominion low, and would raise the Israelites; that he would excel all men in virtue and obtain a glory that would be remembered though all the ages" (*Jewish Antiquities,* Book 1, Chapter 9, v. 3). The fear of that prophecy being fulfilled was enough for the king to take this action.

[217]These are not the only instances where Satan used genocide in an attempt to ruin God's Plan. In the Book of Esther, he used Haman, a high official to King Xerxes of the Persian-Mede empire, to trick the emperor into signing a decree that would allow the death of all the Jews in the empire, thereby eliminating God's chosen people and Jesus' eventual arrival. Queen Esther was made aware of the plan by her uncle, Mordecai, who was a Jewish official at the King's Gate. Esther was able to expose Haman's deceitful plan to her husband, who rescinded his edict and put Haman to death. Genocide avoided.

at the time of the birth of Jesus Christ, working in Herod to kill the babies in Bethlehem."[218]

As with Herod's plan, God intervened in Pharaoh's plot. In Josephus' account, Amram (father to Moses), "one of the nobler sorts of Hebrew, whose wife was with child (Moses), prayed to God for the safety of his people and for that of his own child."[219] God answered his prayer in a dream by reminding Amram of His promise through Abraham to deliver His people to the Promised Land and it would be his son who would lead the Israelites out. Therefore, God protected Moses to ensure the promise was fulfilled.

Three months after Moses was born, his parents could no longer hide the child from the Egyptians. They determined to trust the "safety and care of the child to God, rather than depend on their own concealment of him."[220] This total trust in God's protection was not unlike the trust Abraham displayed when he was ordered to sacrifice his son Isaac. In both cases, the spiritual hearts of the parents placed their respective sons' fates in God's hands, trusting in His ultimate promise. The book of Hebrews recognized his parents' trust in God: "By faith Moses' parents hid him for three months after he was born, because they saw he was no ordinary child, and they were not afraid of the king's edict" (Heb. 11:23).

His mother, Jochebed, constructed a waterproof basket and placed it in the Nile River. Moses's older sister Miriam stood at a distance to see what would happen to him. The basket was discovered by Pharaoh's daughter while she was bathing in the river; God was obviously working in the background. Miriam popped onto the scene to offer the assistance of a Hebrew wet nurse to help the princess wean the child, which turned out to be Jochebed, Moses's mother. She had a strong spiritual heart and Moses was taught under the Hebrew faith and traditions rather than exposed to Egyptian pagan practices of the king's court.

---

[218]James Boice, *The Life of Moses*, 2018, p. 26

[219]Josephus, *Jewish Antiquities*, Book 2, Chapter 9, v. 3:211.

[220] Ibid., v. 4:219.

Scriptures are silent regarding Moses's life in the Egyptian court for the next 40 years. We get some information of this period from Stephen's testimony at his trial before the Sanhedrin in the New Testament. He recounted the life of Moses as he did for Abraham. "When he was placed outside, Pharaoh's daughter took him and brought him up as her own son. Moses was educated in all the wisdom of the Egyptians and was powerful in speech and action" (Acts 7:21–22). Moses was raised in the Egyptian court under protection of the princess.[221] He was well educated and, according to Stephen's account, was quite the oral presenter and military leader.

By Stephen's characterization of Moses being powerful in action, we may draw on Josephus to fill in the gaps.[222] Despite the protection of Pharaoh's daughter, the king's court watched his development with a wary eye. When he reached a mature age, Egypt was attacked by the neighboring nation of Ethiopia. The military attack was successful, and the Ethiopians took over several provinces of Egypt. Josephus tells us that God wanted Pharaoh to make Moses a general in the Egyptian army and launch a counterattack. The princess rebuked those who wanted to kill Moses and they now were ashamed to admit they needed his help. However, they secretly hoped that Moses would be killed during the battle.

God was with Moses and helped him beat the Ethiopians back, recovering all the territory lost plus the spoils of victory. While the populace rejoiced over Moses's victory, the king's court grew angrier

---

[221]Josephus tells us that, when the princess brought Moses into the court, the scribes who foretold of the Hebrew that would bring the nation low identified Moses as the very one who would cause Egypt's hardships. They urged Pharaoh to kill the child to prevent the prophecy from coming true. The princess grabbed Moses before harm could be done. "And the king was not hasty to slay him. God himself, whose providence protected Moses, inclined the king to spare him." *Jewish Antiquities,* Book 2, Chapter 9, v. 4:236.

[222]Josephus, *Jewish Antiquities,* Book 2, Chapter 10.

with his success and feared him taking up the Hebrews in a rebellion to overthrow the government.[223]

When Moses was 40 years old, he killed an Egyptian for beating one of the Hebrew slaves. Fearful of being caught, Moses buried the Egyptian in the sand. Pharaoh was made aware of the situation, and he sought to kill Moses, likely for the reasons Josephus provided in his account, but Pharaoh also had legal justification to be rid of him. Moses fled to Midian and remained there until God called him. He left all his connections to Egypt and the enslaved, oppressed Israelites behind.[224]

While in Midian, Moses married and had two children. He was tending his flock in Pithom when God commissioned him to lead His people out of Egypt to the Promised Land. This journey would hone their spiritual hearts, test their trust in God, and correct their rebellious behavior. But first, God had to prepare Moses for leadership and to give him the spiritual tools to take on Pharaoh and the Egyptian military.

Out of Egypt – Lessons for a Trusting Heart

As you read through the Scriptures, it becomes apparent that the men God chose for specific tasks were unlikely candidates. Abraham was a childless, 75-year-old whose trust in God was tentative at best, yet he would be the father of the nation of Israel. Gideon, a simple farmer with no military training, led a small army against the Midianites and defeated them. In the New Testament, Jesus selected ordinary men like fishermen and tax collectors to be His apostles rather than learned

---

[223]The jealousy and fear of his military success sounds similar to Saul's envy of David's military success which will be discussed in Chapter 8. Note that both Saul and the Pharaoh sought to have their potential 'rivals' killed.

[224]The book of Hebrews treats this account in a more positive light. "By faith Moses, when he had grown up, refused to be known as the son of Pharaoh's daughter. He chose to be mistreated along with the people of God rather than to enjoy the fleeting pleasures of sin" (Heb. 11:24–25). Moses removed himself from his courtly persona and identified with the oppression of his own people. He forwent the life of the "rich and famous" and returned to his people as God commanded him.

scholars or speakers. Saul of Tarsus, persecutor of the early church, was selected to spread the gospel to the Gentiles. However, these and others demonstrated the power in God's plans.

Moses was reluctant in his initial meeting with God. The 40 years in Midian and living in the Egyptian court must have softened Moses's resolve and sense of authority. When God appeared to him in the burning bush and tasked him to lead the nation of Israel out of Egypt (emphasizing that He would be with him all along the way), Moses balked at the thought of the undertaking. He gave several excuses for why God may have picked the wrong man for the task, but each time, God reassured Moses that He would protect and assist him. God had to strengthen Moses's spiritual heart to lead His people and minister to their spiritual development.

"But Moses said to God, 'Who am I that I should go to Pharaoh and bring the Israelites out of Egypt?'" (Exod. 3:11). God responded, "I will be with you" (v. 12). Still not comfortable with the assignment, Moses said, "'Suppose I go to the Israelites and say to them, "The God of your fathers has sent me to you," and they ask me, "What is his name?" Then what shall I tell them?'" (v. 13). God responded, "I AM WHO I AM" and told Moses that He was fulfilling the promise made to Abraham, Isaac, and Jacob to lead the people out of bondage into the land of Canaan. God revealed His plan for Moses to entreat Pharaoh to let the people go but warned Moses that Pharaoh would resist releasing the Israelites. This resistance, however, would allow God to demonstrate His power over the Egyptians and that His people could trust in Him to deliver them. By the time God was finished with the Egyptians, they were paying the Israelites to leave Egypt.

Despite God's reassurance that He was fulfilling His promise, Moses was still not comfortable with his role saying, "'What if they do not believe me or listen to me and say, "The LORD did not appear to you"?'" (Exod. 4:1). God gave Moses two signs: He changed Moses's staff into a snake and back into his staff, and He made the skin on his hand leprous and restored it. A third sign for the Israelites would be for Moses to take water from the Nile and it would turn to blood when poured on dry ground.

Moses continued with yet another excuse: "Moses said to the LORD, 'Pardon your servant, Lord. I have never been eloquent, neither in the past nor since you have spoken to your servant. I am slow of speech and tongue'" (v. 10). God responded that He would help him speak and teach him what to say. "But Moses said, 'Pardon your servant, Lord. Please send someone else'" (v. 13). This last pushback must have irritated God (if that's possible) because God's anger burned against Moses, and He told Moses to use his brother Aaron as his spokesman. God would speak to Moses directly and he would use Aaron to speak to the people.

Moses returned to Egypt (by that time, those who wanted to kill him were dead) and was reunited with his brother Aaron. Together, they met with the leaders of the Hebrews to relay God's message and plan for them. "Moses and Aaron brought together all the elders of the Israelites, and Aaron told them everything the LORD had said to Moses. He also performed the signs before the people, and they believed. And when they heard that the LORD was concerned about them and had seen their misery, they bowed down and worshiped" (Exod. 4:29–31).

Moses and Aaron delivered God's command to Pharaoh to let the Hebrews go into the wilderness to offer sacrifices and worship Him. As a divine leader of the Egyptians, Pharaoh claimed he had no knowledge of their God and for them to ask for three days off to worship Him indicated that the Hebrew slaves were lazy and had too much time on their hands. He dismissed Moses and Aaron and directed the labor supervisors to stop providing the Hebrews with straw to make bricks. "'You are no longer to supply the people with straw for making bricks; let them go and gather their own straw. But require them to make the same number of bricks as before; don't reduce the quota'" (Exod. 5:7–8). The burden on the Hebrews increased because of Moses and Aaron's message to Pharaoh.

The spiritual heart of the Hebrews phased in and out, depending on the circumstances. When Moses and Aaron said that God would answer their prayers, they were relieved that He would intervene and, in their gratitude, they worshiped Him. Despite the news that

God would fulfill His promise to deliver them to the Promised Land, the people's faith failed them because of their increased hardships in having to maintain their quota for bricks without being supplied the straw to make them.

God told Moses and Aaron that, despite revealing displays of His might, Pharaoh's heart would remain hard, and he would refuse to free the Hebrews. In his next meeting with Pharaoh, Moses threw his staff to the ground in front of Pharaoh and his court, and it turned into a snake, just as God had shown Moses earlier. The magicians of the court duplicated Moses's actions, but Moses's snake devoured all of theirs. Pharaoh was unimpressed (or deliberately denied) the authority of God and refused the request to let the people go.

God sent ten devastating plagues against Pharaoh and his people to show them He was mightier than any of their gods. In addition to the destruction caused by each plague to the land, livestock, agriculture, economic structure, and population, each one was targeted toward the gods the Egyptians worshiped. James Boice writes "...the plagues were not a case of God's simply being arbitrary in his choice of scourges. The plagues were all directed against the gods of Egypt. Every single plague showed that the God of the Hebrews—the true God, Jehovah—was more powerful than Apis the bull or Hathor the cow, down through all the gods and goddesses of the Egyptian pantheon."[225]

For the first plague, God instructed Moses and Aaron to confront Pharaoh while he was bathing at the Nile (the source of fertility and agriculture for the nation), and to place his staff in the water, causing it to turn to blood. Oddly, Pharaoh's magicians compounded the pollution to demonstrate they could duplicate this "trick." The main source of the Egyptians' water supply was polluted beyond use. "The fish in the Nile died, and the river smelled so bad that the Egyptians could not drink its water. Blood was everywhere in Egypt" (Exod. 7:21). Regardless of this miracle, Pharaoh remained unimpressed and refused to let the Hebrews go.

---

[225]James Boice, *The Life of Moses*, 2018, p. 9.

God sent a plague of frogs all over Egypt, getting into everyone's homes, kitchens, pots, and food. Even though the magicians duplicated this action as well, the frogs proved too much for the people. Pharaoh conceded to let the Hebrews go if God would end the plague of frogs. God granted the request, but Pharaoh immediately had a change of heart and refused to honor his promise.

A pattern developed as God sent seven more plagues[226] upon the Egyptians. With each plague, Pharaoh could not deal with the consequences, so he pretended to repent and begged Moses to remove the plague on the promise of releasing his people. But each time God ended the plague, Pharaoh reneged on his promise. The court magicians are unable to duplicate the last several plagues and God limited these remaining plagues to affect only the Egyptians. The Hebrews, isolated in the Goshen area, were spared the consequences of each plague, demonstrating His protection of them. "'But on that day I will deal differently with the land of Goshen, where my people live; no swarms of flies will be there, so that you will know that I, the LORD, am in this land. I will make a distinction between my people and your people. This sign will occur tomorrow.'" (Exo. 8:22-23) The Hebrews and Egyptians were well aware that the plaques were targeted at the Egyptians, but Pharaoh remained adamantly opposed to letting the Hebrews leave Egypt.

Before His last plague (the death of all firstborn children and animals throughout Egypt), God gave instructions to Moses to prepare His people to leave Egypt for good. To protect the Hebrews and identify their allegiance to God, Moses instructed the Hebrews to sacrifice one-year-old unblemished lambs and use the blood to cover the mantles of their doors so the angel of death would pass over their homes. Anyone without the blood on their doorframes would suffer the loss

---

[226]As the creator of all things, God used elements of nature to demonstrate He is in total control. He sent swarms of gnats, followed by flies covering the land; a plague causing livestock to die, followed by festering boils on all the Egyptian people; then hailstones that killed anyone outside of their dwelling and destroyed animals and crops. He sent swarms of locust to eat the remaining crops, and finally, caused darkness in Egypt for three days.

of their firstborn, just like the Egyptians. Those who followed God's instructions would be delivered out of Egypt to the Promised Land.[227]

When the final plague took place, death covered all of Egypt, including Pharaoh's oldest son. Pharaoh finally allowed Moses and the Hebrews to leave. As God foretold Abraham, the Egyptians provided them with gold and jewelry, probably because they were happy to see them leave and end the plagues. When the people left Egypt, God protected them from the desert elements day and night. "By day the LORD went ahead of them in a pillar of cloud to guide them on their way and by night in a pillar of fire to give them light, so that they could travel by day or night. Neither the pillar of cloud by day nor the pillar of fire by night left its place in front of the people" (Exod. 13:21–22).

When Pharaoh recovered from the last plague, he realized the consequences of letting the Hebrew slaves go. He sent his army in pursuit, and they caught up with the Israelites as they reached the Red Sea. When the Israelites saw the army closing in on them, their faith in God and His promise immediately failed them, despite witnessing the ten plagues and having Him deliver them out of Egypt. All they could think of was their impending doom. "They said to Moses, 'Was it because there were no graves in Egypt that you brought us to the desert to die? What have you done to us by bringing us out of Egypt? Didn't we say to you in Egypt, "Leave us alone; let us serve the Egyptians"? It would have been better for us to serve the Egyptians than to die in the desert!'" (Exod. 14:11–12).

How quickly their trust in God left them; their hearts were weak. But God showed the Hebrews one more demonstration of His power and protection. Using Moses as his medium, God parted the Red Sea to allow the entire nation of Israel to cross through it, a spectacular miracle. The Egyptian army followed, then God released the waters, drowning the entire army "That day the LORD saved Israel from the hands of the Egyptians, and Israel saw the Egyptians lying dead on

---

[227]This is symbolic of Jesus and His mission to deliver mankind from sin and the spiritual death that goes with it. The blood around the mantle resembles the cross and the blood of the sacrificial unblemished lamb is like Jesus who is the Lamb of God, perfect and sinless, providing us a way from death to eternal life.

the shore. And when the Israelites saw the mighty hand of the LORD displayed against the Egyptians, the people feared the LORD and put their trust in him and in Moses his servant" (Exod. 14:30–31).

Their trust in God was short-lived. For three days they traveled in the desert without water. When they did find water, it was undrinkable and instantly they started to complain. This was the beginning of a series of complaints that demonstrated how quickly the Hebrews forgot everything God had shown them. Their physical needs overpowered their spiritual growth.

Walter Kaiser observes, "One would think that the mighty demonstration of God's power at the crossing at the Red Sea would quiet all grumbling and bad-mouthing of God or his servant Moses, but not so!"[228] Josephus also makes note of this in his account: "And by fixing their attention upon nothing but their present misfortunes, they were hindered from remembering what deliverances they had received from God, and those by the virtue and wisdom of Moses also..."[229]

On God's instruction, Moses threw a log into the water to make it pure and the complaining temporarily ceased. When they reached an oasis and settled in, Moses reminded the people that if they obeyed God's commands and trusted in His will, they would be protected.

A month later, the complaining was renewed. "The Israelites said to them, 'If only we had died by the LORD's hand in Egypt! There we sat around pots of meat and ate all the food we wanted, but you have brought us out into this desert to starve this entire assembly to death'" (Exod.16:3). Complaining that they had better eating conditions as slaves in Egypt and were drawn out to the desert to die, they again forgot all of God's prior miracles because of their immediate physical needs. There was no "waiting upon the Lord." Their spiritual hearts were overridden by their physical desires. This view that God had essentially abandoned them and wanting to return to their comfortable lifestyle in Egypt was not unusual in the Old Testament. I mentioned earlier how Lot sought to return to Sodom after Abraham

---

[228]Walter Kaiser, *The Promise-Plan of God,* 2008, p. 452.

[229]Josephus, *Jewish Antiquities,* Book 3, Chapter 1, v. 3:12.

rescued him. He preferred the material comfort that Sodom provided rather than life as a tent-dwelling livestock tender.

In his commentary on the prophet Zechariah, George Klein observes that the exiles returning to Jerusalem from Babylon had the same feelings of abandonment demonstrated by the Israelites on their way to the Promised Land. Prior to their captivity, the exiles trusted that God dwelled with them in the temple and would never destroy it or the city of Jerusalem. They didn't recognize that it was a judgement for their sin. "Thus, many understood the exile as God's breach of covenant, a divine act of abandoning his people forever. Moreover, on a socio-political level, life in Babylon for Judah's descendants was often better economically than the exiles had ever experienced before. The lure of materialism proved too strong for many who went into exile, just as it does today."[230]

Again, there was the lack of trust that God would continue to provide for their physical needs as the Israelites continued their journey across the desert. God did hear their cries, and in the morning, they discovered manna, a bread-like substance that God provided for them the entire time they were in the wilderness. He sent them bread for life, with instructions to take what they needed on a daily basis and not to store any of it except for the Sabbath. This was another lesson in trust; storing any of it for later indicated greed and implied that they didn't trust God's promise to take care of their daily needs.[231]

Not long after, the Israelites were without water and again the people leveled their complaints against Moses. God told Moses to strike a rock and water would come out of it for the people to drink. In

---

[230]George Klein, *The New American Commentary – Zechariah*, 2008, p. 118.

[231]As God provided manna for physical life for the Israelites, He sent His Son Jesus to provide spiritual life to those who put their faith in Him. After Jesus fed the 5,000, his followers asked what other signs He would show them. "'Our ancestors ate the manna in the wilderness; as it is written: "He gave them bread from heaven to eat."' Jesus said to them, "Very truly I tell you, it is not Moses who has given you the bread from heaven, but it is my Father who gives you the true bread from heaven. For the bread of God is the bread that comes down from heaven and gives life to the world." "Sir," they said, "always give us this bread." Then Jesus declared, "I am the bread of life. Whoever comes to me will never go hungry, and whoever believes in me will never be thirsty"'" John 6:31–35).

each of these three cases of complaining, the Hebrews did not repent of their bad behavior after their needs were met; instead, they were ready to stone Moses for the poor conditions.

God continued to protect His complaining people. During their journey, the Amalekites attacked from the rear of the procession where the weaker people were lagging. In the counterattack, Joshua, Moses's military leader, was successful as long as Moses raised his arms toward heaven. When he grew tired, Aaron and Hur held up his arms until the Amalekites are defeated. In all of these situations, God continued to show His people how He would protect them, but their level of trust lasted only until the next crisis.

The Law and the Beginning Rebellion

Three months after leaving Egypt, the people arrived at Mount Sinai where they set up camp. God gave Moses the Ten Commandments and additional instructions to make them a holy people. God also revealed His covenant with them: "'You yourselves have seen what I did to Egypt, and how I carried you on eagles' wings and brought you to myself. Now if you obey me fully and keep my covenant, then out of all nations you will be my treasured possession. Although the whole earth is mine, you will be for me a kingdom of priests and a holy nation'" (Exod. 19:4–6).[232]

The role of God's nation as a "kingdom of priests" was to set the bar for morality and righteousness for the rest of the world and, in doing so, to "help those around you to experience His grace, mercy, love, and forgiveness."[233] In essence, to demonstrate the virtues of the Second Great Commandment to the rest of the nations. Capturing Williams' summary, Jay Sklar adds, "As a kingdom of priests, Israel is

---

[232]The concept of a royal priesthood is repeated in the New Testament by the apostle Peter to followers of Jesus. In his first Epistle, he writes, "But you are a chosen people, a royal priesthood, a holy nation, God's special possession, that you may declare the praises of him who called you out of darkness into his wonderful light" (1 Peter 2:9).

[233]Jay Sklar, *ESV Expository Commentary (Volume 7): Daniel–Malachi (Jonah)*, 2018, p. 420.

called to represent the nations before God, to mediate God's redemptive purpose in the world. A priest stands between God and the people, representing each to the other...Yahweh here summons Israel as an entire nation to act as a priest, a covenantal mediator between Him and the rest of the world. In this priestly service, He expects Israel to pray for, love, minister to, and witness to the nations."[234]

God told Moses to ascend Mount Sinai to get the first set of instructions for the spiritual development of His people so that they may represent Him in the priestly manner He intended. During this time, Moses received the Ten Commandments written in God's hand. In giving Moses the Commandments, God also provided Moses with additional conditions and various situations that spell out each individual Commandment in more detail.[235]

For example, regarding worshiping Him exclusively, God warned Moses that when the people reached the Promised Land, they were to eliminate any foreign element and resist adopting pagan practices to keep them pure in their special relationship with God. "'I will establish your borders from the Red Sea to the Mediterranean Sea, and from the desert to the Euphrates River. I will give into your hands the people who live in the land, and you will drive them out before you. Do not make a covenant with them or with their gods. Do not let them live in your land or they will cause you to sin against me, because the worship of their gods will certainly be a snare to you'" (Exod. 23:31–33).

To demonstrate "loving one's neighbor as oneself," the Israelites were instructed to show respect for each other and for individual property (land and livestock). Improving the people's spiritual development reinforced the Second Great Commandment. God repeatedly stressed the importance of taking care of those in need, namely, the widows and orphans. "'Do not mistreat or oppress a foreigner, for you were foreigners in Egypt. Do not take advantage of the widow or the

---

[234] Ibid.

[235] Some of the situations God described are repeated in the book of Deuteronomy. The repetition is for the spiritual development of the second generation of Israelites. The first generation died while wandering in the desert as punishment for their lack of trust in God's will, to be discussed in the next section on Numbers.

fatherless. If you do and they cry out to me, I will certainly hear their cry'" (Exod. 22:21–23).[236] Social justice was a key ingredient to being God's representatives in the pagan world.

God provided further guidance in respecting the reputation of others (do not bear false witness) and avoiding personal biases (show kindness and compassion); they were to seek and demonstrate true and proper justice. "'Do not spread false reports. Do not help a guilty person by being a malicious witness. Do not follow the crowd in doing wrong. When you give testimony in a lawsuit, do not pervert justice by siding with the crowd, and do not show favoritism to a poor person in a lawsuit.'... 'Do not deny justice to your poor people in their lawsuits. Have nothing to do with a false charge and do not put an innocent or honest person to death, for I will not acquit the guilty. Do not accept a bribe, for a bribe blinds those who see and twists the words of the innocent'" (Exod. 23:1–3, 6–8).

God laid the initial groundwork for showing compassion when interacting with one another. He encouraged consideration and thoughtfulness toward their enemies and foreigners. It was not enough to show compassion toward those they got along with; but also, to those they didn't know or hated.[237] "'If you come across your enemy's ox or donkey wandering off, be sure to return it. If you see the donkey of someone who hates you fallen under its load, do not leave it there; be sure you help them with it...Do not oppress a foreigner; you yourselves know how it feels to be foreigners, because you were foreigners in Egypt'" (Exod. 23:4–5, 9). This was the behavior Joseph demonstrated

---

[236]In addition to rampant idolatry, ignoring this instruction was a failing of Israel that the prophets admonished religious leaders and authorities for, which eventually led to the nation's dissolution by Assyrian and Babylonian captivity (discussed in Chapter 11).

[237]Jesus reinforced this guidance in His teachings while here on earth. "'But to you who are listening I say: Love your enemies, do good to those who hate you, bless those who curse you, pray for those who mistreat you...If you love those who love you, what credit is that to you? Even sinners love those who love them. And if you do good to those who are good to you, what credit is that to you? Even sinners do that'" (Luke 6:27–28, 32–33). This will be discussed in more detail in Volume II.

in the last chapter; the development of the spiritual heart was not necessarily dependent upon a codified set of instructions.

After receiving these instructions, Moses returned to the camp to present them to the people. "When Moses went and told the people all the LORD's words and laws, they responded with one voice, 'Everything the LORD has said we will do'" (Exod. 24:3). Moses built an altar at the foot of the mountain, offered burnt offerings, and worshiped God.

God called Moses to return to Mount Sinai and he stayed on the mountain for forty days and forty nights. During this time, God gave Moses instructions for constructing His sanctuary so He could dwell among the people. These instructions also included the ark of the covenant, the tabernacle, an altar for worship, and the Tent of Meeting where Moses would communicate with God within the camp. God specified individuals for priesthood, their garments, how they were to be consecrated, and how to lead the people to worship and sacrifice.

His absence from the camp caused the Israelites to get restless. Despite agreeing to the spiritual guidance that they received a month earlier, their impatience resulted in their disobedience once again. They yearned to return to Egypt, which was a constant plague on their spiritual development. "When the people saw that Moses was so long in coming down from the mountain, they gathered around Aaron and said, 'Come, make us gods who will go before us. As for this fellow Moses who brought us up out of Egypt, we don't know what has happened to him'" (Exod. 32:1). Walter Kaiser says that this demand for false images "...reveals their inadequate faith in a time of waiting." He adds that their snide remark regarding "this fellow Moses" demonstrated a total lack of respect for God's appointed leader.[238]

Faced with impatient Israelites, Aaron caved to their demands. He collected their gold and fashioned it into an idol in the form of a calf. When in doubt, Moses was quick to ask the Lord for guidance. But with Moses out of the picture, Aaron acquiesced to the people who wanted something (an idol) to worship. "He took what they handed

---

[238]Walter Kaiser, *The Promise-Plan of God*, 2008, p. 540.

him and made it into an idol cast in the shape of a calf, fashioning it with a tool. Then they said, 'These are your gods, Israel, who brought you up out of Egypt'" (Exod. 32:4). It's rather disheartening that the Israelites would declare the idols were responsible for delivering them out of Egypt.[239]

The next day, the people indulged in revelry and profane worship of the idol, all under Aaron's consenting eyes. God brought this violation of His basic commandment to Moses's attention. "Then the LORD said to Moses, 'Go down, because your people, whom you brought up out of Egypt, have become corrupt. They have been quick to turn away from what I commanded them and have made themselves an idol cast in the shape of a calf. They have bowed down to it and sacrificed to it and have said, "These are your gods, Israel, who brought you up out of Egypt."' 'I have seen these people,' the LORD said to Moses, 'and they are a stiff-necked people'" (Exod. 32:7–9).

God disassociated Himself from the Israelites, labeling them Moses's people rather than His. Walter Kaiser writes, "The fact that they are 'quick to turn away' (v. 8) shows that Israel has apostatized from the truth revealed in word and events they themselves witnessed. A 'stiff-necked people' will not bow under God's authority, even though they have readily 'bowed down' to the calf and worshipped it."[240] G. K. Beale says that the term "stiff-necked people" is referred to several times in the Old Testament and alludes to the worshipers of the golden calf or sometimes to later idolaters. This metaphor...would seem to be a picture of a cow that does not want to go in the direction its master desires but responds with a stiff neck and wanders from the desired way."[241]

God told Moses He was finished with the people and would destroy them. God would make Moses individually into a great nation,

---

[239]This scene would be replicated by Jeroboam, first king of the divided kingdom of Israel, some 600 years later in a political move to keep his reign intact, as described in Chapter 9. Another lesson not learned.

[240]Walter Kaiser, *The Promise-Plan of God,* 2008, p. 541.

[241]G. K. Beale, *We Become What We Worship,* 2008, p. 82.

similar to what He told Abraham. This was a test to see how Moses would react. Moses advocated on behalf of the people and stated that such a punishment would void God's glory in the view of the pagan nations who would readily question the conviction of the Hebrews' God. Could He not see His plan to fruition? The Egyptians would think God took His people out to the desert to see them die. He reminded God of His covenant made with Abraham, Isaac, and Jacob. Moses passed God's challenge; he made the arguments God expected from the spiritual leader of His people and God relented from His threat.

However, Moses's advocacy did not prevent the consequences for the people's failure to adhere to the most basic requirement of their faith. Moses himself was angry with the people and with Aaron for resorting to idolatry. He destroyed the golden calf, admonished Aaron for his participation in the sin, and called upon those who were with him, not those participating in the revelry. The Levites sided with Moses, and he instructed them to kill those responsible for the rebellion, which resulted in about 3,000 deaths. This sounds harsh to today's Christians, but it was intended to purify the people from corruption. When Moses returned to God, he pled to God to forgive them for their sins. God did so but struck the people with a plague because of what they did. If these people were to be God's chosen, they must focus on spiritual develop and not fall back on the "safe and comfortable" ways of the Egyptian lifestyle. That behavior was reminiscent of Lot longing for Sodom after his capture.

The Book of Leviticus: Defining Holiness and Purity

Leviticus is the third book of the Pentateuch. There was a pause in the journey to the Promised Land and the focus was on defining holiness and purity for the Israelites. They were in the wilderness for about a year and the construction of the tabernacle for the Lord's dwelling was complete. But, as He is holy, the people must be clean and pure for God to dwell among them. Kevin Vanhoozer tells us that Leviticus sets the tone for how the Israelites were to prepare themselves for God's dwelling among them. "First, *the people are to worship God*...Second, *the Aaronic priests are to direct the worship*... Third, *the people are to avoid ritual impurity and make atonement when they fail*...Fourth, *the people are to be holy.*"[242]

Leviticus details each of these components. Worship practices included the types of offerings (burnt, grain, etc.) to be made and the meaning behind each type of offering. Richard Hess states that "sacrifices (and more generally, offerings) provided a means of commitment of all that the people received as gifts from God (burnt and grain offerings). They provided access for the Israelites and their families to enjoy feasts and communion with God in a physical manner (fellowship offerings)."[243]

The priests directing the worship oversaw the offerings and God outlined the duties required for each offering. Detailed descriptions of the ordinance and services of the priests included their dress code within the sanctuary and the protocol for anointing and consecrating those initiated into the service. With those instructions in place, Moses consecrated his brother Aaron as the initial priest, who then consecrated his sons to follow.

The final two instructions God provided Moses were for the people. Paul House indicates that these instructions set Israel apart from other nations and maintain their closeness to God. "The chief benefit was God's presence among them, which separated them from other nations."[244] God intended the nation of Israel to be His representatives and serve as priests to set the moral standard for the rest of the nations, so the rules of purity and holiness were a necessity. House continues, "It would be pointless for God to deliver Israel so that the chosen people could engage in the same practices that caused the world to sink into ever-greater depravity. One more nation like all the others hardly improve the moral climate on earth...Rather

---

[242]Kevin Vanhoozer, *Dictionary for Theological Interpretation of the Bible*, 2005, p.448–449.

[243]Richard Hess, *The Expositor's Bible Commentary – Leviticus*, 2008, p. 573.

[244]Paul House, *Old Testament Theology*, 1998, p. 137.

than adopting corrupt nations as their model, Israel must emulate their holy God's character and resultant behavior."[245]

God made it clear that His people were to be holy. "You are to be holy to me because I, the LORD, am holy, and I have set you apart from the nations to be my own" (Lev. 20:26). They were to set their moral code high above the pagan nations and avoid participating in the idolatry and immorality of the nations around them. In his commentary, Richard Hess states, "Israel's holiness requires distinction from the practices of foreign nations and adherence to a separate way, whether in deity worship or sexual practices. By avoiding activities that would tie Israel with the deities of other peoples, they recognize their God alone."[246]

It was because of their worshiping of false gods and their immorality (an abomination to God) that He used the Israelites to march into their pagan lands and destroy them. As to the nature of sin on behalf of His own people, whether intentional or not, God provided the sacrificial mechanism for atonement. Hess continues, "The sacrificial system demonstrates God's justice in providing a means for dealing with sin and its guilt without denying it or showing favoritism."[247]

Additional guidelines that shadow the Ten Commandments helped define their expected behavior. For example, God described prohibitions against adultery to preserve the sanctity of marriage between a man and a woman. "That is why a man leaves his father and mother and is united to his wife, and they become one flesh" (Gen. 2:24).

The sanctity of marriage and the structure of the family is foundational for God's people, so any deviation in sexual practices would be an attack on the very first sacrament God created. Again, from Hess, "Adultery tears apart the fundamental building block of human society – marriage and the family. It is the most dangerous

---

[245] Ibid., p. 143.

[246] Richard Hess, *The Expositor's Bible Commentary – Leviticus,* 2008, p. 761.

[247] Ibid., p. 573.

of conventional violations and one that the prophets connect with idolatry."[248] James Boice concurs: "The family is the smallest but most important unit in society. Where the family stands, the culture stands; where the family breaks down, the culture breaks down."[249]

Secondly, it was God's intent that the Israelites (and in our present times, we Christians) strive toward a spiritual heart and not be led away by the physical pleasures of the world. Falling into sexual practices outside of marriage chain you to the physical realms of this earth and take your focus away from God.

In Genesis, God commanded Adam and Eve to be fruitful and multiply to occupy the earth. The command was repeated to Noah after the flood. Abraham was promised descendants that would be as countless as the stars. To indulge in the sexual practices of the pagans around them would lead to idolatry, destroying their trust in God to multiply their descendants.

God prohibited the sexual deviations indulged in by the pagans occupying the Promised Land that the Israelites were to enter.[250] The sexually oriented worship practices and immoral behavior of the pagan nations (including incest, homosexuality, and bestiality) were prohibited in order to keep them spiritually clean.

Of the many guidelines provided in Leviticus, I find that the provisions for following the Second Great Commandment fit well within the theme of this text. God's instructions cover immoral behavior, social interactions, and kindness and consideration for all, particularly for those in need. Christopher Wright points out that beyond the description of ritual practices, food laws and others found in Leviticus, we also find that "it shows that the kind of holiness God has in mind, the kind that reflects God's own holiness, is thoroughly practical and down to earth...'to love your neighbor as

---

[248] Ibid., p. 742.

[249] James Boice, *The Life of Moses*, 2018, p. 148.

[250] It didn't take long for the Israelites to forget this fundamental statute. In the book of Numbers, Moabite women led some of the men into sexual promiscuity and the worship of the pagan god Baal.

yourself' is not a revolutionary new love ethic invented by Jesus. It was the fundamental ethical demand of Old Testament holiness, which Jesus reaffirmed and sharpened in some cases."[251]

Once in the Promised Land, obedience to God would result in prosperity for His people; however, greed could overcome those with underdeveloped spiritual hearts, and they could take advantage of the less fortunate. As John Fuellenbach notes, "Israel was an egalitarian society in which all were regarded as equal on the basis of land and inheritance. The danger always existed that the thriftier and shrewder would get ahead and gradually establish an autocracy. Consequently, the egalitarian society would give way to an order where peasants would become dependent upon and ultimately exploited by the aristocrats."[252]

To protect the underprivileged, God provided instructions in regard to harvesting at the end of the planting season. "'When you reap the harvest of your land, do not reap to the very edges of your field or gather the gleanings of your harvest. Do not go over your vineyard a second time or pick up the grapes that have fallen. Leave them for the poor and the foreigner. I am the LORD your God'" (Lev. 19:9–10). God was ensuring that the Israelites would be blessed and should be content with the bounty He provided. They should not be greedy but show compassion toward the poor and extend that charity to those in need. The guidelines also included caring for and respecting the elderly. The goal was to have a giving nature because of what God had provided, and to have a compassionate heart that would easily give to those in need.

Richard Hess points out that the extension of charity to foreigners was unique to Israel and he connects it to the story of the good Samaritan. Jesus extended the concept of "love your neighbor" to anyone who is in need, including the Gentiles.[253] Throughout

---

[251]Christopher Wright, Knowing God Through the Old Testament, 2019, p. 171.

[252]John Fuellenbach, *The Kingdom of God,* 1995, p. 52.

[253]Richard Hess, *The Expositor's Bible Commentary – Leviticus,* 2008, p. 750.

Leviticus, God reminded Israel to care for the sojourner since they themselves were once sojourners in Egypt.

The lessons continued as reiterations of the Ten Commandments. "'Do not steal.' 'Do not lie.' 'Do not deceive one another.' 'Do not swear falsely by my name and so profane the name of your God. I am the LORD.' 'Do not defraud or rob your neighbor.' 'Do not hold back the wages of a hired worker overnight'" (Lev. 19:11–13). Honesty and respect for one another are indicators of a pure heart. Never put yourself in a position to lie to others; always be truthful, which demonstrates your own humility and honesty. It also makes you accountable. If you are in the wrong, be responsible and own up to it, don't tell lies to cover a wrongdoing. There is no need to deceive or defraud people to gain an advantage in business or society.

"'Do not curse the deaf or put a stumbling block in front of the blind but fear your God. I am the LORD.' 'Do not pervert justice; do not show partiality to the poor or favoritism to the great but judge your neighbor fairly.' 'Do not go about spreading slander among your people.' 'Do not do anything that endangers your neighbor's life. I am the LORD.' 'Do not hate a fellow Israelite in your heart. Rebuke your neighbor frankly so you will not share in their guilt'" (Lev. 19:14–17). These are all about respect for one another; do not humiliate or bear false rumors against others that would harm their standing in the community.

Finally, God summarized these instructions with words from the Second Great Commandment: "'Do not seek revenge or bear a grudge against anyone among your people *but love your neighbor as yourself.* I am the LORD'" (v.18, emphasis mine).

Within Leviticus, God reiterated the conditions of His covenant with His people. Put simply, if the Israelites remained faithful and obedient to His commandments, God would bless them, and they would prosper. God would protect them from their enemies and give them peace in their land. Most importantly, they would be a holy people and God would dwell among them. "'If you follow my decrees and are careful to obey my commands, I will send you rain in its season, and the ground will yield its crops and the trees their fruit. Your threshing will continue until grape harvest and the grape harvest will continue until planting, and you will eat all the food you want and live in safety in your land. I will grant peace in the land, and you will lie down, and no one will make you afraid. I will remove wild beasts from the land, and the sword will not pass through your country...I will put my dwelling place among you, and I will not abhor you. I will walk among you and be your God, and you will be my people'" (Lev. 26:3–6, 11–12).

These ideal conditions were much like what God provided to Adam and Eve before their sin. In both cases, all their needs were provided to them by God, and they lacked nothing. God wanted to dwell with the Israelites; He desired to walk among them as He walked with Adam and Eve in the Garden of Eden.

The flip side of the covenant was that if the Israelites fell into disobedience and worshiped false gods, God would take the Promised Land from them. Just as Adam and Eve's disobedience caused their expulsion from the Garden of Eden, so the disobedience of the Israelites led to the expulsion from the Promised Land.

"'...and if you reject my decrees and abhor my laws and fail to carry out all my commands and so violate my covenant, then I will do this to you: I will bring on you sudden terror, wasting diseases and fever that will destroy your sight and sap your strength. You will plant seed in vain because your enemies will eat it. I will set my face against you so that you will be defeated by your enemies; those who hate you will rule over you, and you will flee even when no one is pursuing you... And I will bring the sword on you to avenge the breaking of the covenant. When you withdraw into your cities, I will send a plague among you, and you will be the flesh of your sons and the flesh of your daughters.[254] I will give into enemy hands...You will eat destroy your high places, cut down your incense altars and pile your dead bodies on the lifeless forms of your idols, and I will abhor you. I will turn your cities into ruins and lay waste your sanctuaries, and I will take no delight in the pleasing aroma of your offerings...I will scatter you among the nations and will draw out my sword and pursue you. Your land will be laid waste, and your cities will lie in ruins...You will perish among the nations; the land of your enemies will devour you'" (Lev. 26:15–17, 25, 29–31, 33, 38).

The Book of Numbers: The Rebellion Continues

With God's commandments and instructions revealed to His people and the priesthood and formal worship initiated, the journey to the Promised Land continued. The book of Numbers tells the tragic story of how the first generation of Israelites continued to rebel against God's will. Despite the many miracles God performed to save and protect them, complaints began only a week out of Egypt, and they mount in the book of Numbers. Their lack of faith prevented them from entering the Promised Land and they wandered for the next 38 years and died in the desert.[255] Ironically, this occurred when they were only days away from their destination. As Dale Brueggemann

---

[254]As horrifying as this curse sounds, it occurred in the northern nation of Israel during the time of Elisha the prophet and during king Joram's rule (circa 852–841 BC). War broke out between Syria and Israel. From Richard Patterson and Hermann Austel's account of 2 Kings 6, "The Arameans were eminently successful—they penetrated the gates of Samaria itself and put the city under a dire siege. The lengthy siege evoked a severe famine...as the king was on tour about the embattled city's wall, he stumbled upon a case of cannibalism." *The Expositor's Bible Commentary – 1 and 2 Kings,* 2009, p. 839. "As the king of Israel was passing by on the wall, a woman cried to him, 'Help me, my lord the king!'...Then he asked her, 'What's the matter?' She answered, 'This woman said to me, "Give up your son so we may eat him today, and tomorrow we'll eat my son." So, we cooked my son and ate him. The next day I said to her, "Give up your son so we may eat him," but she had hidden him'" (2 Kgs. 6:26, 28–29).

[255]Quoting David Olson, Provan, Long, & Longham note, "...the entire book of Numbers is structured around this theme of the death of the original exodus generation and the rise of a second generation, a generation of hope." *A Biblical History of Israel,* 2015, p. 188.

writes, "Numbers tells a story that should never have happened, a story that warns against the rejection of God's plans. Nevertheless, the story reveals that God remains faithful to his gracious promise, even when his people neglect the means and aims of grace."[256]

The book begins with God instructing Moses to take a census of the men over 20 years of age who would be eligible to serve in the army. The men were numbered by the twelve tribes (descendants of each of the sons of Jacob), except for the Levites, who God designated to serve Him as priests and to take care of the tabernacle and the ark. Excluding them, the men ready for war numbered 603,500. Each tribe was grouped around the ark and the tabernacle and when it was time to travel, the groups would proceed in an ordered fashion.

As for the Levites, God assigned individual clans within the tribe to specific religious functions related to the care of the tabernacle, the ark, preparation of the altar for sacrifices, and the furnishings and utensils that went with the ceremonies. The organization and duties would provide structure for the nation when it settled in the Promised Land.

God instructed Moses on maintaining purity among the people, since His holy presence was to dwell with them. There were directions for those with leprosy, keeping them away from others to prevent infection from spreading. The instructions also dealt with unfaithfulness and how to manage jealousy in a marriage. Purity rights were described for those wishing to take the vow of a Nazarite, a separate and special form of dedication to the Lord. (Samson, the last judge in the book of Judges, was a Nazarite.) There was a consecration for the tabernacle whereby each day, one tribe at a time brought before Moses a prescribed offering. On the first month of their second year out of Egypt, God instructed Moses to renew the Passover ceremony, commemorating their exodus out of Egypt.

God continued to dwell with the people as they traveled, guiding them by providing cloud cover during the day to keep the heat of the desert away and as a fire in the evening to light their way and keep

---

[256]Dale Brueggemann, *Cornerstone Biblical Commentary: Leviticus, Numbers, Deuteronomy,* 2008, p. 215.

them warm during cold desert nights. The people did not travel until God's glory rose and moved forward and they didn't stop until God's glory stopped. They were in obedience to God, following Him as He led the way to Canaan.

But the people continued to grumble about the hardships of their traveling conditions and God sent fire to destroy some of the complainers. That didn't stop them, though; they complained about eating nothing but manna and yearned for the days in Egypt where they had a variety of food to eat. "Moses heard the people of every family wailing at the entrance to their tents. The LORD became exceedingly angry, and Moses was troubled" (Num. 11:10).

Moses lamented to God that dealing with their constant complaining was too much for him to handle; he was ready to give up on all of them. God told him He would send so much meat it would come out of their nostrils. As for lightening his load, God had Moses appoint 70 elders to share the burden. God was displeased with the people's lack of faith and constant complaining. They had only been on the road for a year, and He provided everything they needed along the way. Had the people forgotten God's power and how they were delivered from the Egyptians? Did He not feed them and provide water for them when they cried out? Did He not give them the victory over the Amalekites? In the slightest discomfort, their physical needs were outweighing their trust in God.[257]

God instructed Moses, "'Tell the people: "Consecrate yourselves in preparation for tomorrow when you will eat meat. The LORD heard you when you wailed, 'If only we had meat to eat! We were better off in Egypt!' Now the LORD will give you meat, and you will eat it. You will not eat it for just one day, or two days, or five, ten or twenty days, but

---

[257]In His sermon on the Mount, Jesus preached about relying on God to take care of His people and not to be overly concerned with the daily cares of the world. "'So do not worry, saying, "What shall we eat?" or "What shall we drink?" or "What shall we wear?" For the pagans run after all these things, and your heavenly Father knows that you need them. But seek first his kingdom and his righteousness, and all these things will be given to you as well. Therefore, do not worry about tomorrow, for tomorrow will worry about itself. Each day has enough trouble of its own'" (Matt. 6:31–34).

for a whole month—until it comes out of your nostrils and you loathe it—because you have rejected the LORD, who is among you, and have wailed before him, saying, 'Why did we ever leave Egypt?'"" (Num. 11:18–20). The next day, God sent quail to the Israelites; there were so many quail dropping from the sky that they laid three feet high around the camp and the people gathered almost two tons of meat from them. But before they could finish eating, God sent a plague, killing those who complained about the lack of Egyptian delights.

The rebellion continued, but instead of coming from the people, it came from Aaron and Miriam, the brother and sister of Moses. His own family challenged God's leadership structure. The complaints started with Moses taking a Cushite wife, but really, they envied Moses's position with the Lord. "'Has the LORD spoken only through Moses?' they asked. 'Hasn't he also spoken through us?' And the LORD heard this" (Num. 12:2).

Even though they both had positions of authority (Aaron oversaw the priests, Levites, and religious structures, while Miriam was a prophetess), they felt they should be on equal footing with Moses. God called out all three of them, chastising Aaron and Miriam for challenging His relationship with Moses. God spoke to Moses as a friend, face to face and not through visions or dreams. To reinforce that He was in charge, God struck Miriam with leprosy. Aaron and Miriam realized their sin and Aaron pled for forgiveness. Miriam was removed from the camp, but Aaron's pleading coupled with Moses's intercession reduced her punishment to seven days outside of the camp until she was cleansed. For Miriam and Aaron, it was a lesson learned; a minor rebellion quelled.

As Moses and the people approached Canaan, the land that God had promised for them, Moses sent a member from each tribe (including Joshua and Caleb) on a reconnaissance mission to check out the land, the status of the crops, and any potential opposition. After the 40-day mission, they reported that, while the crops were bountiful and the land fertile, "'...the people who live there are powerful, and the cities are fortified and very large. We even saw descendants of Anak there. The Amalekites live in the Negev; the Hittites,

Jebusites and Amorites live in the hill country; and the Canaanites live near the sea and along the Jordan'" (Num. 13:28–29).

The descendants of Anak were like the Nephilim, giants among men.[258] The Promised Land was at hand, but the scouts feared the odds ahead of them. They already forgot how God delivered them from Egypt, the mightiest of nations at the time, just one year earlier. Despite the perilous nature of the report, Caleb and Joshua appealed to the crowd (who practically turned into a mob because of the "bad" news) to remind them that they had God on their side. They were the only two scouts who still had strong faith and trust in God's deliverance.

"Then Caleb silenced the people before Moses and said, 'We should go up and take possession of the land, for we can certainly do it.' But the men who had gone up with him said, 'We can't attack those people; they are stronger than we are.' And they spread among the Israelites a bad report about the land they had explored. They said, 'The land we explored devours those living in it. All the people we saw there are of great size. We saw the Nephilim there (the descendants of Anak come from the Nephilim). We seemed like grasshoppers in our own eyes, and we looked the same to them'" (Num. 13:30–33).

The fear of taking on the Nephilim frightened the Israelites to the point that they were prepared to revolt against Moses and Aaron. The people were not moved by Caleb's plea that God was with them, which showed their complete lack of faith in God. They were afraid and gave in to emotional hysteria. "All the Israelites grumbled against Moses and Aaron, and the whole assembly said to them, 'If only we had died in Egypt! Or in this wilderness! Why is the LORD bringing us to this land only to let us fall by the sword? Our wives and children will be taken as plunder. Wouldn't it be better for us to go back to Egypt?' And they said to each other, 'We should choose a leader and go back to Egypt'" (Num. 14:2–4).

---

[258]In Chapter 8, David's encounter with Goliath is recounted. Goliath was also a related to the Nephilim, as he was over 9 feet tall.

Every element of the Israelites' faith had evaporated. They were just miles from having the Promised Land handed over to them and there was no trust in God for those final steps. All the miracles God performed were a distant memory. Caleb and Joshua continued to counter their fears. "'If the LORD is pleased with us, he will lead us into that land, a land flowing with milk and honey, and will give it to us. Only do not rebel against the LORD. And do not be afraid of the people of the land, because we will devour them. Their protection is gone, but the LORD is with us. Do not be afraid of them'" (Num. 14:8–9). Their pleas fell upon deaf ears.

God told Moses that He'd had enough of the rebellious people. "The LORD said to Moses, 'How long will these people treat me with contempt? How long will they refuse to believe in me, in spite of all the signs I have performed among them? I will strike them down with a plague and destroy them, but I will make you into a nation greater and stronger than they'" (Num. 14:11–12). The Lord was testing Moses to see if his leadership skills had improved, and Moses came through. He advocated for the Israelites, saying that God's name was at stake. What would the neighboring pagans think if God delivered His people out of Egypt and then gave up on them just miles from their destination?

God forgave His people, but their bad behavior was met with severe consequences. God made the nation wander in the wilderness for another 38 years until all the complaining and rebellious adults died of natural causes.[259] Those who railed against God's protection didn't live long enough to see the Promised Land, except Caleb and Joshua who stayed strong in their faith. "'As for your children that you said would be taken as plunder, I will bring them in to enjoy the land you have rejected. But as for you, your bodies will fall in this wilderness. Your children will be shepherds here for forty years, suffering for your unfaithfulness, until the last of your bodies lies in the wilderness. For forty years—one year for each of the forty days you explored the

---

[259]"'For forty years I was angry with that generation; I said, "They are a people whose hearts go astray, and they have not known my ways." So, I declared on oath in my anger, "They shall never enter my rest"'" (Ps. 95:10–11).

166

land—you will suffer for your sins and know what it is like to have me against you'" (Num. 14:31–34).

God's punishment can be likened to the flood where He wiped out everyone but Noah and his family, or destroying Sodom and Gomorrah, saving only Lot and his daughters. He rid the Israelites of the detractors who would lead them in the wrong direction. He hit the reset button by getting rid of the bad apples before they polluted the rest of the nation.[260] And those ten scouts who caused the panic in the first place? They were struck down that morning by a plague sent by God.

Still, the people's disobedience did not end. Even though they recognized their sins, they decided they could make it to the Promised Land without God's help. Moses warned them that this wasn't God's plan, but their stubborn hearts ignored the warning. They decided to march into the Promised Land anyway, thinking their repentance would be rewarded with victory, but they repented too late. They were attacked by the Amalekites and Canaanites and were driven back to Hormah, soundly defeated.

Obedience to God's will continued to be overlooked. Members of the tribe of Levite grew tired of roaming the wilderness even though it was the result of the people's own disobedience. Korah, a member of the Kohite[261] clan led the rebellion along with Dathan and Abiram from the tribe of Rueben and they were joined by 250 elders. Like Miriam and Aaron, Korah challenged Moses's authority, stating Moses lorded his role over the people. He demanded to know where was the land of milk and honey the people were promised? Did Moses lead the

---

[260]In Chapter 10, God hits the reset button again by using the Assyrians and Babylonians to purge His people because of their rebellious idolatry that had them worshiping everything on earth but Him. The remnant exiles brought back from the Babylonian captivity are those who learned to remain obedient and faithful to God, at least temporarily.

[261]The Kohites had the highest level of responsibility with the Tent of Meeting. They were responsible for the holiest articles in the tent along with taking it down when traveling and setting it up when they stopped.

people into the wilderness to die? They were forgetting it was because of their sin that they were wandering.

Moses was angry at their insubordination. The next day, they met outside Moses's tent. Moses instructed the crowd to step away from Korah and his rebels and he called on the Lord to swallow them up. The earth opened and the three rebel leaders and their families fell into the earth and the earth resealed itself. As for the 250 elders who joined Korah, God sent a fire to destroy them all.

The next day, Korah supporters grumbled against Moses for killing his own people and a mob surrounded Moses and Aaron. In their disobedience and weak faith, they challenged God any time there was discomfort in the camp. God told Moses to step aside so he could wipe everyone out. Moses interceded for those not involved and God sent a plague upon the rebels, killing 14,700 people. Moses immediately told Aaron to offer the Lord a sacrifice to appease Him, which stopped the plague.

Despite not reaching the Promised Land, God continued to provide instructions for the priesthood and their portion of the offerings, regulations for sacrifices and tithing, and maintaining purity and cleansing among the people. He showed His mercy because eventually, the people entering the Promised Land would need to be prepared spiritually, unlike the first generation.

The camp ran out of water and once again lamented that Moses brought the people out of Egypt to die. No one seemed to trust that God would provide, and the weakness of their spiritual hearts remained. Moses was reaching his own level of frustration with his people, so God told Moses to speak to a nearby rock and water would pour from it. "He and Aaron gathered the assembly together in front of the rock and Moses said to them, 'Listen, you rebels, must we bring you water out of this rock?'" (Num. 20:10). Moses did not put God first, but said "must we bring you water?" And instead of speaking to the rock, he struck it twice in frustration with his people. While water did come forth, God was upset with Moses for demonstrating anger and not obeying His instructions. After all, Moses was God's representative to the people and his actions should have reflected God. As a result of his disobedience, Moses was not allowed to take the people into the Promised Land.

Not long after, a tribe of Canaanites attacked a group of the Israelites. The people implored the Lord to be with them in a counterattack, claiming if God was with them, they would wipe out the army and the surrounding cities. God heard their pleas and backed them up. Though they were granted victory by God's hand, they soon started complaining about their conditions and speaking out against God and Moses.

As punishment, God sent poisonous snakes into the camp and many Israelites died from being bitten. The spiritual hearts of the people seemed to have improved, and they repented of their sins. God told Moses to make a bronze snake and put it on a pole. Anyone who was bitten could look at the snake and live. The cure, then, was to show obedience and trust that God's intervention would save them. Even though they sinned, they immediately repented and trusted God.

Somewhat similar is the image of Jesus on the cross; those who believe in Him are forgiven of their sins and granted eternal spiritual life. Jesus Himself said, "'Just as Moses lifted up the snake in the wilderness, so the Son of Man must be lifted up, that everyone who believes may have eternal life in him'" (John 3:14–15).

Fast forward through the remaining years of their wandering and the malcontents were eliminated through attrition. The hearts of the people seemed to be on the right path, and they proceeded to the Promised Land. God granted them military victory over Sihon, king of the Amorites, and Og, king of Bashan, and the Israelites took all the surrounding cities that belonged to the two kings.

As the Israelites continued forward, Balak, the king of Moab, feared his kingdom would be conquered next. He summoned the local prophet Balaam to put a curse on the army so he could be victorious over the Israelites. Balaam was not a prophet in the same sense as those for the Israelites, but he did have the ability to convey divine messages and interpret omens. He was certainly interested in financial gain and his moral compass was not one of a righteous man. However, he understood the power of the Hebrews' God.

Scriptures do not account for how, as a pagan, Balaam had an understanding of God, but in this sequence, God used Balaam to confirm His blessing on Israel. Three times Balaam asked God what he should say, and each time God responded with blessings on the Israelites rather than curses. The untrusting generation had died off and the remaining Israelites were trusting and obedient and in God's good favor. Balak was angry that God wouldn't let Balaam curse the Israelites and he returned to Moab.

While the Israelites were resting (when they should have been praying and preparing themselves to enter the Promised Land), there is one final act of disobedience that proved problematic. "While Israel was staying in Shittim, the men began to indulge in sexual immorality with Moabite women, who invited them to the sacrifices to their gods. The people ate the sacrificial meat and bowed down before these gods. So Israel yoked themselves to the Baal of Peor. And the LORD's anger burned against them" (Num. 25:1–3). This sexual practice had long been incorporated into the pagan worship to the idol Baal and the local Moabite women enticed a group of Israelites into taking part. Sexual promiscuity corrupted these men; they totally forgot (or ignored) several of the Ten Commandments given to them 40 years earlier. We learn later in Scriptures that Balaam was responsible for undermining the spiritual integrity of the Israelites in this situation.[262]

God sent a plague on the people because of those who strayed off the compound, so to speak, with the pagan women (Scriptures refer to Moabites and Midianites interchangeably). Moses had everyone involved in the idol worship executed. Zimri, a leader of the Simeonite family, brought Kozbi, the daughter of a Midianite leader, into the camp before the eyes of Moses and the whole assembly. Phinehas, the

---

[262]In Peter's second letter, he writes "They have left the straight way and wandered off to follow the way of Balaam son of Bezer who loved the wages of wickedness" (2 Peter 2:15). From the book of Revelation, we find John writing of Balaam in Jesus' critique of the Church in Pergamum, "'Nevertheless, I have a few things against you: There are some among you who hold to the teaching of Balaam, who taught Balak to entice the Israelites to sin so that they ate food sacrificed to idols and committed sexual immorality'" (Rev. 2:14).

grandson of Aaron, defending the honor and faith of God's people, drove a spear into both. He displayed righteous anger toward the sinners in his fervor for the Lord, like David when he slew Goliath for his disrespect to God and His army. With that action, God ended the plague that killed 24,000 people. God continued to cleanse His people to maintain the purity and holiness intended from them.

God instructed Moses to attack the Midianites for trying to lead His people astray, so 1,000 men from each tribe were sent into battle and the Midianite army was destroyed, including Balaam the prophet. The victory was accomplished without losing a single Israelite in combat. The Israelite army went on to destroy all the surrounding cities, claiming a great deal of gold and livestock. They also returned with the women of Midian. Moses was angry with the generals for bringing them into the camp. "'Have you allowed all the women to live?' he asked them. 'They were the ones who followed Balaam's advice and enticed the Israelites to be unfaithful to the LORD in the Peor incident, so that a plague struck the LORD's people'" (Num. 31:15–16). Moses ordered all the non-virgins and any boys in the group to be killed; only the girls who never slept with a man were spared.

By modern standards, these actions seem cruel or immoral, but they were to keep the people of Israel holy and pure. God continued to warn His people about these influences that led them into sinful methods, like we witnessed while they were in Shittim.

When the fighting was over, God gave the Israelites further instructions for the different festivals to be held for national worship, specifying the number and types of animals to be offered as sacrifices daily, weekly, monthly, and annually, including Passover and the Day of Atonement. The formal instructions were designed to maintain frequent offerings and worship to the Lord. All these instructions were in preparation for the Promised Land and setting their standards above the pagan nations around them.

As the book of Numbers ends, God gave the people final instructions before leading them into the Promised Land. First and foremost, the Canaanites were to be driven from the land along with all their carved idols, pagan shrines, and any other semblance of idolatry. He also set the boundaries of land to the north, south, east, and west. Land was designated for the Levites, and cities of refuge were established for people who accidentally killed someone. God recognized the need for justice as well as opportunities for His people to show mercy when required; loving your neighbor can be demonstrated through offering a haven when necessary.

The Book of Deuteronomy: Hitting the Reset Button Once More

Deuteronomy is the last of the Pentateuch (the books of Genesis, Exodus, Leviticus, Numbers, and Deuteronomy), all of which are generally believed to be written by Moses. Kevin Vanhoozer summarizes the theme of the book: "...Deuteronomy functions as a theological manifesto, calling Israel to respond to God's grace with unreserved loyalty and love."[263] Bruce Waltke writes that "Deuteronomy is the most important book in the Old Testament for writing an Old Testament theology...The regulations of *I AM*'s covenant are the first to establish universal education and health for all members of a nation and fixes the only welfare system that was in existence in ancient times."[264]

As he was nearing death, Moses gave his last set of instructions to the Israelite nation before they entered the Promised Land. He had to reteach the second generation the rules and statutes that were laid out at Mount Sinai for the first generation. This generation could not afford to make the same mistakes. Moses needed to repeat and expand upon the instructions to prepare their spiritual hearts to make sure they didn't reject God's word.

The foundation for Moses's instructions was the Two Great Commandments. Warnings against idolatry and adopting pagan practices were plentiful throughout Deuteronomy; the Israelites were to maintain their holy and pure character and exhibit social responsibility. "The principle is articulated that the covenant between Yahweh

---

[263]Kevin Vanhoozer, *Dictionary for Theological Interpretation of the Bible,* 2005, p. 165.

[264]Bruce Waltke, *An Old Testament Theology*, 2007, p. 479.

and Israel also has horizontal dimensions. To love God is to love God's people, no matter their rank or station."[265] Special attention is levied for the care and protection of widows, orphans, strangers, and the poor—all of whom lack social representation. Christopher Wright notes, "The poor as a particular group in society receive God's special attention because they are the ones who are on the 'wronged' side of a situation of chronic injustice – a situation God abhors and wished to have redressed."[266]

Taking the land they were about to enter required the Israelite army to succeed in driving out the seven nations of Canaanites; the Israelites had to trust God with the mission and their obedience was critical to overcome their being out-manned militarily. To prepare them spiritually and emotionally, Moses reminded them how the Israelites became God's chosen people and how God fulfilled His promises to the patriarchs to lead and protect the people. He recapped their exodus from Egypt and how the plagues and destruction of the Egyptian army were ample proof of His ability to protect them. All they needed to do was trust and obey.

He also reminded them how God protected them from the elements, provided food and water during their journey, and prevented their clothes and shoes from wearing out. God granted them military victories along the way, including Sihon king of the Amorites, and Og king of Bashan.[267] All of this was to show His love for His people and Moses stressed the need for them to appreciate that love by dedicating themselves to Him exclusively. Kevin Vanhoozer writes, "While the Canaanites posed a formidable military threat, the spiritual threat (falling into the idolatry practices of those around them) was more serious. Accordingly...emphasis is on exclusive devotion to Yahweh, demonstrated in grateful obedience. If they would do so,

---

[265]Eugene Merrill, *Kingdom of Priests*, 2008, p. 459.

[266]Christopher Wright, *Old Testament Ethics for the People of God*, 2004, p.268.

[267]Og was a descendent of the Nephilim and nine feet tall. This second generation of Israelites had more trust in God's protection than did their fathers who were afraid to confront the giants 38 years earlier. Their spiritual growth continued to exceed the earlier generation; they were ready to serve as God's holy people.

Moses envisioned the people of Israel and the land they would occupy as flourishing."[268]

Moses revisited the Ten Commandments so that the second generation was well aware of God's statutes before entering the Promised Land. He also warned the generation against the sin of idolatry and recalled how the Moabite women seduced some of the men to worship Baal, which resulted in their deaths. It was imperative that they keep themselves pure and not fall victim to the practices of the pagan nations they were about to pass through.[269]

Moses drove home the point that the Israelites were God's holy people, and they must remain obedient to Him. That God appointed the Israelites to represent Him as priests to all other nations was a key element of the covenant. "See, I have taught you decrees and laws as the LORD my God commanded me, so that you may follow them in the land you are entering to take possession of it. Observe them carefully, for this will show your wisdom and understanding to the nations, who will hear about all these decrees and say, 'Surely this great nation is a wise and understanding people'" (Deut. 4:5–6).

Idolatry and pagan worship had to be purged from the land lest it infiltrate the people and spread like a cancer, detracting from God, and derailing their priestly role. God was sending His people against several nations, all mightier in numbers, but God will be with them in victory. "When the LORD your God brings you into the land you are entering to possess and drives out before you many nations—the Hittites, Girgashites, Amorites, Canaanites, Perizzites, Hivites and Jebusites, seven nations larger and stronger than you—and when the LORD your God has delivered them over to you and you have defeated

---

[268]Kevin Vanhoozer, *Dictionary for Theological Interpretation of the Bible*, 2005, p. 169.

[269]In his warning, Moses spoke of the consequences of Israel falling victim to pagan practices and idolatry. "The LORD will scatter you among the peoples, and only a few of you will survive among the nations to which the LORD will drive you" (Deut. 4:27). This warning comes to fruition. In Chapter 10, I'll share how Israel was scattered among the Assyrians when they destroyed the nation of Israel, and later Judah was driven into captivity by the Babylonians. Only a remnant remained to return to Jerusalem after the latter exile ended.

them, then you must destroy them totally. Make no treaty with them and show them no mercy. Do not intermarry with them. Do not give your daughters to their sons or take their daughters for your sons, for they will turn your children away from following me to serve other gods, and the LORD's anger will burn against you and will quickly destroy you'" (Deut. 7:1–4).

The rules were clear and specific: no peace treaties and no intermarrying. God's holy people must not be turned to worship pagan gods because of their spouses. As we'll see in Chapter 9, this is precisely the rule Solomon violated; he had 700 wives and 300 concubines who led him to worship their gods.[270]

Moses also warned against self-proclaimed prophets who tried to convince the people to go the way of their pagan neighbors; such a prophet should be put to death. Friends or relatives who tried to entice them to worship other gods should be stoned to death. Moses went so far as to say that if an entire village or a city engaged in idolatry, it would be razed and burned to a heap, and all in the city should be put to death. The city would never be rebuilt.

Moses repeated what God said to him on the mountain: "Now if you obey me fully and keep my covenant, then out of all nations you will be my treasured possession. Although the whole earth is mine, you will be for me a kingdom of priests and a holy nation'" (Exod. 19:5–6).

Strict standards were necessary to keep God's people from the infection of idolatry. They were a rebellious people, as was demonstrated in the desert, so they needed to understand the consequences for disobeying God's commandments, idolatry being the most dangerous violation. For all that God had done for them, it was logical for them to appreciate His protection and love and dedicate their

---

[270]Moses reiterated the need to eliminate all evidence of the nation's they were about to take over because of the pagan practices. "However, in the cities of the nations the LORD your God is giving you as an inheritance, do not leave alive anything that breathes. Completely destroy them—the Hittites, Amorites, Canaanites, Perizzites, Hivites and Jebusites—as the LORD your God has commanded you. Otherwise, they will teach you to follow all the detestable things they do in worshiping their gods, and you will sin against the LORD your God" (Deut. 20:16–18).

lives to Him alone. Their spiritual hearts had to be focused on Him. Their trials were a test to see if their spiritual hearts were improving: "Remember how the LORD your God led you all the way in the wilderness these forty years, to humble and test you in order to know what was in your heart, whether or not you would keep his commands. He humbled you, causing you to hunger and then feeding you with manna, which neither you nor your ancestors had known, to teach you that man does not live on bread alone but on every word that comes from the mouth of the LORD" (Deut. 8:2–3).[271]

Why was God testing the hearts of His people at this point? Eugene Merrill provides the answer: "...that the people themselves might know how committed they were and to acknowledge how dependent they must be upon God. Testing frequently comes to God's children so that they can mature in faith as they confront it and by God's Grace, overcome it."[272] God then emphasized that selecting them as His chosen people was based on His everlasting love for them as Abraham's descendants. "For you are a people holy to the LORD your God. The LORD your God has chosen you out of all the peoples on the face of the earth to be his people, his treasured possession. The LORD did not set his affection on you and choose you because you were more numerous than other peoples, for you were the fewest of all peoples. But it was because the LORD loved you and kept the oath he swore to your ancestors that he brought you out with a mighty hand and redeemed you from the land of slavery, from the power of Pharaoh king of Egypt" (Deut. 7:6–8).

Robert Jenson agrees that God's selection of Israel was not due to any factor other than His grace and "that Israel is elected to his holiness in the strictly theological sense of closeness to God."[273] The selec-

---

[271]Jesus quoted this last verse when tested by Satan after 40 days in the wilderness. "The tempter came to him and said, 'If you are the Son of God, tell these stones to become bread.' Jesus answered, 'It is written: "Man shall not live on bread alone, but on every word that comes from the mouth of God"'" (Matt. 4:3–4). When Moses went up to Mount Sinai to get the Ten Commandments, he also fasted 40 days.

[272]Eugene Merrill, *Biblical Commentary - Deuteronomy*, 2008, p. 527.

[273]Robert Jenson, *Commentary on the Bible – Ezekiel*, 2009, p. 156.

tion was also the promise given to Abraham's descendants reiterated to both Isaac and Jacob.

God chose the Israelites over other nations to occupy the Promised Land. Through Moses, they were made aware that it was not because of their righteousness or integrity, but because of the wickedness of the other nations. God was granting them military victories because of the promise He made to them, but He was also punishing the pagan nations and ridding the land of their wickedness and pagan practices.

They had to stay focused on their obedience to God's will and avoid idolatry at all costs. Moses reminded them of the principles behind the First Great Commandment. "And now, Israel, what does the LORD your God ask of you but to fear the LORD your God, to walk in obedience to him, to love him, to serve the LORD your God with all your heart and with all your soul, and to observe the LORD's commands and decrees that I am giving you today for your own good?" (Deut. 10:12–13).

Moses described the methods for worshiping God and reminded them of the role of the Levites and how tithes were their means of support. Moses warned the people against worshiping anywhere they pleased, which was one of the trappings of pagan worship. Rather, they would gather in an area where God's presence would be among them.

"Destroy completely all the places on the high mountains, on the hills and under every spreading tree, where the nations you are dispossessing worship their gods. Break down their altars, smash their sacred stones and burn their Asherah poles in the fire; cut down the idols of their gods and wipe out their names from those places. You must not worship the LORD your God in their way. But you are to seek the place the LORD your God will choose from among all your tribes to put his Name there for his dwelling. To that place you must go; there bring your burnt offerings and sacrifices, your tithes, and special gifts, what you have vowed to give and your freewill offerings, and the firstborn of your herds and flocks. There, in the presence of the LORD your God, you and your families shall eat and shall rejoice in everything you have put your hand to, because the LORD your God has blessed you" (Deut. 12:2–7).

God was guiding the people to gather together in corporate worship so that all could participate, including sojourners, widows, and those in need. Eventually, the center of worship that God chose was the temple constructed by Solomon in Jerusalem. Before its construction, there was mention in the book of Judges and in First Samuel that the center of worship took place in Shiloh, north of the city of Bethel. There, a temple of the Lord had been constructed that housed the tabernacle and the ark of the covenant. It was the earliest central spot where worship and the festivals were held.[274]

Moses recognized that, at some point, the people would require a king to rule once they settled into Canaan.[275] Moses said the king's duties included coping the law on scrolls so that he may lead the people by God's law. In Chapter 10, I'll share how the king's spiritual heart would be the barometer of how the people obeyed God and remained faithful to His will.

Moses realized the importance of the king being well-versed in the Law, and not seeking gold and wealth or relying on Egypt for military supplies. He also warned against the king having many wives who would steer him away from God. Eugene Merrill writes, "These instructions for royal behavior seemed tailor-made for Solomon. He had a virtual monopoly on the horse market...he had an enormous harem of wives and concubines who caused his heart to turn from Yahweh; and he was fabulously wealthy, more than anyone else in the known world."[276]

God described behavior regarding social justice to hone His people's hearts and ensure the Israelites extended worship to one and all. This social equality was a mainstay of God's instructions. It was demonstrated later when the Israelites were led into the Promised Land.

---

[274]Note in the next chapter in the section on Hannah, it was there the family went annually for worship and the place the prophet Samuel was brought for his early religious training by Eli.

[275]This took place after the book of Judges when the Israelites rejected theocracy in favor of monarchy so they could be like the nations around them. In Chapter 8, we'll see that this began with Saul's appointment, followed by David.

[276]Eugene Merrill, *Biblical Commentary – Deuteronomy*, 2008, p. 581.

Property was distributed in an equitable manner so that there were no undo distortions in the allocations. Property was to be kept in the family and no selling the land to anyone outside the clan was allowed.

Christopher Wright contrasts Israel's equitable property ownership against their pagan neighbors. "Kings owned the land of the small city-states they ruled. But such a notion was strongly resisted among the Israelites. The gift of the land percolated, so to speak, down to the lowest social level, so that each individual household could claim that its right to the land it possessed was guaranteed by the Lord himself."[277]

Provisions for distribution of the agricultural output continued with the motif of social justice. One-tenth of the crop production, new wine, olive oil, flocks, and herds were to be stored up and, at the end of the third year, given as a tithe to the Levites "so that the Levites (who have no allotment or inheritance of their own) and the foreigners, the fatherless and the widows who live in your towns may come and eat and be satisfied, and so that the LORD your God may bless you in all the work of your hands" (Deut. 14:29). Tithing did not just support the Levites, but also those without means.

Once settled, God hoped the people would realize that His blessings allowed enough prosperity for all to enjoy. "However, there need be no poor people among you, for in the land the LORD your God is giving you to possess as your inheritance, he will richly bless you..." (Deut. 15:4).

Having said that, Moses understood that God would allow the people to prosper in the Promised Land, but there was the danger of selfish or greedy attitudes when God blessed His people. In that event, those with means were not to exploit those less fortunate, but to show them compassion in their plight. "If anyone is poor among your fellow Israelites in any of the towns of the land the LORD your God is giving you, do not be hardhearted or tightfisted toward them. Rather, be openhanded and freely lend them whatever they need" (Deut. 15:7–8). Respecting the ownership rights of others and not charging interest

---

[277]Christopher Wright, *Old Testament Ethics for the People of God*, 2004, p. 81.

on loans to fellow Israelites was also meant to keep greed in check and the Second Great Commandment in mind.

Particularly important was to protect those whose social standing exposed them to being exploited. Moses laid down the ground rules for the care of those in need. "Be careful not to harbor this wicked thought: 'The seventh year, the year for canceling debts, is near,' so that you do not show ill will toward the needy among your fellow Israelites and give them nothing. They may then appeal to the LORD against you, and you will be found guilty of sin. Give generously to them and do so without a grudging heart; then because of this the LORD your God will bless you in all your work and in everything you put your hand to. There will always be poor people in the land. Therefore, I command you to be openhanded toward your fellow Israelites who are poor and needy in your land" (Deut. 15:9–11).[278]

God laid the foundation for the Israelites to be conscious of the poor and needy of the land, to show them compassion and provide for them spiritually and physically. As Christopher Wright aptly points out, "Vertical thanksgiving for God's goodness must be matched by horizontal action for the needy."[279]

It is interesting that God made them aware that there would always be poor people in the land. These instructions warned against avarice and begrudging the canceling of debt every seven years. Focused on the heart, Moses wanted his people to be kind and compassionate toward those who are indebted and not complain about what they owed. "Do not take advantage of a hired worker who is poor and needy, whether that worker is a fellow Israelite or a foreigner residing in one of your towns. Pay them their wages each day before sunset because they are

---

[278]In Psalm 112, we read how generosity flowed from those who were obedient to and revered God: "Good will come to those who are generous and lend freely, who conduct their affairs with justice. Surely the righteous will never be shaken; they will be remembered forever. They will have no fear of bad news; their hearts are steadfast, trusting in the LORD. Their hearts are secure, they will have no fear; in the end they will look in triumph on their foes. They have freely scattered their gifts to the poor, their righteousness endures forever; their dignity will be lifted high in honor" (vv. 5–9).

[279]Christopher Wright, *Old Testament Ethics for the People of God*, 2004, p. 41.

poor and are counting on it. Otherwise, they may cry to the LORD against you, and you will be guilty of sin" (Deut. 24:14–15).

Allowing the needy to glean remnants of crops was described in Leviticus and reiterated for the benefit of the second generation of Israelites. "When you are harvesting in your field and you overlook a sheaf, do not go back to get it. Leave it for the foreigner, the fatherless and the widow, so that the LORD your God may bless you in all the work of your hands. When you beat the olives from your trees, do not go over the branches a second time. Leave what remains for the foreigner, the fatherless and the widow. When you harvest the grapes in your vineyard, do not go over the vines again. Leave what remains for the foreigner, the fatherless and the widow. Remember that you were slaves in Egypt. That is why I command you to do this" (Deut. 24:19–22).

Moses reiterated the special relationship they had with God; a relationship reserved for them among all nations and to continue in their spiritual walk with Him. "You have declared this day that the LORD is your God and that you will walk in obedience to him, that you will keep his decrees, commands and laws—that you will listen to him. And the LORD has declared this day that you are his people, his treasured possession as he promised, and that you are to keep all his commands." (Deut. 26:17–18).

Moses laid out situations that targeted the purity of the nation, including marital relationships, proper behavior for worshiping, personal hygiene, and the treatment of slaves. As God is holy and pure, so should His people be.

In Leviticus, God identified the blessings for obedience to His will and the curses if they failed to uphold their end of the covenant. They would either dwell in the Promised Land and be blessed forever, or they would worship false idols and be cursed. This message was given to the first generation out of Egypt, and it was important that the second generation receive the same lesson.

Moses gave his final instructions, hoping that the second generation would live and walk with God, not rebel and suffer the consequences of being driven from the Promised Land. (This is reminiscent of Adam and Eve being cast out of the Garden.) If the second generation returned to God in repentance and obedience, they would not be cursed forever; God would forgive them, and the relationship would continue.

"For I command you today to love the LORD your God, to walk in obedience to him, and to keep his commands, decrees, and laws; then you will live and increase, and the LORD your God will bless you in the land you are entering to possess. But if your heart turns away and you are not obedient, and if you are drawn away to bow down to other gods and worship them, I declare to you this day that you will certainly be destroyed. You will not live long in the land you are crossing the Jordan to enter and possess. This day I call the heavens and the earth as witnesses against you that I have set before you, life and death, blessings, and curses. Now choose life, so that you and your children may live and that you may love the LORD your God, listen to his voice, and hold fast to him. For the LORD is your life, and he will give you many years in the land he swore to give to your fathers, Abraham, Isaac and Jacob" (Deut. 30:16–20).

These instructions would certainly set Israel apart from the practices and behavior of the pagan nations around them. Worship and obedience to the one, true living God, social equity and proportional land distribution, and instructions for caring for the less fortunate were clearly different cultural practices that were unlike those of the nations around them. The formula and structure for pure and holy hearts had been laid out. The core ingredients were there to fulfill their role just as God designed; it was up to God's people to apply those guidelines in their hearts. The formula and structure are not too different for all of mankind moving forward. In fact, these are presented to us in the words and actions of Jesus while He was on earth, the Two Great Commandments in play for all to adhere to.

Chapter 6

Book of Judges: Eroding Hearts

T he previous chapter ended with Moses giving final instructions
before the Israelites entered the Promised Land. When Moses died,
Joshua inherited the leadership. He was an equally strong, central force
for the Israelites and, under his military guidance and with God's assistance, the Israelites slowly took over the land from the pagan nations
occupying the territory. The conquered territory was allocated to each
tribe and the nation of Israel established roots. However, it wasn't long
after Joshua and his generation passed away that the next generation
fell out of favor with God.

For the next several hundred years,[280] the people sputtered along
in their walk with God, falling off the path much of the time. This was
the period of the judges, a theocracy of sorts whereby God appointed
various leaders to get the sinful Israelites back on track. There was no
unity in the collective spiritual heart of the people. The intended role
of holy priests did not materialize and there was no corporate worship of any kind. In fact, the Israelites fell into pagan practices and
worshiped false gods.

---

[280]There are several accounts for calculating the period of the time that took place within
the book of Judges. Stone (2012, p. 204) puts a table together resulting in a total of
410 years. Provan et al., in the *Biblical History of Israel* (2012, p. 222), make note of the
potential overlap between Samson's career and time of oppression under the Philistines,
resulting in a shorter time period of 350 years. Merrill (*Kingdom of Priests*, p. 169–170)
initially suggests 235 years or 311 depending upon the starting point. But, Merrill adds,
in consideration of Paul's calculations in Acts 13:19–20, 450 years (including Eli's 40-year
career) is possible. Kitchen (*On the Reliability of the Old Testament*, 2008, p. 207), has a
chart from Othniel to the end of Sampson's rule spanning 232 years, a bit more in line
with Merrill's lower estimate.

In the Midst of Disobedience and Chaos

After Joshua led the twelve tribes of Israel into the Promised Land and they settled into their allotted land, they were at peace with neighbors in the surrounding territory. However, following Joshua's death, the "Deuteronomy Cycle" began.

The covenant God made with Moses and his people included the land promised to the patriarchs Abraham, Isaac, and Jacob. This new nation would prosper if the people obeyed God and His commandments, but if they disobeyed God's commands and worshiped other gods, curses and calamity would befall them. This is precisely the warning Moses gave his people toward the end of the book of Deuteronomy.

The book of Judges describes the cycle of the people's disobedience, followed by judgement and repentance, and returning to God through an appointed judge. Obedience lasted only while the judge was alive, and the cycle began all over again after the judge's death.

While the Israelites were successful in occupying the Promised Land, they were not successful in totally driving out the pagan tribes (Canaanites, Amorites, and Asherites). This was problematic because the remnant pagans, who were utilized as forced labor or slaves, began to influence the worship practices of the Israelites.

Lawson Stone observes that putting their enemies into slave conditions led to some ironic conclusions. "Here Israel actually participates in the very social evils from which they themselves were delivered by Yahweh. Moreover...forced labor characterized the Egyptian-Canaanite management style. It directly contradicted the central ethos of the covenant; the Israelites had begun to operate like their former oppressors and their current enemies."[281]

Not long after settling in the Promised Land, the surrounding pagan culture and worship practices infected the nation, and the Israelites succumbed to idolatry like their forefathers did in the golden

---

[281]Lawson Stone, *Cornerstone Biblical Commentary: Joshua, Judges, Ruth*, 2012, p. 219.

calf incident. Falling away from God and worshiping false gods began almost immediately after Joshua's death.

"After that whole generation had been gathered to their ancestors, another generation grew up who knew neither the LORD nor what he had done for Israel. Then the Israelites did evil in the eyes of the LORD and served the Baals. They forsook the LORD, the God of their ancestors, who had brought them out of Egypt. They followed and worshiped various gods of the peoples around them. They aroused the LORD's anger because they forsook him and served Baal and the Ashtoreths" (Judg. 2:10–13).

Just one generation removed from Joshua and the elders, the Israelites were disconnected from their unique relationship with God. Rather than be His holy people and fulfill their role as a nation of priests, they absorbed the pagan culture. Thomas Schreiner writes, "They (the Israelites) had a mandate: to live as the people of the Lord, to trust in God, and do his will...[and] they failed miserably."[282]

No one remembered the miracles God performed to get the Israelites out of Egypt, how He protected and fed them as they wandered in the desert for 40 years, or the covenant to deliver them to the Promised Land. The lessons of their forefathers and the consequences of worshiping the golden calf were totally forgotten. They never established their role as royal priests.

To compound the problem, the Israelites intermarried with their pagan neighbors, a prohibition God and Moses adamantly stressed. Rather than convert the pagans to their own faith as a nation of priests should have, the Israelites converted to the idol practices of the tribes they occupied. "The Israelites lived among the Canaanites, Hittites, Amorites, Perizzites, Hivites and Jebusites. They took their daughters in marriage and gave their own daughters to their sons and served their gods" (Judg. 3:5–6).

Stone points out that "intermarriage with the Canaanites constitutes a cultural surrender that, though not specifically mentioned... seems the logical outcome of the military failure and the making of

---

[282]Thomas Schreiner, *New Testament Theology: Magnifying God in Christ*, 2008, p. 42.

185

covenants with the Canaanites. This is a clear expression of compromise and a failure of the test of 3:4"[283] (Judges 3:4 says, "They [the pagan remnants] were left to test the Israelites to see whether they would obey the LORD's commands, which he had given their ancestors through Moses.")

Because of their disobedience, God allowed (or sent) raiders from surrounding nations to attack different regions of Israel. These nations subjected the tribes to slave-like conditions. Eugene Merrill argues this was purposeful on God's part: "An important reason Israel could not expel all its Canaanite enemies was that they might remain in the land whereby Yahweh could discipline it. They also remained to provide a test of Israel's loyalty to Yahweh and to teach the new generation of Israelites the skills of warfare."[284]

The conquered tribes recognized their sins and pled for God to deliver them. God selected a series of judges to be the spiritual and (in most cases) military leaders for the Israelites. These judges were not juridical in nature, but governors or generals whose responsibility was to protect the people and, hopefully, lead them back to God. While the judges were alive, they delivered the Israelites out of bondage and back to the covenant promises and peace prevailed.

Rather than leading the entire nation, the appointment of judges was limited to the geographic region being oppressed; only certain tribes were affected rather than the nation as a whole. There was no rallying cry from the rest of Israel to rescue the oppressed tribe, so unity was clearly lacking. In some cases, with the death of the judge and no direct line of succession ("these individuals were selected and empowered by Yahweh alone...and their office was not hereditary"[285]), the leadership gap resulted in the return of doing evil in God's eyes and adopting the pagan ways of their neighboring nations. The cycle started all over again.

---

[283]Lawson Stone, *Cornerstone Biblical Commentary: Joshua, Judges, Ruth,* 2012, p. 233.

[284]Eugene Merrill, *Kingdom of Priests,* 2008. pp. 177–78.

[285] Ibid., p. 181.

This cyclical behavior by God's chosen people continued throughout the book of Judges. As Ronald Youngblood summarizes: "After the conquest of Canaan by Joshua, the people of Israel experienced the normal range of problems that face colonizers of newly occupied territory. Exasperating their situation, however, was not only the resilience of the conquered but also the failures—moral and spiritual, as well as military—of the conquerors. Their rebellion against the covenant that God established with them at Sinai brought retribution, and the restoration that resulted from their repentance lasted only until they rebelled again...The dreary cycle of rebellion-retribution-repentance-restoration-rebellion is repeated throughout the book of Judges, which in many respects rehearses the darkest days of Israel's long history."[286]

The ease at which the Israelites fell into pagan practices, despite the demonstration of God's power to protect them and bring them out of Egypt, was an indication of how weak their spiritual hearts were. There was no leader to unite the tribes, spiritually or politically.

It is curious that the spiritual nature of the people diminished within a generation of settling in the Promised Land. In his lecture notes for Judges from his summary of the Old Testament, Dr. Douglas Stuart of the Gordon-Conwell Theological Seminary highlights several reasons why the Israelites easily adopted the worshiping practices of neighboring pagan cultures. For one, God was an invisible presence to them, while idols (carved or metal images) were physical and defined; therefore, a physical awareness made it easier to identify with an idol. The pagan cultures had a different purpose for each god; how could the one God do everything for the Jewish people?

The pagan nations were seen as economically successful; their agriculturally based businesses were more prolific than Israel's. The perception was that their gods blessed their land better than what the Jewish

---

[286]Ronald Youngblood, *Expositor's Bible Commentary: 1 Samuel – 2 Samuel*, 2009, p. 24–25. While it appears as a cyclical pattern, it's more of a spiritual "death spiral." The pattern would continue in both the northern kingdom of Israel and subsequently, the southern kingdom of Judah after King Solomon, as described in Chapter 10.

God provided. Perhaps worshiping the pagan gods specializing in fertility, like Baal, would help close the economic gap.

The pagan religions required no ethical behavior or moral discipline, while God's covenant relationship seemed too onerous, complex, and inconvenient to the Israelites. In addition, pagan practices could take place any time or anywhere, while the Israelites were required to participate in corporate worship on the Sabbath exclusively at Shiloh. They were also required to meet there three times a year for festivals that required extensive travel.

Pagan practices were physically (worldly) indulgent; sexual promiscuity was promoted, male and female prostitutes were provided within their temples, and sex was a regular part of the worship practice. In addition, frequent feasts and heavy drinking were in vogue and making images of their idols for art were encouraged. God explicitly prohibited image making: "'You shall not make for yourself an image in the form of anything in heaven above or on the earth beneath or in the waters below. You shall not bow down to them or worship them; for I, the LORD your God, am a jealous God, punishing the children for the sin of the parents to the third and fourth generation of those who hate me'" (Exod. 20:4–5 and Deut. 5:8–9).

In short, pagan practices lent themselves to worldly pleasures with no moral discipline. God, however, wanted His chosen people to be spiritually pure and holy, to be one with Him and not of this world, and to adhere to a higher moral standard than the pagan cultures around them. If they indulged in pagan practices, what difference in this world could they possibly make? How could they represent the holiness of God if they were no different in behavior or actions than the pagan nations around them?

This moral deterioration spirals out of control as the book of Judges progresses. The early judges proved to be morally strong and defenders of the faith, relying strictly on God to provide military success over their oppressors. Othniel, the first judge, was the nephew of Caleb, the only one other than Joshua from the first generation who remained faithful to God. Scripture says the Spirit of the Lord came upon him and he ruled peacefully for 40 years. Of the next judges, Lawson Stone writes, "The stories of Ehud, Shamgar and Deborah present Israel successfully overcoming its oppressors under divinely prompted and enabled leadership...they fully embody the 'heroic qualities.'"[287]

The judges who followed them had difficulty maintaining the corporate heart of God's covenant. In some cases, they were deficient in their own faith. For example, Gideon was slow to recognize God's calling and displayed reluctance just as Moses did when he was commissioned for God's work.

Gideon's appointment began when the angel of the Lord appeared to him while he was threshing wheat. When Gideon asked why God abandoned His people and handed them over to the Midianites, the Lord said, "'Go in the strength you have and save Israel out of Midian's hand. Am I not sending you?'" (Judg. 6:14). (This is a preincarnate appearance of Jesus.)

Gideon was not prepared to take on this assignment. He argued that he was from a small family and had no military training. Further demonstrating his lack of confidence, when he was commanded by the Lord to tear down his father's altar to Baal and cut down the Asherah pole, Gideon did it under cover of darkness for fear of being found out. Once God instilled His Holy Spirit however, Gideon became a faithful warrior, giving God credit for their victory over the Midianites.

The military victory was a huge success. Gideon started with 32,000 men, but God whittled it down to 300 so that the Israelites would realize what a powerful ally they had in Him. According to Scriptures, the Midian army numbered 135,000 against Gideon's 300. God assisted Gideon's nighttime attack by causing confusion among the Midianites, who turned and attacked each other. Gideon pursued the remaining 15,000 men for over 26 miles with the same 300 men, slaughtering them all. Clearly, the victory belonged to God and not Gideon's tiny army.

The grateful Israelites wanted to make Gideon king, failing to realize to whom the victory belonged. "The Israelites said to Gideon, 'Rule over us—you, your son and your grandson—because you have

---

[287]Lawson Stone, *Cornerstone Biblical Commentary: Joshua, Judges, Ruth,* 2012, p. 245.

saved us from the hand of Midian.' But Gideon told them, 'I will not rule over you, nor will my son rule over you. The LORD will rule over you'" (Judg. 8:22–23).

Gideon did ask each of the Israelites for a gold earring from their plunder. He made the gold into an ephod, "which he placed in Ophrah, his town. All Israel prostituted themselves by worshiping it there, and it became a snare to Gideon and his family" (v. 27). Despite God's hand in the victory and the apparent lip service from the Israelites, there was no real revival from witnessing God's glory and blessings.

After Gideon's death, his son Abimelek took over without God's appointment and an intrafamily rivalry ensued for leadership. He slaughtered his 70 brothers in his drive for authority. He spent most of the time of his leadership removing rivals to his authority. When he attacked Shechem, the townspeople fled to the tower, which he set on fire, killing over 1,000 people.

When he attacked the next town, the entire population also retreated to its tower. However, when he attempted to set it ablaze, he was too close to the wall and a woman in the tower dropped a millstone on him, mortally wounding him.[288] Rather than die at the hands of a woman, he urged his armor bearer to finish him off, which he did.

There are two minor judges, Tola and Jair, who followed Abimelek; peace in the land lasted 46 years, the sum of their combined leadership. Though little is mentioned of their leadership, no mention of any deviant behavior implied that they adhered to the covenant. Stone notes the significance of their rule: "...the minor judges show us intrinsic leadership...In each case, some outstanding point of competence or achievement will be noted, upon which their rule is grounded. It will never be coercion or violence, but likely prestige and respect

---

[288]This military defeat remains as folklore in Jewish history. In Chapter 9, we'll read that David had Uriah murdered in battle by ordering him too close to the walls of the city being attacked by David's army. David must have had Abimelek's death in mind as he ordered Uriah's death.

well-earned...they succeed one another without any intervening sin or oppression."[289]

After Jair's leadership, the Israelites fell out of their covenant commitment. "Again, the Israelites did evil in the eyes of the LORD. They served the Baals and the Ashtoreths, and the gods of Aram, the gods of Sidon, the gods of Moab, the gods of the Ammonites and the gods of the Philistines. And because the Israelites forsook the LORD and no longer served him, He became angry with them. He sold them into the hands of the Philistines and the Ammonites, who shattered and crushed them. For eighteen years they oppressed all the Israelites on the east side of the Jordan in Gilead, the land of the Amorites. The Ammonites also crossed the Jordan to fight against Judah, Benjamin and Ephraim; Israel was in great distress" (Judg. 10:6–9).

Under dire conditions, the Israelites realized their sin once again and begged for God to forgive them for worshiping other idols. This time, God refused to immediately rescue them from their plight. He reminded the errant people of all the times He rescued them in the past and how each time they returned to their sinful ways. He was done saving them; let the gods they were happily worshiping do it. Stone writes, "Only under the pressure of oppression, with the Ammonite fist locked around their throats and the Philistine dragon about to leap from its lair did they cry out to Yahweh. Even then, they proved arch hypocrites."[290]

They continued to plead for forgiveness and promised to rid themselves of their idols. God capitulated but didn't provide them the peace that was promised when they entered the Promised Land. That did not take place until David's reign as king when God established a covenant with him. (His reign as king is covered in Chapters 8 and 9; the Davidic Covenant is discussed in Appendix B).

Jephthah became the next major judge who, through God's assistance, was able to release the grip of the Ammonites. Jephthah was

---

[289]Lawson Stone, *Cornerstone Biblical Commentary: Joshua, Judges, Ruth,* 2012, pp. 327–28.

[290] Ibid., p. 337.

referred to as a mighty warrior but was the son of a prostitute.[291] Although he was the firstborn, he was driven from the family by his half-brothers because of his mother's status. He became a leader of a criminal gang, but when the Ammonites waged war against Israel, the people were desperate for his leadership. He accepted the responsibility but made a rash oath. "And Jephthah made a vow to the LORD: 'If you give the Ammonites into my hands, whatever comes out of the door of my house to meet me when I return in triumph from the Ammonites will be the LORD's, and I will sacrifice it as a burnt offering'" (Judg. 11:30–31).[292]

It can be surmised that the house he referred to was his estate rather than his home and that Jephthah was assuming that an animal from his herd would be the first thing he would see. Lawson Stone writes, "Jephthah's vow, seen almost universally as an attempt to manipulate Yahweh, was probably a tragically misguided, but well-intentioned attempt to honor Yahweh."[293]

At any rate, Scriptures tell us that the Spirit of the Lord came to him, and he mustered an army, much like Saul did in his first military encounter. God granted him the victory, but when he returned home, the first thing he saw was his daughter, his one and only child, who came dancing out of the house to greet him in his victory. The celebration turned to tragedy as Jephthah had to follow through on his vow.

Stone doubts that Jephthah offered his daughter as a burnt human sacrifice, which Yahweh would find an abomination. Rather, he suggests that Jephthah offered his daughter as a virgin in lifelong service to God, much like Hannah did with Samuel. Stone suggests that Jephthah's daughter "was consigned to a lifetime of service at the

---

[291]Stone notes the Hebrew word for prostitute "also signifies any woman having sex outside of marriage. The later reference to Jephthah as the 'son of another woman' suggests his origin in an irregular union, not prostitution." Ibid., p. 340.

[292]In Chapter 8, Saul made a similar foolish oath that his army should not eat until he had victory over the Philistines, under punishment by death. His son Jonathan didn't hear the order and violated his father's command. If not for the intercession of his military leaders, Saul would have ordered Jonathan's death.

[293]Lawson Stone, *Cornerstone Biblical Commentary: Joshua, Judges, Ruth*, 2012, p. 357.

sanctuary and required to remain a virgin till her death."[294] Since he had no other children, the tragedy for Jephthah would be the end of his progeny to carry on his name, estate, and land holding, a critical loss for any ancient Israelite.

Conflicts among the Israelites escalated after the Ammonites were defeated. The tribe of Ephraim mobilized an army to challenge Jephthah's decision to fight the Ammonites without them. "Then the men of Ephraim gathered together, crossed over toward Zaphon, and said to Jephthah, 'Why did you cross over to fight against the people of Ammon, and did not call us to go with you?'" (Judg. 12:1, NKJV). According to David Guzik, "The tribe of Ephraim felt slighted by Jephthah, and was angry that they did not have a central and prestigious role in the victorious battle over the Ammonites."[295] They even threatened to burn down Jephthah's house with him in it. Rather than seek peace with his fellow Israelites, Jephthah marched his army in battle against them. "Forty-two thousand Ephraimites were killed at that time" (Judg. 12:6).

The murders Abimelek committed were limited to members of his own family and potential rivals, but we see tribal unity starting to disintegrate as they wage war with each another. While the number of deaths caused by Jephthah may be an exaggeration, it's likely more than their enemies the Ammonites inflicted upon them. Just as Levi and Simeon's revenge on the city of Shechem for their sister's rape far exceeded that offense (as discussed in Chapter 4), Jephthah's reprisal against the Ephraim tribe was equally excessive. "While the Ephraimite grievance falls far short of a justification for war, Jephthah's response here appears extreme as he subjected his fellow Israelites to virtual annihilation."[296]

---

[294] Ibid., p. 358.

[295] David Guzik, "Study Guide for Judges 12 by David Guzik," Blue Letter Bible, last modified February 21, 2017, https://www.blueletterbible.org/Comm/guzik_david/StudyGuide 2017-Jdg/Jdg-12.cfm.

[296] Lawson Stone, *Cornerstone Biblical Commentary: Joshua, Judges, Ruth,* 2012, p. 362.

Four minor judges followed Jephthah without incident (that is, no mention of apostasy or doing evil in God's eyes) spanning about 30 years. But when their governance ended, "the Israelites did evil in the eyes of the LORD, so the LORD delivered them into the hands of the Philistines for forty years" (Judg. 13:1).

In His mercy and compassion, God appointed Samson, the last judge mentioned in the book of Judges. The angel of the Lord appeared to his mother (another Christophany) to announce her pregnancy, despite her inability to have children, and that she was to raise him as a Nazirite. That is, he would be placed in special service to God and "take the lead in delivering Israel from the hands of the Philistines" (Judg. 13:5).

A Nazirite pledged an oath to dedicate him or herself to God. "'As long as they remain under their Nazirite vow, they must not eat anything that comes from the grapevine, not even the seeds or skins. During the entire period of their Nazirite vow, no razor may be used on their head. They must be holy until the period of their dedication to the LORD is over; they must let their hair grow long'" (Num. 6:4–5). In Samson's case, he was a Nazirite until his death, but he did not adhere to the holiness and purity intended for a Nazirite.

True to His word, God provided a child to Manoah's wife (she remained unnamed in Scriptures), just as He did with Sarah, Rebecca, and Hannah, the mother of the prophet Samuel. "The woman gave birth to a boy and named him Samson. He grew and the LORD blessed him, and the Spirit of the LORD began to stir him while he was in Mahaneh Dan, between Zorah and Eshtaol" (Judg. 13:24–25).

Samson, who was from the tribe of Dan, had significant character failings despite being a Nazirite, particularly in relationships with women. He found a Philistine woman to his liking and told his parents that he wanted to marry her. When his parents questioned him about marrying a pagan woman rather than one from Israel, Samson responded, "'Get her for me! She's the right one for me'" (Judg. 14:3). Israelites were prohibited from marrying pagans and Samson's demand sounded disrespectful to his father. (Samson also failed to adhere to the fifth commandment of honoring his parents.)

Stone notes the similarity of Samson's demands to the end of the book of Judges "...where everyone did 'whatever seemed right in their own eyes.' The parallel is deliberate: Samson parallels and personifies the nation in its willful determination to do what it pleases and defines its own standard of conduct."[297]

The marriage festivities were a disaster and led to a long-standing feud between Samson and the Philistines. It began with Samson's self-serving riddle to the Philistines at the wedding party. If they solved the riddle within seven days of the wedding feast, Samson would provide the family with thirty linen garments and thirty sets of clothes; otherwise, the Philistines would owe him the same. Pressured by her family to get the answer, Samson's wife nagged him until he provided her the answer. When the Philistines revealed the answer to his riddle, he realized his wife had betrayed him. In a rage, he murdered thirty Philistines in town to pay off the wager and returned home without his wife.

The feud escalated when, months later, Samson returned to his father-in-law with reconciliation in mind, only to find out his wife had been given to his best man in the interim. Samson perceived his honor had been sullied, so he destroyed the grain, vineyards, and olive groves of the Philistines. When the townspeople learned what Samson had done, they took his father-in-law and wife and burned them to death. Samson retaliated by killing several of the townspeople and retreated to a cave outside town. The human carnage continued; it seemed the spiritual heart was nowhere in sight.

Samson's feud was personal, not an effort to free Israel from the control of their enemies. The tribe of Judah was under Philistine jurisdiction at the time and Samson's private war with the Philistines endangered Judah's position with them. "Then three thousand men from Judah went down to the cave in the rock of Etam and said to Samson, 'Don't you realize that the Philistines are rulers over us? What have you done to us?' He answered, 'I merely did to them what they did to me'" (Judg. 15:11). As a Danite, Samson should not have put a

---

[297] Ibid., p. 388.

fellow Israelites in danger. His response of revenge was reminiscent of Lamech's boasting. He forgot that vengeance belonged to God: "It is mine to avenge; I will repay. In due time their foot will slip; their day of disaster is near and their doom rushes upon them" (Deut. 32:35).

Samson agreed to let Judah's representatives bind him with ropes and lead him to the Philistines to appear cooperative with their oppressors. When the Philistines were about to take him captive, Samson broke his bonds and killed 1,000 Philistines with the jawbone of a donkey.

Later, Samson fell in love with Delilah, another pagan woman. Philistine leaders bribed her to find out the secret of his strength so they could finally capture him. Each time she asked him, Samson gave Delilah a deceptive answer about his source of strength. Delilah nagged him and Samson yielded. "So, he told her everything. 'No razor has ever been used on my head,' he said, 'because I have been a Nazirite dedicated to God from my mother's womb. If my head were shaved, my strength would leave me, and I would become as weak as any other man'" (Judg. 16:17).

With the secret revealed, Delilah lulled Samson to sleep, the Philistines cut off his hair, and his strength and Nazirite connection with God were gone. They gouged out his eyes and enslaved him to grinding grain in the prison mill. Those were the consequences of his intermarriage and coexistence with pagans.

While he did not worship pagan idols, Samson never recognized God's role in his strength, nor did he ever demonstrate a real relationship with God while he was a judge. The only time Samson appealed to God at all was at the time of his death. The Philistines were offering sacrifices to their god and called for Samson to entertain them, not recognizing that his hair grew back, and that he had repented before God. His strength had returned as he stood between pillars of the temple. "Then Samson prayed to the LORD, 'Sovereign LORD, remember me. Please, God, strengthen me just once more, and let me with one blow get revenge on the Philistines for my two eyes.' Samson said, 'Let me die with the Philistines!' Then he pushed with all his might, and down came the temple on the rulers and all the people in it. Thus, he killed many more when he died than while he lived" (Judg. 16:28, 30).

Several spiritual components were missing from Samson while he was a judge. Despite having the Spirit of the Lord and pledging himself as a Nazirite, there was no mention of him eliminating Israel's enemies or leading his people back to God. Samson was more interested in foreign women than saving Israel; he was motivated by self-gratification and personal revenge. His heart was not an example for us to follow. Samson didn't deliver his fellow tribesmen of Judah from the hands of the Philistines; he died as one of their captives.

The tragedy of Samson's failure was a microcosm of the tribes of Israel during the times of the judges. Iain Provan et al., write, "Webb highlights the story of Samson as 'the climatic realization of the major themes' providing a mirror of Israel's own experience: 'Samson's awareness of his separation from God, and yet his disregard for it, his fatal attraction to foreign women, his willfulness and his presumption all hold the mirror up to the behavior of Israel itself. So too does his fate.'"[298]

Despite their character failings, these men were not without faith; rather, God used these flawed men to deliver the nation. That is God's grace at its best, but these judges were supposed to be the spiritual leaders.

This progressive moral decay continued and by the closing chapters of Judges, we see how far away from God the Israelites had drifted. In fact, there seemed to be no real connection to God at that point and the carnage and immorality within Israel was hardly different from their neighboring pagan communities. Unity among the tribes had come completely unraveled.

In one story, a man from the tribe of Ephraim stole money from his mother to buy a mold for an idol and appointed his son to be a priest for the family. "Now this man Micah had a shrine, and he made an ephod and some household gods and installed one of his sons as his

---

[298]Iain Provan, Phillip Long, & Tremper Longham, *A Biblical History of Israel*, 2015, p. 216.

priest. In those days Israel had no king; everyone did as they saw fit" (Judg. 17:5–6). When a traveling Levite passed by his home, Micah offered him a full-time position as the official priest of the family. With utter hubris, Micah thought, "'Now I know that the LORD will be good to me, since this Levite has become my priest'" (v. 13).

Meanwhile, the tribe of Dan was still roaming the land after all those years. Lawson Stone writes that they "had actually failed to secure their very lush and fecund territory because they were no match for the fierce Amorites who hemmed them up in the hill country."[299] They sent scouts into parts of Ephraim. The scouts found the town of Laish to be prosperous, peaceful, and more importantly, defenseless. They also found the priest at Micah's house and all his household idols.

When the men returned from scouting the land, they encouraged the Danites to attack the unsuspecting people. The scouts went to Micah's house while an army of 600 men waited at the city gate. They took Micah's idols and his priest, and they destroyed the town and everything in it. When the Danites rebuilt the city, they "set up for themselves the idol, and Jonathan, son of Gershom, the son of Moses, and his sons were priests for the tribe of Dan until the time of the captivity of the land. They continued to use the idol Micah had made, all the time the house of God was in Shiloh" (Judg. 18:30–31). Bruce Waltke notes, "The narrator saves the best irony for last: the Levite is Moses' great-grandson Jonathan. Younger comments, 'Thus, the problems of religious syncretism and spiritual decay have infected the very institution designed to combat these problems, not to mention one of most revered households in ancient Israel.' The fatal contagion of the Levites infects all the tribes"[300]

The tribes were collapsing on each other for worldly gain and apostasy ruled the day. Iain Provan et al., states, "These events are rife with irony. Israel was to have eradicated debased religion by dispossessing

---

[299]Lawson Stone, *Cornerstone Biblical Commentary: Joshua, Judges, Ruth*, 2012. p. 436. He also suggests that the Danites ended up in two groups; the southern part where Samson was and this northern group still searching for a settlement.

[300]Bruce Waltke, *An Old Testament Theology*, 2007, p. 614.

the Canaanites, whose iniquity was full, and to have established true Yahwistic religion. Instead, the Danites attack and dispossess 'the quiet, and unsuspecting' people outside their allotted territory and institute their own debased religion, replete with idols."[301]

In another story, a Levite from the Ephraim tribe brought home a woman from Bethlehem to be his concubine. There was an unexplained marital dispute whereby the woman returned to her father's house. After four months, the Levite traveled back to retrieve her. As they made their way back to Ephraim, they stopped in Gibeah (another town in the land of Benjamin), but no one took them in for the night. In a scene right out of Lot's story, a man found them in the town square. "'You are welcome at my house,' the old man said. 'Let me supply whatever you need. Only don't spend the night in the square'" (Judg. 19:20).

That was the same warning Lot gave the two visiting angels and for the same reason. The ensuing events almost literally follow Lot's dilemma. While they were enjoying their meal, troublemakers surrounded the house demanding to have sex with the Levite. Like Lot, the older man tried to appease the mob by offering his virgin daughter and the Levite's concubine, but the people were adamant until the Levite finally pushed his concubine out and they had their way with her. It was horrible enough when it happened in the pagan city of Sodom, but this was one of the tribes of Israel, the nation intended to be holy and pure priests! The depravity and disintegration of Israel's morality was astonishing.

The Levite found the concubine the next morning at the doorstep and callously ignored what happened to her (which could have happened to him). He put her on his donkey and took her home. Realizing she was dead and with no remorse for his selfish actions that caused her horrible death, he cut her limb by limb and sent them into all the areas of Israel as a call to arms to avenge his situation. In the only scene in Judges where there was any semblance of unity among the tribes, they

---

[301]Iain Provan, Philip Long, and Tremper Longham, *A Biblical History of Israel*, 2015, p. 215.

all met with their respective troops to decide the fate of the tribe of Benjamin. Lawson Stone notes the irony of this sudden urge to unify. "For the entire book of Judges, the tribes have shown little inclination to unite...Against the enemies oppressing them, they found little unity, but against one of their own tribes, they come together almost spontaneously 'as one man.'"[302] With a force of 400,000, the army marched toward Bethlehem and a message was sent to the leaders of Benjamin to deliver the guilty parties over to them.

Rather than capitulate, the Benjamites mobilized more than 26,000 men. The army of Israel attacked first, but the Benjamin warriors killed 22,000 of the attackers. The tribes of Israel attacked again the next day, but the Benjamin warriors successfully warded off the attack, killing another 18,000. In the third attack, Israel ambushed Bethlehem by drawing them away from the city and attacking from the rear.

It was a slaughter; 25,100 Benjamites were killed and all those in Gibeah were annihilated. The carnage was extended: "The men of Israel went back to Benjamin and put all the towns to the sword, including the animals and everything else they found. All the towns they came across they set on fire" (Judg. 20:48).

The tragedy continued without logic. First, the Israelites made a rash oath that none of their daughters would marry a Benjamite. However, when the battle was over, remorse set in. They wondered how the tribe of Benjamin would repopulate without wives. They decided that anyone who did not make the vow would be put to death and their women would be "donated" to the remnants of Benjamin. In accounting for who was there to take the oath, they realized that no one from Jabesh Gilead had participated, so 12,000 men were sent to kill all the males in the town and any woman who wasn't a virgin. Only 400 virgins were found and given to the Benjamites, which was obviously not enough to provide mates to their remaining male population.

The next plan made even less sense and displayed no moral integrity at all. The elders of the assembly told the men of Benjamin to ambush young women on their way to the annual festival of the Lord

---

[302]Lawson Stone, *Cornerstone Biblical Commentary: Joshua, Judges, Ruth*, 2012, p. 471.

in Shiloh. The Benjamites hid in the vineyards and when the women were in sight, they carried them off to be wives for them. And since these women would be from the other tribes, what about that being in violation of the vow? The rationale was that the daughters were not given to the Benjamites, they were forcibly taken. "When their fathers or brothers complain to us, we will say to them, 'Do us the favor of helping them, because we did not get wives for them during the war. You will not be guilty of breaking your oath because you did not give your daughters to them'" (Judg. 21:22).

In a disingenuous application of semantics, it was okay if the women were kidnapped and taken against their will as long as they were not given voluntarily in marriage by members of their family. Stone writes, "Now, instead of one woman violated to save the skin of one cold hearted Levite, 400 women have their lives and families ripped from them...in order to preserve the lineage of 600 men who put their lives at risk to defend a town full of rapists."[303]

The book of Judges ends with the simple but telling commentary: "In those days Israel had no king; everyone did as he saw fit" (Judg. 21:25). This is reminiscent of the behavior we witnessed in Lamech's story; he defined his own sense of morality, lived by his own rules and murderous behavior, and was totally detached from God and His will. Unlike Lamech's excuse of being six generations removed from God's presence, the nation of Israel had no such excuse for their lack of moral fortitude.

Thomas Schreiner writes, "Judges ends on a dour note. The behavior of the tribe of Dan in attacking a quiet and peaceful people and hiring a priest to support their own agenda was a far cry from what the Lord commanded. The rape and murder of the Levite's concubine and then the subsequent support from the tribe of Benjamin relay the depth to which Israel had fallen."[304] No real demonstration of love for God or man seemed to exist.

---

[303] Ibid., p. 484.

[304]Thomas Schreiner, *New Testament Theology*, 2008, p. 42.

The Israelites had fallen away from God, disobeyed His commandments, worshiped false gods, killed at random, and had no sense of morality or unity. Instead of representing Him as His pure and holy priests here on earth, they acted no different than the pagan nations; if it's even possible, their behavior was worse.

It caused Charles Scobie to remark, "Politically, during this period the Israelites form at best, a loose confederation of tribes. The at-times, anarchic political, social, and religious conditions are attributed to the fact that, 'in those days, there was no king in Israel; all the people did what was right in the own eyes."[305]

---

[305]Charles Scobie, Charles, *The Ways of Our God,* 2003, p. 196.

Chapter 7

WOMEN OF HEART

We continue to move sequentially through the books of the Old Testament. While the last chapter showed us how the spiritual hearts of the Israelites were nearly empty, Scriptures provide us with the stories of two women of great faith: the story of Ruth from the book of Ruth and the story of Hannah from First Samuel. While apostasy was taking place during this time, Ruth and Hannah, both living at the tail end of the era of judges, demonstrated the core ingredients for remaining obedient to God's will and showing love toward their neighbors. Their stories provided a small but brilliant light during Israel's dark beginnings. Their faith and trust in God stood in stark contrast to all others.

Ruth's history of faith began with leaving her pagan life behind to care for her widowed Israeli mother-in-law, both returning to Bethlehem in near poverty. She became one of the earlier recorded converts of faith, and her story ended happily with her marriage to Boaz, a noble man in every sense of the word. From their lineage came King David and our savior Jesus Christ.

Hannah, like Sarah and Rachel before her, was a barren woman of faith who prayed for a child that she would dedicate to serving God. Her prayers were answered, and she became the mother of the great prophet Samuel who oversaw the anointing of King Saul and King David. These were the beginnings of the monarchy and the establishment of a united nation.

Boaz and Ruth: A Love Story

The book of Ruth is one of the shorter books in the Bible, much like the book of Jonah. And like Jonah, Ruth is a familiar story that those with a rudimentary knowledge of the Bible are likely to remember. Both stories also have deeper truths that may not be obvious in a casual reading.

Jonah's story has some amusing moments and his three days in the belly of the large fish for not proclaiming the Lord's message to the Ninevites was referenced by Jesus in respect to His own mission and eventual resurrection.

The story of Ruth is a tender and genuine love story. The character traits of Boaz, Ruth, and her mother-in-law Naomi readily fit the theme of the spiritual heart.

There are several reasons for including the book of Ruth in this discussion. For one, it recounts a pure and compassionate love story between Boaz and Ruth, which is somewhat unique in the Scriptures. In addition, there is a loving and loyal relationship between Ruth and her mother-in-law, Naomi. Their relationship was so strong that Ruth was willing to leave her homeland behind and declare her faith in following God. Ruth was one of the Bible's earliest displays of Gentile conversion and augments the concept that the spiritual heart is not limited to just the Israelites.

In Boaz, we find nobility, integrity, morality, and spirituality. He was obedient and faithful to God's will. He cared for the widow and foreigner as outlined by Moses. In Boaz's compassion and thoughtful treatment of Ruth, Bruce Waltke contrasts his behavior with the men described in Judges: "Unlike the men in Judges, he does not treat her as a piece of property...He immediately addresses her as 'my daughter,' signaling that he too accepts her as a true Israelite." [306]

Naomi, Ruth, and Boaz exhibited the best characteristics of the heart that reflected an almost perfect representation of the Two Great Commandments.

---

[306]Bruce Waltke, *An Old Testament Theology*, 2007, p. 855.

Finally, while the book of Ruth is in the middle of the Old Testament, there is a New Testament flavor to it. In the latter, we find that most of Jesus's ministry and teachings were intended for the masses with a universal message for those who would listen, all of which is just as meaningful and important in today's world.

There is a message for all in this story as well. In the book of Ruth, we've moved away from the patriarchs, early leaders, and prophets in the Old Testament to find a message for the heart that doesn't require an elaborate formula or sets of rules to follow. We see the spiritual heart in action through the lens of ordinary life. We see the characteristics of three individuals who were not the pillars of the Old Testament. This is ordinary life providing an excellent example of how a spiritual heart can be demonstrated without having to being among the scriptural elite like David or Abraham. In fact, when Jesus gave his lesson on the Good Samaritan, I can readily see Him tell the story of Ruth as a sequel to reemphasize the lesson of compassion and kindness to one's neighbor.

It is this kindness that Christopher Wright correctly uses the story of Ruth as the epitome of its description. It speaks "of committed faithfulness within a relationship, a commitment which is willing to take on costs or burdens for the sake of the other party and to do so for the long haul...As a human characteristic, it is modeled in the book of Ruth. Ruth is commended for her remarkable *hesed* [a Hebrew word that is a slightly weak translation for kindness] to the family of her widowed mother-in-law Naomi and her own deceased husband. Similarly, Boaz is commended for his *hesed* to Naomi's family by fulfilling the duties of a kinsman-redeemer, at a cost to himself."[307]

Robert Hubbard makes a similar characterization behind the simplicity of Ruth's story. "Unlike other books, it treats on episode in the life of an ordinary family from Bethlehem, not the exploits of Israel's leaders. It also lacks the miracles and wonders—angelic visitors,

---

[307]Christopher Wright, Knowing God Through the Old Testament, 2019, p.341.

burning bushes, parted seas, trembling mountains, holy wars—so typical of OT narratives."[308]

In previous chapters, I contrasted the heart of a faithful individual with a contemporary to demonstrate the range of spiritual hearts abiding by God's commandments. In this chapter, we have individual hearts for God in direct contrast to the Israelite community described in the last chapter. The behavior and actions of the individuals in Ruth are defined by a moral fiber and obedience to God in contrast to that of Israel at large that was in rapid decline.

As background, Ruth's story took place during the latter stages of the judges, the period in Israel's history following Joshua's death and prior to the start of the monarchy. In Josephus' account of Ruth, he notes that the story took place after Samson's death, with Eli as the acting high priest and governor.[309] Eli would eventually be instructor to Samuel, who would be the last of the judges in Israel's history as discussed in the next chapter.

Kevin Vanhoozer cites two purposes for the book of Judges: "(1) to demonstrate the failure of Israel's leadership to pass on the knowledge of God to the next generation or to lead them in covenant-keeping... and (2) to argue for a better leader; a covenant-keeping king, not a judge."[310] Instead of setting the spiritual bar for the nations around them, the time of the judges was marked by phases of chaos, violence, apostasy, and lack of unity—both spiritually and politically—among the tribes of Israel. The following chapter will demonstrate that it would take King David to unite the nation and keep the covenant relationship between God and His people.

In contrast to this failing of the spiritual heart, Jason Driesbach notes that in Bethlehem, the location for the story of Ruth, "...society is unified in common values and people look out for each other. This is unexpected for readers familiar with the stories of judges and causes the virtues of Ruth's main characters, as well as the evidence of God's

---

[308]Robert Hubbard, *The Book of Ruth,* 1988, p. 66.

[309]Josephus, *Jewish Antiquities,* Book 5 Chapter 9, v. 318, p. 192.

[310]Kevin Vanhoozer, *Dictionary for Theological Interpretation of the Bible,* 2005, p. 412.

ongoing, purposeful providence, to stand out against the images of moral and religious chaos and accompanying judgement that dominate the book of Judges."[311]

It is within this backdrop of unfaithfulness and disobedience to God and their leanings toward paganism that we have the book of Ruth, which is a breath of fresh air with their obedient hearts. Lawson Stone makes a similar assessment when contrasting spiritual hearts: "The minor judges remind us of the book of Ruth, which transpires in 'the days when the judges ruled' (Ruth 1:1). In that book, each character behaves with dignity, honor, and integrity. In the human network of faithfulness, every person in the story finds redemption, and that without a single miracle."[312]

The story begins with Naomi and her husband Elimelek leaving Bethlehem with their two sons on account of a famine in the land. Robert Hubbard notes that famines were common in the Old Testament and "despite tragic appearances, often advance God's plan for his people." To substantiate this, he adds in a footnote, "Famines sent Abram to Egypt and Isaac to Philistia where both experienced divine protection (especially their wives) and emerged much wealthier than before. ...Similarly, famine drove Jacob and his sons to Egypt where their descendants also prospered and experienced the miraculous Exodus of a new nation, Israel."[313]

Naomi and Elimelek headed for Moab, hoping to escape the hard times. On the face of it, it was odd that they chose Moab as their refuge, a nation that proved a thorn in the moral side of the Israelites for centuries. While the Israelites wandered in the wilderness, Balak, king of Moab, tried to attack the Israelites to prevent them from taking over his land, but was not successful. And it was the Moabite women that led some of the second generation of Israelite men into sexual

---

[311]Jason Driesbach, *Cornerstone Biblical Commentary: Joshua, Judges, Ruth,* 2012, p. 501.

[312]Lawson Stone, *Cornerstone Biblical Commentary: Joshua, Judges, Ruth,* 2012, p. 327.

[313]Robert Hubbard, *The Book of Ruth,* 1988, p. 85.

immorality and worship of their idols at Shittim.[314] There had been bad blood between Israel and Moab since then. Despite this animosity between the nations, there was no mention of any danger or conflicts while Naomi and Elimelek resided there; however, they were in a predominately pagan environment.

While in Moab, Elimelek died and their two sons married Moabite women, Ruth and Orpah. After living there for ten years, both sons died, leaving no children behind and Naomi had no means of support. While this posed a very difficult situation for Naomi, her faith in God was not severed. "When Naomi heard in Moab that the LORD had come to the aid of his people by providing food for them, she and her daughters-in-law prepared to return home from there" (Ruth 1:6). While God is never mentioned directly in the book of Ruth, we see His hand "directing" behind the scenes. As the verse implied, Naomi still had her faith and understood that God would end the famine and return things back to normal. As she prepared to return to Bethlehem, she insisted that she return alone and that her daughters-in-law remain with their own families.

"Then Naomi said to her two daughters-in-law, 'Go back, each of you, to your mother's home. May the LORD show you kindness, as you have shown kindness to your dead husbands and to me. May the LORD grant that each of you will find rest in the home of another husband.' Then she kissed them goodbye, and they wept aloud" (Ruth 1:8–9).

Naomi's blessing over Ruth and Orpah revealed a few things about her faith in God. First, she obviously shared her faith with the women; after ten years, they would be familiar with the teachings of Israel's God to understand the blessing she left with them. Note that Naomi said "the" Lord, not "my" Lord, which implies her faith was not exclusive to her. It was obviously a shared faith; Naomi was obedient and faithful to God's will, and her heart was true to the First Great Commandment.

---

[314]"While Israel was staying in Shittim, the men began to indulge in sexual immorality with Moabite women, who invited them to the sacrifices to their gods. The people ate the sacrificial meal and bowed down before these gods" (Num. 25:1–2).

There was a lot of love, tenderness, caring, and kindness in this family. Naomi wanted God to bless them with the same kindness Orpah and Ruth provided to her two sons and to her. Hubbard adds, "Powerless to repay their kindness, her only recourse was to turn them over to God's care."[315]

The women obviously treated Naomi with love and respect, so much so that they wept in the face of having to part ways. God gave mankind the ingredients for the spiritual hearts they demonstrated. While her daughters-in-law weren't of the Jewish faith, they certainly had kind, thoughtful, and loving hearts. The other interesting point about Naomi's faith was that it stayed strong even though she lived in the pagan land of Moab for ten years and lost her beloved husband and their two sons. Her faith in God wasn't watered down by the catastrophic events in her life, the lack of a synagogue nearby, or being surrounded by those of Jewish faith. Keeping a strong faith despite living in an exclusively pagan environment was demonstrated by Abraham in Ur and Joseph in Egypt. Naomi's faith was certainly in good company, and it rubbed off on her daughters-in-law.

Naomi's selflessness was apparent as she tried to convince the women to return to their own home and family in Moab. There's was nothing to be gained from them following her back to Israel; Naomi had no other sons for them to marry, nor did she have any visible means of financial support. She was a widow without sons to care for her; she was totally on her own. Still, she wasn't just thinking of her own welfare, she wanted the women to start a new life without feeling obligated to help her.

Orpah reluctantly chose to return home to her family, but Ruth couldn't bear the thought of giving up her relationship with Naomi. In fact, she was willing to adopt Naomi's ways to remain with her. Ruth also demonstrated selflessness, willing to sacrifice her own happiness and future to remain loyal to Naomi. As she placed her trust in Naomi, she said, "'Don't urge me to leave you or to turn back from you. Where you go I will go, and where you stay I will stay. Your people

---

[315] Ibid., p. 103.

will be my people and your God my God. Where you die I will die, and there I will be buried. May the LORD deal with me, be it ever so severely, if even death separates you and me'" (Ruth 1:16–17). Bruce Waltke observes that her confession "...gives the classic expression to true faith, loyalty, and love to God and his people, who are inseparable. According to the calculus of faith, not of sight, she found her security in God and the people of God, not in Moab and her own pagan family...Like Abraham, Ruth leaves her county and family to follow *I AM* to an unseen land."[316]

It was truly a tender and loving entreaty. Ruth was willing to dedicate her life to Naomi's faith. It was a life-changing decision for Ruth. To give up her friends, family, and country without knowing how the future would play out showed total loyalty and trust in Naomi and God. Giving up her own faith was equally dramatic. As Jason Driesbach notes in his commentary regarding faith in those days, "religious belief was rarely viewed as subject to personal choice and was instead a critical part of cultural identity."[317] Ruth was giving up her identity as a Moabite and adopting Naomi's cultural heritage. She witnessed the Lord's power and blessings in Naomi's life and was ready to accept Him into her own life. So Ruth the Moabite adopted the faith of Israel; quite the contradiction of what was taking place in the nation she was headed toward with Naomi.

Abandoning a lifestyle to adopt one of faith was a basic tenet for the disciples of Jesus in the New Testament. Ruth's decision to leave with Naomi and follow in her faith cannot be overstated; it was prophetic because it was exactly what Jesus required of his disciples. George Ladd writes that "the most basic demand Jesus laid upon people if they would be his disciples was for a radical, unqualified decision. A person must make a decision so radical that it involves turning his or her back upon all other relationships. It may involve forsaking one's home."[318]

---

[316]Bruce Waltke, *An Old Testament Theology*, 2007, p. 855

[317]Jason Driesbach, *Cornerstone Biblical Commentary: Joshua, Judges, Ruth*, 2012, p. 518.

[318]George Ladd, *A Theology of the New Testament*, 1993, p. 130.

Robert Hubbard makes a similar comparison to the apostles who followed Jesus. "Ruth's renunciation foreshadows Jesus's teaching: to be his disciple requires one to renounce family ties for the sake of the kingdom of God."[319] They left everything behind to follow Him on His mission and their entire lives were reshaped. When we accept Jesus as our Savior, are we not following the same pattern? That is, are we not leaving a former life behind and following a new path?

Naomi and Ruth returned to Bethlehem and were excitedly greeted by Naomi's friends as they hadn't seen her in ten years. While they expressed happiness for her return, Naomi lamented that she left with a full life (a husband and two sons) and returned empty; she had no family but Ruth and no prospects of being provided for in the future. "'I went away full, but the LORD has brought me back empty. Why call me Naomi? [Her name meant pleasant, but she wanted to be called Mara, which meant bitter.] The LORD has afflicted me; the Almighty has brought misfortune upon me'" (Ruth 1:21). Naomi recognized God's hand in her fate, so this should not be taken as her condemning God for her circumstance. Jason Driesbach says that she is "characterizing her grief and emptiness and setting the stage so that we may also recognize the Lord's hand behind the scenes in restoring her condition."[320] As Hubbard points out, "In effect, Naomi joined Job is questioning God's mysterious justice."[321]

When it was time to harvest the barley crops, Ruth went to the fields to pick up anything that was left over from the initial harvesting. Knowing that Naomi had no other support, she took it upon herself to support the two of them.

Ruth demonstrated the same care that Naomi must have shown her when they lived in Moab. She didn't leave Naomi to fend for herself or to seek out her own fortune. Unwittingly, Ruth was observing God's desire for the Jewish community to care for its own widows. "He defends the cause of the fatherless and the widow, and loves

---

[319]Robert Hubbard, *The Book of Ruth*, 1988, p. 118.

[320]Jason Driesbach, *Cornerstone Biblical Commentary: Joshua, Judges, Ruth*, 2012, p. 521.

[321]Robert Hubbard, *The Book of Ruth*, 1988, p. 124.

the foreigner residing among you, giving them food and clothing" (Deut. 10:18).

Through Moses, God instructed the Israelites to care for widows and orphans so they would be conscious of their social responsibilities and provide for the less fortunate. "When you are harvesting in your field and you overlook a sheaf, do not go back to get it. Leave it for the foreigner, the fatherless and the widow, so that the LORD your God may bless you in all the work of your hands" (Deut. 24:19). And again, in Exodus 22, "'Do not take advantage of the widow or the fatherless. If you do and they cry out to me, I will certainly hear their cry'" (vv. 22–23).

While Ruth wasn't raised in the Jewish faith or familiar with these scriptures, she had it in her heart to carry out God's instructions. It appears to be her innate spirit to behave in this manner. This aligns with one of our basic themes: Ruth has the core ingredients to reflect God's image with her loyalty, care, and thoughtfulness.

Ironically, Naomi's friends and neighbors didn't rush to her aid despite their initial, excited greeting. However, Boaz, being a true Israelite, provided Ruth with extra food and grain to take to Naomi when he found out about her gleaning in his fields. (Gathering the leftover grain is called gleaning.)

As mentioned, God had long ago directed the Israelites to care for widows and orphans, the poor, and the sojourners crossing their territory. "For six years you are to sow your fields and harvest the crops, but during the seventh year let the land lie unplowed and unused. Then the poor among your people may get food from it, and the wild animals may eat what is left. Do the same with your vineyard and your olive grove" (Exod. 23:10–11).

Farm owners were given a second command to allow leftovers that were missed during the harvest to be picked by the poor and travelers, "'When you reap the harvest of your land, do not reap to the very edges of your field, or gather the gleanings of your harvest. Do not go over your vineyard a second time or pick up the grapes that have fallen. Leave them for the poor and the foreigner. I am the LORD your God'" (Lev. 19:9–10).

It was a lesson in mercy and compassion toward those who had little to support themselves. God blessed landowners and farmers well enough to allow for extra. Think of it as a form of tithing, but instead of an offering to the Lord, it was reserved for the less fortunate. It was a practice that lent itself to the Second Great Commandment: charity and mercy to those in need.

We discover that Ruth was gleaning in a field owned by Boaz, a man of wealth and property who also happened to be a relative of Naomi's husband, Elimelek. As I mentioned earlier, God was not seen directly in this story, but His guiding hand was. It's no small coincidence that of all the farmland in the area, Ruth finds herself in a field owned by Boaz.[322]

"Just then Boaz arrived from Bethlehem and greeted the harvesters, 'The LORD be with you!' 'The LORD bless you!' they answered" (Ruth 2:4). A simple but profound entrance. Boaz was a wealthy landowner with hired hands taking in the harvest for him. While he was obviously a man of authority, he entered his field with a greeting that demonstrated his zeal and comfort in faith. He didn't ask how the harvesting was going, he greeted his workers with a blessing much like Naomi demonstrated her faith in her blessings. He also allowed those less fortunate to glean from his fields with no questions asked. His faith and obedience in abiding by the instructions for harvesting mentioned above revealed ingredients of both Great Commandments.

Boaz's staff returned his greeting in a manner that was equally enthusiastic and cheerful. He obviously had a good rapport with his workers to have such an exchange; it must have been the norm. You get the feeling that he and his employees share the same enthusiasm of faith.

As Thomas Schreiner observes, "Boaz is a model of a man who fears Yahweh. He invokes Yahweh's blessing on his workers, and they wish the same for him (2:4). It appears that the relationship between

---

[322]As we saw with Joseph in Chapter 4, it was no coincidence that he was sold as a slave to Potiphar, who oversaw prisons. While he was falsely accused of rape by Potiphar's wife, it was no coincidence he was sent to the prison where he would eventually interpret the cup bearer's dream that would eventually lead to his release and future fortune. God's plan underlies what may appear as coincidence or luck, just as in this case with Ruth.

employer and employees is just and righteous in accord to the will of Yahweh."[323] It appears to be a spiritually healthy workplace, which is the opposite of what we saw with the Israelites in the book of Judges.

For Boaz to bless his staff in this way shows that he was not a proud, authoritative, or vain man, but a thoughtful, good-hearted boss who treated his employees with kindness and respect. He was cheerful and comfortable in his position and certainly had the charity to allow for gleaning in his fields.

Boaz already had a group of gleaners picking up behind the harvesters when he spotted Ruth in the group and asked who she was. He was told that it was Ruth, the Moabite woman who returned to Bethlehem with Naomi. She had asked for permission to work the fields. Boaz must have been struck by her; rather than send the message to her through his subordinates, he eschewed his social status and spoke to her directly. Boaz welcomed Ruth to his fields and advised her to work no other fields than his. He also instructed her to stay with the women who worked for him. He essentially took her under his protection and reassured her that none of his male workers would trouble her.

"At this, she bowed down with her face to the ground. She asked him, 'Why have I found such favor in your eyes that you notice me—a foreigner?' Boaz replied, 'I've been told all about what you have done for your mother-in-law since the death of your husband—how you left your father and mother and your homeland and came to live with a people you did not know before. May the LORD repay you for what you have done. May you be richly rewarded by the LORD, the God of Israel, under whose wings you have come to take refuge.' 'May I continue to find favor in your eyes, my lord,' she said. 'You have put me at ease by speaking kindly to your servant—though I do not have the standing of one of your servants'" (Ruth 2:10–13).

This lovely exchange between the two projected the nature and character of their hearts. Ruth provided a blessing of Israel's God to Boaz, so her knowledge of the Jewish faith was keen enough to know

---

[323] Thomas Schreiner, *The King in His Beauty*, 2013, p. 133.

how blessings were exchanged. She was sincerely grateful to Boaz to allow her, one of lowly status, to glean in order to survive and help provide for Naomi. There was no sense of being selfish; in fact, she was the epitome of humility. She understood the gap in their social status and respected Boaz for his authority. She worked diligently and did not take a break or talk to the others in the field. She was not angry, bitter, or too proud to glean and she was grateful to Boaz for this small opportunity.

Boaz recognized her for her loyalty, charity, and love and returned her blessing to acknowledge her kindness toward Naomi. There was a sense of dignity and nobility in both individuals, along with kindness and thoughtfulness. A spark of love between them was beginning to take root, but it was the characteristics of their hearts that was coming to the forefront.

Boaz invited Ruth to join him and his workers for dinner, a genuine and generous offer from a man of higher social standing. He wanted to keep her in his company; he was attracted to her character and demeanor. Boaz made sure she had plenty to eat, then gave her additional food to take back to Naomi.

Jason Driesbach captures the quality of their hearts: "As the scene closes, we see the fruits of virtue. Boaz's generosity with his means, coupled with Ruth's diligent labor, bring a satisfying reward that will benefit both Ruth and Naomi. As we have already seen, Ruth's behavior was most expected, but Boaz was unknown before this point. His honorable and kind character shows through this scene and the result is a surprisingly positive outcome for Ruth's effort to provide for herself and Naomi."[324]

When Ruth returned from the dinner, she told her mother-in-law all about Boaz and his generosity. "'The LORD bless him!' Naomi said to her daughter-in-law. 'He has not stopped showing his kindness to the living and the dead.' She added, 'That man is our close relative; he is one of our guardian-redeemers'" (Ruth 2:20).

---

[324]Jason Driesbach, *Cornerstone Biblical Commentary: Joshua, Judges, Ruth*, 2012, p. 527.

Boaz's reputation for kindness and generosity was well known in the community and Naomi was aware of his character since she remembered their kinship. Again, she asked for the Lord's blessing on him; her spiritual heart was given a boost as she remembered Boaz as a guardian-redeemer.

At this juncture, Naomi considered Ruth as her daughter and not an in-law. With the turn of good fortunes, Naomi didn't feel as desperate as when they first arrived in Bethlehem. No longer bitter because of her circumstances, she saw great hope for her and Ruth though Boaz and his generosity. Of course, this was all according to God's long-term plan.

Guardian-redeemer is an Old Testament term for one who delivers a family member from an outstanding debt or loan. It was usually the person's closest living relative who could pay the debt or loan. According to William Elwell, "Property sold under similar conditions could likewise be redeemed, thus keeping it in the family."[325] A fuller description of the protocol for property rights are discussed in the following pages.

In essence, a guardian-redeemer took over the debt of a family member in order to save them. Jesus is called our redeemer because, through His death, he cancelled our debt of sin for our own salvation.

The property in question must have been the land they left behind when she and Elimelek escaped to Moab from the famine. However, Naomi was impoverished; she owned the property but had no means of maintaining it, so it was a relief knowing a man of Boaz's wealth and position was in line to help her out of debt.

Several weeks went by and the wheat harvesting followed the barley crops. All that time, Ruth continued to work in the fields of Boaz for him to get familiar with her and for her to stay under his protection. Note that she continued to live with Naomi rather than stay with the other young women who gleaned Boaz's fields. Her loyalty to Naomi continued.

---

[325]William Elwell, *Theological Dictionary of the Bible,* 1996, p. 664.

When the harvesting neared completion, Naomi came up with a scheme (a mother intervening to speed up the romance). It was not exactly proper and could have put them both in a compromising position if caught. She instructed Ruth to get cleaned up, put on perfume and her best clothes, and go to the threshing floor. She knew that Boaz would return there when the harvesting was complete. When Boaz finished eating and drinking, Ruth was to wait for him to fall asleep. "'When he lies down, note the place where he is lying. Then go and uncover his feet and lie down. He will tell you what to do'" (Ruth 3:4).

Without hesitating or being concerned with how this would all work out, Ruth obediently followed Naomi's instructions. Given the virtue of both Ruth and Boaz, Naomi must have known nothing untoward or improper would take place, but it is a bit curious she came up with such a risky plan.

Naomi was aware that there was mutual fondness between Boaz and Ruth and with harvesting completed, Ruth wouldn't have an opportunity or excuse to stay in Boaz's company any longer. Naomi was trying to get them together with no outside interference and let love work its magic. She counted on Boaz's honor, integrity, and nobility (in terms of his personality, not his rank) to see this situation in the manner it was intended, and he would act accordingly.

Ruth went to the threshing floor and followed Naomi's instruction to the letter. The plan worked. When Boaz woke up in the middle of the night to find Ruth at his feet, he was startled. "'Who are you?' he asked. 'I am your servant Ruth,' she said. 'Spread the corner of your garment over me since, you are a guardian-redeemer of our family'" (Ruth 3:9).

Ruth understood that Boaz, as the guardian-redeemer, was her protector. Her request for Boaz to spread his covering over her was a marriage request. Robert Hubbard notes that "Ruth acted neither from passion nor greed. Rather, sacrificially, setting aside personal preferences, she chose a marriage of benefit to her family. She reckoned her own happiness as secondary to provision of an heir for her late husband and Naomi."[326]

The manner of proposal (spreading of the garment) had a similar reference in Ezekiel where God used the metaphor for Israel as a young woman growing up and Israel's early relationship with Him. "Later I passed by, and when I looked at you and saw that you were old enough for love, I *spread the corner of my garment over you* and covered your naked body. I gave you my solemn oath and entered into a covenant with you, declares the Sovereign LORD, and you became mine'" (Ezek. 16:8, emphasis mine). Spreading the corner of the garment was the proposal and the oath similar to one taken in matrimony. In Ezekiel, God was reminiscent of His earlier covenant with the Israelites as He recounts the nation's history in His view.[327]

With Ruth suggesting that he propose, Boaz recognized that she wanted to fulfill Naomi's family line and was flattered that she chose him over any of the younger men of her age. "'The LORD bless you, my daughter' he replied. 'This kindness is greater than that which you showed earlier. You have not run after the younger men, whether rich or poor. And now, my daughter, don't be afraid. I will do for you all you ask. All the people of my town know that you are a woman of noble character. Although it is true that I am a guardian-redeemer of our family, there is another who is more closely related than I. Stay here for the night, and in the morning if he wants to do his duty as your guardian-redeemer, good; let him redeem you. But if he is not willing, as surely as the LORD lives, I will do it. Lie here until morning'" (Ruth 3:10–13).

---

[326]Robert Hubbard, *The Book of Ruth*, 1988, p. 215.

[327]There are many instances in the Old Testament where God used a marriage (covenant or contract) metaphor to describe His special relationship with His chosen people. The spreading of the garment was a pledge for marriage. Jesus used the same marriage metaphor when He spoke of the church as His bride and He as the Bridegroom. Just as an aside, it is in the confines of this metaphor of marriage that God condemned Israel of adultery when they worshiped other idols; they broke their vows to love only Him by seeking false gods. That is addressed in Chapter 12.

A few observations are warranted here. First, while I painted a bleak picture of the Israelites turning to pagan ways during the time of the judges, that is not to say that everyone was disobedient the entire time. The people of Bethlehem recognized the quality of Ruth's character, so they must have had a good sense of moral standards to see her in this manner. In fact, she was well greeted when she returned with Naomi, Naomi's friends accepted her, even though she was a Moabite. There was no hint of anyone worshiping Baal or other idols, and no murderous behavior, so it's safe to say the people of Bethlehem in this story were righteous, good-hearted, and faithful.

Secondly, what was it about Ruth that people quickly found her to be of noble character? She was in town for only a few months, so her quality of heart must have been easily discernible. Her actions and behavior earned her the respect of the townspeople. She worked hard in the fields instead of idly talking with the other women. Her care and kindness toward Naomi were recognized by Boaz and close friends of Naomi. Ruth always returned to Naomi with extra food after gleaning the fields. She was totally dedicated to her mother-in-law and demonstrated the character of a virtuous woman.

Finally, Boaz did not feel any pressure to marry Ruth. He knew she was virtuous and kind, but with his wealth and status, he could have married anyone. It was probably love at first sight, but he kept his feelings for Ruth in his heart. He was pleasantly surprised to find out she felt the same for him and that she wanted to marry him. That she was a Moabite and a gleaner in his fields was irrelevant to Boaz. Ruth's character, kindness, and care are what captured his heart.

And what does that say about the character Boaz, that he was willing to marry someone of her social standing and nationality? He wasn't concerned with either, nor was he driven by the need to marry into wealth. God provided him with all he needed, and he was satisfied with what he had been given. He was in love with a woman that had a heart equal to his. Even with the distance in their social status and age, Boaz was flattered that Ruth was willing to spend her life with him. He realized that she could have been attached herself to any of the young men in the fields or in town, but she chose him.

For her protection, Boaz kept Ruth with him until early morning so she could leave before any of the field hands arrived. Nothing immoral occurred between them; they remained virtuous, as was their nature. But Boaz knew he was not the first in line to be guardian-redeemer. Another relative had first rights of refusal to redeem Naomi's property. He promised Ruth if this relative wouldn't pay off the debt, then he would. He filled her shawl with food and sent her back to Naomi before the field hands returned to work.

Robert Hubbard shares how, once again, Boaz demonstrated his honesty and integrity. Rather than rush off to get married, Boaz abided by Jewish law and met with the other man in town who had first rights of refusal in acting as Naomi's redeemer; Boaz was only next in line. Boaz put their romance at risk by giving the other relative an opportunity to claim the property...and Ruth. Robert Hubbard writes, "Evidently, in Israelite custom, this duty (redeemership) fell upon the closest male relative or, if he waived his right, to others in order of priority...As an upright Israelite, Boaz bowed before that custom rather than scheme or circumvent it. Personal preference gave way to priority rights of other relatives...it presented Boaz as a model of integrity... Indeed, that very integrity may explain why Boaz did not exercise the duty of redeemer earlier; he knew that the right belonged to someone else and was not to be infringed upon."[328]

Boaz went to the city gate (which served as a court-like setting) and waited for the relative to pass by so that he would be aware of the offer of Naomi's property. Boaz knew the cultural rules regarding the redeemer's duties and protocol. Naomi was not at liberty to sell it to anyone for the highest bid.[329] Christopher Wright explains the reason for this; "...according to Israel's ancient land laws, agricultural land

---

[328]Robert Hubbard, *The Book of Ruth*, 1988, p. 217.

[329]Property rights and ownership guidelines were established in the book of Leviticus. "'The land must not be sold permanently, because the land is mine, and you reside in my land as foreigners and strangers. Throughout the land that you hold as a possession, you must provide for the redemption of the land. If one of your fellow Israelites becomes poor and sells some of their property, their nearest relative is to come and redeem what they have sold'" (Lev. 25:23–25).

belonged to the extended families living on it, is to be passed down by inheritance through the generations. It was no to be bought and sold simply as a commercial commodity, for profit or speculation."[330]

When the nearest relative to Naomi arrived, Boaz set the stage by calling together several of the town elders as witnesses and informed the relative that Naomi needed to sell her property, which the relative was in line to purchase. Boaz stated that if the relative declined, then he had the next right-of-refusal. He was going by the book, making this presentation in front of the witnesses.

The relative initially agreed to the proposal; he was happy to do so, as it would add to his asset portfolio. Then Boaz added the proviso that with the property, he would have to acquire Ruth in order to maintain the name of the dead (Elimelek) with his property. "At this, the guardian-redeemer said, 'Then I cannot redeem it because I might endanger my own estate. You redeem it yourself. I cannot do it'" (Ruth 4:6).

With this added condition of having to take Ruth (and most likely Naomi, too) along with the property, the relative backed out of the deal, likely because he already has his assets designated for his existing family upon his death. Adding Ruth to the mix would cause a further complication for the division of assets than he was willing to undertake. Further, he was allowed to hold on to the property only until any descendant from Ruth he sired was old enough to claim the property as the rightful heir; it would not be divided among his other children. So, not only would he eventually lose the property, he would also lose the money he paid for it.

Additionally, he would incur the cost to maintain Ruth, Naomi, and any children they had, who would be entitled to a portion of his existing estate that would have gone exclusively to his current children.[331]

With all that in mind, he told Boaz to redeem the property himself. Christopher Wright comments on the complexity of redeeming the property. "Now, even under normal times, such an act of

[330]Christopher Wright, *The Message of Jeremiah*, 2014, p. 342.

[331]Robert Hubbard, *The Book of Ruth*, 1988, p. 245.

kinship-redemption was a costly and potentially risky thing to do. That is why Boaz is commended for exercising it when the nearer kinsman declined."[332]

While the kinsman was initially happy to acquire the property, additional beneficiaries and complications was too much of a problem for him. It's not that he was an evil man, just a practical one that didn't want to take the risk that Boaz was willing to take.

Was it a coincidence that he backed out of the deal? Again, God was in the background, ready to reward Ruth and Boaz with each other for their dedication to Him and those around them.

With the transaction settled, Boaz announced, "'Today you are witnesses that I have bought from Naomi all the property of Elimelek, Kilion and Mahlon. I have also acquired Ruth the Moabite, Mahlon's widow, as my wife, in order to maintain the name of the dead with his property, so that his name will not disappear from among his family or from his hometown. Today you are witnesses!'" (Ruth 4:9–10).

The people in town were pleased with the union and they blessed the outcome of the marriage; another indication that the townsfolk were also of good, moral character. How many Jewish mothers would have wanted Boaz to marry their daughters instead of this outsider? But you don't see any resentment or jealousy from the community, just happy wishes for the union of two noble individuals.

There was a communal blessing for Ruth to have the same success as Rachel and Leah (the progeny of Jacob's wives) and to Boaz: "'May you have standing in Ephrathah and be famous in Bethlehem'" (Ruth 4:11). They were married and Ruth was blessed with a son they named Obed.

The women of Bethlehem were very happy for Naomi, who returned to Bethlehem in dire straits but had her fortunes reversed, blessed with a grandchild. "'He will renew your life and sustain you in your old age. For your daughter-in-law, who loves you and who is better to you than seven sons, has given him birth'" (Ruth 4:15).

---

[332]Christopher Wright, *The Message of Jeremiah*, 2014, 342.

We could end the book of Ruth with "and they all lived happily ever after." It is a stark contrast with the ending of the book of Judges, where the nation of Israel was so self-invested that everyone did as they saw fit. Obed was the father of Jesse, who was the father of David. David became the greatest king of Israel, spiritually attuned with God's will and, as I'll discuss in the next chapter, a man after God's own heart.

As we found in the story of Enoch regarding the good seed following the lineage from Seth to Enoch, the same good seed of Boaz flowed to David, his great-grandson, and ultimately to the Perfect Seed in Jesus. In his account of the story of Ruth, Josephus writes that King David "left his dominions to his sons for one and twenty generations. I was therefore obligated to relate this history of Ruth, because I had a mind to demonstrate the power of God, who, without difficulty, can raise those that are of ordinary parentage of dignity and splendor, to which he advanced David, though he were born of such mean parents."[333]

To summarize the love story, we saw three individuals who demonstrated trust, faith, and obedience in God—more clearly in Boaz in recognition of God's rules—and all three called upon God's blessing for others. Naomi and Ruth showed great trust in God, and Ruth in particular because she was a Moab who was willing and eager to trust God.

In his review of Ezekiel's condemning oracle against Moab, Christopher Wright lists Moab's sins, Balak's attempt to curse and attack Israel, and Balaam leading the Israelites into idolatry and sexual immorality. Despite all Moab's sins against Israel, Wright observes, "This makes the story of Ruth, a Moabitess, even more remarkable in that not only is she adopted by conversion into the faith of Israel, but she marries into an Israelite family and becomes an ancestress of king David (Ruth 4:13–22), as well as entering the genealogy of the Messiah Jesus (Matt. 1:5)."[334]

---

[333]Josephus, *Jewish Antiquities* Book 5 Chapter 9, v. 337, p. 192.

[334]Christopher Wright, *The Message of Ezekiel*, 2001, p. 234.

Their adherence to the First Great Commandment was implicit, but the character of heart toward each other was a clear indication of how to "love thy neighbor." All three had the ingredients of a pure, loving heart (the structure of God's image mentioned earlier), but it was their actions and behavior and the functioning of those gifts that made this story a happy example of the pure hearts God designed for us at creation. All of this happened in the midst of a disobedient nation.

Hannah and the Sons of Eli

While the story of Ruth and Boaz was a brief interlude in the history of God's people, it took place in a time when judges still had authority over the Israelites. (Josephus places the story of Ruth in the time of Eli's judgeship.)

The book of Judges comes to near conclusion following the death of Samson, although further deterioration of the spiritual heart continued in the final chapters. Eli was the judge who succeeded Samson and the chronology of Israel's history continues in the next two books of Samuel following Ruth.

The first book begins with the life of the great prophet Samuel, followed by the anointing of Saul as the first king, and ends with establishment of David's rule over Israel. The history of the monarchy continues into the second book of Samuel, recalling David's complete reign. The two books cover some 120 years in Israel's chronology. The history of Israel and the monarchy continues through the books of Kings and Chronicles[335] which will lead us to the end of Israel as a nation. This period will be described in the next several chapters.

The prophet Samuel was the last of the judges and the first prophet to counsel the monarchy established because of the Israelites' desire for a king. Samuel's place in the line of prophets ranks highly. Ronald Youngblood notes, "If Moses is rightly celebrated as Israel's lawgiver

---

[335]First and Second Chronicles cover the same history as First and Second Kings; however, First and Second Chronicles exclusively trace the lineage of David and shine a positive light on the southern nation of Judah. While covering the same time frame, Chronicles often provides more detail.

par excellence, so also Samuel is justly heralded as the prototypical prophet...standing at the head of the prophetic line...As priest, judge, prophet, counselor, and anointer of Israel's first two rulers, Samuel takes his place as one of ancient Israel's greatest and most godly leaders."[336]

Despite the apostasy in Israel's history, the spiritual heart was alive and well, as demonstrated through individuals like Boaz and Ruth. As the first book of Samuel begins, we are given another example of divergent spiritual hearts; Eli, the last of the judges and his two wicked sons are measured against the dedication to God by Samuel's parents, particularly his mother Hannah. The range of the heart is depicted through these individuals by their obedience (or lack thereof) to God's commandments.

The first book of Samuel begins with Elkanah, Samuel's father, who had two wives: Peninnah and Hannah. Elkanah was a man of means and had a very strong faith; Scriptures note that he observed the annual trek to Shiloh where he took his entire family to worship and sacrifice to the Lord.[337] Hannah was childless as "the LORD closed her womb" (1 Sam. 1:5). Elkanah may have married his second wife Peninnah to carry on his progeny, which she did.

Overlooking her inability to bear children, Elkanah loved Hannah more and showed compassion for her situation. He provided her double the portions she was entitled to during festivals and because she was so remorseful, he asked, "'Hannah, why are you weeping? Why don't you eat? Why are you downhearted? Don't I mean more to you than ten sons?'" (1 Sam. 1:8). He clearly was concerned with Hannah's condition and hoped his love for her could overcome her feeling of hopelessness. But as D. A. Carson points out in his footnotes, "Elkanah is concerned for Hannah's welfare, but he does not

---

[336]Ronald Youngblood, *Expositor's Bible Commentary: 1 Samuel –2 Samuel*, 2009, p. 272.

[337]Shiloh was the location of the tabernacle and the ark of the covenant, hence the annual trek to worship and offer sacrifices to God. "They continued to use the idol Micah had made, all the time the house of God was in Shiloh" (Judg. 18:31).

understand the depth of her despair. For many married women, the inability to have children is a source of considerable grief."[338]

We saw this situation with Abraham and Sarah, and Jacob and Rachel; the inability to bear children was catastrophic for women in ancient Israel. Ronald Youngblood writes, "Barrenness in ancient times was the ultimate tragedy for a married woman, since her husband's hopes and dreams depended on her providing him with a son to perpetuate his name and inherit his estate."[339]

As her rival in marriage, Peninnah compounded Hannah's misery by making fun of her condition. This clearly demonstrated the range of their hearts; Peninnah took delight in Hannah's desperate condition, showing a complete lack of compassion, while Elkanah did all he could to brighten Hannah's spirits. Peninnah's haughty attitude revealed the true nature of her heart by contributing to Hannah's misery. "So Peninnah would taunt Hannah and make fun of her because the Lord had kept her from having children" (1 Sam. 1:6, NLT) This harassment and taunting went on for years.

With great effort, Hannah rose above the grief of her condition and Peninnah's ridicule and harassment, which demonstrated her true spiritual heart. While she anguished over her situation, she did not blame her husband for her condition, nor did she show anger toward Peninnah's taunting. Youngblood notes, "The devout Hannah, in the spirit of Deuteronomy 32:35,[340] is content to allow the Lord to avenge the wrong committed to her."[341]

This was reminiscent of Rachel, also barren, and her sister Leah, who had no problem bearing children. Rachel was Jacob's true love as Hannah was to Elkanah. In Abraham's story, Sarah was also barren

---

[338]D. A. Carson, *NIV Zondervan Study Bible,* 2015, p. 492.

[339]Ronald Youngblood, *Expositor's Bible Commentary: 1 Samuel – 2 Samuel,* 2009, p. 45–46.

[340]"It is mine to avenge; I will repay. In due time their foot will slip; their day of disaster is near and their doom rushes upon them." Again, in Deuteronomy, "when I sharpen my flashing sword and my hand grasps it in judgment, I will take vengeance on my adversaries and repay those who hate me'" (32:41).

[341]Ronald Youngblood, *Expositor's Bible Commentary: 1 Samuel – 2 Samuel,* 2009, p. 46.

and she allowed Abraham to have a child through her servant Hagar. Hagar showed contempt for Sarah once she got pregnant, taunting Sarah just as Peninnah taunted Hannah. However, unlike Rachel and Sarah's attitude to their respective rival, Hannah took the spiritual high road by turning to God and not seeking vengeance.

Hannah did what anyone with a strong heart for the Lord would do in a crisis: she dutifully appealed to God (rather than blame Him for her situation) in thoughtful prayer. On one of their trips to the tabernacle in Shiloh, Hannah pled her case to God in solitude. "In her deep anguish Hannah prayed to the LORD, weeping bitterly. She made a vow, saying, "'LORD Almighty, if you will only look on your servant's misery and remember me, and not forget your servant but give her a son, then I will give to the LORD for all the days of his life, and no razor will ever be used on his head'" (1 Sam. 1:10–11).

If God answered her prayer, Hannah was willing to dedicate her only child to be placed into God's service rather than enjoy the pleasure of raising him in the family. This was an act of extreme sacrifice; it was somewhat reminiscent of Abraham's willingness to sacrifice his only son Isaac. Hannah volunteered her son to God's service rather than God requiring it. To go all those years without having a child and then giving him up to serve God as a priest was the ultimate sense of selflessness and gratitude for God's favor.

Appealing to God in prayer demonstrated her faith that He would be with her. Youngblood continues, "Hannah's prayer reveals her conscious intimate relationship with God...she prays 'in her heart' and she prays silently. Hannah is a woman of prayer; indeed, she is the first and only woman in the Bible to utter a formal, spoken prayer and have her prayer quoted in the text for us to read."[342] It was a demonstration of her dedication to the First Great Commandment.

As it happened, Eli the high priest was on duty when Hannah was praying so earnestly. Her lips were moving but no sound was coming from her mouth. Eli mistook her devoted actions for drunkenness and rebuked her. Eli's misinterpretation revealed his lack of sensitivity as

---

[342] Ibid., p. 48.

their religious leader. Stephen Dempster observes, "This is an amazing irony, since this is the priest who will not rebuke his own sons for blatant immorality."[343]

Hannah candidly explains, "'Do not take your servant for a wicked woman; I have been praying here out of my great anguish and grief'" (1 Sam. 1:16). Satisfied by her response, Eli sent her off with a blessing of peace with the hope that God would answer her prayer. Feeling a sense of relief, Hannah's disposition turned to joy. As the family prepared to return home the next day, the first thing they did was worship before the Lord; another example of their strong faith.

Hannah's faith was undeterred as she patiently waited for the Lord to grant her a child and her prayers were soon answered. By the time the next festival arrived, she had a son, Samuel. God had rewarded her faith after several years of childlessness.

True to her word, after Samuel was weaned the family returned to Shiloh to leave him in Eli's care to raise a man of God. "'I prayed for this child, and the LORD has granted me what I asked of him. So now I give him to the LORD. For his whole life he will be given over to the LORD.' And he worshiped the LORD there" (1 Sam. 1:27–28).

In thanksgiving and praise, Hannah offered a beautiful prayer to God, the Song of Hannah. It was a hymn of praise that recognized God's power and love; that all people and situations were subject to His will. Those who were obedient would be rewarded and those who opposed Him would be cursed. Ronald Youngblood suggests that Hannah's song may have served "as the seed plot for Mary's Magnificat (Luke 1:46–55). Both Hannah and Mary became pregnant miraculously...and both sang a hymn of thanksgiving and praise to the Lord."[344]

Walter Brueggemann adds, "The faithful are those who trust God's promises, receive God's gifts, and keep vows to God—people like

[343]Stephen Dempster, *Dominion and Dynasty*, 2003, p. 135.

[344]Ronald Youngblood, *Expositor's Bible Commentary: 1 Samuel – 2 Samuel*, 2008, p. 55.

Hannah. The wicked are those who rely on their own strength, people like Peninnah or the Philistines."[345]

The prayer ended prophetically: "'The Most High will thunder from heaven; the LORD will judge the ends of the earth. He will give strength to his king and exalt the horn of his anointed'" (1 Sam. 2:10). This may have been a prelude to David's reign as king, but as David Guzik notes, "At this time Israel did not have a king and didn't seem to want one. So when Hannah spoke of His king she looked ahead to the Messiah, who will finally set all wrongs right. He is His anointed."[346]

In his characterization of the Messiah in the Old Testament, George Ladd comes to the same conclusion. "This prophecy looks beyond its immediate fulfillment in the house of David and Solomon to its eschatological fulfillment in the greater messianic King, the Son of David."[347]

In the following year of festival, the family again made their way to Shiloh for worship and to give Samuel into Eli's hands.[348] With each passing year, Hannah and Elkanah returned to Shiloh to worship and visit Samuel. On their visits, "Eli would bless Elkanah and his wife, saying, 'May the LORD give you children by this woman to take the place of the one she prayed for and gave to the LORD.' Then they would go home. And the LORD was gracious to Hannah; she gave

---

[345]Walter Brueggemann, *Interpretation: First and Second Samuel,* 1990, p. 20.

[346]David Guzik, "Study Guide for 1 Samuel 2 by David Guzik," Blue Letter Bible, last modified February 21, 2017, https://www.blueletterbible.org/Comm/guzik_david/StudyGuide 2017-1Sa/1Sa-2.cfm. Guzik also observes that this is the first place in the Bible where Jesus is referred to as the Messiah and adds, "Zechariah, the father of John the Baptist, quoted Hannah in Luke 1:69 ['He has raised up a horn of salvation for us in the house of his servant David'] when he prophetically called Jesus a *horn of salvation,* quoting from 1 Samuel 2:10."

[347]George Ladd, *A Theology of the New Testament,* 1978, 1993, p. 135.

[348]In Josephus' account, he notes, "They therefore came to the tabernacle to offer sacrifice for the birth of the child and brought their tithes with them." (*Jewish Antiquities* Book 5, Chapter 10 v. 346). This is just a subtle notation, but it adds validation of the family's devotion to God. They strictly adhered to God's instructions for worship. Josephus' notation includes the fact that they brought their tithes as required, in addition to the worship and sacrifices they were to offer.

birth to three sons and two daughters. Meanwhile, the boy Samuel grew up in the presence of the LORD" (1 Sam. 2:20–21).

This is one of the many examples describing God's blessings on those who are faithful and obedient. A similar blessing was given the midwives who obeyed God rather than the murderous edict of the Pharaoh described in Chapter 5.

As for her son Samuel, his heart for the Lord continued to grow under the education and training of Eli. Scripture records two other times where Samuel dedicated himself to God's service, "But Samuel was ministering before the LORD—a boy wearing a linen ephod" (1 Sam. 2:18).

Eli's sons were officials of the temple, eventually replacing Eli as high priest. Josephus tells us that, "Phinehas officiated already as high priest, his father having resigned his office to him by means of his great age."[349] Rather than demonstrate the appropriate spiritual leadership of their positions, both sons took advantage of their authority by exploiting the men and women who attended the temple for worship and sacrifice.

Josephus summarizes their wicked and debased hearts: "These sons of Eli were guilty of injustice toward men and of impiety toward God and abstained from no sort of wickedness. Some of their gifts they carried off, as belonging to the honorable employment they had; others they took away by violence. They also were guilty of impurity with the women that came to worship God (at the Tabernacle), obligating some to submit to their lust by force and others by bribes; in fact, the whole course of their lives was no better than tyranny."[350]

The Bible is equally condemning: "Eli's sons were scoundrels; they had no regard for the LORD" (1 Sam. 2:12). Scriptures recount their taking the choicest sacrifices by force rather than following the ritual. "But even before the fat was burned, the priest's servant would come and say to the person who was sacrificing, 'Give the priest some meat to roast; he won't accept boiled meat from you, but only raw.' If the

---

[349] Ibid., Book 6, Chapter 11, v. 355, p. 194.

[350] Ibid., Book 6, Chapter 10, v. 340. p. 193.

person said to him, 'Let the fat be burned first, and then take whatever you want,' the servant would answer, 'No, hand it over now; if you don't, I'll take it by force.' This sin of the young men was very great in the LORD's sight, for they were treating the LORD's offering with contempt" (vv. 15–17).

Stephen Dempster captures the severity of their behavior. "The dark nature at the end of Judges is continued, but now the moral and spiritual anarchy has contaminated the holy site and the priesthood. Aged Eli and his sons have become corrupt, and the place of sanctuary and enlightenment has become a place of exploitation and darkness."[351]

Taking offerings by force showed total disregard for their positions as well as the regulations for sacrificial offerings to the Lord. Their words are reminiscent of Lamech's evil behavior described in Chapter 2. The wickedness of his sons was not overlooked by Eli, but he did little to correct their behavior. Although he rebuked them, they totally ignored their father. It's likely their bad behavior went unchallenged for years, so Eli's attempt at proper parenting was futile at that point.

He was also very aware that their reputation was spreading among the people. "Now Eli, who was very old, heard about everything his sons were doing to all Israel and how they slept with the women who served at the entrance to the tent of meeting. So he said to them, 'Why do you do such things? I hear from all the people about these wicked deeds of yours. No, my sons; the report I hear spreading among the LORD's people is not good. If one person sins against another, God may mediate for the offender; but if anyone sins against the LORD, who will intercede for them?' His sons, however, did not listen to their father's rebuke, for it was the LORD's will to put them to death" (1 Sam. 2:22–25).

The sons taking the women was no different than rape, yet Eli's chastisement was half-hearted at best. Eli was even warned by a man of God of their wickedness, especially as members of the Levite tribe. They were the priests who were supposed to lead the spiritual nature

[351]Stephen Dempster, *Dominion and Dynasty*, 2003, p. 135.

of God's people. His sons' behavior, however, was no better than the pagans around them. The rebuke by the man of God ended with the eventual judgement for their actions. "'Every one of you that I do not cut off from serving at my altar I will spare only to destroy your sight and sap your strength, and all your descendants will die in the prime of life. And what happens to your two sons, Hophni and Phinehas, will be a sign to you—they will both die on the same day'" (1 Sam. 2:33–34).

Eli's sons were destined for doom and the "priesthood would be transferred into the family of Eleazar: for Eli has loved his sons more than he has loved My worship, and to such a degree as is not for their advantage."[352] By Josephus's account, Eli would rather indulge his sons wicked lifestyle than obey God's rules for priestly behavior.

The prophecy of judgement was also relayed to Samuel in a vision as a young man still under Eli's tutelage (Josephus places Samuel at 12 years of age). 1 Samuel 3:1 tells us this occurred at a time when God's communication with His people was rare due to the general state of apostasy. And, according to Guzik, "because of the hardness of heart among the people of Israel and the corruption of the priesthood. God will speak, and guide, when His people seek Him, and when His ministers seek to serve Him diligently."[353]

Eli and his lineage were on the way out and God's focus was on Samuel's spiritual growth. He revealed His will in a vision to Samuel that was similar to the one Eli received from the man of God. The message to Samuel was that the day of judgement against Eli and his sons was near at hand. No amount of atonement or sacrifice would alter their destiny; their sinful nature had gone on long enough.

Eli instructed Samuel to give him a full account of God's message (Eli knew it was the Lord speaking to Samuel in the vision). Samuel reluctantly revealed the prophecy to Eli, and he accepted the fatal news.

[352]Josephus, *Jewish Antiquities*, Book 1, Chapter 10, v. 351, p. 194.

[353]David Guzik, "Study Guide for 1 Samuel 3 by David Guzik," Blue Letter Bible, last modified February 21, 2017, https://www.blueletterbible.org/Comm/guzik_david/StudyGuide 2017-1Sa/1Sa-3.cfm.

The torch of spiritual leadership was passed to Samuel. "The LORD was with Samuel as he grew up, and he let none of Samuel's words fall to the ground. And all Israel from Dan to Beersheba recognized that Samuel was attested as a prophet of the LORD. The LORD continued to appear at Shiloh, and there he revealed himself to Samuel through his word" (1 Sam. 3:19–21). The judgement against Eli and his sons was soon fulfilled, as described in the next chapter.

Despite the high placement of Eli's sons in the clergy, their behavior exemplified the same disobedience and disregard for God's commandments as in the time of the judges. This debase and evil attitude was in stark contrast to the heart displayed by Hannah.

J. Robert Vannoy writes, "One cannot but be struck by the contrast between Hannah and the sons of Eli. Hannah is a humble and godly woman, while the sons of Eli are priestly officials who are dishonest and immoral. Hannah and her house are elevated while the house of Eli is ultimately removed from priestly responsibility."[354]

The end of the judges' authority over Israel was partly due to the ineffective spiritual leadership of the clergy. By contrast, Hannah's spiritual devotion to God—like Boaz and Ruth's faith—was a shining example during the same period of time.

---

[354]J. Robert Vannoy, *Cornerstone Biblical Commentary (Book 4): 1 – 2 Samuel*, 2009, p.55.

Chapter 8–

SAUL AND DAVID: KINGS FOR ISRAEL

As we move forward in Israel's history, the people wanted a king to rule over them, just as the nations around them had. The books of Samuel, Kings, and Chronicles capture the period of the monarchy, marking the times when Israel remained faithful to the covenant and when she fell away. This request would take them from a theocracy, in which God's hand directly led the tribes, toward a monarchy that would unite and stabilize the nation. When Moses received the commands and rules of the Law, God allowed that a king could rule His people, subject to several conditions. The most important condition was that the king maintain the people's covenant with God.

In this chapter, I'll compare the faith and obedience of the first two kings by comparing the hearts of Saul and David. David was an example for all kings; he faithfully kept God's covenant from the time he was introduced in the Scriptures until his death. Saul, on the other hand, showed no sign of a sincere relationship with God. Instead, his tepid obedience was based on fear of losing his throne, an obsession that drove him to an irrational frenzy to murder David and anyone who protected him.

It was David's heart for the Lord that inspired me to gather these examples scattered throughout the Scriptures to demonstrate the nature of heart and way of life God wanted us to follow. Of all the individuals presented in the Bible, there is more material dedicated to the life of David (found in both books of Samuel, First Kings, First

Chronicles, and the Psalms) than any other. His faith and obedience to God set the bar for all the kings who followed him.[355]

Because of his love for and faith in God, David was promised that Jesus the Messiah would come directly from his lineage. The fulfillment of the plan for mankind's salvation would come from David's seed. This promise would become a central theme throughout the messages of the prophets following David's reign.

That is not to say that David's behavior was iconic or that he didn't falter; far from it. Like all the main characters in the Old Testament, David made mistakes in his life that made him very much human. He committed adultery with Bathsheba while her husband Uriah was fighting the Philistines (where David himself should have been). She got pregnant with David's child and after two failed attempts to bring Uriah back from battle so he could sleep with his wife to make it appear the child was his, David ordered his general to put Uriah in the heat of the battle and for the troops to draw back, essentially causing Uriah's death.[356]

David relied on the protection of Israel's sworn enemy, the Philistines, to protect him from Saul's anger rather than rely on God's protection. Like Eli's lack of parental structure with his sons, David took no punitive action against his oldest son Amnon for raping his half-sister Tamar. This led to his second son Absalom taking the law into his own hands by murdering Amnon and, much later, trying to oust his own father from the throne. Despite those failings, David continued in his obedience and faithfulness to God. While David

---

[355]For example, in a rebuke to Jeroboam's disobedience as the newly appointed king of Israel (discussed in Chapter 10), God spoke through Ahijah, "'I tore the kingdom away from the house of David and gave it to you, but you have not been like my servant David, who kept my commands and followed me with all his heart, doing only what was right in my eyes'" (1 Kgs. 14:8).

[356]With Uriah out of the picture, David married the widow. When Nathan his prophet confronted him with his sin, David immediately recognized his falling out with God, asked for His forgiveness, and repented. However, he suffered the consequences of his sin and the child died soon after his birth.

was a man after God's own heart, he did occasionally have "lapses and departs from this identity but...he does come back to his true self."[357]

Even with these drawbacks, the thing that separated David from the individuals described so far was the immediate recognition of his sins and his sincere concern with getting back in God's good graces by atoning for his sins. By recognizing and repenting of his sins, we see the full range of his spiritual heart in action. It's easy to see why David was thought to be a man after God's own heart.

In contrast, Saul, Israel's first king, did not have a heart dedicated to God's will. Saul was appointed by God in response to the Israelites' demand for a king, but Saul was not who He had in mind for them. Initially, Saul was not an evil or wicked man like Lamech (in Chapter 2), but he often followed his own intuition rather than trust God's authority. Saul was jealous of David's military successes and adoration from the people, which developed into a paranoia regarding the security of his throne. Finally, it was his lack of obedience that led to his falling out of God's favor. In fact, God would leave Saul's presence in the same manner as He left Cain's, and with similar results.

Cain's faulty spiritual heart was the result of his envy of God favoring Abel, while Saul's heart was tormented by jealous and evil thoughts toward David and his successes despite David's unwavering loyalty to him. Saul's insecurity and wrongful thinking led to a spiritual decline of such magnitude that he sought nothing but David's death toward the end of his reign; it resembled near madness. He reached such a low point spiritually that he attempted to end his own son Jonathan's life, demanded the murder of an innocent priest and his entire household, and succumbed to pagan practices to save his life from the Philistine army.

The main difference between Saul and David was that Saul often resorted to his own instincts rather than relying on God's direction for him. As a result, he disobeyed God's commands and those given to him by the prophet Samuel. On the other hand, David adhered to

---

[357]Walter Brueggemann, *Interpretation: First and Second Samuel*, 1990, p. 355.

the direction of God's will and maintained the covenant commitment that a king was instructed to fulfill.

Background

We concluded the book of Judges with the twelve tribes in total disarray, both spiritually and politically. When they weren't attacking each other, they were constantly at battle with the surrounding nations, particularly the Philistines. There was no peace in the land.

As the first book of Samuel begins, Eli and his sons were the lead authorities of the tribes and the Philistines waged war on Israel. The judgement of Eli and his sons mentioned in the last chapter came to fruition as the Philistines positioned themselves to attack Israel. A call to arms came to Israel and, thinking that God was still with them, Phineas and Hophni led the army, taking the ark of the covenant with them into the fray. To their dismay, the ark did not provide victory.

Iain Provan writes, "God never fights on Israel's side at all; the question is always whether Israel is going to fight on God's side—on the side of justice and righteousness. Thus in 1 Samuel 4, e.g., when Israel tries to manipulate God into fighting against the Philistines by bringing the ark of the covenant into the camp, God demonstrates his independence of them by seeing to it they are routed."[358]

Ronald Youngblood writes, "What the elders failed to understand, however, was that the ark was neither an infallible talisman nor a military palladium that would ensure victory. If God willed defeat for his people, a thousand arks would not bring success...They mistakenly assumed however, that wherever the ark was, the Lord was."[359] J. Robert Vannoy adds, "What Israel's leaders forgot was that the Ark was the symbol of divine presence in the context of the covenant. When the covenant was scorned, the Ark was of no significance...So

---

[358]Iain Provan, *Seriously Dangerous Religion,* 2014, p. 420, footnote 47.

[359]Ronald Youngblood, *Expositor's Biblical Commentary: 1 Samuel –2 Samuel,* 2009, pp. 71–72.

the response of the leaders of the nation was not one of repentance and faith, but rather one of superstition."[360]

True to His word of judgement, both of Eli's sons died in battle, the army was routed, and worst of all, the Philistines captured the ark. When the catastrophic news reached Eli, he took the death of his sons in stride but when he was told of the loss of the ark, "...Eli fell backward off his chair by the side of the gate. His neck was broken, and he died, for he was an old man, and he was heavy. He had led Israel forty years" (1 Sam. 4:18).

While the Philistines were victorious, taking the ark as a trophy to the temple of their idols was disastrous. Not only was the statue of their god Dagon destroyed by God in the presence of the ark, but a plague also descended on the city where the ark was being held. "The LORD's hand was heavy on the people of Ashdod and its vicinity; he brought devastation on them and afflicted them with tumors" (1 Sam. 5:6). Josephus is more graphic when describing the nature of the plague. "At length, God sent a very destructive disease upon the city and country of Ashdod, for they died of the dysentery or flux, a sore sickness that brought death upon them very suddenly; for before the soul could leave...they brought up their entrails and vomited up what they had eaten...And as to the fruits of their country, a great multitude of mice arose out of the earth and hurt them and spared neither the plants nor the food."[361]

Realizing this had to be the work of the Hebrew's God, the people in Ashdod (where the ark was first taken) were in a panic. They sent the ark to four different cities to rid themselves of it.

Moving the ark from one city to another only made matters worse; the same plague descended on each one. In desperation, the leaders from each city decided to set the ark on a cart driven by cows with no one to lead to cart. They placed five gold tumors and five gold rats in the ark, hoping it would appease the Hebrews' God. The plan was

---

[360]J. Robert Vannoy, *Cornerstone Biblical Commentary (Book 4): 1–2 Samuel,* 2009, p. 68.

[361]Josephus, *Jewish Antiquities,* Book 6, Chapter 1, v.3. p. 195.

simple; if it was God's desire to have His ark back, He would direct the cows back to the land of Israel and take the plague with it.[362]

The ark returned to the people of Israel, who rejoiced in its return. "So the men of Kiriath Jearim came and took up the ark of the LORD. They brought it to Abinadab's house on the hill and consecrated Eleazar his son to guard the ark of the LORD. The ark remained at Kiriath Jearim a long time—twenty years in all. Then all the people of Israel turned back to the LORD" (1 Sam. 7:1–2).

Samuel, who became Israel's spiritual and military leader when he transitioned from the last judge to prophet, took advantage of this restoration of faith. He led the nation into a state of corporate worship, asking them to pledge themselves back to God and rid themselves of all their idols.[363] This revival got their spiritual hearts back on track. The people were contrite, sincerely repentant, and ready and willing to be obedient. J. Robert Vannoy observes, "Their mourning and sorrow showed itself not to be merely an expression of resentment or self-pity but rather a true remorse that led to genuine repentance."[364]

It had been a long time since the people were redirected to the covenant promises by a spiritual leader. Samuel was the catalyst for Israel's holiness and obedience to God.

Knowing that the Hebrews were assembled at Mizpah, the Philistines realized this presented a great opportunity to attack them. As we'll see again later, the devoted and obedient Hebrew leaders consistently prayed to God for guidance and assistance in battle against their enemy. Samuel's faith was in that vein; he prayed and asked for God to assist them in battle against the Philistines and God granted

---

[362]The significance of this mode of delivery will become apparent in the next chapter when David attempts to bring the ark into Jerusalem and there was a fatal delay.

[363]"Samuel is summoned by Yahweh to call Israel back to its primary loyalty, to its single reliance, and to shun other modes of life, security, and well-being." Walter Brueggemann, *First and Second Samuel*, 1990, p. 49.

[364]J. Robert Vannoy, *Cornerstone Biblical Commentary (Book 4): 1–2 Samuel*, 2009. p. 80. He continues, "Ritual without obedience and repentance is an abomination to the Lord and repentance without public ritual privatizes religious faith and gives insufficient recognition in the corporate nature of the people of God."

them victory. Peace finally settled into the region and Samuel led his people for many years after. "Samuel continued as Israel's leader all the days of his life. From year to year, he went on a circuit from Bethel to Gilgal to Mizpah, judging Israel in all those places. But he always went back to Ramah, where his home was, and there he also held court for Israel. And he built an altar there to the LORD" (1 Sam. 7:15–17).

Samuel's military success over the Philistines was due to his faith; God was with him and his people. However, in his old age, he appointed his sons to follow in his footsteps as judges for Israel, the natural successors. "But his sons did not follow his ways. They turned aside after dishonest gain and accepted bribes and perverted justice" (1 Sam. 8:3).

It's a bit ironic that Samuel's spiritual teacher Eli also had two wicked and corrupt sons. Eli tried to rebuke their behavior, but he was ignored, and it led to the demise of all three. Samuel was dedicated to God all his life and was obedient and faithful, despite his sons' bad behavior.[365] However, unlike Eli and his sons, no judgement was made against them. Perhaps this was due to Samuel's lifetime of devotion and closeness with God. God never spoke to Eli directly as He did with Samuel; Samuel was found more righteous in God's eyes.

Israel's Desire for a King: The Rise and Fall of Saul

The elders and leaders of the Israelites were aware that Samuel's sons did not walk in the ways of their father. They told Samuel they wanted a king, just as nations around them had, to provide military stability. This would also provide a succession of governance through the king's descendants. However, a system of succession through the monarchy would be wrought with the same problems as with Eli's or Samuel's sons and their lack of a spiritual compass. In fact, it became very apparent that after Solomon, a righteous king would typically be

---

[365]"The failure of Samuel's sons reminds us of the failure of Eli's except that the affront with Samuel's sons is not cultic exploitation but a distortion of the judicial process. In taking bribes and perverting justice, the sons violate the Torah (cf. Exod. 23:6–8; Deut. 16:18–20)." Walter Brueggemann, *First and Second Samuel*, 1990, p. 61.

followed by a son who did evil in the eyes of God, which I'll discuss in Chapter 10.

Instead of a theocracy, a system of government whereby priests ruled in the name and direction of God, the people demanded a king; the Israelites were willing to rely on a governing system just like the other nations, rather than rely on God. However, monarchy as a system of ruling itself was not the real issue. Walter Brueggemann explains, "The supreme obligation of the children of Israel had not changed with the establishment of the monarchy. Their duty, as it always had been, was to follow after the Lord—to worship him with all their hearts."[366]

Moses instructed that if a king ruled the Israelites, he would be required to maintain the covenant with God on behalf of His people. Paul House writes, "Reverence for God will keep the king mindful of his true relationship to his fellow Israelites, which is as an equal, not a lord. Seen this way, kings are public servants, not masters of the masses. They are accountable to the covenant and are responsible for embodying and enforcing its principles. Thus, though kingship has secular duties, it is truly a religious institution that touches the heart and soul of the nation."[367]

Ronald Youngblood notes, "According to the Deuteronomist, the political success or failure of a king was entirely dependent upon the degree to which Israel obeyed the covenant. Political success could thus only be achieved by a king through fulfilling his responsibility as a covenant administrator."[368] Lawson Stone's assessment is similar: "The king's first obligation is to be a student of the law of Yahweh, to live in fear of Yahweh, and lead as a humble servant of Yahweh with a heart not exalted over his brothers and sisters."[369]

Those, then, were the requirements God commanded of any king over His people. Reflecting on the motivation of Israel's first two kings, we will see that Saul relied on his own thought process and did little

---

[366] Ibid., p. 113.

[367] Paul House, *Old Testament Theology*, 1998, p,185,

[368] Ronald Youngblood, *Expositor's Bible Commentary: 1 Samuel –2 Samuel*, 2009, p. 28.

[369] Lawson Stone, *Cornerstone Biblical Commentary: Joshua, Judges, Ruth*, 2012, p. 485.

to reinforce the covenant obligations with his people. Consequently, he quickly fell out of favor with God and failed as a spiritual leader for Israel. On the other hand, Youngblood continues, "To the extent that David understood that his role as a human king was to implement the mandates of the divine King, blessing would follow."[370]

J. Robert Vannoy makes a similar observation: "The human king in Israel was to be an agent of Yahweh's rule over his people. He was not an autonomous king, like kings of the surrounding nations. He was obligated to obey the requirements of the Mosaic laws and take the instructions of the prophets."[371] This was the most significant difference between the reigns of Saul and David and reflected the true nature of their respective hearts; Saul was consumed with trying to preserve his earthly rule at the expense of his relationship with God, while David's heart stayed true to the Lord's will and commandments as he fulfilled his covenantal duty as king.

Matthew Henry felt that the elders, in their push for a king, jumped the gun by demanding a king ahead of what God had planned based on His timeline. "God designed them a king, a man after his own heart, when Samuel was dead; but they would anticipate God's counsel and would have one now that Samuel was old. They had a prophet to judge them, that had immediate correspondence with heaven, and therein they were great and happy above any nation, none having God *so nigh unto them* as they had (Deut. 4:7)."[372]

Adds Thomas Schreiner, "It seems that the Lord ultimately wants Israel to have a king, so why the reluctance? The best answer seems to be that the problem with Israel was its motives: it desired a king not in order to serve and cling to the Lord, but rather to be like all

---

[370]Ronald Youngblood, *Expositor's Bible Commentary: 1 Samuel –2 Samuel*, 2009, p. 32.

[371]J. Robert Vannoy, *Cornerstone Biblical Commentary (Book 4): 1–2 Samuel,* 2009, p. 299.

[372]Matthew Henry, "Commentary on 1 Samuel 8 by Matthew Henry," Blue Letter Bible, last modified March 1,1996, https://www.blueletterbible.org/Comm/mhc/1Sa/1Sa_008.cfm?a=244001. "What other nation is so great as to have their gods near them the way the Lord our God is near us whenever we pray to him?" (Deut. 4:7).

other nations and to find security in their battles. Thereby they were rejecting Yahweh's reign over them."[373]

Paul House concurs: "...though they are in no current danger, they want a king so they can be like other nations, which is a direct repudiation of their calling as a nation of priests, set apart as holy to Yahweh."[374]

God granted their desires, recognizing that their rejection fell on Him and not their leader Samuel. In His instructions to Moses, God allowed for a king to rule the nation as long as the king adhered to the guidelines of the covenant and led the nation in its obedience and trust in God's design for them.[375] Samuel explained this caveat to the people and warned them of what the Israelites could expect with a king (be careful what you wish for). Walter Brueggemann summarized the downside of having a king as the "culmination of political power and social organization in a state brought by the redistribution and concentration of wealth, the monopoly of land control, and the nullification of local initiatives for justice and well-being."[376]

God revealed to Samuel that He had someone in mind to anoint as king. "'About this time tomorrow I will send you a man from the land of Benjamin. Anoint him ruler over my people Israel; he will deliver them from the hand of the Philistines. I have looked on my people, for their cry has reached me'" (1 Sam. 9:16). This man was Saul, a Benjamite, who was "as handsome a young man as could be found anywhere in Israel, and he was a head taller than anyone else" (1 Sam. 9:2).

When Saul and Samuel met, Samuel told Saul of his appointment to lead the nation of Israel. Instead of understanding this to be God's

---

[373]Thomas Schreiner, *The King in His Beauty, A Biblical Theology of the Old and New Testament*, 2013, p. 143.

[374]Paul House, *Old Testament Survey*, 1992, p. 233.

[375]"When he takes the throne of his kingdom, he is to write for himself on a scroll a copy of this law, taken from that of the Levitical priests. It is to be with him, and he is to read it all the days of his life so that he may learn to revere the LORD his God and follow carefully all the words of this law and these decrees and not consider himself better than his fellow Israelites and turn from the law to the right or to the left. Then he and his descendants will reign a long time over his kingdom in Israel" (Deut. 17:18–20).

[376]Walter Brueggemann, *First and Second Samuel*, 1990, p. 63.

will, Saul, like Moses and Gideon before him, was skeptical of this divine appointment. He was unsure of his selection and questioned whether he was the right man for the job. "'But am I not a Benjamite, from the smallest tribe of Israel, and is not my clan the least of all the clans of the tribe of Benjamin? Why do you say such a thing to me?'" (1 Sam. 9:21).

Saul was aware that Samuel was a prophet and spoke for God, yet he was not convicted by God's direction. If he'd had an obedient heart, he wouldn't have questioned his appointment; he would have accepted it without question. Unlike David's obedience and commitment to God throughout his life, we don't see the same from Saul.

After anointing Saul as king (in private, a few days before sending Saul back to Bethlehem), Samuel told Saul, "'The Spirit of the LORD will come powerfully upon you, and you will prophesy with them [a procession of prophets he was about to encounter]; and you will be changed into a different person'" (1 Sam. 10:6).

Samuel gave Saul two charges: "'Once these signs are fulfilled, do whatever your hand finds to do, for God is with you. Go down ahead of me to Gilgal. I will surely come down to you to sacrifice burnt offerings and fellowship offerings, but you must wait seven days until I come to you and tell you what you are to do'" (1 Sam. 10:7–8).

The first charge was an implicit command to deal with the Philistines militarily and God would be with him. The second was for Saul to wait for Samuel when he arrived in Gilgal. At this, they parted ways. "As Saul turned to leave Samuel, God changed Saul's heart, and all these signs were fulfilled that day" (1 Sam. 10:9).

In order to have the quality of leadership that Saul obviously lacked, God had to infuse His Spirit upon him so that his heart was prepared to become king. As I see it, this infusion of the *Spirit of the Lord* had to happen, as this spirit (or we could insert "this heart") was obviously not with Saul up to that point in his life; God strengthened him spiritually to help him prepare for his appointment as king. In describing the function of the Spirit in the Scriptures, James Hamilton writes, "The Old Testament speaks of the Spirit 'rushing upon' someone not to describe a conversion experience...but rather the Spirit's empowering leaders who will deliver the nation."[377] J. Robert Vannoy makes a similar observation: "In this context, it would appear to be a reference to the Lord's equipping Saul with the necessary disposition of mind and will to assume the responsibilities of kingship."[378]

But Saul's changed heart did not stick for very long. J. Vernon McGee points out, "Samuel anoints Saul king (v. 1). Was Saul (v. 6) converted? This verse is not the final proof. The Spirit of God came upon Balaam also, but he was not converted. Succeeding events in Saul's life indicate that he was not. Verse 9 does not mean he had a *new* heart, only *another* heart. God equipped him for the office of king."[379]

There was little evidence up to this point that Saul possessed the conviction of heart to place his trust in God. Samuel was prepared to proceed with a lottery process to select a king before the people, knowing in advance that it would lead to Saul. When Samuel assembled the Israelites together at Mount Mizpah to officially anoint Saul as their king, Saul was nowhere to be found. Walter Brueggemann observes, "Saul clearly is not an eager candidate for the throne. He was not even present for 'the drawing.'"[380]

"So, they inquired further of the LORD, 'Has the man come here yet?' And the LORD said, 'Yes, he has hidden himself among the supplies'" (1 Sam. 10:22). The newly appointed and first king of Israel was found hiding behind luggage. Had he trusted in God and known his appointment was divinely sanctioned, he would have been bold and confident to accept his kingship with dignity and honor.

Did that lack of conviction and confidence dissuade the people of Israel? Apparently not. They were desperate to have any man for a king. "They ran and brought him out, and as he stood among the people, he was a head taller than any of the others. Samuel said to all the people,

[377]James Hamilton, *God's Indwelling Presence,* 2006, p. 31.

[378]J. Robert Vannoy, *Cornerstone Biblical Commentary (Book 4): 1–2 Samuel,* 2009, p. 95.

[379]J. Vernon McGee, "Comments for 1 Samuel by Dr. J. Vernon McGee," Blue Letter Bible, last modified November 15, 2017, https://www.blueletterbible.org/Comm/mcgee_j_vernon/notes-outlines/1samuel/1samuel-comments.cfm.

[380]Walter Brueggemann, *First and Second Samuel,* 1990, p. 79.

'Do you see the man the LORD has chosen? There is no one like him among all the people.' Then the people shouted, 'Long live the king!'" (1 Samuel 10:23–24).

The crowd was excited that a man of Saul's physical stature would be their leader. "Though God actually appointed Saul, Saul did not in the final analysis represent God's choice, but the people's choice...the Israelites...wanted...one who was grand in appearance and in whom they could rejoice with fleshly pride (1 Sam. 8:20). So, God picked for them the man who in all Israel came nearest to fulfilling their idea of what a king should be."[381]

After he was appointed king, Saul experienced military success against the Ammonites who besieged Jabesh Gilead. He established an army of 3,000 men and showed some leadership potential as the Spirit of the Lord came upon him once again. In a righteous rage driven by the Ammonite attack, he urged the Israelites to join him in battle against the enemy. With God's power, he achieved his military victory, rescued his people, and dispersed what was left of the Ammonite army. Still, it took the Spirit of the Lord to get him to muster the courage and retaliate.

That courage would be short-lived. The Philistines, who were a constant threat during Saul's reign, amassed an army to attack the Israelites and positioned themselves in the valley at Gilgal. Saul found himself greatly outnumbered and his troops grew anxious as they watched the Philistine army positioning for attack. They feared the Philistine forces, despite the recent success they had against the Ammonites. "The Philistines assembled to fight Israel, with thirty thousand chariots, six thousand horsemen, and soldiers as numerous as the sand on the seashore.[382] They went up and camped at Mikmash, east of Beth Aven" (1 Sam. 13:5).

Recall that two years earlier at his private anointing, Samuel had instructed Saul to wait for him for a week when he found himself in

---

[381]Ronald Youngblood, *Expositor's Bible Commentary: 1 Samuel –2 Samuel*, 2009, p. 98.

[382]Josephus identified a much larger force: 300,000 footmen, 30,000 chariots, and 6,000 calvary. Book 6, Chapter 6 verse 97, p. 206.

Gilgal. "'Go down ahead of me to Gilgal. I will surely come down to you to sacrifice burnt offerings and fellowship offerings, but you must wait seven days until I come to you and tell you what you are to do'" (1 Sam. 10:8).

According to Eugene Merrill and others, "What the prophet is saying is that if Saul should ever go to Gilgal, Samuel would go there, too. Whenever this might occur, Saul should wait at least seven days for Samuel to arrive. That Saul did not go to Gilgal until two years had passed is immaterial."[383] C. Phillip Long adds clarity to this directive. "Samuel...commissions Saul to challenge Philistine domination by an initial act of defiance, assuring him of divine assistance in the accomplishment of this feat...And since it must not commence independent of Yahweh's spokesperson [i.e., Samuel], Saul is commanded in 10:8 to follow-up his first action by repairing to Gilgal to await the arrival of Samuel, who will come not only to consecrate the battle but also to instruct the new appointee as to what he should do."[384]

Saul waited for Samuel to get the Lord's blessing for the attack, thinking that he would repeat his success against the Ammonites. However, the week was almost up, and Samuel still had not arrived, nor had the Spirit of the Lord. With the mounting numbers of Philistines in full view, some of the Israeli troops began to desert their positions. Acting without thought, Saul totally ignored priestly protocol. Rather than wait for Samuel or pray to the Lord for assistance, Saul took matters into his own hands. He offered a sacrifice on his own, an action reserved only for the priests.

J. Robert Vannoy explains why Saul's actions were so egregious. Citing V. P. Long, he states that "there needed to be a clear 'division of labor between the king and prophet' that was inherent in the newly restructured theocracy. The king had the responsibility for the execution of military affairs, 'but only as directed by the prophet whose responsibility it was to receive and communicate the divine initiate. The command of [1 Sam.] 10:8 that Saul should await Samuel's arrival

---

[383]Eugene Merrill, *Kingdom of Priests: A History of Old Testament Israel*, 2008, p. 220.

[384]C. Phillip Long, *The Reign and Rejection of King Saul*, 1989, p. 64.

in order to consecrate battle and receive instructions was designed to safeguard this theocratic structure.' It is for this reason Saul's disobedience was treated as such a serious offense."[385]

Samuel arrived just as Saul finished making the offering and the prophet immediately reprimanded Saul. When Samuel asked for an explanation, Saul responded with excuses: the Philistine army was assembling in large numbers for battle, his own forces were fleeing, and Samuel was late to offer a sacrifice before battle (implying that Saul's action was Samuel's fault). "So I felt compelled to offer the burnt offering" (1 Sam. 13:12).

In other words, he panicked, made a rash decision, and deliberately acted on his own. Guzik notes that, had he merely trusted in God, he wouldn't have panicked. He paraphrases Saul's reason for acting hastily: "'We really needed God's help against the Philistines, and we needed it now, so I had to do it.' But if Saul would have obeyed and trusted God, the Lord would take care of the Philistines. Saul could have made supplication to the Lord in any number of ways. He could have cried out [to] the Lord for the whole nation with a humble heart, but instead he did the *one* thing he must not do: offer a sacrifice."[386]

Ronald Youngblood writes, "Saul therefore felt the urgent need to seek God's favor, or at least that was his excuse. What he apparently failed to realize, however, is that animal sacrifice is not a prerequisite for entreating God."[387]

Of course, this caused Samuel to chastise Saul. "'You have done a foolish thing,' Samuel said. 'You have not kept the command the LORD your God gave you; if you had, he would have established your kingdom over Israel for all time. But now your kingdom will not endure; the LORD has sought out a man after his own heart and

---

[385]J. Robert Vannoy, *Cornerstone Biblical Commentary (Book 4): 1–2 Samuel*, 2009, p. 123.

[386]David Guzik, "Study Guide for 1 Samuel 13 by David Guzik," Blue Letter Bible, last modified February 21, 2017, https://www.blueletterbible.org/Comm/guzik_david/StudyGuide 2017-1Sa/1Sa-13.cfm.

[387]Ronald Youngblood, *Expositor's Bible Commentary: 1 Samuel –2 Samuel*, 2009, p. 136.

appointed him ruler of his people, because you have not kept the LORD's command'" (1 Sam. 13:13–14).

This coincides with our running theme of what constitutes a heart for the Lord. In Samuel's chastisement for Saul's disobedience, we are given the reference to that herein, God will seek out a replacement for Samuel who will be a man after His own heart. In line with Genesis 1:26–27 where the image of God is characterized by doing His work here on earth, Samuel said there would be a successor to Saul who would reflect those virtues. This person would lead God's people in faithfulness, obedience, devotion, and righteousness. This new king would restore the nation of Israel spiritually and strengthen their position in the Promised Land.

However, Saul made a unilateral decision and did not rely on God for His protection of His people against the Philistines. Solomon may have had this in mind when he wrote, "A person may think their own ways are right, but the LORD weighs the heart. To do what is right and just is more acceptable to the LORD than sacrifice. Haughty eyes and a proud heart—the unplowed field of the wicked—produce sin" (Prov. 21:2–4).

Solomon's proverb is exactly the condemnation Samuel leveled against Saul's actions and behavior. Saul convinced himself that his actions made sense and justified them. His disobedience led to sin, just as the proverb predicted. The state of Saul's spiritual heart was becoming evident. In the beginning, he was reluctant to be king because of his own lack of conviction. Eventually, he used his own judgement rather than trusting in God to rule Israel.

The prophet Jeremiah delivered a similar rebuke to the leaders of his time. It reflected the same criticism regarding those who trust in their own judgement rather than trust in God and obey His will. "This is what the LORD says: 'Cursed is the one who trusts in man, who draws strength from mere flesh and whose heart turns away from the LORD. That person will be like a bush in the wastelands; they will not see prosperity when it comes. They will dwell in the parched places of the desert, in a salt land where no one lives. But blessed is the one who trusts in the LORD, whose confidence is in him. They will be like a tree planted by the water that sends out its roots by the stream. It does not fear when heat comes; its leaves are always green. It has no worries in a year of drought and never fails to bear fruit'" (Jer. 17:5–8).

Jeremiah's point is well taken; trusting in the Lord will provide confidence during adversity or challenges. In one respect, the contrasting approaches mentioned by Jeremiah seem to fit the respective hearts of Saul and David. Saul continued to turn away from God and relied on his own resources, only to find that he would fall out of God's graces. On the other hand, David totally relied on God, regardless of the adversities he had to face. He did not retreat from a challenge, seen especially in his confrontation with Goliath.

Saul's rebuke of Samuel signaled the beginning of the end of Saul's reign as king and the departure of God's protecting grace.

Samuel was correct to point out that, by his actions, Saul ignored God's order. Iain Provan et al., write, "Our own view is that...Saul has failed to keep his two-part first charge, given at the time of his anointing. Jonathan eventually fulfills the first part (providing victory against the Philistines in verse 13:3), and it falls to Saul only to fulfill the second (waiting for Samuel in verse 10:8). His failure to do so, his failure to wait until Samuel arrives, even if tardy (13:8–9) is no trifling matter for Saul's first charge was designed to test his suitability to be a king not like those of the nations' but one who would rule in submission to the word of the Great King."[388]

As a consequence, Saul lost the kingdom that was established for him along with any succession of kingship for his descendants. Samuel let Saul (and us, the readers) know that Saul did not have the heart to follow God's commands; God would seek out a "man after his own

---

[388]Iain Provan, V. Phillips Long, and Tremper Longham, *A Biblical History of Israel*, 2015, p. 284.

heart"[389] as the new leader. This is instrumental in describing David as the leader that God had in mind for Israel.

While the main forces of the Philistine army remained in position, they sent a detachment to set up post at the outskirts of the encampment. Saul had a smaller force of 600 men moving in their direction. Unbeknownst to his father, Jonathan and his armor-bearer encroached the area of the outpost, ready to attack it. Jonathan had a practical and spiritual heart for the Lord, more so than his father. He told his armor-bearer that the two of them would attack the outpost if God would provide them a sign. "Jonathan said to his young armor-bearer, 'Come, let's go over to the outpost of those uncircumcised men. Perhaps the LORD will act in our behalf. Nothing can hinder the LORD from saving, whether by many or by few'" (1 Sam. 14:6).

Jonathan's faith was soon rewarded. He received the sign from God and attacked the garrison. With God's assistance (the earth shook and the troops in the garrison panicked), the entire army of the Philistines took to fleeing in the chaos that followed.[390] From his vantage point, Saul witnessed the confusion taking over the enemy, so he ordered his men to attack. "Then Saul and all his men assembled and went to the battle. They found the Philistines in total confusion, striking each other with their swords" (1 Sam. 14:20). The Israelites routed the Philistines, who fled the area.

This was clearly a victory achieved by God's hand following Jonathan's initial assault. Note that this is the first charge Samuel had

---

[389]"This phrase is commonly understood to mean that David's heart, that is, he himself, was so upstanding in the eyes of the Lord that he was considered eligible to be king...Since 'heart' usually refers to the will and intellect, the text is teaching that the Lord exercised elective grace in his choice of David." Eugene Merrill, *A Commentary on 1 & 2 Chronicles*, 2015, p. 180, footnote 36.

[390]While it is clear God was behind their confusion, Josephus provides a secular reason as to why the Philistine army fought among themselves. "So, they (Jonathan and his armor-bearer) fell upon them as they were asleep, and killed about twenty of them and thereby, filled them with disorder and surprise...but the greatest part, not knowing one another, because they were of different nations, suspected one another to be enemies (for they did not imagine there were only two of the Hebrews who came up)." Josephus, *Jewish Antiquities*, Book 6, Chapter 6, v.114, p. 207.

given Saul earlier, but it was Jonathan's actions that delivered victory to Israel. As the Philistine army fled, Saul's forces pursued but were exhausted by the battle and the fast march needed to overtake the fleeing Philistine army. Saul made another rash oath: under penalty of death, no man could eat until they had vanquished the enemy. Or, as Josephus stated it, "That if anyone put a stop to the slaughter of the enemy, and fell on eating, and left off the slaughter or pursuit before night came on...he should be accursed."[391]

The army feared Saul and his mandate, so they slugged it out to near exhaustion. However, Jonathan had not heard his father's orders and ate some honey he found on the march, which invigorated him. Saul's army continued their battle with the enemy and were successful. The routed Philistines continued to flee. Meanwhile, his army was so exhausted and hungry, they began eating the cattle left behind, including the blood, which was prohibited by the law.[392] When this was brought to Saul's attention, he halted the march. Fearing that God would punish the army for violating the statute prohibiting eating blood, Saul built an altar and offered a burnt offering.[393] When they were finished with the sacrifice, he asked his priest to seek a sign from God as to whether they should continue to pursue the enemy, but God did not respond.

Saul did not realize that God had abandoned him spiritually, so he looked for someone to blame. "Saul therefore said, 'Come here,

---

[391] Ibid., v. 117.

[392] "I will set my face against any Israelite or any foreigner residing among them who eats blood, and I will cut them off from the people. For the life of a creature is in the blood, and I have given it to you to make atonement for yourselves on the altar; it is the blood that makes atonement for one's life. Therefore, I say to the Israelites, "None of you may eat blood, nor may any foreigner residing among you eat blood"'" (Lev. 17:10–12).

[393] This is the first time Saul bothered to set up an altar to the Lord. In his footnotes to Josephus' account, Whiston notes "Here we have still more indications of Saul's taking on of despotic power, and of his encroaching upon the priesthood, and making and trying to execute a rash vow or curse, without consulting Samuel or the Sanhedrin. In this view, it is also that I look upon this erection of a new altar by Saul and his offering of burnt offerings himself upon it, and not as any proper instance of devotion or religion, with other commentators." Josephus, *Jewish Antiquities,* 1999, p. 209.

all you who are leaders of the army, and let us find out what sin has been committed today. As surely as the LORD who rescues Israel lives, even if the guilt lies with my son Jonathan, he must die.' But not one of them said a word" (1 Sam. 14:38–39). When it was revealed that it was indeed Jonathan who had disobeyed his father's edict, Saul's hand was forced by his own sense of piety to sacrifice his own son, all because of his foolish bravado in making such an impractical mandate.

Fortunately for Jonathan, the army intervened; they were mortified that Saul would demand the death of his own son, the man who led them to victory. Ronald Youngblood writes, "Unable to contain themselves any longer in the face of gross injustice, Saul's men remind him how cruel it would be to execute Israel's deliverer."[394] Saul acquiesced to the potential mutiny and Jonathan was spared. Youngblood adds, "Distracted by his determination to execute his own son, Saul loses his best opportunity to deal the Philistines a lethal blow."[395]

Saul was losing face with his people. Because of his God-inspired actions, Jonathan's image was raised at Saul's expense. Thus began the slow erosion of Saul's good-will, especially with his troops. God's abandonment and the impact on Saul's heart became more evident as he moved further away from God. Walter Brueggemann notes, "Public opinion and the affirmation of Jonathan's bravery overpower the threat of the violated oath. Saul holds to a primitive religious view of his situation longer than his compatriots, who are more pragmatic."[396] C. Phillip Long is not so gracious in assessing Saul's actions. "Rebuked by Yahweh, forsaken by Samuel, at odds with Jonathan, Saul ultimately finds himself alienated by his obduracy even from his own troops."[397]

Later, the Scriptures describe Samuel giving Saul specific instructions from God to attack the Amalekites: destroy everything that belonged to them, and do not spare a living thing. Saul stated the reason for this directive was to punish them for their treatment of

---

[394]Ronald Youngblood, *Expositor's Bible Commentary: 1 Samuel – 2 Samuel*, 2009, p. 149.

[395] Ibid.

[396]Walter Brueggemann, *First and Second Samuel*, 1990, p. 105.

[397]C. Phillip Long, *The Reign and Rejection of King Saul*, 1998, p.129.

the Israelites when they came up from Egypt. "Remember what the Amalekites did to you along the way when you came out of Egypt. When you were weary and worn out, they met you on your journey and attacked all who were lagging behind; they had no fear of God. When the Lord your God gives you rest from all the enemies around you in the land he is giving you to possess as an inheritance, you shall blot out the name of Amalek from under heaven. Do not forget!" (Deut. 25:17–19). Now was the time to fulfill God's judgement of the Amalekites.

In a previous chapter, we saw how easily the Israelites fell into pagan practices. While paganism would be a problem late into Solomon's reign and thereafter (described in following chapters), Saul's task was to keep this from happening now. Israel's formulation of a nation was on the rise, so the complete destruction of the Amalekites would eliminate the opportunity to let their pagan religious influences affect the people. Therefore, it was necessary that God's instructions be carried out to the fullest. With that in mind, I believe there may have been an additional reason for this command; perhaps it was a test of Saul's obedience, to see if he learned from his mistakes. Just as God gave Cain an opportunity to repent for his disobedience, this may have been an opportunity for Saul to redeem himself in God's eyes.

Where God called for total destruction of an enemy tribe or nation, including women and children, Eugene Merrill notes that it is "...repugnant to many people who find it incompatible with the message of the gospel. However, the gospel also speaks of severe divine judgement against all who spurn the overtures of God's Grace...A holy God has no recourse in the face of hopeless unrepentance but to destroy such wickedness from his presence. This included even 'innocent' children because, these people, God foreknew, would never embrace the true and living one, but to the contrary, would become a trap ensnaring God's own people in idolatry and apostasy."[398]

Similarly, J. Robert Vannoy observes that "...the conquest of Canaan is not viewed in the OT as simply an aggressive war of

---

[398]Eugene Merrill, *Biblical Commentary – Deuteronomy*, 2008, p. 490.

territorial expansion of Israel against the Canaanites, but rather as God's judgement for their wickedness...it is to be understood as a portrayal of divine wrath against the ungodly people that anticipates the eschatological Day of the Lord."[399]

While his troops were victorious in the battle, Saul once again disobeyed God's orders. Rather than follow through with the annihilation of the Amalekites and their possessions, Saul allowed the army to keep the best of the spoils and he himself spared Agag, the Amalekite king, from death.[400] Of course, once again, Saul was thinking on his own and disregarding God's direct order.

"Then the word of the LORD came to Samuel: 'I regret that I have made Saul king, because he has turned away from me and has not carried out my instructions'" (1 Sam. 15:10–11). This news was troubling to Samuel. He left the next day to confront Saul, only to find out that Saul left for Carmel.

To make matters worse, Saul erected a monument in his own honor there and proceeded to Gilgal. Not only had he disobeyed God's instructions, but Saul was so pleased with "his" victory that he raised a monument as if he earned the victory without God's assistance. This hubris was not unlike the people who erected the Tower of Babel to recognize their own self-righteous attitude; and like them, Saul suffered the consequences.

When Samuel reached Saul and confronted him about his disobedience, Saul argued that he did everything God commanded. When Samuel pointed out the evidence of his disobedience (the bleating of sheep and the lowing of cattle in the background), Saul made excuses. "'The soldiers took sheep and cattle from the plunder, the best of what was devoted to God, in order to sacrifice them to the LORD your God at Gilgal'" (1 Sam. 15:21).

---

[399]J. Robert Vannoy, *Cornerstone Biblical Commentary (Book 4): 1–2-Samuel*, 2009, p. 148, footnote 1.

[400]Josephus writes that Saul spared Agag because he was struck by his "...beauty and tallness of whose body he admired so much that he thought him worthy of preservation... as if he preferred the fine appearance of the enemy to the memory of what God had sent him about." Book 6, Chapter 7, verse 139, p. 210.

Rather than taking responsibility, Saul first blamed his troops for the disobeying the command, and then said it was for the purpose of making a sacrifice to God. Note that Saul said "your" God, as if He was the God of Samuel only. J. Robert Vannoy writes, "He did not say, the 'Lord our God' but the 'Lord *your* God.' By putting it in this way, it appears that Saul did not include himself among the followers of Yahweh"[401] Walter Brueggemann makes the same observation: "From what we have seen of Saul's almost superstitious piety (cf. 14:24), it is likely that he imagines himself innocent. His defense is reminiscent of that of Adam, who seeks to shift the blame for his actions (cf. Gen. 3:12). Second, the sacrifice is intended for the 'Lord your God,' not 'our' God or 'my' God. Saul seems almost to remove himself from the sphere of God's reign, defending himself by rhetorically removing himself from the event."[402]

Did Saul neglect to order his troops to destroy the Amalekites and their possessions, or did they disobey his order? In either case, Saul showed a lack of leadership over his own men. Or perhaps he planned to enjoy the fruits of victory himself. Youngblood likens the disobedience of Saul and his men to the wickedness of Eli and his reprobate sons. "As the latter had sinfully fattened themselves on the 'choicest parts' of Israel's offerings [1 Sam. 2:29], so Saul's troops had stubbornly kept the 'best' of the plundered animals."[403]

You can sense Samuel's outrage at Saul's excuses. "But Samuel replied: 'Does the LORD delight in burnt offerings and sacrifices as much as in obeying the LORD? To obey is better than sacrifice, and to heed is better than the fat of rams. For rebellion is like the sin of divination, and arrogance like the evil of idolatry. Because you have rejected the word of the LORD, he has rejected you as king'" (1 Sam. 15:22–23).

---

[401]J. Robert Vannoy, *Cornerstone Biblical Commentary (Book 4): 1 – 2 Samuel*, 2009, p. 144.

[402]Walter Brueggemann, *First and Second Samuel*, 1990, p. 112.

[403]Ronald Youngblood, *Expositor's Bible Commentary: 1 Samuel –2 Samuel*, 2009, p. 159.

We read about this attitude and motivation for sacrifice in the story of Cain in Chapter 2. God was always more interested in obedience than sacrifice. As Vannoy puts it, "God is not interested in the displays of outward piety that are used as a cover for disobedience. Religion or ritual acts that are performed in the absence of a heart to desire to live in obedience to the Lord's commands are not only unacceptable, but they are also an abomination."[404] This was the catalyst for Cain falling out of favor with God. It was the obedience of Saul's heart, not the sacrifice, that God sought.

Samuel's condemnation finally resonated with Saul. He sensed his kingship slipping away and sought to save himself through repentance. "Then Saul said to Samuel, 'I have sinned. I violated the Lord's command and your instructions. I was afraid of the men and so I gave in to them'" (1 Sam. 15:24). You could easily conclude that Saul's recognition of his transgressions was for fear of the consequences rather than a true admission of his sin. His insincerity and excuses were evidence of his lack of faith in God's provision for him and his troops. How could he be king? Wasn't he in charge of the troops and weren't they to obey his every command? Saul had no inner strength or confidence and certainly no conviction to trust God.

Saul's disobedience was at the turning point. He lost his connection with God and his reign as king would have to move forward without His backing. God told Samuel to find Saul's successor which would be David, the youngest son of Jesse. When Samuel reached David later to anoint him privately (Saul would still officially be the king), the Spirit of the Lord departed from Saul at that point. "So Samuel took the horn of oil and anointed him [David] in the presence

---

[404]J. Robert Vannoy, *Biblical Commentary: 1–2 Samuel*, 2009, p. 145. Vannoy cites Isaiah 66:2b–4: "'These are the ones I look on with favor: those who are humble and contrite in spirit, and who tremble at my word. But whoever sacrifices a bull is like one who kills a person, and whoever offers a lamb is like one who breaks a dog's neck; whoever makes a grain offering is like one who presents pig's blood, and whoever burns memorial incense is like one who worships an idol. They have chosen their own ways, and they delight in their abominations; so I also will choose harsh treatment for them and will bring on them what they dread. For when I called, no one answered when I spoke, no one listened. They did evil in my sight and chose what displeases me.'"

of his brothers, and from that day on the Spirit of the LORD came powerfully upon David. Samuel then went to Ramah. *Now the Spirit of the LORD had departed from Saul, and an evil spirit from the LORD tormented him*" (1 Sam. 16:13–14, emphasis mine).

Just as Cain and Lamech spiritually regressed when they were removed from the presence of God, so did Saul as he succumbed to the same influence of jealousy, anger, and insecurity. As the book of 1 Samuel continues, Saul slipped into a spiritual death spiral as he became more and more self-consumed. Walter Brueggemann captures the self-destruction of Saul's heart: "Indeed, before our very eyes, the narrator [writer of 1 Samuel] diminishes, depreciates, and finally destroys Saul, episode by episode. All that is left, when the narrator completes the dismantling, is an empty shell of hate, no longer a king. Saul is portrayed as finished with power, legitimacy, and authority long before his death."[405]

The downfall of his spiritual heart began in earnest as David was introduced to the story. Initially, Saul placed him in charge of the army (after David's defeat of Goliath), and because of his faith and obedience, God granted David many military successes. With each victory, he gained popularity with the troops and the people. Saul became more jealous of David as the nation's adoration for him grew. "Whatever mission Saul sent him on, David was so successful that Saul gave him a high rank in the army. This pleased all the troops, and Saul's officers as well. When the men were returning home after David had killed the Philistine, the women came out from all the towns of Israel to meet King Saul with singing and dancing, with joyful songs and with timbrels and lyres. As they danced, they sang, 'Saul has slain his thousands, and David his tens of thousands'" (1 Sam. 18:5–7).

This public adoration of David's accomplishments added to Saul's envy. Much like Cain, his angry, envious heart deteriorated into hatred and murderous thoughts that gnawed away at any spiritual ingredients he had left. It was clear to him that the throne would be handed over to David and Saul was consumed with plans to eliminate him. What Saul

---

[405]Walter Brueggemann, *First and Second Samuel*, 1990, p. 146.

didn't realize was that this succession of authority was part of God's plan and while Saul sought to eliminate David, he would be unsuccessful. With each failure to eliminate David, his heart grew darker, and he was more desperate to save his kingdom.

As an example of his condition, on two separate occasions Saul was entertaining dinner guests (which included David) and Saul fell into a fit of rage. Saul threw a spear at David in an attempt to kill him. On each occasion, the spear missed, and David fled. Later, Saul learned that his son Jonathan had bonded in friendship with David. In Saul's mind, he believed Jonathan was willing to yield his birthright of the throne to David and was a co-conspirator against Saul's throne. He was enraged and attempted to kill his own son in the same manner.

Several chapters in 1 Samuel are devoted to Saul's pursuit of David, who fled for his own safety. Saul was so consumed by David's perceived threat that his loyalty to Saul didn't seem to matter. It also appeared that Saul's duties and responsibility to maintain the covenant relationship with God went by the wayside. No mention of leading his people spiritually was made during this pursuit (of madness, it would appear).

David went to Ahimelek the priest in Nob. He did not explain to the priest the real reason he was there (fleeing from Saul) but that he was on a secret mission for the king. Ahimelek provided him and his men with bread and a place to stay, little realizing he was aiding and abetting a fugitive and enemy of the king.

Meanwhile, no one could tell Saul where David was, and Saul's paranoia kicked into high gear. He accused own his men of conspiring with and protecting David. He assumed David had bribed his military leaders with the promise of land and vineyards, which was precisely what Saul himself had done previously.

An Edomite who was seeking favor from the king spoke up to say he witnessed David at the Shrine in Nob. With that information, Saul immediately summoned Ahimelek, his family, and supporting priests to appear before him. When they arrived, Saul asked Ahimelek if the report from the Edomite was true; did Ahimelek provide aid to David and his small band of men? Not realizing David was considered an enemy of the crown, he innocently admitted that he had helped David, and Saul accused the priest of harboring a criminal. The priest asked Saul what crime David had committed. How could the king's most loyal military leader have earned the king's wrath that he would hunt down David to kill him?

That was the question on everyone's mind since no one knew about the demons in Saul's head and heart. After his daughter Michal married David and learned of her father's intent to kill David, she lowered David out of their bedroom window to help him escape. She placed a dummy in the bed and said that David was a sick in order to buy him time to escape. The king was furious that David had escaped, and his daughter couldn't understand why the king sought to have him killed.

It was the same question his son Jonathan asked that provoked Saul to hurl a spear at him. It was the same question David asked (from a distance) on two separate occasions when Saul was close to tracking him down. It was the same question Ahimelek asked.

Saul was not convinced of Ahimelek's ignorance regarding David's offense. Brueggemann, commenting on Saul's state of mind, says, "Saul is completely and obviously beyond reason...From Saul's perspective, anyone who deals with David is by definition guilty, no matter what they do or why."[406] Ronald Youngblood makes a similar point: "In his paranoia, Saul assumes that all his men (1 Samuel 22:8) —indeed, the priest Ahimelek as well (22:13) are co-conspirators with David against him."[407] In an uncontrolled fit of rage, he ordered his men to kill the priest and his entire household, but his troops were reluctant to obey the order.

First, they understood that Saul was beyond rational thinking. Second, they realized that Ahimelek was innocent of any crime, let alone something demanding instant execution. They refused to act because no one in their right mind would strike a priest of God. "In ancient Israel, the anointed one, whether priest or king, stood in the place of God before his people. To attack an anointed one, therefore,

---

[406] Ibid., p. 160.

[407] Ronald Youngblood, *Expositor's Bible Commentary: 1 Samuel –2 Samuel*, 2009, p. 230.

was equivalent to an attack on God."[408] This explains why David did not kill Saul on the two occasions where he had perfect opportunities to rid himself of his tormentor.

While his own troops refused to follow through on his orders, the Edomite was more than eager to curry favor with the king, and he followed Saul's execution order to completion. In addition to Ahimelek's execution, Saul was responsible for the murder of an entire innocent household and the holy priests as well.[409] Vannoy writes, "Saul gave the order; he exhibited no fear of God and had no scruples about exterminating the Lord's priests. His sin was conscious and deliberate."[410] Saul's heart was beyond redemption.

Much later, Saul was faced with a Philistine army that vastly outnumbered his troops and he needed help from God, but there was no one for Saul to turn to. Samuel had long passed away, and there was no mention of a religious counsel to replace him. Also, unbeknownst to Saul, God was no longer in his presence. He pled directly to God, but to no avail. It was way too late as God was no longer listening. Ironically, Saul sought out a medium to assist him when previously, he decreed that all mediums, witchcraft, and other occult practices were illegal and outlawed by edict of death. These practices were also considered an abomination by the law of Moses. Surprisingly, the medium conjured up the spirit of Samuel who told Saul he would soon be joining him; he was done as king. The spiritual prophecy was fulfilled; Saul and his son Jonathan were both killed in battle the very next day.

In summary, it was evident right from the beginning that Saul's heart was not committed to God. He was reluctant to be king and it took the Lord infusing His spirit to prepare Saul for his appointment. Saul never completely trusted in God or obeyed His will. Unlike

---

[408]J. Robert Vannoy, *Cornerstone Biblical Commentary (Book 4): 1–2 Samuel*, 2009, p. 215.

[409]In Josephus' account, the total number of deaths In Abimelech's household were 385. In addition, Saul sent his troops into the city and killed all that were there, including women and children. *Jewish Antiquities,* Book 6, Chapter 12, v. 260, p. 220.

[410]J. Robert Vannoy, *Cornerstone Biblical Commentary (Book 4): 1–2 Samuel*, 2009, p. 208.

David, Saul never consulted God before battle, but only when it was too late. He took matters into his own hands and was in denial of his own deficiencies and disobedience. He was so obsessed by the idea that David was out to take his crown (and not realizing it was God's will to replace Saul), that during the latter part of his reign, he was consumed with murderous and evil thoughts. Vannoy adds, "There is no mention of either his own covenant faithfulness nor of the Lord's blessing on his reign…In addition, there is no statement about Saul that corresponds to the statement in the summary of David's reign that he did what was 'just and right for all his people.'"[411]

God turned away from Saul after his constant disobedience and we witnessed the decline in Saul's heart to his own demise. It was unfortunate because God provided the prophet Samuel for spiritual guidance, but Saul ignored God's will and constantly took matters into his own hands.

When God left Saul to his own devices, his heart turned to jealousy, anger, rage, and in some regard, almost mad. Fortunately for Israel, Saul's evil ways were directed solely toward David. That is, Saul did not lead the nation in pagan ways. Still, it's telling what happens to human behavior when God is not present in the heart, as in Cain and Lamech's case (in Chapter 2).

David: A Man After God's Own Heart

I mentioned earlier how God instructed Samuel to seek out David to replace Saul as king. God's approach was different than the selection process He used for Saul; rather than a man of stature, God looked for the quality of spirit in David's heart. Ronald Youngblood observes that Saul was more the people's choice as king than God's since they insisted on having a king before Samuel's passing. "Unlike Saul's abortive rule, a complex admixture resulting from popular demand and divine choice, David's reign was sovereignly instituted by God alone."[412]

---

[411] Ibid., p. 136.

[412] Ronald Youngblood, *Expositor's Bible Commentary: 1 Samuel –2 Samuel*, 2009, p. 162.

God sent Samuel to select the one He had in mind from the family of Jesse from Bethlehem. Remember, this was the lineage of Boaz, who was Jesse's grandfather. Jesse had eight sons, including David. Samuel asked for Jesse's sons to come one at a time before him so he could determine which one God had in mind for king.

Samuel was impressed with Eliab, Jesse's first born, and mistakenly thought God would choose him based on being the first-born and tall in stature. Samuel may have forgotten that God would be looking for a man after His own heart. It is a lesson from the Scriptures applicable to us all: you can't discern the character of a person by their outward appearance. Appearance can be altered in many ways, but character is defined by the heart.

"When they arrived, Samuel saw Eliab and thought, 'Surely the Lord's anointed stands here before the Lord.' But the Lord said to Samuel, 'Do not consider his appearance or his height, for I have rejected him. The Lord does not look at the things people look at. People look at the outward appearance, but the Lord looks at the heart'" (1 Sam. 16:6–7).

God was interested in a strong moral character, but above all else, dedication and obedience, the traits necessary for a covenantal king. As we will see, David's heart reflected God's image mentioned throughout this text.

After going through seven brothers, Jesse was asked to bring his youngest, David, who was out tending sheep. When he arrived, God directed Saul to anoint him as king. "So Samuel took the horn of oil and anointed him in the presence of his brothers, and from that day on the Spirit of the Lord came powerfully upon David" (1 Sam.16:13, ESV). God infused His spirit into David's heart as He did for Saul. The difference being that the Spirit was removed from Saul permanently, but it remained with David all his life because God knew the nature of David's devotion to Him and the strength of his faith and trust.

Although he was anointed, it would be some time before David officially became king. During that time, David demonstrated his loyalty and respect for Saul as God's anointed. He maintained this honorable behavior during Saul's entire reign, even while Saul sought

David's death. Like Joseph before him, David endured several trials (and attempts on his life) and all the while, his walk with God never wavered.

What clearly demonstrated David's heart for the Lord was his confrontation with Goliath, a story we all know well. The Philistines had assembled an army for another attack against the Israelites at the Valley of Elah. Both armies were pitched against each other, with the valley separating them. Goliath challenged the Israelites to one-on-one combat; the winner would claim victory for his respective army. Goliath was a giant of a man (9 feet, 9 inches tall) and wore bronze armor from head to toe. There wasn't a single Israelite among Saul's troops who had the courage to take him on. Neither did King Saul have the courage to accept the challenge or lead his army into battle. By that time, Saul was spiritually and physically abandoned by God and Samuel.

David's father sent him with bread and cheese to check on his three oldest brothers, who were enlisted in the army and encamped with Saul. While there, David witnessed Goliath's taunting of the Israelite army. Goliath repeated his scorn of them and of their God, continuing his challenge.

"Whenever the Israelites saw the man, they all fled from him in great fear. Now the Israelites had been saying, 'Do you see how this man keeps coming out? He comes out to defy Israel. The king will give great wealth to the man who kills him. He will also give him his daughter in marriage and will exempt his family from taxes in Israel.' David asked the men standing near him, 'What will be done for the man who kills this Philistine and removes this disgrace from Israel? Who is this uncircumcised Philistine that he should defy the armies of the living God?' They repeated to him what they had been saying and told him, 'This is what will be done for the man who kills him'" (1 Sam. 17:24–27).

Checking the information three separate times, David was told of the great reward that would be granted to the one who slayed Goliath. Saul sought a worldly victory of wealth rather than implore God for His aid. David's motivation for taking on the giant was not for earthly rewards. When he heard Goliath's disrespect toward God, he asked rhetorically, "Who is this uncircumcised Philistine that he should defy the armies of the living God?" David's aim was to defend the honor of God from the disrespect and taunting of this pagan. His motivation was reminiscent of Abraham refusing the king of Sodom's reward after defeating the Assyrians. It wasn't for his own glory, but for the glory of God.

David's older brothers overheard his inquiries and told him to go back to watching the sheep where he belonged; he had no business on the battlefield. When Saul heard that David was willing to accept Goliath's challenge, he sent for him. Upon inspection, Saul assumed David was not up to the task, since he was small and wasn't trained in the art of war. But David was not discouraged by his brothers or the doubting king. His faith in God was stronger than anyone in the king's army, especially Saul himself.

In his own defense, David responded, "'Your servant has been keeping his father's sheep. When a lion or a bear came and carried off a sheep from the flock, I went after it, struck it, and rescued the sheep from its mouth. When it turned on me, I seized it by its hair, struck it and killed it. Your servant has killed both the lion and the bear; this uncircumcised Philistine will be like one of them, because he has defied the armies of the living God. The LORD who rescued me from the paw of the lion and the paw of the bear will rescue me from the hand of this Philistine'" (1 Sam. 17:34–37).

It is striking that with this argument, Saul let David take on Goliath. The outcome of the entire war hinged on this winner-take-all situation. Saul's weak leadership allowed him to let a young shepherd with no military experience take on the enemy's champion warrior. But, after 40 days of no one stepping forward to accept Goliath's challenge, Saul ceded his nation's fate to David and his faith in God.

Here is the earliest indication that David's obedience and trust in God was in his heart all along. He was ready to defend God's honor while the Israelite army hung back in fear of the giant. Just as God protected David from wild beasts, He protected David from the heathen who mocked God. You can sense David's righteous anger—how dare a pagan defile God's name and His chosen army. His indignation was also fueled by the army not having the fortitude and faith in God to take on the giant themselves. Ronald Youngblood writes, "In short, the men of Israel see an insuperable, fearsome giant who is reproaching Israel. David sees merely an uncircumcised Philistine who has the audacity to reproach the armies of the living God."[413]

As Goliath approached David on the battlefield, he mocked David as if he represented the best of Israel's army. "He looked David over and saw that he was little more than a boy, glowing with health and handsome, and he despised him. He said to David, 'Am I a dog, that you come at me with sticks?' And the Philistine cursed David by his gods" (1 Sam. 17:42–43).

David remained undaunted; he knew God was with him and he responded accordingly. "David said to the Philistine, 'You come against me with sword and spear and javelin, but I come against you in the name of the LORD Almighty, the God of the armies of Israel, whom you have defied. This day the LORD will deliver you into my hands, and I'll strike you down and cut off your head. This very day I will give the carcasses of the Philistine army to the birds and the wild animals, and the whole world will know that there is a God in Israel. All those gathered here will know that it is not by sword or spear that the LORD saves; for the battle is the LORD's, and he will give all of you into our hands'" (1 Sam. 45–47).

Josephus tells us that through God's power, David would prevail. In his victory over Goliath, "...all men shall learn that God is the protector of the Hebrews, and that our armor and our strength is in his providence; and that without God's assistance, all other warlike preparations and power are useless."[414]

Just as Abraham credited God with his victory over the Assyrians when they took Lot captive, David's victory over Goliath would be for the glory of God. Walter Brueggemann says, "Everything David does is derivative from and permitted by this theological premise...

---

[413] Ibid., p. 181.

[414] Josephus, *Jewish Antiquities,* Book 6, Chapter 9, v. 187, p. 216.

The purpose of David's victory is not simply to save Israel or to defeat the Philistines. The purpose is the glorification of Yahweh in the eyes of the world."[415]

With that, David took out his slingshot and struck Goliath in the forehead before the giant could make a move against him. When Goliath collapsed to the ground from the blow, David took the giant's sword and beheaded him, thus ending (temporarily) the Philistines' threat to Israel. David succeeded in providing a great victory to the Israelites because of his faith.

David's Obedience and Faith

With David's victory over Goliath, Saul sent David out on other military campaigns, all with the same victorious results. God was with David as He was with Joseph; their faith and obedience to His will resulted in them being blessed with success. God's plan for each was to prepare them to be leaders over His people. As David's fame grew, Saul's jealousy and anger grew worse. Saul sent David on several more campaigns against the Philistines hoping he would be killed in battle, but each time, David returned in victory.

Later, when Saul tried several times to kill him, David had to be confused about why; he had shown nothing but loyalty to Saul. David never hesitated to follow Saul's orders. David went into hiding for fear of Saul's desire to see him dead. He consulted Jonathan, with whom David had become as close as a brother. "Then David fled from Naioth at Ramah and went to Jonathan and asked, 'What have I done? What is my crime? How have I wronged your father, that he is trying to kill me?'" (1 Sam. 20:1). David was not seeking revenge or to return evil for evil against the king. Nor was he indignant or angry at what could be seen as Saul's ungratefulness. He brought great victories to Saul, yet he had to flee for his life.

I say all of this to show that, while David didn't understand Saul's assault on his life, he never blamed or questioned God. This is

[415]Walter Brueggemann, *First and Second Samuel*, 1990, p. 138.

somewhat similar to Joseph's story; the obedient son who was almost killed by his brothers, sold into slavery, falsely accused of rape, and sent to prison unjustly. He experienced all these adversities without challenging God's will. David's faith was not shaken by his misfortune, either.

There was further evidence that he continued to rely on God while escaping from Saul. When he fled to Moab, he asked the king, "'Would you let my father and mother come and stay with you until I learn what God will do for me?'" (1 Sam. 22:3). While fleeing from Saul with his small band of followers, David found out the Philistines attacked the city of Keilah. He inquired of the Lord if he should counterattack to save the city and the Lord spoke to him twice to give His permission. After God granted him victory, David found out Saul was in hot pursuit and again inquired of the Lord. David's military success and knowledge at that point was never by his own volition; he demonstrated total obedience to God to do as he was instructed. This was the opposite of Saul, who rarely maintained communication or reliance on God.

David's rapport with God continued after Saul was killed in battle and David became king. In preparation for his anointing as king of Judah, "...David inquired of the LORD. 'Shall I go up to one of the towns of Judah?' he asked. The LORD said, 'Go up.' David asked, 'Where shall I go?' 'To Hebron,' the LORD answered" (2 Sam. 2:1).

When David was officially anointed king, he initially only controlled Judah and Jerusalem; the rest of nation was still under the reign of Saul's surviving son, Ish-Bosheth. Despite the dual monarchy, David performed his duties in a covenantal manner. From J. Robert Vannoy, "The writer of Samuel later characterizes David as doing what was just and right for all his people (8:15). In writing Psalm 101, David himself described the aspiration that he brought to the royal office. He pledged to reign in a righteous manner, defend the cause of the faithful and to remove the wicked from the land."[416]

---

[416]J. Robert Vannoy, *Cornerstone Biblical Commentary (Book 4): 1–2 Samuel*, 2009, p. 267.

After he ruled over Judah for seven years, circumstances allowed David to become king over all Israel. Soon after, the Philistines planned another attack. Once again, David inquired of the Lord if he should attack them first and would the Lord grant him victory. God responded yes to both. Josephus remarks, "but the king of the Jews, who never permitted himself to do anything without prophecy and the command of God...directed the high priest to foretell to him what was the will of God."[417] In his footnote to Josephus' translation, William Whiston adds, "Saul very rarely, and David very frequently consulted God by Urim; and...David aimed always to depend, not on his own wisdom or abilities, but on the divine direction, as against Saul's practices."[418]

Walter Brueggemann writes, "What is central is David's open and trusting communication with Yahweh. David knows to inquire and is ready to listen and obey," which was in total contrast with Saul's approach.[419]

Much later in David's reign, his son Absalom attempted to overthrow his throne. Absalom's propaganda disparaged his father's leadership and connection to the people. After a few years of sowing the seeds of doubt, Absalom was able to convince a large group living around Jerusalem that David had become ineffective as king and led a coup against his father.

You may be wondering what prompted Absalom to do this. The backstory is that years earlier, Absalom murdered his brother Ammon for raping their sister Tamar. There were no consequences for Ammon's wicked actions; David essentially swept it under the rug, perhaps because he felt hypocritical concerning his affair with Bathsheba.

When Tamar told Absalom what happened, he was calm. "Her brother Absalom said to her, 'Has that Amnon, your brother, been with you? Be quiet for now, my sister; he is your brother. Don't take this thing to heart.' And Tamar lived in her brother Absalom's house,

---

[417]Josephus, *Jewish Antiquities,* Book 7, Chapter 4, verse 71, p. 237.

[418] Ibid., footnote on page 239.

[419]Walter Brueggemann, *First and Second Samuel,* 1990, p. 201.

a desolate woman…And Absalom never said a word to Amnon, either good or bad; he hated Amnon because he had disgraced his sister Tamar" (2 Sam. 13:20, 22).

As second in line to be king, Absalom may have thought all along about eliminating Amnon to get to the throne and this may have been the excuse he needed to carry it out. Patterson & Austel make the same observation: "Absalom's later actions make it appear likely that it was his aspirations to the throne, not the desire to avenge his sister, that motivated him in slaying his older brother Ammon."[420]

Absalom waited two years to carry out his revenge. He invited Amnon and his other brothers to a feast and had Amnon murdered in front of all his guests. This time, David took action. He banished Absalom for four years after the murder, but then he was allowed to return to Jerusalem where he spent the next two years planning to take over as king.

When the coup began, David was fearful that his son would succeed, so he fled Jerusalem with his most loyal military and court members. Upon leaving Jerusalem, he was taunted by Shimei, a leading citizen and a holdover loyalist to Saul. He cursed David for the bloodshed and death of Saul's family, even though David was not responsible. When one of his generals sought to kill Shimei for his disrespect, David left the curses unchallenged as an indication of God's will. "David then said to Abishai and all his officials, 'My son, my own flesh and blood, is trying to kill me. How much more, then, this Benjamite! Leave him alone; let him curse, for the LORD has told him to. It may be that the LORD will look upon my misery and restore to me his covenant blessing instead of his curse today'" (2 Sam. 16:11–12).

David still relied on God and trusted that the outcome of the coup would be in accordance with His plan. He prayed to God in his flight from Absalom: "'LORD, how many are my foes! How many rise up against me! Many are saying of me, "God will not deliver him." But you, LORD, are a shield around me, my glory, the One who lifts my

---

[420]Richard Patterson and Hermann Austel, *The Expositor's Bible Commentary: 1 and 2 Kings*, 2009, p. 643.

head high. I call out to the LORD, and he answers me from his holy mountain. I lie down and sleep; I wake again because the LORD sustains me. I will not fear though tens of thousands assail me on every side. Arise, LORD! Deliver me, my God! Strike all my enemies on the jaw; break the teeth of the wicked. From the LORD comes deliverance. May your blessing be on your people'" (Ps. 3:1–8).

Note the stark contrast in the hearts of David and Saul and their behavior to the challenge to their kingship. Absalom's coup was real, and he had no problem if the coup resulted in his father's death. In an act of defiance, he took David's concubine in the view of the public. This display of disrespect showed the people that Absalom was now in charge.[421] This act was similar to Reuben sleeping with his father Jacob's concubines, which resulted in Rueben losing his birthright and inheritance. Absalom lost all of that and his life because of his actions.

And what of David's reaction considering his son's betrayal? He did not seek Absalom's life before or after the coup, trusting in God for how the events would unfold. In fact, when his troops were about to engage Absalom's army, he ordered his generals not to harm his son, even though they were effectively at war with each other. When these orders were disobeyed by his general Joab, David wailed and grieved for the loss of Absalom as a father, and not as a victorious leader squashing a rebellion.

Bruce Waltke notes that up to this point, "David has been blind and indecisive about his son, but nevertheless a man of faith who looks outward and is concerned with the kingdom of *I AM*. But now, he becomes a man who apart from faith in *I AM* and praise looks

---

[421]This fulfilled Nathan's prophecy of the consequences of David's sin with Bathsheba. When Nathan confronted the king for his transgressions, he revealed the judgement from the Lord: "'Now, therefore, the sword will never depart from your house, because you despised me and took the wife of Uriah the Hittite to be your own.' This is what the LORD says: 'Out of your own household I am going to bring calamity on you. Before your very eyes I will take your wives and give them to one who is close to you, and he will sleep with your wives in broad daylight. You did it in secret, but I will do this thing in broad daylight before all Israel'" (2 Sam. 12:10–12).

inward and yearns for the well-being of his sons more than for the kingdom of God."[422]

David's emotional display had a demoralizing effect on his own troops. "Then Joab went into the house to the king and said, 'Today you have humiliated all your men, who have just saved your life and the lives of your sons and daughters and the lives of your wives and concubines. You love those who hate you and hate those who love you. You have made it clear today that the commanders and their men mean nothing to you. I see that you would be pleased if Absalom were alive today and all of us were dead. Now go out and encourage your men. I swear by the LORD that if you don't go out, not a man will be left with you by nightfall. This will be worse for you than all the calamities that have come on you from your youth till now'" (2 Sam. 19:5–7). David heeded his general's advice, but only reluctantly.

In all of this, David's heart did not seek vengeance, but instead left his fate to God's will.

Contrast this to King Saul's behavior when he perceived David as a threat. David never threatened Saul's leadership; he waited on the Lord until His appointed time. But Saul was so paranoid that he sought to kill David (in effect, trying to derail God's plan for the nation). The threat was a product of Saul's imagination and unlike the real situation that David faced with Absalom.

In his long pursuit of David, Saul left himself vulnerable to David on two occasions. In both cases, David had a clear and open opportunity to kill Saul, end the threat of the chase, and take over as king. Both times David was encouraged by his troops to take advantage of the opportunity, but David refused, stating Saul was still king and God's anointed. In David's heart, he knew the whole situation was in God's hands and He would take care of Saul, not David. David even presented himself (from a safe distance) to Saul in these two cases just to let him know how close Saul was to losing his life, but that David had spared him because of his loyalty to the king. This evidence of David's loyalty still did not rid Saul of his paranoid thoughts.

---

[422]Bruce Waltke, *An Old Testament Theology*, 2007, p. 671.

David's heart, like Hannah's described earlier, recognized that vengeance belonged to God. Saul, on the other hand, sought to pursue his own thought processes and ignored God altogether.

In a final example of David's devotion to God, I refer to First Chronicles, which overlaps some of David's story described in First and Second Samuel. The later chapters in the first book capture the end of David's reign and the transition to his son Solomon. Frederick Mabie notes that the end of First Chronicles "makes a clear shift...from a focus on David to a focus on David and his son (and designated heir) Solomon. This focus on David and Solomon is one of transition, largely within the context of David's expansive preparations for the Jerusalem temple and the requisite personnel."[423]

As we'll see later in this section, David's respect and dedication to God had him envisioning a temple for the Lord. However, the prophet Nathan revealed that it would not be David who would build the temple, but Solomon. David was still able to prepare the materials and plans for Solomon as his contribution to honoring God.

I bring this up to show, once again, how strong David's spiritual heart was for the Lord, especially toward the end of his reign. As we'll see in the next chapter, many of the Judean kings who followed David's example, including Solomon, allowed their spiritual heart to fade toward the end of their reign. This was not the case for David; the final chapters of his reign demonstrated that his heart for the Lord was as strong as it was from the start.

The resources David dedicated to build the temple were enormous: 100,000 talents of gold, one million talents of silver,[424] iron and bronze in quantities too large to measure, and all the craftsmen needed to build it. David instructed all the leaders in his court to help Solomon in the effort. "He said to them, 'Is not the LORD your God with you? And has he not granted you rest on every side? For he has given the

---

[423]Frederick Mabie, *The Expositor's Bible Commentary – 1 and 2 Chronicles*, 2010, p. 127.

[424]The amount of gold David dedicated to the temple was equivalent to 3,750 tons of gold. At today's price of $1,300/ounce, the values of the gold in today's terms would be $156 billion in gold. The amount of silver dedicated was 37,500 tons. At $16/ounce for silver, the value in today's dollars would be $19 billion.

inhabitants of the land into my hands, and the land is subject to the LORD and to his people. Now devote your heart and soul to seeking the LORD your God. Begin to build the sanctuary of the LORD God, so that you may bring the ark of the covenant of the LORD and the sacred articles belonging to God into the temple that will be built for the Name of the LORD'" (1 Chron. 22:18–19).

David reminded his court how everything Israel had achieved—peace, wealth, and the lands of the nation—were all gifts from God. Even as king, David's humble heart took no credit for how Israel had succeeded. David took his spiritual leadership to heart by instructing his people to continue in their faith and obedience to God, taking the tenants of the First Great Commandment to heart, and devoting their "heart and soul to seeking the Lord your God" (v. 19).

Close to the time Solomon became king, David exhorted his counselors and court to continue their spiritual leadership for Israel and obedience to God's will. The instructions were reminiscent of those Moses gave his people who were about to enter the Promised Land. David emphasized what God's covenant had been all along: Israel would maintain the land and their status with God as promised from Abraham to Moses as long as they remained faithful and obedient. "'So now I charge you in the sight of all Israel and of the assembly of the LORD, and in the hearing of our God: Be careful to follow all the commands of the LORD your God, that you may possess this good land and pass it on as an inheritance to your descendants forever'" (1 Chron. 28:8).

David gave final instructions to Solomon to fulfill God's instructions given to Moses for the king of Israel: to love and serve God as the spiritual leader of the nation. God would be with him, but failure to stay faithful to the Lord would have consequences. "'And you, my son Solomon, acknowledge the God of your father, and serve him with wholehearted devotion and with a willing mind, for the LORD searches every heart and understands every desire and every thought. If you seek him, he will be found by you; but if you forsake him, he will reject you forever'" (1 Chron. 28:9).

The account of David in First Chronicles concludes with David giving his final dedication to God, which was part of Solomon's public coronation. Sacrifices and burnt offerings were made for all of Israel. The corporate worship demonstrated a unified, spiritual heart for God by all the people, as it was intended. This was orchestrated by David and his spiritual leadership and, even at the end of his reign, he provided the template for all to follow.

Chapter 9

DAVID REDUX:
A NEW TESTAMENT HEART?

After some thoughtful consideration and prayers for guidance, I decided to add a second chapter on David's life to include material that would further demonstrate the nature of his heart for God. In the previous chapter, we saw that David's faith and obedience to God was in stark contrast to the deficient spiritual heart of King Saul.

But the description of David's spiritual nature was unique among the individuals discussed in the Old Testament thus far. The accounts of Adam and Eve, Abraham, Jacob and his sons, many of the judges, and to some extent Moses, each demonstrated room for improvement while God patiently waited on their spiritual growth. David, too, stumbled spiritually as we will see in this chapter.

I think David's story is different. Scripture describes how he reacted remorsefully to his sins and sought quickly to atone and repent of them, which I believe serves as a template for our own behavior when we sin against God.

Scripture doesn't tell us how Abraham atoned for the times he strayed from God's plan, or that Jacob acknowledged his deceit to his father or brother. When Moses was reprimanded for striking the rock for water, he showed no remorse for his offense. Cain complained about the severity of judgement for murdering his brother, and Joseph's brothers were more concerned with God's judgement of their sin than restoring their relationship with Him.

However, in David's story, he atoned for his sins to restore his relationship with God. He took ownership of his sins, and his repentance came from his heart. He admitted his failings and his remorse was driven by his fear of offending God, not by the fear of judgement.

David likely felt that he lost face with God and was ashamed of the potential fracture in their relationship. In his sin with Bathsheba, David pled for God's forgiveness. "Do not cast me from your presence or take your Holy Spirit from me" (Ps. 51:11). Where Saul and Cain suffered in the consequences of their disobedience by God's departure, David feared losing his close relationship with God. David did suffer the judgement for his transgressions, but he knew to ask for God's forgiveness despite his failings. Of course, God forgave David (as He does with all sincere repentance), and David continued in his covenantal leadership; the faith of the nation stayed on course.

Writers of the Old Testament don't describe the depth of repentance in any other individual than we see in David's life. Maybe it's the amount of material dedicated to his story, but David's life had a New Testament element that reflected the same lessons in Jesus's mission of repentance, forgiveness, and return to God. In Chapter 12, we'll see how the prophets warned Israel and Judah to follow the message of repentance to avoid judgement, but it was David's personal relationship with God that remained strong throughout his life.

For this reason, God saw David as a man after His own heart and the writers of the books of Kings and Chronicles (discussed in the next two chapters) would refer to faithful Judean kings as doing "what was right in the eyes of the LORD, just as [their] father, David had done" (2 Kgs. 18:3). David's example set the bar for all the kings to follow. While the faithful kings did much to restore the nation's faith in God, only Josiah and perhaps Hezekiah managed to maintain their connection with God throughout their reign as David did.

David's Heart Danced for the Lord

David's relationship with God was truly a personal one, as described in the previous chapter with examples of his prayers and entreaties. He followed the requirements of a covenantal king so when he did sin, his remorse and atonement were driven by his desires to maintain his relationship with God. His righteous anger against Goliath's taunts was the first indication of that bond. We see another dimension to this kinship when David returned the ark of the covenant to Jerusalem after he was declared king in Judea. His worship of the Lord in this example was exemplary.

How extensively can we show our praise and honor to God? As we are directed in the last prayer in the book of Psalms: "Praise the LORD. Praise God in his sanctuary; praise him in his mighty heavens. Praise him for his acts of power; praise him for his surpassing greatness. Praise him with the sounding of the trumpet, praise him with the harp and lyre, praise him with timbrel and dancing, praise him with the strings and pipe, praise him with the clash of cymbals, praise him with resounding cymbals. Let everything that has breath praise the LORD. Praise the LORD" (Ps. 150:1–6).

The reasons to give praise to God are countless. We closed the last section with how David gave thanks to God for all His blessings, even up to his final days, which is a great lesson to us all. One who is obedient to Him and has a heart for the Lord should not be restricted in their praise to God. In fact, the Psalmist urges us to sing and dance in praise of Him. David danced when he returned to Jerusalem with the ark of the covenant after defeating the Philistines following Saul's death.

Recall the battle with the Philistines that resulted in the death of Eli's wicked sons, and, to the horror of Israel, the ark of the covenant captured by the Philistines. Samuel recovered the ark and left it with Abinadab in the town of Kiriath Jearim where it remained for several years. It was somewhat revealing of Saul's heart for the Lord that there was no further mention of the ark during his reign. J. Robert Vannoy observes, "During the entire duration of Saul's reign, the ark had remained in obscurity at the house of Abinadab in Kiriath Jearim... Saul's subsequent failure to provide the ark with a visible and prominent place in Gibeah, his capital city, was symptomatic of his failure to fully recognize the sovereignty of Yahweh as Israel's divine king."[425]

---

[425] J. Robert Vannoy, *Cornerstone Biblical Commentary (Book 4): 1–2 Samuel*, 2009, p. 300.

Saul's military preoccupation with the Philistine army and obsession with eliminating David's perceived threat to his crown distracted him from setting the spiritual pace for the nation. His heart was set on the death of David rather than being a righteousness leader in God's eyes.

This was not the case with David. Following the deaths of Saul and Jonathan, David was recognized as king of Judah (Saul's surviving son Ish-Bosheth temporarily ruled the remaining northern tribes). One of David's initial acts as king was to bring the ark back to Jerusalem. Frederick Mabie writes that "David's immediate attention to bringing the ark of the covenant to a position of physical and spiritual centrality for the community implies that David's reign will be marked by seeking God and by a concern for the covenant," which was in sharp contrast to Saul. In fact, Mabie suggests that the neglect of the ark during Saul's reign "is a subtle but significant negative commentary on the spiritual priorities reflected in Saul's reign."[426]

By bringing the ark back to Jerusalem, Walter Brueggemann observes, "David here gets back in touch with the most elemental dimension of Israel's traditional faith."[427] He was keenly aware that one of his primary duties as king was to keep the heart of his people in line with God's covenant, making it clear to the people that, while David was their earthly king, God was their true ruler. Vannoy notes, "Implicit in bringing the Ark to Jerusalem was David's recognition that Yahweh was Israel's divine sovereign. In fact, by this act, David and the people were publicly acknowledging that Yahweh was their Great King."[428] Graeme Goldsworthy adds, "David's religious masterstroke was to bring the ark to Jerusalem and make the city the focal

---

[426]Frederick Mabie, *The Expositor's Bible Commentary – 1 and 2 Chronicles,* 2010, pp. 101–102.

[427]Walter Brueggemann, *First and Second Samuel,* 1990, p. 248.

[428]J. Robert Vannoy, *Cornerstone Biblical Commentary (Book 4): 1 – 2 Samuel,* 2009, p. 300. Vannoy continues in a footnote "In my view the chapter should be taken as an authentic account of the bringing of the Ark to Zion/Jerusalem by David in order to celebrate the kingship of Yahweh over his covenantal people...not the legitimization of David's royal office." p. 303.

point of the covenant relationship with God. All the promises of God concerning his relationship to his people and the land given them are concentrated in Jerusalem."[429]

There was a large celebration in anticipation of the ark's arrival; David had 30,000 troops in tow and the best of his immediate military leaders for the procession. The ark was placed on a new cart and Uzzah and Ahio, sons of Abinadab in whose home the ark had remained all those years, walked ahead of it. The rest of the procession followed, giving thanks and praise to the Lord. "David and all Israel were celebrating with all their might before the LORD, with castanets, harps, lyres, timbrels, sistrums and cymbals" (2 Sam. 6:5).

Unfortunately, the ox carrying the cart stumbled and, earnest to protect the ark from hitting the ground, Uzzah took hold of the ark to hold it up. "The LORD's anger burned against Uzzah because of his irreverent act; therefore, God struck him down, and he died there beside the ark of God" (2 Sam. 6:7). David was angered by the severity of God's punishment, but at the same time, gained a renewed respect or fear of the Lord. He came to realize that God's holiness and glory demanded the utmost respect and reverence. God's holiness required strict adherence to His instructions to maintain distance between our unholy beings and His presence. As Mabie points out, "Although David's reaction to Uzzah's death includes anger (v. 8), David also gains a greater degree of the fear of the Lord and a greater recognition of the separation between a holy God and unholy humanity (v. 9)."[430] Brueggemann adds, "The holiness of God is indeed present in the Ark, but that holiness is not readily available. To touch the Ark is to impinge on God's holiness, to draw too close and presume too much."[431]

One of the reasons for God's wrath was the mode of transportation for the ark. By bringing the ark to Jerusalem in a cart, David was

[429]Graeme Goldsworthy, *According to Plan: The Unfolding Revelation of God in the Bible,* 1991, p. 169.

[430]Frederick Mabie, *The Expositor's Bible Commentary – 1 and 2 Chronicles,* 2010, p. 102.

[431]Walter Brueggemann, *First and Second Samuel,* 1990, p. 249.

showing a lack of reverence and respect to God's holiness. As we read in Chapter 8, the pagan Philistines rid themselves of the ark by placing it and their guilt offering on a cart pulled by two cows and sent them away. Eugene Merrill writes, "Why the men of Beth Shemesh should have died for mishandling the ark whereas the Philistines could do so with relative impunity is quite clear: Yahweh's expectations of his own holy people are not incumbent on those who are not his. That is, the ark was holy only to holy people."[432]

Both Youngblood[433] and Mabie[434] agree that the mode of transportation followed the pagan methods rather than the proper Levitical procedure.[435] Levitical priests were to be the sole carriers of the ark, using the poles to carry it on their shoulders as the proper means of transportation so that no human hands would touch the ark. "'After Aaron and his sons have finished covering the holy furnishings and all the holy articles, and when the camp is ready to move, only then are the Kohathites to come and do the carrying. But they must not touch the holy things, or they will die. The Kohathites are to carry those things that are in the tent of meeting'" (Num. 4:15). David's celebration disobeyed God's instructions to Moses for managing the ark's transportation with the reverence it deserved.

In the time between Moses and David, God hadn't changed His mind about how His people were to maintain their purity as His representatives. Uzzah's death may have seemed harsh, but it was a reminder that strict obedience to God's commands were still a priority and as their king, David was to set the example. In fact, it was Saul's lack of obedience that made God replace him with David as king in the first place.

---

[432]Eugene Merrill, *Kingdom of Priests*, 2008, pp. 196–197.

[433]Ronald Youngblood, *Expositor's Bible Commentary: 1 Samuel – 2 Samuel*, 2009, p. 367.

[434]Frederick Mabie, *The Expositor's Bible Commentary: – 1 and 2 Chronicles,* 2010, p. 102.

[435]In Exodus, God describes the construction of the ark along with poles that are to be used to carry the ark. "Cast four gold rings for it and fasten them to its four feet, with two rings on one side and two rings on the other. Then make poles of acacia wood and overlay them with gold. Insert the poles into the rings on the sides of the ark to carry it. The poles are to remain in the rings of this ark; they are not to be removed" (Exod. 25:12–15).

After a three-month cooling off period, David realized he needed to move the ark in the proper manner. David declared, "It was because you, the Levites, did not bring it up the first time that the LORD our God broke out in anger against us. We did not inquire of him about how to do it in the prescribed way" (1 Chron. 15:13). David redirected the procession by ordering the Levites to carry the ark properly. "'No one but the Levites may carry the ark of God, because the LORD chose them to carry the ark of the LORD and to minister before him forever'" (1 Chron. 15:2).

Walter Kaiser notes that David and the religious leaders should have realized the proper method for transporting the ark at the outset; "...these men were aware of the prescribed method of treating the holiness of God. Thereby, they stood under the greater condemnation than the Philistines, who had touched the ark and had used a cart to transport it in ignorance."[436] David directed the high priests and the Levites to consecrate themselves to carry the ark into Jerusalem properly. "So the priests and Levites consecrated themselves in order to bring up the ark of the LORD, the God of Israel. And the Levites carried the ark of God with the poles on their shoulders, as Moses had commanded in accordance with the word of the LORD" (1 Chron. 15:14–15).

With the proper mode of carrying the ark in place, David continued the procession into Jerusalem. It had been some time since the nation of Israel worshiped and sacrificed to God en masse and David orchestrated this service out of joy and happiness inspired by God. Thus began the practice of corporate worship God intended for His people to perform; a unified, centrally located formal worship for all.[437] David continued the practice through the end of his reign. His son Solomon led the nation in corporate worship before and after

---

[436]Walter Kaiser, *The Promise-Plan of God,* 2008, p. 125.

[437]1 Chronicles 15 provides greater detail of the key individuals participating in the celebration, from the priests and Levites to the musicians and singers. The author stresses that the whole community of Israel was involved in the worship process, and King David would maintain Israel's corporate obedience to God. The author adds that the ceremony included burnt and fellowship offerings in worship and praise to God. David gave praise and thanks to God in a psalm that includes verbiage from Psalms 96, 105, and 106.

the temple was built. As will be discussed in the next chapter, several of the good kings of Judah continued in their efforts to restore the corporate heart of the nation after a generation of apostasy that took place before each of them.

The celebration in God's name continued with David and those with him. "When those who were carrying the ark of the LORD had taken six steps, he sacrificed a bull and a fattened calf. Wearing a linen ephod, David was dancing before the LORD with all his might, while he and all Israel were bringing up the ark of the LORD with shouts and the sound of trumpets. As the ark of the LORD was entering the City of David, Michal daughter of Saul watched from a window. And when she saw King David leaping and dancing before the LORD, she despised him in her heart" (2 Sam. 6:13–16).

The worship continued as the ark was placed in the tabernacle tent David set up for it. In his account, Josephus says that David "offered costly sacrifices and peace offerings, and treated the whole multitude, and dealt both to the women and the men and the infants a loaf of bread and a cake and another cake baked in a pan, with the portion of sacrifice."[438] When worship was completed, David sent the people home with those gifts and returned to his palace.

I find the last few verses to be very demonstrative of David's love and dedication to the Lord; he had a heart for the Lord. He was so joyful that *he danced before the Lord with all his might*. The king of all Israel led the people in joyful praise and honor to God, celebrating in His name.

I believe that, when we are filled with love from the Holy Spirit, our joy allows us to sing and dance in happiness for being one with God. When we are walking in God's presence, there is peace and contentment knowing we are in His care and protection. We can be so filled with the Holy Spirit that we bask in God's glory and love and can feel a sense of euphoria. With all the anecdotes that show David's heart for the Lord, dancing and loving God with all his strength is one of the clearest and simplest examples in all of David's story.

---

[438]Josephus, *Jewish Antiquities*, Book 7, Chapter 4, verse 86, p. 238.

In contrast to this overwhelming joy, his wife Michal was extremely critical and embarrassed by the king's actions and "she despised him in her heart" (2 Sam. 6:16). Call it jealousy or envy, Michal's spiritual heart was nowhere near her husband's. She was disgusted by David's euphoric display. As Saul's daughter and being raised in his court, she was more likely accustomed to rigid decorum and an overindulged sense of dignity that goes with being king.

"When David returned home to bless his household, Michal daughter of Saul came out to meet him and said, 'How the king of Israel has distinguished himself today, going around half-naked in full view of the slave girls of his servants as any vulgar fellow would!' David said to Michal, 'It was before the LORD, who chose me rather than your father or anyone from his house when he appointed me ruler over the LORD's people Israel—I will celebrate before the LORD. I will become even more undignified than this, and I will be humiliated in my own eyes. But by these slave girls you spoke of, I will be held in honor.' And Michal daughter of Saul had no children to the day of her death" (1 Sam. 16:20–23).

Michal's greeting to her husband was delivered with sarcasm and loathing. She could not grasp how deep was David's love for the Lord that he danced with abandon. Michal was embarrassed by David's actions and angry because his socially unbecoming behavior could reflect on her. Perhaps she was accustomed to the pomp and self-righteousness of her father's reign, which was devoid of leading the spiritual hearts of the nation.

David was unashamed of his praise to the Lord, despite his wife's criticism. In fact, he was only concerned with how the Lord perceived his actions. Michal was more concerned with dignity, protocol, and appearances (and maybe jealous of what the slave girls might think) than she was with the sincerity of David's love and devotion to God. Ronald Youngblood notes that the "narrator pauses to inject a discordant note (v.16). "Michal...is depicted as being critical of David and is therefore "acting like a true daughter of Saul...she reacts with disdain. Once, Michal, Saul's daughter, had helped David escape through a window (1 Sam. 19:12); now, peering at him through a window, she despises him in her heart."[439]

Responding to Michal's sarcastic greeting, David said he was willing to become even more undignified in order to celebrate the Lord. Youngblood writes, "In his rebuke of Michal, David takes pains to dissociate himself from Saul ('your father') and the Saulides by asserting that God has chosen him rather than them...David, of course, knows that the Lord had in fact chosen Saul...but he also knows that Saul's abortive kingship has been replaced by his own anointed reign."[440] Further, he was not going to be bound or limited in demonstrating his love for God in public. Unabashed and unashamed, David's heart for the Lord was joyful and happy; he was willing to leap and dance in the Holy Spirit.

It is revealing that Michal's disdain and criticism of David's behavior resulted in her having no other children from that point onward. It can be taken as irreverence to God since she had no sense of worship; the apple didn't fall far from the tree. The consequences were apparent.[441] As we read in previous chapters, particularly in Hannah's story, the inability to bear children was a social stigma or seen as a curse in the culture; the more children a woman bore, the more blessed she was deemed to be. Being barren was the worst thing to happen to a woman.

Because of her lack of faith and her hard-heartedness, Michal was punished by no longer bearing children. Brueggemann concludes by saying, "The exchange with Michal reflects a total inversion. David, who is thought to be despised by Michal, is in fact honored in Israel

---

[439]Ronald Youngblood, *Expositor's Bible Commentary: 1 Samuel – 2 Samuel*, 2009, p. 371.

[440] Ibid., p. 374.

[441]J. Robert Vannoy observes that this sequence also demonstrates the "change of rule from the northern leadership of the house of Saul to the Judaic family of Jesse and the house of David...Michal's childlessness is not only seen as reflecting her own personal tragedy but must also be understood as the definitive destiny of the family of Saul, which there can be no possibility of a return to the throne." *Cornerstone Biblical Commentary (Book 4): 1–2 Samuel*, 2009, p. 304.

and by Yahweh. Michal, who thinks she is in a position of strength, is dismissed by the narrative as barren and hopeless."[442]

David's Example of a Repentant Heart

While David certainly exemplified having a heart for God, like all of us, he was not without sin. The story of his affair with Bathsheba is well-known and likely his most serious offense. Scriptures tell us that it was spring, a time when kings were out at battle (fighting was more conducive during the spring when the weather was favorable). However, David remained in Jerusalem when he should have been with his troops in their battle against the Ammonites.

From his rooftop, David saw Bathsheba the wife of Uriah the Hittite, bathing naked. Uriah was a pagan but one of David's top military leaders. He was engaged with Joab (David's general) in their assault against the Ammonites at Rabbah. Bathsheba was a beautiful woman and Scripture notes that David desired her, violating the tenth commandment: "You shall not covet your neighbor's house. You shall not covet your neighbor's wife, or his male or female servant, his ox or donkey, or anything that belongs to your neighbor" (Exod. 20:17).

He ordered her to come to his bedroom, violating the seventh commandment: "You shall not commit adultery" (Exod. 20:14). There are consequences associated with sinful behavior and Bathsheba became pregnant as a result of the affair and David tried to cover his sin. Josephus states that David could not overcome his desires for her and when she became pregnant, Bathsheba "sent to the king that he should contrive some way for concealing her sin (for according to the laws of their fathers, she who had been guilty of adultery ought to be put to death)."[443]

He sent orders to have Uriah return home from battle and tried to get him to sleep with his wife so that Uriah (and likely, everyone else) would expect that he was the father. David wined and dined Uriah

---

[442]Walter Brueggemann, *First and Second Samuel,* 1990, p. 253.

[443]Josephus, *Jewish Antiquities*, Book 7, Chapter 6, Verse 132, p. 243.

and sent him home to be with Bathsheba. But Uriah was more honorable than David anticipated. As a long-term military man, Uriah felt it would be disrespectful if he stayed in the comfort of his home with his wife while his troops were still fighting. Instead, he slept outside the entrance of the palace with the rest of the servants. David's plan was frustrated Uriah's noble actions so he tried again. He invited Uriah over the next day and got him drunk, thinking he would certainly return home to sleep with his wife, but this plan also failed.

Falling deeper into a sinful thought process, David sent Uriah back into battle. He instructed his commanding officer Joab to put Uriah in the heat of the battle and withdraw troops to ensure his death. Joab followed David's instructions to the letter. In Josephus' account, Joab sent some of his best troops with Uriah and ordered Uriah to siege one of the walls so they could enter the city of Rabbah. When the battle ensued, the Ammonites dispatched the best of their fighting men. Josephus tells us, "When those that were with Uriah saw this, they all retreated backward, as Joab directed them beforehand; but Uriah was ashamed to run away and leave his post, faced the enemy, and received the violence of their onset. He killed many of them but being surrounded, and caught in the midst of them, he was killed and some of his companions were killed with him."[444]

In Scripture and in Josephus' account, Uriah demonstrated integrity, bravery, and loyalty when he refused to take his rest at home with Bathsheba while his troops were still fighting. He refused to retreat in battle when the odds were against him. I see his death as one taken in honor for his king even though he was a Hittite and not an Israelite. Still, David planned Uriah's death and was responsible for the other soldiers who died with him, thus violating the sixth commandment: "You shall not murder" (Exod. 20:13).

Joab dispatched a messenger to deliver the news to the king regarding the battle. Since David possessed a wealth of military knowledge through his years of experience in the field of battle, Joab was concerned that David would question the military tactic of sending

---

[444] Ibid., v. 140, p. 243.

Uriah too close to the enemy's fortified wall. He worried that it could be perceived by David as a classic blunder in military strategy. Joab was conscious of the lesson of Abimelech, the son of the judge Gideon described earlier who was killed for being too close to the wall he was attacking. David would certainly be mindful of this and could be angry that Joab would repeat such a foolish tactic.

Joab told the messenger that if David raised the issue, to respond to the king with, "Uriah the Hittite is dead" and the king would understand. David reacted as Joab expected and, when given the news about Uriah, he shrugged off his death as the inevitability of the war. There was no remorse in David's heart; he felt he was clear of the guilt of his affair and resulting love child. As far as anyone knew, Uriah was a casualty of war. But war or not, David's tactics were deliberate.

David took Bathsheba as his wife and carried on without remorse, even after the baby was born. David must have thought he got away with his sinful behavior. Soon after, the prophet Nathan presented David with a situation requiring the king's judgement. He related an account (much like a parable) that characterized David's sin: A rich man wishing to entertain and feed his guest stole his poor neighbor's only lamb, one that he raised with loving care and treated as a member of the family. The rich man obviously could have chosen any sheep in his own flock but abused his social position by preying on the defenseless, poorer neighbor, taking his treasured possession to serve his guest.

Initially, David didn't understand that Nathan was describing the king's sin and angrily replied that the rich man in Nathan's account should be killed. Nathan declared, "'You are the man! This is what the LORD, the God of Israel, says: "I anointed you king over Israel, and I delivered you from the hand of Saul. I gave your master's house to you, and your master's wives into your arms. I gave you all Israel and Judah. And if all this had been too little, I would have given you even more. Why did you despise the word of the LORD by doing what is evil in his eyes? You struck down Uriah the Hittite with the sword and took his wife to be your own. You killed him with the sword of the Ammonites'" (2 Sam. 12:8–9).

The rebuke was very revealing; Nathan reminded David that God gave him all sorts of blessing and protection throughout his life. God appointed David as king over all His people and all that comes with a royal title. Anything God didn't given him, all David had to do was ask and He would have granted David anything. "And if all this had been too little, I would have given you even more." God effectively had given David a blank check to ask for anything, yet he felt compelled to take what was not his. Ronald Youngblood writes, "Master of all he surveys, David has everything—and yet does not have enough." Youngblood notes the comparison to Adam in the Garden of Eden, who had it all in Eden, yet took the one thing God told him not to take.[445]

Nathan revealed the consequences of his sins: the death of the child and calamity to his household. "'This is what the LORD says: "Out of your own household I am going to bring calamity on you. Before your very eyes I will take your wives and give them to one who is close to you, and he will sleep with your wives in broad daylight. You did it in secret, but I will do this thing in broad daylight before all Israel'" (2 Sam. 12:11–12). This is precisely what occurred when Absalom chased David out of Jerusalem and took his father's concubine in view of everyone.

So, what was David's reaction when he saw himself in Nathan's mirror? Did he make excuses or blame Bathsheba for his actions? Did he deny his actions or shirk his responsibility like Saul did when confronted with his disobedience? No. Immediately we see David's remorse: "Then David said to Nathan, 'I have sinned against the Lord'" (2 Sam. 12:13). David did not make any excuses for his sins, nor did he ignore his own responsibility. Brueggemann notes that, as king, David didn't need to own up to his sin. "A lesser man—perhaps his son Solomon—would not have confessed but would have eliminated the prophet instead. The elimination of Nathan could have easily been done, but David did not move against Nathan."[446] Youngblood makes the same observation: "Though he could have vacillated or indignantly

---

[445]Ronald Youngblood, *Expositor's Bible Commentary: 1 Samuel –2 Samuel,* 2009, p. 431.

[446]Walter Brueggemann, *First and Second Samuel,* 1990, p. 282.

denied Nathan's accusation or ridded himself of Nathan in one way or another, David accepts full responsibility for his actions."[447]

David contrasted Saul, who refused to admit to the responsibility of his actions, blaming others for why he disobeyed God. Like Nathan, Samuel made Saul aware of his offenses, but Saul denied them. House states, "Unlike Saul's, David's admission of guilt contains no excuses or hopes for retaining governmental power. Rather, the psalmist owns the sin, recognizes its effect on the one praying and those around him and realizes that all sins are ultimately against God."[448]

David recognized the horror of his own sin, and he was truly repentant. His reaction was sincere, and he accepted full responsibility for his actions. He was sorry and his actions expressed his desire to be forgiven by God. This is the first time in the Old Testament where someone convicted of their actions realized their offense against God. (While Joseph's brothers eventually repented, it took years for them to show the same remorse.)

The good news is that David was forgiven by God, just as we are today when we confess our sins and ask the Lord for forgiveness. Sincere acknowledgement of sin and repentance has always been the formula to restore our spiritual hearts. That's the lesson John the Baptist preached ahead of Jesus's ministry and the message Jesus preached while on earth. It was the lesson available to Cain and Saul, but neither of them accepted it in their hearts, either as a result of pride or abandonment of God.

Through his repentance, David's heart for the Lord was restored. However, there were still consequences for his sin; David and Bathsheba's son fell ill. For seven days David fasted, laid prostrate on the ground, and pled for the child's health. This was a prayer that God did not answer; the prophet's words were fulfilled.

David gave us a template for atoning for our sins. It was captured in Psalm 51, where he dedicated the entire prayer to this occasion. In it,

---

[447]Ronald Youngblood, *Expositor's Bible Commentary: 1 Samuel – 2 Samuel*, 2009, pp. 447–48.

[448]Paul House, *Old Testament Theology*, 1998, p. 245.

he recognized his sin, identified his remorse, and pled for forgiveness. I find that it has universal appeal and serves as a prayer for our own sins and for that, I find it valuable to provide in its entirety.

"Have mercy on me, O God, according to your unfailing love; according to your great compassion blot out my transgressions. Wash away all my iniquity and cleanse me from my sin. For I know my transgressions, and my sin is always before me. Against you, you only, have I sinned and done what is evil in your sight; so, you are right in your verdict and justified when you judge. Surely, I was sinful at birth, sinful from the time my mother conceived me. Yet you desired faithfulness even in the womb; you taught me wisdom in that secret place. Cleanse me with hyssop, and I will be clean; wash me, and I will be whiter than snow. Let me hear joy and gladness; let the bones you have crushed rejoice. Hide your face from my sins and blot out all my iniquity. Create in me a pure heart, O God, and renew a steadfast spirit within me. Do not cast me from your presence or take your Holy Spirit from me. Restore to me the joy of your salvation and grant me a willing spirit, to sustain me. Then I will teach transgressors your ways, so that sinners will turn back to you. Deliver me from the guilt of bloodshed, O God, you who are God my Savior, and my tongue will sing of your righteousness. Open my lips, Lord, and my mouth will declare your praise. You do not delight in sacrifice, or I would bring it; you do not take pleasure in burnt offerings. My sacrifice, O God, is a broken spirit; a broken and contrite heart you, God, will not despise. May it please you to prosper Zion, to build up the walls of Jerusalem. Then you will delight in the sacrifices of the righteous, in burnt offerings offered whole; then bulls will be offered on your altar" (vv. 1–19).

This is a complete prayer we can all use when we sin against God. In it, David recognized his sin and how God desired him (and us) to be faithful. He pled for a pure heart, to be cleansed from his sin, and most of all, to not be cast from God's presence. David did not want to forgo the grace God has granted him through the Holy Spirit. Matthew Henry writes, "That he might never be deprived of God's grace: *Take not thy Holy Spirit from me.* He knew he had by his sin grieved the Spirit and provoked him to withdraw, and that because he also was flesh, God might justly have said that his Spirit should no more strive with him nor work upon him (Gen. 6:3). This he dreads more than anything. We are undone if God take his Holy Spirit from us. Saul was a sad instance of this. How exceedingly sinful, how exceedingly miserable, was he, when the Spirit of the Lord had departed from him!"[449]

In this portion of his prayer, David most certainly had Saul in the back of his mind. He may also have had Cain and Cain's descendants in mind, for we have described a heart that was removed from God. It is more fitting, though, that David's love for God was great and he didn't want to fall out of favor or lose face. In the conclusion of the prayer, David continued to sing praises to God and made the same observation Samuel made to Saul: God does not delight in ceremonial sacrifices for the atonement of sin, rather He desires a contrite heart. Because of his love for God and desiring to stay in his favor despite his sins, David wrote this wonderful prayer for us to follow.

A second recollection of David's transgressions took place later in his reign. Returning to the throne after Absalom's failed coup, David's army defeated an attempted rebellion and won a few more victories against the Philistines, then there was peace in the land. However, 2 Samuel 24 opens with the narrative for David's sin. "Again, the anger of the LORD burned against Israel, and he incited David against them, saying, 'Go and take a census of Israel and Judah' So the king said to Joab and the army commanders with him, 'Go throughout the tribes of Israel from Dan to Beersheba and enroll the fighting men, so that I may know how many there are'" (vv. 1–2).

A first reading implies that God directed David to take a sinful action, which is counterintuitive as God will not lead anyone into sin. 1 Chronicles 21 provides us with overlapping information for the same situation and it begins with "Satan rose up against Israel and incited David to take a census of Israel" (v. 1).

The combination of the two verses indicates that Satan tempted David into taking a census of Israel and that God allowed David to

---

[449]Matthew Henry, "Commentary on Psalms 51 by Matthew Henry," Blue Letter Bible, Last Modified March 1, 1996, https://www.blueletterbible.org/Comm/mhc/Psa/Psa_051.cfm.

take whatever action that was in his heart. This is not unlike God allowing Satan to tempt Job to demonstrate his faithfulness and obedience. God allowed Satan to tempt David into a moment of pride, to which David succumbed and instructed his general Joab to take a census of the land.

Now the census in itself was not the sin; it's what was in David's heart that drove him to follow through with it. Perhaps it was his pride that made him marvel at the number of subjects in his kingdom, the greater the number of people, the greater his honor as king. Josephus offers an alternative explanation of why taking the census was wrong. "Now King David was desirous to know how many tens of thousands there were of the people but forgot the commands of Moses, who told them beforehand, that if the multitude were numbered, they should pay a shekel to God for every head,"[450] a command that David neglected to mention in his orders to Joab.

The more likely reason, however, may be that in numbering his people, David was trying to determine how large an army he could rely upon. In Mabie's and Youngblood's commentaries, they imply that David was measuring his military strength, and not so much the total population. From Youngblood's commentary, he notes, "Concentrating only on the 'fighting men,' they were not only to count them but also to enroll them (vv. 2, 4), an act with purpose more military than statistical."[451] Mabie agrees: "While David's motivation for ordering this census is unspecified, the repeated connection to troops and elements of warfare implies a level of trust on David's part in his troops rather than complete trust in God."[452]

Before he understood the magnitude of his sin, David's pride led him to find out how many fighting men he had at his disposal; he was

---

[450]Josephus, *Jewish Antiquities, Book 7*, 13.318. Whiston cites in his footnote, "The words of God by Moses sufficiently satisfy the reason here given by Josephus for the great plague mentioned in this chapter. 'When you take a census of the Israelites to count them, each one must pay the LORD a ransom for his life at the time he is counted. Then no plague will come on them when you number them' (Exod. 30:12)."

[451]Ronald Youngblood, *Expositor's Bible Commentary: 1 Samuel –2 Samuel,* 2009, p. 307.

[452]Frederick Mabie, *The Expositor's Bible Commentary – 1 and 2 Chronicles,* 2010, p. 125.

thinking about how strong his forces were, as if the sheer number of men would matter. Instead of relying on God's strength for protection, David marveled at how large his army was. The earlier lessons such as Abraham's army of 318 men to recover his nephew Lot from the Assyrians, or Gideon's army of 300 routing the Midianites was a clear indication that God wanted His people to rely on His strength and not their own in claiming victory over their enemies. You wonder why David would have forgotten God's hand throughout Israel's history this late in his life.

J. Robert Vannoy points out, "the Lord did not want his people to trust military might as the basis for national security...the Lord did not want Israel to create a military establishment. This was one of the provisions of the 'law of the king' in Deuteronomy that prohibited the king from building up a 'large stable of horses for himself'"[453] "The king, moreover, must not acquire great numbers of horses for himself or make the people return to Egypt to get more of them, for the LORD has told you, 'You are not to go back that way again'" (Deut. 17:16).

This was somewhat substantiated by the response David received from Joab when he ordered Joab to take the census. "But Joab replied to the king, 'May the LORD your God multiply the troops a hundred times over and may the eyes of my lord the king see it. But why does my lord the king want to do such a thing?'" (2 Sam. 24:3). Ironically, Joab was the one who realized it was a mistake to disregard God's protection. Joab was far from being enlightened spiritually[454] but he was cognizant of God's ability to provide victory to His people.

---

[453]J. Robert Vannoy, *Cornerstone Biblical Commentary (Book 4): 1–2 Samuel*, 2009, p. 213.

[454]Joab was a brutal but effective leader of the army, but his moral compass had always been way off. He assisted David in ensuring that Uriah didn't make it back from the campaign against the Ammonites. He murdered Abner, Saul's military leader, to avenge his brother's death at Abner's hand. He convinced David to let his son Absalom return from exile, which later leads to Absalom's attempted coup. It was Joab who killed Absalom in the counterattack while Absalom was caught in the trees, despite David's order not to kill him. And it was Joab who murdered Amassa, the general David chose over Joab later during his reign. Not quite the paradigm of morality, but even Joab saw the folly of David's census.

Joab's reluctance to carry out the king's order should have been cause for David to reconsider and see the error of his way. A challenge to his thinking by his military leader could have made David pause to see the sin he was about to commit and perhaps take the opportunity to do the right thing. However, it was a lost opportunity. He did not see the warning behind Joab's plea, David overruled his general, and the census took place.

The census itself was no easy undertaking, considering the territory Joab had to cover. "After they had gone through the entire land, they came back to Jerusalem at the end of nine months and twenty days" (2 Sam. 24:8). It took almost a year to complete the census and even at that, Joab did not include the tribes of Levite or Benjamin. "Joab reported the number of the fighting men to David: In all Israel there were one million one hundred thousand men who could handle a sword, including four hundred and seventy thousand in Judah. But Joab did not include Levi and Benjamin in the numbering, because the king's command was repulsive to him" (1 Chron. 5–6).

Only when the report came back to David did he realize his lack of trust in God. This time, he did not need his prophet (Gad, at that point) to tell him of his transgression. He immediately begged for God's forgiveness for his lack of faith. "David was conscience-stricken after he had counted the fighting men, and he said to the LORD, 'I have sinned greatly in what I have done. Now, LORD, I beg you, take away the guilt of your servant. I have done a very foolish thing'" (2 Sam. 24:10).

David had no one to blame but himself for this sin, but unlike Saul, David realized his error, took responsibility for it, and asked for God's forgiveness. Ronald Youngblood writes that "David's confession...is the ideal repentance of the ideal king...David's insight into the seriousness of his error in relying on numerical strength instead of on the Lord's power who can 'save by many or save by few.'"[455]

There were usually consequences for bad behavior and this was no exception. Through his prophet Gad, God gave David three choices of

---

[455]Ronald Youngblood, *Expositor's Bible Commentary: 1 Samuel–2 Samuel*, 2009, p. 609.

punishment: three years of famine in the land, three months of David being hunted by his enemies, or three days of plague in the land. David chose the plague and 70,000 people died as a result. David took ownership of his sin once again. "Then David and the elders, clothed in sackcloth, fell facedown. David said to God, 'Was it not I who ordered the fighting men to be counted? I, the shepherd, have sinned and done wrong. These are but sheep. What have they done? LORD my God, let your hand fall on me and my family, but do not let this plague remain on your people'" (1 Chron. 21:16–17).

David admitted he took the census for military purposes: "Was it not I who ordered the fighting men to be counted?" He begged for mercy on behalf of his sheep, as he affectionately referred to his people, and he was their shepherd who was supposed to protect them from harm. It was David's sin that caused their plight; they were innocent of any wrongdoing. He pled for God to punish him and his house instead. Still, it was not only David; the elders also participated in the confession.

Unlike Saul, David was sincerely remorseful for the pain and suffering his people had endured because of his sin. Was this not similar to the love, compassion, and self-sacrifice for his people that we witnessed when Judah asked Joseph to absolve Benjamin of the theft he didn't commit and enslave Judah instead? David was willing to put himself in harm's way rather than see his people suffer any longer. Youngblood notes "David's loving concern for and care of 'sheep,' whether literal or metaphorical, has characterized him from his first appearance in the books of Samuel (cf. 1 Sam. 16:11[456]) to his last. Rather than witness further destruction of his men, he calls on the wrath of God down on himself and his own family."[457]

God forgave David because of his sincere repentance. "Then the angel of the LORD ordered Gad to tell David to go up and build an

---

[456]"So he asked Jesse, 'Are these all the sons you have?' 'There is still the youngest,' Jesse answered. 'He is tending the sheep.' Samuel said, 'Send for him; we will not sit down until he arrives.'"

[457]Ronald Youngblood, *Expositor's Bible Commentary: 1 Samuel –2 Samuel,* 2009, p. 611.

altar to the LORD on the threshing floor of Araunah the Jebusite" (1 Chron. 21:18). David responded immediately and offered to buy the site so he could build the altar and end the plague. While Araunah was willing to give David everything for free, David refused. "But the king replied to Araunah, 'No, I insist on paying you for it. I will not sacrifice to the LORD my God burnt offerings that cost me nothing.' So David bought the threshing floor and the oxen and paid fifty shekels of silver for them. David built an altar to the LORD there and sacrificed burnt offerings and fellowship offerings. Then the LORD answered his prayer on behalf of the land, and the plague on Israel was stopped" (2 Sam. 24:24–25).

When making a sacrifice, God puts more emphasis on what's in the heart than on what is being offered. This was yet another demonstration that David put God's will ahead of his own desires.

After building the altar and offering the sacrifice, David once again called upon the Lord who heard his prayer and ended the plague. "Then David said, 'The house of the LORD God is to be here, and also the altar of burnt offering for Israel'" (1 Chron. 22:1). By his edict, the threshing floor would be the exact location that Solomon would build the temple. Interestingly, this location (Mount Moriah) was also the same place Abraham was to sacrifice his son Isaac.

In these two examples, the difference between Saul and David recognizing their sins shows the range of their spiritual hearts. Saul had great difficulty admitting his errors, took exception that any transgressions were a result of his own actions, and struggled with being held accountable for his sin. I think part of his behavior was a lack of conviction and honesty with himself; he was more concerned with concealing his deficiencies than admitting to them. It is difficult to admit mistakes when your spiritual heart is running on empty, which was Saul's condition. Pride and self-preservation were the catalyst for his jealousy, and envy of David's popularity led to Saul's murderous thoughts. Once God left his presence, it was impossible for Saul to restore the dying embers of God's image in his heart.

On the other hand, David's behavior provided a template for us to follow. We all sin, we all lose face with God, and we all fall short of the mark. Sin itself does not condemn us forever if we recognize it, atone for it, repent of it, and ask for God's forgiveness. J. Robert Vannoy writes, "It is in these responses that the most significant difference between Saul and David is found. David did not always walk in the ways of the Lord, but in contrast to Saul, when David failed to do so he repented for his sin and sought the Lord's forgiveness by casting himself on divine mercy and making proper atonement through sacrifice."[458]

These actions call for true humility that admits character flaws exist. David showed us that, no matter how egregious the sin, God will forgive us if we follow that example. It is no wonder that God referred to David as a man after His own heart. Because we are all created in His image, we all have the core ingredients to ask for forgiveness just as David did.

God knew that David would be obedient to His will and, even when he strayed from that path, David's restored heart would put him back on track.

David and the Second Great Commandment

As Jesus shared with the disciples, we are to ask God to "[f]orgive us our sins, for we also forgive everyone who sins against us" (Luke 11:4). Joseph set an example by forgiving his brothers for their attempt to end his life. Implicitly, he forgave Potiphar, his wife, and the cupbearer. In David's story, we read brief accounts of his willingness to forgive those who sought to harm him at a time when loving his enemies was considered exceptional behavior. David continued to prove that he was a man after God's own heart.

Despite his military success and the adoration of the people, David remained humble and faithfully dedicated to Saul. He was not puffed up, conceited, or proud because of his success, not unlike Joseph when

---

[458]J. Robert Vannoy, *Cornerstone Biblical Commentary (Book 4): 1–2 Samuel*, 2009, p. 427.

Pharaoh placed him second over all of Egypt.[459] Even though he was anointed to be king well before Saul's death, he respected Saul as God's anointed and showed no ambition to get the throne. David was Saul's servant despite his own popularity. On the contrary, David's son Absalom used his contrived popularity to dethrone his own father.

A primary attribute of showing love to your fellow man is the ability to care for those who want to do you harm: your enemies. In the New Testament, Jesus teaches: "'You have heard that it was said, "You shall love your neighbor and hate your enemy." But I say to you, love your enemies, bless those who curse you, do good to those who hate you, and pray for those who spitefully use you and persecute you, that you may be sons of your Father in heaven; for He makes His sun rise on the evil and on the good, and sends rain on the just and on the unjust'" (Matt. 5:43–45, NKJV).

Jesus made that known 1,000 years after David's reign. Like Joseph in his lifetime, the popular theme in David's day would have been to take revenge on your enemies; to strike back and get even. But David showed love and respect to Saul despite Saul's attempts to kill him. David was certainly considered an enemy by Saul, even though Saul was constantly at war with the Philistines. And how did David react to Saul's anger? By showing him respect as king, not seeking revenge, and not seeking a way to have Saul taken out so he could take the throne which he had already been anointed by Samuel.

When Saul died at the hands of the Philistines and the news of his death reached David, he reacted as if a member of his immediate family had died; one whom he truly loved and respected. "Then David and all the men with him took hold of their clothes and tore them. They mourned and wept and fasted till evening for Saul and his son Jonathan, and for the army of the LORD and for the nation of Israel, because they had fallen by the sword" (2 Sam. 1:11–12).

---

[459]It is interesting to note the similarities between Joseph and David. Both were the youngest (although Joseph had a younger brother, Benjamin) in large families of boys, both came from humble beginnings, both were scorned by their brothers, and both were chosen by God to be leaders over His people. Like Joseph, David did not show any revenge on his transgressors later in life.

This goes to show where David's heart was in comparison to Saul's. J. Robert Vannoy notes, "Even though Saul had waged a longstanding vendetta against him, and in spite of the fact that Saul had even sought to take his life, David showed no vindictiveness toward him when he learned of his death...David showed only respect and honor for the person whom he continued to recognize as the Lord's anointed, notwithstanding his abuse of the office with which he was entrusted."[460]

When the people of Jabesh Gilead (Saul loyalists) recovered Saul's body from the Philistines, "he sent messengers to them to say to them, 'The LORD bless you for showing this kindness to Saul your master by burying him. May the LORD now show you kindness and faithfulness, and I too will show you the same favor because you have done this'" (2 Sam. 2:5–6). David harbored no grudge and honored those who had great respect for Saul.

There were two other accounts that demonstrated David's mercy and kindness. After taking control of Israel and following several military victories, David asked, "'Is there anyone still left of the house of Saul to whom I can show kindness for Jonathan's sake?'" (2 Sam. 9:1). David's success brought peace in the kingdom, and he wanted to make good a pledge he made to Jonathan, which was to care for his family if he died before David. He showed compassion to Jonathan's son Mephibosheth, a cripple from birth, by restoring his property and allowing him to dine with the king at any time. He extended his generosity to Mephibosheth's servant Ziba and his family by allowing them to farm the land for their master, who David treated as a son.

The second account occurred when David dealt with Shimei when he returned to Jerusalem after Absalom was killed. I mentioned that even though Shimei cursed and spat at the fleeing king, David spared him from his aides who would have killed Shimei for his disrespect. After the attempted coup was thwarted, David and his army returned to Jerusalem. As he and his army passed through Gilgal, Shimei presented himself to the victorious king, fell prostrate before him, and begged for

[460]J. Robert Vannoy, *Cornerstone Biblical Commentary (Book 4): 1–2 Samuel*, 2009, p. 271.

mercy. He repented of his actions against David and wanted to be the first before the king on his return to show the sincerity of his repentance and remorse. "'For I your servant know that I have sinned, but today I have come here as the first from the tribes of Joseph to come down and meet my lord the king'" (2 Sam. 19:20).

When his men asked why Shimei shouldn't be killed for his prior actions, David replied that there had been enough bloodshed for the day (thinking of the death of his son, Absalom) and was looking forward to bringing the nation back together. David forgave Shimei for his behavior and spared his life once again. This was another lesson in David showing mercy and kindness to one who wished him harm; someone who reviled David when he was down and out, but begged for mercy and forgiveness when David returned to power. It would be easy to be revengeful and within his right to punish Shimei for his hatred, but David was mindful of how God forgave him for his sins.

When David pled with God to spare his sheep for the punishment for which he himself was responsible, he showed great compassion for his people. He didn't want to see his people suffer any harm and was willing to take on God's wrath and lose his position or life for their sake. As Jesus said to His apostles near the end of his ministry, "'My command is this: Love each other as I have loved you. Greater love has no one than this: to lay down one's life for one's friends'" (John 15:12–13).

David and Joseph had spiritual hearts that were ahead of their time and the concept is the same today: that we all have the ingredients to reflect God's image and likeness in our own hearts. David did not hear the messages Jesus would teach about loving one's enemy, nor did the individuals in Genesis know the commandments given to Moses. Those characteristics are innate; we all have the basic ingredients to love God and mankind as God intended, although not in the purity and holiness that existed before Adam's sin. It's just a question of acting on those ingredients.

So far in this text, we've seen that there are varying degrees of how these gifts were inherent within the individuals in the Old Testament and David provided the best overall example. No one else in the Old

Testament was said to have a heart like God's, which is precisely the reason God chose him to lead His people and to establish an everlasting dynasty from his lineage.[461]

---

[461]See Appendix B for a discussion of God's covenant with David that includes Jesus as part of David's lineage and final ruler of His Kingdom.

Chapter 10–

KING SOLOMON:
A TALE OF TWO HEARTS

D avid made great strides getting Israel back to God and away from the idolatry characterized in the book of Judges. He united the tribes into a solid nation that worshiped and gave praise to God. Under David's reign, the spiritual heart of his people reflected his own. David's rule over Israel was about 40 years and God granted him and the nation prosperity and military success to secure its borders. There was peace in the land by the start of his son Solomon's reign.

A monarchy was established and the kings that succeeded him were to set the example of a spiritual heart for the people. In some cases, the king focused on following the covenant requirements as David did during his reign, but that was the exception rather than the rule. Only eight of the forty kings who ruled the bifurcated nation followed in David's footsteps. The remainder were described as doing evil in God's eyes.

Solomon set the tone for things to come. Early in his reign, he maintained a spiritual plateau inherited from David, but as he prospered, he fell out of obedience to God and led the nation back into idolatry. Unlike David, Solomon did not repent when made aware of his transgression, nor did he attempt to right himself in his walk with God. The consequence of his sin saw the nation torn in half and the splendor achieved in his early years slowly dissolved. In the following chapter, the Judean kings who initially followed in David's footsteps typically suffered from the same pattern as Solomon. There was a falling away from God in sin, which by human nature, was to be expected. But rather than realize their sin, ask God for forgiveness, and follow His will, those kings, like Solomon, rarely showed the level of repentance that David demonstrated. I think that is one reason David's spiritual life set the bar for the kings that followed.

At the beginning of his reign, Solomon began where David left off. Solomon was to build the great temple in Jerusalem as God instructed, so that all of Israel could worship God in a central location and fulfill what God decreed to Moses just before the people crossed the Jordan into the Promised Land. "Then to the place the LORD your God will choose as a dwelling for his Name—there you are to bring everything I command you: your burnt offerings and sacrifices, your tithes and special gifts, and all the choice possessions you have vowed to the LORD" (Deut. 12:11). Prior to the construction of the temple, regular worship was held at various places, but the main festivals were held in Shechem. These were referred to as altars in high places.

The central location was necessary for the nation to worship as one. This corporate worship enabled the people to praise and worship God as a unified body, which Jesus and Paul taught during their missionary journeys. Without a central location for worship, there was the danger of falling into the pagan practice of worshiping many false gods, each with its own altar for worship scattered throughout the land. Israel had only one God who was to be worshiped in unity at one altar, the temple of Jerusalem. Paul House notes that the temple would provide continuity from one generation to the next and provide an orderly structure to their faith. "The centralizing of worship in this one place is intended to bring order and uniformity to Israel's religion, without suppressing love and devotion for God."[462]

While David was precluded from building the temple, he dedicated a lot of the resources and materials that Solomon needed, including the blueprints, so that Solomon was well-prepared for its construction.[463]

---

[462]Paul House, *Old Testament Survey,* 1992, p. 153.

[463]David received the instructions from God. "He gave him the plans of all that the Spirit had put in his mind for the courts of the temple of the LORD and all the surrounding rooms, for the treasuries of the temple of God and for the treasuries for the dedicated things" (1 Chron. 28:12).

The temple would be the culmination of the Israelites' finest spiritual moment, one of spiritual unity among its people. It would be a time of independence and self-determination. Peace would finally prevail, and the nation would be the richest and strongest nation in the region because of its faithfulness and obedience to God. In all of Israel's history, it was a period when the corporate spiritual heart of the nation would be close to the priestly function intended for Adam; it would be temporarily restored under Solomon's early reign.

Solomon was blessed with great wisdom and demonstrated expertise in many subjects. He was obedient and faithful to God at the beginning of his reign, and he followed the instructions given to him by his father. The nation grew even closer to God once the temple in Jerusalem was complete and it became the center of all Jewish worship. Love and obedience to God dwelt once again in the hearts of His people. It reflected the covenant made with Moses and his people centuries prior when God said, "'you shall be my treasured possession among all peoples...and you shall be to me a kingdom of priests'" (Exod. 19:5–6). As G. K. Beale reflects, "The entire nation was to live in the midst of God's presence and were all to become like priests standing in the presence of God in his temple and reflecting his glorious light, being the intermediaries for the nations living in darkness and apart from God."[464]

Their relationship with God as a nation, however, was short-lived. It wasn't long before leadership failed to keep their covenantal relationship with God, and they fell again into the cycle of idolatry and pagan worship. The decline started toward the end of Solomon's reign; his many pagan wives influenced him to worship their many idols. With Solomon's death, the nation would be split between the ten tribes of the north (Israel) and Judah and Benjamin to the south, as judgement for Solomon's disobedience to God's commands.

[464]G. K. Beale and Mitchell Kim, *God Dwells Among Us,* 2004, p. 115.

The Rise of Solomon's Heart

Recall that David was told by his prophet Nathan that the temple he wanted to build for God would be built by Solomon instead. While David was obedient to God's command, he wanted to contribute to its success, so David made great efforts to simplify Solomon's task. "David said, 'My son Solomon is young and inexperienced, and the house to be built for the LORD should be of great magnificence and fame and splendor in the sight of all the nations. Therefore, I will make preparations for it.' So, David made extensive preparations before his death" (1 Chron. 22:5). David also ensured that Solomon was surrounded by the best counsel to advise him on its construction.

Solomon had the benefit of spiritual direction from his father and David conveyed the lessons that he learned in doing God's will: "'And you, my son Solomon, acknowledge the God of your father, and serve him with wholehearted devotion and with a willing mind, for the LORD searches every heart and understands every desire and every thought. If you seek him, he will be found by you; but if you forsake him, he will reject you forever'" (1 Chron. 28:9).

David imparted the words of the First Great Commandment, which were to love and serve God with his whole heart and mind. God knows what's in man's heart; Solomon was advised to keep God close and not forsake him. David was keenly aware that as king, Solomon must lead the spiritual heart of his people by keeping God's commandments and staying obedient to them as David had. He passed along the same warning God passed on to him: if you forsake Him, He will forsake you.

Solomon's ascension to the throne was not a smooth one.[465] Toward the end of David's life, Adonijah, Solomon's oldest surviving half-brother, declared himself king. He repeated some of Absalom's tactics

---

[465] That God had selected Solomon to succeed David and not any other of his brothers was revealed when Solomon was born. "Then David comforted his wife Bathsheba, and he went to her and made love to her. She gave birth to a son, and they named him Solomon. The LORD loved him; and because the LORD loved him, he sent word through Nathan the prophet to name him Jedidiah" (2 Sam. 12:24–25).

when he tried to wrestle the throne from his father David. Adonijah had the backing of two key figures in David's court, his long-time general Joab and Abiathar the priest. "Now Adonijah, whose mother was Haggith, put himself forward and said, 'I will be king.' So, he got chariots and horses ready, with fifty men to run ahead of him. Adonijah conferred with Joab son of Zeruiah and with Abiathar the priest, and they gave him their support" (1 Kgs. 1:5, 7). Patterson and Austel write, "his ambition was in direct contravention of God's will and David's explicit wishes. He did not wait for prophetic anointing or a royal proclamation."[466]

Nathan was fully aware that God had selected Solomon to succeed David and not Adonijah. With the help of Solomon's mother Bathsheba, Nathan revealed to David Adonijah's plan to take the throne and reminded David that he had already designated Solomon as his successor. David, in his weakened condition due to his old age, didn't immediately recall that he made that declaration, but appointed Solomon as king. Adonijah's plan was thwarted, his supporters fled, and he had to beg Solomon to spare his life.

Solomon took action to secure his throne. He removed Abiathar from the priesthood and put him under house arrest. He had Joab killed for the innocent blood that he shed. He also eliminated Shimei (a Saul loyalist) who cursed David during Absalom's insurrection. When Adonijah went through Bathsheba to ask King Solomon to give him Abishag (David's last concubine) as his wife, Solomon was angry that he could use the marriage to eventually claim the throne, so he had Adonijah killed. Solomon viewed Adonijah's request as a power play similar to what his older brother Absalom did with their father's concubine. Both actions were similar to Rueben taking his father Abraham's concubine as we read in Chapter 4.

These actions don't cast Solomon in a great light morally, but there are several times in Israel's history where God allowed for such tactics in order for His long-term plan to stay on track. On the other hand,

[466]Richard Patterson and Hermann Austel, *The Expositor's Bible Commentary – 1 and 2 King,* 2009, p. 641.

the actions may have been an early indication of the flaws in Solomon's character.

Even though threats to his kingship were eliminated, the first thing Solomon did was make an alliance with Pharaoh king of Egypt and marry his daughter. "He brought her to the City of David until he finished building his palace and the temple of the LORD, and the wall around Jerusalem" (1 Kgs. 3:1b). There was no explanation for why he made the alliance with the king of Egypt; relying on God's protection would have been sufficient. In fact, centuries earlier, Moses warned against relying on Egypt for any military assistance. "The king, moreover, must not acquire great numbers of horses for himself or make the people return to Egypt to get more of them, for the LORD has told you, 'You are not to go back that way again'" (Deut. 17:16).

In addition, Moses gave instructions against intermarriage to prevent the influence of pagan worship. "'Do not intermarry with them. Do not give your daughters to their sons or take their daughters for your sons, for they will turn your children away from following me to serve other gods, and the LORD's anger will burn against you and will quickly destroy you'" (Deut. 7:3–4). Solomon's choice of a pagan wife rather than one from the nation of Israel was the catalyst for his spiritual downward spiral.

It was four years into his reign when Solomon turned his attention to building the temple. In the religious ceremony dedicated to the commencement of the temple's construction, Solomon brought all the commanders, leaders, and judges to lead them in prayer and burnt offerings before God at Gibeon. "Solomon showed his love for the LORD by walking according to the instructions given him by his father David, except that he offered sacrifices and burned incense on the high places.[467] The king went to Gibeon to offer sacrifices, for that

---

[467]High places were associated with pagan worship later in the Old Testament. Prior to the building of the temple, Gibeon, Shiloh, and a few other main sites were acceptable places for worshiping God. Once the temple was complete, however, there would be no reason or excuse to continue worshiping anywhere else. What is curious is that the wording includes "except that he offered...on the high places."

was the most important high place, and Solomon offered a thousand burnt offerings on that altar" (1 Kgs. 3:3–4).

Solomon's faith continued in the manner of his father David; this was a welcome demonstration of the king leading his people to worship and praise the Lord. He led his people in sacrificing on the high place at Gibeon because the temple was not yet built.[468]

God was pleased with Solomon's initial spiritual leadership and appeared to him in a vision after the temple dedication ceremony. "That night God appeared to Solomon and said to him, 'Ask for whatever you want me to give you.' Solomon answered God, 'You have shown great kindness to David my father and have made me king in his place. Now, LORD God, let your promise to my father David be confirmed, for you have made me king over a people who are as numerous as the dust of the earth. Give me wisdom and knowledge, that I may lead this people, for who is able to govern this great people of yours?'" (2 Chron. 1:7–10).

Conscious of the enormous responsibility of leading God's people, Walter Brueggemann notes, "the king asks for an 'understanding mind.' This conventional translation is scarcely adequate; it would be better to render a 'hearing heart' or even an obedient heart."[469] In a show of humility and wanting to do right in leading God's nation, Solomon asked God to grant him the wisdom to lead Israel properly. God was pleased with an answer that showed a true, spiritual heart. Frederick Mabie notes, "Solomon's request for wisdom is connected to his ability to govern (judge) God's people and facilitate an ordered, God-honoring society...In order to judge wisely, Solomon

---

[468]Solomon was not only preparing to build the temple, but also his palace and one for the queen. Scriptures note that the completion of the temple came after these other projects. Iain Provan suggests that this delay in completing the temple may have been influenced by his pagan wife who "...living in temporary accommodations while her new palace is being built, has a vested interest in the progress of the building program." *1 & 2 Kings*, 1995, p. 45. Provan adds, "The continuation and proliferation of worship at these shrines, unchecked by royal intervention, is one of the main concerns of Kings." p. 48.

[469]Walter Brueggemann, *1 and 2 Kings*, 1990, p. 47.

must be able to discern and apply God's will."[470] Essentially, Solomon was asking for the ability to rule as a covenantal king that was prescribed through Moses.

Solomon could have asked for anything that would benefit him personally, such as riches, long life, or fame. These gifts would be indications of self-gratifying rewards of this world. But Solomon asked for something that would benefit his people: to lead Israel justly and fairly as a benign ruler. It seemed likely that God would have wanted Adam to do the same given his authority over all the earth; but this is a snapshot of what may have been through Solomon. He was not a man full of pride or selfishness, nor was he a cruel man. Solomon adhered to his father's instructions and continued in David's footsteps by following God in obedience and in faith. At that point in his reign, Solomon's spiritual heart was in line with David's.

God not only granted Solomon's request for wisdom, but because he did not request on his own behalf, God granted him the things for which he did not ask. "'Moreover, I will give you what you have not asked for—both wealth and honor—so that in your lifetime you will have no equal among kings. And if you walk in obedience to me and keep my decrees and commands as David your father did, I will give you a long life.' Then Solomon awoke—and he realized it had been a dream. He returned to Jerusalem, stood before the ark of the Lord's covenant, and sacrificed burnt offerings and fellowship offerings. Then he gave a feast for all his court" (1 Kgs. 3:13–15). Solomon's immediate response was to offer sacrifices before the ark to give thanks and praise for His blessing.

Solomon proceeded to establish his court and government administration and designated twelve district governors to help rule over Israel. There was prosperity and the food was plentiful. "The people of Judah and Israel were as numerous as the sand on the seashore; they ate, they drank, and they were happy" (1 Kgs. 4:20). There was enough wealth to go around for all to enjoy. While the physical requirements to support his government were extensive, "The district governors,

---

[470]Frederick Mabie, *The Expositor's Bible Commentary – 1 and 2 Chronicles*, 2010, p. 161.

each in his month, supplied provisions for King Solomon and all who came to the king's table. They saw to it that nothing was lacking. They also brought to the proper place their quotas of barley and straw for the chariot horses and the other horses" (1 Kgs. 4:27–28).

While Solomon constructed the temple, he continued the trade agreement that his father David initiated with Hiram king of Tyre, who provided the cedar. Solomon shared with Hiram his intention of building a great house for God but recognized that no ornate building could capture the greatness and glory of God. "'The temple I am going to build will be great, because our God is greater than all other gods. But who is able to build a temple for him, since the heavens, even the highest heavens, cannot contain him? Who then am I to build a temple for him, except as a place to burn sacrifices before him?" (2 Chron. 2:5–6). Solomon clearly understood that the temple would not contain God; rather, it will be the center of worship for God, a place where God could commune with His people.

When construction was complete, Solomon held a nationwide ceremony to dedicate the temple to God. As their spiritual leader, he called all Israel to participate in the consecration and dedication of the temple. This was the second time Solomon led his people to show gratitude for the Lord's blessing and offer praise to Him. The corporate worship of praise and thanksgiving to God culminated with the ark of the covenant being installed in the inner sanctuary in the temple. "When the priests withdrew from the Holy Place, the cloud filled the temple of the LORD. And the priests could not perform their service because of the cloud, for the glory of the LORD filled his temple" (1 Kgs. 8:10–11). God's glory returned in the presence of His faithful people, just as He did to lead Moses and his people out of Egypt and into the wilderness. This was Israel's faithfulness and obedience to God at its finest.

Solomon made a prayer of dedication in the presence of the whole assembly as part of the temple's consecration. In his prayer, he asked God to recognize one of the major roles of the temple: to serve as a conduit for the people to come to God to forgive their sins. Solomon described several scenarios where the people might find themselves in sin and the temple was to be used to confess those sins. He stressed that there had to be recognition and admission of sin followed by sincerity in their atonement. And while it was not necessary to be within the physical confines of the temple to ask for God's forgiveness, they could offer their prayers in the direction of the temple.

Solomon declared the temple a center of worship where the sins of Israel would be forgiven and their faith renewed during times of falling out with God.[471] At the conclusion of his prayer, he asked for God's continued blessings on the nation. "'May the LORD our God be with us as he was with our ancestors; may he never leave us nor forsake us. May he turn our hearts to him, to walk in obedience to him and keep the commands, decrees and laws he gave our ancestors. And may these words of mine, which I have prayed before the LORD, be near to the LORD our God day and night, that he may uphold the cause of his servant and the cause of his people Israel according to each day's need, so that all the peoples of the earth may know that the LORD is God and that there is no other. And may your hearts be fully committed to the LORD our God, to live by his decrees and obey his commands, as at this time" (1 Kgs. 8:57–61).

Solomon implored his people to dedicate their hearts totally to God and only Him and keep his commandments. This was a reinstatement of the covenant commitment the nation pledged after Moses comes down from Mount Sinai. In their commentary, Patterson and Austel reiterate one of the themes of this text: sincerity of heart is what God recognizes as the motivation behind atonement and obedience. "Notice the emphasis on the heart, that is, one's inner being rather than ritual. God, who knows the heart, will respond to a person's prayer in accordance with the realty of his repentance."[472]

---

[471]The temple being a conduit for the Israelites to atone and ask for God's forgiveness is important to remember. Jesus will replace the function of the temple. He foretells the destruction of the temple itself, but He represents the new temple and sins will be forgiven through Him. This will be discussed in Volume II.

[472]Richard Patterson and Hermann Austel, *The Expositor's Bible Commentary – 1 and 2 King,* 2009, p. 708.

Faith and obedience to God were the order of the day and the people responded affirmatively to Solomon's call to faith. God showed His approval for the entire ceremony by His presence in His new home. "When Solomon finished praying, fire came down from heaven and consumed the burnt offering and the sacrifices, and the glory of the LORD filled the temple" (2 Chron. 7:1).

The prayers of dedication and worship were a strong spiritual showing of Solomon's leadership; the people of Israel followed his lead in faith and dedication to God. There was a huge congregation of the nation to offer prayers and sacrifices for God to consecrate the temple and the people. "It is surely true that Solomon had it in his heart and mind the thought of a covenant renewal, a personal and national rededication to God. It is not the ritual that is emphasized but the outpouring of Solomon's heart to God."[473]

The seven days of corporate worship was followed by seven days of feasting, praise, and blessings. When it was over, Solomon sent the people home. "They blessed the king and then went home, joyful and glad in heart for all the good things the LORD had done for his servant David and his people Israel" (1 Kgs. 8:66). Solomon and his people were in unison; their hearts reflected the gratefulness and joy of being in God's grace. They had a corporate spiritual heart for God. It was reminiscent of the joy David and his people had when the ark was brought back to Jerusalem. As Paul House notes, "All the people participate in a joyful feast and then return happily to their homes. Few moments in biblical history surpass this scene in hope, gladness and glory."[474]

When the dedication was over and the people returned to their homes, God appeared to Solomon a second time to let him know his prayers had been heard. God also extended the covenant promise He made with David to establish the throne forever if Solomon remained in obedience to Him. The Lord said to Solomon, "'As for you, if you walk before me faithfully with integrity of heart and uprightness, as

---

[473] Ibid., p. 700.

[474] Paul House, *The New American Commentary: 1, 2 Kings*, 1995, p. 149.

David your father did, and do all I command and observe my decrees and laws, I will establish your royal throne over Israel forever,[475] as I promised David your father when I said, 'You shall never fail to have a successor on the throne of Israel'" (1 Kgs. 9:4–5). By these instructions, God defined the character that He expected from Solomon. God wanted him to be a man of integrity and uprightness, following God's commands and keeping David's lineage on the throne forever. Above all, obedience to His commandments was key to keeping the dynasty intact.

However, as with all God's covenants, there were consequences for disobedience to His will: "But if you or your descendants turn away from me and do not observe the commands and decrees I have given you and go off to serve other gods and worship them, then I will cut off Israel from the land I have given them and will reject this temple I have consecrated for my Name. Israel will then become a byword and an object of ridicule among all peoples'" (1 Kgs. 9:6–7). This disobedience will come to pass toward the end of Solomon's reign.

The dedication of the temple before the Lord was to be the spiritual high point in the nation's history. The temple became God's new dwelling place among His people and its function at this point in Israel's history cannot be overstated. As Graeme Goldsworthy notes, "The temple is a witness to all the nations that God dwells in Israel and that he is found through the name he is revealed...a foreigner can be joined to the people of God only by coming to the temple, for it is here that God chooses to deal with those who seek him."[476] From N. T. Wright, "The Temple was the sign and focus and means of God's presence with his people, a presence at once dangerously holy and wonderfully encouraging. The regular sacrifices, day by day and hour by hour, and the regular festivals, season by season but always with a climax at Passover, gave the Temple its inner life and meaning, as the

---

[475]This is the second mention by God regarding Solomon's commitment to be obedient to His will. In his first vision where Solomon asks for wisdom, God responded, "And if you walk in obedience to me and keep my decrees and commands as David your father did, I will give you a long life" (1 Kgs. 3:14).

[476]Graeme Goldsworthy, *The Son of God and the New Creation*, 2015, p. 161.

Israelites journeyed to Jerusalem to be in the very presence of God who had promised to live there and to celebrate his promise of ultimate deliverance."[477]

God allowed continued peace between Israel and the other nations for Solomon. In fact, the other nations would send emissaries to Jerusalem with gifts, gold, and jewels to pay homage to Solomon because his reputation for wisdom and wealth was known throughout the region. Jerusalem would become the epicenter of the Near East; the nation's power, wealth, and fame spread, and God's blessings came to fruition. Solomon continued with his massive plan for urban development. He constructed several government buildings,[478] a palace for himself, and one for his Egyptian wife. He rebuilt several surrounding cities and, through his arrangements with Hiram, he gained access to sea trade and built a fleet of trading ships. "And Hiram sent him ships commanded by his own men, sailors who knew the sea. These, with Solomon's men, sailed to Ophir and brought back four hundred and fifty talents of gold [$700 million delivered for each three-year journey], which they delivered to King Solomon" (2 Chron. 8:18).

Solomon also gained access to several trade routes allowing economic growth for his people. The wealth obtained throughout all these activities was unprecedented. "The weight of the gold that Solomon received yearly was 666 talents (over $1 billion in today's value), not including the revenues from merchants and traders and from all the Arabian kings and the governors of the territories" (1 Kgs. 10:14–15). This says nothing of the gold, silver, bronze, and jewels that were inlaid in the temple's construction, which had enormous value.

Upon her visit, the Queen of Sheba was astonished by Solomon's wisdom and overwhelmed by the amount of wealth she witnessed. She was wise enough herself to recognize that Israel's success was due to the blessing of their God. "Praise be to the LORD your God, who has

---

[477]N. T. Wright, *How God Became King,* 2012, p. 101.

[478]Eugene Merrill, *Kingdom of Priests: A History of Old Testament Israel,* 2008, p. 313. The author credits David Ussishkin who "identifies at least six separate structures, some of which were joined together into complexes."

delighted in you and placed you on the throne of Israel. Because of the LORD's eternal love for Israel, he has made you king to maintain justice and righteousness" (1 Kgs 10:9). She brought him gifts from her region: "And she gave the king 120 talents of gold ($187 million in today's value), large quantities of spices, and precious stones. Never again were so many spices brought in as those the queen of Sheba gave to King Solomon" (1 Kgs. 10:10). That Solomon's reputation spread throughout the Near East was indicative of how far the Queen of Sheba was willing to travel to see him. Sheba is located in the vicinity of today's Yemen, some 1,500 miles from Jerusalem.

Eugene Merrill notes, "the queen concluded that the real reason for Solomon's giftedness and prosperity is that his God loved him and Israel, and therefore cared for him and preserved his nation under Solomon's benevolent care. In many respects, her understanding of the ways of Israel's God far surpassed that of his own people as the Scriptures eloquently testify."[479]

The nation was at peace and appeared to be one with God. Just as God promised, Solomon's reign, wealth, and fame continued to spread. "King Solomon was greater in riches and wisdom than all the other kings of the earth. All the kings of the earth sought audience with Solomon to hear the wisdom God had put in his heart. Year after year, everyone who came brought a gift—articles of silver and gold, and robes, weapons and spices, and horses and mules...He ruled over all the kings from the Euphrates River to the land of the Philistines, as far as the border of Egypt" (2 Chron. 9:22–24, 26).

The Fall of Solomon's Heart

There were early warning signs that Solomon's dedication and obedience to God's commands would diminish. A curious observation made by Graeme Goldsworthy was, despite being at the high point of their religious dedication to God after completing the temple, "there is neither a great program of evangelism driving Israel nor a mass

---

[479]Eugene Merrill, *A Commentary on 1 & 2 Chronicles,* 2015, p. 370.

conversion of Gentiles."[480] If it was God's intent that Israel reflect His purity and holiness as His priests here on earth, spreading the faith to pagan nations around them would be in line with that role. As with the Great Commission, Jesus instructed His apostles to spread His message after the resurrection; Solomon should have taken the opportunity to share the knowledge of his faith to the surrounding nations after the temple was finished.

The nations around them indeed witnessed God's presence through His blessings on Israel, which should have led them to realize how God rewarded His chosen. It was the point made earlier in Chapter 5 by Gentry and Wellum, "They are supposed to witness a group of people who demonstrate a right relationship to the one and only true God, a human way of treating each other, and a proper stewardship of the earth's resources."[481]

Unfortunately, no conversions in the surrounding nations ever took place. The Queen of Sheba was overwhelmed by what she had seen and marveled that God had blessed Solomon. But even this realization was not enough to cause her to take up the Jewish faith. She recognized the blessings of God, but she was not given a lesson of faith by Solomon. He readily displayed all his wealth and demonstrated the breadth of his wisdom and knowledge, but Scriptures are silent whether Solomon shared his faith with her. We assume he did not, as she did not walk away in faith. Faithful outreach to the nations simply was not on Solomon's mind, but building up Jerusalem and wealth to display certainly was.

According to David Guzik, "If we take the Queen of Sheba as an example of a *seeker*, we see that Solomon impressed her with his wealth and splendor, and also impressed her personally. But she returned home without an evident expression of faith in the God of Israel. This shows that impressing seekers with facilities and programs

---

[480]Graeme Goldsworthy, *Christ-Centered Biblical Theology*, 2012, p. 202.

[481]Peter Gentry and Stephen Wellum, *Kingdom Through Covenant*, 2018, pp. 297–98.

and organization and professionalism isn't enough."[482] The nation of priests had not carried out their mission to convert by example or through instruction.

Another indication of the chinks in Solomon's armor was his effort in building the palaces for himself and his Egyptian queen ahead of completing the Temple for God. Scriptures say that after seven years of detailed and ornate work, the temple was finished. "In the eleventh year in the month of Bul, the eighth month, the temple was finished in all its details according to its specifications. He had spent seven years building it" (1 Kgs. 6:38). However, Iain Provan suggests, "The temple is not really 'complete' until all the work on its interior is finished and is being worshiped in. This does not happen until...[1 Kgs.] 7:51,[483] when Solomon's own contribution to the interior is 'finished.'"[484]

His point is verse 38 references the structure of the temple being complete but more work on the interior was necessary. The criticism relates to Solomon's priorities. Provan points to 1 Kings 7:1 ("Solomon was building his own house thirteen years, and he finished his entire house") to illustrate Solomon's home was completed before God's home was finished. Quoting Provan, Bruce Waltke says the implication is that "Solomon not only spent more time on the palace project, but also pushed it through to completion before fully finishing his work on the temple."[485]

Scriptures continue with the description of the King's palace, including the amount of detail in the ornate design of its interior, along with the resources required for the interior. All this was written before the author returned to describing Solomon's effort in undertaking the finishing touches on the temple. The suggestion is Solomon may have

---

[482]David Guzik, "Study Guide for 1 Kings 10 by David Guzik," Blue Letter Bible, last modified February 21, 2017, https://www.blueletterbible.org/Comm/guzik_david/StudyGuide 2017-1Ki/1Ki-10.cfm.

[483]"When all the work King Solomon had done for the temple of the LORD was finished, he brought in the things his father David had dedicated—the silver and gold and the furnishings—and he placed them in the treasuries of the LORD's temple."

[484]Iain Provan, *1 & 2 Kings*, 1995, p. 70.

[485]Bruce Waltke, *An Old Testament Theology*, 2007, p. 121.

had a higher priority in finishing his own abode; another indication that his character of heart may not reflect the same attention to God that his father David demonstrated. In Chapter 12, we will find the same criticism targeting the remnant Jews returning from their exile to Babylon. The prophet Haggai criticized the people for focusing on building their own homes before restoring the temple. "Is it a time for you yourselves to be living in your paneled houses, while this house remains a ruin?" (Haggai 1:4).

A further indication of Solomon falling away from the guidelines of the covenantal king was his emphasis of building up chariots and horses for the defense of the nation. "(...Solomon rebuilt Gezer.) He built up lower Beth Horon, Baalath, and Tadmor in the desert, within his land, as well as all his store cities and the *towns for his chariots and for his horses*—whatever he desired to build in Jerusalem, in Lebanon and throughout all the territory he ruled" (1 Kgs. 9:17–19, emphasis mine).

Solomon was dedicating towns for the purpose of housing the number of horses and chariots in his possession. Towns?? How massive was his collection of horses and chariots that he needed multiple towns to store them? This action goes beyond David taking a census and trusting in the sheer number of his army. This investment in military hardware goes directly against the specific guidelines for the monarchy provided by Moses. "The king, moreover, must not acquire great numbers of horses for himself or make the people return to Egypt to get more of them, for the LORD has told you, 'You are not to go back that way again'" (Deut. 17:16).

J. Robert Vannoy notes "...the Lord did not want Israel to create a military establishment...Saul had no chariots or horses. David had only a few. However, his son Solomon built cities to house his numerous chariots and horses...Solomon's policy established a pattern in Israel that continued to plague the nation throughout its history (Isa. 2:6–7[486])."[487]

To compound his error, Solomon received some of these horses from Egypt, which went against God's instructions to not rely on Egypt for any military assistance. "Solomon's horses were imported from Egypt and from Kue—the royal merchants purchased them from Kue at the current price. They imported a chariot from Egypt for six hundred shekels of silver, and a horse for a hundred and fifty. They also exported them to all the kings of the Hittites and of the Arameans" (1 Kgs. 10:28–29). Solomon clearly ignored the prohibition; he had so much wealth that he indulged in the activities of the pagan nations that served him.

Year after year, the amount of gold provided to Solomon increased beyond what anyone in modern times could image; so much so that silver was considered a common metal, not a precious metal. The gold itself seemed to be for Solomon's own personal purposes and not for the benefit of the nation. "King Solomon made two hundred large shields of hammered gold; six hundred shekels of gold went into each shield. He also made three hundred small shields of hammered gold, with three minas of gold in each shield. The king put them in the Palace of the Forest of Lebanon. Then the king made a great throne covered with ivory and overlaid with fine gold...All King Solomon's goblets were gold, and all the household articles in the Palace of the Forest of Lebanon were pure gold. Nothing was made of silver, because silver was considered of little value in Solomon's days" (1 Kgs. 10:16–18, 21).

Rather than easing the tax burdens on his people to fund his construction projects or redistributing income to the people, Solomon's use of gold was self-indulgent. In this regard, Iain Provan notes, "...the authors go out of their way in (chapters) 4–5 to emphasize that the

---

[486]"You, LORD, have abandoned your people, the descendants of Jacob. They are full of superstitions from the East; they practice divination like the Philistines and embrace pagan customs. Their land is full of silver and gold; there is no end to their treasures. Their land is full of horses; there is no end to their chariots."

[487]J. Robert Vannoy, *Cornerstone Biblical Commentary (Book 4): 1–2 Samuel*, 2009, p. 313.

prosperity of the king was shared with his subjects (cf. 4:20, 25 cited earlier). This theme is notable for its absence in 9:10–10:29, where all the emphasis lies upon the luxury of the royal court."[488] It would appear that his riches and splendor eventually caused him to lose site of the characteristics of the covenantal king that he established earlier in his reign.

His covenantal transgressions built up over time and led to Solomon abandoning God, driven mostly by the influence of his many pagan wives. "King Solomon, however, loved many foreign women besides Pharaoh's daughter—Moabites, Ammonites, Edomites, Sidonians and Hittites. They were from nations about which the LORD had told the Israelites, 'You must not intermarry with them, because they will surely turn your hearts after their gods.' Nevertheless, Solomon held fast to them in love" (1 Kgs. 11:1–2).

The accumulation of wealth and wives was precisely the prohibition Moses defined in Deuteronomy 17:17: "He must not take many wives, or his heart will be led astray. He must not accumulate large amounts of silver and gold."

It's difficult to imagine that, with all his wisdom and previous desire to serve God like his father David, Solomon would lose sight of Israel's fundamental commandment to not worship other idols. God's warning against intermarriage with pagans was reemphasized prior to the Israelites entering the Promised Land.[489] But Solomon's weakness for women caused him to fall away from both directives. Besides the Pharaoh's daughter, Solomon married women from all the surrounding pagan nations, the same nations God warned the Israelites not to intermarry. God was trying to protect His people from themselves.

The king was required to lead his people spiritually, but Solomon failed to maintain the First Great Commandment: to love God with

---

[488]Iain Provan, *1 & 2 Kings*, 1995, p. 85.

[489]"Be careful not to make a treaty with those who live in the land; for when they prostitute themselves to their gods and sacrifice to them, they will invite you and you will eat their sacrifices. And when you choose some of their daughters as wives for your sons and those daughters prostitute themselves to their gods, they will lead your sons to do the same'" (Exod. 34:15–16).

all your heart, soul, and strength. The fact that Solomon loved many foreign women clearly showed his heart was divided. It's no wonder Jesus warned against straddling the fence between loving God and loving things of this world. "'No one can serve two masters. Either you will hate the one and love the other, or you will be devoted to the one and despise the other. You cannot serve both God and money'" (Matt. 6:24). While He used the pursuit of money in this saying, it's applicable to Solomon and his love for women.

G. K. Beale observes that "God's command to Israel not to inter-marry was to protect them ultimately from intermarrying spiritually with idols and to enable them to be a faithful wife to Yahweh."[490] The warning came to fruition with Solomon. Early in his reign, Solomon appeared to be on the right path with God. His dedication to building the temple and the grand religious ceremony showed his heart had been with God. But even with all his wisdom, prosperity, and military power, God's gifts apparently were not enough to satisfy Solomon's earthly desires. He had seven hundred wives and three hundred con-cubines[491] and was only a matter of time before his wives led him astray. In fact, Josephus says of Solomon's pagan wives, "he soon was governed by them, until he came to imitate their practices. He was forced to give them this demonstration of his kindness and affection to them, to live according to the laws of their countries."[492]

---

[490]G. K. Beale, *We Become What We Worship,* 2008, p. 239.

[491]The number of women for Solomon is likely an exaggeration. David also had multiple wives (none of whom altered his devotion to God) and 10 concubines. Walter Brueggemann suggests, "It must have been galling to the traditional north that the king in Jerusalem has concubines. The presence of concubines suggests how much the monarchy has embraced the royal ideology of the Near East, which is inimical to the old covenant tradition...as a concession and a conciliatory gesture to the north...David moves visibly away from the royal ideology in the direction of the old requirements of covenant." *First and Second Samuel,* 1990, p. 330.

[492]Josephus, *Jewish Antiquities,* Book 8, Chapter 7, verse 193, p. 284. In his footnote, Whistone observes "...those very one thousand women intimated elsewhere by Solomon himself, when he speaks of his not having found one (good) woman among that very number." ("...while I was still searching but not finding—I found one upright man among a thousand, but not one upright woman among them all" [Eccl. 7:28]).

Walter Brueggemann suggests that the number of wives and concubines could indicate the king's preoccupation with sexuality. "It is more likely the case, however, that the many women in his court reflect endless political arrangements that are sealed and made visible by political marriages."[493] If that was the case, then Solomon was forgetting that it was God's blessing to provide peace in the land and political alliances through marriage were not necessary.

Patterson and Austel take another angle: "The many wives and concubines seem to be far more than necessary for diplomatic purposes and betray in Solomon a desire to display his wealth and grandeur. This necessarily increased the financial burden on his subjects and sowed seeds of rebellion, which came to fruition when his son became king."[494] I'll discuss this in the next chapter.

The real failing, however, was that Solomon's heart for God disappeared altogether; he resorted to worshiping the pagan idols proffered by his many wives. "As Solomon grew old, his wives turned his heart after other gods, and his heart was not fully devoted to the LORD his God, as the heart of David his father had been. He followed Ashtoreth the goddess of the Sidonians, and Molek the detestable god of the Ammonites...On a hill east of Jerusalem, Solomon built a high place for Chemosh the detestable god of Moab, and for Molek the detestable god of the Ammonites. He did the same for all his foreign wives, who burned incense and offered sacrifices to their gods" (1 Kgs. 11:4–5, 7–8).

The many wives were not necessarily the problem; turning Solomon's heart away from God was the real sin. All those years of dedication and obedience to God slowly eroded. He allowed himself to be influenced by his pagan wives, built altars at their request, and participated in the worship. From the spiritual heights at the opening of the temple to the nadir of pagan worship toward the end of his life, it's as if his mighty accomplishments on behalf of God never happened.

---

[493]Walter Brueggemann, *1 & 2 Kings,* 2000, p. 142.

[494]Richard Patterson and Hermann Austel, *The Expositor's Bible Commentary – 1 and 2 Kings,* 2009, p. 729.

The nation of Israel was dragged down with him. As Thomas Schreiner notes, "David's sin with Bathsheba and the murder of Uriah was egregious, but he never turned to other gods as Solomon did."[495]

You don't need to wonder how wealth, fame, authority—anything that satisfies worldly desires—would affect you over time. Solomon had God's love and blessings all those years, but he chose the trappings this world offered and still couldn't be satisfied. He finished his economic and urban development program; perhaps there was no further drive to build anything else. He was world renown for his wisdom, so additional fame would be moot. He didn't need to build up his wealth, it was already beyond measure.

Even Jesus referred to Solomon and his level of riches: "Consider how the wildflowers grow. They do not labor or spin. Yet I tell you, *not even Solomon in all his splendor* was dressed like one of these" (Luke 12:27, emphasis mine). Despite this nod to Solomon, T. W. Manson makes a condemning observation: "It is noteworthy that Jesus says nothing whatever about the other features of Solomon's greatness—his wealth, the splendor of his court, his magnificent buildings—although according to the Old Testament account, these also threw the Queen into ecstasies. Judging from what Jesus says elsewhere about the glories of Solomon, this omission would seem to be deliberate."[496]

Did Solomon have no challenges left in life and just allow himself to waste away? Robert Jamieson points to how having it all led to the downfall of Solomon's spiritual heart. "No sadder, more humiliating, or awful spectacle can be imagined than the besotted apostasy of his old age...A love of the world, a ceaseless round of pleasure, had insensibly corrupted his heart, and produced, for a while at least, a state of mental darkness. The grace of God deserted him; and the son of the pious David—the religiously trained child of Bathsheba...and pupil of

---

[495]Thomas Schreiner, *The King in His Beauty*, 2013, p. 175.

[496]T. W. Manson, *The Teaching of Jesus*, 2008, p. 271.

Nathan, instead of showing the stability of sound principle and mature experience became at last an old and foolish king."[497]

Paul House adds a similar insight. "'His heart was not fully devoted to the LORD his God, as the heart of David his father had been.' In other words, his heart was no longer wholly God's. The Lord had ceased to be the major factor in his life. Once this shift occurred, the next steps into idolatry became more natural and easier to accept."[498]

Eugene Merrill offers a bit more insight in the contradiction between Solomon's wisdom and his eventual spiritual demise. "[I]n the face of his preeminent wisdom, we must simply make the point that it is possible to be wise in the biblical sense of the term[499] and yet fail to live out the implication of this wisdom. Solomon's sin in multiplying wives and in turning after other gods does not vitiate the fact of his wisdom, but it certainly undercuts any claim on his part that he ordered his own life and that of his kingdom according to its principles."[500]

Iain Provan continues, "Wisdom and obedience to God are always in tension in the Solomon story, and ultimately, they become completely divorced. Solomon becomes, in fact, the very picture of a typical ancient Near Eastern god-king. He is no longer the Israelite king of Deuteronomy 17 who keeps the law of God constantly beside him and does not turn from it 'to the right or to the left.'"[501]

Then came God's rebuke of Solomon's sin: "The LORD became angry with Solomon because his heart had turned away from the LORD, the God of Israel, who had appeared to him twice. Although he had forbidden Solomon to follow other gods, Solomon did not

---

[497]Jamieson, Fausset & Brown, "Commentary on 1 Kings 11 by Jamieson, Fausset & Brown," Blue Letter Bible, last modified February 19, 2000, https://www.blueletterbible.org/ Comm/jfb/1Ki/1Ki_011.cfm.

[498]Paul House, *The New American Commentary: 1, 2 Kings,* 1995, p. 167.

[499]"The ability to live life in a skillful way—an ability, the Bible insists, that is possessed only by the individual who knows and fears God." Eugene Merrill, *Kingdom of Priests,* 2008, p. 329.

[500] Ibid., p. 330.

[501]Iain Provan, *Seriously Dangerous Religion,* 2014, p. 115.

keep the LORD's command" (1 Kgs. 11:9–10). He built altars and high places to several pagan idols and worshiped them in the same fashion as his wives. His dedication and obedience to God were forgotten or fell out of his heart, going totally against what both his father David had taught him and what God commanded him to do in His second communication with Solomon.

As God had promised, there would be consequences for Solomon's sinful behavior. "So the LORD said to Solomon, 'Since this is your attitude and you have not kept my covenant and my decrees, which I commanded you, I will most certainly tear the kingdom away from you and give it to one of your subordinates. Nevertheless, for the sake of David your father, I will not do it during your lifetime. I will tear it out of the hand of your son. Yet I will not tear the whole kingdom from him but will give him one tribe for the sake of David my servant and for the sake of Jerusalem, which I have chosen'" (1 Kgs. 11:11–13).[502] The judgement against Solomon led to the dissolution of the nation; God stripped his successor of all but one tribe (Judah) and gave the rest to a servant of Solomon. While the bulk of the nation was given to a mere servant and not a relative or member of society worthy of ruling them, God preserved David's dynasty for David's sake, and he preserved Jerusalem for the same reason.

Interestingly, Scripture makes no mention of Solomon recognizing his sin or asking God for forgiveness. Judgement came to him directly from God and not through a prophet or through his own realization like his father David. David's spiritual heart helped him to immediately realize his sin. He didn't want to lose face with God, and he was remorseful for having caused a fracture in their relationship. On the contrary, when Cain murdered his brother Abel, God afforded Cain the opportunity to beg for forgiveness, which he did not do. Solomon was given the same opportunity, but there is no mention of remorse or atonement from Solomon. Scriptures are silent as to

---

[502]To portray David's descendants in a positive light, the books of Chronicles do not include Solomon's disobedience, just as it doesn't report David's sin with Bathsheba.

Solomon's reaction to God's condemnation, which indicates how numb Solomon's heart had become.

God defers his ultimate judgment of splitting the nation until Solomon's son Rehoboam reigned; however, Solomon did not escape other consequences. God allowed the Edomites and tribes from Syria (that had earlier been subdued by David) to rise up and wage war against Solomon. The peace that Israel enjoyed for years was replaced by wars and threats of war. Hadad, a member of Edomite royalty, was a survivor of those earlier battles against David and Joab but escaped to Egypt as a young boy with some of his father's officials. The reigning Pharaoh took them in and provided shelter and an alliance. Years later, when the news of Joab and David's deaths reached him, Hadad returned to Israel to wage war as vengeance on Solomon toward the end of Solomon's reign (yet another instance of Egypt's influence that plagued Israel).

God sent another adversary that caused problems from the north. "And God raised up against Solomon another adversary, Rezon son of Eliada, who had fled from his master, Hadadezer king of Zobah. When David destroyed Zobah's army, Rezon gathered a band of men around him and became their leader; they went to Damascus, where they settled and took control. Rezon was Israel's adversary as long as Solomon lived, adding to the trouble caused by Hadad. So Rezon ruled in Aram and was hostile toward Israel" (1 Kgs. 11:23–25).

Amid the military conflicts, Jeroboam, the servant who took over the 10 northern tribes, was sent to the south to be in charge of the work force in that area. Solomon had previously assigned him to be in charge of the labor forces during construction of the government buildings and his work ethic was admired by the king. On his way, Jeroboam was met by Ahijah, a prophet from Shiloh. Ahijah told him that God was about to split the nation of Israel; the ten tribes in the north would be taken from Solomon and given to Jeroboam. "'I will do this because they have forsaken me and worshiped Ashtoreth the goddess of the Sidonians, Chemosh the god of the Moabites, and Molek the god of the Ammonites, and have not walked in obedience to me, nor done what is right in my eyes, nor kept my decrees and laws as David, Solomon's father, did'" (1 Kgs. 11:33).

God promised Jeroboam he would reign over Israel and prosper, subject to one simple caveat: "If you do whatever I command you and walk in obedience to me and do what is right in my eyes by obeying my decrees and commands, as David my servant did, I will be with you. I will build you a dynasty as enduring as the one I built for David and will give Israel to you" (v. 38). This was the same covenant God made with Solomon that he failed to keep; but if Jeroboam remained obedient and faithful, God would reward him.

Solomon found out that God appointed Jeroboam and sought to have him killed. Jeroboam escaped to Egypt where he remained until Solomon's death. Solomon's frame of heart resembled Saul's attempt to eliminate David. Solomon was concerned for his throne even though God told him the split would take place during his son's reign. Just like Saul tried to circumvent God's plan to have David rule, Solomon attempted to take things into his own hand. His heart had truly turned from God at that point.

Despite Solomon's wisdom, Graeme Goldsworthy accurately notes, "Solomon is suddenly portrayed as a covenant-breaker, a philanderer, a political opportunist and an idolator...Solomon's reversal becomes the trigger for all subsequent national acts of renewed idolatry and rebellion against God. Thus, the supremely tragic irony of Solomon is that he who glorified Zion by building the temple became the architect of its ultimate destruction."[503] This brings to mind the condition of Samson from the book of Judges, whose demise was also caused by his love for women above his dedication to God. The difference between them, however, was that Samson asked for God's forgiveness at the end and dedicated his last, self-sacrificial act to God. Solomon did not repent but allowed his heart to lose all the grace he demonstrated earlier. In fact, he sought to murder the one to whom God would give the northern nation of Israel.

---

[503]Graeme Goldsworthy, *Christ-Centered Biblical Theology*, 2012, p. 127.

Solomon's fall from grace resounded throughout the nation of Israel. Some 500 years later when the returning exiled Israelites were rebuilding Jerusalem, Nehemiah, governor of the Hebrews at the time, used Solomon's marriages to foreigners as a warning to his people. This practice was still occurring, and it was one of the spiritual reforms he and the high priest Ezra tried to correct. "Was it not because of marriages like these that Solomon king of Israel sinned? Among the many nations there was no king like him. He was loved by his God, and God made him king over all Israel, but even he was led into sin by foreign women. Must we hear now that you too are doing all this terrible wickedness and are being unfaithful to our God by marrying foreign women?" (Neh. 13:26-27).[504]

---

[504]The Jews returning to Jerusalem from their captivity in Babylon spend several years rebuilding the temple under Zerubbabel their governor and the spiritual leadership of the prophets Haggai and Zechariah. The temple was completed around 516 BC. There was still more work to be done, both spiritually and in the reconstruction of Jerusalem. Around 50 years later, Ezra, who was a scribe and was learned in the wisdom of the Mosaic law, requested permission from the King Artaxerxes (Persian emperor) to return to Jerusalem to revive their hearts for God. Nehemiah followed 12 years later to help restore the city and its wall to keep their enemies out. When the wall was completed, both Ezra and Nehemiah focused their attention on the moral level of the people and restored their total obedience to God. The purpose was not to repeat the sins of the past and one of the most blatant examples was the widespread intermarriage, even among the Levites and priests. By decree, all such marriages were prohibited and those who were involved had to rid themselves of their spouses.

Chapter 11

WHERE THE KING'S HEART GOES,
SO GOES THE NATION

M oving beyond Solomon's reign, Scriptures revealed that kings with faith and obedience like David's lead the hearts of the people to follow in the same direction. The king kept the covenantal obligation to direct the people along their spiritual path and reflect God's holy representatives on earth. Richard Patterson and Hermann Austel tell us that, "As kings, Solomon and his successors were responsible for the whole nation. Failure on the king's part affected all the people. Israel's subsequent history amply illustrates this principle: As the king went, so went the people."[505]

From the beginning of the monarchy, writes J. Robert Vannoy, "Israel's kinship was established by the word of a prophet...The king was required to submit to the laws of the Sinai covenant as well as the Lord's word through his prophet."[506] In the case of Saul, while he didn't lead the Israelites to worshiping false gods, he did not have the spiritual heart required to focus on his role as the spiritual leader of his people; he did not adhere to the law and definitely did not obey the words of the prophet Samuel. In contrast, David excelled in leading the nation in unity to worship and sacrifice to God and followed the words of his prophets, albeit not perfectly.

---

[505]Richard Patterson and Hermann Austel, *The Expositor's Bible Commentary – 1 and 2 Kings,* 2009, p. 715. (The wording in this reference and the title of the chapter are a happy coincidence.)

[506]J. Robert Vannoy, *Cornerstone Biblical Commentary (Book 4): 1 – 2 Samuel,* 2009, p. 28.

Solomon followed in the spiritual heart of his father David and his people continued their dedication to the Lord. At the beginning of his reign, he pulled the nation together to worship God in unison as his father had and led the people spiritually. By building the temple of Jerusalem, he created the single focal point for the nation's worship as God directed Moses.[507] Solomon led his people in corporate worship and the nation enjoyed the height of its spirituality and prosperity. But it was that prosperity and his many wives that eventually led to Solomon's downfall. Consequently, God's judgement stripped a large part of the nation away from David's lineage. However, God did not totally abandon David's ancestors as He did with Saul.

The introduction of idolatry, which Solomon initiated at the end of his reign (a practice that had ceased from Saul's time through much of Solomon's reign, totaling more than 100 years), would be the cancer afflicting the Israelites' culture that would last 400 years. Despite the many prophets sent to rescue it, the northern nation of Israel never experienced a spiritual revival. The people followed the same pagan practices that plagued them since the time of Moses in the wilderness. There were some remnants of the faithful during this time, but for the most part, the nation followed the king's lead. For the next 250 years, the northern nation of Israel would be led by 20 kings, all of whom did evil in the eyes of the Lord and paganism and idolatry spread throughout the culture. God's punishment for the northern nation was their destruction by the Assyrians who obliterated the northern nation in 722 BC and led the survivors out of Israel into captivity.

The southern nation of Judah faired a bit better; they also had 20 kings, eight of whom followed in David's faithfulness and obedience to God's will. These faithful kings did their best to return the people of Judah back to God, all with limited success. That success lasted only while they ruled over Judah, similar to the circumstances of the judges in Chapter 6. When the kings worshiped pagan gods, the people followed suit. This disobedience ended when Babylon captured Jerusalem,

---

[507]"But you are to seek the place the LORD your God will choose from among all your tribes to put his Name there for his dwelling. To that place you must go" (Deut. 12:5).

destroyed the temple, and led the people into exile in the same manner as the Assyrians captured their northern kin 140 years earlier. After 70 years in captivity, the remnant of the Jewish population returned to their homeland and slowly rebuilt everything that was lost.

In this chapter, we'll see that obedience to God was highly driven by the king's heart. In the southern nation of Judah, where the king was faithful to God's word, pagan worship was terminated and there was a revival in the spiritual hearts of the people. When the faithful king died, he was typically followed by one who led the people back into idolatry. Anthony Hoekema refers to these as national conversions, which he notes "...were short-lived. They certainly did not bring about the true conversion of every member of the nation. In the case of Israel, after the godly ruler had been succeeded by an evil one, the people went back to their sinful ways."[508]

The Nation's Heart is Divided

When Solomon died, his son Rehoboam traveled to Shechem, located in the area of the northern tribes, where he sought their endorsement as king. David Guzik observes that Rehoboam's political position in the north was tenuous at best. Shechem was the place where Abraham and Jacob built altars and it was where Joseph was buried. "Shechem was also the geographical center of the northern tribes. All in all, it showed that Rehoboam was in a position of weakness, having to meet the ten northern tribes on *their* territory, instead of demanding that representatives come to Jerusalem."[509] Frederick Mabie concurs: "Rehoboam's journey to Shechem implies the importance of securing the support of the northern tribes—and that such support was not automatic."[510]

---

[508] Anthony Hoekema, *Saved by Grace,* 1994, p. 116.

[509] David Guzik, "Study Guide for 1 Kings 12 by David Guzik," Blue Letter Bible, Last Modified February 21, 2017, https://www.blueletterbible.org/Comm/guzik_david/StudyGuide 2017-1Ki/1Ki-12.cfm.

[510] Frederick Mabie, *The Expositor's Bible Commentary – 1 and 2 Chronicles,* 2010, p. 204.

It was difficult to keep the tribes unified when David was made king following Saul's death. David's base of followers was initially limited to just the tribe of Judah, and he had to work hard to get the northern tribes united under his authority because they were loyal to king Saul. Eugene Merrill notes, "Only by the most creative and winsome kind of diplomacy was David able to extend his rule over the north, even so it took over seven years. But the apparent unity he thereby achieved was nothing more than a facade, for Absalom instigated his rebellion by fanning the flames of the smoldering Judah-Israel antagonism."[511]

Robert Hubbard concurs: "Absalom's nearly successful coup suggests how shaky was David's power base in his own homeland of Judah. (Hubbard notes that Absalom's co-conspirators included some of David's close supporters; the high priest Ahithophel and his general Amassa). Those still loyal to Saul, especially his fellow Benjamites, apparently viewed David as a callous usurper who had entirely connived his way to power."[512]

There were a few instances under David's united reign where the fragile unity showed signs of fracture. Shimei was a loyalist to Saul, as were many other Benjamites who weren't happy that David took over the throne. When Absalom was killed and the coup ended, David returned to Jerusalem. During the trek, there was a serious argument among the troops (most of whom were David's troops, but part of the army was from the northern tribes) whether it should be Judah or Israel leading David back to Jerusalem. Judah prevailed, but not without hard feelings from the men of the northern tribes.

Later in David's reign, there was another rebellion in the north refusing to recognize his authority. Sheba, a member of Saul's tribe, was their leader. "Now a troublemaker named Sheba son of Bikri, a Benjamite, happened to be there. He sounded the trumpet and shouted, 'We have no share in David, no part in Jesse's son! Every man to his tent, Israel!' So all the men of Israel deserted David to follow

---

[511]Eugene Merrill, 2008, *Kingdom of Priests,* 2008, p. 334.

[512]Robert Hubbard, *The Book of Ruth,* 1988, p. 44.

Sheba son of Bikri. But the men of Judah stayed by their king all the way from the Jordan to Jerusalem" (2 Sam. 20:1–2).

J. Robert Vannoy notes, "that Sheba could convince the northern troops to abandon David at such a crucial moment demonstrates the vulnerability of David's status as a ruler over a united kingdom including both Judah and the northern tribes...The underlying weakness of northern support for David had apparently never been fully overcome and Sheba was able to exploit a long-simmering discontent."[513]

David successfully put down the rebellion, but the underlying friction continued. There was no explicit reference to continued resentment of the northern tribes under Solomon's reign. However, all of the urban development for the nation took place in Jerusalem, which included the temple, Solomon's palace, and several government buildings. There had to be considerable jealousy on behalf of the northern tribes because Jerusalem and all its glory was centered in Judah.

It was also quite possible that the northern tribes bore a disproportionate share of Solomon's urban development in Jerusalem by way of taxes and forced labor during construction. Eugene Merrill suggests that the southern tribe of Judah may have escaped that burden and identifies it as the key for the schism. "Given Solomon's Judahite ancestry, exemption from taxation, forced labor and other burdens is understandable, but such exemption also may have been the single most contributing factor in the division after his death."[514] Merrill continues that during the development, Solomon deliberately exempted Judah from his labor and taxation. In 1 Kings 4:7, "Solomon had twelve district governors over all Israel, who supplied provisions for the king and the royal household. Each one had to provide supplies for one month in the year." Scriptures list each of twelve districts and Judah

---

[513]J. Robert Vannoy, *Cornerstone Biblical Commentary (Book 4): 1–2 Samuel,* 2009, pp. 390–91.

[514]Eugene Merrill, *Kingdom of Priests,* 2008, p. 324. Merrill adds in his footnote that the discriminatory treatment was in fact a major issue in the division of the kingdom.

is conspicuously absent from the list.[515] This tax and labor burden had to be on the minds of the northern tribes when Rehoboam met with them in Shechem.

Adding to this perspective, Paul House quotes J. A. Soggin who argues that "the northern tribes began to feel that they were shouldering more than their share of the tax and conscripted burden. Perhaps they believed Judah received special treatment for being David's clan."[516] Despite Scriptures noting that Solomon did not make slaves of any of the Israelites, House states, "The distinction is a technical one. The Canaanites were *permanent* corvee workers, while the Israelites were temporary draftees. Regardless of the technical differences, the northern tribes came to resent the practices bitterly, as later texts reveal."[517]

Meanwhile, when Jeroboam heard of Solomon's death, he returned from his self-imposed exile in Egypt and joined the representatives of the northern tribes. The leaders of Israel assembled before the new king and asked Rehoboam how he will rule, cognizant of the burden his father had previously placed upon them. "'Your father put a heavy yoke on us, but now lighten the harsh labor and the heavy yoke he put on us, and we will serve you'" (2 Chronicles 10:4).

The northern tribes were willing to continue their alliance with the king if he would reduce the fiscal and labor oppression under Solomon's massive building efforts. In fact, Jeroboam initially came back to lend his support to Rehoboam, even though God promised he would get to rule the northern tribes. As J. D. Pentecost notes, "Jeroboam demonstrated no rebellion or threat to become king over part of the nation, nor did he aspire to rule over the whole nation. He showed submission to Rehoboam and came with the rest of the assembly to crown Rehoboam."[518] Rehoboam told the northern representatives that he would respond to their inquiry in three days.

---

[515] Ibid., p. 391.

[516] Paul House, *The New American Commentary: 1, 2 Kings,* 1995, p. 156.

[517] Ibid.

[518] J. Dwight Pentecost, *Thy Kingdom Come,* 1995, p. 160.

Rather than listen to the advice of his father's experienced counselors who advocated for a more benign rule, Rehoboam followed the advice of the younger court members; those he grew up with. They suggested that he should rule the northern tribes with more severity than his father Solomon to keep them in line. Nowhere in this discussion did Rehoboam consider what God wanted him to do. Rather than show a kind and compassionate heart to the tribes in the north, he ignored the guidelines of the covenantal king.

When he announced that his rule would be much more severe than his father, the people of the north rebelled. "When all Israel saw that the king refused to listen to them, they answered the king: 'What share do we have in David, what part in Jesse's son? To your tents, Israel! Look after your own house, David!' So the Israelites went home" (1 Kgs. 12:16). Eugene Merrill adds, "Theirs is a complaint about not only the heavy burdens per se but also the discriminatory burdens. The very silence of the people of Judah regarding this oppression says clearly they were not its victims."[519]

The northern tribes returned to their homes and refused to recognize Rehoboam as king. For them to refuse his authority so readily demonstrated how fragile the relationship was between the two states. Rather than offer an olive branch, Rehoboam further aggravated the situation by sending Adoniram back into the northern lands. Even though he was in charge of forced labor for non-Israelites, the northern tribes took his presence as a message of Rehoboam's mandate. They killed Adoniram and Rehoboam fled to Jerusalem.

The northern tribes anointed Jeroboam as king and the nation was divided. The seeds of discontent from the northern tribes that began under David's reign came to full bloom. God's prophecy of punishment for Solomon's disobedience was now a reality. Rehoboam wanted to show a strong hand against the northern tribes and his actions backfired. House writes, "One incredibly poor decision tears down in a few days what David and Solomon labored eighty years to build."[520]

---

[519]Eugene Merrill, *Kingdom of Priests,* 2008, p. 324.

[520]Paul House, *The New American Commentary: 1, 2 Kings,* 1995, p. 182.

In realty, he could not have prevented the split of the nation; it was God's will. Showing no real heart for the Lord proved that he was the right man to cause the fulfillment of God's punishment.

Meanwhile, as the newly appointed king in the north, Jeroboam made the monumental mistake of not trusting God's promise that, if he walked in David's footsteps, his rule over Israel would be secure. Rather than rely on God's word, he devised his own plan to secure his kingship. He feared that the people in the north would continue to flock to Jerusalem to worship in the temple and while there, fall back into allegiance with Rehoboam. Jeroboam feared a counter-revolution and that it would undermine his rule and lead to his own death. "Jeroboam thought to himself, 'The kingdom will now likely revert to the house of David. If these people go up to offer sacrifices at the temple of the LORD in Jerusalem, they will again give their allegiance to their lord, Rehoboam king of Judah. They will kill me and return to King Rehoboam'" (1 Kgs. 12:26–27).

To keep his people from traveling south to worship during the many festivals, he created two separate places of worship in the north: one in Bethel and one in Dan. These altars would keep the people worshiping in the north instead of traveling to Jerusalem. In addition, he created his own festivals and established his own system for appointing the clergy. "Jeroboam built shrines on high places and appointed priests from all sorts of people, even though they were not Levites. He instituted a festival on the fifteenth day of the eighth month, like the festival held in Judah, and offered sacrifices on the altar. This he did in Bethel, sacrificing to the calves he had made. And at Bethel he also installed priests at the high places he had made" (1 Kgs. 12:31–32).

Relying on his own plan rather than trusting in God was reminiscent of the mistakes made by Saul, who often took matters into his own hands. Christopher Wright describes Rehoboam's motivation, "His intention was clearly to protect his own nascent kingdom from any popular hankering after the splendor of Jerusalem (vv. 26–27). To make completely sure, he elaborated an alternative cultic system for the northern kingdom, totally designed, appoint, and run by himself an all to serve the interest of his state (vv. 31–33).”[521]

Placing altars in both cities violated God's long-standing command to worship in one place, and this transgression was further compounded in his placement of an altar in Bethel. Historically, it was the site of several altars placed in honor of and worship to God and it was somewhat ironic that Jeroboam placed an unauthorized, pagan altar there. It was the sacred site where God spoke to Abraham and Jacob: a hallowed ground. Abraham placed his first altar there. Jacob dreamt of angels ascending to heaven and built altars to God there twice. In the book of Judges, the people of Israel asked the Lord who should march against the Benjamites for the sin against a traveling Levite. Samuel the prophet used the city as the starting point for his annual circuits throughout Israel in his role as a judge. Despite the sanctity of the site, Jeroboam set up false idols to worship, instead of the one true God.

Creating these altars led to the northern nation of Israel worshiping false idols for the next two centuries until it was destroyed by the Assyrians in 722 BC. As one of many prophets who later warned Israel against idolatry, Amos[522] condemned these practices. “‘Hear this and testify against the descendants of Jacob,’ declares the LORD, the LORD God Almighty. ‘On the day I punish Israel for her sins, I will destroy the altars of Bethel; the horns of the altar will be cut off and fall to the ground’” (Amos 3:13–14).

Behold Jeroboam's disastrous actions. “After seeking advice, the king made two golden calves. He said to the people, ‘It is too much for you to go up to Jerusalem. Here are your gods, Israel, who brought you up out of Egypt.’ One he set up in Bethel, and the other in Dan” (1 Kgs. 12:28–29). The errors of Jeroboam continued. “And this thing became a sin; the people came to worship the one at Bethel and went as far as Dan to worship the other. Jeroboam built shrines on high places and appointed priests from all sorts of people, even though they

---

[521]Christopher Wright, *Old Testament Ethics for the People of God*, 2004, p.235.

[522]C. Hassell Bullock, *An Introduction to the Old Testament Prophetic Books,* 2007, pp. 80–81.

were not Levites. He instituted a festival on the fifteenth day of the eighth month, like the festival held in Judah, and offered sacrifices on the altar. This he did in Bethel, sacrificing to the calves he had made. And at Bethel he also installed priests at the high places he had made" (1 Kgs. 12:30–32).

Jeroboam clearly violated God's instructions even though He guaranteed his position. As Iain Provan is right to point out: "The new king has built a temple outside Jerusalem that infringes the prohibition in Deuteronomy 12; created a priesthood that has blurred the important distinction between those set apart by God for priestly service (here **Levites**) and those simply of the **people** (cf. Num. 3–4) and invented a festival celebrated on a date with no divine significance whatsoever."[523]

On his own, Jeroboam did nothing to deserve being king over Israel; it was a judgment against Solomon's transgressions. God required His people to have one, central place of worship: Jerusalem. He wanted corporate worship from the people. Jeroboam not only set up two worship sites, but other temples in high places and appointed priests who were not of the tribe of Levi. All of this was prohibited by God during Israel's wandering in the desert centuries before.

Jeroboam's most egregious sin was that he made two golden calves as idols and said to the people, "'Here are your gods, O Israel, who brought you up out of the land of Egypt'" (1 Kgs. 12:28). This was the same mistake the Israelites made in the desert while Moses was at Mount Sinai, with virtually the same words. "So all the people took off their earrings and brought them to Aaron. He took what they handed him and made it into an idol cast in the shape of a calf, fashioning it with a tool. Then they said, '*These are your gods, Israel, who brought you up out of Egypt.*' When Aaron saw this, he built an altar in front of the calf and announced, 'Tomorrow there will be a festival to the LORD'" (Exod. 32:3–5, emphasis mine).

Scripture doesn't tell us how long Jeroboam was in Egypt where he fled from King Solomon, but it must have been long enough to influence his religious persona. He was selected by God to take

---

[523]Iain Provan, *1 & 2 Kings*, 1995, p. 111.

the northern kingdom from Solomon's successors. God even gave Jeroboam the same governance guarantee that He granted to Solomon if he remained obedient to God's commandments. But Jeroboam's heart was geared for the secular world and not the spiritual dedication that was demonstrated by David. Like Saul, Jeroboam followed his own heart to make his decisions and totally ignored the gift God had provided him. In essence, Jeroboam did not trust that God would keep His promise to him.

God even provided Jeroboam with an opportunity to repent by sending him a prophet who brought judgement against his altars. "By the word of the LORD he cried out against the altar: 'Altar, altar! This is what the LORD says: "A son named Josiah will be born to the house of David.[524] On you he will sacrifice the priests of the high places who make offerings here, and human bones will be burned on you"'" (1 Kgs. 13:2). When the king heard the condemnation, he ordered the prophet be arrested. As he reached out to seize the prophet, God caused the king's hand to shrivel with paralysis. It was restored upon the king's pleadings, but Scriptures say, "Even after this, Jeroboam did not change his evil ways, but once more appointed priests for the high places from all sorts of people. Anyone who wanted to become a priest he consecrated for the high places. This was the sin of the house of Jeroboam that led to its downfall and to its destruction from the face of the earth" (1 Kgs. 13:33–34).

Jeroboam's heart was unchanged, even in the face of his own personal miracle. He disregarded the covenant God arranged with him and sought to preserve his kingdom through his own actions rather than be obedient to God's commandments. His heart was consumed by his desire to keep his throne, much like Saul; however, Saul did not

---

[524]Josiah was the last of the Judean kings faithful to God and would appear 300 years after this prophecy. "Then Josiah looked around, and when he saw the tombs that were there on the hillside, he had the bones removed from them and burned on the altar to defile it, *in accordance with the word of the LORD proclaimed by the man of God who foretold these things*" (2 Kgs. 23:16, emphasis mine). As Walter Brueggemann notes, "Josiah is portrayed as the ultimate Torah keeper who gives closure to the historic narrative, a closure that corresponds the Torah-keeping piety of Moses at the outset of the history." *1 & 2 Kings*, 2000, p. 168. Josiah's contribution will be discussed later in this chapter.

turn to worshiping idols. Jeroboam did not stop his downward spiral with building temples for false idols. He appointed anyone at will to be priests and erected additional altars in high places for his people to worship idols.

As a result of his maneuvers, Jeroboam stripped the northern nation of all its religious connections to God. In a significant display of their spiritual hearts, all the priests, Levites, and righteous laymen that were still in the north left their property and possessions in Israel to return to Jerusalem where God's commands were still the order of the day. "The priests and Levites from all their districts throughout Israel sided with him [Rehoboam]. The Levites even abandoned their pasturelands and property and came to Judah and Jerusalem, because Jeroboam and his sons had rejected them as priests of the LORD when he appointed his own priests for the high places and for the goat and calf idols he had made. Those from every tribe of Israel who set their hearts on seeking the LORD, the God of Israel, followed the Levites to Jerusalem to offer sacrifices to the LORD, the God of their ancestors" (2 Chron. 11:13–16).

Think about the significance of this. The spiritual hearts of these people were so strong that they readily gave up their land, property rights, and possessions to continue in their faith in God rather than remain behind to fall into sin. I mentioned earlier that not all of Israel fell into idolatry when apostasy settled in the land. This speaks volumes for those who continued in faith rather than remain in economic and physical comfort. Sacrificing all of their worldly possessions cannot be understated. Lot could not give up the comfort of his secular life to return with Abraham, but Ruth left her life in Moab to stay with Naomi. The strength of these Israelites' faith was beyond the physical trappings of the world. It is the same strength of faith the apostles and disciples demonstrated in following Jesus during His mission. It bears repeating: "For where your treasure is, there your heart will be also" (Luke 12:34).

Jeroboam's plan to prevent people emigrating back to Jerusalem backfired. Those in obedience to God left Israel and the remaining Israelites fell in line with worshiping the golden calves that had been erected in those temples. Jeroboam not only left himself and his family at risk for his sins, but more damning, he led the entire northern nation into a spiritual death spiral that resulted in its destruction by Assyria less than 200 years later.

In the south, Judah fared no better under Rehoboam. He had the benefit of the returning Levites and priests, as well as God's faithful who emigrated from Israel, and for three years he stayed on the right track. But in a sudden change of heart, once he felt his throne was secure, he picked up where Solomon left off. Rather than lead the people in faith, Rehoboam allowed for the same pagan practices as seen in the north. "After Rehoboam's position as king was established and he had become strong, he and all Israel with him abandoned the law of the LORD" (2 Chron. 12:1). The spiritual heart of Judah fell under the same disobedient practices that plagued the Israelites from the days of Moses. Rehoboam was following in his father's footsteps by installing altars in high places and allowing prostitution to be part of the worshiping process.

Judah replicated the sins of their forefathers during the period of the judges. Worse yet, their behavior was no different than the pagan nations God drove out when putting the nation together under Saul and David's reign. "Judah did evil in the eyes of the LORD. By the sins they committed they stirred up his jealous anger more than those who were before them had done. They also set up for themselves high places, sacred stones and Asherah poles on every high hill and under every spreading tree. There were even male shrine prostitutes in the land; the people engaged in all the detestable practices of the nations the LORD had driven out before the Israelites" (1 Kgs. 14:22–24).

There were huge economic consequences of Judah turning to idolatry a scant three years into Rehoboam's reign. God allowed the Egyptians to invade the southern nation and strip it of its wealth. Egypt attacked the southern nation with a huge army: "With twelve hundred chariots and sixty thousand horsemen and the innumerable troops of Libyans, Sukkites and Cushites that came with him from Egypt, he captured the fortified cities of Judah and came as far as Jerusalem" (2 Chron. 12:3–4). Egypt would have carried their attack into Jerusalem itself, but Rehoboam's prophet urged the king and his court to repent of their sins, citing that the success of the invasion was evidence of God's judgement for their transgressions. God spared the temple from destruction as the king and his court humbled themselves in repentance, but He did allow the Egyptians to strip Judah of its wealth. All the treasures that David and Solomon accumulated were taken as pillage. "In the fifth year of King Rehoboam, Shishak king of Egypt attacked Jerusalem. He carried off the treasures of the temple of the LORD and the treasures of the royal palace. He took everything, including all the gold shields Solomon had made" (1 Kgs. 14:25–26).

Thus, Rehoboam led Judah into sin the last 17 years of his reign and suffered at the hands of the Egyptians; however, neither the king nor the people returned to God. As Scriptures close the book on his reign, "He did evil because he had not set his heart on seeking the LORD" (2 Chron. 12:14). The nation of Israel that David built, and Solomon solidified was permanently divided and both nations were headed for destruction for their disobedience and lack of faith.

The Northern Tribes' Failure to Restore Their Hearts

The northern nation of Israel had set a course for their spiritual destruction. While Judah regained its faith sporadically under David's lineage, Israel no longer had ties to the dynasty, the temple, Jerusalem, or with God. Eugene Merrill writes, "With its moorings to the temple and the Davidic dynasty now loosened, the northern kingdom of Israel found itself adrift in a sea of paganism, acting precisely like all the other nations."[525] With no connection to the Davidic dynasty and the promise of God's protection gone, there was only chaos in the monarchy in the north. There were periods of succession but any passing of authority by generation did not endure for any length of

---

[525]Eugene Merrill, *A Commentary on 1 & 2 Chronicles*, 2015, p. 436.

time.[526] What was consistent was those successive kings did evil in the sight of God. Apostasy, idolatry, and social injustice were the norm as their spiritual hearts flickered then totally died out when the Assyrians destroyed the nation.

God did not abandoned Israel altogether; prophets were sent to warn the kings and leaders to repent and reform, but they didn't. For example, during the Omri dynasty[527] God dispatched the prophets Elijah, Micaiah, and Elisha to what may be acknowledged as the spiritually worst of the northern kings. Regarding Elijah and Elisha, Walter Kaiser notes their "direct involvements into the political arena of the northern kingdom were more pronounced in their actions than in their speaking... Elijah's work featured the divine judicial power opposing a rebellious people who were set on bringing themselves wholesale destruction; Elisha was the dispenser of divine blessing when the people repented."[528]

In the decades prior to Israel's fall, the prophets Amos, Micah, and Isaiah warned the nation of its inevitable doom. They were great prophets in their time, but their warnings were ignored. God even granted military success against great odds to demonstrate He was still with them. Despite these victories, the kings continued in their pagan practices.

When Jeroboam died, the succession of kings resembled a Shakespearian tragedy. His son Nadab took the throne and continued the pagan worship begun by his father. "He did evil in the eyes of the LORD, following the ways of his father and committing the same sin his father had caused Israel to commit" (1 Kgs. 15:26). He was on the throne only one year when he was killed by a conspirator named Baasha while Israel was involved in a military campaign against the Philistines. Baasha became king (reigning for 24 years) and continued

---

[526]There are four distinct dynasties during the first 175 years and myriad kings in the last 30 years of Israel's existence. Jeroboam began his reign around 930 BC and the nation survived until 722 BC.

[527]Omri was followed in family succession by Ahab, Ahaziah, and Joram. The dynasty lasted from 865 BC through 817 BC.

[528]Walter Kaiser, *The Promise-Plan of God*, 2008, p. 155.

eschewing God's favor. Scriptures say he spent most of his reign in war against Judah. When Baasha died, he was succeeded by his son Elah who continued to follow in his father's pagan ways.

Elah was on the throne two years when one of his military commanders, Zimri, killed him and the entire royal family, thereby claiming the throne for himself. "As soon as he began to reign and was seated on the throne, he killed off Baasha's whole family. He did not spare a single male, whether relative or friend" (1 Kgs. 16:11). However, the military was still loyal to Baasha's family and when they learned of the assassination, they marched against Zimri under the command of their general, Omri. When Zimri found out that there was a countercoup heading toward him, he committed suicide by setting his palace on fire and died within it. He was only on the throne for a week when Omri replaced him as king.

Israel's spiritual vacuum continued. Omri reigned 12 years, continuing the pagan practices of the past. When he died, his son, Ahab inherited the throne, reigning for the next 22 years. Ahab had the reputation for being the least spiritual leader of all the kings of Israel. "Ahab son of Omri did more evil in the eyes of the LORD than any of those before him. He not only considered it trivial to commit the sins of Jeroboam son of Nebat, but he also married Jezebel daughter of Ethbaal king of the Sidonians and began to serve Baal and worship him. He set up an altar for Baal in the temple of Baal that he built in Samaria. Ahab also made an Asherah pole and did more to arouse the anger of the LORD, the God of Israel, than did all the kings of Israel before him" (1 Kgs. 16:30–33). Ahab, more than any other king, led the nation in worshiping everything but God. However, the real driver behind the throne was Ahab's wife Jezebel.[529] As Solomon succumbed to following the practices of his pagan worshiping wives, Ahab did his wife's bidding and led the nation into a spiritual abyss.

---

[529]Richard Patterson and Hermann Austel, *The Expositor's Bible Commentary – 1 & 2 Kings*, 2009, p. 782. "Her personality was so forceful that even Ahab feared her and was corrupted by her." And according to 1 Kings 21:25: "(There was never anyone like Ahab, who sold himself to do evil in the eyes of the LORD, urged on by Jezebel his wife.)"

Through God, Elijah brought judgement on Ahab; a drought that brought a severe famine in the land.[530] After three years of no rain, God sent Elijah to confront Ahab, who believed Elijah was the cause of this curse. Elijah was the moral conscience of Israel and Jezebel was annoyed that he preached against the gods she worshiped.

Ahab was equally vexed by Elijah's messages from God. The king brought along one of his court administrators, Obadiah, who was secretly faithful to God despite the official pagan practices of the court. While Jezebel purged the nation of the priests, Obadiah hid 100 of them in caves and provided them with food and protection.[531]

When Elijah and Ahab met up at Mount Carmel. Elijah issued a challenge to the king. He suggests a contest to determine whether God or Baal should be worshiped in Israel. Two altars were erected—one for God and one for Baal—and Ahab called on all 450 Baal prophets (all favorites of Jezebel). Each team (actually, it was just Elijah and God against everyone else; not good odds for the bad guys) was to slaughter a bull to burn on the altar as a sacrifice, but each team must rely on their deity to set fire to the wood. Ahab's team prayed to Baal, and danced around their altar for hours, to no avail. "And at noon Elijah mocked them, saying, 'Cry aloud, for he is a god. Either he is musing, or he is relieving himself, or he is on a journey, or perhaps he is asleep and must be awakened'" (1 Kgs. 18:27, ESV).

Elijah mocked the Baal priests for their fruitless efforts and then he demonstrated God's power. After drenching his altar with water three times, he called upon God, who sent fire down, consuming the entire altar site. "When all the people saw this, they fell prostrate and cried, 'The LORD—he is God! The LORD—he is God!'" (1 Kgs. 18:39). Elijah ordered the people to slay all of Ahab's prophets and told

---

[530] Ahab worshiped Baal, the god of fertility. Pagans also expected Baal to provide rain. God caused a draught to prove how impotent their false idol was. (When God sent the ten plagues upon Egypt during Moses's time, each plague targeted a specific deity the Egyptians worshiped.

[531] In the introduction to this chapter, I mentioned that despite the nationwide apostasy, there were those whose hearts were still connected to God. Obadiah and the faithful prophets were some of those examples.

Ahab to return to his palace; God, in His mercy, will send rain and the nation will be agriculturally restored. Despite God defeating the pagan deity and ending the drought, there was no effort by Ahab to give up his pagan ways. In fact, when Ahab told Jezebel what occurred, she was enraged that her prophets were killed and issued a death warrant for Elijah.

Elijah fled and spent 40 days at Mount Horeb hiding. When God asked him why he was hiding, Elijah explained that he failed in his mission and was the only one left in Israel faithful to God, and now he had a contract out on him. God told him to go back to Damascus, anoint Jehu as king, and appoint Elisha to take over as prophet (not as a punishment, just to continue in God's message to the Israelites). God reminded him that he was not the only faithful one in Israel: "'Yet I reserve seven thousand in Israel—all whose knees have not bowed down to Baal and whose mouths have not kissed him'" (1 Kgs. 19:18).

God gave Ahab another opportunity to turn his heart back to Him. The king of Syria led a large army against Ahab and Israel and Israel's military was seriously outnumbered. "Meanwhile a prophet came to Ahab king of Israel and announced, 'This is what the LORD says: "Do you see this vast army? I will give it into your hand today, and then you will know that I am the LORD"'" (1 Kgs. 20:13). God assured Ahab that He would protect Israel against the enemy. Ahab commanded his troops to go down from the hills and they routed the Syrian army despite their smaller number. The same prophet warned Ahab that the Syrians would return in the spring and attack in the valley. Again, the Israelite military was seriously outnumbered, but they routed the Syrians because God provided them with the victory.

In the second battle, the king of Syria was captured and brought to Ahab. The king pled for his life and promised to give Ahab back the land he took from Israel. Rather than put him to death, Ahab agreed and released the king, but this was not in God's plan; He sent the prophet back to bring judgement on Ahab. "He said to the king, 'This is what the LORD says: "You have set free a man I had determined should die. Therefore it is your life for his life, your people for his people.'" Sullen and angry, the king of Israel went to his palace in Samaria" (1 Kgs. 20:42–43).

Ahab made the same mistakes as Saul. Neither of them realized how God provided them victories against a greater army and yet both of them decided to act on their own rather than consult God for guidance. Ahab never did connect his heart to God, so it's easy to see how his pagan practices kept him from seeking God, even though God sent several prophets to prove to Ahab that he hadn't been abandoned. The fact that he returned vexed and sullen demonstrated he had the core ingredients to resuscitate his heart, but it wasn't enough to convict and commit himself to God's will.

God granted Ahab another opportunity to show some signs of repentance. In an account similar to the parable Nathan gave David in his rebuke of David's sin with Bathsheba, Ahab desired an adjacent property that would expand his vineyards. When he told Naboth the landowner that he was willing to buy the land, Naboth respectfully refused the king because it was family property and the law prevented him from selling to anyone outside the clan. The king returned home, pouting that he didn't get what he wanted. Jezebel rebuked him when she heard why he was upset. He was the king, after all, why can't he just take what he wanted? Taking the matter into her own hands, she had Naboth falsely accused of cursing God and the king at a dinner Naboth was hosting. He was found guilty by the gathering, taken out, and stoned. Jezebel's mission was accomplished, and Ahab took the property as his own.

God dispatched Elijah to confront Ahab of his sin and to pass God's judgement on him. "'Behold, I will bring calamity on you. I will take away your posterity, and will cut off from Ahab every male in Israel, both bond and free.'...And concerning Jezebel the LORD also spoke, saying, 'The dogs shall eat Jezebel by the wall of Jezreel.'...So it was, when Ahab heard those words, that he tore his clothes and put sackcloth on his body, and fasted and lay in sackcloth, and went about mourning" (1 Kgs. 21:21, 23, 27). Ahab's dejected actions were just another feeble show of repentance, an action with no call out to God and no atonement or rejection of his pagan worship. However, God revealed to Elijah that because of this act of humility, He would withhold Ahab's judgement and pass it on to his descendants.

After three years of peace with Syria, Ahab hosted Jehoshaphat, the king of Judah (brothers-in-law by marriage) at that time and described how he wanted to attack Syria to regain additional land that Ahab believed still belonged to Israel. Jehoshaphat was a king obedient to God and agreed to aid Ahab, subject to inquiring of the Lord for guidance. The inquiry was not Ahab's idea. Ahab summoned all 400 of his prophets (of Jezebel's idol Asheroth) who unanimously agreed that God told them Ahab would be successful in his military effort. "But Jehoshaphat asked, 'Is there no longer a prophet of the LORD here whom we can inquire of?' The king of Israel answered Jehoshaphat, 'There is still one prophet through whom we can inquire of the LORD, but I hate him because he never prophesies anything good about me, but always bad. He is Micaiah son of Imlah.' 'The king should not say such a thing,' Jehoshaphat replied" (1 Kgs. 22:7–8).

Micaiah was another prophet of God sent for Ahab's benefit. He was summoned before both kings and initially told Ahab what he wanted to hear. Ahab was skeptical and pressed Micaiah for what God had really revealed to him. Micaiah then prophesied that Ahab would be killed in battle and the Israelite army would return home. He also revealed that God allowed one of His angels to put a lying spirit in the mouths of Ahab's prophets to convince Ahab to attack Syria, which would lead to his death. Ahab was furious with Micaiah's prophecy and sent him to his city to be imprisoned until Ahab returned in victory.[532] Ignoring the prophecy, Ahab went ahead to take on the Syrian army. The king was killed in battle by an errant arrow and when the news of his death spread to the army, they disbanded from the battle and returned to their homes.

---

[532]Ahab did not put Micaiah to death for predicting his defeat and death but sentenced him to prison instead. Centuries later, Jeremiah made a similar prediction to his king and the court regarding the Babylonian attack on Jerusalem. His king sought to have Jeremiah killed for this prophecy, but some of the members of the court reminded the king that Micaiah was spared for the same type of prophecy, thereby Jeremiah was spared as well.

Despite the pagan direction in which Ahab led Israel, he was offered on several occasions God's merciful intervention. While he exhibited moments of regret or remorse, it was never enough to overcome his wife's control of the faith of the nation. Paul House summarizes, "Ultimately, he is judged as a man who heard from God yet did not act on the revelation he received. This character thereby allows more wickedness than he intended, perhaps, yet an amount of wickedness Israel could not afford."[533]

Ahab's son Ahaziah took over the throne and continued in the same pagan practices as his father. He ruled Israel for only two years. After having an accident that placed him on his sickbed, he sent his messengers to inquire of the god Baal if he would recover from the accident. That apostasy led to his early death because he turned to idols rather than God for his recovery. "But the angel of the LORD said to Elijah the Tishbite, 'Go up and meet the messengers of the king of Samaria and ask them, "Is it because there is no God in Israel that you are going off to consult Baal-Zebub, the god of Ekron?" Therefore, this is what the LORD says: "You will not leave the bed you are lying on. You will certainly die!"' So Elijah went" (2 Kgs. 1:3–4). Elijah delivered the message to the king and true to God's judgement, the king died.

His brother Joram (or Jehoram) took the throne and he reigned for 12 years, still leaving Israel in a state of apostasy. Elisha was the prophet for Israel and his relationship with the king was not as contentious as his father's was with Elijah. When the king of Moab rebelled against Israel after Ahab died, Joram joined forces with Jehoshaphat and the king of Edom to fight against Moab. After seven days marching without finding water or the Moabites, Elisha was summoned to assist

---

[533]Paul House, *The New American Commentary: 1, 2 Kings,* 1995, p. 240.

them with the effort.[534] Elisha foretells of water flowing to them in the morning followed by the victory over the Moabites, both of which God provided.

A Brief Interlude

There was a brief interlude in the confrontations between Aram (Syria) and the nation of Israel where we find an interesting side story of a pagan conversion to the Jewish faith that was in stark contrast to the conditions in Israel. Naaman was presented as the commanding general of the Syrian army and Scriptures tell us he was blessed by the Lord with prior victories over Israel. This blessing, no doubt, was God's judgement on Israel's continued rejection of their own faith.

While he was a great general, Naaman had leprosy, which he was desperate to rid himself of. Not by any coincidence, a servant of Naaman's wife was a young girl captured from Israel who knew of the prophet Elisha. She told Naaman's wife that Elisha could heal him. Getting permission from his king, Naaman took money and gifts to Joram (the king of Israel) with a message from the king of Syria asking for healing. When he received the message, Joram tore his clothes in anguish as he claimed he wasn't God and couldn't heal Naaman. He thought this was a trap to give Syria an excuse to attack Israel. It didn't occur to Joram to seek out Elisha for help.

Elisha heard of the circumstances and sent for Naaman so that "he will know that there is a prophet in Israel" (2 Kgs. 5:8). When Naaman reached Elisha's house, the prophet sent a messenger to tell Naaman to bathe seven times in the Jordan River and he would be healed. Naaman was enraged that Elisha didn't greet him as a man of authority and instead was sending him out of his way to the Jordan River. His

---

[534]Elisha agreed to help only because Jehoshaphat was aligned with Joram. "Elisha said to the king of Israel, 'Why do you want to involve me? Go to the prophets of your father and the prophets of your mother.' 'No,' the king of Israel answered, 'because it was the LORD who called us three kings together to deliver us into the hands of Moab.' Elisha said, 'As surely as the LORD Almighty lives, whom I serve, if I did not have respect for the presence of Jehoshaphat king of Judah, I would not pay any attention to you'" (2 Kgs. 3:13–14).

servants convinced him to follow the instructions. He had come this far, what could he lose? When he got over his pride, Naaman followed Elisha's instructions, and he was immediately and completely healed.

"Then Naaman and all his attendants went back to the man of God. He stood before him and said, 'Now I know that there is no God in all the world except in Israel'" (2 Kgs. 5:15). In gratitude, he offered Elisha gifts, which the prophet rightfully refused for doing God's work. Then Naaman announced his commitment to worship God instead of his pagan gods. "'If you will not,' said Naaman, 'please let me, your servant, be given as much earth as a pair of mules can carry, for your servant will never again make burnt offerings and sacrifices to any other god but the LORD. But may the LORD forgive your servant for this one thing: When my master enters the temple of Rimmon to bow down and he is leaning on my arm and I have to bow there also—when I bow down in the temple of Rimmon, may the LORD forgive your servant for this'" (2 Kgs. 5:17–18).

With this confession, Richard Patterson and Hermann Austel recognize "a soul for whom God was concerned was at stake. God's blessing had been designed for Naaman's response in repentance and faith, Gentile though he was."[535] Naaman asked forgiveness for having to participate with his king in a ceremonial practice; he still had a position to maintain in Aram, but his heart belonged to God. D. A. Carson writes, "Naaman was truly converted to worship the God of Israel, but he asked for forbearance on the occasions when he would be forced to bow in a pagan temple while serving his master. Though his body would bow down, Naaman's heart would be committed to the Lord only."[536]

Naaman exhibited more faith in God than those living in Israel. Joram's father, Ahab, had witnessed God's miracles, yet he continued to worship other idols. And those who witnessed the altar contest seemed to follow their leader. Like the story of Ruth, this episode

---

[535]Richard Patterson and Hermann Austel, *The Expositor's Bible Commentary – 1 & 2 Kings,* 2009, p. 831.

[536]D. A. Carson, *NIV Zondervan Study Bible,* 2015, p. 663, footnote.

highlights once again the theme that in being created in God's image, even Gentiles have the ingredients in their hearts to allow God's healing to create a faith that was otherwise non-existent. And, as pointed out earlier, there was still a remnant of faith in Israel despite the general condition of the nation.

However, examples of Israel representing God as a nation of priests were limited to the servant girl and Elisha. Paul House notes, "This text contains one of the great Gentile accounts in the Old Testament. Like Rahab (Josh. 2:9–13), Ruth (Ruth 1:16–18) and the sailors and Ninevites in Jonah (Jonah 1:16, 3:6–10), Naaman believes in the Lord. From Genesis 12:2–3 onward in the Old Testament, God desires to bless all nations through Israel. This ideal becomes a reality here due to the witness of the Israelite servant girl and the work of the Israelite prophet...Sadly, Naaman's confession of faith condemns most Israelites of that era since they have rejected the one true God and embraced gods that cannot heal."[537]

The story ended with another contrast of faith. Gehazi, Elisha's servant for many years, decided that while Elisha refused Naaman's gifts, he wanted to get something from Naaman. "So Gehazi hurried after Naaman. When Naaman saw him running toward him, he got down from the chariot to meet him. 'Is everything all right?' he asked. 'Everything is all right', Gehazi answered. 'My master sent me to say, "Two young men from the company of the prophets have just come to me from the hill country of Ephraim. Please give them a talent of silver and two sets of clothing."' 'By all means, take two talents', said Naaman. He urged Gehazi to accept them, and then tied up the two talents of silver in two bags, with two sets of clothing. He gave them to two of his servants, and they carried them ahead of Gehazi" (2 Kgs. 5:21–23).

Patterson and Austel note the nature of their spiritual hearts. "What a contrast can be seen in the meeting between Naaman and Gehazi! Naaman's descent from his chariot to meet Elisha's servant is a mark of his being a changed man. No longer a proud, arrogant person (vv. 9–12), but the grateful (v. 15), reverent (v. 17), and humble

---

[537]Paul House, *The New American Commentary*, 1995, p. 273.

(v. 18) Aramean came down from his honored place to meet a prophet's servant. He who had been a fallen, hopeless sinner displayed the true believer's grace. Contrariwise, Gehazi, who had enjoyed all the privileges of his master's grace, was about to abuse them and fall from that favor."[538]

Gehazi tried to hide the gifts and when Elisha asked where he had been, Gehazi lied again by saying, "'Your servant didn't go anywhere'" (2 Kgs. 5:25). Of course, nothing was hidden from Elisha. In an ironic turn of events, as punishment for deceiving Naaman, showing how greed had overtaken him, and lying to one of the greatest prophets in Israel, Elisha inflicted Naaman's leprosy upon Gehazi. Provan notes, "The fierceness is unsurprising, given the heinousness of the crime. Gehazi has sought to cash in on an act of God."[539]

Back to the Battles

When Ben-Hadad, the king of Aram, waged war against Israel, Elisha warned Joram of the time and location of the invasion. In fact, Elisha provided Joram information each time the Aramian army moved, which enraged the attacking king. He sent some of his troops to Dothan where Elisha was staying, and Elisha asked God to strike the army with blindness. God answered Elisha's prayer and Elisha led the blinded troops to Joram who was in Samaria. Rather than kill them all as Joram asked, Elisha told him to feed the army and send them home.

Later, Ben-Hadad laid siege to Israel while it was suffering from a severe famine. When Joram toured the city, he encountered chilling evidence of cannibalism among his citizens. He was horrified and blamed Elisha for the calamity, little realizing it was the result of his own apostasy. Once again, Elisha foretold that the Lord would intervene, and the famine would cease.

---

[538]Richard Patterson and Hermann Austel, *The Expositor's Bible Commentary – 1 & 2 Kings*, 2009, p. 831.

[539]Iain Provan, *1 & 2 Kings*, 1995, p. 195.

The next morning, the entire Aramean army abandoned its position, leaving all of their supplies behind. "...for the Lord had caused the Arameans to hear the sound of chariots and horses and a great army, so that they said to one another, 'Look, the king of Israel has hired the Hittite and Egyptian kings to attack us!' So they got up and fled in the dusk and abandoned their tents and their horses and donkeys. They left the camp as it was and ran for their lives" (2 Kgs. 7:6–7).

Through Elisha, God intervened on behalf of the Israelites when disaster was about to befall them and despite His show of power, Joram did nothing to change the spiritual path of the nation, just as his father Ahab failed to do. The next time he was involved in war with the Arameans, he was wounded in battle and did not gain the victory.

Elisha instructed one of his followers to anoint Jehu, a commander in the Israelite army, as king of Israel. Jehu was instructed to wipe out Ahab's family, particularly Jezebel. The messenger reached Jehu in the city of Ramoth Gilead with God's instructions. "You are to destroy the house of Ahab your master, and I will avenge the blood of my servants the prophets and the blood of all the LORD's servants shed by Jezebel. The whole house of Ahab will perish. I will cut off from Ahab every last male in Israel—slave or free" (2 Kgs. 9:7–8). Jehu was declared king by his followers, and he killed Joram in battle. When he arrived at the Ahab's palace, Jehu had Jezebel's servants throw her out the window from which she taunted Jehu and she fell several stories to her death.

Jehu seemed to be on the verge of righteousness when he destroyed the temple of Baal and killed all the ministers to Baal, but he continued to worship the golden calves at Bethel and Dan. He followed God's plan to rid Israel of Ahab's family, "Yet Jehu was not careful to keep the law of the LORD, the God of Israel, with all his heart. He did not turn away from the sins of Jeroboam, which he had caused Israel to commit" (2 Kgs. 10:31). Jehu continued to rule Israel for 27 years and three more generations of kings continued the practice of pagan worship.

Jeroboam II, three generations removed from Jehu, had military success against Israel's enemies and expanded the borders of Israel. He ruled for 40 years but, like his predecessors, did nothing to lead his nation back to God. However, God showed mercy toward Israel, despite their lack of heart to do His will. "The LORD had seen how bitterly everyone in Israel, whether slave or free, was suffering; there was no one to help them. And since the LORD had not said he would blot out the name of Israel from under heaven, he saved them by the hand of Jeroboam son of Jehoash" (2 Kgs. 14:26–27).

Patterson and Austel note, "But God's blessings are too often taken for granted[540]...Spiritually, the lives of God's people degenerated into open sin in the northern kingdom and into empty formalism in the south...When Jeroboam II died in 752 BC, he left behind a strong kingdom but, unfortunately, one whose core foundation was so spiritually rotten that the edifice of state would not long withstand the rising tides of international intrigue and pressure."[541]

Jeroboam's son succeeded him but only managed to reign one year before he was assassinated by Shallum in full view of the people. Only when the heart of the nation has reached such a level of apathy could the king be disposed of so easily in public without an outcry. Shallum reigned only a month, then he was assassinated by a man from Tirzah named Menahem. The assassin became king and ruled Israel for ten years, all in the manner of the preceding kings. When Assyria attacked a weakened Israel, Menahem (the reigning king at the time) placed a tax on the wealthy to bribe the king of Assyria from going further in the land. Patterson and Austel continue, "Although Menahem had thought to buy time, perhaps even Israel's independence, his policy was to spell the beginning of the end. A totally apostate Israel was to reap the harvest of her spiritual wickedness at the hands of the very ones whom Menahem had trusted for deliverance."[542]

Menahem's son succeeded him and ruled for two years. Another military coup took place and again a king was appointed from the

---

[540]"When I fed them, they were satisfied; when they were satisfied, they became proud; then they forgot me" (Hosea 13:6).

[541]Richard Patterson and Hermann Austel, *The Expositor's Bible Commentary – 1 & 2 Kings*, 2009, pp. 877–878.

[542] Ibid., p. 884.

assassination party. The next king continued to do evil in the eyes of the Lord and his reign lasted eight years. Meanwhile, God allowed Israel's enemies to claim parts of the land and maintain military success over them. The country slowly eroded, spiritually and geographically. The Assyrians took cities and land from around Galilee and deported the people to Assyria. The king at that time was Pekah, who was assassinated by Hoshea, the last of the kings of Israel. At that same time, Assyria took the city of Damascus and Israel became a vassal state to Assyria.

The king of Assyria found out that Hoshea had stopped making tribute payments and sought military protection from Egypt (trouble originates from Egypt once again). Rather than rely on God for protection, Hoshea made the same mistakes his predecessors did in seeking protection from a foreign military source. The king of Assyria took Hoshea prisoner, and the nation of Israel was finally dissolved.

Scriptures summarize the northern nation of Israel's entire history of apostasy.[543] "All this took place because the Israelites had sinned against the LORD their God, who had brought them up out of Egypt from under the power of Pharaoh king of Egypt. They worshiped other gods and followed the practices of the nations the LORD had driven out before them, as well as the practices that the kings of Israel had introduced...They set up sacred stones and Asherah poles on every high hill and under every spreading tree...They worshiped idols, though the LORD had said, 'You shall not do this.'...They forsook all the commands of the LORD their God and made for themselves two idols cast in the shape of calves, and an Asherah pole. They bowed down to all the starry hosts, and they worshiped Baal. They sacrificed their sons and daughters in the fire. They practiced divination and sought omens and sold themselves to do evil in the eyes of the LORD,

---

[543]Eugene Merrill summarizes 2 Kings 17:7–33 as the downfall of the northern tribes; "(1) They sinned by forsaking Yahweh for the customs and traditions of the pagans who lived among them (vv. 7–12); (2) they disregarded the adjurations of the Lord and his prophets who attempted to bring about their repentance (vv.13–14); and (3) they broke the sacred covenant God had mad with them at Sinai and in the plains of Moab (vv.15–18). *A Commentary on 1 & 2 Chronicles*, 2015, p. 236.

arousing his anger...The Israelites persisted in all the sins of Jeroboam and did not turn away from them until the LORD removed them from his presence, as he had warned through all his servants the prophets. So, the people of Israel were taken from their homeland into exile in Assyria, and they are still there" (2 Kgs. 17:7–8, 10, 12, 16–17, 22–23).

Asa Restores Judah's Faith

While the northern nation of Israel continued its death spiral of idolatry and disregard for God's commandments, the southern nation of Judah had spurts of spiritual revival by eight different kings who followed in the heart of David. They destroyed the altars (not always completely) dedicated to the false gods and brought the people back in line with God's commands; hence, they restored or recharged the corporate spiritual heart. There were varying degrees of success; some had a more complete return to David's ways than others and each of them had some problems maintaining their spiritual heart for the duration of their reign. However, as was the case in Judges, when the faithful king's reign was over, the succeeding king led the people back to pagan worship.

Rehoboam, the son of King Solomon, was succeeded by his son, Abijah, who "...committed all the sins his father had done before him; his heart was not fully devoted to the LORD his God, as the heart of David his forefather had been" (1 Kgs. 15:3). The idolatry practices from the end of Solomon's reign were passed to Rehoboam and continued during Abijah's reign. Obedience and faith were abandoned, and the priesthood envisioned for people of Judah was nowhere to be seen. Luckily, Abijah only reigned for three years.

With the death of his father Abijah, Asa reigned over Judah forty-one years in Jerusalem. Unlike his father and grandfather, Asa did what was right in the eyes of the LORD, as David had done. He was righteous and obedient to God's will. Eugene Merrill writes, "Asa was a man whose works were good in Yahweh's eyes and whose goodness was inextricably linked to his being a person of unquestioned integrity."[544] He was the first king to clean out the pagan practices from the end of Solomon's reign. He ended the practice of cult prostitutes being part of the worship practices and drove them out of the land, and he removed all the idols that his fathers had made. He removed the foreign altars from the high places along with all the incense altars in the cities in Judah, smashed the sacred stones, and cut down the Asherah poles.

The account in First Kings mentions that he did not remove the high places entirely. "Nevertheless, the heart of Asa was wholly true to the LORD all his days" (1 Kgs. 15:14, ESV). Asa's heart followed David's and he was dedicated to God in obedience his entire life. After ridding Judah of pagan worship, "He commanded Judah to seek the LORD, the God of their ancestors, and to obey his laws and commands" (2 Chron. 14:4). With that decree, there was a return to the corporate worship that David and Solomon instituted earlier, adhering to God's covenant for His kings. With his heart of obedience and faith to God, Asa led his people back into the fold; the people of Judah returned to following in the Lord's will and the religious revival began. Because of his faithfulness and obedience, the people of Judah followed, and God provided peace in Judah for the first ten years of his reign.

During that span of peace, Asa built up the cities of Judah to fortify them. He called the people's attention to the fact that God granted them peace from the neighboring nations. "'The land is still ours, because we have sought the LORD our God; we sought him and he has given us rest on every side.' So they built and prospered" (2 Chron. 14:7). Not only was there peace in Judah, but they also prospered. The spiritual heart of the people had been reinvigorated by following Asa's strong, faithful leadership. The prosperity was no different than when David and Solomon reigned in faith and obedience to God; Asa and Judah likewise found favor with God because of their actions and behavior.

---

[544] Ibid., p. 401.

When war did break out, Asa continued to reflect David's behavior. He called upon God to lead his army to victory rather than put trust in his forces alone. Asa had an army of almost six hundred thousand men from Judah and from Benjamin that warded off an attack from Zerah the Cushite, who had a superior force which included three hundred chariots. As the two armies faced each other in battle, Asa prayed before God, "LORD, there is no one like you to help the powerless against the mighty. Help us, LORD our God, for we rely on you, and in your name we have come against this vast army. LORD, you are our God; do not let mere mortals prevail against you'" (2 Chron. 14:11). Asa demonstrated total faith and reliance in God. He knew he was seriously outnumbered, but like David, Asa realized that no enemy was too large to defeat when you trust in God. In his obedience, he turned to God's will and had the faith to know the outcome.

God responded to Asa's prayer by striking down the Cushites before the battle even commenced. They fled the battle, with Asa's army right behind them. The Cushite army was crushed, and Asa's army carried off a large amount of the spoils. Asa destroyed and looted the nearby villages of the Cushites and returned to Jerusalem. God was clearly with Asa and his faithful people of Judah.

God spoke through the prophet Azariah in the manner of a pep talk so that Asa's faith would stay strong and not waiver. Azariah encouraged Asa to continue to lead his people in their faith and obedience to God, warning Asa that troubling times would affect the safety of Judah and Israel as the result of not having any spiritual leadership. There would be violence and potential for war with other nations, but as long as Asa was with God, God would be with him, and his work would be rewarded.

With this shot of encouragement, Asa continued to remove all aspects of pagan worship from his kingdom. He removed any remaining idols from the land of Judah and Benjamin and from the towns he had captured in the hills of Ephraim. He repaired the altar in front of the portico of the Temple. He also deposed his grandmother Maakah from her position as queen mother, because she kept an image for the worship of Asherah. Asa cut it down, broke it up, and burned it in the Kidron Valley. He also brought into the temple of God the silver and gold and the articles that he and his father had dedicated.

Asa assembled the people of his kingdom, including those from Ephraim, Manasseh, and Simeon from the northern nation of Israel. He reached out to Israel in the hope of bringing them back to God, a missionary effort that God expected from His nation of priests. Apparently, Asa's faith and that of Judah spread to the nation of Israel and many who saw that God was with him came down from the north to settle in Judah. Despite the influence of the kings of Israel who continued to do evil in God's eyes, there was still a faithful remnant from Israel who wished to maintain their faith rather than succumb to the spread of idolatry that infected the north. Frederick Mabie notes the similarity in religious reforms enacted by Asa, Hezekiah, and Josiah: "...about two centuries later the Judean King Hezekiah will likewise invite those situated within the northern kingdom to assemble in Jerusalem and publicly declare their loyalties to his ways. Such assemblies...marked significant moments in the spiritual life of the community of God's people."[545]

In the fifteenth year of Asa's reign, faithful citizens from both nations gathered in Jerusalem for praise, worship, and a renewal of their covenant with God. "They entered into a covenant to seek the LORD, the God of their ancestors, with all their heart and soul. All who would not seek the LORD, the God of Israel, were to be put to death, whether small or great, man or woman" (2 Chron. 15:12–13). Thus, in keeping with the First Great Commandment, the people sought the Lord with all their heart and soul. Those who did not were purged in order to keep the people pure, just as God intended with the Israelites.

The joy and jubilation of the ceremony resembled David's triumphant return of the ark of the covenant into Jerusalem and the spiritual uplifting at the opening of the temple by Solomon. The spiritual heart of Judah returned to God in worship and obedience. The people of Judah took an oath to God to renew their covenant amidst shouting and trumpets and rejoiced at the sincerity with

---

[545]Frederick Mabie, *The Expositor's Bible Commentary – 1 and 2 Chronicles*, 2010, p. 225.

which the oath was made. They sought God with enthusiasm and they found Him. Because of their faith, God granted them peace for another 20 years.

Despite his reliance on God's grace and trusting in His word to protect his people, Asa's spiritual heart eventually failed. After 20 years of peace, Baasha king of Israel went up against Judah and fortified the city of Ramah to prevent anyone from leaving or entering Asa's territory, most likely in response to the people of Israel emigrating to Judah for religious purposes. God was likely testing Asa's faith, which also happened to Hezekiah.

Rather than placing his trust in God for this potential invasion, Asa took the silver and gold out of the treasuries of the temple and delivered it to Ben-Hadad, who was the king of Syria ruling in Damascus. The treasure was given as a military alliance payment to thwart Baasha's effort to fortify Raman. Ben-Hadad agreed to the alliance and attacked the Israelite towns in the area around Raman; the military action and potential threat from Damascus caused Baasha to abandon his plan.

For Asa, this was a Pyrrhic victory. Why would Asa resort to paying a pagan king to prevent Israel from invading Judah? "At that time Hanani the seer came to Asa king of Judah and said to him: 'Because you relied on the king of Aram and not on the LORD your God, the army of the king of Aram has escaped from your hand. Were not the Cushites and Libyans a mighty army with great numbers of chariots and horsemen? Yet when you relied on the LORD, he delivered them into your hand. For the eyes of the LORD range throughout the earth to strengthen those whose hearts are fully committed to him. You have done a foolish thing, and from now on you will be at war'" (2 Chron. 16:7–9).

H. G. M. Williamson notes, "What the prophet means is that if Asa had remained faithful, he would have not only conquered Baasha, but also the Syrians who were in league with him."[546] Up to that point, Asa had followed David's example and had done well in God's eyes;

---

[546] H. G. M. Williamson, *1 and 2 Chronicles,* 2010, p. 274.

however, his poor judgement and overdose of pride showed his lack of trust in God's ability to help him. Recall that when Nathan rebuked David for his affair with Bathsheba, David immediately recognized his sin and was completely remorseful and repented. Asa, however, didn't measure up to David's total loyalty to God.

Rather than see his error in judgement, Asa was angry with Hannai's rebuke and threw the prophet in prison. To compound matters, Asa brutally oppressed some of the people who supported Hanani. There is no explanation for this sudden turn of events or why Asa turned from God. Three years later, Asa was afflicted with a severe disease in his feet. Even with this illness, he did not seek help from God (unlike Hezekiah, who we will see, asked for God's help in his illness), but sought help from his personal physicians. Asa died two years later, having reigned in Judah for 41 years.

Asa's timeline of his obedience and trust in God was similar to Solomon's. Throughout most of his reign, Asa demonstrated the same character of heart that David and Solomon had in their love for the Lord. Like David, Asa implored the Lord when taking on the might of the Cushite army and, with God's help, was granted a great victory. Like David's return of the ark of the Lord and Solomon's dedication of the temple, Asa led his people in a nationwide celebration to God and a spiritual revival that lasted for several years.

And like Solomon, all of these good efforts were for not because he turned away from God and collapsed into self-indulgence instead of life-long dedication to God. Solomon yielded to idolatry because of the influence of his pagan wives that led his nation down the path of destruction. Asa did not lead his people into idolatry at the end of his reign, but he did abandon his own personal faith in God. It may have been his own pride for failing to admit his sin, or maybe he lost faith because of the pain associated with his illness. In either case, Asa did demonstrate that he had the right ingredients to be faithful and obedient to God for most of his life but was unable to see it to the end, just like Solomon before him. As Thomas Schreiner aptly points out, "It seems that Asa functions as a parable of Judah, which started well and trusted in the Lord but later departed from him and thereby suffered the consequences."[547]

Therein lies the lesson for us as well. We all have hearts that will fail God, but we have the benefit of Jesus's sacrifice for our sins to establish our walk with God and maintain that relationship through Christ.

In the Old Testament there was always the ability to repent and ask God for forgiveness of sin as we saw in David's life, but Asa's spiritual heart failed.

Judah's Cyclical Restoration: In and Out of God's Favor

Jehoshaphat son of Asa became king and, early on, followed in the manner of his father by being obedient and faithful to God. Scriptures mention that the Lord was with him because he did not succumb to the Baal worshiping of the northern nation of Israel. He refortified cities in Judah and removed the remaining cult prostitution and the Asherah poles that were left behind from his father's reign. "In everything he followed the ways of his father Asa and did not stray from them; he did what was right in the eyes of the LORD. The high places, however, were not removed, and the people continued to offer sacrifices and burn incense there...He rid the land of the rest of the male shrine prostitutes who remained there even after the reign of his father Asa" (1 Kgs. 22:43, 46).

Jehoshaphat sent out Levites, priests, and officials to all the towns in Judah to teach his people the book of the Law, which was a revival of the priestly role originally intended for all of Israel. Frederick Mabie observes, "It is noteworthy that these individuals go out to teach God's Word (in analogy to *going forth* built in the Great Commission: cf. Matt. 28:19–20), rather than expecting the people to come to them."[548] Jehoshaphat's missionary efforts reminded the people of their covenantal obligations and it was noteworthy that he sent the Levites

---

[547]Thomas Schreiner, *The King in His Beauty*, 2013, p. 202.

[548]Frederick Mabie, *The Expositor's Bible Commentary – 1 and 2 Chronicles*, 2010, p. 234.

and priests to reteach the covenant tenets to those who needed it most. As he devoted his heart to God, his kingdom was established; Judah was respected as being under God's protection and he and all Judah prospered. Richard Patterson and Hermann Austel commend Jehoshaphat's dedication to God's will: "Jehoshaphat's spiritual condition was basically sound and largely commended by God...His concern for spiritual things manifested itself in religious and social reforms."[549]

The character flaw for Jehoshaphat was that he was aligned with Ahab king of Israel through marriage. As mentioned earlier, Ahab was one of Israel's worst kings in driving his people away from God. Despite the northern nation's pagan practices, Jehoshaphat maintained communication with Ahab because of their relationship. On one of Jehoshaphat's visits to Ahab in Damascus, Ahab convinced him to join in a military attack against Ramoth Gilead. Ahab was killed in the battle and Israel was defeated. Jehoshaphat returned to Judah where he was rebuked by his prophet Jehu for allying himself with Israel, who was in God's path of wrath. "Jehu the seer, the son of Hanani, went out to meet him and said to the king, 'Should you help the wicked and love those who hate the LORD? Because of this, the wrath of the LORD is on you. There is, however, some good in you, for you have rid the land of the Asherah poles and have set your heart on seeking God'" (2 Chron. 19:2–3). Eugene Merrill writes, "... as Jehu the seer observed, even a good king might have flaws that result in catastrophic judgement. Jehoshaphat sold out his privileges as a Davidic king by allying himself with a man who hated God, namely, King Ahab."[550]

Jehoshaphat later redeemed himself when a large army of Moabites and Ammonites prepared to attack Jerusalem. Like his father Asa before him, he gathered all of Judah together to pray to God for help because they were vastly outnumbered. When he and his army were about to advance toward the enemy force, he called upon the

---

[549]Richard Patterson and Hermann Austel, *The Expositor's Bible Commentary – 1 and 2 Kings*, 2009, p. 803.

[550]Eugene Merrill, *A Commentary on 1 & 2 Chronicles*, 2015, p. 420.

Lord to lead them to victory. God intervened and caused the enemy army to attack itself to such an extent that when Jehoshaphat's army arrived, there was no one left to fight. God rewarded Judah for its faith in Him.[551]

Jehoshaphat ruled for 25 years and for the most part remained obedient to God. He did make the mistake of agreeing to a shipping trade pact with Ahab's son Ahaziah the king of Israel. Instead of relying on God to provide prosperity, he allied himself with wickedness from his northern neighbor. The venture was disastrous; all the ships were lost at sea. As Merrill notes, "This judgement fell because Jehoshaphat apparently learned nothing from his alliance with Ahab and thus must pay for doing the same with his equally paganized son."[552]

Jehoshaphat's next two successors fell back into idol and pagan worship, eschewing the restoration of spiritual hearts that Asa and Jehoshaphat accomplished. Jehoram succeeded his father and ruled for eight years. "He followed the ways of the kings of Israel, as the house of Ahab had done, for he married a daughter of Ahab. He did evil in the eyes of the LORD...He had also built high places on the hills of Judah and had caused the people of Jerusalem to prostitute themselves and had led Judah astray" (2 Chron. 21:6, 11). After ignoring the prophet Elijah's warning of judgement if he continued in his pagan ways, Jehoram was inflicted with a horrible and painful disease of the bowels that led to his death two years later.

Jehoram's youngest son Ahaziah ruled in his place and followed the pagan practices of his father. He reigned only one year. He was traveling with king Joram of Israel and they were both killed by Jehu who was sent by God to end the rule of Ahab's descendants. Ahaziah happened to be in the wrong place at the right time.

The next king in line, Joash, did well under the tutelage of the high priest Jehoiada; he restored the temple and did right in God's eyes. But

---

[551]Having their enemies attack each other in confusion rather than directly against His people was a common tactic God used to provide victory to His people. With Gideon against the Midianites and again with Saul's son Jonathan against the Philistines, we saw the same manner of providing victory to the His people.

[552]Ibid., p. 433.

as a soon as the high priest died, Joash was left to his own evil counsel and he fell back into the bad practices that plagued Israel. His son, Amaziah didn't fare much better. He took favorable actions in obedience to God, but his pride got in the way of his obedience. After being granted victory over the Edomites, he brought back their idols and started to worship them. Even though his prophet tried to warn him of God's anger for doing so, he shut the prophet down. With pride overwhelming his heart from the victory God granted him earlier, he unilaterally decided to take on the northern nation of Israel, boasting of an easy victory (without God's help, obviously). He and his army were routed on account of his pride, pagan worshiping, and displaying a lack of confidence in God. He was killed in battle by the Israelites.

Uzziah (also known as Azariah in 2 Kings 15) followed next in line and, like his father Amaziah, he started his reign in obedience to God. He was tutored by the prophet Zechariah and remained faithful to the Lord. "As long as he sought the LORD, God gave him success" (2 Chron. 26:5). As with the kings who kept their faith in God, Judah continued to be blessed by God and the southern nation prospered. Uzziah continued to build up his military forces and the nations around him respected his military strength.

Like his father, Uzziah's success and power led to his own pride. He took it upon himself to take incense in the temple, which only the priests were allowed to do. This act was similar to Saul's self-appointed sacrificial actions. When the priests tried to stop him, he raged against them over their perceived insubordination, rather than acknowledge he was the one who was out of line. God struck Uzziah with leprosy for his disobedience and pride. Regarding Uzziah's transgression, Eugene Merrill writes, "...there is no hint of moral failure but what appears to be an egregious crossing of well-marked boundaries of authority and responsibility. He became 'haughty'..." [553] The disease stayed with him until he died, secluded from the rest of the court because of it. As with the other good kings whose hearts waned at the end of their

---

[553]Eugene Merrill, *A Commentary on 1 & 2 Chronicles,* 2015, p. 477.

reign, Uzziah's sin of pride was a personal failing, but he did not lead his people back to idolatry.

Jotham followed Uzziah and while he did walk in obedience to God, Scriptures tell us that the people still continued their corrupt practices, so he did not lead the people back into community prayer and worship. Here was an example of a good-hearted king whose people did not totally follow his example. God did, however, grant him success because of his earlier obedience.[554] He led Judah for 16 years and was followed by his son, Ahaz, who also led Judah for 16 years. However, Ahaz followed the path of Israel by taking Judah back into pagan practices. "He followed the ways of the kings of Israel and also made idols for worshiping the Baals. He burned sacrifices in the Valley of Ben Hinnom and sacrificed his children in the fire, engaging in the detestable practices of the nations the LORD had driven out before the Israelites. He offered sacrifices and burned incense at the high places, on the hilltops and under every spreading tree" (2 Chron. 28:2–4).

Ahaz's idolatry practices in Judah seemed to match those of Ahab in the north, clearly one of the most wayward kings of either nation. Walter Brueggemann notes that "Ahaz is rated unqualifiedly bad. Indeed, he is as negatively judged as any Northern kind."[555] He was the first king of Judah to sacrifice his children to idols, an atrocity beyond comprehension.[556]

As punishment for his turning away from God and practicing like the pagan culture around him, Ahaz was attacked by Israel and Aramean armies, suffering huge losses in trying to defend Jerusalem. Against the advice of his prophet, Ahaz appealed to Assyria for help

---

[554]Frederick Mabie, *The Expositor's Bible Commentary – 1 and 2 Chronicles,* 2010, p. 275. "Jotham's success as king is based on his relationship with God and God's subsequent blessings...because he walked steadfastly before the Lord...suggesting his intentional effort to live in a manner pleasing to God."

[555]Walter Brueggemann, *1 & 2 Kings: Smyth & Helwys Bible Commentary & 2 Kings,* 2000, p.463.

[556]Chapter 12 discusses the atrocity of child sacrifice undertaken by Judean authorities during Jeremiah's prophecies, including the original command against it from God through Moses.

ahead of a second attack coming from the Philistines and Edomites. Rather than seek God's help as the faithful kings did before him, Ahaz plundered the temple in order to pay the Assyrians. "The LORD had humbled Judah because of Ahaz king of Israel, for he had promoted wickedness in Judah and had been most unfaithful to the LORD...Ahaz took some of the things from the temple of the LORD and from the royal palace and from the officials and presented them to the king of Assyria, but that did not help him" (2 Chron. 28:19, 21). Because of his evil heart, Ahaz did not seek God to help him out of his troubles nor did he understand he was being punished for his pagan practices. The people of Judah suffered the consequences as well.

As a matter of fact, when Ahaz suffered his earlier defeat by the Arameans, rather than turn to God, he decided it was the pagan gods of his enemies that defeated him. He figured their gods must be superior to his. He even took a clue from the Assyrians by copying their altar configuration and placing it in the temple. As the Philistines and Edomites took hold of surrounding towns and took his people prisoner, Ahaz resorted to worshiping the gods he set up, thinking their previous success was based on their gods favoring them. He set up altars for these foreign gods all over Judah, but to no avail; he only incurred God's anger and died unceremoniously after reigning in Judah for 16 years.

Hezekiah Revives Judah's Faith

Hezekiah became the king of Judah when he was 25 years old and reigned for 29 years. Like the good kings before him, Hezekiah did what was right in the eyes of God and faithfully followed the Lord with the same spiritual heart that David demonstrated. He was obedient to God's commandments and relied on God to lead him to military success. "Hezekiah trusted in the LORD, the God of Israel. There was no one like him among all the kings of Judah, either before him or after him. He held fast to the LORD and did not stop following him; he kept the commands the LORD had given Moses. And the LORD was with him; he was successful in whatever he undertook. He rebelled against the king of Assyria and did not serve him. From watchtower to fortified city, he defeated the Philistines, as far as Gaza and its territory" (2 Kgs. 18:5–8).

Like his faithful predecessors, Hezekiah led the nation of Judah in a revival of service and worship to God. He reopened the temple and repaired the damage that it sustained. He called upon the priests and Levites to consecrate themselves and the temple so he could restore worship in Jerusalem and reverse the practices instituted by his father Ahaz. When the work was accomplished, he held a worship service and invited all of Judah to attend. This led to another restoration of faith and corporate worship in the temple.

Hezekiah reinstated the previously ignored structure and duties of the priests and Levites. He also restored tithing, which was given to the priests and Levites so they could devote themselves to the Law of the Lord. The people obeyed willingly and enthusiastically. So much was offered that there was a great surplus that was put into storerooms. God was blessing the faithfulness and obedience of His people, with Hezekiah leading the effort. "In everything that he undertook in the service of God's temple and in obedience to the law and the commands, he sought his God and worked wholeheartedly. And so he prospered" (2 Chron. 31:21).

Most importantly, Hezekiah reached out to the remnant left behind in his northern neighbor Israel (this was after the Assyrians had taken over the territory) to join the celebration of the Passover. He sent out a proclamation throughout Israel, from Beersheba to Dan, calling the people to come to Jerusalem and celebrate the Passover to the Lord, the God of Israel. The Passover had not been celebrated in large numbers for quite some time, so Hezekiah attempted to bring in fellow Jews from fallen Israel to join in the restoration of faith. A letter went out from the king and religious leaders inviting people from Israel and Judah to join the service to honor and submit to God who "will not turn his face from you if you return" (2 Chron. 30:9). As Eugene Merrill observes, "The message was more than a mere invitation; it was an appeal to Israel as well as Judah to return to the God of their fathers and to renew the covenant commitment to him."[557]

Hezekiah's intent was religiously motivated. Israel had fallen away from God since its separation from Judah and he wanted all of Judah and Israel to return to God. He wanted a return to national worship and purity as it was in David and Solomon's time. He was looking for reconciliation for all God's chosen people. By his behavior and the pure intentions of his heart, he demonstrated compassion and a sense of forgiveness for the wayward manners of his northern neighbors. It was an olive branch to Israel to give up its idolatry and return with Judah in celebration and worship to God. It was a sign of his spiritual heart to show his love for God and Israel, truly reflecting sincere adherence to the Two Great Commandments.

Unfortunately, a majority of those in the north rejected Hezekiah's offer. However, Scriptures mention that some of the people from Asher, Manasseh, and Zebulun humbled themselves and went to Jerusalem. "Also in Judah the hand of God was on the people to give them unity of mind to carry out what the king and his officials had ordered, following the word of the LORD" (2 Chron. 30:12). The spiritual leadership of Hezekiah restored the hearts of his people and, to a limited extent, those in the nation of Israel whose hearts were also rekindled. Hezekiah embodied the spiritual leadership that was required of the covenantal king of God's people.

A very large crowd of people assembled in Jerusalem to celebrate the Passover service. During that time, they removed the pagan altars and threw them into the Kidron Valley. The people who came from Israel were not purified as a result of their long absence from God, so Hezekiah offered a prayer of pardoning so they could participate. "Although most of the many people who came from Ephraim, Manasseh, Issachar, and Zebulun had not purified themselves, yet they ate the Passover, contrary to what was written. But Hezekiah prayed for them, saying, 'May the LORD, who is good, pardon everyone who sets their heart on seeking God—the LORD, the God of their

---

[557]Eugene Merrill, *A Commentary on 1 & 2 Chronicles,* 2015, p. 512.

371

ancestors—even if they are not clean according to the rules of the sanctuary.' And the LORD heard Hezekiah and healed the people" (2 Chron. 30:18–20).

Advocating on behalf of those from the north was a demonstration of loving your enemies as Jesus would teach. Israel had long been a military enemy to Judah, but Hezekiah ignored their past differences. Hezekiah's desire was for them to join in worship and restore their faith in God.

The service included burnt, thank, peace, and drink offerings as prescribed by Moses. Frederick Mabie notes, "These additional offerings are provided by those 'whose hearts were willing' and highlight the image of corporate fellowship."[558] Hezekiah and his people rejoiced in the Lord for how quickly the restoration of faith had been. This was another demonstration that the core ingredients of God's image prompted them to act on their faith.

The Passover service continued for two weeks and Hezekiah provided food out of his own treasury. The same joy given to us by the Holy Spirit when we worship was likely the same euphoria felt by the entire assembly, including all who came from Israel. "There was great joy in Jerusalem, for since the days of Solomon son of David king of Israel there had been nothing like this in Jerusalem. The priests and the Levites stood to bless the people, and God heard them, for their prayer reached heaven, his holy dwelling place" (2 Chron. 30:26–27). The nation's jubilation was recaptured as it was under David, Solomon, and Asa's spiritual leadership. The spiritual revival was a great success; those from Israel returned home to remove the sacred stones and cut down the Asherah poles used for pagan worship. The destruction of the high places and pagan altars extended throughout Judah and Benjamin and as far north as Ephraim and Manasseh.

It was during this spiritual revival early in Hezekiah's reign that the powerful nation of Assyria invaded the northern territory of Israel. After a three-year siege, the Assyrian army succeeded in wiping out the nation and took the survivors into exile; they were led out of their land

---

[558]Frederick Mabie, *The Expositor's Bible Commentary – 1 and 2 Chronicles,* 2010, p. 288.

to towns and cities in Assyria. After more than 200 years of idolatry and pagan worship, God punished Israel and dispersed the survivors.

Eight years later, Assyria set its sights on Judah. Sennacherib king of Assyria attacked all the fortified cities of Judah and captured them on his way to Jerusalem.

Given Hezekiah's efforts for restoring Judah's faithful obedience to God and his lifelong devotion and trust in the Lord, some commentators note that as the Assyrians approached Jerusalem, he had a failure of faith. He became seriously ill and was at the point of death. The prophet Isaiah came to his bedside with the message to get his house in order because he would not recover. This message was obviously from God and, rather than accept His will and be joined with Him, Hezekiah was distraught, turned his face to the wall, and prayed to the Lord to reverse this course. "But Hezekiah's heart was proud, and he did not respond to the kindness shown him; therefore, the LORD's wrath was on him and on Judah and Jerusalem. Then Hezekiah repented of the pride of his heart, as did the people of Jerusalem; therefore, the LORD's wrath did not come on them during the days of Hezekiah" (2 Chron. 32:25–26). No real explanation is given for this since neither Second Kings nor Isaiah refer to it. Eugene Merrill suggests that it "may permit the interpretation that Hezekiah's pride and lack of appreciation for all of Yahweh's goodness to him brought on the disease to begin with. He then cried out to God, who gave him the miraculous sign and then Hezekiah sincerely repented thus bringing about his healing."[559]

In his prayer, he reminded the Lord of his faithfulness and all that he accomplished in his short lifetime and wept bitterly. Some commentators view his reaction to Isaiah's message in a negative sense that, at the age of 39, he still had many years left to serve the Lord. He was bitter that his life was being cut short.

Edward Young makes a positive argument for Hezekiah's actions. He states that there was no mention of Hezekiah having an heir. "If he were to die without issue, how could the Davidic dynasty culminate

---

[559]Eugene Merrill, *A Commentary on 1 & 2 Chronicles*, 2015, p. 528.

in the advent of the Messiah?[560]...He turns to the wall then, not acting childishly, as some commentators suggest, but merely to be alone so as to speak to his God without disturbance...that he may speak undisturbedly to God and pour out his grief unto the One who holds in His hand the issue of life and death."[561] Richard Patterson and HermannAustel have a similar positive opinion: "Because Hezekiah is noted for his trust in the Lord (2 Kings 18:5) and since he pleads with God on the basis of a wholehearted devotion to the Lord, it is perhaps best to give him the benefit of any doubt. The fact that God did answer his prayer instantly and Hezekiah praised God after his recovery (Isaiah 38:9–20) attest to Hezekiah's proper attitude of heart."[562]

The Lord heard Hezekiah's prayers and through Isaiah was told he would recover to live another 15 years. God also promised His continued protection from the Assyrians. Hezekiah asked Isaiah what sign would be given him to verify this promise. This was a challenge to God's grace and Hezekiah should have known better to ask, as if God's word should be called into question. However, Isaiah didn't question his request and told him of the miraculous sign that God would provide.[563] Hezekiah was healed and had a son, Manasseh, three years later. Even though Hezekiah was granted an heir to keep David's line intact, Manasseh would turn out to be Judah's equivalent to Ahab

---

[560]In his account, Josephus makes a similar observation: "...he was childless and was going to die and leave his house and his government without a successor of his own body... he was troubled at the thoughts of his condition, and lamented himself, and entreated of God that he would prolong his life for a little while until he had some children and not suffer him to depart before he was to become a father." *Jewish Antiquities,* Book 10, Chapter 1, vv. 25–26.

[561]Edward Young, *The Book of Isaiah: A Commentary, Volume 2,* 1969, p. 510.

[562]Richard Patterson and Hermann Austel, *The Expositor's Bible Commentary – 1 and 2 Kings,* 2009, p. 923.

[563]"Isaiah answered, 'This is the LORD's sign to you that the LORD will do what he has promised: Shall the shadow go forward ten steps, or shall it go back ten steps? 'It is a simple matter for the shadow to go forward ten steps,' said Hezekiah. 'Rather, have it go back ten steps.' Then the prophet Isaiah called on the LORD, and the LORD made the shadow go back the ten steps it had gone down on the stairway of Ahaz" (2 Kgs. 20:9–11).

in the north; he would do more evil than all other king's before or after him.

With his spiritual heart back on the right track, Hezekiah continued to prosper under the Lord's blessing. He made treasuries for his silver and gold and for his precious stones, shields, and all kinds of valuables. He built storehouses for the harvest of grain, new wine, and olive oil; he made stalls for various kinds of cattle and pens for the flocks; and he built villages because God had given him very great riches and granted him success in everything he did.

After hearing about Hezekiah's miraculous recovery, the prince of Babylon (which was on the rise as a military power) sent an envoy, possibly to hear more about the sun going back ten steps, the sign Hezekiah asked from the Lord, or to learn how the small nation accumulated such riches.

Scripture reveals the importance of this visit. "God left him to test him and to know everything that was in his heart" (2 Chron. 32:31). God used that opportunity to determine where Hezekiah's obedience was at that stage in his life.[564] Was his heart still faithful and trusting or did his pride rule over his heart? Without any communication or warnings from Isaiah, the Lord would see how Hezekiah would react to attention from the powerful (and pagan) nation of Babylon.

Hezekiah made every effort to entertain his guests and proudly revealed everything in his treasury. "Hezekiah received the envoys and showed them all that was in his storehouses—the silver, the gold, the spices and the fine olive oil—his armory and everything found among his treasures. There was nothing in his palace or in all his kingdom that Hezekiah did not show them" (2 Kgs. 20:13). The actions were ill-advised, as Hezekiah soon learned from Isaiah, but he seemed oblivious to his prideful error. Hezekiah also failed to give God credit for the amassed treasure. Instead of relating the great work of God to the pagans, including his miraculous recovery, Hezekiah boasted of

---

[564]"The heart is deceitful above all things and beyond cure. Who can understand it? I the LORD search the heart and examine the mind, to reward each person according to their conduct, according to what their deeds deserve" (Jer. 17:9–10).

his own greatness by way of his accumulated wealth, another blessing from God that went unmentioned.

There are a few reasons for Hezekiah's naivety in showing off his riches to the Babylonian ambassador. With the threat of the Assyrian army looming, he may have sought to form an alliance with Babylon in the near future. That, however, would run counter with covenantal kings relying on God and not on foreign assistance, which was the very mistake his father Ahaz made with Assyria. Eugene Merrill notes, "Hezekiah's opening of the public treasure can mean only that he favored the proposed Chaldean affiliation and that he wished to impress the delegation with the wealth and power of his kingdom. This, the Chronicler says, was an act of pride that brought the wrath of Yahweh on Judah and Jerusalem."[565]

Hezekiah left nothing to the imagination, hiding none of his accomplishments from the Babylonian envoy. Judah was still a small nation in the scheme of things and having a large nation such as Babylon sending their ambassadors to wish him well boosted his ego. Merrill agrees, "...Hezekiah was so flattered by the attention paid him by the Babylonian envoys that he opened up the treasuries and armories of the kingdom so the Babylonians could marvel at the holdings of an otherwise minor monarch."[566]

It may not be a stretch of the imagination to assume the envoy was on more than a well-wishing tour. Judah's military and treasury may have been well-known and the visit may have been a reconnaissance mission to size up Judah's strength and wealth. Hezekiah's boasting of his riches was not a very smart tactic since Babylon would eventually invade Judah and strip it of all that wealth. It's like inviting a thief into your house to show him what's ripe for the taking. Hezekiah had forgotten his trust in God's protection against his enemies.

When word of the visit got to the prophet Isaiah, he asked the king where the envoy came from and what they saw during the visit. Hezekiah responded that they were from Babylon and there was

---

[565]Eugene Merrill, *Kingdom of Priests,* 2008, p. 445.

[566]Eugene Merrill, *A Commentary on 1 & 2 Chronicles,* 2015, p. 541.

nothing in his treasury he did not show them. Isaiah fully understood the folly of Hezekiah's actions and pride. "Then Isaiah said to Hezekiah, 'Hear the word of the LORD: The time will surely come when everything in your palace, and all that your predecessors have stored up until this day, will be carried off to Babylon. Nothing will be left, says the LORD. And some of your descendants, your own flesh and blood who will be born to you, will be taken away, and they will become eunuchs in the palace of the king of Babylon.' 'The word of the LORD you have spoken is good,' Hezekiah replied. *For he thought, 'Will there not be peace and security in my lifetime?'*" (2 Kgs. 20:16–19, emphasis mine).

Hezekiah showing off his treasures (which were a blessing from God and not what he had earned on his own) displayed some ignorance on his part to safeguard Judah from all pagan countries, no matter how innocent this meeting might have appeared. Isaiah was rightfully upset because he knew the future threat Babylon posed for Judah. As J. Daniel Hays notes, "...Isaiah, knowing that the Babylonians will be the ones in the future who will completely destroy Jerusalem and exile the people, rebukes Hezekiah for his foolishness."[567]

Also note that Hezekiah was comfortable with the rebuke, thinking that it won't affect him directly; he knew God had promised him additional years of life and security, so let God's condemnation fall on his descendants. This is a not a sparkling attitude from an otherwise worthy spiritual heart. C. Hassell Bullock remarks, "Hezekiah, shortsighted and insensitive to the future, had rejoiced that exile would not occur in his day, so it remained for the prophet (Isaiah) to take up the cause for the unborn generation."[568] Adds Walter Brueggemann, "Hezekiah's response to the oracle is perhaps shameless, certainly pathos-filled (20:19)...The second part of the response, however, is less noble, suggesting the king reckons his own life and reign will be undisturbed, as though he had no care for what comes after."[569]

---

[567]J. Daniel Hays, *The Message of the Prophets,* 2010, p. 116.

[568]C. Hassell Bullock, *An Introduction to the Old Testament Prophetic Books,* 2007, p. 183.

[569]Walter Brueggemann, *1 & 2 Kings,* 2000, p. 526.

However, other commentaries are not as quick with the negativity. Richard Patterson and Hermann Austel write, "Some interpreters view it as a callous regard for his own safety...Others consider it an acknowledgement of God's grace and goodness...The canonical commendations of Hezekiah as a man of trust tends to indicate that Hezekiah accepts the Lord's rebuke through Isaiah and is grateful that God's judgement of Judah will not come immediately."[570]

Edward Young reaches a similar conclusion: "There is no egoism in this thought, as Penna seems to think, for the king is not attributing these blessings to his own merit. In reality, the words constitute a childlike acknowledgment of the truth of the prophesy and also of the mercy with which it is intermingled...At the same time his very language shows he considered the mitigation of the punishment a blessing for himself, and yet regarded the woes pronounced upon his descendants as a misfortune of his own."[571]

After the visit from Babylon, the Assyrians started advancing its army toward Jerusalem. When Hezekiah saw Sennacherib and his army heading south toward Jerusalem, he consulted with his officials and military staff about blocking off the water from the springs outside the city to prevent the Assyrians from getting access. Hezekiah refortified the walls around the city and rebuilt the armory. As he assembled his army, he encouraged them to not be afraid of the Assyrians' large army because Judah has God on their side.

The Assyrians captured the fortified cities of Judah outside of Jerusalem. In an effort to slow down the siege toward Jerusalem, Hezekiah offered to pay them a large amount of gold and silver taken from the Temple and royal holdings as a peace offering, hoping the

---

[570]Richard Patterson and Hermann Austel, *The Expositor's Bible Commentary – 1 and 2 Kings*, 2009, pp. 925–926.

[571]Edward Young, *The Book of Isaiah: A Commentary, Volume 2*, 1969, p. 539.

Assyrian king would withdraw.[572] As Provan, et al note, "...the king of Assyria did not on this occasion withdraw upon payment of tribute, choosing while Jerusalem's gates remained closed to him to continue to regard Hezekiah as a rebel."[573] The payment didn't slow down Sennacherib at all; however, he was distracted by news of a potential gathering of an Egyptian army at Lachish, so he departed to meet the perceived, imposing threat. This "news" was a divine intervention to split his forces and save Jerusalem. Meanwhile, he sent his delegate and part of his army to the outskirts of Jerusalem to continue the siege against Judah.

As the army settled at the base of the city, the commander of the Assyrians taunted Hezekiah's people (who were watching from the tops of the walls) to surrender. He boasted that God himself told him to march against Jerusalem and destroy it. He tried to instill fear in the people of Judah and dissuade them from listening to Hezekiah. He argued that their king would try to deceive them into believing God would deliver them, thereby blaspheming God's ability to rescue Jerusalem. The mocking speech was reminiscent of Goliath taunting Saul's army, belittling God's chosen people and their reliance of God for help. The taunts went unanswered. Edward Young notes Hezekiah would not stoop to respond to the insults aimed at God. "There are times when the best answer to blasphemy is a disdainful silence, and this seemed to have been such a time. A reproof would have fallen flat before the Rabshakeh (the Assyrian commander)."[574]

---

[572]The payment to stave off the attack is only mentioned in Second Kings. "So Hezekiah king of Judah sent this message to the king of Assyria at Lachish: 'I have done wrong. Withdraw from me, and I will pay whatever you demand of me.' The king of Assyria exacted from Hezekiah king of Judah three hundred talents of silver and thirty talents of gold [amounting to about $56 million in today's currency]. So Hezekiah gave him all the silver that was found in the temple of the LORD and in the treasuries of the royal palace. At this time Hezekiah king of Judah stripped off the gold with which he had covered the doors and doorposts of the temple of the LORD and gave it to the king of Assyria" (2 Kgs. 18:14–16).

[573]Iain Provan, V. Philips Long, and Tremper Longham, *A Biblical History of Israel*, 2015, p. 370.

[574]Edward Young, *The Book of Isaiah: A Commentary, Volume 2*, 1969, p. 471.

When word of these threats were relayed to Hezekiah, rather than rely on military assistance from any of his neighbors (Egypt comes to mind), he went immediately into the temple of the LORD in humility, seeking the wisdom and advice of the great prophet Isaiah. This was truly in line as a covenantal king. Young continues, "Hezekiah knows the right thing to do. Rending his clothes and putting on sackcloth represent a true penitence and contriteness of heart...Hezekiah's piety is truly exemplary, for not only does he himself engage in prayer, but he also seeks the Word of God through the mouth of the prophet."[575]

In his actions, Hezekiah sought God's assistance in prayer and through his prophet Isaiah. His reaction to his enemy's blasphemy against Judah and God was much different than David's reaction to similar taunts by Goliath. Both were confronted with the physical strength of their enemy. David reacted with righteous anger and had no fear of his enemy. Hezekiah feared for his whole nation and trusted that God would come to their aid. Both men totally relied on God to provide victory, not for their own sake but because victory against such odds would reveal God's glory.

Isaiah told the king and his court not to fear the Assyrians, for God would intervene to save his faithful people. From a military perspective, it was a leap of faith for Hezekiah; the Assyrian army continued to gobble up territory from all the nations around him and Judah had no army to combat them. In fact, the Assyrian taunts included providing Judah with horses and chariots to protect themselves, sarcastically recognizing there wasn't a militia to utilize the offer.

But Hezekiah's faith was strong and he trusted God to save the nation, which He does. God sent a spirit to cause the Assyrian commander to return to King Sennacherib who was engaged nearby. Previously, God caused Sennacherib to believe a huge Egyptian army was on their way toward him, which caused the delay in his assault on Jerusalem. Sennacherib sent another blasphemous letter to Hezekiah to have him capitulate Jerusalem to him. (Sennacherib was concerned about an attack from Judah and Egypt at the same time.)

---

[575] Ibid., p. 472.

The letter was intended to shake Hezekiah's confidence in God, maintaining that other nations he conquered also had their gods and they were of no help to them. He essentially was telling Hezekiah that God was deceiving him into thinking He would rescue him, but that He was as weak as the gods of the lands Sennacherib has already conquered. Iain Provan states there was a marked difference in the Assyrians' message. "Here is a much more direct attack on the Lord than the one in Chapter 18, and one that displays monumental arrogance."[576]

Hezekiah once again reach out to the Lord for deliverance from the Assyrian threat. Young reminds his readers how different the spiritual hearts were between Hezekiah and his father Ahaz when confronted with military threats. "The latter will not ask for a sign in obedience to the prophecy given by God. He would rather rely on human defenses such as the aid of Tiglath-Pileser (Assyrian king at the time). Hezekiah, however, betakes himself to prayer."[577]

"That night the angel of the LORD went out and put to death a hundred and eighty-five thousand in the Assyrian camp. When the people got up the next morning—there were all the dead bodies! So Sennacherib king of Assyria broke camp and withdrew. He returned to Nineveh and stayed there. One day, while he was worshiping in the temple of his god Nisrok, his sons Adrammelek and Sharezer killed him with the sword, and they escaped to the land of Ararat" (2 Kgs. 19:35–37). Similar to when God came to the assistance of Jehoshaphat against great military odds, Hezekiah's people were also saved without engaging the enemy army. God again took care of his faithful people and the people were thankful for God's protection; many offerings were brought forth in worship. The spiritual heart of Hezekiah's people was alive and well.

When Hezekiah died, he was succeeded by his son Manasseh, who did not follow in his father's footsteps. He rebuilt all the pagan altars and followed the detestable practices of the pagan nations his father

---

[576]Iain Provan, *Commentary: 1 & 2 Kings,* 1995, p. 258

[577]Edward Young, *The Book of Isaiah: A Commentary, Volume 2,* 1969, p. 482.

had previously driven out. He rebuilt all the high places his father destroyed, built altars to Baal, and worshiped the stars. "But Manasseh led Judah and the people of Jerusalem astray, so that they did more evil than the nations the LORD had destroyed before the Israelites. The LORD spoke to Manasseh and his people, but they paid no attention" (2 Chron. 33:9–10). He desecrated the temple by erecting pagan altars inside the courts. He sacrificed his son Molech to fire, practiced divination, sought omens, and consulted oracles. Unlike his father leading his people to worship God, Manasseh led his people to worship idols in pagan practices so that they did more evil than the pagan nations around Judah.

Josephus notes that Manasseh's actions were no better than the transgressions pursued by the northern nation of Israel prior to its destruction: "...he barbarously killed all the righteous men that were among the Hebrews, nor would he spare the profits, for he every day killed them until Jerusalem was overflowing with blood."[578] It's no wonder that Manasseh's actions rival that of Ahab mentioned earlier.

Regarding Isaiah's judgement on Israel's idolatry, G. K. Beale notes, "Under Manasseh's reign (697–642 BC) and influence, idolatry flourished in Israel to such an unprecedented degree, even to the extent that the king installed idols in the temple and the nation became more idolatrous than its pagan neighbors (2 Kings 21:1–11). As a result, Israel would have to undergo a severe judgement (2 Kings 21:10–18)."[579] Manasseh's reign was the result of Hezekiah's desire to live beyond his appointed time, which God had granted. Judah sinned against God with such magnitude that it caused Ezekiel to write that its sin of idolatry was worse than her sister nation of Israel. "Her sister Oholibah [Judah] saw this, yet in her lust and prostitution she was more depraved than her sister [Israel]" (Ezek. 23:11).

While Second Kings does not record the following event, Second Chronicles does: as judgement for his sins, God punished Manasseh by allowing the Assyrians to capture him and hand him over to the

---

[578]Josephus, *Jewish Antiquities*, Book 10, Chapter 3, verse 38.

[579]G. K. Beale, *We Become What We Worship*, 2008, p. 59, footnote.

Babylonians. Manasseh realized the error of his ways. "In his distress he sought the favor of the LORD his God and humbled himself greatly before the God of his ancestors. And when he prayed to him, the LORD was moved by his entreaty and listened to his plea; so he brought him back to Jerusalem and to his kingdom. Then Manasseh knew that the LORD is God" (2 Chron. 33:12–13).

With his prayers answered and his life spared, Manasseh's faith was reborn. He reversed all the actions that led his people into idolatry. As Josephus states, "...he tried, if it were possible, to cast out his memory of his former sins against God, of which he now repented, to apply himself to a very religious life."[580] He removed the altars he dedicated to idols, restored the temple and its altar, and dedicated it all back to the Lord. He led the people of Judah in the same fashion. God's mercy and forgiveness restored his spiritual heart to lead his people back to God in a rare reversal of events.

Frederick Mabie notes that Manasseh's conversion "shows that God can restore anyone who seeks him in true repentance, regardless of the depth of darkness of that person's ungodliness."[581] Adds Josephus, "And indeed, when he had changed his former course, he so led his life for the time to come, that from the time of his return to piety toward God he was deemed a happy man and a pattern for imitation."[582]

Most commentators feel the story of Manasseh's repentance and restoration was included to prove to the post-exiled Jews (the writer's initial audience) how God can restore His relationship with His people. From H. G. M. Williamson, "The experience of Manasseh is thus to be read as a paradigm of the people's experience, a reflection of their own Babylonian exile, which will aid them in the interpretation of their current situation and encourage them on the way forward toward a regaining of blessings they have lost."[583]

---

[580]Josephus, *Jewish Antiquities,* Book 10, Chapter 3, verse 2:42.

[581]Frederick Mabie, *The Expositor's Bible Commentary – 1 and Chronicles,* 2010, p. 309.

[582]Josephus, *Jewish Antiquities,* Book 10, Chapter 3, verse 45.

[583]H. G. M. Williamson, *1 and 2 Chronicles,* 2010, p. 389.

Eugene Merrill provides another reason for the inclusion of Manasseh's restoration. "Despite Manasseh's unprecedented wickedness, a matter the Chronicler makes no attempt to hide in verses 1–9, he is still the scion of David and as such is a link in that long messianic chain. The inclusion of the account of his repentance and restoration is designed to offer at least some legitimacy to the otherwise embarrassing claims of the king to Davidic succession."[584]

Finally, Williamson makes the case that the amount of restoration activity by Manasseh had to be limited at best, noting that "the idols installed earlier by Manasseh were not removed until Josiah's reign."[585] As evidence of his point, he cites Jeremiah, who was witness to Manasseh's activities (much earlier historically than the Chronicler's writing): "I will make them abhorrent to all the kingdoms of the earth because of what Manasseh son of Hezekiah king of Judah did in Jerusalem" (Jeremiah 15:4), as well as the Chronicler's own words later in Chapter 33: "Amon was twenty-two years old when he became king, and he reigned in Jerusalem two years. He did evil in the eyes of the LORD, as his father Manasseh had done. Amon worshiped and *offered sacrifices to all the idols Manasseh had made*" (2 Chron, 33:21–22, emphasis mine).

Josiah, the Last of Judah's Obedient Kings

Manasseh reigned for 55 years and was succeeded briefly by his son Amon who followed in the idolatry practices of his father before his conversion. Amon led Judah for two years and was assassinated by his own servants. His son Josiah took the reins at 8 years old. Josiah is the last of the faithful kings, as he had it in his heart to live for the Lord in the manner of David; he reigned in Judah for 31 years. Christopher Wright correctly identifies that "Josiah was the only king of Judah to

---

[584]Eugene Merrill, *A Commentary on 1 & 2 Chronicles,* 2015, p. 563.

[585]H. G. M. Williamson, *1 and 2 Chronicles,* 2010, p. 394.

have a virtually unblemished record of faithfulness to God's law in the exercise of practical and compassionate justice."[586]

At the age of 16, Josiah "began to seek the God of his father David" (2 Chron. 34:3). Once again, the core ingredients of the nation's spiritual heart were revived by Josiah as it had been by the other good kings before him. We find in Scriptures, "Neither before nor after Josiah was there a king like him who turned to the LORD as he did—with all his heart and with all his soul and with all his strength, in accordance with all the Law of Moses" (2 Kgs. 23:25).

While it was in his heart to do God's will at such a young age, Josiah had the advantage of the prophet Jeremiah at his service for spiritual guidance in his early twenties. It was at that time Josiah began to reverse the pagan course Judah took under Amon in the same fashion Hezekiah had done ridding the nation of the pagan influence. He tore down the high places of worship, along with removing all images of the pagan gods that had been erected. Wright observes, "At the age of 21, in 629 BC, he launched a program of sweeping reforms that brought about massive religious and social reforms to his nation. He purged all the non-Yahwistic cults and shrines and all Assyrian idolatrous and occult practices."[587]

Josiah extended his spiritual revival program into cities formerly of the nation of Israel, including Bethel (which was the first temple erected by Jeroboam who installed the golden calves when the nations split), Manasseh, Ephraim, and Simeon, and as far as Naphtali. Like Asa and Hezekiah, Josiah carried out the commission God intended for His nation of priests to spread His word beyond the borders of Judah, but Josiah's efforts exceeded those of his predecessors. "Just as he had done at Bethel, Josiah removed all the shrines at the high places that the kings of Israel had built in the towns of Samaria and that had aroused the LORD's anger. Josiah slaughtered all the priests of those high places on the altars and burned human bones on them. Then he went back to Jerusalem" (2 Kgs. 23:19–20). Iain Provan notes, "For

---

[586]Christopher Wright, *The Message of Jeremiah*, 2014, p. 45.

[587] Ibid., p. 19.

the first time since Solomon, a king has been able to treat the northern area of Israel as if it were part of the same kingdom as the south."[588]

When that was complete, he directed his officials to determine the amount of tithing that had been restored under his direction and instructed Hilkiah the high priest to use those funds to repair the neglected temple. Tithing extended beyond Judah's borders into some of the northern cities of Israel, which was indicative of his ability to cause the spiritual revival. Frederick Mabie writes, "Notice that Josiah's desire to hear from God relates not only to his concern for Judah but also for his concern for the remnant of Israel. He truly desired to have all of the Jews return to God's favor."[589] This was another demonstration that the heart of obedience and faith to God was capable of being revived. The northern cities had a long history of pagan idol worship, which Josiah was successful in reversing when he purged the altars dedicated to false gods. With the removal of those places of worship, he returned the cities to obedience and faithfulness.

In the course of the temple's restoration, Hilkiah discovered the long-lost book of the Law that God had given through Moses.[590] The book was brought to Josiah and read in his presence. When Josiah realized the punishment for all Israel for failing to keep God's word, he tore his garments in repentance, fearful that he and his people may still be out of God's favor. Concerned that God's wrath would fall upon Judah, he immediately dispatched the priest to inquire of the Lord concerning the sins of their fathers.

Josiah's actions were those of a true covenantal king. For the sake of the nation, he had to be sure that Judah was not lacking in its faith. His main concern was for his people; through his actions and motivation, he showed his humility and selflessness. He relied on his priests to plead to God on Judah's behalf. He was willing to repent of any actions or omissions that would put Judah in jeopardy of falling out

---

[588]Iain Provan, *1 & 2 Kings,* 1995, p. 274.

[589]Frederick Mabie, *The Expositor's Bible Commentary – 1 and 2 Chronicles,* 2010, p. 316.

[590]Christopher Wright, *The Message of Jeremiah,* 2014, p. 49. The author notes this was likely the book of Deuteronomy.

of favor with God. He didn't rely on his previous actions for getting Judah's faith restored; had his obedience given him a pass from judgement? For the sake of Judah, he had to be sure, so he sought counsel from the prophetess Huldah.

The response from God was a warning of His wrath to those who continued to forsake him and worship other gods. However, God acknowledged Josiah's actions and the nature of his heart. God was aware of the strides Judah had made in its collective faith and He promised to spare them from impending disaster. The prophet Huldah said, "'Tell the king of Judah, who sent you to inquire of the LORD, "This is what the LORD, the God of Israel, says concerning the words you heard: Because your heart was responsive and you humbled yourself before God when you heard what he spoke against this place and its people, and because you have humbled yourself before me and tore your robes and wept in my presence, I have heard you, declares the Lord. Now, I will gather you to your ancestors, and you will be buried in peace. Your eyes will not see all the disaster I am going to bring on this place and on those who live here." So they took her answer back to the king" (2 Chron. 34:26–28).

With those words of assurance, Josiah took to his faith with renewed vigor. This was similar to Asa getting assurance from God, and Josiah took the same actions as Asa. He called upon the elders and the nation to gather at the temple where he read from the book of the covenant. He made a covenant with God that he would keep His commandments with all his heart and soul (the First Great Commandment) and to perform the actions written in the book. He then involved the nation in making the same pledge: to be obedient and faithful to God and the commandments.

Josiah permanently removed from the temple all the vessels made for pagan idols and burned them. He deposed the priests who made offerings in high places in the cities in Judah, destroyed the houses of cult prostitutes and the altars of pagan gods, and rid Judah of the pagan places built by Manasseh and Solomon.

Eugene Merrill notes, "The exclusion of idolatry from Judah was, however, only one side of the coin of reformation. It was now necessary for Josiah to lead the nation back to Yahweh and restore the structures of worship and service according to Mosaic prescription."[591] Josiah restored the national celebration of the Passover. He and his officials made their own personal contributions for the nation to participate in the ceremony. The service was available to Judah and the remnants of the Israelites that were left behind from the Assyrian exile. Josiah extended Judah's outreach to their northern brethren so God would be known to the lost souls of Israel. Josiah's love for the people was not limited by political boundaries; he fulfilled the Second Great Commandment through his actions as a good king.

Scriptures recount the detail to which Josiah followed the book of the covenant during the Passover service, which had not been celebrated since the days of Samuel the prophet. Robert Jamieson et al., observe that the reason it was unique was "the ardent devotion of the king and people, the disregard of purely traditional customs, and the unusually strict adherence, even in the smallest minutiae, to the forms of observance prescribed in the book of the law, the discovery of an original copy of which had produced so great a sensation."[592] David Guzik adds, "This celebration of Passover was so significant that one had to go back *before* the time of David and Solomon to find a keeping of Passover that was so well organized and joyfully conducted...It was remarkable in its strict obedience to the Law of Moses."[593]

Josiah was bound by God's word, strictly adhering to the guidelines of the covenantal king God gave to Moses centuries before him. He was taken by the Scriptures and strove to put God's words into action; one of the better examples of a spiritual heart like David's. "Moreover, Josiah put away the mediums and the necromancers and the household gods and the idols and all the abominations that were seen in the

---

[591]Eugene Merrill, *Kingdom of Priests,* 2008, p. 456.

[592]Jamieson, Fausset & Brown, "Commentary on 2 Chronicles 35 by Jamieson, Fausset & Brown," Blue Letter Bible, last modified February 19, 2000, https://www.blueletterbible.org/ Comm/jfb/2Ch/2Ch_035.cfm.

[593]David Guzik, "Study Guide for 2 Chronicles 35 by David Guzik," Blue Letter Bible, last modified February 21, 2017, https://www.blueletterbible.org/Comm/guzik_david/ StudyGuide 2017-2Ch/2Ch-35.cfm.

land of Judah and in Jerusalem, that he might establish the words of the law that were written in the book that Hilkiah the priest found in the house of the Lord. Before him there was no king like him, who turned to the Lord with all his heart and with all his soul and with all his might, according to all the Law of Moses, nor did any like him arise after him" (2 Kgs. 23:24–25, ESV).

Josiah was heavily invested in fulfilling the instructions in the book of the Law, which included the practice of gleaning as a means to care for the poor. In addition, there were directions for caring for widows, orphans, and foreigners; for example, "When you finish tithing all your income in the third year (the year of tithing), you must give it to the Levites, the resident foreigners, the orphans, and the widows so that they may eat to their satisfaction in your villages" (Deut. 26:12, NET). These guidelines were intended for the Israelites to care for their own and foreigners. Social justice was key to the Jews being a holy people.

Those actions were important to Josiah, and he was adamant about following the laws regarding social justice and adhering to the Second Great Commandment. Then there is Jeremiah's criticism of Jehoiakim, Josiah's son, who failed to follow his father's example. "'Does it make you a king to have more and more cedar? Did not your father have food and drink? He did what was right and just, so all went well with him. He defended the cause of the poor and needy, and so all went well. Is that not what it means to know me?' declares the LORD" (Jer. 22:15–16). Christopher Wright tells us, "He did righteousness and justice (which God delights in) and he defended the poor and needy (whom God cares for)."[594]

Caring for those in need or of lower social status was a characteristic often missing in the nation of Judah and the northern nation of Israel. The religious and political leaders didn't care for the unrepresented, the weak, and the poor of their nations. The lack of social justice was a common condemnation preached by the prophets as a warning of eventual judgement. As king of Judah, Josiah was the

---

[594]Christopher Wright, *The Message of Jeremiah,* 2014, p. 240.

exception. Wright accurately points out, "Josiah, in short, knew the Lord. And the proof was practical and ethical. And the affirmation that he did know the Lord came not from his own boasting, but post-humously from God himself through his prophet Jeremiah.[595]

Even with this revival moving his people closer to God, Josiah's illustrious spiritual career ended prematurely. Necho king of Egypt and his army were headed toward the Euphrates River to attack Assyria. Josiah thwarted this maneuver by confronting the Egyptian army with his own troops. Since the time of Manasseh's reign, Judah was a vassal to the Assyrian empire; hence, Josiah had some obligation to protect Assyria from Egypt's attack.

However, Iain Provan et al., note, "The Egyptians often appear in texts from the period of Josiah's reign as allies of the Assyrians in the struggle with Babylon, sending them to the north at least from 616 (BC) to join the Assyrians in battle there."[596] The relationship between Assyria and Egypt "...remained friendly throughout this period. Certainly, the Egyptians did not hesitate to support the Assyrians when they later were confronted by the Babylonians."[597] Josiah's moti-vation for his actions was to establish a sense of independence from his father's prior relationship with Egypt in the hopes of currying favor with the Babylonians.[598]

Necho sent an envoy to tell Josiah that the Egyptian army had no intention of attacking Judah, but that God instructed Necho to hurry into battle. He urged Josiah to allow the Egyptian army to get through or it would be seen as opposing God's plan. Necho added that God was with him, so stand aside or be destroyed.

Robert Jamieson et al., write that, "Commentators are not agreed whether it was really a divine commission given him through Jeremiah, or whether he merely used the name of God as an authority that Josiah

---

[595] Ibid., p. 241.

[596] Iain Provan, Phillip Long, and Tremper Longham, *A Biblical History of Israel*, 2015, p. 275.

[597] Ibid.

[598] Ibid., p. 276.

would not refuse to obey. As he could not know the truth of Necho's declaration, Josiah did not sin in opposing him; or, if he sinned at all, it was a sin of ignorance."[599] Frederick Mabie offers an alternate explanation of Josiah intending to align itself with Babylon: "However, it seems most likely that Josiah's action reflected some type of alliance between Judah and Babylon (an attempt to get out from under Assyrian vassalage)...such alliances imply inadequate allegiance to Yahweh...This verse suggests that God was providing Josiah the opportunity to repent of seeking security apart from the Lord."[600]

I offer that God was leaving Josiah to follow his heart; a test of trusting in the Lord only. Like Hezekiah, Josiah did not heed God's word coming from Necho, if indeed it had. In any event, Josiah could have consulted Jeremiah or his priests to call on the Lord for direction. Instead, he took to battle, was fatally wounded, and died on his retreat to Jerusalem. Josiah was greatly revered by his people and his death rippled through his kingdom. "All Judah and Jerusalem mourned for Josiah. Jeremiah also uttered a lament for Josiah; and all the singing men and singing women have spoken of Josiah in their laments to this day. They made these a rule in Israel; behold, they are written in the Laments" (2 Chron. 35:24–25, ESV).

The Fall of Jerusalem and Destruction of the Temple

Josiah's death ended the last spiritual restoration for Judah. His successors returned Judah to evil and idol worshiping, obliterating any progress the nation made through Josiah. In just one generation, Judah's disobedience resulted in its Babylonian captivity and exile, despite the warnings of the prophets, including Jeremiah, Ezekiel, and Zechariah. In fact, under the reign of Zedekiah, the last king of Judah, the apostasy exceeded the direction of the king; it contaminated all of

---

[599] Jamieson, Fausset & Brown, "Commentary on 2 Chronicles 35 by Jamieson, Fausset & Brown," Blue Letter Bible, last modified February 19, 2000, https://www.blueletterbible.org/ Comm/jfb/2Ch/2Ch_035.cfm.

[600] Frederick Mabie, *Commentary on 1 & 2 Chronicles,* 2010, p. 324.

Judah. Mabie adds, "Sadly, the depth of unfaithfulness is not limited to the ungodly reign of Zedekiah but likewise, seen in the hearts of both people and priest."[601]

Scriptures note that Zedekiah's lack of political awareness led to Judah's ultimate destruction. "He also rebelled against King Nebuchadnezzar, who had made him take an oath in God's name. He became stiff-necked and hardened his heart and would not turn to the LORD, the God of Israel. Furthermore, all the leaders of the priests and the people became more and more unfaithful, following all the detestable practices of the nations and defiling the temple of the LORD, which he had consecrated in Jerusalem" (2 Chron. 36:13–14).

As described in more detail in the next chapter, God revealed to the prophet Ezekiel the depths to which worship took place within the temple itself. It had become so depraved that God decided He'd had enough; He left the temple and the city, never to return. Not long after, the Babylonians destroyed Jerusalem and the temple. Zedekiah was captured trying to leave through the back door, so to speak. Nebuchadnezzar executed Zedekiah's sons in front of him before blinding the Jewish king and leading most of the survivors back to Babylon. The destruction of Judah was complete.

After all of this and with most of Judah taken into exile by the Babylonians, the small remnants left behind learned nothing from God's judgement. They were so fearful of the Babylonians that, after an internal coup against the Babylonian-installed government, they asked Jeremiah what God wanted them to do next. Jeremiah gave them God's final warning to stay faithful and remain in the land.

This command fell on hardened hearts and deaf ears. Rejecting Jeremiah's command from God to remain in Judah, the people responded with the worst apostasy: "'We will not listen to the message you have spoken to us in the name of the LORD! We will certainly do everything we said we would: We will burn incense to the Queen of Heaven and will pour out drink offerings to her just as we and our ancestors, our kings and our officials did in the towns of Judah and

---

[601] Ibid., p. 331.

in the streets of Jerusalem. At that time, we had plenty of food and were well off and suffered no harm. But ever since we stopped burning incense to the Queen of Heaven and pouring out drink offerings to her, we have had nothing and have been perishing by sword and famine'" (Jer. 44:16–18).

Why did they bother to ask Jeremiah for God's input when they pledged their continued allegiance to the Queen of Heaven? She hadn't let them down like God had. Stay behind and get slaughtered by the Babylonians? No way! The deserters won out; the small group decided to flee to Egypt for refuge, dragging Jeremiah with them. As we've seen, any time Egypt was involved, bad things happened to God's chosen people when not instructed by God to go there. They were destroyed (God's judgement against their disobedience) when the Babylonians attacked Egypt and wiped out the nation.

The nation that had reached its spiritual zenith under Solomon's reign was now displaced, both Judah and Israel were completely destroyed, and God's chosen people were scattered throughout the region as a result of their sins. As G. K. Beale notes, "Israel's spiritual separation from God due to their intractable idolatry is partly pictured by their removal from the land where God said He would be intimately present with his people. This is not only a picture of their spiritual condition but a judgement for it."[602] Interestingly, Stephen Dempster remarks that in taking the Promised Land several hundreds of years earlier, only through obedience to God would the Israelites be allowed to keep the land. "Residence in the land will depend upon obedience, and disobedience will mean expulsion from the land, just as it was in the garden of Eden at the beginning."[603] In effect, God's people had come full circle from the beginning of creation: cast out of Eden and cast out of the Promised Land.

The plan God had for the nation of Israel to represent His holiness here on earth had only momentary signs of fulfilling that role. Michael

---

[602]G, K. Beale, *We Become What We Worship,* 2008, p. 50.

[603]Stephen Dempster, *Dominion and Dynasty: A Theology of the Hebrew Bible,* 2003, p. 129.

Vlach writes, "In sum, the nation chosen by God to be a kingdom of priests, a holy nation and a chosen people, failed its mission. Israel was supposed to be a holy witness to the nations but instead became just like the nations, even serving their gods. As a result, dispersion to the nations occurred just as God predicted (Deuteronomy 30). Yet this dispersion to the nations would not be permanent. With the decline of the monarchy, the prophets became prominent as they preached repentance and future restoration of Israel."[604]

The promise of restoration revealed through the prophets will be discussed in the last two chapters.

---

[604]Michael Vlach, *He Will Reign Forever,* 2017, p. 124.

Chapter 12

THE PROPHETS PART I

The Message for a Circumcised Heart

Although the guidelines for spiritual living were given through Moses (see Chapter 5), God continued to speak to His people through His prophets. Allan Harman writes that one of the primary messages of the prophets was obedience to God as part of their obligation to the Mosaic covenant. "They were not originators of new teaching but rather called to challenge the commitment to God's covenantal requirements in the Mosaic law."[605] God's messages were intended to guide them to clear the worldly clutter from their hearts so they could better serve Him and care for one another. In many cases, God called for them to "circumcise their hearts" and remove the physical trappings of the world that got in the way of them following God's commandments willingly and faithfully.

In addition to the prophets identified in the books of Chronicles and Kings, there are sixteen books in the Old Testament written by prophets: four from the Major Prophets (Isaiah, Jeremiah, Ezekiel, and Daniel) and twelve from the Minor Prophets (Jonah, Amos, Hosea, Micah, Zephaniah, Habakkuk, Nahum, Obadiah, Zechariah, Joel, Haggai, and Malachi).[606] It is not my intention to review all sixteen

---

[605]Harman, Allan, *Expository Commentary - Joel*, 2008, p. 266.

[606]The distinction between major and minor prophets is merely the amount of written material provided in the Scriptures by the individual prophet and not as a distinction of their relative importance. Note that all sixteen prophets wrote during the period after the nation was divided following Solomon's reign and in some cases after the return of the exiles from Babylon.

prophets and the range of their messages. Instead, I'll focus on the common message of repenting and cleansing the heart and returning to the covenant commitment. I'll give a brief overview of the prophets in terms of history, the relevance of their messages, and their target audiences. These messages are universal in that they speak to the constant struggle to maintain a healthy spiritual heart. While the messages were directed to the people of that time, they may easily apply to our lives as well.

The Role for the Prophets

There were many prophets throughout the Old Testament, including Moses and Abraham. In some cases, the prophets were used by God to communicate instructions to kings, such as Nathan advising David, or Samuel attempting to advise Saul. The messages from these prophets were often targeted toward a specific situation faced by the king. Other prophets, like Elijah and Elisha, were used to warn the king and religious leaders in the northern nation of Israel against worshiping false idols.

J. Robert Vannoy writes that the primary task of the prophets from Samuel's time forward "...was to hold Israel's kings accountable to the (Mosaic) covenant. To a large degree the prophets functioned as messengers of the covenant."[607] He notes that the prophets had a vested interest in holding the kings responsible for keeping the covenant since "the kingship was established by the word of the prophet."[608] The prophet Samuel established the kingships for Saul and David, Nathan disclosed God's anointment for Solomon, and Abijah was sent to reveal Jeroboam's kingship for Israel when the nation is divided.

After the kingdom was divided, the role of the prophets expanded. Graeme Goldsworthy succinctly summarizes the message of these prophets: "The writing of the prophets all do three things. First, they identify the specific way in which Israel has broken the covenant.

---

[607] J. Robert Vannoy, *Biblical Commentary: 1–2 Samuel,* 2009, p. 29.

[608] Ibid., p. 28.

These include social injustice, oppression, insincere worship of God, mixing pagan religion with the true faith...Second, they pronounce the judgment of God on this unfaithfulness to the covenant...Third, they speak a message of comfort to the faithful: God will yet save them completely, finally, and gloriously."[609]

I described how peace was lost after the country was divided following Solomon's reign. It seemed that the two nations were constantly attacked by one force or another when they were not attacking each other. During those assaults, the prophets warned against relying on military support from other nations. Time and again, God protected against heavy opposing odd, *if the leaders prayed and sought his aid*. Jeremiah and Ezekiel in particular warned against continual reliance on Egypt for military aid against the impending threat of the Babylonian army headed for Jerusalem. Jenson notes that, "It is as if Israel had never really come out of Egypt...Israel, says the Lord by Ezekiel, was from the start and always remained a liberated and chosen people who did not want to be free or different."[610]

The format for this and the next two chapters follows the three common elements cited by Goldsworthy. First, a review of the call for repentance of the sins being committed, which centered on the worshiping of false idols and mixing the worship of God with pagan practices. In either case, the people took their cues from the religious leaders, and the king and his administration.

Another sin the prophets commonly addressed was social injustice, where the needs of the widows, the orphans, and the poor were neglected by those with means, particularly those in power who had the ability to care for the unrepresented. C. Hassell Bullock says that the prophets were to intercede for those who had no representation in Jewish society. "Nowhere was the decay of the society better registered than the neglect of the indigent poor and nowhere was the true nature of Israel's God more faithfully conveyed than in the words of

---

[609]Graeme Goldsworthy, *According to Plan: The Unfolding Revelation of God in the Bible*, 1991, p. 189.

[610]Robert Jenson, *Commentary on the Bible: Ezekiel*, 2009, p. 191.

the prophets for the disadvantaged and oppressed."[611] In effect, the guidelines of the Two Great Commandments were ignored during the reign of the kings who did evil in the eyes of the Lord. The prophets' messages were to warn the nation of the consequences if they did not repent.

The second common element of the prophets' messages was to identify the consequences of refusing to abide by the covenant promises. Judgement resulted in the destruction of Israel by the Assyrians, the fall of Jerusalem, and the destruction of the temple by the Babylonians 140 years later. The judgement led to their eviction from the Promised Land and resulted in captivity for both nations.

Despite the oncoming judgements, the prophets pointed to a silver lining. The third common element was a message of hope after the consequences were issued. There was hope for Israel that God would restore the nation and have them return to Him. In terms of this text, that focus would be the restoration of the heart and the personal relationship with God through His everlasting ability for forgiveness.

The key to the restoration of the heart was the promised path of salvation through the Messiah in Jesus (Chapter 13), followed by the infusion of the Holy Spirit (Chapter 14) to restore the spiritual heart. The salvation promised to Israel was not limited to just that nation. As described earlier, this promise was revealed to Abraham whereby all nations would be blessed through him, and restoration of the heart would be available to all. This will be described more fully in Volume II, but for now, the target audience for the prophets' messages was God's chosen people.

Apostasy: Violation of The First Great Commandment

Throughout this text we've seen how the Scriptures describe the difficulty of Israel remaining faithful to God. Without a strong leader to help them maintain their faith, pagan influence from the nations around them infiltrated their hearts and idolatry quickly and easily

---

[611]C. Hassell Bullock, *An Introduction to the Old Testament Prophetic Books,* 2007, p. 30.

led the Israelites astray. The intended role of God's nation of priests seldom materialized; their spiritual hearts were indistinguishable from the pagan nations to whom they were supposed to provide a guiding light. This role seemed to be the main thrust of the prophets' messages: We are God's chosen people. Repent of idolatry and pagan practices; be holy and pure as God intended for us to be. God's special relationship with Israel required effort on the part of the nation to maintain that connection.

Since much of the prophets' warnings and guidance were similar in focus, I won't delve into each prophet's writing separately, but will provide a sampling of their messages.

Amos

Amos was an early minor prophet, addressing the sins of the northern nation of Israel around 780–745 BC, but there were also implicit warnings for the southern nation of Judah. Like his successors, Amos called attention to idolatry and social injustice. Michael McKelvey writes, "Since idolatry was at the heart of the nation's unfaithfulness, it is not surprising that their turning from God led them away from his moral standard (his law) of righteousness, goodness and equity. Since they failed to love God, they inevitably failed to love their fellow man...The rich were oppressing the poor, corruption was pervasive, self-aggrandizement was the norm, and remarkable indifference to the plight of others and the immoral state of society was common."[612]

Amos addressed the widespread practice of worshiping false gods and defaming the Sabbath. Speaking on God's behalf, he chastised the people of Israel for their hypocrisy and lack of sincerity in their feeble respect for worshiping God. "'I hate, I despise your religious festivals; your assemblies are a stench to me. Even though you bring me burnt offerings and grain offerings, I will not accept them. Though you bring choice fellowship offerings, I will have no regard for them. Away with

---

[612]Michael McKelvey, *ESV Expository Commentary: Daniel–Malachi (Amos)*, 2018, p. 307.

the noise of your songs! I will not listen to the music of your harps. But let justice roll on like a river, righteousness like a never-failing stream! Did you bring me sacrifices and offerings forty years in the wilderness, people of Israel?'" (Amos 5:21–25).

Amos chastised the Israelites for merely going through the motions in their attempt to worship God by rote. They attended all the festivals, and praised God with lip service, but they lacked justice and compassion; there was no righteousness or sincerity. Their worshiping was in vain, while God required obedience and love in their hearts. David Guzik notes that Amos' audience was completely oblivious to their lack of faith. "This [condemnation of false worship] would have amazed—and offended—those in Israel who heard Amos say this. They told themselves that they were really honoring God and pleasing Him by their observance of the feasts and sacred assemblies, but God was offended by their religious ceremonialism, disconnected from the heart and justice toward one another."[613]

Adherence to religious ceremonies with a lack of heart meant nothing to God. In Chapter 2, Cain's lack of a righteous heart was cause for God to reject his sacrifice. Centuries later, nothing changed in God's attitude toward worship; it must be sincere, obedient, and from the heart with no underlying selfish motive. As Bullock notes, "Religion that is confined to the sanctuary is worse than no religion at all, for it is false. Amos and the prophets generally issued their most stinging rebukes against those who practiced pseudo-piety. Hypocrisy is worse than atheism for it camouflages the sickness that grace is meant to heal...(Such) hypocrisy is not even recognized by its adherents."[614]

Hosea

There isn't a lot of background information for Hosea; indications are that he was in the northern nation of Israel and wrote during

---

[613]David Guzik, "Study Guide for Amos 5 by David Guzik," Blue Letter Bible, last modified February 21, 2017, https://www.blueletterbible.org/Comm/guzik_david/StudyGuide2017-Amo/Amo-5.cfm.

[614]C. Hassell Bullock, *An Introduction to the Old Testament Prophetic Books*, 207, p. 95.

the period prior to the Assyrian captivity in 722 BC, making him a contemporary to Amos. As noted in Chapter 11, there were no religious revivals or restoration in the north because every king from Jeroboam forward encouraged idol worship, even though a remnant stayed faithful to worshiping God. However, taking their cue from the king, the people in the north practiced polytheism; they didn't focus on God alone. From Kevin Vanhoozer, "...idolatry was rampant, respect for the law was nonexistent and the people were in effect treating Yahweh as an idol or a Baal who could be pacified by presents and bribed into acting on Israel's behalf."[615] The sin of idolatry was referred to as adultery in Hosea's writings, who used the analogy of being married to a prostitute to describe Israel's unfaithful relationship with God.

Hosea joined the other prophets in his rebuke against Israel for being more concerned with religious ritualism than adhering to the Two Great Commandments. Similar to Amos, Hosea's audience was equally oblivious to their lack of faith. J. Daniel Hays comments, "the people believed that if they performed religious rituals, then everything would be all right. They could sin as much as they wanted to and worship other gods if they wanted to as long as they kept the basic religious rituals of Yahweh worship."[616]

Speaking on God's behalf, Hosea went directly to the core of this problem: "For I desire mercy, not sacrifice, and acknowledgment of God rather than burnt offerings" (Hosea 6:6). Jesus dealt similarly with the same hypocrisy of the Pharisees. "'But go and learn what this means: "I desire mercy, not sacrifice." For I have not come to call the righteous, but sinners'" (Matt. 9:13).

The issue was not the manner of worship or how it was performed, but the motivation behind the action. That is, what was the condition of the heart during community worship? The question of the heart was what Amos and Hosea were addressing: what was the motivation for worshiping the Lord? Earlier we read that Samuel admonished

---

[615]Kevin Vanhoozer, *Dictionary for Theological Interpretation of the Bible,* 2005, p. 308.

[616]J. Daniel Hays, *The Message of the Prophets,* 2010, p. 270.

Saul for an unauthorized sacrifice; it was obedience to God's will that was required. Hosea reminded his audience that worship required sincerity and obedience that came from the heart.

Israel's disobedience in worshiping false gods was problematic because they were no different than the nations around them. It happened when Moses led his people out of Egypt, and it continued through the time of the judges, Solomon's reign, and the Babylonian captivity. It was a stumbling block that destroyed the nation of Israel.

Micah

Micah's writing took place around the same time as Isaiah, in the years just before the northern nation of Israel was destroyed by the Assyrians in 722 BC. He followed the theme Amos and Hosea discussed regarding ritualistic worship, with Micah's focus on pagan practices mixed into the Jewish services. Apparently, Israel didn't think such a mixture was a problem or that it would lead to God's judgement. Vanhoozer noted that the people addressed in Micah's message "assumed that God's presence in their midst exempted them from adversity."[617] Micah rebuked those in authority who held this opinion. "'Hear this, you leaders of Jacob, you rulers of Israel, who despise justice and distort all that is right; who build Zion with bloodshed, and Jerusalem with wickedness. Her leaders judge for a bribe, her priests teach for a price, and her prophets tell fortunes for money. Yet they look for the LORD's support and say, "Is not the LORD among us? No disaster will come upon us"'" (Mic. 3:9–11).

Micah reiterated the message of his predecessors: God was not interested in ritualistic sacrifices, whereas the Israelites believed that was all that was needed to appease God. "They thus give sacrifices and expect them to be sufficient to appease if not to please God, rather than seeing what God requires."[618] As Hosea expounded upon earlier, Micah's message was that the Lord expected something more significant than that. God expected obedient characteristics that are the core

---

[617]Kevin Vanhoozer, *Dictionary of Theological Interpretation of the Bible,* 2005, p. 514.
[618] Ibid.

of spiritual hearts. God looks for a heart that exhibits just living and shows mercy. He is happy with humble hearts and quality of worship.

Micah set out the criteria for what God was expecting of His people. "With what shall I come before the LORD and bow down before the exalted God? Shall I come before him with burnt offerings, with calves a year old? Will the LORD be pleased with thousands of rams, with ten thousand rivers of olive oil? Shall I offer my firstborn for my transgression, the fruit of my body for the sin of my soul? He has shown you, O mortal, what is good. And what does the LORD require of you? *To act justly and to love mercy and to walk humbly with your God*" (Mic. 6:6–8, emphasis mine). God emphasized actions based on a spiritual hear that showed compassion, mercy, and humility before God.

J. Daniel Hays notes, "Yahweh desires of his people that they do justice, that they love *hesed* (loyal, faithful love), and that they walk humbly with Yahweh (a daily relationship). Here, Micah pulls together several major themes of prophetic literature." Hays continues that through Micah message, God was more concerned with having justice shown rather than zealous rituals, and to show mercy toward one another and to be humble before Him.[619]

Jeremiah

Jeremiah's role as a prophet began during the latter half of King Josiah's reign in Judah and his commission lasted 45 years, through the fall of Jerusalem and the destruction of temple by the Babylonians. His initial calling to serve the Lord was in the thirteenth year of King Josiah's reign in 627 BC, the last of the obedient kings of Judah. Jeremiah survived Jehoiakim[620] and Zedekiah's reign, the latter ending in 587 BC when Judah was destroyed by the Babylonians. Even though

---

[619]J. Daniel Hays, *The Message of the Prophets,* 2010, p. 315.

[620]Two other kings came before Jehoiakim, Jehoahaz and Jehoiachin, but their reigns only lasted a matter of weeks, both of whom were deposed and exiled by Egypt and Babylon, respectively.

Josiah would lead the nation back to worshiping God, his descendants fell back into apostasy and God's judgement.

Jeremiah was in Jerusalem until the siege, warning those in power that God was punishing Judah for failing to live up to the covenant commitment. Idolatry was at its worst after Josiah died and God was ready to use the Babylonians to carry out His judgement. Jeremiah warned the kings what God was about to do if Judah did not repent and return to Him in repentance.

In his criticism of their behavior, Jeremiah pointed out how Judah's disobedience to God was worse than the pagan nations around them. "'Has a nation ever changed its gods? (Yet they are not gods at all.) But my people have exchanged their glorious God for worthless idols. Be appalled at this, you heavens, and shudder with great horror,' declares the Lord" (Jer. 2:11–12). God was with His people all along, yet they did something that even the pagans had never done: they discarded their own faith to worship worthless idols.

The frustration was evident. Despite everything God had done for His people, they continued to ignore His blessings and turn to other gods, yet they were not gods at all. Even pagans were consistent with whom they worshiped; they didn't turn their backs on their gods as Israel had done. "Be appalled at this...and shudder with great horror" is an accurate reaction when observing how badly God's people behaved.

Jeremiah's warnings were totally ignored. The religious leaders and the king's court continued to disobey God's covenant, thinking that God wouldn't treat them the way He treated the northern nation of Israel. How could God not protect them? Jerusalem was His city, and the temple was His dwelling place. They relied on those tokens like their ancestors relied on the ark of the covenant to assist them in battle during the period of the judges. They were all in denial of their sins because of this false sense of protection. Jeremiah warned them, "'This is what the LORD Almighty, the God of Israel, says: Reform your ways and your actions, and I will let you live in this place. Do not trust in deceptive words and say, 'This is the temple of the LORD, the temple of the LORD, the temple of the LORD!'" (Jer. 7:3–4).

So what was the solution? Jeremiah offered the same advice as the other prophets: "'Circumcise yourselves to the LORD, circumcise your hearts, you people of Judah and inhabitants of Jerusalem, or my wrath will flare up and burn like fire because of the evil you have done—burn with no one to quench it'" (Jer. 4:4). Here was the call for repentance and for cleansing their hearts to be obedient to the Lord. Christopher Wright notes, "Jeremiah insists, like Deuteronomy 10:16 and 30:6 [see the discussion in Chapter 13] that this must be a circumcision of the heart...in effect saying 'Start again. Come through the door again.'"[621] He adds that the repentance God was calling for would be "a fresh surrender of heart, mind and will, of worship and life, to him as covenant Lord."[622]

Jeremiah was also asking his people to extend their hearts to God and repent of their lack of compassion for those in need. Like the other prophets, Jeremiah recognized that those in power neglected the unrepresented. Their hearts were hardened by their own selfish tendencies as he warned them: "Jerusalem, wash the evil from your heart and be saved. How long will you harbor wicked thoughts?" (Jer. 4:14).

Turning the tide against impending punishment should have started with turning their hearts to God instead of rebelling against His will. But the prophet could only do so much. As we saw in Chapter 11, it took the king's leadership to get the population back in obedience to God. In addition to hardened hearts, Jeremiah observed, "But these people have stubborn and rebellious hearts; they have turned aside and gone away" (Jer. 5:23).

Jeremiah had the same things to say about the nation of Judah that Amos leveled against the northern nation of Israel. Those in Jerusalem were more concerned with the rituals of sacrifice (and typically, for idol worshiping) than being obedient to the commandments. "'For when I brought your ancestors out of Egypt and spoke to them, I did not just give them commands about burnt offerings and sacrifices, but I gave them this command: Obey me, and I will be your God and you

---

[621]Christopher Wright, *The Message of Jeremiah*, 2014, p. 90.

[622] Ibid.

will be my people. Walk in obedience to all I command you, that it may go well with you. But they did not listen or pay attention; instead, they followed the stubborn inclinations of their evil hearts. They went backward and not forward" (Jer. 7:22–24).

Wright reiterates that Jeremiah's message clarified the difference between sacrifice and obedience. Even from Moses's time, God did not require the people from the exodus to bring sacrifices. "What was the first thing God required of Israel when he redeemed them out of Egypt? That they should set up a sacrificial system? No, that they should listen to him, obey him (same word in Hebrew) and walk in his ways as set out in the covenant law.[623]

When it appeared that there was no returning to God, Jeremiah tried to convince those in authority to surrender to Babylon. He said that God's judgement was inevitable, so they should accept their punishment and yield to the Babylonians; otherwise, death would be the only alternative. This was in direct opposition to the message given by the court prophets who convinced the king that God would not allow the destruction of the city or the temple. Not surprisingly, Jeremiah suffered both physically and emotionally for his unique stand.

The worst behavior condemned by Jeremiah was not disobedience or even mixing pagan practices with their worship to God, it was the abominable practice of sacrificing children to the Canaanite god Molek.

God condemned this practice in his instructions to Moses in the desert. "'Do not give any of your children to be sacrificed to Molek, for you must not profane the name of your God. I am the LORD'" (Lev. 18:21). The consequence was death by stoning: "'Say to the Israelites: "Any Israelite or any foreigner residing in Israel who sacrifices any of his children to Molek is to be put to death. The members of the community are to stone him"'" (Lev. 20:2). God rightfully sets this practice apart from any other worship of false gods, "for by sacrificing his children to Molek, he has defiled my sanctuary and profaned my holy name" (v. 3).

---

[623]Christopher, Wright, *The Message of Ezekiel*, 2014, p. 116.

Children are the most innocent yet most defenseless members of society. They need protection more than the widows and the poor. "If the members of the community close their eyes when that man sacrifices one of his children to Molek and if they fail to put him to death, I myself will set my face against him and his family and will cut them off from their people together with all who follow him in prostituting themselves to Molek" (Lev. 20:4–5).

It's difficult to imagine that such an atrocity took place in Jerusalem. It was a practice undertaken by the northern nation of Israel, but now the corruption was tearing away at Jerusalem's moral fabric.[624] Toward the end of Zedekiah's reign, Jeremiah was quick to point out the depraved conditions in Jerusalem. It's as if no one was worthy of being saved from God's judgement. "The people of Israel and Judah have provoked me by all the evil they have done—they, their kings and officials, their priests and prophets, the people of Judah and those living in Jerusalem" (Jer. 32:32).

And then comes the horror of their actions: "They set up their vile images in the house that bears my Name and defiled it. They built high places for Baal in the Valley of Ben Hinnom to sacrifice their sons and daughters to Molek, though I never commanded—nor did it enter my mind—that they should do such a detestable thing and so make Judah sin" (Jer. 32:34–35). You can sense God's exasperation; He cannot even conceive that such an action would come to His mind. Yet there it was for all to know. David Guzik, quoting Feinberg makes this point, "So abhorrent was this practice that the Lord by a strong

---

[624]Scriptures say that King Ahaz introduced the practice in Judah: "He followed the ways of the kings of Israel and even sacrificed his son in the fire, engaging in the detestable practices of the nations the LORD had driven out before the Israelites" (2 Kgs. 16:3). The practice was picked up later by his grandson, Manasseh: "He sacrificed his own son in the fire, practiced divination, sought omens, and consulted mediums and spiritists. He did much evil in the eyes of the LORD, arousing his anger" (2 Kgs. 21:6).

anthropomorphism says that it had never entered his mind that his favored people would stoop so low."[625]

Ezekiel

Like Jeremiah, Ezekiel's prophecies were made immediately before the destruction of Jerusalem and the temple. His condemnation of Judah's apostasy was the most damning of all the prophets. Like Hosea, Ezekiel used the metaphor of an initially faithful wife who gave in to idolatry and prostituted herself to pagan practices, forgetting all God's blessings. Ezekiel compared Jerusalem to an orphan girl God rescued (taking the people out of Egypt) and watched as the child grew to full beauty in her womanhood, and who God blessed with riches and adornment (the height of Solomon's reign). All these gifts were thrown away as Jerusalem left God's comfort for pagan gods. "'But you trusted in your beauty and used your fame to become a prostitute. You lavished your favors on anyone who passed by, and your beauty became his'" (Ezek. 16:15).

Ezekiel also condemned the practice of child sacrifice that Jeremiah spoke of earlier. "'And you took your sons and daughters whom you bore to me and sacrificed them as food to the idols. Was your prostitution not enough? You slaughtered my children and sacrificed them to the idols'" (Ezek.16:20–21). Their apostasy was bad enough, but human sacrifice was horrifyingly wicked.

Ezekiel listed one by one the pagan nations that Jerusalem ran to for protection instead of relying on God. "'You engaged in prostitution with the Egyptians...I stretched out my hand against you and reduced your territory; I gave you over to the greed of your enemies, the daughters of the Philistines, who were shocked by your lewd conduct. You engaged in prostitution with the Assyrians too, because you were insatiable; and even after that, you still were not satisfied. Then you increased your promiscuity to include Babylonia, a land of merchants, but even with this you were not satisfied'" (Ezek. 16:26–29).

---

[625]David Guzik, "Study Guide for Jeremiah 32 by David Guzik," Blue Letter Bible, last modified February 21, 2017, https://www.blueletterbible.org/Comm/guzik_david/ StudyGuide 2017-Jer/Jer-32.cfm.

Ezekiel made a shocking comparison: Jerusalem was more immoral than both Israel (Samaria) and Sodom, the latter of which Scripture uses as the poster child for depravity and corruption. "'As surely as I live, declares the Sovereign LORD, your sister Sodom and her daughters never did what you and your daughters have done. Now this was the sin of your sister Sodom: She and her daughters were arrogant, overfed, and unconcerned; they did not help the poor and needy. They were haughty and did detestable things before me. Therefore, I did away with them as you have seen. Samaria did not commit half the sins you did. You have done more detestable things than they and have made your sisters seem righteous by all these things you have done'" (Ezek. 16:48–51).

Christopher Wright observes, "Not only does Jerusalem share a family resemblance to the likes of Samaria and Sodom by the fact that she has sunk to the same level of wickedness; she has actually plumbed the depths of depravity to such an extent that she has made even Sodom look *righteous* in comparison."[626]

What exactly were Judah's sins of apostasy identified by Ezekiel? Wright tells us, "The charge sheet includes bloodshed, idolatry contempt of parents, oppression of aliens, orphans, and widows (the landless, familyless and homeless), desecration of the Sabbath, slander, sexual perversions including adultery and incest, bribery, corruption, taking interest, dispossession, and confiscation of property ('devouring people'), neglect of religious traditions, vicious bureaucracy, murder for profit, false prophecy justifying the status quo, extortion and robbery."[627] It's no wonder Ezekiel found Jerusalem's spiritual vacuum worse than Samaria, or even Sodom!

Ezekiel returned to his graphic metaphor to depict the infidelity of Israel (Oholah) and Judah (Oholibah), characterizing them as sisters who prostituted themselves by yielding to everyone but God. Ezekiel began with both nations appearing to be faithful to God as married wives, but both were led astray by the trappings of worldly pleasures

---

[626]Christopher Wright, *The Message of Ezekiel*, 2001, p. 149.

[627] Ibid., p. 150.

and assimilated the pagan practices surrounding them. "'She gave herself as a prostitute to all the elite of the Assyrians and defiled herself with all the idols of everyone she lusted after. She did not give up the prostitution she began in Egypt, when during her youth men slept with her, caressed her virgin bosom, and poured out their lust on her. Therefore, I delivered her into the hands of her lovers, the Assyrians, for whom she lusted. They stripped her naked, took away her sons and daughters and killed her with the sword. She became a byword among women, and punishment was inflicted on her'" (Ezek. 23:7–10).

Worshiping false gods started in Egypt and continued in Israel when the nation adopted the pagan ways of the Assyrians. The Assyrians stripped Israel of everything and took the people into captivity; the nation was no longer. Now only a memory and a byword among women (v.10). David Guzik notes, "We imagine the small kingdom of Israel looking with awe and envy upon the mighty empire of the Assyrians. Though they feared them, they also noticed their power and wealth, their influence and fame. Israel thought that by worshipping Assyria's gods, adopting their morals, and embracing their customs they also could gain some of that power and fame. It was a foolish rejection of their covenant God and embrace of idolatry."[628]

Ezekiel condemned the nation of Judah for the same practices. He declared that Judah was more immoral than Israel because it witnessed the destruction of Israel 140 years earlier and learned nothing from it. "'Her sister Oholibah saw this, yet in her lust and prostitution she was more depraved than her sister. She too lusted after the Assyrians—governors and commanders, warriors in full dress, mounted horsemen, all handsome young men. I saw that she too defiled herself; both of them went the same way. But she carried her prostitution still further'" (Ezek. 23:11–14). Ezekiel described how Judah held Babylonia with the same esteem and pagan practices that Israel had with Assyria, little realizing they would both be consumed by the very nations they admired. God was nowhere in their sight.

---

[628]David Guzik, "Study Guide for Ezekiel 23 by David Guzik," Blue Letter Bible, last modified February 21, 2017, https://www.blueletterbible.org/Comm/guzik_david/StudyGuide 2017-Eze/Eze-23.cfm.

Robert Jenson notes, "Jerusalem sees what happens to Samaria but does not learn from it. She too submits to the Assyrians, then calls on the Babylonians to deliver her from them...So she submits to Babylon. But then she dumps Babylon...Even this does not wean her from entangling alliances, and she turns to her original seducers in Egypt."[629]

The most devastating revelation from Ezekiel, however, was that God was so disgusted by the apostasy within the temple that He departed from it and Jerusalem, never to return. In a vision, Ezekiel was made privy to this abominable behavior in the temple and God showed him four levels of apostasy. Christopher Writer tells us that "each stage is simultaneously closer to the holiest part of the temple and, for that reason, increasingly offensive in the idolatry being practiced at each stage."[630] Jenson adds "Each station has its 'abomination,' that is, a pollution that makes it impossible for the Lord to remain in Jerusalem. Thus, the vision will end with the Lord's departure."[631]

The first level of apostasy was a statue at the north entrance of the temple, an idol of jealousy. "And he said to me, 'Son of man, do you see what they are doing—the utterly detestable things the Israelites are doing here, things that will drive me far from my sanctuary? But you will see things that are even more detestable'" (Ezek. 8:6). It's possible that this was a statue of Asherah. If so, says Write, "then it represented all the degraded sexuality of the fertility cult associated with the worship of Baal and Asherah."[632]

The second level of apostasy was the wicked and detestable things taking place in the temple. "In front of them stood seventy elders of Israel, and Jaazaniah son of Shaphan was standing among them. Each had a censer in his hand, and a fragrant cloud of incense was rising. He said to me, 'Son of man, have you seen what the elders of Israel are doing in the darkness, each at the shrine of his own idol? They say,

---

[629]Robert Jenson, *Commentary on the Bible – Ezekiel*, 2009, pp. 190–191.

[630]Christopher Wright, *The Message of Ezekiel*, 2001, p. 99.

[631]Robert Jenson, *Commentary on the Bible – Ezekiel*, 2009, p. 81.

[632]Christopher Wright, *The Message of Ezekiel*, 2001, p. 101.

"The LORD does not see us; the LORD has forsaken the land"'" (Ezek. 8:11–12). These influential members of society absolved themselves from sinning, thinking that because God let the land decline by His absence, they can do whatever they want. But the Lord did see their abominations.

The third level of apostasy that God showed Ezekiel in his vision was women mourning over the god Tammuz. "He said to me, 'Do you see this, son of man? You will see things that are even more detestable than this'" (Ezek. 8:15). David Guzik comments, "This was another example of pagan worship, and Tammuz was a deity worshipped by many in neighboring nations, often with immoral or impure rites. Ezekiel was dismayed because women were there, in the holy place reserved only for priests, and because of their immoral idolatry."[633]

The fourth level of apostasy was priests in the inner sanctuary, the holiest part of the temple, participating in the most irreligious practice of all. "He then brought me into the inner court of the house of the LORD, and there at the entrance to the temple, between the portico and the altar, were about twenty-five men. With their backs toward the temple of the LORD and their faces toward the east, they were bowing down to the sun in the east" (Ezek. 8:16).

These practices were so depraved that God revealed to Ezekiel that He would depart from the Temple. "Then the glory of the LORD departed from over the threshold of the temple and stopped above the cherubim...Then the cherubim, with the wheels beside them, spread their wings, and the glory of the God of Israel was above them. The glory of the LORD went up from within the city and stopped above the mountain east of it" (Ezekiel 10:18, 11:22–23).[634]

With God's presence totally out of the temple, the judgement against Judah neared completion. Zedekiah rebelled against Babylon

[633]David Guzik, "Study Guide for Ezekiel 8 by David Guzik," Blue Letter Bible, last modified February 21, 2017, https://www.blueletterbible.org/Comm/guzik_david/StudyGuide 2017-Eze/Eze-8.cfm.

[634]Despite the rebuilding of the temple by the remnant Jews returning from Babylon and its splendid renovation under Herod the Great centuries later, God's presence in the temple was never restored.

by refusing to maintain tribute payments and sought Egyptian assistance to protect Judah against the army of Babylon. Reacting to this attempted rebellion, the king of Babylon waged a three-pronged attack against Jerusalem, tore down the walls of the city, and destroyed the temple. Like the northern kingdom before it, Judah, Jerusalem, and the temple were all destroyed, and a majority of the survivors were taken back to Babylon. Zedekiah was captured while trying to flee the city, then blinded after seeing his sons killed right before his eyes.

Of all the consequences of their sin, I think losing the temple was the most devastating to the people in Jerusalem. It was the center of worship for all of Israel and the leaders of Judah quite wrongly assumed that nothing would befall Jerusalem since God would never let His temple be destroyed. It was God's dwelling, and the city of Jerusalem was precious in His eyes. This was precisely the resistance Jeremiah encountered when he tried to convince his leaders to surrender to the Babylonian army. Their enemy was being used by God to punish Judah for its sins.

God had already departed from the temple. Though it was restored by the returning exiles from Babylon and returned to splendor under Herod the Great 500 years later, God still did not return. The destruction of the temple was a key component in God's plan to infuse the Holy Spirit in each believer through Jesus so that we would become God's dwelling place, a temple in our hearts (see Chapter 14). With the completion of Jesus's mission here on earth, Thomas Schreiner notes, "The temple no longer represents the place of God's presence where atonement is offered. Jesus is the new temple (John 2:19–20; 20:20–24), and believers are the temple of the Holy Spirit (1 Cor. 3:16, 2 Cor. 6:16)."[635]

Haggai and Zechariah

The prophets Haggai and Zechariah began their public ministries about the same time, during the post exilic period around 520 BC. It was after the Persians, led by their king Cyrus, defeated the

---

[635]Thomas Schreiner, *The King in His Beauty*, 2013, p. 61.

Medes (in 550 BC) and took over the Babylonian empire in 539 BC. Under Cyrus' reign, the remnant of Israelites was allowed to return to Jerusalem and rebuild the city and the temple. Isaiah spoke about Cyrus 200 years earlier saying he would allow the Israelites to return and rebuild the temple. "'He is my shepherd and will accomplish all that I please; he will say of Jerusalem, 'Let it be rebuilt,' and of the temple, 'Let its foundations be laid'" (Isa. 44:28).[636]

While the foundation for the temple was completed three years after the returning Israelites began, political adversaries and changes in Persian leadership halted the reconstruction. Cyrus exhibited enormous religious tolerance by allowing those in his empire to practice their own religion. However, his son Cambyses II was not as tolerant when he took over his father's reign in 530 BC. Meanwhile, the nations around Jerusalem deterred the reconstruction of the city, most likely in fear of how powerful Israel was under David and Solomon's reign. The temple reconstruction was delayed until Darius ruled the empire in 522 BC.

Michael Stead tells us that Haggai's preaching was targeted to give God "the whole-hearted reverence and respect he deserves as the one and only Lord…Through the preaching of Haggai, the Lord reorients the hearts of the people, who turn from indifference and disobedience to reverence and obedience. *This change of heart leads to changed behavior* (emphasis mine)."[637]

Haggai and Zechariah were concerned with the reconstruction of Jerusalem and the spiritual hearts of the returning exiles. They recognized that the first call to order for the returning remnant was getting

---

[636]From the book of Ezra, there is more detail regarding Cyrus and the returning Israelites: "In the first year of Cyrus king of Persia, in order to fulfill the word of the LORD spoken by Jeremiah, the LORD moved the heart of Cyrus king of Persia to make a proclamation throughout his realm and also to put it in writing: 'This is what Cyrus king of Persia says: "The LORD, the God of heaven, has given me all the kingdoms of the earth and he has appointed me to build a temple for him at Jerusalem in Judah. Any of his people among you may go up to Jerusalem in Judah and build the temple of the LORD, the God of Israel, the God who is in Jerusalem, and may their God be with them"'" (Ezra 1:1–3).

[637]Michael Stead, *Expository Commentary Volume 7: Daniel–Malachi (Haggai)*, 2018, p. 614.

the temple rebuilt. They urged the people to return to building the house of the Lord that would be their vehicle to reconnect with God. In fact, Haggai argued that national renewal could not take place until the temple was rebuilt.

Haggai rebuked the people for focusing on rebuilding their own homes rather than rebuilding the temple. "'Is it a time for you yourselves to be living in your paneled houses, while this house remains a ruin?'" (Haggai 1:4). By building their own homes first, the people were self-serving and disobedient to their covenant obligation of serving the Lord in the fashion of the First Great Commandment.

Haggai continued with God's command to rebuild the temple. "'Go up into the mountains and bring down timber and build my house, so that I may take pleasure in it and be honored,' says the LORD" (Haggai 1:8). Stead continues, "The reason for building the temple is not for their own blessing but for God's pleasure and glory...By rebuilding the temple, the people could restore it both to where God takes pleasure in sacrifice and where he dwells in glory amid his people."[638]

In addition to rebuilding God's house, both prophets were concerned that there could be a repeat of the sins of the past; repentance and honoring God's will would be tantamount to returning to the fold of His blessings. This was another reset button for the returning exiles; restoration of their spiritual hearts would prevent another abandonment by God. The challenge for both prophets was to rekindle the hearts of the people after the punishment from which they just escaped. There was a sense that God was no longer with them because they erroneously put too much faith in the first temple thinking, as George Klein states, "that the temple itself would protect the nation from any foreign intruder because the Lord 'dwelled' within."[639]

That was precisely the warning Jeremiah gave prior to the Babylonians ransacking the city and destroying the temple. With the destruction of the temple and being taken into captivity, the returning exiles were demoralized, thinking God terminated the covenant

---

[638] Ibid., p. 613.

[639] George Klein, *The New American Commentary – Zechariah*, 2008, p. 68.

with them, rather than understanding they were being punished for their sins.

This was the mentality of the people Zechariah sought to correct. God was going to restore the nation once again, although not with the splendor of David and Solomon. Through Zechariah and the other prophets, God promised His return to them if they obeyed His will and remained faithful to Him.

Expressing the same message given to the Israelites by Moses, Zechariah gave the remnant exiles instructions with respect to the Second Great Commandment. "'This is what the LORD Almighty said: "Administer true justice; show mercy and compassion to one another. Do not oppress the widow or the fatherless, the foreigner or the poor. Do not plot evil against each other." But they refused to pay attention; stubbornly they turned their backs and covered their ears'" (Zech. 7:9–11).

This compassion continued in the messages of the prophets, which is the core of the Second Great Commandment. It was not merely the actions Zechariah prescribed, but the motivation behind them. In Anthony Petterson's commentary on Zechariah, he writes, "Furthermore, justice is not merely external acts but extends to thoughts and motivations: Let none of you devise evil against another in your hearts, where the 'heart' is the seat of will in Hebrew thought."[640]

Malachi

Malachi is the last prophet presented in the Old Testament and is the last book before transitioning to the New Testament. It is generally believed Malachi was a contemporary to Nehemiah, which places his writing around 450 BC,[641] long after the return of the exiles to

---

[640]Anthony Petterson, *Expository Commentary: Daniel-Malachi (Zechariah)*, 2018, p. 681.

[641]C. Hassell Bullock notes that the spiritual decline of the city and priesthood, lack of enthusiasm for tithing, and marriage issues that Malachi addressed may place him ahead of the reforms enforced by Ezra and Nehemiah. He suggests Malachi could be placed between Haggai and Zechariah. *An Introduction to the Old Testament Prophetic Books*, 2007, p. 408.

Jerusalem from the Babylonian captivity. In that time, the city and the temple were restored by Ezra, Nehemiah, and the governor Zerubbabel. The prophets Haggai and Zechariah helped restore the temple and the role of the priests.

The question Malachi (as well as Haggai and Zechariah) tried to answer was, had anything changed since the return of the exiles and the restoration of Jerusalem and the temple? The answer was, not yet. Apparently, the Israelites finally removed the influence of idolatry, but compassion for the weaker class was yet to be addressed. As for worshiping God, their hearts went from worshiping too many gods to getting so formalized that religious legalism was the new idolatry. J. Daniel Hays states, "The nation is apparently cured of idolatry (except for the danger of intermarriage with people who worship idols) but it quickly slides into extreme legalism, embracing religious ritualism while excusing social justice. The social and theological issues that Malachi struggles against reveal the early forms of Judaism that Jesus encounters in Israel when he appears."[642]

This latter point is important because religious platitudes began to percolate under Malachi's witnessing. The people had it down to a science 400 years later when Jesus was frustrated with the legalism displayed by the hardened hearts of the religion leaders.

Social Justice: The Second Great Commandment

The book of Deuteronomy contains the instructions the Lord provided to His people to care for those in need. Israel was not to ignore the problem of poverty nor blame it on the indigent for causing their own problem. As Christopher Wright tells us, "Israel's law puts the focus instead on those who actually have the power to do something, or whose powers must be constrained in some way for the benefit of the poor."[643] To separate Israel from their pagan counterparts, those

---

[642]J. Daniel Hays, *The Message of the Prophets*, 2010, p. 360.

[643]Christopher Wright, *Old Testament Ethics for the People of God,* 2004, p.171.

who were able were to take a compassionate, active role to protect and care for those falling through the cracks.

The messages given to the people of Israel and Judah by the prophets included the issue of social justice; that is, reminding the nation to show compassion for the unrepresented because of their lower social status. Generally, this was the motivation for spiritual hearts to care and tend to the needy, widows, and orphans. "The righteous care about justice for the poor, but the wicked have no such concern" (Prov. 29:7). Obviously, the need for the prophets' messages was caused by lack of consideration by those in authority who took advantage of their power to increase their worldly possessions rather than share their blessings with others. God's instructions were to prevent greed and promote compassion for those in need.

Amos

The insincerity of the nation's heart by ignoring the instructions behind the First Great Commandment resulted in the Israelites' lack of respect and compassion for each other, and those with means took away from the less fortunate. God commanded Moses to care for the poor and needy and to not take advantage of those who were socially inferior.

J. Daniel Hays writes that Amos, like the other prophets, spoke to "the importance of social justice and underscored that the religious rituals of Israel cannot replace the requirement to live justly, especially in regard to the poor."[644] Noting the practices of the wealthy in his society, Amos had harsh words for the rich women in Israel: "Hear this word, you cows of Bashan on Mount Samaria, you women who oppress the poor and crush the needy and say to your husbands, 'Bring us some drinks!'" (Amos 4:1).

Michael McKelvey writes that "these affluent women were being compared to cows that graze constantly on the abundance of the land. The women's lives of indulgence have made them voluminous, slothful, and demanding. They 'oppress the poor' and 'crush the needy,' the

---

[644]J. Daniel Hays, *The Message of the Prophets*, 2010, p. 290.

same type of injustice of which the nation is accused in Amos 2:7, highlighting those women as well as men are guilty of exploitation and cruelty."[645]

Amos assailed those in power who abused their position. "'You levy a straw tax on the poor and impose a tax on their grain...For I know how many are your offenses and how great your sins. There are those who oppress the innocent and take bribes and deprive the poor of justice in the courts'" (Amos 5:11–12). David Guzik notes that Amos passed along God's judgement for "the terrible way that the people of Israel treat one another, especially how the strong take advantage of the weak. The weak has no voice in the gate [the courts], is robbed by oppressive taxes. The rich take advantage with bribes and pay off the system to drive the poor from justice."[646]

Amos continued with his condemnation of the wealthy who took advantage of the poor, almost to the point of driving the victims out of the land. The rebuke included the stark practices of conducting business, as if they could wait for the festivals and the Sabbath to end so business could resume. Amos called out their avarice: cheating, swindling by using dishonest scales, and extracting higher prices for their goods than warranted. "Hear this, you who trample the needy and do away with the poor of the land, saying, 'When will the New Moon be over that we may sell grain, and the Sabbath be ended that we may market wheat?'—skimping on the measure, boosting the price and cheating with dishonest scales, buying the poor with silver and the needy for a pair of sandals, selling even the sweepings with the wheat" (Amos 8:4–6).

Extracting the highest price possible and dishonestly measuring out grain sounds like Charles Dickens's Ebenezer Scrooge before his conversion. Matthew Henry's comment on the Israelites' treatment of the poor was equally condemning. "They valued themselves so much

---

[645]Michael McKelvey, *Expository Commentary Daniel – Malachi (Amos)*, 2018, pp. 330–331.

[646]David Guzik, "Study Guide for Amos 5 by David Guzik," Blue Letter Bible, last modified February 21, 2017, https://www.blueletterbible.org/Comm/guzik_david/StudyGuide2017-Amo/Amo-5.cfm.

on their wealth that they looked upon all that were poor with the highest contempt imaginable; they hated them, could not endure them, but abandoned them, and therefore did what they could to make them cease, not by relieving them to make them cease to be poor, but by banishing and destroying them to make them cease to be, or at least to be in their land."[647]

It was mentioned that through their obedience, God would allow His people to prosper. That prosperity should have been enough, making it unnecessary to be greedy and take more than they needed. God knew there would always be the poor, and the Israelites were supposed to take care of them. It was apparent to Amos and the other prophets crying out against social injustice that profiteering and gathering up wealth was the focus. Physical comfort trumped spiritual compassion.

Warning the nation that judgement followed an unrepentant heart, Ronald Youngblood references spiritual famines foretold by Amos "that were soon to come—a prophecy fulfilled not only as a result of the disaster of 722 BC, but also in the exilic and post-exilic periods."[648] "'The days are coming,' declares the Sovereign LORD, 'when I will send a famine through the land—not a famine of food or a thirst for water, but a famine of hearing the words of the LORD. People will stagger from sea to sea and wander from north to east, searching for the word of the LORD, but they will not find it" (Amos 8:11–12).

Hosea

Similar to Amos's condemnation of social injustices, Hosea writes, "Hear the word of the LORD, you Israelites, because the LORD has a charge to bring against you who live in the land: 'There is no faithfulness, no love, no acknowledgment of God in the land. There is only cursing, lying and murder, stealing and adultery; they break all

[647]Matthew Henry, "Commentary on Amos 8 by Matthew Henry," Blue Letter Bible, last modified March 1, 1996, https://www.blueletterbible.org/Comm/mhc/Amo/Amo_008.cfm.

[648]Ronald Youngblood, *Expositor's Bible Commentary: 1 Samuel –2 Samuel*, 2009, pp. 66–67.

bounds, and bloodshed follows bloodshed'" (Hosea 4:1–2). Without the love of God in their hearts, the Israelites forwent obeying any of the commandments and followed a lifestyle of violence and bloodshed. George Schwab observes, "Notice that God's first complaint is not that Israel is worshipping Baal; instead, he addresses Israel's moral compass. To deviate from the revealed moral code is to lose any connection or relationship with the Lord. Bloodshed has become a defining characteristic of God's people...Violence had become the order of the day."[649]

Hosea laid the root of Israel's transgressions at the feet of religious leaders who failed to provide adequate spiritual guidance. He spoke the words of the LORD: "'my people are destroyed from lack of knowledge. Because you have rejected knowledge, I also reject you as my priests; because you have ignored the law of your God, I also will ignore your children. The more priests there were, the more they sinned against me; they exchanged their glorious God for something disgraceful. They feed on the sins of my people and relish their wickedness'" (Hosea 4:6–8). The people had no one to lead them in the ways of the Lord because the religious authorities had no real knowledge of God. Schwab continues, "Prophets are lumped together with priests as those who claim to know but in fact, only deceive...Their spiritual state of affairs was so bad that Amos was embarrassed to be called a prophet (Amos 7:14) while Micah soundly criticized them (Mic. 3:11)...The whole religious and political system has failed to preserve God and has in fact rejected him."[650]

Micah

Micah also condemned those in authority for their lack of compassion for the socially unrepresented. In fact, the authorities allowed the wealthy to strip those in need from what little they possessed. "Woe to those who plan iniquity, to those who plot evil on the beds! At morning's light they carry it out because it is in their power to do

---

[649]George Schwab, *Expository Commentary Volume 7: Daniel–Malachi (Hosea)*, 2018, p. 201.

[650] Ibid., pp. 202–203.

it. They covet fields and seize them, and houses, and take them. They defraud people of their homes; they rob them of their inheritance" (Mic. 2:1–2).

Micah condemned the rich who had the power to take from the poor because they controlled the system. They coveted fields and homes, which violated the tenth commandment. Robbing them of their inheritance was against God's guidelines for the people entering the Promised Land. Stephen Dempster writes, "Their wickedness is thus clear; instead of helping those who suffer, they take advantage of them...The key theological word here is 'covet.' This stresses that the theft and social oppression both originate in the heart."[651]

Micah turned his attention to those in authority for their exploitations. "Then I said, 'Listen, you leaders of Jacob, you rulers of Israel. Should you not embrace justice, you who hate good and love evil; who tear the skin from my people and the flesh from the bones; who eat my people's flesh, strip off their skin and break their bones in pieces; who chop them up like meat for the pan, like flesh for the pot?'" (Mic. 3:1–3). The leaders were condemned for treating people no better than cannibals, a metaphor for how vicious the leaders were. David Guzik writes, "'You who hate good and love evil'...If this description isn't bad enough, Micah goes on to illustrate how terribly the leaders of Israel and Judah 'use' the people – as if they were cannibals feasting on the people of God."[652]

Micah continued with the root cause of Israel's lack of connection with God. "Her leaders judge for a bribe, her priests teach for a price, and her prophets tell fortunes for money. Yet they look for the LORD's support and say, 'Is not the LORD among us? No disaster will come upon us'" (Mic. 3:11). Of this indictment, Dempster notes, "The heads—the judicial officials—are bought with bribes, and so their verdicts are unjust; the priests likewise have 'sold out' to money as

[651]Stephen Dempster, *Expository Commentary: Daniel–Malachi (Micah)*, 2018, p. 447.

[652]David Guzik, "Study Guide for Micah 3 by David Guzik," Blue Letter Bible, last modified February 21, 2017, https://www.blueletterbible.org/Comm/guzik_david/StudyGuide 2017-Mic/Mic-3.cfm.

well, tailoring their teaching to the monetary payments they desire. The prophets' activity has become so bankrupt that it is compared to pagan divination."[653]

Micah also pointed to the lack of sincerity in Israel's practice of worship; that God was not concerned with the quality or quantity of burnt offerings. As noted throughout this text, God is interested in the nature of our hearts. "He has shown you, O mortal, what is good. And what does the LORD require of you? To act justly and to love mercy and to walk humbly with your God" (Mic. 6:8).

Micah listed the ingredients God seeks in our hearts when it comes to our worship of Him. To act justly, not like the corrupt court officials of his time, but in Dempster's words, "To do justice is often to help someone in need (i.e., to be an advocate for those whose rights are violated)...One must be committed to helping those in need."[654] Micah continued with "to love mercy" or kindness, qualities that lead to compassion, thoughtfulness, and forgiving those who have offended.

Finally, Micah addressed "to walk humbly with God." Dempster adds, "To walk with God is to accept his vision and values for life, to fellowship with him. Thus, one does this humbly, recognizing one's place before God on high."[655] These attributes were articulated by others prior to Micah and were explained by Jesus during His mission: that of mercy justice and humility.

Isaiah

Isaiah had a ministry of about 64 years, starting in approximately 740 BC, and was a contemporary to Micah. Beginning in the latter part of King Uriah (Ahaziah)'s reign, his preaching and spiritual leadership went well into King Hezekiah's reign. Even with Hezekiah's reforms, Isaiah found it necessary to send the same warnings of repentance as his predecessors.

---

[653]Stephen Dempster, *Expository Commentary: Daniel–Malachi (Micah),* 2018, pp. 464–65.

[654] Ibid., p. 486.

[655] Ibid.

With regard to social justice, Isaiah gave a simple set of instructions. "Wash and make yourselves clean. Take your evil deeds out of my sight; stop doing wrong. Learn to do right; seek justice. Defend the oppressed. Take up the cause of the fatherless; plead the case of the widow" (Isa. 1:16–17). For Isaiah, the type of repentance God was expecting required not only the admonishment of sins, but it had to be coupled with a change of heart. He outlined the very actions required to change social oppression. To take up the cause of the widows and orphans goes back to the instructions God gave to Moses.[656]

As mentioned in the previous chapter, the people took their cues from those in charge of the nation. Isaiah was quick to point out their wickedness. "Your rulers are rebels, partners with thieves; they all love bribes and chase after gifts. They do not defend the cause of the fatherless; the widow's case does not come before them" (Isa. 1:23). At the expense of the poor, there was more concern for personal wealth by the ruling class, the very people who were responsible for maintaining the covenant requirements with God.

Later, Isaiah ridiculed Israel's attempt to seek the moral high ground through fasting, all the while missing the point of ignoring the less fortunate. "'Why have we fasted,' they say, 'and you have not seen it? Why have we humbled ourselves, and you have not noticed?' Yet on the day of your fasting, you do as you please and exploit all your workers. Your fasting ends in quarreling and strife, and in striking each other with wicked fists...'Is not this the kind of fasting I have chosen: to loose the chains of injustice and untie the cords of the yoke, to set the oppressed free and break every yoke? Is it not to share your food with the hungry and to provide the poor wanderer with shelter—when you see the naked, to clothe them, and not to turn away from your own flesh and blood?'" (Isa. 58:3–4, 6–7).

Isaiah called out their motivation for fasting and acting humble, which was to gain the attention and admiration of the populace, not to glorify God. This is the puffed-up insincerity of piety that Jesus

---

[656]There are ten verses in Deuteronomy alone dedicated to the care of widows. For example, "He defends the cause of the fatherless and the widow, and loves the foreigner residing among you, giving them food and clothing" (Deut. 10:18).

criticized the religious leaders for in His time. "'When you fast, do not look somber as the hypocrites do, for they disfigure their faces to show others they are fasting. Truly I tell you, they have received their reward in full'" (Matt. 16:6).

Isaiah adds that their fasting led to anger, arguments, and violence. Was that the purpose of their righteous fasting? Where was the compassion shown for those who were oppressed? Where was the love to help those without shelter, food, or clothing? Isaiah rightly pointed out the true path of a spiritual heart: to show true justice to the oppressed, to clothe and feed the poor, and to not ignore those in need. He was referring to fellow Israelites that fell by the wayside. Clearly, those he chastised missed the very essence of God's command to care for those who were just as much His chosen as those who had social advantages.

Jeremiah

Jeremiah delivered a similar message of repentance when he addressed the king's court. Jeremiah rebuked king Jehoiakim for his lack of compassion for the less fortunate, especially compared to the compassion that his father Josiah had shown. Jeremiah's advice to the king was similar to the advice God gave Cain for restoring fellowship with Him. "'If you really change your ways and your actions and deal with each other justly, if you do not oppress the foreigner, the fatherless or the widow and do not shed innocent blood in this place, and if you do not follow other gods to your own harm, then I will let you live in this place, in the land I gave your ancestors for ever and ever. But look, you are trusting in deceptive words that are worthless'" (Jer. 7:5–8).

The message addressed the same two problems that the earlier prophets addressed: social injustice and idolatry. Jeremiah's message gave the people of Judah the opportunity to turn their hearts and follow the rules to show love for God and the weaker members of the community. If they followed these simple instructions, God would spare them, and they would live in Jerusalem without being taken into captivity by the Babylonians. Jeremiah spelled out the consequences:

"'and if you do not listen to the words of my servants the prophets, whom I have sent to you again and again (though you have not listened), then I will make this house like Shiloh and this city a curse among all the nations of the earth'" (Jer. 26:5–6).

Christopher Wright adds that the demand was aimed at the "practical, social and ethical level of everyday life in the public arena...do justice with another in the community; no oppression of the weak and vulnerable – the homeless and the familyless; no violence against the innocent; and no self-destructive hankering after the false gods of surrounding cultures."[657] Those were the initial covenant conditions God required before entering the Promised Land and for continuing to live there.

Just like Isaiah and Micah, Jeremiah railed against the wicked who had enriched themselves at the expense of the weak. They had "grown fat and sleek. Their evil deeds have no limit; they do not seek justice. They do not promote the case of the fatherless; they do not defend the just cause of the poor" (Jer. 5:28). The guidelines Moses provided for the care of those in need were neglected and greed was rampant.

Jeremiah also addressed actions that would demonstrate righteousness and correct this injustice: "'Hear the word of the LORD to you, king of Judah, you who sit on David's throne—you, your officials and your people who come through these gates. This is what the LORD says: Do what is just and right. Rescue from the hand of the oppressor the one who has been robbed. Do no wrong or violence to the foreigner, the fatherless or the widow, and do not shed innocent blood in this place'" (Jer. 22:2–3). As Paul House points out, Jeremiah was reminding them that "it was the king's responsibility to protect the weak and helpless against oppressors."[658] As God's prophet, it was Jeremiah's role to remind them of the covenant requirements for the nation.

Unfortunately, Jeremiah's words were received with self-righteous anger. The priests and the officials of the temple were enraged by the

---

[657]Christopher Wright, *The Message of Jeremiah*, 2014, p. 109.

[658]Paul House, *Old Testament Theology*, 1995, p. 361.

condemnation and wanted to put Jeremiah to death. The voices of reason in the group argued that Jeremiah's preaching of the impending judgement was no different than Micah's prophecy[659] of destruction during King Hezekiah's reign. The same warning made decades earlier did not result in Micah being persecuted, which saved Jeremiah from being put to death for his warnings.

Jeremiah's warnings to repent fell on deaf ears. He was aware of the impending doom coming to Judah because of its disobedience; those in power were leading the people off the cliff. He was critical of the arrogance among the political and religious elite because they boasted of their worldly blessings rather than what the Lord really delighted in: compassion and righteous living. He compared the disobedient (uncircumcised) hearts of Israel to the pagan cultures around them. God was going to punish all the nations for their rebellion against him, including the whole house of Israel.

"This is what the LORD says: 'Let not the wise boast of their wisdom or the strong boast of their strength or the rich boast of their riches but let the one who boasts boast about this: that they have the understanding to know me, that I am the LORD, who exercises kindness, justice and righteousness on earth, for in these I delight,' declares the LORD. 'The days are coming,' declares the LORD, 'when I will punish all who are circumcised only in the flesh—Egypt, Judah, Edom, Ammon, Moab and all who live in the wilderness in distant places. For all these nations are really uncircumcised, and even the whole house of Israel is uncircumcised in heart'" (Jer. 9:23–26).

Jeremiah's message is relevant to all. As Paul addressed in his epistles, physical circumcision gains nothing; it is the circumcised heart that matters. The continuation of a hardened heart against God led

---

[659]Micah of Moresheth prophesied in the days of Hezekiah king of Judah. He told all the people of Judah, "'This is what the LORD Almighty says: "Zion will be plowed like a field, Jerusalem will become a heap of rubble, the temple hill, a mound overgrown with thickets." Did Hezekiah king of Judah or anyone else in Judah put him to death? Did not Hezekiah fear the LORD and seek his favor? And did not the LORD relent, so that he did not bring the disaster he pronounced against them? We are about to bring a terrible disaster on ourselves!'" (Jer. 26:18–19).

to the judgement against Israel and Judah, but this condition is very much applicable in today's world. To rely on yourself and not be dependent on God's will reflects an uncircumcised heart. The concept that God delights in kindness, justice, and righteousness has been revealed throughout the Bible; it is not new. Without a spiritual heart, selfishness and boasting can rule your actions and behavior, as Lamech demonstrated in Chapter 2 and those in authority who Jeremiah was addressing. Knowing God and living righteously and compassionately is His simple request. The apostle Paul cites Jeremiah's message[660] directly in his second letter to the Corinthians, "But, 'Let the one who boasts boast in the Lord.' For it is not the one who commends himself who is approved, but the one whom the Lord commends" (2 Cor. 10:17–18).

Ezekiel

Ezekiel's message was primarily for the benefit of the first group of exiles in Babylon, some 1,000 miles away from Jerusalem. However, his warnings were intended to get the exiles to understand that Jerusalem and the temple's demise were the result of their sins, neither of which the exiles nor the people still in Jerusalem believed God would allow to happen. In their minds, Jerusalem and the temple were God's home; He wouldn't let it be destroyed. They failed to recognize how deep their sins were.

"'Say to rebellious Israel, "This is what the Sovereign Lord says: Enough of your detestable practices, people of Israel! In addition to all your other detestable practices, you brought foreigners uncircumcised in heart and flesh into my sanctuary, desecrating my temple while you offered me food, fat, and blood, and you broke my covenant. Instead of carrying out your duty in regard to my holy things, you put others in charge of my sanctuary. This is what the Sovereign Lord says: No foreigner uncircumcised in heart and flesh is to enter my sanctuary, not even the foreigners who live among the Israelites."'" (Ezek. 44:6–9).

---

[660]"...but let the one who boasts boast about this: that they have the understanding to know me, that I am the Lord, who exercises kindness, justice, and righteousness on the earth, for in these I delight,' declares the Lord" (Jer. 9:24).

In summary, the prophets' warnings to Israel called for repentance and recognition of the nations' sins and the restoration of their hearts to God in obedience. The warnings were primarily aimed at the religious leaders and the rulers; they were responsible for leading the people back to the covenantal obligations given during Moses's time. God sent several prophets, but the message never resonated with the people. The consequences of their disobedience led to the judgement revealed as early as Moses's time in the destruction of the nations and their removal from the Promised Land. It came to fruition as the nations of Israel and Judah were taken into captivity and Jerusalem and the temple were destroyed. Only a remnant of God's people remained.

However, the prophets also proclaimed that God would not abandon His people forever. The promise of their restitution was not dependent on their actions, but as an intervention by God. This is the promise of a redeemer (in Jesus), and the promise of the Holy Spirit to restore the hearts of mankind.

Chapter 13

THE PROPHETS PART II

Not everyone in Israel followed the sinful nature of the religious leaders or of the kings who did evil in the eyes of the Lord. God told Elijah that there were 7,000 still faithful to God in Israel during Ahab's rule, and he was the worst of the unfaithful kings in the north. Obadiah saved 100 faithful priests from Jezebel's murderous campaign against them. Still, you have to wonder what was going on in the minds of this remnant as they witnessed the northern nation falling into the hands of the Assyrians, never to be restored.

Like the faithful few in the north, Ezekiel commented that there was still a remnant in the southern nation who were appalled by the evil and idolatry practiced by their religious leaders. When God was about to send His angels to kill those who corrupted the temple, He deliberately protected those who remained faithful to Him. "Now the glory of the God of Israel went up from above the cherubim, where it had been, and moved to the threshold of the temple. Then the LORD called to the man clothed in linen who had the writing kit at his side and said to him, 'Go throughout the city of Jerusalem and put a mark on the foreheads of those who grieve and lament over all the detestable things that are done in it'" (Ezek. 9:3–4).

Those in the southern nation of Judah who remained faithful to God must have been even more devastated by the conditions prior to their captivity, particularly because of the religious status of Jerusalem and the temple. They were witnesses to the sieges undertaken by the Babylonian army. Together with the initial group taken into exile before the destruction, they must have wondered what happened to the glory days of David and Solomon.

Of course, all the events of Israel's history were anticipated. God warned them as early as Moses's time that the nation would be destroyed if His people rebelled against Him by worshiping other gods and taking advantage of the socially inferior. After several centuries, Israel had proven that, on its own, it could not maintain the covenants God promised them, but God would intervene and send the Messiah, Jesus, to atone for the sins of mankind and put the Holy Spirit into their hearts. This was the promise of hope that the prophets declared.

The Promise of a Restored Heart

From the very beginning, it was God's plan to send Jesus for our salvation; to redeem us from our sins and spiritual death. In the theme of this text, this is the promise God gave us to restore our hearts; not to its original intent, which will be reached in the Second Coming and the New Jerusalem, but to guide us while we are still here on earth.

The other key element in the restoration of our hearts is the indwelling of the Holy Spirit, Who will help us understand His saving grace bestowed upon us so we can reflect the image of God.

As mentioned earlier, this promise was not made exclusively to the Israelites, but to all mankind, as God had promised Abraham, "I will surely bless you and make your descendants as numerous as the stars in the sky and as the sand on the seashore. Your descendants will take possession of the cities of their enemies, and through your offspring all nations on earth will be blessed, because you have obeyed me'" (Gen. 22:17–18).

Christopher Wright states, "God's plan and purpose (or God's mission) is to bring the whole of creation, spoiled and broken by human and satanic evil, into unity in Christ, through whom he has accomplished its reconciliation by the blood of the cross. And that new creation will be populated by people from every tribe and nation and language and people, who will have been redeemed through the Lord Jesus Christ, in fulfillment of God's promise to Abraham that through him and his descendants all nations on earth would enter into God's blessings."[661]

This promise was revealed from the beginning. When Adam and Eve rationalized their disobedience in the Garden of Eden by blaming the serpent for their transgression, God delivered the consequences to each of them (and for all mankind). But to the serpent, He said, "'Because you have done this, cursed are you above all livestock and all wild animals! You will crawl on your belly, and you will eat dust all the days of your life. And I will put enmity between you and the woman, and between your offspring and hers; *he will crush your head, and you will strike his heel*" (Gen. 3:14–15, emphasis mine).

There was God's plan revealed. The serpent was Satan and the woman's offspring included Jesus. Jesus's crucifixion was where Satan struck his heel, but Satan was crushed by His death and resurrection, the victory over sin and death. D. A. Carson writes, "This promise anticipates Revelation 12 (especially 12:9: 'The great dragon was hurled down—that ancient serpent called the devil, or Satan, who leads the whole world astray. He was hurled to the earth, and his angels with him') and the victory in Revelation 19–20 (especially 20:2: 'He seized the dragon, that ancient serpent, who is the devil, or Satan, and bound him for a thousand years')."[662]

David Guzik writes, "There is no doubt this is a prophecy of Jesus' ultimate defeat of Satan. God announced that Satan would wound the Messiah (you shall bruise His heel), but the Messiah would crush Satan with a mortal wound (He shall bruise your head). The heel is the part within the serpent's reach. Jesus, in taking on humanity, brought Himself near to Satan's domain so Satan could strike Him. This prophecy also gives the first hint of the virgin birth, declaring

---

[661]Christopher Wright, *The Message of Jeremiah,* 2014, p. 35.

[662]D. A. Carson, *NIV Zondervan Study Bible,* 2015, p. 31, footnote.

the Messiah – the Deliverer – would be the Seed of the Woman, but not of the man."[663]

Given the previous references to the covenants God made with the nation of Israel, this was God's ultimate promise because He knew they did not have the capability to honor the covenants on their own. Israel's spiritual heart was constantly sidetracked by the physical desires and pleasures of this world. The ultimate violation was the abomination of pagan worship in the temple (described in Ezekiel's vision in Chapter 12). J. Daniel Hays tells us these activities were so horrific that "Yahweh has had enough and declares, 'This will drive me from my sanctuary.' Ezekiel 10 then describes the actual departure of Yahweh from the temple. The departure has profound theological implications for it significantly alters the covenant arrangement between Yahweh and his people defined in Deuteronomy."[664]

Hays continues that with this departure and, despite the return from Babylonian captivity, there was no reference to His return when the temple's reconstruction was complete. Nothing is mentioned in any of the accounts of Ezra, Nehemiah, or Haggai, and there was no mention of God's presence returning to the temple when the massive restoration was undertaken by Herod the Great centuries later. "This absence is a clear indication that this return to the Land did not result in a return of blessing of life in the land promised in Deuteronomy. The old covenant arrangement was gone with the wind."[665]

The messages from the prophets addressed Israel's disobedience to God's commandments, particularly with respect to idolatry and social injustice. With that call for repentance came the prophecies of punishment if the warnings went unheeded (which came in the form of Assyrian and Babylonian captivities and the destruction of Jerusalem

---

[663]David Guzik, "Study Guide for Genesis 3 by David Guzik," Blue Letter Bible, last modified February 21, 2017, https://www.blueletterbible.org/Comm/guzik_david/StudyGuide 2017-Gen/Gen-3.cfm.

[664]J. Daniel Hays, *The Message of the Prophets*, 2010, p. 64.

[665] Ibid., p. 72.

and the temple). In the third of Goldsworthy's prophet motifs, the promise of hope and restoration was provided.

In this chapter I'll give you a sampling of the messages for the coming of Jesus and the Holy Spirit that would restore peoples' hearts for God, which is the key to salvation. In Chapter 14, we'll see how God intends to restore hardened hearts with the infusion of the Holy Spirit.

The Prophecies of the Messiah's Arrival

A few pages earlier, I referred to the book of Genesis revealing God's plan to send His Son for our salvation and to defeat Satan. That promise was implicitly revealed on Jacob's deathbed as he blessed each of his twelve sons. Judah, because of the restoration of his heart after plotting against Joseph, received the inheritance of the first born. Jacob also prophesied that Judah's lineage would trace down to King David and Jesus. "The scepter will not depart from Judah, nor the ruler's staff from between his feet, until he [Shiloh in the King James version] to whom it belongs shall come and the obedience of the nations shall be his" (Gen. 49:10).

David Guzik notes that "these refer to the *ruling* position Judah will have among his brethren. He inherited the leadership aspect of the firstborn's inheritance. This leadership position among his brothers meant that the eventual kings of Israel would come from Judah and that the Messiah – God's ultimate leader – would eventually come from the tribe of Judah...The leadership prophecy took some 640 years to fulfill *in part* with the reign of David, first of Judah's dynasty of kings. The prophecy took some 1600 years to *completely* fulfill in Jesus. Jesus is referred to as **Shiloh**, the name meaning, *He whose right it is,* and a title anciently understood to speak of the Messiah."[666]

In Zechariah's prophecy, he mentioned that the Messiah will come from Judah, "From Judah will come the cornerstone, from him the

---

[666]David Guzik, "Study Guide for Genesis 49 by David Guzik," Blue Letter Bible, last modified February 21, 2017, https://www.blueletterbible.org/Comm/guzik_david/StudyGuide 2017-Gen/Gen-49.cfm.

tent peg, from him the battle bow, from him every ruler" (Zech. 10:4). George Klein notes, "Verse 4 focuses on the primary outcome of the Lord's visitation of his flock, the introduction of the Messiah described as the cornerstone, the tent peg and the bow of war. Each of these three metaphors are different aspects of the Messiah's character and role... Zechariah began by reminding his hearers that the Messiah would rise from Judah. Genesis 49:10 first proclaims the relationship between the tribe of Judah and the Messiah."[667]

The book of Deuteronomy describes the rules and commandments for how the Israelites were to conduct themselves. Moses taught them that they should be blameless before God and not practice the ways of the pagan nations whose lands God would dispossess. He also warned against false prophets and laid the foundation for Jesus and His appointed mission: "'I will raise up for them a prophet like you from among their fellow Israelites, and I will put my words in his mouth. He will tell them everything I command him. I myself will call to account anyone who does not listen to my words that the prophet speaks in my name'" (Deut. 18:18–19).

We know this foretells of Jesus because Peter used this verse when he cured a lame man at the temple gates shortly after Pentecost. The crowd was astonished by the miracle, but Peter credited Jesus and admonished the religious leaders for crucifying the very One God sent to save them: Jesus. He referred to Jesus as the prophet Moses spoke of. "For Moses said, 'The Lord your God will raise up for you a prophet like me from among your own people; you must listen to everything he tells you. Anyone who does not listen to him will be completely cut off from their people. Indeed, beginning with Samuel, all the prophets who have spoken have foretold these days'" (Acts 3:22–24).

Jesus Himself drew upon God's words to Moses when He cured a man who was crippled for 38 years. Typical of the religious leaders and their hard hearts, they objected to Jesus curing someone on the Sabbath. Jesus called them out on their blind devotion to the Law and literal interpretation of Moses. "'If you believed Moses, you would

---

[667]George Klein, *The New American Commentary – Zechariah*, 2008, p. 293.

believe me, for he wrote about me. But since you do not believe what he wrote, how are you going to believe what I say?'" (John 5:46–47). From the earliest writings, God revealed His promise for our salvation. The prophets that God sent to His people centuries after Moses continued to offer the Israelites hope that God would not totally abandon them.

There are many passages that relate to this promise because the primary focus of the Bible is to reveal God's plan for our salvation, which is based on the ministry of Jesus. This is just a small sample of the prophets' messages of the Messiah restoring Israel and all who accept Jesus as their Savior.

<u>Isaiah</u>

There is a wealth of information regarding Jesus's arrival and saving grace in Isaiah's writings. Kevin Vanhoozer refers to several historic commentaries on Isaiah's writings, citing Jerome in particular. "According to Jerome, Isaiah should be called an evangelist rather than a prophet because he describes all the mysteries of Christ and the church so clearly that one would think he is composing a history of what already happened rather than prophesying what is to come."[668] While the references to the coming Messiah are scattered throughout the book of Isaiah, Chapters 49–55 in particular are dedicated to "The Suffering Servant," referencing how Jesus will serve mankind and suffer death on our behalf. Too numerous to cite here, I will limit the examples of Isaiah's messages regarding the arrival of Jesus.

During King Ahaz's reign over Judah, there was an impending attack posed by Syria and Israel prior to Israel's Assyrian captivity. Isaiah instructed the king to ask for a sign from God as to how this attack would turn out. Ahaz initially refused, not wanting to test God for a sign. Frustrated, Isaiah said that God would give him a sign anyway. "'Therefore, the Lord himself will give you a sign: The virgin will conceive and give birth to a son and will call him Immanuel'" (Isa. 7:14; Immanuel meaning "God is with us").

---

[668]Kevin Vanhoozer, *Dictionary for Theological Interpretation of the Bible*, 2005, p. 336.

Isaiah was referring to the immediate need of Ahaz, but also fore-telling Jesus's arrival here on earth. David Guzik reiterates this point: "This is one of the most famous prophecies regarding the birth of Jesus the Messiah in the Bible. It also illustrates a principle of prophecy, that prophecy may have both a *near fulfillment* and a *far fulfillment*...The *near fulfillment* of this prophecy centered around Ahaz, Jerusalem, and the attack from Israel and Syria...Simply put, God would give Ahaz a sign that within a few years, both Israel and Syria would be crushed. This was a sign of deliverance to Ahaz."[669]

Guzik continues, "Many commentators think that this was imme-diately fulfilled when a young woman in the royal household shortly married, conceived a son, and unknowingly naming him '*Immanuel*.' Before this boy came to eat solid food, Israel and Syria would be defeated. It is also possible that God is just referring in a figurative way to a year or two period of time. 'The name "Immanuel" was a rebuke to Ahaz. If "God is with us," then why should he have feared the enemy?' (Wolf). 'The "sign" of the child, therefore, constitutes an indication that the all-sovereign and all-knowing God has the sit-uation completely in hand, and it rebukes the king's lack of faith in him.' (Grogan). The *far* or *ultimate fulfillment* of this prophecy goes far beyond Ahaz, to announce the miraculous virgin birth of Jesus Christ. We know this passage speaks of Jesus because the Holy Spirit says so through Matthew: 'Behold, the virgin shall be with child, and bear a Son, and they shall call His name Immanuel,' which is translated, 'God is with us' (Matthew 1:23)."[670]

Isaiah continued with a prophecy that reflected end-time condi-tions, where Jesus's millennial reign of His kingdom takes place prior to the New Jerusalem. "For to us a child is born, to us a son is given, and the government will be on his shoulders. And he will be called Wonderful Counselor, Mighty God, Everlasting Father, Prince of

[669]David Guzik, "Study Guide for Isaiah 7 by David Guzik," Blue Letter Bible, last modified February 21, 2017, https://www.blueletterbible.org/Comm/guzik_david/StudyGuide 2017-Isa/Isa-7.cfm.

[670] Ibid.

Peace. Of the greatness of his government and peace there will be no end. He will reign on David's throne and over his kingdom, establishing and upholding it with justice and righteousness from that time on and forever. The zeal of the LORD Almighty will accomplish this" (Isa. 9:6–7).

In reference to "a child is born, to us a son is given," Edward Young notes that, "He is, of course, a son of David, a legitimate heir to David's throne, for He is to bear the government with all its responsibilities, and this He will do upon David's throne...This government is a kingdom of grace, but also in the widest extent the kingdom of nature and power."[671] That He will maintain the government with justice and righteousness forever describes no ordinary king, but Jesus the Son of God, who will rule the kingdom with peace, justice, and righteousness. No earthly king can rule in this manner. As Barry Webb notes, "There can be little doubt, then, that this oracle points directly to the coming of the Messiah, the great Son of David and the true light."[672]

Isaiah continues his prophesy of the Messiah's arrival, the one whom God had promised for His coming kingdom. "Comfort, comfort my people, says your God. Speak tenderly to Jerusalem and proclaim to her that her hard service has been completed, that her sin has been paid for, that she has received from the LORD's hand double for all her sins. A voice of one calling: 'In the wilderness prepare the way for the LORD; make straight in the desert a highway for our God. Every valley shall be raised up, every mountain and hill made low; the rough ground shall become level, the rugged places a plain. And the glory of the LORD will be revealed, and all people will see it together. For the mouth of the LORD has spoken'" (Isa. 40:1–5).

God's mercy and compassion came through the words of the prophet as he provided comfort and assurance to God's people and Jerusalem that their sins were paid in full. This is also a message for the future, that the coming of the Messiah will remove the debt of sin and all will witness the glory of God. Young writes, "When the way has

---

[671]Edward Young, *The Book of Isaiah, Vol. 1*, pp. 330–31.

[672]Barry Webb, *The Message of Isaiah*, 1996, p. 96.

been fully prepared, then will be revealed the glory of the Lord in His appearance among men; and this glory will be universally witnessed."[673] Young continues that Isaiah implies that this glory is the incarnation of Jesus and supports this with the quote Jesus gave in response to Phillip asking to see the Father. "Jesus answered: 'Don't you know me, Philip, even after I have been among you such a long time? Anyone who has seen me has seen the Father. How can you say, "Show us the Father"?'" (John 14:9).[674]

The voice in the wilderness to which Isaiah referred was John the Baptist, who preached that Isaiah's prophesy was fulfilled in Jesus and warned the people (and the religious leaders in particular) to repent and prepare their hearts for Him.[675] John quoted almost verbatim from Isaiah that he was the voice.

Isaiah described the Messiah's dispatch by God the Father. "'Here is my servant, whom I uphold, my chosen one in whom I delight; I will put my Spirit on him, and he will bring justice to the nations.'... 'I, the LORD, have called you in righteousness; I will take hold of your hand. I will keep you and will make you to be a covenant for the people and a light for the Gentiles, to open eyes that are blind, to free captives from prison and to release from the dungeon those who sit in darkness'" (Isa. 42:1, 6–7).

In the first verse, Isaiah described the telling of Jesus's baptism by John, where the heavens were opened, and Jesus was filled with the Holy Spirit. Matthew captured the event almost verbatim in his gospel. "As soon as Jesus was baptized, he went up out of the water. At that moment heaven was opened, and he saw the Spirit of God descending like a dove and alighting on him. And a voice from heaven said, 'This

---

[673]Edward Young, *The Book of Isaiah, Vol. 3,* 1972, p. 30.

[674] Ibid., p. 31.

[675]"He went into all the country around the Jordan, preaching a baptism of repentance for the forgiveness of sins. As it is written in the book of the words of Isaiah the prophet: 'A voice of one calling in the wilderness, "Prepare the way for the Lord, make straight paths for him. Every valley shall be filled in, every mountain and hill made low. The crooked roads shall become straight, the rough ways smooth. And all people will see God's salvation"'" (Luke 3:3–6).

is my Son, whom I love; with him I am well pleased'" (Matt. 3:16–17). Note the similarity between Isaiah and Matthew regarding God's delight of his Son and the pouring of the Holy Spirit; Isaiah's words were fulfilled.

Isaiah 42:6 describes Jesus's mission "to be a covenant for the people [the Israelites] and a light for the Gentiles." Matthew drew upon Isaiah's prophecy when referring to the many people Jesus healed, "This was to fulfill what was spoken through the prophet Isaiah: 'Here is my servant whom I have chosen, the one I love, in whom I delight; I will put my Spirit on him, and he will proclaim justice to the nations'" (Matt. 12:17–18). In referring to the Messiah as God's servant, David Guzik observes in Jesus's role of the servant: "He serves us; not only in what He did in the past, but also He serves us every day through His constant love, care, guidance, and intercession."[676]

In Isaiah 42:6–7, Isaiah noted the connection between God and His servant by declaring the latter as righteous and providing fatherly protection by taking hold of his hand. Isaiah also spoke of the servant being made a covenant between God and His people. Edward Young notes, "To say that the servant is a covenant is to say that all the blessing of the covenant are embodied in, have their root and origin in, and are dispensed by him. At the same time he is himself, at the center of all these blessings and to receive them is to receive him, for without him there can be no blessing."[677]

Finally, Isaiah states that the mission of the servant included being a light for the Gentiles, to release people from prison and the darkness of the dungeon. This is a metaphor for sin; salvation is provided to those who are imprisoned by sin and darkness but repent and ask Jesus for forgiveness. The light for the Gentiles returns us to the promise made to Abraham, that all nations would be blessed through his name.

---

[676]David Guzik, "Study Guide for Isaiah 42 by David Guzik," Blue Letter Bible, last modified February 21, 2017, https://www.blueletterbible.org/Comm/guzik_david/StudyGuide 2017-Isa/Isa-42.cfm.

[677]Edward Young, *The Book of Isaiah, Vol. 3*, 1972, pp. 120–121.

This message of salvation is for all, not just the Israelites. Isaiah later repeated that the servant would provide light to the Gentiles: "he says: 'It is too small a thing for you to be my servant to restore the tribes of Jacob and bring back those of Israel I have kept. I will also make you a light for the Gentiles, that my salvation may reach to the ends of the earth'" (Isa. 49:6).

Jesus himself said that salvation is for everyone in the world. "When Jesus spoke again to the people, he said, 'I am the light of the world. Whoever follows me will never walk in darkness but will have the light of life'" (John 8:12).

The inclusion of the Gentiles starts early after Jesus's death. When their message of Jesus was rejected by the Jews, two apostles referred to Isaiah's prophecy. "Then Paul and Barnabas answered them boldly: 'We had to speak the word of God to you first. Since you reject it and do not consider yourselves worthy of eternal life, we now turn to the Gentiles. For this is what the Lord has commanded us: 'I have made you a light for the Gentiles, that you may bring salvation to the ends of the earth'" (Acts 13:46–47).

The latter chapters of Isaiah are dedicated to the "Suffering Servant." It's commonly accepted that Isaiah was referring to the promised Messiah and His mission of our salvation. In one prophecy, Isaiah depicted how the Messiah would be received by the nation of Israel. "He was despised and rejected by mankind, a man of suffering, and familiar with pain. Like one from whom people hide their faces he was despised, and we held him in low esteem. Surely, he took up our pain and bore our suffering, yet we considered him punished by God, stricken by him, and afflicted. But he was pierced for our transgressions, he was crushed for our iniquities; the punishment that brought us peace was on him, and by his wounds we are healed" (Isa. 53:3–5).

Isaiah described how the servant would be rejected and scorned by those He was sent to save and how He was pierced for our transgressions. He was speaking of the rejection and scorn Jesus would face from the religious leaders and the suffering that He would undertake so that we would be healed from sin through His death. This was the plan of salvation that God designed from the beginning of time; the perfect sacrifice to atone for the sins of the world. Thomas Schreiner observes, "He suffered not because of his own sins but rather to bring healing to his people."[678]

In reference to, "Surely, he took up our pain and bore our suffering," Young points us to Matthew 8:17 where Jesus healed the sick and drove out demons: "This was to fulfill what was spoken through the prophet Isaiah: 'He took up our infirmities and bore our diseases.'" Young writes, "The reference in Matthew 8:17 is appropriate, for although the figure of sickness here refers to sin itself, the verse also includes the thought of the removal of the consequence of sin. Disease is the inseparable companion of sin."[679]

Isaiah tells us that Jesus was pierced for our transgressions. This prophesy regarding the Suffering Servant was fulfilled at His crucifixion. "But when they came to Jesus and found that he was already dead, they did not break his legs. Instead, one of the soldiers pierced Jesus' side with a spear, bringing a sudden flow of blood and water" (John 19:33–34). Barry Webb notes that "the punishment that brought us peace" refers to the reconciliation of God's people as a result of His death. Webb tells us that "the peace of God, the healing of their broken relationship with him, was secured by the Servant's death. He *was pierced for* their *transgressions* and *crushed for* their *iniquities*. The comfort they have received, the good news of their pardon, has been procured at tremendous cost."[680]

My final example of Isaiah's prophecy defining the mission of the Suffering Servant is this: "The Spirit of the Sovereign LORD is on me, because the LORD has anointed me to proclaim good news to the poor. He has sent me to bind up the brokenhearted, to proclaim freedom for the captives and release from darkness for the prisoners, to proclaim the year of the LORD's favor and the day of vengeance of our God, to comfort all who mourn, and provide for those who grieve in Zion—to bestow on them a crown of beauty instead of ashes, the oil

---

[678]Thomas Schreiner, *The King in His Beauty*, 2013, p. 343.

[679]Edward Young, *The Book of Isaiah, Vol. 3*, 1972, p. 345.

[680]Barry Webb, *The Message of Isaiah*, 1996, p. 212.

of joy instead of mourning, and a garment of praise instead of a spirit of despair. They will be called oaks of righteousness, a planting of the LORD for the display of his splendor" (Isa. 61:1–3).

Webb notes that the speaker of these verses "is both the Servant of chapters 40–55 and the Messiah of chapters 1–35—for this is what we must notice—these are one and the same person."[681] The Jews would later use these verses in Isaiah to identify the coming of the Messiah.

Isaiah said that the Spirit of God was given to the servant, which is the prophecy of Jesus being baptized by John the Baptist and the Holy Spirit descending upon Him. Jesus would declare the message of God's kingdom, particularly to the poor. He proclaimed freedom from the darkness and imprisonment of sin and comfort to God's suffering people.

Isaiah's prophecy was centered on the mission and message of Jesus during His brief ministry. The mission of the Messiah was to heal the brokenhearted and announce the freedom from sin ("release from darkness for the prisoners" [Isa. 61:1]). Young writes, "The people were captives to sin and bound with the fetters of iniquity...Isaiah is not speaking of deliverance from a physical prison but from the spiritual darkness which the people had been imprisoned."[682]

Attending the synagogue while in Nazareth, Jesus read this direct quote from Isaiah. "Then he rolled up the scroll, gave it back to the attendant and sat down. The eyes of everyone in the synagogue were fastened on him. He began by saying to them, 'Today this scripture is fulfilled in your hearing'" (Luke 4:20–21). Jesus announced to the stunned audience that He was, in fact, the one Isaiah wrote about.

Again, from Webb, "He (Jesus) knew that Isaiah's vision of a suffering Messiah was to be fulfilled in him; indeed, it had already begun to be fulfilled that day...The poor to whom the message is preached are not just those, but the poor in spirit everywhere. The comfort they receive is not just from the release from exile, but release from

---

[681] Ibid., p. 234.

[682] Edward Young, *The Book of Isaiah, Vol. 3,* 1972, p. 460.

condemnation through the forgiveness Jesus has won for them."[683] Those who heard Jesus's proclamation were astounded and indignant that the carpenter from Nazareth proclaimed himself to be the Messiah and they drove Him from town.

Zechariah

The book of Zechariah was written around 520 BC, following the return to Jerusalem after the Babylonian exile. Although his message was targeted to the community to rebuild the temple, he also had a forward-looking message regarding the coming of God's kingdom. The Israelites held the popular belief that, through the promised Messiah, God would rid His people of their military enemy, reinstate them in their land, and establish a king like David; in a sense, this was their perception of God's kingdom.

In contrast to this misunderstanding of God's plan, Zechariah's message was in line with the spiritual kingdom that Jesus would announce, not a kingdom based on military conquests like David. C. Hassell Bullock summarizes Zechariah's message, "Yahweh will cut off the implementations of war and establish his kingdom of peace through the humble king who makes his royal entry riding on a donkey."[684] "Rejoice greatly, Daughter Zion! Shout, Daughter Jerusalem! See, your king comes to you, righteous and victorious, lowly, and riding on a donkey, on a colt, the foal of a donkey. I will take away the chariots from Ephraim and the warhorses from Jerusalem, and the battle bow will be broken. He will proclaim peace to the nations. His rule will extend from sea to sea and from the [Euphrates] River to the ends of the earth" (Zech. 9:9–10).

Zechariah's prophecy was fulfilled prior to the Passover when Jesus returned to the city for the last time. Jesus instructed two of his disciples to go ahead of them to the village and retrieve the donkey He would ride into Jerusalem. "This took place to fulfill what was spoken through the prophet: 'Say to Daughter Zion, "See, your king comes to

---

[683]Barry Webb, *The Message of Isaiah*, 1996, pp. 234–35.

[684]C. Hassell Bullock, *An Introduction to the Old Testament Prophetic Books*, 2007, p. 388.

you, gentle and riding on a donkey, and on a colt, the foal of a donkey" (Matt. 21:4–5).

I previously mentioned that the Messiah was characterized as the cornerstone, the tent peg, and the battle bow. Of the three, "cornerstone" was the most significant reference to the Messiah. "I will give you thanks, for you answered me; you have become my salvation. The stone the builders rejected has become the cornerstone" (Ps. 118:21–22). In the New Testament, Jesus referred to this very quote: "'Have you never read in the Scriptures: "The stone the builders rejected has become the cornerstone; the Lord has done this, and it is marvelous in our eyes"?'" (Matt. 21:42).[685]

Further, Peter made a similar statement after receiving the Holy Spirit on Pentecost when he addressed the Sanhedrin. "'Jesus is "the stone you builders rejected, which has become the cornerstone"'" (Acts 4:11). In his first letter to the church, Peter quoted both Isaiah 28:16 and Psalm 118:22: "For in Scripture it says: 'See, I lay a stone in Zion, a chosen and precious cornerstone, and the one who trusts in him will never be put to shame.' Now to you who believe, this stone is precious. But to those who do not believe, 'The stone the builders rejected has become the cornerstone'" (1 Pet. 2:6–7).

Later in his writing, Zechariah spoke of the blessings received as a result of the death of the Messiah: "'And I will pour out on the house of David and the inhabitants of Jerusalem a spirit of grace and supplication. They will look on me, *the one they have pierced*, and they will mourn for him as one mourns for an only child and grieve bitterly for him as one grieves for a firstborn son'" (Zech. 12:10, emphasis mine).

Zechariah's prophecy for the people of Israel was fulfilled. God's grace was indeed poured out for Israel and those in Jerusalem when Jesus was resurrected and ascended into heaven. We see "the one they have pierced" in John's gospel when the Roman guards came to break the legs of those being crucified to speed up their death. "But when they came to Jesus and found that he was already dead, they did not

---

[685]See also Mark 12:10–11 and Luke 20:17.

break his legs. Instead, one of the soldiers pierced Jesus' side with a spear, bringing a sudden flow of blood and water" (John 19:33–34).

Zechariah prophesied the selling out of Jesus by Judas Iscariot's betrayal. "'If you think it best, give me my pay; but if not, keep it.' So they paid me thirty pieces of silver. And the LORD said to me, 'Throw it to the potter'—the handsome price at which they valued me! So I took the thirty pieces of silver and threw them to the potter at the house of the LORD" (Zech. 11:12–13). Zechariah was addressing the value of the shepherd to whom he was referring. From George Klein, "The money the shepherd received was tantamount to slave wages.[686] The exchange drips with the peoples' disdain for their estimation of the value of the shepherd...The monetary value ascribed to the shepherd forcefully spoke of the trifling attitude of the nation to their shepherd and their God who had sent him."[687]

Clearly, this was the attitude Jesus faced from the religious authorities. The reference to the thirty pieces of silver foretold the payment to Judas Iscariot by the Jewish authorities for his betrayal of Jesus. "Then one of the Twelve—the one called Judas Iscariot—went to the chief priest and asked, 'What are you willing to give me if I deliver him over to you?' So, they counted out for him thirty pieces of silver" (Matt. 26:14–15).

When Judas realized the error of his betrayal, he tried to return the money. The leaders at the temple were apathetic to his grief-struck conscience and Judas committed suicide in his despair. "When Judas, who had betrayed him, saw that Jesus was condemned, he was seized with remorse and returned the thirty pieces of silver to the chief priests and the elders. 'I have sinned,' he said, 'for I have betrayed innocent blood.' 'What is that to us?' they replied. 'That's your responsibility.' So Judas threw the money into the temple and left. Then he went away and hanged himself" (Matt. 27:3–5).

---

[686]Note that thirty pieces of silver was historically the price for a slave. "If the bull gores a male or female slave, the owner must pay thirty shekels of silver to the master of the slave, and the bull is to be stoned to death" (Exod. 21:32).

[687]George Klein, *The New American Commentary – Zechariah*, 2008, p.338.

"The chief priests picked up the coins and said, 'It is against the law to put this into the treasury, since it is blood money.' So they decided to use the money to buy the potter's field as a burial place for foreigners. That is why it has been called the Field of Blood to this day. Then what was spoken by Jeremiah the prophet was fulfilled: 'They took the thirty pieces of silver, the price set on him by the people of Israel, and they used them to buy the potter's field, as the Lord commanded me'" (Matt. 27:6–10).

Zechariah delivered another prophecy pointing to the aftermath of the death of Jesus. He spoke of the shepherd who was stricken and how the sheep were scattered. "'Awake, sword, against my shepherd, against the man who is close to me!' declares the LORD Almighty. 'Strike the shepherd, and the sheep will be scattered, and I will turn my hand against the little ones'" (Zech. 13:7). This was the condition of the disciples when Jesus was arrested. Jesus referred to Zechariah's prophecy when speaking to them at the Last Supper: "Then Jesus told them, 'This very night you will all fall away on account of me, for it is written: "I will strike the shepherd, and the sheep of the flock will be scattered"'" (Matt. 26:31; see also Mark 14:27).

Malachi

Malachi is the last book of the prophets before the beginning of the New Testament. Along with identifying continued disobedience to God's commandments, Malachi also delivered messages in anticipation of the Messiah in the New Testament. For example, he announced John the Baptist as the one who would prepare the Israelites for the coming of the Messiah.

"'Behold, I send my messenger, and he will prepare the way before me. And the Lord whom you seek will suddenly come to His temple, even the messenger of the covenant, in whom you delight. Behold, He is coming,' says the LORD of hosts. 'But who can endure the day of His coming? And who can stand when He appears? For He is like a refiner's fire and like launderers' soap. He will sit as a refiner and purifier of silver; He will purify the sons of Levi, and purge them as gold and silver, that they may offer to the LORD and offering in righteousness'" (Mal. 3:1–3, NKJV).

After John's apostles asked Jesus if He was the One they were waiting for, he sent them back and spoke to the remaining crowd, "This is the one about whom it is written: 'I will send my messenger ahead of you, who will prepare your way before you'" (Matt. 11:10). Jesus was drawing from Malachi's message.[688] Malachi described the coming of the Messiah, the one with the message of the new covenant that Jeremiah and Ezekiel announced. Malachi also described the Messiah as the one who would act as a refiner's fire to purify the heart like gold or silver so they would be righteous once again.

Malachi's message spoke of John the Baptist, but in a larger sense, the coming of Jesus with words about the compassion for one another that had been missing for some time. "See, I will send the prophet Elijah to you before that great and dreadful day of the LORD comes. He will turn the hearts of the parents to their children, and the hearts of the children to their parents; or else I will come and strike the land with total destruction" (Mal. 4:5–6).

While I have limited this chapter to the prophets' messages of the Messiah, there are other references in the Old Testament that predict the events of Jesus, including His death. As one example, "All my bones are on display; people stare and gloat over me. They divide my clothes among them and cast lots for my garment" (Ps. 22:17–18). We also see this in John's recounting of the crucifixion: "When the soldiers crucified Jesus, they took his clothes, dividing them into four shares, one for each of them, with the undergarment remaining. This garment was seamless, woven in one piece from top to bottom. 'Let's not tear it,' they said to one another. 'Let's decide by lot who will get it.' This happened that the scripture might be fulfilled that said, 'They divided my clothes among them and cast lots for my garment.' So this is what the soldiers did" (John 19:23–24).

---

[688]See also Mark 1:2, "'I will send my messenger ahead of you, who will prepare your way'" and Luke 7:27, "'This is the one about whom it is written: 'I will send my messenger ahead of you, who will prepare your way before you.'"

From the Branch of David

Of all the kings who ruled over the nations of Israel and Judah, David was clearly the paragon of the covenant king. Despite his sins, he had a zealous love for God, constantly sought God's will, and kept the nation connected to God because of his spiritual leadership. God had chosen him from all of Israel because his heart was in line with God's. He was cited time and again in Scriptures as the model to whom all other kings were compared.

It is no wonder that a descendant of David would rule the kingdom that would last forever. As God promised him; "'Your house and your kingdom will endure forever before me; your throne will be established forever'" (2 Sam. 7:16). Jesus the Messiah would be the ruler over God's kingdom.[689] The promise of Jesus descending (in human form) from the house of David has several references in the New Testament (which will be discussed in Volume II), but the clearest examples are taken from the gospels of Matthew and Luke that trace Jesus's genealogy directly to David.

There are numerous prophesies regarding this promise, but again, I will limit the text to a few examples of how the prophets foretold the familial connection. One Psalmist reiterates God's promise to establish David's line forever: implicitly referring to the reign of Jesus. "'Once for all, I have sworn by my holiness—and I will not lie to David—that his line will continue forever and his throne endure before me like the sun; it will be established forever like the moon, the faithful witness in the sky'" (Ps. 89:35–37).

Another Psalmist repeats the pledge to keep David's line intact forever. "For the sake of your servant David, do not reject your anointed one. The LORD swore an oath to David, a sure oath he will not revoke: 'One of your own descendants I will place on your throne. If your sons keep my covenant and the statutes I teach them, then their sons will sit on your throne for ever and ever'" (Ps. 132:10–12).

---

[689]See Appendix B for the description of God's covenant with David.

When the apostle Peter spoke to the crowd in Jerusalem having received the Holy Spirit at Pentecost, he referred to Jesus as fulfilling God's promise to David. "'Fellow Israelites, I can tell you confidently that the patriarch David died and was buried, and his tomb is here to this day. But he was a prophet and knew that God had promised him on oath that he would place one of his descendants on his throne. Seeing what was to come, he spoke of the resurrection of the Messiah, that he was not abandoned to the realm of the dead, nor did his body see decay'" (Acts 2:29–31).

The prophet Hosea called for the repentance of sin in the northern nation of Israel because of the impending punishment for failing to heed the warning. But as with the other prophets, Hosea ended his writing with the message of hope that Israel would return to God in obedience and faith. "Afterward the Israelites will return and seek the LORD their God and David their king. They will come trembling to the LORD and to his blessings in the last days" (Hos. 3:5). "David their king" was a veiled reference to Jesus who would fulfill that hope in the future.

Isaiah

One of Isaiah's messages concerned the coming of the Messiah, who would rule over God's kingdom. Isaiah described how His rule would establish peace over the earth and maintain justice and righteousness. "For to us a child is born, to us a son is given, and the government will be on his shoulders. And he will be called Wonderful Counselor, Mighty God, Everlasting Father, Prince of Peace. Of the greatness of his government and peace there will be no end. He will reign on David's throne and over his kingdom, establishing and upholding it with justice and righteousness from that time on and forever. The zeal of the LORD Almighty will accomplish this" (Isa. 9:6–7). Isaiah's message was about the end times where Jesus rules over the millennial kingdom rather than His incarnate mission in Israel.

Isaiah continued the message of Jesus coming from the seed of David and described how the Spirit of the Lord would descend upon Him, giving Him wisdom and counsel. "A shoot will come up from the stump of Jesse; from his roots a Branch will bear fruit. The Spirit of the LORD will rest on him—the Spirit of wisdom and of understanding, the Spirit of counsel and of might, the Spirit of the knowledge and fear of the LORD—and he will delight in the fear of the LORD. He will not judge by what he sees with his eyes or decide by what he hears with his ears; but with righteousness he will judge the needy, with justice he will give decisions for the poor of the earth. He will strike the earth with the rod of his mouth; with the breath of his lips he will slay the wicked" (Isa. 11:1–4).

The shoot coming up from the stump of Jesse is a reference to David's father Jesse. David Guzik writes that, "The royal authority of the house of David had lain dormant for 600 years when Jesus came as King and Messiah. When Jesus came forth, it was like a new green **Branch** coming from an apparently dead stump."[690]

Isaiah also used the metaphor of the Branch that will bear fruit. Barry Webb adds that from Isaiah 4:2,[691] "...the full-grown Branch was a general image of the Lord's saving work for his people at last come to fruition. Here, the shoot/Branch is a metaphor for the Messiah, through whose advent and rule this will be accomplished."[692] Jesus would later refer to Himself as the vine (the main stem) and His followers as the branches; they would bear no fruit if not with Him. "'Remain in me, as I also remain in you. No branch can bear fruit by itself; it must remain in the vine. Neither can you bear fruit unless you remain in me. I am the vine; you are the branches. If you remain in me and I in you, you will bear much fruit; apart from me you can do nothing'" (John 15:4–5).

In one other example, Isaiah declared how God would establish the throne of His kingdom by placing a descendant of David on it. "In love a throne will be established; in faithfulness a man will sit on

---

[690]David Guzik, "Study Guide for Isaiah 11 by David Guzik," Blue Letter Bible, last modified February 21, 2017, https://www.blueletterbible.org/Comm/guzik_david/StudyGuide 2017-Isa/Isa-11.cfm.

[691]"In that day the Branch of the LORD will be beautiful and glorious, and the fruit of the land will be the pride and glory of the survivors in Israel."

[692]Barry Webb, *The Message of Isaiah,* 1996, p. 74.

it—one from the house of David—one who in judging seeks justice and speeds the cause of righteousness" (Isa. 16:5). I like the fact that God establishes this throne "in love." With compassion and love for His people, He will place the perfect ruler over us: His own Son Jesus, "the one from the house of David." He will bring peace to all in God's kingdom.

Jeremiah

Jeremiah condemned the practices of Judah's king Jehoiakim who ignored the good practices of his father Josiah. Jeremiah addressed the lack of social justice under Jehoiakim and his court: "'Rescue from the hand of the oppressor the one who has been robbed. Do no wrong or violence to the foreigner, the fatherless or the widow, and do not shed innocent blood in this place'" (Jer. 22:3). The king and those around him ignored this message; they were more concerned with providing themselves with the best of the land than taking care of the weak and needy.

The bad shepherds (kings) who allowed the flock (God's people) to be scattered and ignored were punished with the fall of Jerusalem and Babylonian captivity. But God would bring back the remnant, which is most likely referring to the return from exile to rebuild the city and the temple.

"'The days are coming,' declares the LORD, "when I will raise up for David a righteous Branch, a King who will reign wisely and do what is just and right in the land. In his days Judah will be saved and Israel will live in safety. This is the name by which he will be called: The LORD Our Righteous Savior'" (Jer. 23:5–6).

J. Daniel Hays characterizes Jeremiah's prophecy as "a forward-looking promise as Yahweh declares that he himself will gather the scattered flock (Jer. 23:3). Furthermore, Yahweh declares that he will raise up a righteous "Branch" from the lineage of David who will do what is just and right (in contrast to the current rulers). This text is messianic, looking forward to the coming of a righteous Davidic King and Shepherd."[693]

In one sense, this was an eschatological (end times) prophecy for the nation of Israel when they returned from exile. It was also the first arrival of the incarnate Jesus when He came to save mankind from sin. Christopher Wright observes, "At some unspecified future date God himself will raise *up to David a righteous Branch*. And *this* son of David will be the one who will combine a reign of righteousness and justice with the blessing of salvation."[694]

Jeremiah brought to the forefront the message of restoration that will provide peace to Israel and protection from their enemies. "'In that day,' declares the LORD Almighty, 'I will break the yoke off their necks and will tear off their bonds; no longer will foreigners enslave them. Instead, they will serve the LORD their God and David their king, whom I will raise up for them'" (Jer. 30:8–9). This is similar to a promise made by Hosea. In both cases, this is not the physical structure of the monarchy witnessed under David's reign, but a return to serving and seeking the Lord. Wright notes, "Only in that state of repentance and obedience would they know the benign rule of a true *David their king*, issuing in 'his blessing in the last days' (from Hosea's verse)." This prophecy is targeted for the period of Jesus's first coming and ultimately to the end-time period.[695]

Ezekiel

Ezekiel conveyed the message that the leaders of Judah neglected the spiritual needs of the flock and that there would be the promise of one from the line of David who would better care for God's people "'I will place over them one shepherd, my servant David, and he will tend them; he will tend them and be their shepherd. I the LORD will be their God, and my servant David will be prince among them. I the LORD have spoken'" (Ezek. 34:23–24).

---

[693]J. Daniel Hays, *The Message of the Prophets*, 2010, p. 167.

[694]Christopher Wright, *The Message of Jeremiah*, 2014, p. 244.

[695] Ibid., p. 306.

Ezekiel tied together the role of the shepherd with the lineage of David, a similar link that is explored in the next section. In his commentary on Ezekiel, David Thompson writes, "The ruler's Davidic lineage indicates that Ezekiel expected Yahweh to keep the promise regarding an unending Davidic dynasty...There will be one shepherd. That is, there will be no divided monarchy with a Davidic house in Judah and random dynasties in the house of Israel." Thompson continues that in the New Testament, "Luke tells us that devout Jews (like Zechariah and Mary) believed that God's definitive rescue of his people would come from a son of David who would restore the kingdom with unprecedented blessings. Ezekiel here and other similar passages...supports such expectation. These expectations were fulfilled in Jesus, the son of David, who claimed to be the Good Shepherd, caring for God's flock, and uniting them under his royal leadership."[696]

In Ezekiel's reference to the Shepherd/David line regarding the dried bones, God restored muscle, tendons, and flesh to the field of bones and breathed new life into them. This was a vision of the restoration of Israel; spiritual renewal following God's promise. (This will be discussed in Chapter 14.) With the restoration of His people, God will send a king (David) to rule over them, again with the reference to one shepherd. "'My servant David will be king over them, and they will all have one shepherd. They will follow my laws and be careful to keep my decrees'" (Ezek. 37:24).

Arrival of the Good Shepherd

Scriptures often referred to Israelite leadership as a shepherd caring for his flock, a metaphor that easily related to readers. In this vein, Christopher Wright notes that "...a metaphor for kingly rule, was that of a *shepherd*. Kings were shepherds of their people. Sheep need to follow their shepherd, but the primary responsibility of the shepherd is to care for the sheep, not exploit them."[697]

---

[696]David Thompson, *Cornerstone Biblical Commentary (Ezekiel),* 2010, pp. 208–09.

[697]Christopher Wright, *Old Testament Ethics for the People of God,* 2004, p.122.

David often referred to this role of the shepherd and spoke of his people as sheep. For example, when David sinned by taking the census to assess his potential military strength, he witnessed the consequence of his failure to trust in God. As judgement, God sent the plague among his people. "When David saw the angel who was striking down the people, he said to the LORD, 'I have sinned; I, the shepherd, have done wrong. These are but sheep. What have they done? Let your hand fall on me and my family'" (2 Sam. 24:17).

In the famous Twenty-Third Psalm, David, who was a shepherd in his early life, wrote of how the Lord cared for him as a shepherd cared for his flock. "The LORD is my shepherd; I shall not want. He makes me to lie down in green pastures; He leads me beside the still waters. He restores my soul; He leads me in the paths of righteousness for his name's sake" (Ps. 23:1–3). God protected David, gave him peace of mind, refreshed his soul (in our context, his spiritual heart), and kept him on the path of righteousness.

As sheep need the protection of their shepherd, so too the people of Israel needed the king to protect them spiritually and militarily. In their condemnation of the kings and their inability to protect their people, the prophets spoke of a better shepherd, an ideal shepherd that God would provide, which would be Jesus. In the New Testament, Jesus says several times that He is the shepherd who cares for His sheep.

Micah

Micah, like some of the later prophets, proclaimed peace for Israel that would come from a shepherd who would protect His flock. "'But you, Bethlehem Ephrathah, though you are small among the clans of Judah, out of you will come for me one who will be ruler over Israel, whose origins are from of old, from ancient times.' Therefore, Israel will be abandoned until the time when she who is in labor bears a son, and the rest of his brothers return to join the Israelites. He will stand and shepherd his flock in the strength of the LORD, in the majesty of the name of the LORD his God. And they will live securely, for then his greatness will reach to the ends of the earth" (Mic. 5:2–4).

Micah's prophecy announced that the Messiah would come from the small town of Bethlehem. This was the same town where Boaz and Ruth lived, whose lineage led to David and Jesus. Coming from a small town indicates His humble beginnings. I maintain that humility is a key ingredient to a spiritual heart and Jesus certainly exemplifies that trait.

J. Daniel Hays comments on the shepherd coming out of Bethlehem, the same town where David was born: "so Micah's prophecy not only identifies the town in which the Messiah will be born but also connects the Messiah to the Davidic covenant."[698] Micah's prophecy is referenced in the New Testament when the Magi asked, "'Where is the one who has been born king of the Jews? We saw his star when it rose and have come to worship him'" (Matt. 2:2). Of course, the Magi were headed to witness the arrival of Jesus. Troubled by the thought that his kingship was threatened, Herod sought an answer from his religious leaders for what this was all about. They rightly responded that the Messiah would come from Bethlehem, as Micah's prophecy foretold some 700 years earlier.

There were earlier references of hope for this shepherd who would take over God's flock to provide care, compassion, peace, and security. Micah, a contemporary to Isaiah, shared this promise: "Therefore Israel will be abandoned until the time when she who is in labor bears a son, and the rest of his brothers return to join the Israelites. He will stand and shepherd his flock in the strength of the LORD, in the majesty of the name of the LORD his God. And they will live securely, for then his greatness will reach to the ends of the earth" (Mic. 5:3–4). Micah's forward-looking prophecy told the people of the new shepherd who rule in God's glory and peace would extend to the ends of the world.

Isaiah continued with the hope of a covenantal leader; a great shepherd who would treat his flock with tenderness and compassion. "See, the Sovereign LORD comes with power, and he rules with a mighty arm. See, his reward is with him, and his recompense accompanies

---

[698]J. Daniel Hays, *The Message of the Prophets,* 2010, p. 315.

him. He tends his flock like a shepherd: He gathers the lambs in his arms and carries them close to his heart; he gently leads those that have young" (Isa. 40:10–11). I like the visual Isaiah's words bring to mind; that of Jesus carrying a lost lamb back to the fold. It represents the loving concern for lambs who have lost their way, just as sinners have lost their way from God.

Jeremiah also used the shepherd metaphor, but in a military sense that described the misuse of the power prior to the fall of Jerusalem and its capture by the Babylonian army. "'Woe to the shepherds who are destroying and scattering the sheep of my pasture!' declares the LORD. Therefore, this is what the LORD, the God of Israel, says to the shepherds who tend my people: 'Because you have scattered my flock and driven them away and have not bestowed care on them, I will bestow punishment on you for the evil you have done,' declares the LORD" (Jer. 23:1–2).

Ezekiel

Ezekiel made extensive use of the shepherd analogy throughout his writings. He began with his criticism of the same regime that Jeremiah targeted. "'Son of man, prophesy against the shepherds of Israel; prophesy and say to them: 'This is what the Sovereign LORD says: Woe to you shepherds of Israel who only take care of yourselves! Should not shepherds take care of the flock? You eat the curds, clothe yourselves with the wool and slaughter the choice animals, but you do not take care of the flock. You have not strengthened the weak or healed the sick or bound up the injured. You have not brought back the strays or searched for the lost. You have ruled them harshly and brutally'" (Ezek. 34:2–4).

The leaders of Judah (bad shepherds) allowed themselves to prosper at the expense of the weak. This lack of social justice was called out by the prophets to the ones who should have demonstrated charity to the poor. Leadership in Jerusalem was only concerned for its own selfish needs and the weak and injured were ignored. Rather than lead the wayward people back into God's arms, the religious leaders allowed the people to wonder away from Him, often getting spiritually lost.

Christopher Wright notes, "Basically, they had served themselves at the expense of their people, rather than serving the people at any cost to themselves...Those who have been entrusted with leading the people of God have always been exposed to the temptation of 'fleecing' the flock for their own advantage in terms of money or status, rather than the genuine and costly work for caring for the lost, the sick, the wounded and the strays."[699] With the lack of care and protection, the flock was scattered throughout the nations (the disparate remnants).

Ezekiel continued to compare the leadership in Judah to ineffective shepherds. "'As surely as I live, declares the Sovereign LORD, because my flock lacks a shepherd and so has been plundered and has become food for all the wild animals, and because my shepherds did not search for my flock but cared for themselves rather than for my flock, therefore, you shepherds, hear the word of the LORD: This is what the Sovereign LORD says: I am against the shepherds and will hold them accountable for my flock. I will remove them from tending the flock so that the shepherds can no longer feed themselves. I will rescue my flock from their mouths, and it will no longer be food for them'" (Ezek. 34:8–10).

God intervened and took His neglected flock from the hands of those in charge to protect them from enemy nations. Robert Jenson notes, "Shepherds necessarily live at least in part from the products of the flock, but the calling for which they receive these privileges is to live *for* the flock, which the princes of Israel have not done." In his footnote to this, Jenson adds "Since Israelite shepherds were not permitted to slaughter for food, the wicked shepherds taking of meat from the flock was not only selfish, but illegal."[700] But from Ezekiel's message, God will rescue His people by providing a better shepherd: Himself through His Son, Jesus.

Jeremiah and Ezekiel both note that God will personally intervene with His people to place His own shepherd to care for them. "'I myself will gather the remnant of my flock out of all the countries where I

---

[699]Christopher Wright, *The Message of Ezekiel*, 2001, p. 275.

[700]Robert Jenson, *Commentary on the Bible – Ezekiel*, 2009, p. 264.

have driven them and will bring them back to their pasture, where they will be fruitful and increase in number. I will place shepherds over them who will tend them, and they will no longer be afraid or terrified, nor will any be missing,' declares the LORD" (Jer. 23:3–4). God will gather His flock from the four corners of the world, bring them home, and they will prosper. No longer will they have to fear their enemies.

Ezekiel's prophecy complemented Jeremiah's. "'For this is what the Sovereign LORD says: I myself will search for my sheep and look after them...I will tend them in a good pasture, and the mountain heights of Israel will be their grazing land. There they will lie down in good grazing land, and there they will feed in a rich pasture on the mountains of Israel. I myself will tend my sheep and have them lie down, declares the Sovereign LORD. I will search for the lost and bring back the strays. I will bind up the injured and strengthen the weak, but the sleek and the strong I will destroy. I will shepherd the flock with justice'" (Ezek. 34:11, 14–16).

In much the same way David described the rest and peace God provided to him, Ezekiel's message extended this rest and comfort to all God's people. Searching for the lost and bringing back the strays fell in line with part of Jesus's ministry. Those who were lost in sin or had strayed from God's grace will be targeted by Jesus to forgive them of their sins. He will fulfill God's promise to heal the injured and give strength to those weak in faith.

Ezekiel described how the shepherd would separate the good sheep from the bad sheep in judgement over the entire flock. "'As for you, my flock, this is what the Sovereign LORD says: I will judge between one sheep and another, and between rams and goats'" (Ezek. 34:17). This prophecy will be fulfilled when Jesus returns to rule. "When the Son of Man comes in his glory, and all the angels with him, he will sit on his glorious throne. All the nations will be gathered before him, and he will separate the people one from another as a shepherd separates the sheep from the goats. He will put the sheep on his right and the goats on his left. Then the King will say to those on his right, "Come, you who are blessed by my Father; take your inheritance, the kingdom prepared for you since the creation of the world"'" (Matt. 25:31–34).

Like the earlier prophets, Ezekiel identified the shepherd that God would provide as a descendent from David. "'I will save my flock, and they will no longer be plundered. I will judge between one sheep and another. I will place over them one shepherd, my servant David, and he will tend them; he will tend them and be their shepherd. I the LORD will be their God, and my servant David will be prince among them. I the LORD have spoken'" (Ezek. 34:22–24).

Jesus used the shepherd metaphor several times in John's gospel. He would save and protect those who believe in Him (His flock) in the same manner the Lord looked over David in Psalm 23. Jesus Himself referred to His role as the Good Shepherd in fulfilling the promises that the prophets relayed: "'I am the good shepherd. I know my own and my own know me, just as the Father knows me, and I know the Father; and I lay down my life for the sheep. And I have other sheep that are not of this fold. I must bring them also, and they will listen to my voice. So there will be one flock, one shepherd'" (John 10:14–16, ESV).

Jesus verified the identity given in Jeremiah's message and that His role was to die on behalf of His flock. This was not restricted to the nation of Israel alone, but also the Gentiles ("other sheep that are not of this fold") so that the blessings of all Abraham's descendants (beyond the nation of Israel) are fulfilled. One shepherd, one flock.

Seeking the lost and bringing back those that strayed is what Jesus does for the sinners of the world. His mission is to save those lost in sin so that their damaged spiritual hearts can be restored. He revealed this to the Pharisees in a parable: "'What man of you, having a hundred sheep, if he has lost one of them, does not leave the ninety-nine in the open country, and go after the one that is lost, until he finds it? And when he has found it, he lays it on his shoulders, rejoicing. And when he comes home, he calls together his friends and his neighbors, saying to them, 'Rejoice with me, for I have found my sheep that was lost.' Just so, I tell you, there will be more joy in heaven over one sinner who repents than over ninety-nine righteous persons who need no repentance'" (Luke 15:4–7).

In Ezekiel's message, the Shepherd would bind up the injured and strengthen the weak. When we get to the New Testament in Volume II, it will be obvious that the accounts of Jesus's mission include healing everyone with afflictions, not just the crippled. He particularly targets the weak, poor, widows, and orphans—those who the leaders of Israel failed. This is the point made by Robert Jenson, "The Lord will personally do what Israel's rulers were supposed to do and did not and what Jesus in a parable (Matt. 18:12) describes as his own mission. The Lord will search for the lost sheep and bring them back."[701]

The salvation that God promised to Adam and Eve is echoed throughout the Old Testament. While this text isolates the spiritual heart and the plan for its promised restoration, the Scriptures are about God's plan of salvation through His Son Jesus, with the restoration of the spiritual heart being the benefit of that plan. The prophets' messages reinforced God's initial promise. God revealed that, while Israel sinned and judgement was levied against them, the prophets shared the promise to have His people rejoin Him by providing the Messiah, the Suffering Servant, as the only way to salvation. He will rule over them in peace and justice and care for them like the Good Shepherd. In order for that salvation to take hold, God will intervene and begin the restoration of the core ingredients to love God and our neighbor by writing the law directly into our hearts, which is the focus of the next chapter.

---

[701]Robert Jenson, *Commentary on the Bible – Ezekiel*, 2009, p. 265.

Chapter 14–

THE PROMISE OF A "NEW HEART"

The Circumcised Heart

I n Chapter 3, recall that God made His covenant with Abraham to make a great nation from his descendants and to deliver the people from Egypt to the Promised Land. As part of this covenant, God required Abraham and his people to obey His will and to be circumcised as a sign of their agreement. Circumcision thereby became an important symbol of the Israelites' commitment to this covenant and obedience to God.

While circumcision is the physical removal of the foreskin, Scriptures often refer to a spiritual circumcision; that of the circumcised heart. It is a metaphor to represent removing physical or worldly distractions that get in the way of our dedication to God. James Hamilton relates the circumcised heart to that of a regenerated heart or renewed spirit, one that Jesus would later refer to as being reborn or a spiritual rebirth.[702] "The New Testament's metaphor of 'new birth' matches the Old Testament's metaphor of heart circumcision. That is,

---

[702]"Jesus replied, 'Very truly I tell you, no one can see the kingdom of God unless they are born again'" (John 3:3).

I take circumcision of the heart to be the same experience as regeneration (Rom. 2:29,[703] Col. 2:11–13[704])."[705]

In many instances, an uncircumcised heart refers to the hardened rejection of God's commandments or of God Himself. This described the Israelites' own failing relationships with God and Pharaoh's position before the exodus from Egypt. Moses made several attempts to have Pharaoh release the Israelites, all of which were rebuffed because God hardened Pharaoh's heart. God didn't cause Pharaoh to be set in his stubborn ways; God merely allowed Pharaoh to dig into his stubbornness without any interference on His part.[706]

After leaving Egypt for the Promised Land and having been instructed on the Ten Commandments, God continued to remind His people to keep their hearts open to Him, to trust in His care and protection. In His mercy, He tolerated their intermittent bad behavior. The first reference to a circumcised heart is found in the book of Deuteronomy. "Yet the LORD set his affection on your ancestors and loved them, and he chose you, their descendants, above all the nations—as it is today. Circumcise your hearts, therefore, and do not be stiff-necked any longer" (Deut. 10:15–16).

---

[703]"No, a person is a Jew who is one inwardly; and circumcision is circumcision of the heart, by the Spirit, not by the written code. Such a person's praise is not from other people, but from God."

[704]"In him you were also circumcised with a circumcision not performed by human hands. Your whole self ruled by the flesh was put off when you were circumcised by Christ, having been buried with him in baptism, in which you were also raised with him through your faith in the working of God, who raised him from the dead. When you were dead in your sins and in the uncircumcision of your flesh, God made you alive with Christ. He forgave us all our sins..."

[705]James Hamilton, *God's Indwelling Presence: The Holy Spirit in the Old & New Testament*, 2003, p. 2.

[706]We read in Chapter 3 that God did intercede with Pharaoh and Abimilech regarding them taking Sarah, believing her to be Abraham's sister rather than his wife. God intervenes through a dream to nip it in the bud to keep His plan from being derailed. In this case, God allowed Pharaoh to wallow in his own stubbornness rather than reveal His plan in a dream. His hardened heart was allowed in order to demonstrate God's power over Pharaoh's until he finally acquiesced.

God reminded the Israelites that they were His chosen people based on the covenant He made with Abraham, Isaac, and Jacob. Eugene Merrill writes, "Just as the removal of the flesh testified to obedience and covenant allegiance, so circumcision of the heart reflects an internal commitment to belong to and serve Yahweh unreservedly."[707] God was instructing them to get rid of the rebellious attitude they displayed many times in the desert. He wanted them to clear their hearts of the things of this world and to keep them open for Him.

John Sailhamer notes that the author of the Pentateuch wanted to show that God's promise to restore the blessing given to mankind at creation would ultimately succeed because "none other than God ensures the obedience seed through a new covenant (Deut. 29). By that covenant God will give them a new heart to engender their trust and obedience."[708] Robert Jenson adds to this characterization, "Circumcision, like baptism, was the entry point into the covenant relationship." But in context to this chapter, Jenson makes a universal point that is relevant for all the biblical references for the circumcised heart. In part, it requires repentance. "Repentance involves a radical new beginning with God, with a fresh surrender of heart, mind and will, of worship and life, to him as covenant Lord."[709] God was giving the Israelites the opportunity to give up their idols and repent of their disobedience. Moving forward in their walk with Him required them to recognize their sins, atone for them, and not repeat them.

This call to cleanse their hearts was reiterated later in Deuteronomy to emphasize the importance of the First Great Commandment. "He will bring you to the land that belonged to your ancestors, and you will take possession of it. He will make you more prosperous and numerous than your ancestors. The LORD your God will circumcise your hearts and the hearts of your descendants, so that you may love him with all your heart and with all your soul, and live" (Deut. 30:5–6). God spoke plainly that cleansing their hearts would allow them to love

---

[707]Eugene Merrill, *Bible Commentary – Deuteronomy*, 2008, p. 547.

[708]John Sailhamer, *The Expositor's Bible Commentary; Genesis*, 2008, p. 40.

[709]Robert Jenson, *Commentary on the Bible: Ezekiel*, 2009, p. 90.

Him and that they have the responsibility to pass these instructions on to their children. God would forgive His people of their transgressions through their repentance so they could restore their relationship with Him.

Anthony Hoekema notes, "In Deuteronomy 30:6 we find our spiritual renewal figuratively described as a circumcision of the heart...That since the heart is the inner core of the person, the passage teaches that God must cleanse us within before we can truly love him."[710] Regarding the direction God gave Israel, G. K. Beale states that God promised He would dwell with them, and in response to God's promise, "Israel was to 'walk in His ways and keep his commandments' in order to reach the Promised Land." Beale adds: "Ultimately, only if God 'circumcised their heart' would they be able to love and obey him, continuing in his presence and inherit the promise and truly 'live.'"[711]

God's promise to lead the Israelites to Canaan (at the time of this verse, they were still on their way) included making them prosperous and fruitful in their endeavors. Michael Vlach writes that the circumcised heart referred to in verse 6 "...is related to the concept of regeneration in which God causes a person to become alive spiritually." The caveat was that the Promised Land was contingent on spiritual renewal; "...but the regathering and restoration of Israel to the land of promise can only occur with spiritual salvation and a new heart." Vlach identifies Deuteronomy 30:6 as "the first reference to the New Covenant in the Bible [Vlach refers to Jeremiah's prophecy later in this section] ...Israel did not obey the Mosaic Covenant because they were sinful. Yet the day is coming when God will remedy the heart problem by circumcising hearts."[712]

God's rewards are great when the heart is open and available to Him. In Chapters 8 and 10, these rewards were clearly demonstrated through the prosperity of David and Solomon, which continued during the reign of the good kings of Judah. Indeed, the Israelites had

---

[710]Anthony Hoekema, *Saved by Grace,* 1994, p. 95.

[711]G. K. Beale, *The Temple and the Church's Mission,* 2004, p. 114.

[712]Michael Vlach, *He Will Reign Forever,* 2017, pp. 105–106.

the Ten Commandments committed to memory, but as we saw in the last chapter, the pratfalls of idolatry caused those blessings to get lost in the muddle of pagan worship. Jesus would preach that obeying the commandments and following Him would allow us to live in God's kingdom forever. At the genesis of the nation, God made the same promise: keep your heart open to love God with all your effort and live.

Failure to keep their hearts open to God caused the Israelites to falter time and again and to fall into the coziness of idolatry. G. K. Beale cites several passages in the Old Testament (Psalm 106:20, Hosea 4:7, and Jeremiah 2:11) where Israel had given up their representation of His presence on earth in exchange for the lifeless image of the idols they worshiped. In speaking of their own personal glory, Beale states that it is "a reference to God's presence and his glorious attributes demonstrated toward Israel [that] they were to reflect in themselves."[713] He goes on to state that "Israel's faithfulness was to bring them into such close proximity to God and his glory so that it was to result in a reflection of this glory, but they exchanged it for not merely another god but for a reflection of that god's inglorious nature."[714]

Indeed, warnings identified within the "Deuteronomy Curse" were initiated in Leviticus where the prophecy of Israel's captivity by the Assyrians and Judah's Babylonian captivity were anticipated centuries before they occurred. The warnings were laid out well in advance that sinful behavior would lead Israel into the hands of their enemies. But, as we will see in this chapter, repentance and atonement lay the foundation for restoration with God.

The formula for their return to the Promised Land was simple and had an end-times ring to it. "'Those of you who are left will waste away in the lands of their enemies because of their sins; also because of their ancestors' sins they will waste away. But if they will confess their sins and the sins of their ancestors—their unfaithfulness and their hostility toward me, which made me hostile toward them so that I sent them into the land of their enemies—then when their uncircumcised

---

[713] G. K. Beale, *We Become What We Worship*, 2008, p. 94.

[714] Ibid.

hearts are humbled and they pay for their sin, I will remember my covenant with Jacob and my covenant with Isaac and my covenant with Abraham, and I will remember the land'" (Lev. 26:39–42).

God's plan to directly intervene with Israel's wayward behavior began with removing their reliance on the temple as protection against the world. By the time of the Babylonian invasion, the people in Judah had relied so heavily on the temple for their protection that they couldn't imagine God would allow it to be destroyed. But that didn't stop them from the abominations of pagan practices that went on during the last years following King Josiah's earlier reforms. Jeremiah's message to the authorities at that time was to prepare to surrender to the invading army as it was God's judgement against their sinful behavior.

Walter Kaiser summarizes that Jeremiah's message to Judah prior to its destruction was their failure to worship God with their hearts. "Jeremiah announced three propositions: (1) attendance at the house of God was no substitute for real repentance, (2) observance of religious rituals was no substitute for obedience to the Lord and (3) possession of the word of God was no substitute for responding to what that word said."[715]

Ezekiel's description of God's presence leaving the temple prior to the fall of Jerusalem in 587 BC was an important piece in God's plan. Initially, the temple was the place where God dwelt with His people and could hear their repentance and prayers. By the time of its destruction, apostasy within the temple reached such a depraved level, that God had no choice but to leave it all behind. His departure, as announced by Ezekiel, was the turning point for modifying His dwelling position with His people. "Then the glory of the LORD departed from over the threshold of the temple and stopped above the cherubim" (Ezek. 10:18). With the return of the remnant Jews from their Babylonian captivity, both the city and the temple would slowly be rebuilt. However, there was no mention of God's presence

---

[715]Walter Kaiser, *The Promise-Plan of God,* 2008, p. 198.

returning at any time after the construction of the second temple, for good reason; God planned a more personal dwelling with mankind.

With His departure from the temple and its destruction, God established His ultimate plan to wean Israel from the temple as a mere icon and to forego His presence in a man-made structure. The single-minded focus on the temple structure itself and the sacredness it promoted created a false practice of worship and not a personal relationship with God. Jesus found that this focus on the temple had not changed, which was one of the reasons He faulted the religious leaders; they put up barriers to prevent worshipers from having a relationship with God.

Rather than have His people bound in the temple confines, God promised to dwell within each of us through the Holy Spirit. This message of promise came through Isaiah, Jeremiah, Ezekiel, and Joel. Ezekiel revealed God's redemptive promise: "'Therefore say: "This is what the Sovereign LORD says: Although I sent them far away among the nations and scattered them among the countries, yet for a little while I have been a sanctuary for them in the countries where they have gone"'" (Ezek. 11:16).

The warnings of the prophets to get the people back on track were unsuccessful. If man could not open his heart to obey God and be faithful in his own abilities, then God would have to intervene and implant that obedience in individuals' hearts. In their messages, the prophets must have understood at that point in Israel's history, the instructions for circumcised hearts could not be fulfilled by man's own will, but only through God's grace. This would be accomplished through God's promise of the new covenant, and it would be all-inclusive.

This concept is echoed by the authors, Peter Gentry and Stephen Wellum. "However, as redemption history unfolds, the Prophets anticipate a day when the Messiah will come, and *all* his people will experience heart circumcision by the Spirit. What is promised is that *all* the people of the new covenant will have the inward reality of a new heart, who in relation to Christ, the covenant head, and by the Spirit will live in service and obedience to God…the Lord will bring about a *spiritually* renewed covenant people."[716] Thus, the new covenant incorporates the two-stage process of Jesus's salvation through His death on the cross in coordination with the infusion of the Holy Spirit that was mentioned at the outset of this text.

This was the good news from Isaiah, Jeremiah, and Ezekiel, along with the prophet Joel. God's law would be written in the hearts of individuals and become the foundation of a new covenant. The covenant established at Mount Sinai through Moses could not be adhered to by the Israelites' efforts alone. We witnessed the failures of His people from the time they entered the Promised Land until their return from exile. God's promise to come directly to individuals' hearts was required. As Christopher Wright notes, "It is no longer merely that Israel should wholeheartedly obey the law when they read or hear it (Deuteronomy clearly called for that), but that they should live by an inner impulse coming from within, from God's word written on their own hearts."[717]

Jeremiah, Ezekiel, and Joel relayed similar messages regarding God's plan to send the Holy Spirit to restore our hearts to the holy and pure nature that better and more consistently reflects His image. D. A. Carson's introductory text to Ezekiel tells us that "Jesus' blood cleanses us from all sins and unrighteousness (1 John 1:9[718]). In doing so he saves us by performing heart surgery (a heart surgery that with God's Spirit enables a spiritually transformed life), fills us with the new life of his Spirit who empowers us of holy transformation from death to life."[719] This was the promise that the prophets revealed to us: the promise of restored hearts and a new covenant with God and mankind. The difference was that this new covenant would be all-inclusive and not restricted to the descendants of Abraham.

---

[716] Peter Gentry and Stephen Wellum, *Kingdom Through Covenant*, 2018, p. 156.

[717] Christopher Wright, *The Message of Jeremiah*, 2014, p. 327.

[718] "If we confess our sins, he is faithful and just and will forgive our sins and purify us from all unrighteousness."

[719] D. A. Carson, *NIV Zondervan Study Bible*, 2015, p. 1601.

Hosea gave a hint to the promise of this new arrangement. Under the covenant, God would bring peace to all living creatures. "'In that day I will make a covenant for them with the beasts of the field, the birds in the sky and the creatures that move along the ground. Bow and sword and battle I will abolish from the land, so that all may lie down in safety. I will betroth you to me forever; I will betroth you in righteousness and justice, in love and compassion. I will betroth you in faithfulness, and you will acknowledge the LORD'" (Hosea 2:18–20).

In his commentary on Hosea, George Schwab writes, "The covenant...is depicted as a cosmic renewal. The (new) covenant will bind the people in justice and righteousness, and they will 'know' the Lord. To 'know' is often a marital term, a euphemism for conjugal bliss. They will be intimate with their God—they will be true to the covenant and in their hearts, they will love him...this future state is the promise that those who had been excluded from the covenant will be included."[720]

Isaiah will pick up on this theme of inclusiveness in his message which would progressively be developed by the prophesies of Jeremiah, Ezekiel, and Joel. No longer would God's family be restricted to those of Jewish descent; there would be opportunities for the Gentiles under the new covenant.

Isaiah

Isaiah mentioned the arrival of the Spirit that renews: "The fortress will be abandoned, the noisy city deserted; citadel and watchtower will become a wasteland forever, the delight of donkeys, a pasture for flocks, till the Spirit is poured on us from on high, and the desert becomes a fertile field, and the fertile field seems like a forest" (Isa. 32:14–15). All that was great in the nation of Israel was destined to become an uninhabited wasteland until the Spirit was provided by God. Isaiah continued with the metaphor for a thirsty land renewed by the Spirit. "'For I will pour water on the thirsty land, and streams on the dry ground; I will pour out my Spirit on your offspring, and my blessing on your descendants'" (Isa. 44:3).

---

[720]George Schwab, *Expositors Commentary: Daniel–Malachi (Hosea)*, 2018, p. 193.

Isaiah described Israel's spiritual condition as an arid wasteland. Things that were once considered dead or deserted (like the spiritual heart of the sinful man) would be totally refreshed when the Holy Spirit comes to renew all things. Mankind's salvation is augmented by the Holy Spirit, the life-giving source, just as water gives life to dry land. The blessings God promised will be passed on to descendants, just like the blessings God promised to Abraham's descendants.

With respect to the renewal of life the Spirit brings, Edward Young notes, "Only the Spirit will be able to restore what the sin of man had destroyed."[721] Barry Webb adds that this prophecy points to the new age of the Spirit which "was inaugurated at Pentecost and will be here in its fullness when Jesus the Messiah – who is both Spirit-endowed and the one who bestows the Spirit – returns in power to reign.[722]

To Webb's point, we are reminded that Jesus was endowed with the Holy Spirit when baptized by John the Baptist. Isaiah spoke of this in his prophecy regarding the Suffering Servant: "Here is my servant, whom I uphold, my chosen one in whom I delight; I will put my Spirit on him, and he will bring justice to the nations" (Isa. 42:1) In Mark's gospel, this prophecy was fulfilled. "As Jesus came up out of the water, he saw the heavens splitting apart and the Holy Spirit descending on him like a dove. And a voice from heaven said, 'You are my dearly loved Son, and you bring me great joy'" (Mark 1:10–11, NLT).

Isaiah later proclaimed that God would give comfort and assurance to a restored Israel that would be initiated through resurrected hearts. "'Though the mountains be shaken, and the hills be removed, yet my unfailing love for you will not be shaken nor my covenant of peace be removed,' says the LORD, who has compassion on you" (Isa. 54:10).

Peter Gentry and Stephen Wellum define this as a new covenant of peace because God's faithfulness and love will never be taken away. "There will be a new covenant, called a covenant of peace in [Isaiah] 54:10 to emphasize the fact of reconciliation...The new covenant renews and restores the broken old covenant. But it is more than that.

---

[721]Edward Young, *The Book of Isaiah, Vol. 2*, 1969, p. 400.

[722]Barry Webb, *The Message of Isaiah*, 1996, p. 139.

It is a new covenant, different from the old one and superior to it, because it depends not on God's people but instead on the everlasting kindness of God."[723] The authors also identify the benefit of this covenant. It is unlike the covenant with Abraham where one could be born into the Israelite community but still be an unbeliever. This "new covenant community, the believing community and the covenant community will be perfectly coextensive."[724]

Young further defines Isaiah's covenant of peace. "This is a covenant that brings peace to man and is an equivalent expression for *my mercy*. The reference is to a covenant of grace, wherein God freely offers life and salvation to sinners."[725] Given the achievement of salvation by way of the Suffering Servant in Isaiah 53, Webb states, "The witnesses in [Isaiah] 53:5[726] are aware that their relationship with God has been fully restored, not by anything they have done, but by what the Servant has done for them...Israel is assured that the peace which has so long eluded her because of her failure to obey will now be hers because of what the Servant will accomplish."[727]

Isaiah described the characteristics that lead to salvation. We read about them all throughout the Old Testament and they are reiterated by Jesus, especially in His Sermon on the Mount (discussed in Volume II). "This is what the LORD says: 'Maintain justice and do what is right, for my salvation is close at hand and my righteousness will soon be revealed. Blessed is the one who does this—the person who holds it fast, who keeps the Sabbath without desecrating it, and keeps their hands from doing any evil'" (Isa. 56:1–2).

This call for righteousness and treating others with compassion and fairness is not new; it goes back to "love your neighbor as yourself"

---

[723]Peter Gentry and Stephen Wellum, *Kingdom Through Covenant*, 2018, p. 498.

[724] Ibid., p. 499.

[725]Edward Young, *The Book of Isaiah, Volume 3*, 1972 p. 368.

[726]"But he was pierced for our transgressions, he was crushed for our iniquities; the punishment that brought us peace was on him, and by his wounds we are healed."

[727]Barry Webb, *The Message of Isaiah*, 1996, p. 215.

(Lev. 19:18). God blesses those who stay on the right path. "My salvation is close at hand" tells us that we should not wait to do His will.

No one would be excluded from God's family. God's kingdom is not limited to the Israelites alone, but all who hold fast to His covenant. "Let no foreigner who is bound to the LORD say, 'The LORD will surely exclude me from his people.' And let no eunuch complain, 'I am only a dry tree.' For this is what the LORD says: 'To the eunuchs who keep my Sabbaths, who choose what pleases me and hold fast to my covenant—to them I will give within my temple and its walls a memorial and a name better than sons and daughters; I will give them an everlasting name that will endure forever. And foreigners who bind themselves to the LORD to minister to him, to love the name of the LORD, and to be his servants, all who keep the Sabbath without desecrating it and who hold fast to my covenant—these I will bring to my holy mountain and give them joy in my house of prayer. Their burnt offerings and sacrifices will be accepted on my altar; for my house will be called a house of prayer for all nations'" (Isa. 56:3–7).

Foreigners and eunuchs were excluded from entering the inner sanctuary of the temple, but those restrictions were based on religious leaders thinking that the temple would be contaminated by them. Gentry and Wellum note that, "not only are individuals who are extreme examples of excluded people now characterized as true worshipers of the Lord, but also they are considered to be included in the covenant community."[728]

God announced that those excluded from the temple by man-made restrictions would not be excluded from His Kingdom. The obedient and faithful would be His servants and those who hold fast to the Sabbath and the covenant would all be welcome in His Kingdom. Edward Young comments on the removal of all barriers to God's Kingdom: "Inasmuch as the Lord's salvation is near; all personal and national distinctions and disabilities are abolished."[729] In addition to observing the Sabbath, "the eunuchs must choose those things in

---

[728]Peter Gentry and Stephen Wellum, *Kingdom Through Covenant*, 2018, p. 501.

[729]Edward Young, *The Book of Isaiah, Vol. 3*, 1972, pp. 390–391.

which God delights, namely the humble walking in obedience to his commands...they must carry out the responsibilities that devolve upon members of God's covenant people. What is required is the same thing that is required of all who would come to God, a heart of obedience."[730]

Foreigners and eunuchs were on the fringe of Jewish society, yet they possessed the same core ingredients to be obedient to God as those who were indoctrinated in Jewish faith. They, too, would be included in His Kingdom. No longer would social barriers or exclusive lineage prevent anyone from participating, for God's house would be called a house of prayer for all nations. God's kingdom is for all nations, just as He promised Abraham, "and all peoples on earth will be blessed through you" (Gen. 12:3b).

Isaiah offered comfort and peace to those who have the Spirit within them, the new covenant that Jeremiah, Ezekiel, and Joel addressed. Understanding the covenant was enabled by the Holy Spirit's presence. "'As for me, this is my covenant with them,' says the LORD. 'My Spirit, who is on you, will not depart from you, and my words that I have put in your mouth will always be on your lips, on the lips of your children and on the lips of their descendants—from this time on and forever,' says the LORD" (Isa. 59:21).

Young cites John's gospel to indicate Isaiah was speaking of the tutorial role of the Holy Spirit. "But when he, the Spirit of truth, comes, he will guide you into all the truth. He will not speak on his own; he will speak only what he hears, and he will tell you what is yet to come" (John 16:13). Young notes, "The gift of the Spirit (cf. John 16:13) who will instruct the Church in all truth and in the comforting, saving words that God has given her, will abide with her and her seed forever."[731]

Jeremiah

Jeremiah's prophecies set the stage for God to dwell in the hearts of mankind rather than in the temple or the ark. In fact, the southern

---

[730] Ibid., p. 391.

[731] Edward Young, *The Book of Isaiah, Volume 3,* 1972, p. 442.

nation of Judah's heavy reliance on the temple as symbolic protection against all enemies gave them a false sense of security and Jeremiah's message of repentance went unheeded. But Jeremiah saw God's plan for His future dwelling place. "'In those days, when your numbers have increased greatly in the land,' declares the LORD, 'people will no longer say, "The ark of the covenant of the LORD." It will never enter their minds or be remembered; it will not be missed, nor will another one be made'" (Jer. 3:16).

Jeremiah is implying that the presence of God will no longer be located in the temple and therefore, the ark will "no longer have a central role to play... Ultimately, Jeremiah's prophecy finds fulfillment in the New Testament era when God's presence dwells within each believer through the Holy Spirit rather than in the temple around the ark."[732] Walter Kaiser comes to the same conclusion regarding the temple. "Amazingly, no longer would that most central object of all in Israel's worship be significant, nor would it even come into anyone's mind; for God's presence would no longer need a symbol when he himself was plainly discernible."[733]

Jeremiah revealed to the people of Israel God's new covenant to restore their spiritual hearts. Up to this point, they had yet to be obedient to God's will. This was the promise given to the exiles returning from Babylon, but more importantly, it foretells the days of Jesus and His mission. "'The days are coming,' declares the LORD, 'when I will make a new covenant with the people of Israel and with the people of Judah. It will not be like the covenant I made with their ancestors when I took them by the hand to lead them out of Egypt, because they broke my covenant, though I was a husband to them,' declares the LORD. 'This is the covenant I will make with the people of Israel after that time,' declares the LORD. 'I will put my law in their minds and write it on their hearts. I will be their God, and they will be my people. No longer will they teach their neighbor, or say to one another, "Know the LORD," because they will all know me, from the least of them

---

[732]J. Daniel Hays, *The Message of the Prophets*, 2010, p. 153.

[733]Walter Kaiser, *The Promise-Plan of God*, 2008, p. 199.

to the greatest,' declares the LORD. 'For I will forgive their wicked-ness and will remember their sins no more'" (Jer. 31:31–34). Graeme Goldsworthy refers to Jeremiah's prophecy as a remarkable passage that "speaks of a renewed covenant written on peoples' hearts so that they will truly know the Lord and perfectly keep his will."[734]

This is a major paradigm shift in God's relationship with His people and, eventually, with all mankind. As we have witnessed from the time of Moses to Jeremiah, the Israelites were incapable of maintaining the covenant agreement with God, no matter how the prophets pled with them to return to the fold. Bruce Waltke is one of many com-mentators who identifies the need for the new covenant over the one given to Moses. "But the Sinai covenant has a glaring weakness: Israel attempted to keep it by their own resolve. Many Jews regarded it as a covenant of works. But if the covenant of works failed in the Garden of Eden before the fall, how much more will the Sinai covenant fail by human resolve in defiled Canaan."[735]

Through Jeremiah, God announced a new covenant whereby He would personally intervene and write His law directly into their hearts. Thomas Schreiner states this new covenant would "be different from the Sinai covenant for although the Lord was gracious to his people in liberating them from Egypt, Israel did not abide by the stipulations of the covenant...The new covenant is of a different character, for now the Lord will write his law on the hearts of his people so that they will obey him." Schreiner continues, "The old covenant was 'tribal' in that representatives—such as prophets, priests and kings—mediated the Lord to the people (cf. 31:29–30). But now God's people will relate to him more directly, since the law is planted on each member's heart."[736] Gentry and Wellum write, no longer will those included under the new covenant be members through birth (descendants of

---

[734]Graeme Goldsworthy, *According to Plan*, 1991, p. 194.

[735]Bruce Waltke, *An Old Testament Theology*, 2007, p. 437.

[736]Thomas Schreiner, *The King and His Beauty*, 2013, p. 361–362.

Abraham), "but by the new birth, which requires faith on the part of every person."[737]

In quoting Conrad Orelli, Walter Kaiser adds: "The human heart, the source of all volition and inclination of all desires and effort, is unfit for God's service (Gen. 8:21[738]), God will give His accepted people a new heart, related to the former one as flesh to stone, i.e., instead of a heart hard, stubborn, unreceptive, one sensitive to God's word and will, receptive to all good, or as Jeremiah says, like a soft table on which God can write His holy law. And the new Spirit that is to fill theses receptive hearts will be God's spirit, who impels to the keeping of divine commands."[739]

According to Gentry and Wellum, "what is new about the new covenant is the ability of both partners to keep the covenant."[740] In quoting Youngblood, the authors continue that Jeremiah's message indicated that "the new covenant will be stored, not in a piece of cultic furniture but in the very hearts of YHWH's people."[741]

Even though Ezekiel and Joel had the same message of changing hearts, Jeremiah was the only one to identify this as a "new" covenant. According to J. Daniel Hays, this new covenant was given against the broken one that God made with Moses at Mount Sinai because the latter was annulled by decades of idolatry. "The new covenant will be characterized by an internal change, for this covenant will be written on their hearts rather than written on stone, and the law will be placed within each person. Recall that in the Hebrew of the Old Testament, the term 'heart' usually refers to one's seat of volition. That is, one's

---

[737]Peter Gentry and Stephen Wellum, *Kingdom Through Covenant*, 2018, p. 555.

[738]"The LORD smelled the pleasing aroma and said in his heart: 'Never again will I curse the ground because of humans, even though every inclination of the human heart is evil from childhood. And never again will I destroy all living creatures, as I have done.'"

[739]Walter Kaiser, *The King and His Beauty*, 2008, p. 209.

[740]Peter Gentry and Stephen Wellum, *Kingdom Through Covenant*, 2018, p. 551.

[741] Ibid., p. 552.

heart is where one makes decisions, especially whether to follow Yahweh in obedience or not."[742]

Kevin Vanhoozer notes that the pattern of judgement to salvation in the book of Jeremiah reflects what was presented in Deuteronomy, particularly in reference to the circumcised heart. Rather than rely on man to make this happen, God Himself would intervene. "The Law and the Prophets share an analysis of the human problem (persistence in sin) call for the thorough moral and spiritual reconstruction (from the 'heart') and point to the grace of God, ultimately, as the source of revelation."[743]

We cannot rely on our own abilities to circumcise our hearts or restore them based on our own merits. We must rely on God to do that for us. Christopher Wright correctly observes that "Jeremiah has made it clear that the human heart is incapable of curing itself (Jer. 17:9).[744] He has also made it clear that the people's only hope lies in a true turning back to God. But how can a people who *cannot* turn, actually turn? Only if God gives them a heart to do so. But that is exactly what God says now that he *will* do. God will give the new heart with which 'they will turn back to me with their whole heart.' God's sovereign grace will create a new reality that breaks out of the prison of human failure and inability."[745]

Circumcision of the heart allows for spiritual barriers to be removed so we can restore the basic ingredients of God's image. This will be made possible as we will have the Holy Spirit living within us. James Hamilton makes the distinction that, while the Holy Spirit was present in the Old Testament, there was no specific indwelling in individuals as was promised under the new covenant. "That there were believers under the old covenant demonstrates the Spirit had an interior ministry in the Old Testament. Consequently, although not indwelt, old covenant believers had circumcised hearts (i.e., they

[742]J. Daniel Hays, *The Message of the Prophets,* 2010, p. 180.

[743]Kevin Vanhoozer, *Dictionary for Theological Interpretation of the Bible,* 2005, p. 354.

[744]"The heart is deceitful above all things and beyond cure. Who can understand it?"

[745]Christopher Wright, *The Message of Jeremiah,* 2014, p. 262.

were regenerate)."[746] In a footnote, Hamilton adds, "According to Neh. 9:20,30,[747] the Spirit instructed and warned the people, working on their minds and hearts. Such an interior ministry is not equivalent to indwelling. The Spirit can operate upon the heart without taking up residence within a person."[748]

With his prophecy, Jeremiah implied the infusion of the Holy Spirit that was explicitly stated in Ezekiel's prophecy. Hamilton notes that, "Circumcision of the heart appears equivalent to regeneration (restoration of the heart) while writing the law on the heart involves the indwelling of the Holy Spirit, making the recipient into a spiritual temple. Whereas circumcision of the heart was possible for Jeremiah's contemporaries, writing the law on their hearts would await the new covenant."[749]

T. W. Manson recognized that Israel's corporate failure to become a holy nation was, in part, their reliance on a "public administrative act which required the private choice of the individual."[750] He adds that the new heart reflects the nature of inwardness, individualism, and forgiveness of sins. "Here it is emphasized again that membership of the true people of God will be a matter of disposition and character rather than birth."[751] This is the same point made by Gentry and Wellum cited earlier and repeated in their summary of Ezekiel's message: "that the renewed Israel is no longer based on ethnic parameters but defined as those who are reconciled to the Lord and believing in

---

[746]James Hamilton, *God's Indwelling Presence,* 2006, p. 45.

[747]"You gave your good Spirit to instruct them. You did not withhold your manna from their mouths, and you gave them water for their thirst...For many years you were patient with them. By your Spirit you warned them through your prophets. Yet they paid no attention, so you gave them into the hands of the neighboring peoples.

[748] Ibid.

[749] Ibid., p. 47.

[750]T. W. Manson, 2008, *The Teachings of Jesus,* p. 178.

[751] Ibid. This is the same position John the Baptist took with the Pharisees and scribes who believed that being sons of Abraham was sufficient, character of the heart notwithstanding. See Chapter 13.

him...In the new covenant, the old divisions of Israel are healed, and Gentiles are included."[752]

With this new covenant, sins will be forgiven and forgotten. Jeremiah made this prophecy clear in quoting the Lord: "'For I will forgive their wickedness and will remember their sins no more'" (Jer. 31:34). The prophet Micah made a similar proclamation. "Who is a God like you, who pardons sin and forgives the transgression of the remnant of his inheritance? You do not stay angry forever but delight to show mercy. You will again have compassion on us; you will tread our sins underfoot and hurl all our iniquities into the depths of the sea" (Mic. 7:18–19). It bears repeating that sins being both forgiven and *forgotten* should put us all at ease; God will not hold over our heads the sins of our past as we ask for forgiveness and leave our life of sin; we will be spiritually renewed. It is a lesson for Christians that, just as God forgives and forgets our sins, we also should forgive those who trespass against us.

The promise underlying this new covenant was repeated to Ezekiel as he wrote of God changing men's hearts: "'I will sprinkle clean water on you, and you will be clean; I will cleanse you from all your impurities and from all your idols'" (Ezek. 36:25). J. D. Pentecost notes, "One of the major blessings of the New Covenant, then, would be the provision of a way for God to put away sins and receive sinners to Himself."[753]

Continuing in Jeremiah's message, Paul House writes that the old paradigm of merely being a descendant of Abraham would no longer cause one to be "in the definition of the elect...now, in effect, the whole covenant group will be believers, or what has been called the remanent up to now. All will receive the future blessings because none will fail to have had God place the covenant on their hearts."[754] John the Baptist and Jesus reiterated that being sons of Abraham wasn't enough. The

---

[752]Peter Gentry and Stephen Wellum, *Kingdom Through Covenant*, 2018, pp. 592–593.

[753]J. D. Pentecost, *Thy Kingdom Come*, 1995, p. 179.

[754]Paul House, *Old Testament Theology*, 1998, p. 318.

new covenant would be fulfilled when Jesus died on the cross for our sins, then all who believe will be members of His kingdom.

Jeremiah's message was about the restoration of Israel, but it also anticipated the arrival of Jesus. Contributing author Stanton R. Norman writes, "The new covenant was not instituted in the day of Jeremiah. The prophet only foresaw the promise. The new covenant was sealed by the incarnation, death, and resurrection of Jesus Christ... The new covenant, like the Abrahamic and Davidic covenants, was originally given to Israel. Yet salvation is offered to all under the new covenant. That salvation provides not only forgiveness of sins, but also inner transformation, and is expressed by Jeremiah as putting the law of God in believers' minds and writing that law on their hearts."[755]

The need to augment the Sinai covenant with this new covenant is reiterated in the book of Hebrews. "For if there had been nothing wrong with that first covenant, no place would have been sought for another. But God found fault with the people and said: 'The days are coming, declares the Lord, when I will make a new covenant with the people of Israel and with the people of Judah. It will not be like the covenant I made with their ancestors when I took them by the hand to lead them out of Egypt, because they did not remain faithful to my covenant, and I turned away from them, declares the Lord. This is the covenant I will establish with the people of Israel after that time, declares the Lord. I will put my laws in their minds and write them on their hearts. I will be their God, and they will be my people'" (Heb. 8:7–10).

By His death on the cross, all who believe in Jesus are absolved of their sins; God forgives and forgets our sins. This is the good news of the gospel revealed in the New Testament, which I'll expound upon in Volume II. Jeremiah's revelation anticipates the work of the Holy Spirit when we receive Him in our hearts. The infusion of the Holy

---

[755]David Allen and Steve Lemke, eds., *The Return of Christ: A Premillennial Perspective,* 2011, p. 126. In an earlier chapter from the same text, Allen makes a similar observation: "The new covenant emphasizes forgiveness and cleansing of sin, along with the re-creation of human hearts indwelt with God's Holy Spirit and inscribed by God's law." p. 79.

Spirit restores the pure attributes that were originally intended to let us faithfully walk with God.

Ezekiel

The book of Ezekiel began around 593 BC when the prophet was first called by God. He was among the Israelites taken into captivity by the Babylonians during the first exile in 597 BC and his ministry spanned 22 years. He was a contemporary of Jeremiah, and Ezekiel's messages highlighted the period prior to the final siege and destruction of Jerusalem by the Babylonians. Jeremiah wrote during the same time, only he was in Jerusalem prior to the final assault by Nebuchadnezzar when the city fell and God's judgement on the southern nation of Judah was complete.

Like Jeremiah, the earlier chapters of Ezekiel point to the rampant idolatry that overran what was left of Judah, particularly among the very religious leaders who were to keep God's people holy. Their rebellious and stubborn hearts were leading the people down the path of destruction. In his commentary on Ezekiel, David Thompson notes the degradation of the national heart in Ezekiel's writing and how hardened they had become. "The heart is the faculty where they should render moral judgments and make steadfast commitments, but that heart has become impervious to impression, perhaps beyond being moved. In the final analysis, they are simply not willing to hear and do the will of God."[756]

J. Daniel Hays points out that after the exile to Babylon and the return from captivity to rebuild the city and the temple, "there is no mention of the presence of Yahweh returning to dwell in the Temple."[757] The purpose of the temple for God's dwelling had ended. We are God's new temple, and He will write His law on our hearts through the coming of His Son Jesus.

However, following His departure from the temple, Ezekiel repeated God's promise of hope: "'Therefore say: "This is what the

---

[756]David Thompson, *Cornerstone Biblical Commentary (Ezekiel)*, 2010, p. 53.

[757]J. Daniel Hays, *The Message of the Prophets*, 2010, p. 206.

Sovereign LORD says: I will gather you from the nations and bring you back from the countries where you have been scattered, and I will give you back the land of Israel again." They will return to it and remove all its vile images and detestable idols. I will give them an undivided heart and put a new spirit in them; I will remove from them their heart of stone and give them a heart of flesh. Then they will follow my decrees and be careful to keep my laws. They will be my people, and I will be their God'" (Ezek. 11:17–20).

In earlier references to the circumcised heart, God asked His people to take it upon themselves to renew their spiritual hearts. God promised to gather his people in the Promised Land and help them restore their hearts by removing the impediments to faithfulness to His word. The people must make the effort to return to God and rid themselves of false idols, then God will instill the new spirit in them. This was Ezekiel's first reference to God intervening and helping to restore their hearts to Him.

Another lesson God conveyed through Ezekiel was that no one would be condemned for the actions of anyone but themselves. The popular thinking was that sins of the fathers fell to the next generation regardless of their own behavior. In fact, Christopher Wright notes that the exiles Ezekiel addressed "were blaming their fate on previous generations. They were trying to argue that it was all very unfair that God had now let his judgement fall on their generation, after so many generations of wickedness before them. They were being made to suffer innocently for the sins of others, they protested."[758] Not so, Ezekiel responded, they were just as guilty as the generations that preceded them. Not that this was a revelation; we've seen several instances in this text where individuals were held accountable for their transgressions.

However, judgement was levied against the nation for widespread sinning, hence the exile to Babylon. Ezekiel reminded them that their individual behavior contributed to the problem and he tried to dislodge the idea that the Israelites were being punished because of the sins of their leaders. Peter Gentry and Stephen Wellum also refer to

---

[758]Christopher Wright, *Old Testament Ethics for the People of God*, 2004, p.347.

the idea of this national sin. "Under the old covenant, the corporate solidarity between the people and their fallible human leaders meant that they could suffer for the sins of another, but this will not be true under the new covenant."[759]

Each person was accountable for the actions of their own hearts. God's judgement fell on individuals for their sins, but He recognized the good behavior of the righteous as well as the sinners who turned to a life of righteous living. Thompson rightly argues that with this direction, "None can use an earlier generation's behavior as an excuse for their own sins, and none need conclude that their destiny is fixed, and all hope of change and redemption is lost."[760]

In God's mercy and compassion, those who sin, repent, and return to God will not die but live, just as the righteous will live. Renewing your relationship with God is based on your commitment to that life-changing choice. "'But if a wicked person turns away from all the sins they have committed and keeps all my decrees and does what is just and right, that person will surely live; they will not die. None of the offenses they have committed will be remembered against them. Because of the righteousness things they have done, they will live'" (Ezek. 18:21–22).

As with Jeremiah's promise stated earlier, God not only forgives our sins, He forgets them. That's good news! How many of us continue to dwell in the past by carrying the guilt of our sins when God forgives and forgets? Worse yet, how often do we hold on to hurt feeling, wallow in defeat, or try to get even with those who sinned against us? We saw the outcome of harboring anger in the story of Cain and Abel. We even ask God in the Lord's Prayer to forgive our trespasses as we forgive those who trespass against us.

With these messages of individual accountability, Ezekiel was paving the way for Israel (and eventually all mankind) to return to God through repentance. They could restore their hearts and renew their relationship with God. "'Therefore, you Israelites, I will judge

---

[759]Peter Gentry and Stephen Wellum, *Kingdom Through Covenant*, 2018, p. 589.

[760]David Thompson, *Biblical Commentary: Ezekiel*, 2010, p. 123.

each of you according to your own ways, declares the Sovereign LORD. Repent! Turn away from all your offenses; then sin will not be your downfall. Rid yourselves of all the offenses you have committed and get a new heart and a new spirit. Why will you die, people of Israel?'" (Ezek. 18:30–31). God is asking why should they not live in His grace? Why should they die in sin?

God's message of hope through a new covenant came through Jeremiah and Ezekiel. They preached that those who turned away from their sins and walked with Him would receive a new heart and a new spirit. Restoring their hearts in obedience to God and walking away from their sinful past would bring renewal. A new creation is no longer anchored by sins of the world. This, however, requires repentance and ridding yourself of old habits. Says Christopher Wright, "It would require a whole new attitude and mindset, virtually a new 'person' within."[761]

In John's gospel, he wrote of an adulteress who was caught in the act and brought before Jesus for His judgement. Jesus responded, "'Let any one of you who is without sin be the first to throw a stone at her.'... At this, those who heard began to go away one at a time... 'Woman, where are they? Has no one condemned you?' 'No one, sir,' she said. 'Then neither do I condemn you,' Jesus declared. 'Go now and leave your life of sin'" (John 8:7, 9, 10–11). The instructions to her were the same as Ezekiel's message: your sins will be forgiven, but don't return to the former life of sin.

But this restoration of the heart cannot happen without God's intervention through the Holy Spirit. As we read in Ezekiel 11:17–20, God intended to change the hearts of His people so they would be obedient to His will. Paul House indicates that this message adds to Jeremiah's prophesy in that "at the same time God will give the remnant a new spirit, a point not made by Jeremiah yet clearly central to Ezekiel's theology. The new spirit is totally unmerited and a free gift of God. Together with the new heart it will produce covenant obedience

---

[761]Christopher Wright, *The Message of Ezekiel*, 2001, p. 205.

and a renewed relationship with the Lord."[762] Gentry and Wellum add, "The Lord will change the intractable stubbornness and unfaithfulness of the human partners by giving them a new heart and a new spirit...The divine Spirit will enable and motivate the human partners to follow the divine instructions."[763]

The promise of hope through this new covenant was repeated later in Ezekiel's message from God, once again stressing the benefits of this renewed relationship. "'I will take you from the nations and gather you from all the countries and bring you into your own land. I will sprinkle clean water on you, and you shall be clean from all your uncleanness, and from all your idols I will cleanse you. And I will give you a new heart, and a new spirit I will put within you. And I will remove the heart of stone from your flesh and give you a heart of flesh. And I will put my Spirit within you and cause you to walk in my statutes and be careful to obey my rules. You shall dwell in the land that I gave to your fathers, and you shall be my people, and I will be your God. And I will deliver you from all your uncleanness. And I will summon the grain and make it abundant and lay no famine upon you'" (Ezek. 36:24–29, ESV).

J. D. Pentecost writes that, in Ezekiel's message, God expanded on the promise of a new heart, promising that "the Holy Spirit would be given as His gift to those who enter into the New Covenant."[764] Thomas Schreiner takes notice of Ezekiel's new element in God's promise of renewed hearts. "The new feature is the pronounced emphasis on the indwelling of the Spirit ([Ezek.] 36:27), who will enable Israel to fulfill the Lords commands."[765] David Thompson adds, "Jeremiah's 'new covenant' (Jer. 31:31–34) and 'everlasting covenant' (Jer. 32:36–44) feature the distinctive promise of character transformation...Without repeating Jeremiah's 'new covenant' language, Ezekiel carried forward

---

[762]Paul House, *Theology of the Old Testament*, 1998, p. 333.

[763]Peter Gentry and Stephen Wellum, *Kingdom Through Covenant*, 2018, pp. 590–591.

[764]J. D. Pentecost, *Thy Kingdom Come*, 1995, p. 170. Pentecost adds that this is an expansion of Joel's prophecy (Joel 2:28–29), which will be discussed in the next section.

[765]Thomas Schreiner, *The King in His Beauty*, 2013, p. 380.

his theological claim and advanced it, explaining *how* the promised transformation would occur."[766]

With respect to the return of the Jewish remnant from Babylonian captivity, God promised to cleanse them of the idolatry and social injustice that plagued them from the division of the nation in Ezekiel's time. Richard Patterson and Hermann Austel write, "he who would approach God and serve him needs to be cleansed from the pollution of the world. In that great passage speaking of the future conversion of Israel (Ezekiel 36:25–28), Ezekiel speaks of the cleansing that God will perform for Israel, removing all filthiness and idolatry from them, giving them a new heart and causing them to live in the land of God's appointment."[767]

Their hearts of stone were replaced with hearts of flesh as a result of God infusing the new spirit; the same spirit alluded to in Jeremiah and revealed to Joel. The undivided heart would be a single-minded commitment to God, no longer in conflict with idol or pagan worship. Joel provided more details about the prophecy, but Ezekiel and Jeremiah provided the groundwork for the arrival of the Holy Spirit.

Using the story of Joseph and the Patriarchs, John Sailhamer points to their narratives in Genesis to describe the balance between God's faithfulness and the need for an obedient and faithful response. "The theological emphasis is remarkably similar to that of the "new covenant theology" of Jeremiah 31:31–34 and Ezekiel 36:22–32, where the two themes of divine sovereignty and human responsibility are woven together by means of the concept of God's Spirit giving to a person a "new heart"—a new heart, given by God, that responds with obedience and faith."[768] Anthony Hoekema notes that, "Ezekiel uses a figure to describe regeneration which, though reflecting Old Testament modes of thought, we still often use today: I will give you

---

[766]David Thompson, *Biblical Commentary: Ezekiel*, 2010 p. 32.

[767]Richard Patterson and Hermann Austel, *The Expositor's Bible Commentary: 1 and 2 Kings*, 2009, p. 693.

[768]John Sailhamer, *Expositors Commentary – Genesis*, 2008, p. 281.

a new heart and put a new spirit in you, I will remove from you your heart of stone and give you a heart of flesh [Ezek. 36:26]."[769]

Several commentators referred to Ezekiel's message as God performing heart surgery: replacing the stubborn, rebellious heart for one that knows and obeys God. Christopher Wright notes the progression of his messages regarding the circumcised heart. "For Jeremiah it was the promise of the new covenant which God would write his own law on hearts that had been engraved with sin but would now be cleansed with forgiveness. For Deuteronomy it was the promise of heart circumcision in which God's grace would give what God's law demanded – the love and obedience of heart. For Ezekiel, it was the promise of even more radical heart surgery – a complete heart transplant that would replace hard hearts of stone with hearts of flesh that would be moved to the obedience by the regenerating power of the Holy Spirit."[770] The culmination of this progression is complemented in Joel's address of the heart where he links restoration of the heart with the infusion of the Holy Spirit and the ability to understand and act on God's direction.

In Ezekiel's vision of the Valley of Bones, God revealed how the faith of Israel would be brought back to life. Israel's spirituality was all but dead, but God's intervention caused the bones to come back to life. "Then he said to me, 'Son of man, these bones are the whole house of Israel. Behold, they say, "Our bones are dried up, and our hope is lost; we are indeed cut off." Therefore prophesy, and say to them, Thus, says the LORD GOD: Behold, I will open your graves and raise you from your graves, O my people. And I will bring you into the land of Israel. And you shall know that I am the LORD, when I open your graves, and raise you from your graves, O my people. And I will put my Spirit within you, and you shall live, and I will place you in your own land.

---

[769]Anthony Hoekema, *Saved by Grace,* 1994, p. 96.

[770]Christopher Wright, *The Message of Jeremiah*, 2014, p. 197.

Then you shall know that I am the LORD; I have spoken, and I will do it, declares the LORD'" (Ezek. 37:11–14, ESV).[771]

Bruce Waltke writes, "Ezekiel's vision pictures the spiritual state of the Babylonian exiles, who are dead in cynicism and despair, but are revived to hope through God's word and God's spirit, a hope that lifts them from their graveyard in Babylon and lands them in the Sworn Land."[772] Following this restoration of the faith and health of the nation, the renewed nation would have inner peace and the perfect ruler to govern them. "'My servant David will be king over them, and they will all have one shepherd. They will follow my laws and be careful to keep my decrees...I will make a covenant of peace with them; it will be an everlasting covenant. I will establish them and increase their numbers, and I will put my sanctuary among them forever'" (Ezek. 37:24, 26). Paul House adds that, "Ezekiel pins these hopes on a Davidic ruler who serves under a new covenant."[773] This, of course, speaks to the arrival of Jesus ruling over God's kingdom.

C. Hassell Bullock summarizes Ezekiel's hope of good news. "So Yahweh, whose grace can never be outdone by man's sin, would do what Israel could not accomplish. He would give the people a new heart and a new spirit. It is that theme that is illustrated in Chapter 37, associating the new spirit with the return from captivity (v.14). The valley of the dry bones and their resuscitation primarily constitute a messaged of the return from captivity and restoration to the land, although the overtones of physical resurrection may be read from the text."[774]

---

[771]It is interesting that in Matthew's gospel, the revival of the dead depicted in Ezekiel's vision actually occurred following Jesus's death. "And Jesus cried out again with a loud voice and yielded up his spirit. And behold, the curtain of the temple was torn in two, from top to bottom. And the earth shook, and the rocks were split. The tombs also were opened. And many bodies of the saints who had fallen asleep were raised and coming out of the tombs after his resurrection they went into the holy city and appeared to many" (Matt. 27:50–53).

[772]Bruce Waltke, *An Old Testament Theology,* 2007, p. 391.

[773]Paul House, *Old Testament Theology,* 1998, p. 320.

[774]C. Hassell Bullock, *An Introduction to the Old Testament Prophetic Books,* 2007, p. 301.

Kevin Vanhoozer addresses a basic tenet of the New Testament, tying Ezekiel's vision to the mission of Jesus. "Because it is in Christ that the people of God experience death and resurrection, Ezek. 37 [vision in the Valley of Bones] is ultimately fulfilled in Christ's death and resurrection...The central role of the prophetic word in bringing this new creation prefigures the transformation of God's people through the incarnate Word."[775]

Joel

The consensus of modern scholars is that the book of Joel was written between the sixth and fourth century BC, either before the Babylonian captivity or the early post-exile period.[776] There is evidence that Joel was familiar with the writings of the major prophets, so some commentators put him around the time of Nehemiah and Ezra. Little is known about the prophet, but like Jeremiah and Ezekiel, Joel wrote of the Holy Spirit being infused into the hearts of all. All three prophets spoke of Pentecost when the Holy Spirit descended upon the apostles and disciples in Acts 2.

Joel called upon his audience to return to God with a sincere appeal for forgiveness: "'Even now,' declares the LORD, 'return to me with all your heart, with fasting and weeping and mourning.' Rend your heart and not your garments. Return to the LORD your God, for he is gracious and compassionate, slow to anger and abounding in love, and he relents from sending calamity'" (Joel 2:12–13).

Joel appealed to the people to repent from their hearts and not through rending their garments in anguish so their repentance could

---

[775]Kevin Vanhoozer, *Dictionary for Theological Interpretation of the Bible,* 2005, p. 222.

[776]Walter Kaiser, *The Promise-Plan of God.* 2008, p. 158. The author argues that Joel's writing occurred much earlier, during the reign of Joash, king of Judah (835–790 BC).

be seen by all. Such drama was for show and not for God's purpose.[777] Joel stated that God would rather welcome the return of those in sin than send calamity such as captivity by the Assyrians and Babylon. Allan Harman writes, "The call is for all the people to come back to the Lord, not with mere outward display but with an inner change of the heart. No other passage in the OT contains such an instruction regarding rending the heart."[778]

Joel spoke of a plague of locust, which may have been a metaphor for Israel's punishment. But, as with the other prophets, Joel provided the hope of restoration for the repentant heart. God would restore His nation as a new creation, where they would never suffer or be in want again. "'You shall eat in plenty and be satisfied, and praise the name of the LORD your God, who has dealt wondrously with you. And my people shall never again be put to shame. You shall know that I am in the midst of Israel, and that I am the LORD your God and there is none else. And my people shall never again be put to shame'" (Joel 2:26–27, ESV).

Joel then spoke of the universal outpouring of the Spirit: "And afterward, I will pour out my Spirit on all people. Your sons and daughters will prophesy, your old men will dream dreams, your young men will see visions. Even on my servants, both men and women, I will pour out my Spirit in those days...And everyone who calls on the name of the LORD will be saved" (Joel 2:28–29, 32).

As Isaiah alluded to earlier, there would be no discrimination in the distribution of the Spirit; it would be available to all who call on the name of the Lord with salvation being the ultimate gift. The

---

[777]Jesus admonished those hypocrites who prayed or fasted for show so that others would see them. "'And when you pray, you must not be like the hypocrites. For they love to stand and pray in the synagogues and at the street corners, that they may be seen by others. Truly, I say to you, they have received their reward'... 'And when you fast, do not look gloomy like the hypocrites, for they disfigure their faces that their fasting may be seen by others. Truly, I say to you, they have received their reward'" (Matt. 6:5,16, ESV). Joel gave the same warning when asking for forgiveness, which should come from the heart with sincere intentions.

[778]Allan Harman, *ESV Expository Commentary: Daniel–Malachi*, 2018, p. 283.

Spirit will be enlightening, an educational force to better understand God's word and provide the link in restoration of our relationship with Him. In reference to changed hearts by God's intervention presented, David Thompson notes, "Joel 2:28–29 voices a related confidence regarding God's effusion of his Spirit into his people and their consequent capacity to discern and declare his will."[779]

In Joel's message, God would restore what was lost because of Israel's sin through the promise of His Spirit. J. Daniel Hays tells us there is no limit to those who can receive the spirit. "Normally he gave his Spirit to only a few select people at special times in history, people like Moses or King David or the prophets. Now Yahweh is promising to give his Spirit to all of his people, indicating a remarkable shift or change to something new."[780]

Recall that in Chapter 8, God infused Saul with His Spirit to prepare him to be the first king of Israel, which was an example of the Holy Spirit being given to only one individual. Now that Spirit is available to all. Hays points out that with the messages of Joel, Ezekiel, and Jeremiah, "Yahweh proclaims a radically new concept regarding his Spirit and the coming messianic era...Yahweh reveals that in the coming messianic era, he will pour out his spirit on every one of his people. As part of the new covenant, Yahweh promised that he will write his law in the hearts and minds of his people and enable them all to know him [Jer. 31:33–34]."[781]

Allan Harman adds, "The effect of this outpouring, says Joel, will be communication of knowledge to young and old, male and female. In contrast to the limited group of people to whom God revealed himself in OT times, he will now reveal himself much more fully to all his people."[782] James Hamilton reiterates that this prophesy reveals a universal distribution of the Spirit. God will make this gift available to all. "Joel spoke of a future outpouring of the Spirit in terms of a universal

[779]David Thompson, *Biblical Commentary: Ezekiel,* 2010, p. 216.

[780]J. Daniel Hays, *The Message of the Prophets,* 2010, p. 282.

[781] Ibid., p. 281.

[782]Allan Harman, *Expositors Commentary: Daniel – Malachi (Joel),* 2018, p. 290.

gift of prophecy. No longer would the Spirit be reserved for select prophets, but all flesh would experience the Spirit and prophesy."[783]

Kevin Vanhoozer corroborates that the Spirit would be available to all. "Each member in the new community shares in the gift of the Spirit. The democratization by the Holy Spirit transforms the community from a hierocratic (ruled by priests) to a theocratic community... The Spirit as the mark of the new community defines the church as the body of Christ and individual believers as members of his body. He constitutes the new community that awaits the coming of Jesus Christ. The coming of the Spirit on Gentile believers evidences the inclusion of Gentiles as copartners with Israel. All who call on the name of the Lord are not only saved but also receive his Spirit."[784] This is the two-step process of salvation referred to in the introduction; those who believe in Jesus will receive the Holy Spirit, whether Jew or Gentile. Joel's message was the culmination of what God will do to restore our hearts.

C. Hassell Bullock adds that this prophecy speaks to an event of a new age "when Yahweh will pour out His Spirit upon all flesh... The new age will be characterized by a generalization of the phenomenon of prophecy, here described in terms of major manifestations in oracles, dreams and visions."[785] This was fulfilled in the book of Acts when the Holy Spirit came to all who were gathered with the apostles. Immediately after, they started to preach in different languages so that all of Jerusalem could understand the apostles in their own language. "When the day of Pentecost came, they were all together in one place. Suddenly a sound like the blowing of a violent wind came from heaven and filled the whole house where they were sitting. They saw what seemed to be tongues of fire that separated and came to rest on each of them. All of them were filled with the Holy Spirit and began to speak in other tongues as the Spirit enabled them" (Acts 2:1–4).

---

[783]James Hamilton, *God's Indwelling Presence*, 2006, p. 34.

[784]Kevin Vanhoozer, *Dictionary for Theological Interpretation of the Bible*, 2005, pp. 390–391.

[785]C. Hassell Bullock, *An Introduction to the Old Testament Prophetic Books*, 2007, p. 400.

When the doubters in the crowd accused the apostles of being drunk rather than recognize the spectacular event they just witnessed, Peter said to them: "These people are not drunk, as you suppose. It's only nine in the morning! No, this is what was spoken by the prophet Joel" (Acts 2:15–16).

G. K. Beale notes that in Acts 2:1–12, Peter used the episode of tongues to be "an initial fulfillment of Joel's prophecy that God would 'pour out his Spirit upon all flesh' and all classes of people in the covenant community would 'prophesy.'"[786] He goes on to state: "It is important to recognize that Joel 2:28–32 was a prophecy of the pouring out of the Spirit *on all in Israel...* This suggests that, based on Peter's identification of Pentecost as fulfilling Joel 2:28–32, not only ethnic Jewish Christians but also Gentile Christians are the beginning of the Spirit-filled latter-day Israel."[787]

Hays notes that in Jeremiah, God promised that He would write His Law into the hearts and minds of His people so that they will know Him but "does not reveal how this will happen. In Joel 2 and Ezekiel 36, however, the prophecy becomes clear. Yahweh promises to put his Spirit within people, empowering them to know him, to be obedient to him and to speak prophetically of him."[788]

Joel's prophecy predicted the new age where God's Spirit was no longer given on a limited basis but would be available to all. This was a culmination of Isaiah, Jeremiah, and Ezekiel's messages where the Holy Spirit was not limited to kings and prophets. C. Hassell Bullock writes that the Holy Spirit is the vehicle for how God's Law will be "written in human hearts, and no person would say, 'Know the Lord' for the universalization of that knowledge would eliminate the need for its interpersonal communication. It would exude from every transformed heart and fill the world with the knowledge of the Lord as the waters cover the sea."[789]

---

[786]G. K. Beale, *The Temple and the Church's Mission*, 2004, p. 209.

[787] Ibid., p. 222.

[788]J. Daniel Hays, *The Message of the Prophets*, 2010, p. 281.

[789]C. Hassell Bullock, *An Introduction to the Old Testament Prophetic Books*, 2007, p. 402.

I will describe in Volume II how this covenant will put new life into our hearts so that we will know God and better understand how to use the core ingredients of our hearts to renew our relationship with Him. Our ways of sinning will be overwritten by the desire to sincerely follow the Two Great Commandments. As described in the New Testament, the hearts where God has written His law will shed their worldly lives and take on spiritual living. We will become a new creation that reflects the image of God, just as we were originally created to be.

AFTERWORD

Christian parents may find themselves trying to answer this question from their children: "Why did God make me?" The simple answer is God made all of us because He loves just us as a parent loves a child, only infinitely more. He created us out of love with the purpose of being part of His family, so that He might dwell with us in unity to share in His glory. God's love for mankind is boundless and everlasting. As John's gospel so famously and publicly proclaims: "For God so loved the world that he gave his one and only Son, that whoever believes in him shall not perish but have eternal life" (John 3:16).

It was, and always will be, God's intention to be with us to enjoy this personal relationship. This is the crux of our faith. Going to church regularly is an important part of that faith so that we can worship and praise God together as His body in Christ. Corporate worship may have been established as early as Seth. It became an important part of God's blueprint as we saw in Chapter 5, and it reached its height with Solomon and the temple for the nation of Israel. It is with us to this day when Christians around the world celebrate as one in fellowship with Him.

However, our individual relationship with God is just as important as celebrating and worshiping as a group. This text is a snapshot of individuals from the Old Testament who had varying degrees of closeness with God. In contrast to healthy relationships, we witnessed the consequences of those who let their relationship with God wither away.

Despite mankind's sin, the innate core ingredients of our spiritual hearts were never fully extinguished. As evidenced in the Old Testament, there was neither perfect faith nor perfect obedience, but a range of potential righteousness. Sin is here to stay, but that doesn't preclude anyone from being in touch with God. That is an individual's choice based on the nature of their heart and willingness to act on it. In Chapter 14, we saw how God would personally intervene to help us follow His will and understand His words to us; all so that our relationship with Him would continue to grow and He would dwell in our hearts.

The Hope and the Plan

Throughout this text, I showed how faith and obedience were two characteristics that were essential in how love for God was demonstrated in the Old Testament. The earlier chapters addressed the contrast between individuals who acted on their faith and those who rejected God. There were examples of how love was extended to others, like Joseph showing compassion and forgiveness to his brothers, and Ruth showing her loyalty and kindness in caring for her mother-in-law. In later chapters, the spiritual heart of the nation of Israel was shown to be largely in response to the actions of their kings: the good kings revived the nation toward faithful behavior, while the bad kings encouraged paganism and idol worship. Faithfulness, despite the clouds of sin hanging over the earth, made hearts in the Old Testament responsive to God.

It wasn't the Ten Commandments and the law of Moses that started the clock on faith and obedience. There were several centuries between Adam and Moses, but these traits were demonstrated in Enoch, Noah, and Abraham and his immediate descendants. This faith was innate in their hearts. Noah and Abraham in particular were deemed righteous even though the Scriptures mention no formalized education of faith and worship during their lifetimes. Abraham's descendants Isaac, Jacob, and Joseph had the benefit of being raised in a family of faith. Even though there was a direct family link connecting them all, a faithful heart wasn't necessarily based on heredity nor did exposure to the same education of faith produce faithfulness. Solomon was an obvious example of this and was particularly true in Chapter 11 where a righteous king of Judah successfully revived Israel's faith only to be followed by a son who did evil in God's eyes.

Each heart is measured individually. To merely claim "we are sons of Abraham" (a claim made by many of the Israelites in Jesus's time which will be discussed in Volume II) was not a sufficient condition to be counted as righteous. An individual's heart is measured by their own faith and obedience to God. Recall in Chapter 14 how God spoke to Ezekiel regarding each person taking responsibility and being held accountable for their own actions. Heredity had nothing to do with a person being blessed or condemned on account of sins. God recognized the level of each person's spiritual heart, and their own actions would dictate a sinful or a righteous life. As the prophet Habakkuk noted, "'See, the enemy is puffed up; his desires are not upright—but the righteous person will live by his faithfulness" (Hab. 2:4).

In his letter to the Romans, Paul was very clear that righteousness and maintaining a relationship with God came by way of faith and not through adherence to the written law. He used Abraham to demonstrate the significance of faith and obedience. "It was not through the law that Abraham and his offspring received the promise that he would be heir of the world, but through the righteousness that comes by faith...Therefore, the promise comes by faith, so that it may be by grace and may be guaranteed to all Abraham's offspring— not only to those who are of the law but also to those who have the faith of Abraham. He is the father of us all" (Rom. 4:13, 16).

Abraham's faith was innate, and he acted upon it; not perfectly, but well enough to receive an important covenant and be called a friend of God. God extended His promise to Isaac and Jacob because of their faith. While God did not directly interact with Joseph, He was with Joseph all his life because of his unwavering faith despite the many adversities he faced. Because of his enduring obedience, Joseph was blessed by God so that His plan to bring His people to Canaan and dwell with them could continue.

The same was true for Ruth's faith. While most of the Old Testament traced God's plan with the Israelites, the story of Ruth was important to show that the core ingredients of the heart were not limited to them alone. Ruth was exposed to the faith of Naomi and her family, but it was the nature of her heart that enabled her to convert and follow Naomi's God. Beyond that, she exemplified the noble qualities of selflessness, compassion, tenderness, and innocence that are key elements of loving one's neighbor. Ruth was an excellent example of being faithful to God and showing that the core ingredients of the spiritual heart are universal to all mankind.

The most obvious example of faith and obedience was found in the life of David. Noah was the only man in his time who was found righteous; Abraham was deemed a friend of God, and Pharaoh asked of Joseph, "'Can we find anyone like this man, one in whom is the spirit of God?'" (Gen. 41:38). But as the apostle Paul would reiterate the words of God spoken to the prophet Samuel[790] "'I have found David son of Jesse, a man after my own heart; he will do everything I want him to do'" (Acts 13:22).

David was a man after God's own heart; that is, David's heart was closely in sync with God's original design, albeit not in its purest form. God saw that David would be obedient and faithful to rule the nation in the covenantal manner outlined by Moses. David led his people to maintain their relationship with God while putting God above all else.

David's heart was separate and distinct from his seven brothers, just as Jacob's was to Esau, and Joseph's was to his ten brothers. Like the latter two, David had no different education of faith than his older brothers. They all experienced the same faithful upbringing and environment. Yet, like Joseph, David was singled out by God because of his innate ability to demonstrate his love for God.

I spent considerable time discussing David because of this personal relationship with God. Much like Joseph, David's life was one of the best examples of how the spiritual heart in the Old Testament

---

[790]In condemning King Saul for acting on his own, the prophet declared, "But now your kingdom will not endure; the LORD has sought out a man after his own heart and appointed him ruler of his people, because you have not kept the LORD's command" (1 Sam. 13:14).

was at its strongest. In many crossroad situations, David consistently sought God to give him direction rather than rely on his own thought process. To the contrary, Saul came to his own destruction by ignoring God's guidance and seeking his own solutions.

There's a lesson for us, as Christians. All too often we seek to solve our own significant problems without asking God for guidance. How often do we turn to God before trying to figure it out for ourselves? David often turned to God for answers when faced with a crisis and quickly acknowledged his sin and repented. David was willing to accept His will, despite the consequences.

Chapter 12 captured the prophets' warnings to Israel during their downward spiral of apostasy and social injustice following Solomon's reign. Their judgement was captivity and exile, but all was not lost. God promised they could return to Him with His help, and He would welcome them with open arms. Their return was predicated on His promise to write His law into their hearts. This would be the turning point for His people to realize their sin and, through His grace, the restoration of the heart could begin in earnest.

This promise was God's direct intervention so that obedience would not fade away. This was the prophets' messages of hope for Israel (and all of mankind) that was addressed in the last two chapters. "Because the people had broken and violated the Israelite covenant, the prophets announced that God would put in place a new covenant in which not only he would be faithful, but his people would be faithful too."[791] God would send His Son Jesus as the perfect sacrifice to take away the sins of the world and write His law into our hearts by the indwelling of the Holy Spirit. This was the two-step process outlined in the beginning of this text.

God's promise to Abraham that all nations would be blessed through him included all mankind. But first, the effort would be made to restore the hearts of Israel who were still God's chosen people at the close of the Old Testament.

---

[791]Peter Gentry and Stephen Wellum, *Kingdom Through Covenant,* 2018, p. 488.

The Heart of the Bible, Volume II, will describe Jesus's message that changing our hearts happens through faith in God, not through man-made rules such as those that hindered Israel from returning to God. Jesus demonstrated this faith and obedience throughout His ministry, which culminated in his death on the cross so we would have eternal life through Him. How Israel reacted to God's intervention will also be explored in Volume II.

TIME IN EGYPT

There may be a discrepancy regarding the amount of time the Israelites were in Egypt prior to their departure. As noted in Exodus 12:40, "Now the length of time the Israelite people lived in Egypt was 430 years." This is mathematically impossible to verify. The length of time the Israelites lived in Egypt does not start until Jacob arrived there at the age of 130 to be with Joseph (discussed in Chapter 4).

Genesis 46:8–26 lists Jacob's family members who went to Egypt, including "The sons of Levi: Gershon, Kohath and Merari" (v. 11). Kohath was Moses's grandfather who lived to be 133 years old (Exod. 6:18). Kohath's son Amram, Moses's father, lived to be 137 years old (Exod. 6:20) and Moses was 80 years old when the Israelites left Egypt. Assuming Kohath was a newborn when Jacob entered Egypt and he had Amram right before he died at 133 years old and Amram had Moses right before he died at 137 years old, and Moses was 80 years old when the Israelites left Egypt, then the maximum number of years possible from the time Kohath entered Egypt with Jacob to when Moses led his people out of Egypt would be 350 years (133+137+80). So, the 430 years indicated in Exodus 12:40 cannot be mathematically correct.

In Paul's letter to the Galatians, we get clarification of their time spent in Egypt. "The promises were spoken to Abraham and to his seed. Scripture does not say 'and to seeds,' meaning many people, but 'and to your seed,' meaning one person, who is Christ. What I mean is this: *The law, introduced 430 years later, does not set aside the covenant previously established by God and thus do away with the promise*" (Gal.

3:16–17, emphasis mine). Paul stated it is 430 years from the time God made His covenant with Abraham (who at the time was in Canaan and not Egypt) until the time the law (the Ten Commandments) was introduced.

Using this as a starting point, Abraham was 75 years old when he entered the land of Canaan where God made His promise. Twenty-five years later, Isaac was born. Isaac had Jacob when he was 60 years old. Jacob was 130 years old when he entered Egypt. Therefore, when God made His covenant with Abraham in Canaan until the time Jacob arrived in Egypt was 215 years (25+60+130) and Abraham, Isaac, and Jacob were in the land of Canaan.

Paul said that from God's first set of promises to Abraham at 75 years old to when Moses was given the law, was a total of 430 years. We just calculated that, for the first 215 years of that time period, Abraham, Isaac, and Jacob lived in the land of Canaan. That means the other 215 years was the time from Jacob's arrival to when Moses left Egypt and received the law. So, 215 years in Canaan and then 215 years living in Egypt.

Recall that Joseph was about 40 years old when Jacob arrived, and Joseph lived to be 110 years old. While he was alive, he still enjoyed great authority in Egypt, so there was 70 years before the possibility of his descendants being enslaved. At a minimum, the Israelites were in Egypt 145 years after Joseph's death before they left Egypt and it would be hard to imagine that they were enslaved immediately after Joseph died. Therefore, the amount of time the Israelites were in captivity was likely less than 145 years but greater than 80 years, which was Moses's age when they left, because they were enslaved before Moses was born.

This is the same accounting Josephus comes to in his account of Exodus. In Chapter 15, verse 2, he writes "They left Egypt in the month Xanthicus, on the fifteenth day of the lunar month; four hundred and thirty years after our forefather Abraham came into Canaan, but two hundred and fifteen years only after Jacob removed into Egypt." The footnote on this verse from Whiston sees this account agrees with the Samaritan Pentateuch and Greek Septuagint which both report that the 430 years included living in Canaan and Egypt; Whiston is at a loss to explain why Exodus 12:40 makes the 430 years exclusively in Egypt with no mention of the time in Canaan. It is likely "and Canaan" was erroneously left out of the translation of Hebrew Masoretic Leningrad Codex, which all the translated Bible language (King James, NIV, etc.) are based upon.

God's Covenant with David

I n Chapter 3, the covenants and promises the Lord made with Abraham included making a nation from his descendants, returning that nation to the Promised Land, and that all nations would be blessed through him if they remained faithful and obedient. In Chapter 5, God made a covenant with Moses and his people at Mount Sinai that He would be their God, dwell among them, and they would be His people. The covenant called for their obedience to the Ten Commandments, and He would lead them to the Promised Land as revealed through Abraham, Isaac, and Jacob.

When David became king over Israel, God made a covenant with him that would extend his royal lineage as long as they were faithful, and this lineage would endure forever. It is the promise of the kingdom Jesus would establish and rule for eternity. In Chapter 13, the section entitled *"From the Branch of David"* addressed the prophets' announcements that the Messiah would come from David's lineage. In this appendix, I will summarize the actual promise God made to David that the prophets relied upon in their message.

When David was made king, he settled in Jerusalem (the heart of Judea), built a palace for himself, and there was relative peace in the land. While he was content in his palace, it occurred to him that the ark remained in a tent. David decided the ark deserved a permanent place to safeguard it. He told his prophet Nathan that he wanted to build a house for the Lord and place the ark in a temple. His reverence, love, and respect for God were clear. David had been rewarded for his obedience and faith in God and he wanted to give thanks for God's blessings.

I keyed in on faith and obedience as ingredients of a spiritual heart, but not to the exclusion of other attributes. Giving thanks for God's blessings seems like a natural response. There is much to be grateful for and we should acknowledge His love daily. David was going to an extreme, but it was well within his abilities to build a house for God to thank Him for His blessings.

While his heart was in the right place, building the temple at that point in Israel's history was not in God's plans. God said to the prophet Nathan, "'Go and tell my servant David, "This is what the LORD says: You are not the one to build me a house to dwell in...Wherever I have moved with all the Israelites, did I ever say to any of their leaders whom I commanded to shepherd my people, 'Why have you not built me a house of cedar?'"...'When your days are over and you go to be with your ancestors, I will raise up your offspring to succeed you, one of your own sons, and I will establish his kingdom. He is the one who will build a house for me, and I will establish his throne forever'" (1 Chron. 17:4, 6, 11–12).

Ronald Youngblood cites two reasons why David could not build the temple, "1) He is too busy waging war with his enemies, and 2) he is a warrior who has shed much blood."[792] In the first instance, Youngblood cites Solomon's correspondence with Hiram in 1 Kings 5:3: "'You know that because of the wars waged against my father David from all sides, he could not build a temple for the Name of the LORD his God until the LORD put his enemies under his feet.'"

The second reason came from David himself in 1 Chronicles 22:8–9: "'But this word of the LORD came to me: "You have shed much blood and have fought many wars. You are not to build a house for my Name, because you have shed much blood on the earth in my sight. But you will have a son who will be a man of peace and rest, and I will give him rest from all his enemies on every side. His name will be Solomon, and I will grant Israel peace and quiet during his reign."'"

God consoled David by reminding him that He made a king from a shepherd and removed all his enemies. "'Now I will make your name

---

[792]Ronald Youngblood, *Expositor's Bible Commentary, 1 Samuel – 2 Samuel*, 2009, p. 383.

great, like the names of the greatest men on earth. And I will provide a place for my people Israel and will plant them so that they can have a home of their own and no longer be disturbed. Wicked people will not oppress them anymore, as they did at the beginning and have done ever since the time I appointed leaders [judges] over my people Israel. I will also give you rest from all your enemies'" (2 Sam. 7:9–11).

Making David's name great was reminiscent of God's declaration to Abraham: "'I will make you into a great nation, and I will bless you; I will make your name great, and you will be a blessing'" (Gen. 12:2).

God also indicated the fulfillment of the Promised Land given in Abraham's covenant, even though the Israelites settled in the area centuries earlier. God assured David that Israel "will have a home of their own," will no longer be oppressed by "wicked people," and will be granted "rest from all your enemies."

The peace and comfort God promised David was never quite attained in Israel's history. God promised He would give His people a place to call home and bring peace in the land. Walter Kaiser notes, "This 'rest' was a 'place' where Yahweh would 'plant his people—a place where they could live without being disturbed anymore.'"[793] He continues, "Rest was no blank check in which future generations could rest on their ancestors' laurels and slide by God's standards. This promise was to be theirs only if they would appropriate it by faith— that was the spiritual and immediate benefit of 'rest.'"[794] The nation would not be troubled by enemies since they were under the authority of the judges and the people would finally get to settle in comfort.

Since David was already in his palace when God said he would establish a house for him and the throne of Solomon's kingdom, it is commonly understood that God was referring to the dynasty that would come from David's lineage. "For 2 Samuel 7, the meaning of a 'dynasty' was most fitting, especially since the expression 'your house

---

[793]Walter Kaiser, *The Promise-Plan of God*, 2008, p. 96. Kaiser points out this rest was initially promised to Moses when Israel occupied the promised land to Joshua on entering the land, and later in describing Solomon as "a man of peace and rest." He reconciled the separate references as "a contemporaneous installment on the fulfillment."

[794] Ibid., p. 97.

and your kingdom will be made sure forever' (v. 16) could only mean that David's 'dynasty' would rule forever."[795]

This is important for a couple of reasons. First, as described in Chapter 11, once the nation was bifurcated, the succession of all the kings in Judea came from David's lineage. There was no break in succession; each new king ascended the throne of his father. The kings who were faithful to God were compared to the faithfulness of David. Good hearts follow the bloodline. This continuous succession in the monarchy continued until the fall of Jerusalem in 586 BC. However, once the nation was split, the promise was not extended to the northern nation of Israel. Because of its continued disobedience to God's commandments, there would be no continuous succession; kingship was seldom transmitted from father to son. In some cases, the throne was transferred by military coups or through assassination. But J. D. Pentecost notes that "Solomon's seed was not promised perpetuity. The only necessary feature is that the lineage cannot be lost, not that the throne be occupied continuously."[796] This is one reason that Matthew and Luke went to great lengths to trace Jesus's genealogy back to David; to show the lineage had not been severed.

A prophecy typically refers to the period in which it is spoken; for example, God's promise that Solomon would follow David as king and build the temple. The same prophecy also pointed to the coming of the Messiah (Jesus's first arrival). Finally, it's possible that the prophecy reflects an end-time (eschatological) scenario. I take this perspective from Christopher Wright who referred to these as three horizons of the prophetic texts: "Horizon 1 is the Old Testament era itself; Horizon 2 is the New Testament gospel of Messiah Jesus; Horizon 3 is the eschatological vision of new creation."[797]

This was also a prophecy of the coming of Jesus the Messiah (or Anointed One). In saying that God Himself would establish his house,

---

[795] Ibid., p. 118.

[796] J. D. Pentecost, *Thy Kingdom Come*, 1995, p. 147.

[797] Christopher Wright, *Message of Jeremiah*, 2014, p. 84. See also Chapter 12's "The Role of the Prophets."

He did not intend to build a physical house, but a royal dynasty of David's descendants.[798] This line would end with the coming of Jesus, Who was a direct descendant of David. Then, "Your house and your kingdom will endure forever before me; your throne will be established forever" (2 Sam. 7:16). God was not speaking of Solomon, but of Jesus. It refers to Jesus when He arrives to establish His kingdom on earth on His first arrival and also in an eschatological prophecy in His Second coming, where His kingdom will be established for eternity.

In his commentary on the Davidic covenant, David Guzik observes the same type of timing behind the promise: "Each of these great promises was *partially* fulfilled in Solomon, David's son and successor to his throne. [1] Solomon ruled on David's throne, [2] God's mercies never departed from Solomon, though he sinned, [and 3] Solomon built God a magnificent house."[799] This relates to the first horizon, the present or immediate future.

Guzik continues, "But the prophets foretold a greater fulfillment of these promises"[800] and cites the following scriptures. "'Behold, the days are coming,' says the LORD, 'that I will raise to David a Branch of righteousness; a King shall reign and prosper and execute judgment and righteousness in the earth...Now this is His name by which He will be called: The Lord Our Righteousness'" (Jer. 23:5–6, NKJV). "For unto us a Child is born, unto us a Son is given; and the government will be upon His shoulder...Upon the throne of David and over His kingdom, to order it and establish it...from that time forward, even forever" (Isa. 9:6–7, NKJV). "And behold, you will conceive in your womb and bear a son, and you shall call his name Jesus. He will be great and will be called the Son of the Most High. And the Lord

---

[798]D. A. Carson, *NIV Zondervan Study Bible*, 2015, p. 557. In a footnote, Carson references Peter's speech in Acts 2:30: "But he [King David] was a prophet and knew that God had promised him on oath that he would place one of his descendants on his throne."

[799]David Guzik, "Study Guide for 2 Samuel 7 by David Guzik," Blue Letter Bible, last modified February 21, 2017, https://www.blueletterbible.org/Comm/guzik_david/StudyGuide 2017-2Sa/2Sa-7.cfm

[800] Ibid.

God will give him the throne of his father David, and he will reign over the house of Jacob forever, and of his kingdom there will be no end" (Luke 1:31–33, ESV). These verses refer to the second horizon, when Jesus the Messiah would begin His mission here on earth.

Guzik concludes, "God's promise of a house for David is completely fulfilled in Jesus Christ: 1) Jesus does reign and will reign on David's throne forever, 2) the Father's mercies never departed from Jesus, even when He was made sin for us, and 3) Jesus is building the Father a magnificent house (Hebrews 3:3–6)[801] in the sense that we are God's temple (1 Peter 2:5)[802] and the church is God's new house."[803] This relates to third horizon, or the eschatological time frame, when Jesus will rule over all of us for all eternity.

Frederick Mabie makes the same case: "The messianic (and unconditional) application of the Davidic covenant is gleaned from the broader setting of Nathan's prophetic word to David and subsequent biblical revelation. For example, note the details of complete peace... never being oppressed and having all enemies subdued...an everlasting kingdom, and perhaps even of the temple reflected in the person of Christ (cf. Jn 2:18–20[804])." Using the same references to Isaiah and Luke as Guzik, Mabie adds, "Thus God ultimately bases his

---

[801]"Jesus has been found worthy of greater honor than Moses, just as the builder of a house has greater honor than the house itself. For every house is built by someone, but God is the builder of everything. 'Moses was faithful as a servant in all God's house,' bearing witness to what would be spoken by God in the future. But Christ is faithful as the Son over God's house. And we are his house, if indeed we hold firmly to our confidence and the hope in which we glory."

[802]"...you also, like living stones, are being built into a spiritual house to be a holy priesthood, offering spiritual sacrifices acceptable to God through Jesus Christ."

[803]David Guzik, "Study Guide for 2 Samuel 7 by David Guzik," Blue Letter Bible, last modified February 21, 2017, https://www.blueletterbible.org/Comm/guzik_david/StudyGuide 2017-2Sa/2Sa-7.cfm.

[804]"The Jews then responded to him, 'What sign can you show us to prove your authority to do all this?' Jesus answered them, 'Destroy this temple, and I will raise it again in three days.' They replied, 'It has taken forty-six years to build this temple, and you are going to raise it in three days?' *But the temple he had spoken of was his body.*" (v. 21 added, emphasis mine).

commitment to preserve the house of David on account of his Word and his character, rather than on human effort."[805]

Finally, in the book of Revelation, it is revealed that it is indeed Jesus who will reign over the final kingdom. "Blessed and holy are those who share in the first resurrection. The second death has no power over them, but they will be priests of God and of Christ and will reign with him for a thousand years" (Rev. 20:6). Jesus revealed at the end that He will rule.[806]

I wrote about this prophecy of Jesus the Messiah being a descendant of David and establishing His mission in Chapter 10, where the prophets announced the message of His coming.

God's covenant with David required his descendants to fulfill the covenant, just as Abraham's descendants were instructed. "I will be his father, and he will be my son. When he does wrong, I will punish him with a rod wielded by men, with floggings inflicted by human hands. But my love will never be taken away from him, as I took it away from Saul, whom I removed from before you. Your house and your kingdom will endure forever before me; your throne will be established forever'" (2 Sam. 7:14–16).

---

[805]Frederick Mabie, *The Expositor's Bible Commentary – 1 and 2 Chronicles*, 2010, p. 116.

[806]Jesus revealed to John that He is the descendant of David: "'I, Jesus, have sent my angel to testify to you about these things for the churches. I am the root and the descendant of David, the bright morning star'" (Rev. 22:16).

BIBLIOGRAPHY

Alexander, T. Desmond. *From Eden to the New Jerusalem: An Introduction to Biblical Theology.* Grand Rapids, Kregel Academy, 2008.

Allen, David L., and Lemke, Steve W., eds. *The Return of Christ: A Premillennial Perspective.* Nashville, B&H Academic, 2011.

Barclay, William. *The Gospel of Matthew, Volume 1 (3rd Edition),* Louisville, Westminster John Knox Press, 2017.

———. *The Gospel of Matthew, Volume 2 (3rd Edition),* Louisville, Westminster John Knox Press, 2017.

Barnett, Paul. *The Birth of Christianity: The First Twenty Years.* Grand Rapids, Eerdmans, 2005.

———. *Finding the Historical Christ: After Jesus, Volume 3.* Grand Rapids, Eerdmans, 2009.

———. *Jesus & the Rise of Early Christianity: A History of New Testament Times.* Downers Grove, JVP Academic, 1999.

———. *Paul, Missionary of Jesus.* Grand Rapids, Eerdmans, 2008.

Beale, G. K. *A New Testament Biblical Theology.* Grand Rapids, Baker Academic, 2011.

———. *The Temple and the Church's Mission: A Biblical Theology of the Dwelling Place of God.* Downers Grove, InterVarsity Press, 2004.

———. *We Become What We Worship: A Biblical Theology of Idolatry.* Downers Grove, IVP Academic, 2008.

Beale, G. K., and Mitchell Kim. *God Dwells Among Us: Expanding Eden to the Ends of the Earth*. Downers Grove, IVP Academic, 2004.

Bock, Darrell. *A Theology of Luke and Acts: God's Promised Program, Realized for All Nations*. Grand Rapids, Zondervan, 2012.

Boice, James Montgomery. *The Life of Moses: God's First Deliverer of Israel*. Phillipsburg, P&R Publishing, 2018.

Borland, James A. *Christ in the Old Testament: Old Testament Appearances of Christ in Human Form*. Ross-shire, Christian Focus Publications, 2010.

Bruce, F. F. *New Testament History*. New York, Doubleday Dell Publishing Group, Inc., 1969.

Brueggemann, Dale. *Cornerstone Biblical Commentary: Leviticus, Numbers, Deuteronomy*. Carol Stream, Tyndale House Publishers, Inc., 2008.

Brueggemann, Walter. *1 & 2 Kings: Smyth & Helwys Bible Commentary*. Smyth & Helwys Publishing, 2000.

———. *First and Second Samuel: Interpretation: A Bible Commentary for Teaching and Preaching*. Louisville, John Knox Press, 1990.

Bullock, C. Hassell. *An Introduction to the Old Testament Prophetic Books*. Chicago, Moody Publishers, 2007.

Carson, D. A. *Expositor's Bible Commentary: Matthew*. Grand Rapids, Zondervan, 2010.

———. *NIV Zondervan Study Bible*. Grand Rapids, Zondervan, 2015.

Dallman, William. *Jesus, His Words and His Works: According to the Four Gospels*. Milwaukee, Northwest Publishing House, 1914.

Dempster, Stephen G. *Dominion and Dynasty: A Theology of the Hebrew Bible*. Downers Grove, InterVarsity Press, 2003.

———. *ESV Expository Commentary (Volume 7): Daniel–Malachi (Micah)*. Wheaton, Crossway, 2018.

Driesbach, Jason. *Cornerstone Biblical Commentary: Joshua, Judges, Ruth.* Carol Stream, Tyndale House Publishers Inc., 2012.

Dunn, James D. G. *The Theology of Paul the Apostle.* Grand Rapids, Eerdmans, 2006.

Elwell, Walter A., ed. *Theological Dictionary of the Bible.* Grand Rapids, Baker, 1996.

Fuellenbach, John. *The Kingdom of God: The Message of Jesus Today.* Eugene, Wipf and Stock, 1995.

Gentry, Peter J., and Stephen J. Wellum. *Kingdom Through Covenant: A Biblical-Theological Understanding of the Covenants. (2nd Edition),* Wheaton, Crossway, 2018.

Goldsworthy, Graeme. *According to Plan: The Unfolding Revelation of God in the Bible.* Downers Grove, InterVarsity Press, 1991.

———. *Christ-Centered Biblical Theology: Hermeneutical Foundations and Principles.* Downers Grove, IVP Academic, 2012.

———. *The Son of God and the New Creation.* Wheaton, Crossway, 2015.

Hamilton, James M. *God's Indwelling Presence: The Holy Spirit in the Old & New Testaments.* Nashville, B&H Academic, 2006.

Harman, Allan. *ESV Expository Commentary (Volume 7): Daniel–Malachi (Joel),* Wheaton, Crossway, 2018.

Hays, J. Daniel. *The Message of the Prophets.* Grand Rapids, Zondervan, 2010.

Hess, Richard. *The Expositor's Bible Commentary – Leviticus.* Grand Rapids, Zondervan, 2008.

Hitchcock, Mark, *The Complete Book of Bible Prophecy,* Wheaton, Tyndale House Publishers, 1999.120

Hoekema, Anthony A. *Created in God's Image.* Grand Rapids, Eerdmans, 1989.

———. *Saved by Grace.* Grand Rapids, Eerdmans, 1994.

House, Paul R. *The New American Commentary: 1, 2 Kings.* Nashville, B&H Publishing Group, 1995.

———. *Old Testament Survey.* Nashville, B&H Academic, 1992.

———. *Old Testament Theology.* Downers Grove, IVP Academic, 1998.

Hubbard, Robert L., Jr. *The Book of Ruth,* Grand Rapids, Eerdmans, 1988.

Hurtado, Larry W. *Lord Jesus Christ: Devotion to Jesus in Earliest Christianity.* Grand Rapids, Eerdmans, 2003.

Jenson, Robert W. *Commentary on the Bible – Ezekiel,* Grand Rapids, Brazos Press, 2009.

Josephus, *The New Complete Works of Josephus.* Translated by William Whiston Grand Rapids, Kregel Publications, 1999.

Kaiser, Walter C., Jr. *The Promise-Plan of God: A Biblical Theology of the Old and New Testaments.* Grand Rapids, Zondervan Academic, 2008.

Keyes, Nelson B. *Story of the Bible World, (2nd Edition)* Pleasantville, C. S. Hammond, and Company, 1962

Kitchen, Kenneth A. *On the Reliability of the Old Testament.* Grand Rapids, Eerdmans, 2006

Klein, George L. *The New American Commentary – Zechariah.* Nashville, Holman Reference, 2008.

Ladd, George E. *A Theology of the New Testament (Rev. Edition).* Grand Rapid, Eerdmans, 1993.

Liefeld, Walter L., and David W. Pao. *The Expositor's Bible Commentary: Luke.* Grand Rapids, Zondervan Academic, 2007.

Lennox, John C. *Joseph: A Story of Love, Hate, Slavery, Power, and Forgiveness.* Wheaton, Crossway, 2019.

Leupold, H. C. *Exposition of Genesis: Volume 1*. Grand Rapids, Baker House Books, 1942.

Leupold, H. C. *Exposition of Genesis: Volume 2*. Grand Rapids, Baker House Books, 1942.

Long, V. Phillip, *The Reign and Rejection of King Saul; A vase for Literary and Theological Coherence,* Atlanta, Scholar's Press, 1989.

Lumpkin, Joseph. *The Book of Jubilees: The Little Genesis, The Apocalypse of Moses (2nd Edition)*. Blountsville, Fifth Estate Publishers, 2011.

———. *The Books of Enoch: The Angels, The Watchers, and The Nephilim*. Fifth Estate, Inc., 2011.

Mabie, Frederick. *The Expositor's Bible Commentary – 1 and 2 Chronicles*. Grand Rapids, Zondervan, 2010.

Manson, T. W. *Ethics and the Gospel.* New York, Charles Schribner's Sons, 1960.

———. *The Teaching of Jesus: Studies in its Form & Content.* Cambridge, Cambridge University Press, 2008. (Reissued digital edition.)

Manson, T. W., H. D. A. Major, and C. J. Wright. *The Mission and Message of Jesus (2 Edition)*. New York, E. P. Dutton & Co., 1946.

McKelvey, Michael, *ESV Expository Commentary (Volume 7): Daniel–Malachi (Amos)*. Wheaton, Crossway, 2018.

Merrill, Eugene. *Cornerstone Biblical Commentary Genesis – Deuteronomy (Deuteronomy)*. Carol Stream. Tyndale House Publishers, Inc., 2008.

———. *A Commentary on 1 & 2 Chronicles.* Grand Rapids, Kregel Academic, 2015.

———. *Kingdom of Priests: A History of Old Testament Israel*. Grand Rapids, Baker Academic, 2nd edition, 2008.

Oswalt, John N. *Cornerstone Biblical Commentary: Genesis, Exodus (Genesis)*. Carol Stream, Tyndale House Publishers, Inc., 2008.

Patterson, Richard D., and Hermann J. Austel. *The Expositor's Bible Commentary – 1 Samuel - 2 Kings (1, 2 Kings)*. Grand Rapids, Zondervan, 2009.

Pentecost, J. Dwight. *The Words and Works of Jesus Christ: A Study of the Life of Christ*. Grand Rapids, Zondervan Academic, 1981.

———. *Thy Kingdom Come: Tracing God's Kingdom Program and Covenant Promises Throughout History*. Grand Rapids, Kregel Publications, 1995.

Perrin, Nicholas. *The Kingdom of God: A Biblical Theology*. Grand Rapids, Zondervan Academic, 2019.

Petterson, Anthony R. *ESV Expository Commentary (Volume 7): Daniel–Malachi (Zechariah)*. Wheaton, Crossway, 2018.

Provan, Iain W. *1 & 2 Kings (Understanding the Bible Commentary Series)*. Grand Rapids, Baker Books, 1995.

———. *Discovering Genesis: Content, Interpretation, Reception*. Grand Rapids, Eerdmans, 2015.

———. *Seriously Dangerous Religion: What the Old Testament Really Says and Why It Matters*. Waco, Baylor University Press, 2014.

Provan, Iain, V. Philips Long, and Tremper Longman. *A Biblical History of Israel, 2nd Edition*. Louisville, Westminster John Knox Press, 2015.

Ross, Allen. *Cornerstone Biblical Commentary: Genesis*. Carol Stream, Tyndale House Publishers, Inc., 2008.

Sailhamer, John H. *The Expositor's Bible Commentary – Genesis*. Grand Rapids, Zondervan, 2008.

Schreiner, Thomas R. *Evangelical Biblical Theology Commentary: Hebrews*. Bellingham, Lexham Press, 2020.

———. *The King in His Beauty, A Biblical Theology of the Old and New Testaments.* Grand Rapids, Baker Academic, 2013.

———. *New Testament Theology: Magnifying God in Christ.* Grand Rapids, Baker Academic, 2008.

Schwab, George. *ESV Expository Commentary (Volume 7): Daniel–Malachi (Hosea).* Wheaton, Crossway, 2018.

Scobie, Charles H. *The Ways of Our God: An Approach to Biblical Theology.* Grand Rapids, Eerdmans, 2003.

Sklar, Jay. *ESV Expository Commentary (Volume 7): Daniel–Malachi (Jonah).* Wheaton, Crossway, 2018.

Stead, Michael. *ESV Expository Commentary (Volume 7): Daniel–Malachi (Jonah).* Wheaton, Crossway, 2018.

Stibbe, Mark W. G., *Guide to Christian Belief.* Peabody, Hendrickson Publishing, 2007.

Stone, Lawson, G. *Cornerstone Biblical Commentary: Joshua, Judges, Ruth.* Carol Stream, Tyndale House Publishers, Inc., 2012.

Stott, John. *The Message of the Sermon on the Mount.* Downers Grove, InterVarsity Press, 1978.

Thielman, Frank, *The Theology of the New Testament.* Grand Rapids, Zondervan, 2005.

Thompson, David L. *Cornerstone Biblical Commentary: Ezekiel.* Carol Stream, Tyndale House Publishing, Inc., 2010.

Vanhoozer, Kevin J. *Dictionary for Theological Interpretation of the Bible.* Grand Rapids, Baker Academic, 2005.

Vannoy, J. Robert, *Cornerstone Biblical Commentary (Book 4): 1-2 Samuel.* Carol Stream, Tyndale House Publishers, Inc., 2009.

Varkey, Wilson. *Role of the Holy Spirit in Protestant Systematic Theology.* Carlisle, Langham Monographs, 2011.

Vlach Michael J. *He Will Reign Forever: A Biblical Theology of the Kingdom of God.* Silverton, Lampion Press LLC, 2017.

Waltke, Bruce K. *An Old Testament Theology: An Exegetical, Canonical, and Thematic Approach.* Grand Rapids, Zondervan Academic, 2007.

Webb, Barry G. *The Message of Isaiah.* Downers Grove, IVP Academic, 1996.

Williams, Michael. *Hidden Prophets of the Bible: Finding the Gospel in Hosea through Malachi.* Colorado Springs, David C. Cook, 2017.

Williamson, H. G. M. *1 and 2 Chronicles.* Eugene, Wipf and Stock, 2010.

Wright, Christopher J. H. *The Message of Ezekiel: A New Heart and a New Spirit,* Downers Grove, IVP Academic, 2001.

———. *Old Testament Ethics for the People of God.* Downers Grove, InterVarsityPress, 2004.

———. *The Message of Jeremiah.* Downers Grove, IVP Academic, 2014.

———. *Knowing God Through the Old Testament,* Downers Grove, IVP Academic, 2019

Wright, N. T. *Hebrews for Everyone.* Louisville, Westminster John Knox Press, 2004

———. *How God Became King: The Forgotten Story of the Gospels.* New York, HarperCollins Publishers, 2012.

———. *Jesus and the Victory of God.* Minneapolis, Fortress Press, 1996.

———. *The New Testament and the People of God.* Minneapolis, Fortress Press, 1992.

———. *The Resurrection of the Son of God.* Minneapolis, Fortress Press, 2003.

Young, Edward. J. *The Book of Isaiah: A Commentary, Volume 1.* Grand Rapids, Eerdmans, 1965.

———. *The Book of Isaiah: A Commentary, Volume 2.* Grand Rapids, Eerdmans, 1969.

———. *The Book of Isaiah: A Commentary, Volume 3.* Grand Rapids, Eerdmans, 1972.

Youngblood, Ronald J. *Expositor's Bible Commentary: 1 Samuel – 2 Samuel.* Grand Rapids, Zondervan, 2009.

CPSIA information can be obtained
at www.ICGtesting.com
Printed in the USA
LVHW052331230322
714086LV00015B/2758